"Anyone—no matter if they're an old hand or brand-new at the w... a deeper understanding and appreciation of it. I know I did. So deliciously."
—**PIM TECHAMUANVIVIT**, chef, author, and creator of *Chez Pim*

"I've known Kenji as an incredibly talented and multifaceted cook who provides well-researched and -tested recommendations that I could always trust and incorporate into my cooking. He's also approachable, funny, and passionate, which shines through in the knowledge he shares with others."
—**NAMIKO H. CHEN**, author and creator of *Just One Cookbook*

"In this masterful book lies the answers to just about any question you could ask about one of the most ubiquitous, useful, and yet misunderstood tools of the Asian kitchen. My wok is used so frequently it never leaves the stove, but Kenji's scientific approach will benefit beginners and professionals alike."
—**ADAM LIAW**, author and host of *Destination Flavor*

"Kenji has taken on the Herculean task of bringing together techniques and recipes that highlight the versatility of the most important tool in our kitchen: the wok. And he's done it all with his signature ability to translate scientific analysis and thoughtful research into easy-to-follow recipes for the home cook—plus a few choice wok puns!"
—**BILL, JUDY, SARAH,** and **KAITLIN LEUNG**, creators of *The Woks of Life*

"The wok is an essential tool in the kitchens of virtually all Asian restaurants. While it took me many years of grueling hard work in professional kitchens to really learn it, in *The Wok*, you are graciously given all the knowledge you need to master it at home."
—**HOONI KIM**, chef and author of *My Korea*

"Kenji's culinary authority is next level. I've been fortunate to watch his genius in action and I'm proud to be his friend. Enjoy this book and everything this man says, because we are witnessing culinary greatness."
—**ALVIN CAILAN** chef, author, and host of *The Burger Show*

"*The Wok* goes beyond the recipes, which are amazing, into teaching techniques that chefs/home cooks can apply beyond this book. This is a must-have book for cooks of every level."
—**LEAH COHEN**
author of *Lemongrass and Lime*

the
Wok

the
Wok

Recipes and Techniques

J. KENJI LÓPEZ-ALT

W. W. NORTON & COMPANY
Independent Publishers Since 1923

For information about permission to reproduce selections from this book, write to
Permissions, W. W. Norton & Company, Inc., 500 Fifth Avenue, New York, NY 10110

For information about special discounts for bulk purchases, please contact
W. W. Norton Special Sales at specialsales@wwnorton.com or 800-233-4830

Manufacturing by Lakeside Book Company
Book design by Toni Tajima Design
Production manager: Julia Druskin

ISBN: 978-0-393-54121-2

W. W. Norton & Company, Inc., 500 Fifth Avenue, New York, N.Y. 10110
www.wwnorton.com

W. W. Norton & Company Ltd., 15 Carlisle Street, London W1D 3BS

2 3 4 5 6 7 8 9 0

To Adri for putting up with all of this again.

To Alicia for her patience as I finished the noodle chapter.

To Wombat who I can't wait to cook for.

To Fred, Keiko, Pico, Aya, Jita, and Kachan for all the
    great meals we've shared over the years.

To Maria, whose pride I strive to earn, even in her passing.

contents

0 INTRODUCTION

Meet the Most Versatile Pan in Your Kitchen

Since writing my first book, *The Food Lab: Better Home Cooking Through Science*, a lot of things have changed. I spent several years living in San Mateo, California, before moving to Seattle. I now have a normal-sized American kitchen though I dearly miss my small, extraordinarily functional New York galley-style kitchen (I actually have to *walk* between my counter and my stovetop, much to my chagrin). I'm something called a "YouTube Creator" and an "influencer." I've got kids!*

All of these factors mean that fast, fresh cooking is the order of the day, and that's why I reach for my wok more than any other pan in my kitchen.

Do you know the principle of Chekhov's gun? It's a basic rule in good storytelling coined by Russian playwright Anton Chekhov that states that if a loaded gun is introduced to the story, it had better go off before you reach the end.

Dear readers, I apologize, for I broke this rule in *The Food Lab*. My Chekhov's gun? **The wok.** Despite spending two pages expounding on its usefulness, despite declaring that it is the most commonly used pan in my home kitchen, I failed to provide a single recipe for it.† Here I intend to fix that. By the end of this book, not only will you be firing out delicious recipes from your wok left and right; you'll have learned the skills required to throw together a meal using virtually any meat, vegetable, or plant-based protein source you find in your fridge, whether you have a lazy afternoon to cook or a harried half hour while simultaneously handling a toddler.

As far as putting dinner on the table quickly and easily, *nothing* beats stir-frying in a wok. It's the quintessential weeknight supper. Because the actual cooking is so fast, it's also an ideal summer meal—no heating up the house with a hot oven or a long-simmering pot. It's also a fantastic way to showcase good ingredients. Vegetables retain their bright color and crunch, proteins come out tender and flavor-packed.

And there's no reason to stick with just Asian ingredients! Asparagus, corn, zucchini, string beans, peas, fava beans, almost any firm vegetable you can think of makes for wonderful stir-fries. The Asian American restaurant staples of beef, pork, chicken, and shrimp are also only the tip of the iceberg. Firm fish and shellfish are prime stir-fry candidates, as are tofu, seitan, and other vegetarian protein sources.

But it doesn't end there! The wok is also the ideal vessel for deep frying at home (good-bye, stovetop splatter); you can use it to steam vegetables, dumplings, and, well, anything steamable; it doubles as an indoor quick-smoker (home-smoked cheese! Home-smoked duck! Home-smoked whiskey!); and it's great for stovetop-braising meats and vegetables.

When it comes to producing quick, flavorful, and versatile meals, the wok beats every other pan in the kitchen, hands down.

---

* I'm a dad now, which means my punning has gone off the charts. So before we do anything else, let's get all of the wok puns out of our system so that we can avoid them for the rest of the book, OK? Are you nervous to rock out with your wok out? Wok this way and your dinners will be a wok in the park. Not sure where to start? We've all been between a wok and a hard place, but *hei* now, you're a wok star, so just wok the line and by the end of this book you'll be ready to wok around the clock. So gather up your ingredients and quietly whisper to your shrimp "we will, we will wok you."

Wokka wokka wokka.

Feeling better? Good, let's wok on.

† I *did* call out its usefulness for deep frying in my first book, a feature I will expand on here.

Wok History

There are plenty of other books that talk about the history of the wok. I'm a cook with a penchant for science, not a historian, so I see no reason to go into great detail here when other people already do it so much better.

Long story short: The origins of the wok are unclear, but in all likelihood it was introduced to China from a neighboring country sometime during the Han Dynasty (right around the BC to AD changeover) as a clay vessel, designed for drying grains. By the Ming Dynasty, around seven hundred years ago, metal woks used for stir-frying were popularized and have gone on to become the most common cooking method throughout the country.

My own introduction to the wok was during the MacGyver dynasty (right around the eighties-to-nineties changeover) as an infomercial, designed for selling kitchen gadgets. By the MacGyver reboot dynasty, it had gone on to become the most common cooking method throughout my kitchen.

"It's The Great Wok of China!" exclaims Arnold Morris in the middle of his half-hour infomercial. The late 1980s were prime infomercial time, and, along with Mr. Wizard's World and He-Man, they were a staple of my childhood viewing. I loved all those kitchen gadgets, but even then I could see through most of them as a gimmick. Ron Popeil's Chop-o-Matic ("The greatest kitchen appliance ever made!"*), Veg-o-Matic ("Slice tomatoes so thin they only have one side!"†), and Showtime Rotisserie ("Set it and . . ." you can finish the rest, I'm sure) captured my attention, but not my curiosity. But that hand-hammered wok!

I was familiar with woks growing up. My mother, who moved to the United States from Japan in her late teens, had a small carbon-steel number that she used for deep frying gyoza and Japanese-style croquettes or for making fried rice and Chungking Pork (check out page 95 for my updated version of her recipe). But it was through one of those infomercials that I really started getting curious about the wok.

(check out page 95 for my updated version of her recipe)

Why Technique over Recipes?

Don't get me wrong—there are plenty of recipes in this book, and if you're the type who just wants to follow instructions and leave the planning to someone else, that's totally fine. I promise, the recipes will work for you. But if, on the other hand, you have that desire to be in charge of your own destiny, to cook that meal that's custom-suited for future you, then I hope you'll find the lengthy in-between-the-recipes sections of this book even more interesting.

I like to think of cooking as a map. Following a recipe is like getting turn-by-turn instructions, your face buried in your smartphone. Sure, with good recipes, you can get from point A (raw ingredients) to point B (delicious meals), and sometimes that's all you want. But learning the science and technique behind those recipes! That's like being given an atlas. It's full access to all of Google maps, from the biggest bird's-eye view to the details on each street.

With that map at your disposal, you may find a better, more efficient way to get from A to B, custom-suited to your cooking style or kitchen. You may, in fact, find that you'd rather go to B-prime, or maybe even points X, Y, or Z. Sometimes you might plan on going from A to B but find you're up against a roadblock. You're missing one of the ingredients in the list, or perhaps a piece of equipment. No problem. Armed with that map, with those techniques and science, you'll be able to find an alternate route with ease.

If you're just starting out, I'm not gonna kid you, it's gonna take some learning and some commitment. But it's the *fun* kind of learning, and as long as you have a commitment to mapo tofu or tempura, you're going to do just fine.

My current wok is the same one that I've used since buying it in the early 2000s. The quality of my relationship with it is only barely bested by that with my wife, my daughter, and *some* members of my extended family.

If you are ready to start down the path of your own lifelong commitment to an inanimate object, then read on.

---

* Mr. Popeil had obviously never seen a wok or mortar and pestle, undoubtedly the two best kitchen appliances ever made.

† A topological impossibility, unless the Veg-o-Matic somehow produces Möbius strips of tomato—a feat of knifework that is, in fact, relatively easy to perform on a bagel or a doughnut (Google "Möbius Doughnut"; trust me).

Buying a Wok

Woks come in as many shapes, sizes, and materials as Western-style sauté pans and saucepots, but here is my quick and dirty recommendation for anyone who cooks on a standard Western-style range: get yourself a 14-inch, flat-bottomed, carbon steel wok made with material around 2 mm (14 gauge) thick, with a single long handle and a helper-handle on the opposite side. If you happen to live in a city with a sizable Chinese population, your best bet is to hit up a Chinese restaurant supply store. You'll find a variety of woks at really great prices. The Wok Shop in San Francisco's Chinatown has been selling high quality woks for over fifty years. You can browse and order them from wokshop.com.

Want a little more detail? OK, here we go.

WOK MATERIALS

 Q *What metallurgical qualities are important when selecting a wok?*

A Woks come in a variety of materials, thicknesses, and finishes. There are four important qualities to consider in the material for your wok. The first three (specific heat capacity, density, and conductivity) are physical properties of the material itself, while the third (reactivity) is a function of a wok's material, thickness, and geometry. For now we'll focus on the first two.

Specific heat capacity is the amount of energy it takes to raise a specific amount of material a specific number of degrees. In metric, this is measured in kilojoules per kilogram per kelvin. For instance, aluminum has a specific heat of .91. That means that it takes .91 kilojoule of energy to raise 1 kilogram of aluminum by 1 kelvin (about 2°F for those who are imperially inclined). Conversely, this means that for every kelvin a kilogram of aluminum is at, it has 1 kilojoule of energy to give up either to the surrounding environment or the food in the pan. Cast iron, with a heat capacity of .46, holds about half as much energy as aluminum per unit weight. This

means that given identical weights and starting temperatures, an aluminum pan will contain about twice as much heat energy as a cast iron pan. This gets more complicated when you take into account density.

The density of a material is the ratio of weight to size. Aluminum has a density of 2.7 grams per cubic centimeter, whereas cast iron has a density of 7.2. This means that given two pans of identical shape and size, a cast iron pan will weigh about 2.5 times more than an aluminum pan. Thus even though cast iron holds about half as much heat energy per unit weight, given identical shapes and sizes, a cast iron pan will hold about 1.25 times as much heat energy as an aluminum pan. These two concepts, heat capacity and density, can be combined into a more useful concept: volumetric heat capacity.

Volumetric heat capacity is a measure of how much heat energy a given volume of a material will store, given a specific temperature. Conversely, it's also a measure of how much energy you need to add to a fixed volume of material to raise that material's temperature by a fixed number of degrees.

Sound confusing? Here's an easy way to think of it. Every pan in your kitchen acts as a sort of reservoir or bucket of energy. Preheating a pan on a burner is sort of like pouring water into that bucket. The higher the volumetric heat capacity of the pan, the bigger that bucket, the longer it takes to fill up, and the more energy it will hold. A cast iron wok is a heat-storing bucket about 1.25 times (25 percent) bigger than an aluminum wok of the same shape and size.

Conductivity is a material's ability to get heat from one area to another. This applies to its ability to efficiently conduct heat from the heat source to the food, but also to its ability to conduct heat evenly throughout its cooking surface. Conductivity is more or less linear: it will take about twice as long for a 2-millimeter-thick pan to conduct heat from the burner to the food than a 1-millimeter-thick pan.

If we go back to that bucket analogy, you can think of conductivity as the size of the spigot at the

MATERIAL	DENSITY g/cm³	HEAT CAPACITY in J/(g K)	VOLUMETRIC HEAT CAPACITY in J/(cm³ K)	CONDUCTIVITY in W/m K, at room temperature
Carbon steel	7.85	0.49	3.85	54
Stainless steel	7.5	0.5	3.75	45
Cast iron	7	0.46	3.22	80
Aluminum	2.7	0.92	2.48	204
Copper	8.94	0.38	3.40	386

bottom of the bucket. The higher the conductivity, the bigger the spigot, and the faster you can pour energy from inside the bucket into the food you are cooking.

If we were to look purely at heat capacity and conductivity, aluminum is the clear winner here. It stores plenty of heat (nothing has it beat!) and transfers energy quickly (only copper is more conductive). However, aluminum hits a snag in the density department. Because it is so light, you'd need a ludicrously thick aluminum pan to achieve the *volumetric* heat capacity of carbon or stainless steel.

In other words, all else being equal, a 2-millimeter-thick carbon steel pan will hold about 60 percent more energy at a given temperature than a 2-millimeter-thick aluminum pan, though an aluminum pan will be about four times more conductive.

So what about this reactivity thing?

Reactivity is a pan's ability to react quickly to changes in heat input. If I switch off the heat, do the contents of the pan continue to sizzle and sweat, or do they cool rapidly? If I need a quick blast of heat, does the wok react fast enough when I turn the dial up?

With a Western-style pan, we typically value consistency over reactivity. We want the pan to maintain a slow, steady sizzle as we add finely diced vegetables to sauté, and we want it to maintain a vigorous sizzle as we sear. Rarely in

Western cuisine do you find yourself needing to go from a simmer to a sear to a gentle bubble in the course of a few moments. With wok cooking, this is a frequent occurrence.

This quality is related to the conductivity of a wok's material (the more conductive the more reactive) and its thickness (the thinner the more reactive), but more importantly, the geometry of your wok and how it fits with your burner can have a big impact. Ideally, your wok should fit over your hottest burner with a wide enough flat-bottomed area that the ring of flames heats *mostly* the bottom with a little bit of flame riding up the flared sides. This maximizes reactivity in the center of the pan, where you need it the most.

OK, so give it to me: Which material should I choose?

Stainless steel woks are expensive, heavy, difficult to maneuver, and not very reactive. The finish on stainless steel is also designed to be fully cleaned after each use, whereas a wok, like an old-fashioned cast iron pan, should develop a dark patina over time that improves its functionality. I would not recommend a stainless steel wok unless you use your wok primarily for braising.

Clad stainless steel (stainless steel with a layer of aluminum or copper sandwiched in between) is even worse for woks. The layers of bonded metal expand and contract at different rates when heated, so preheating a clad pan to extreme temperatures (as woks frequently are) can cause the metal to split and the layers to separate.

Likewise, solid **copper** woks, with their steel or tin lining, are a waste of money for the same reason (an even bigger waste—copper is significantly more expensive than steel!)

Aluminum distributes heat very evenly, which is a desirable characteristic for Western cooking, but not so much for wok cooking, where distinct cooking zones with different heat levels is desirable. Aluminum, with its low density, does not retain heat very well for a given wok thickness.

Cast iron is a common traditional material, and while it has decent performance stats, its brittleness requires it to be rather thick and heavy in order not to crack or break with regular use. This makes for a heavy, cumbersome wok that isn't very reactive.

Carbon steel is your best bet. Modern carbon steel pans are made of spun steel that is quite durable and unlikely to crack or break. A 14-gauge pan (about 2 millimeters thick) is thick enough to store a good amount of energy for searing, but thin enough that it will react to changes in burner input quickly. It's extremely inexpensive, and when properly used it will end up with a practically nonstick surface.

Q *What about nonstick woks?*

A Most nonstick coatings will begin to break down at around 450°F, and by 650°F they are actively decomposing into toxic vapors. Most should not be heated above 450°F or so. This is an inadequate temperature range for many stir-fries, which rely on higher heat to rapidly cook foods while preserving their color and texture. Moreover, with a nonstick wok you will achieve no *wok hei*—the smoky flavor you find in many restaurant-style dishes. Finally, nonstick surfaces are simply *too* nonstick for effective wok cooking. A small amount of sticking allows you to push food up the sides of the wok to clear space for new ingredients. Avoid nonstick woks.

WOK DESIGN

Q *Round-bottom woks are more authentic than flat-bottom woks, right? Which do you recommend?*

A When it comes to stir-frying at home, flat-bottom woks make the wokin' world go round (er, go flat, that is).

Traditional woks have a deep bowl shape designed to fit into a circular opening directly over the hearth. Most modern home ranges both in the United States and in Asia are designed for flat skillets. Unless you have a custom wok insert in your range, you want to avoid round-bottom or induction woks. They won't work, period, on an electric range, and are tough to use on a gas range—even with one of those wok rings that elevate it and hold it steady. These rings typically raise your wok too high above the heat source. Rather than absorbing all the heat, a lot of it is dissipated or gets deflected away as it travels up from the burner to the sides of the wok. On the other hand, woks with bottoms that are too flat defeat the purpose of a wok, making it tough to flip properly and to move food in and out of the high-heat zone.

Your best bet is a wok with a 4- to 5-inch flattened area at the bottom, with gently sloping sides that flare out to between 12 and 14 inches. This will give you plenty of high-heat space for searing meats and vegetables at the bottom, while still providing ample volume and room to maneuver when flipping.

Q *I've seen woks with long handles and short handles. Which style should I get?*

A Cantonese-style woks have two ear-shaped looped metal handles welded or riveted onto either side. Northern-style woks, also known as *pow* woks, have a single long handle and, frequently, a loop-shaped helper-handle on the opposite side. Either style works, but Northern-style long-handled woks tend to be easier for folks who are used to Western-style long-handled skillets.

Q *So what about those hand-hammered woks from those eighties infomercials? How important is it that a wok be hand-hammered?*

A Woks are made in three ways. Traditional **hand-hammered** woks are an excellent choice. The slight indentations left by the hammering pattern allow you to push cooked food to the sides of the pan while adding ingredients to the center without their slipping. The only problem is that it can be difficult (perhaps impossible?) to find a hand-hammered wok with a flat bottom and a handle.

Stamped woks are made by cutting out a circular piece of thin carbon steel and machine-pressing it into a mold. They are extremely cheap, but completely smooth, which makes it difficult to stir-fry properly in them. They are, without fail, made from low-gauge steel and prone to developing hot and cold spots, as well as feeling flimsy.

Spun woks are produced on a lathe, giving them a distinct pattern of concentric circles. This pattern offers the same advantages as a hand-hammered wok, allowing you to easily keep your food in place against the side of the pan. Spun woks can be found in heavy gauges, with flat bottoms, and with flip-friendly handles.

Fortunately, both spun woks and hand-hammered woks are inexpensive.

Seasoning, Cleaning, and Maintaining a Wok

Q *OK, I've got my new carbon steel wok. It's kinda dull gray and looks like it's coated in oil. What do I need to do to start using it?*

A Just like with a good cast iron or carbon steel pan, a carbon steel wok's performance will improve the more you use it. Most come with a protective film of oil on them to prevent them from rusting or tarnishing in the store, but it's important to remove this layer before using it the first time. First, scrub the wok out with hot, soapy water and dry it carefully. Next, heat up every metal surface over the flame of a gas burner, slowly rotating the pan until it starts to discolor and turn dark brown or black all over. If all you've got is an electric burner, you can achieve this process with a propane or butane torch or over an outdoor grill. This will vaporize any remaining machine oil and get your wok ready for its first layer of seasoning. Finally, give the entire thing another scrub with soapy water, dry it carefully, and rub the surface inside and out with a very light coating of oil (whatever high heat-friendly neutral oil you like to use, such as canola, grapeseed, rice bran, or peanut) using a paper towel held in tongs.

After use, avoid scrubbing the wok unless absolutely necessary. Usually, a rinse and a rubdown with a soft sponge are all that's needed. Purists may tell you not to use soap; I do, and my wok is still well seasoned and completely nonstick. Once it's rinsed, dry the wok with a kitchen towel or paper towels and rub some vegetable oil into the surface to give it a vapor-proof coating that will prevent it from rusting.

Q *So how do I season it, and do I really need to?*

A Meat proteins can form direct chemical bonds with raw iron or steel. This is not good if you don't want your wok to look like a stucco wall after cooking in it. Just as with a cast iron or carbon steel pan, seasoning your wok and keeping it well seasoned will prevent this, but there is a fundamental difference between seasoning a wok and seasoning a Western skillet. It's important to understand the two different products of heating an oiled piece of ferrous material. The first product is black oxide, a reaction that occurs on the surface of the metal, causing it to turn black. The second is the formation of a layer of polymers as oil breaks down with heat.

In a Western skillet, this formation of polymers in increasingly thick layers is what gives it its nonstick properties, and those layers should generally be maintained. With a wok, it's possible to build up those layers as well, but many cooking techniques (such as braising or even rapidly adjusting the heat during a stir-fry) will cause those layers of polymers to break down or flake off. This is OK. The seasoning in a wok mainly comes down to that layer of black oxide, and that layer can be built with each use. With proper preheating and technique, even an omelet should slip and slide without a thick layer of polymers coating the wok.

Some people recommend rigorous extended processes for building up black oxide and polymers, but I suggest you can do it the way I do it: after that initial rubdown with oil, just cook in the darn thing. Stick to relatively dry stir-fries and deep frying for the first several uses to ensure that a decent layer of seasoning has built up. Once your pan is black and shiny, you can safely steam, braise, simmer, or smoke in it.

Q *Wow, my wok is so well seasoned! Thanks! Now how do I keep this lustrous beauty lustrous and beautiful?*

A There's really not much to it. After you're done cooking, clean your wok. This is easiest to do when the wok is still hot and it only takes a matter of seconds. A light scrub with a bamboo brush, a little soap, and water is all it takes. Don't worry; modern soaps are quite mild and will only remove oils without affecting your polymerized seasoning or black oxide.

Once your wok is clean, dry it carefully. Water is the enemy of carbon steel and cast iron, and you don't want it rusting on you. Next, set it over a burner and heat it up empty until every drop of moisture is gone from every part of its surface. Finally, rub it with a little fresh oil using a paper towel to protect it. The thinnest layer is all you want, to prevent your wok from getting sticky. I like to rub oil into it, then pretend I made a mistake and try to wipe off as much oil as I can with a paper towel.

Wok Accessories

The round shape of a wok is not designed for straight, narrow Western cooking implements. So you'll need to outfit your new wok with a couple of inexpensive tools. Here are my recommendations, in order of importance.

- The most important tool is a ***chuan*, or spatula**. These spatulas have a wide head and a gently curved lip designed to fit snugly with your wok, allowing you to easily pick up and flip large quantities of food with minimal effort. Look for spatulas at least 14 inches long made from steel or wood. You can order them online for about $10 apiece.

- **Plenty of bowls** for mise en place. Cooking in a wok is a fast process, but most wok-cooked dishes use more ingredients than your average Western recipe, which means a collection of small bowls for prepared ingredients and sauces is absolutely essential to successful wok cooking. No need to get fancy—I keep a large stack of little metal and ceramic bowls from the restaurant supply shop. They nest and stack, take up very little storage space, and are indestructible (this is important when you inevitably toss a bowl across the kitchen toward the sink after emptying it into your wok).

- **A bamboo brush** is the best tool for scrubbing out your wok (or even your Western skillets) and can be found inexpensively online or at any Asian supermarket.

- A **wire-mesh spider** is essential for deep frying or simmering. I like a stainless steel spider with a basket on the larger side—between 5 and 6 inches—to make it easy to tend to little nuggets of fried chicken or a big mess of noodles.

- A couple of **bamboo steamer baskets** will convert your wok to a multilevel steamer (and they make for great serving vessels as well). I'd recommend a couple of 10- or 12-inch baskets. They're designed to stack, so you can always order another if you find that two isn't enough for your steaming needs.

- A **lid** is not strictly necessary, but it makes tasks that require trapping vapor—such as braising or smoking—easier. You can always use the lid from a large saucepan to cover your wok. Because a wok has tapered sides, pretty much any lid with a diameter less than that of the wok will work. It does not need to fit perfectly.

- In restaurants, you may see Chinese chefs using a **wide ladle called a *hoak*** to add splashes of various sauces to serve soupier dishes, or to break up clumps of rice or noodles when stir-frying. I personally don't find a hoak to be particularly useful in a home setting, where you'll have already measured and mixed your sauces and will be cooking in batches intended to be served all at once instead of ladled out piecemeal. For times when you really need one, a Western ladle will do just fine.

- A **Japanese-style mandoline** will make certain difficult bits of knifework much, much easier. In particular a mandoline is great for making the initial cuts for julienned vegetables, such as the carrots for Sichuan Dry-Fried Beef (page 436) or the ginger matchsticks in Gong Bao Ji Ding (page 64). I use the standard model from Benriner, an inexpensive Japanese brand that is razor-sharp, has minimal moving parts (fancier models with lots of mechanical bits tend to fail pretty quickly), and is infinitely adjustable with a simple screw. It also comes with julienne attachments, though using them drastically increases the odds of injury (I speak from experience).

- **Small plastic squeeze bottles and pour spouts** for commonly used sauces are great once you are comfortable enough to start eyeballing and improvising stir-fries. I keep light and dark soy sauce and sesame oil in their own squeeze bottles, and I top my Shaoxing wine and sake bottles with metal pour spouts for easy access during a cook.

Q *What if I don't have a wok?*

A Most of the recipes in this book will work reasonably well in a larger skillet or, better yet, a large slope-sided saucier pan (a saucepan with gently curved corners), so if that's all you've got, by all means use them. That said, get a wok. They are inexpensive, mostly indestructible, and will make a noticeable difference in the quality of your food.

Knives

A good knife is a tool you'll use virtually every time you cook. Good doesn't have to mean expensive, though! Knives come in a dizzying array of sizes, shapes, and styles. Although many chefs (including me) collect or fetishize knives and pay careful attention to metal types, Rockwell hardness ratings, production methods, and other features, the reality is, once you get past a certain base level of quality, the best knife is the one that you feel comfortable using every day. My advice is to go to a decent knife or kitchen goods store and try a few out to see how they feel.

As a bare minimum, look for knives that are forged rather than stamped. Stamped steel will have a uniform thickness from spine to cutting edge, while forged knives are more carefully shaped for better performance. Forged knives also tend to be better balanced and have harder blades that retain their edge longer.

Your preference in knife is likely going to fall into one of four camps.

WESTERN-STYLE CHEF'S KNIFE

A traditional Western-style chef's knife is an all-purpose knife that has a curved blade designed to allow you to hold your free hand on the top edge of the knife and rock the knife back and forth as you cut. It typically has a relatively thick spine compared to its blade length. These are heavy knives that are great for splitting hard vegetables like squashes or for hacking apart chicken carcasses.

RECOMMENDATION:

- → **My Choice:** Wüsthof Classic 8- or 10-inch chef's knife (about $150)
- → **Best Bang for the Buck:** MAC HB-85 French Chef's Knife (about $70)
- → **Best Budget Knife:** Mercer Culinary Genesis (about $30)

SANTOKU

Santoku knives are the everyday multipurpose knife of Japan. They have blades with either a very gently curving cutting edge or no curve at all. They are designed for more of an up-and-down chopping motion, rather than rocking. They also tend to have thinner, shorter blades than their Western counterparts. Many cooks with smaller hands or who like to feel a little more precision in their knifework prefer santoku knives.

RECOMMENDATION:

- → **My Choice:** Misono UX-10 santoku (about $190)
- → **Best Bang for the Buck:** Tojiro DP 6.7-inch santoku (about $70)
- → **Best Budget Knife:** Mercer Culinary Asian Collection santoku (about $25)

GYUTOU

Gyutou knives are an East-West hybrid that have become increasingly popular among chefs and home cooks. They typically have the length of a Western chef's knife but have a shallower curve and a far thinner, lighter blade. These types of knives are my personal

Got an Electric or Induction Burner? You Can Still Stir-Fry!

For the longest time I didn't think stir-frying was possible on an electric burner, but it is, and in some cases it can even be easier than working with a gas range. You just need to make a few adjustments.

The key difference between electric and gas ranges is that gas ranges have flames that shoot up, heating the wok even if it is not in direct contact with the burner. This means that even while you are shaking and tossing your food, the wok is getting essentially the same amount of heat input as if it were sitting still. An electric or induction range requires direct contact for heating. This means that the wok needs to sit relatively still and flat against the burner for it to have any effect.

Practically, this means for electric or induction cooktops you'll want to cook in even smaller batches—as little as, say, a quarter pound of meat at a time. This is not a problem. It just means your stir-fry will take a little bit longer. Get the wok smoking hot, cook the batch of meat, transfer it to a bowl, wipe out the wok, and repeat until all your meat is seared and in the bowl. Next, do the same for all your vegetables. Finally, heat up the wok again, stir-fry your aromatics, add the meat and vegetables back to the pan along with your sauce, toss to coat and to reduce a bit, and you're good to go.

The other simple solution is to purchase an inexpensive portable gas range. You can find many models that run off butane canisters online or at any Asian supermarket. I'm partial to the 15,000-BTU/hr Iwatani ZA-3HP burner (available online) for its high output and sturdy design. I'm not going to come out and tell you that it's perfectly safe to use them indoors on your kitchen counter, but I'm also not going to come into your home and stop you if you decide to do it. Just make sure you have good clearance around the flame and canister and keep your fire extinguisher handy (a good idea no matter what kind of stir-frying you're doing).

preference, offering a good compromise; they're nearly as precise as a santoku, as long and nearly as powerful as a Western knife, and have the ability to perform both chopping and rocking motions.

RECOMMENDATION:

- → **My Choice:** KAN Core chef's knife (about $140)
- → **Best Bang for the Buck:** Tojiro DP 8.2-inch gyutou (about $80)
- → **Best Budget Knife:** There are not many very cheap gyutou-style knives.

CHINESE CLEAVER

Chinese cleavers are the chef's knives of China. Thinner and lighter than a bulky Western-style cleaver designed to hack through bones, Chinese cleavers have a rectangular shape with a very gently curved cutting edge and a height that can extend to several inches, giving you plenty of knuckle clearance. They take a lot of getting used to if you've never used one. As with a santoku, they're used with a chopping or slicing motion, as opposed to rocking. Their height and wide surface offer a few advantages. They are excellent for smashing ingredients like garlic or ginger before chopping and for transferring prepared ingredients from one place to another.

RECOMMENDATION:

- → You're unlikely to find Chinese-style cleavers at Western cookware stores, but If you've got a good Asian knife shop or a Chinatown nearby, take a look and shop around until you find something that fits you comfortably. I use a Shibazi 9-inch stainless steel Chinese chef's knife, which you can find online for around $40.

A Rice Cooker or Multicooker

There's a reason you'll find big rice cookers in nearly every Japanese or Chinese restaurant and countertop models in Asian kitchens. They're inexpensive and really good at cooking rice. Sure, it's relatively easy to cook rice on the stovetop, but the rice cooker does it perfectly, consistently, and inexpensively at the touch of a button. If you eat rice a few times a week, a rice cooker (or, better yet, an electric countertop multicooker like an Instant Pot) is a worthwhile investment. (See "The Best Way to Cook Rice or, How I Learned to Stop Worrying and Love the Rice Cooker," page 226.)

Stocking a Wok-Friendly Pantry

Many Asian recipes and techniques rely on a large number of seasoning sauces, pastes, pickles, and spices, to add complexity and depth to even the fastest of recipes. There's no way around it: if you're new to Asian cooking, you're gonna have to stock up your pantry. This section covers the ingredients I use most.

The first time you decide to fire up the wok you may have some sticker shock from the number of bottles and sauces you need for even a very basic stir-fry. The good news is that individually most of these ingredients are cheap, and nearly all of them last for a *long* time. With proper storage most will last years without a big loss in quality. Hit an Asian market (or an online source) once to load up and you'll be good to go for

quite a while. If you just want to dip your feet in, your best bet is to browse the chapters, find some recipes that speak to you, and start from there.

In this section I've labeled all of the pantry ingredients as *beginner* (i.e., you'll use them all the time), *intermediate* (nice to have for certain dishes), or *advanced* (used in only very specific cases).

SOY SAUCES

Soy sauce is the staple seasoning of most East Asian countries, and it has been for several thousand years. It's made by inoculating a cooked mixture of soybeans and wheat with *koji* (the Japanese name for the numerous molds of the genus *Aspergillus*), allowing it to incubate, then fermenting it further in a wet brine. The koji breaks down starches into simple sugars and proteins into amino acids, while lactic fermentation in the salt brine further transforms those sugars into lactic acid. The resulting dark brown sludge is pressed to remove solids, and a thin, salty, deeply flavorful dark sauce is the result. High-quality sauces are typically aged after brewing, while more inexpensive sauces may be bottled immediately for sale. The cheapest products sold as soy sauce at the supermarket, such as La Choy brand, are made with hydrolyzed soy protein, corn syrup, and artificial colors. Their flavor only loosely resembles the real deal. I avoid them.

Check the ingredients list, and if it contains any of those, leave it on the shelf. If your bottle says "naturally brewed," you're in good shape.

Japanese soy sauce is made with a mixture of soy and grain, which gives it a thinner texture and sweeter flavor than Chinese sauces. Japanese soy sauce *(shoyu)* comes in two main varieties—*koikuchi* (dark) and *usukuchi* (light). Chinese soy sauces also come in dark and light varieties, but light Chinese soy sauce is more similar in flavor and color to koikuchi sauce than usukuchi (more detail below). For everyday use, I keep a jug of Kikkoman in my fridge, refilling a smaller squeeze bottle as needed, as well as a bottle of Pearl River brand Chinese dark soy sauce.

Once opened, soy sauce can be stored in a cool, dark cabinet for several months or in the fridge for a year or more. It will eventually start to develop unpleasant fishy aromas. Of the varieties of soy sauce listed below, all have some uses, but one bottle of koikuchi shoyu and one bottle of Chinese dark soy sauce will keep you well equipped for nearly any situation.

Usukuchi shoyu (Japan) is useful for when you want to season vegetables or fish without giving them a distinct dark color, but I use it at home only for a few specific uses, such as over cold tofu or in tamago-kake gohan (page 230). It tends to be quite salty and, due to the addition of mirin (a sweet rice wine, see page 20), acidic.

→ **How important is it?** Advanced
→ **Substitute:** None
→ **Brand recommendation:** Yamasa

Koikuchi shoyu (Japan) is the more common variety, and even though it appears darker and thicker, it actually has a lighter flavor than usukuchi soy sauce. It's my Jack-of-all-trades. It can be used in sauces, in marinades, in dips, in stir-fries, or for seasoning soups and broths. I keep a bottle of Kikkoman's All-Purpose in my fridge for cooking and a few fancier bottles for sushi and other situations where soy sauce is the only seasoning.

That bottle, by the way, doesn't say *koikuchi* on it; unless a bottle is specifically labeled *usukuchi*, it's most likely a koikuchi.

→ **How important is it?** Essential
→ **Substitutes:** Chinese light soy sauce or tamari
→ **Brand recommendation:** Kikkoman

Tamari (Japan) is another type of Japanese soy sauce typically made with 100 percent soybeans (or close to it). It has a harsher flavor than shoyu but can be used in place of shoyu for folks with wheat sensitivity. (Check the bottle; some tamari actually contains wheat.)

→ **How important is it?** Essential only for gluten-free cooking
→ **Substitutes:** Koikuchi shoyu or Chinese light soy sauce
→ **Brand recommendation:** San-J

Chinese Light Soy Sauce

Also known as "thin" or "fresh" soy sauce, Chinese light soy sauce is made very similarly to Japanese koikuchi sauces, though often with a lower proportion of wheat. And here's where naming conventions between Japanese and Chinese sauces can get a little confusing. What's labeled "light" soy sauce in the Chinese aisle is more similar to Japanese dark soy sauce (koikuchi) than it is to Japanese light soy sauce (usukuchi). It's the most common sauce for traditional Chinese stir-fries (but you can use shoyu instead).

→ **How important is it?** Intermediate
→ **Substitutes:** Koikuchi shoyu or tamari
→ **Brand recommendation:** Pearl River Bridge

Chinese Dark Soy Sauce

Chinese dark soy sauce is thicker, sweeter, less salty, and, well, darker than light soy sauce. It frequently contains added molasses or caramel coloring to give it its distinct dark color. Tasted raw, it's not particularly pleasant or interesting, but the flavor develops through cooking. Rather than dipping, Chinese dark soy sauce is primarily used for braising or stir-frying.

→ **How important is it?** Essential
→ **Substitute:** None
→ **Brand recommendation:** Pearl River Bridge

Kecap Manis (Indonesia)

Kecap is the Indonesian term for any kind of fermented sauce (and, of Malay origin, is thought to be the source of both the word and the sauce *ketchup* in the West). Kecap manis is the most common form of soy sauce in Indonesia, used in stir-fries like *bami* or *nasi goreng* (fried noodles and rice, respectively) and in stews like *babi kecap* (soy-sauce-braised pork). It's got a thick, syrupy texture and a sweet complex flavor due to the addition of palm sugar and spices

If you can't find it, you can make it yourself quite easily (see the recipe on page 291).

→ **How important is it?** Advanced
→ **Substitute:** Homemade (page 291)
→ **Brand Recommendation:** ABC Indonesian Sweet Soy Sauce

OTHER SAUCES AND PASTES

Oyster Sauce

A thick, slightly sweet sauce made with oyster extract. It has a rich, savory complexity. If you've seen Lee Kum Kee brand products on the supermarket shelf, this is what put them on the map. It was invented in 1888 by the founder of the company, Lee Kum Sheung, apocryphally when he accidentally left a pot of oysters simmering over a burner until it reduced to a rich gravy. It's used widely in Chinese and Thai cuisine, as well as in Vietnam and Malaysia. These days Lee Kum Kee has two grades. The red bottle with a panda on it is made with oyster extract and other flavorings, while the blue bottle with the picture of two boys on a fishing boat labeled "Premium Oyster Sauce" is made the traditional way, with more oyster flavor.

There are many other brands of oyster sauce. So long as oyster extract is listed among the first ingredients, any brand should do fine for the recipes in this book.

Because oysters are so rich in glutamates and inosinates, the family of compounds responsible for umami flavor, it's used to bring out the savoriness of a wide range of dishes, from stir-fried fish (page 137) to steamed or stir-fried green vegetables (pages 205 and 206), or in Chinese American cashew chicken (page 492).

→ **How important is it?** Essential
→ **Substitute:** None
→ **Brand Recommendation:** Lee Kum Kee

Doubanjiang (Sichuan Broad Bean Chile Sauce)

Doubanjiang, or fermented broad bean chile sauce, is an essential sauce in Sichuan cuisine. It's a very salty sauce made with fermented broad beans, soybeans, rice, and chiles (some varieties do not include chiles, but I've never seen a chile-free version sold in the United States). It's the backbone of dishes like mapo tofu (page 598) and *shui zhu niu rou* (Water-Boiled Beef, page 601). It also makes for a quick and easy addition to plain noodles (try stirring a bit into your instant ramen), rice, or tofu. Compared to other jarred sauces, it's extremely salty and powerfully flavored. A little bit goes a long way.

There is a huge difference in quality between the best versions of this sauce, which are made in Pixian, and mass-market ones such as Lee Kum Kee's version. The former is dark red and oily, with whole fermented broad beans and a deep roasty chile flavor, while the latter tend to be more wet and paste-like and will not fry or stain your stir-fry oil red properly. This is the only essential pantry ingredient that you will most likely have to order online. But it's inexpensive and lasts forever in the fridge.

You'll probably come across products with the label "China Time-Honored Brand" on them, which is similar to European traditional product denotations, indicating that it is produced using a stringent set of traditional standards. According to Chris Liang of

Mala Foods, in the case of doubanjiang, that includes the types of chiles (*er jing tiao*, harvested from July to the fifteenth day of lunar autumn), the types of beans (broad beans fermented for at least six months and over a summer), and the period of secondary fermentation (at least three months).

→ **How important is it?** Essential
→ **Substitute:** None
→ **Brand Recommendations:** Juan Cheng Pixian Doubanjiang (A "China Time-Honored Brand"), Dan, or any brand made in Pixian

Hoisin Sauce

One of many sauces based on fermented soybeans, it has a sweet and salty flavor, similar to American-style barbecue sauce. It can be used just like barbecue sauce by painting it onto pork ribs or shoulder toward the end of cooking, though its range of uses goes far beyond roasted meats. It's commonly served with Peking duck or with Moo Shu Pork (page 104). In southern Vietnam you might stir some into your bowl of pho. It pairs great with chile oil (try brushing that mix onto the inside of a tortilla before making a quesadilla. Trust me.)

→ **How important is it?** Essential
→ **Substitute:** None
→ **Brand Recommendations:** Lee Kum Kee or Koon Chun

Tianmianjiang (Sweet Fermented Bean Pastes)

Tianmianjiang translates literally as sweet noodle sauce, and you'll find a wide variety of sweet bean pastes in both Chinese and Korean cuisines. Despite the name, sweet bean pastes typically contain more wheat flour than soybeans. They have a sweet-savory flavor with a funky backbone. Think of tianmianjiang as hoisin sauce for experts. You'll see jars labeled "sweet bean paste" and "ground bean paste," and while subtly different in flavor, I typically keep only one in my pantry.

→ **How important is it?** Intermediate
→ **Substitute:** Hoisin sauce
→ **Brand Recommendation:** Koon Chun Bean Sauce

Douchi (Chinese Black Beans and Black Bean Sauce)

Douchi is the funkiest and oldest (archaeologists have found fermented black beans from 165 B.C.!) of the fermented beans. They're made by fermenting a black variety of soybean with salt. The resulting beans are salty, funky, and semimoist, with a soft texture. You can find them sold whole, in roughly ground sauces flavored with garlic, and in smooth sauces. The whole beans are the most versatile, but if you are going to have only one type of fermented black bean, I'd suggest a jar of Lee Kum Kee black bean garlic sauce, which saves you the trouble of chopping the whole beans yourself and can be incorporated as is into stir-fries and other dishes. (Rare is the occasion when I *don't* want garlic in a dish with black beans.)

→ **How important is it?** Intermediate
→ **Substitute:** Dark miso paste, in a real pinch
→ **Brand Recommendations:** Lee Kum Kee for sauce, Koon Chun for whole black beans

Gochujang (Korean Fermented Chile Paste)

Gochujang, with its deep red color, *looks* like it's going to blow your head off with heat, but this popular Korean sauce is actually only moderately spicy. The fermented chiles that go into it are balanced with sweet glutinous rice and powdered fermented black soybeans. It's great in simple dressings for fresh vegetables (try cucumbers with soy sauce and gochujang), and it's an essential flavor in Soondubu Jjigae (Korean tofu soup, page 539), Tteokbokki (rice cakes simmered with gochujang, page 540), and Bibimbap (topped mixed rice, page 246). It's also a great ingredient to have on hand for sauces and marinades, as its smooth texture allows it to incorporate into sauces easily, while lending them body to cling to food.

→ **How important is it?** Essential
→ **Substitute:** None
→ **Brand Recommendations:** Sunchang or Haechandle

Fish Sauce

Fish sauce is the predominant seasoning in Thai, Vietnamese, Cambodian, Lao, Philippine, Malaysian, Indonesian, and Burmese cuisines. It's made by fermenting anchovies with salt, then straining the resultant liquid. In its raw, undiluted form it can smell . . . powerful. But incorporated into dishes, it brings out a level of flavor you never knew existed. It's loaded with umami-rich compounds—even more than soy sauce—which adds savory depth to all kinds of food ranging from condiments to salad dressings, marinades, soups, stews, and stir-fries.

And it's not just useful for Southeast Asian cuisine! I regularly add a bit of fish sauce to any meaty Western-style stew, like beef stew, chili, or even ragù Bolognese (just don't tell your Italian grandmother), where its fishy aroma blends completely into the background. Chili with fish sauce doesn't taste like fish; it just tastes like extra-tasty chili.

- → **How important is it?** Essential
- → **Substitute:** None
- → **Brand Recommendations:** Tiparos, Red Boat, Golden Boy, or Tra Chang, though honestly most any brand will do

Miso

All miso is made through the same basic process. A grain or a pulse—typically soybeans, though barley, rice, millet, rye, and, more recently, chickpeas and quinoa—is ground and fermented with salt and the fungus *Aspergillus oryzae* (*koji* in Japanese). The resulting protein-rich paste has a salty-savory flavor that can range from heavy and funky to light and mildly sweet. Typically, the darker the color of the miso, the higher the proportion of soybeans used and the stronger the flavor. (More on miso on page 240.)

- → **How important is it?** Essential
- → **Substitute:** Korean doenjang
- → **Brand Recommendations:** Eden Foods, Shirakiku, Miso Boom, or Miko

Doenjang (Korean Fermented Soybean Paste)

Similar in appearance and flavor to Japanese dark miso, *doenjang* is a Korean fermented paste made from 100 percent soybeans. On its own it can be used in marinades and soup bases, but you'll most frequently see it combined with gochujang, garlic, sesame oil, sugar, and scallions to make the sauce *ssamjang*, the sauce that you've probably dabbed onto the leafy greens you eat with Korean barbecue.

- → **How important is it?** Advanced
- → **Substitute:** Miso paste
- → **Brand Recommendations:** Sunchang or Haechandle

Sambal Oelek (Indonesian Chile Sauce)

Traditional Indonesian sambals are similar to Thai nam prik: thick, relish-like condiments made in a mortar and pestle. The simplest are made with chiles and salt, though they can become far more complex with other ingredients like garlic, ginger, and shrimp paste. The California-based Huy Fong (yes, the same company with the green rooster logo that makes the ubiquitous sriracha) makes a version that is fresh, spicy, and great as a table condiment. I use it as a table condiment to add fresh heat to a wide variety of dishes, from noodles and stir-fries to Western dishes like fried eggs or grits.

- → **How important is it?** N/A. I use it as a condiment, not for cooking
- → **Substitute:** Any bright, chunky, chile-forward hot sauce you like
- → **Brand Recommendation:** Huy Fong

Roasted Sesame Paste

A thick paste made from toasted sesame seeds that is widely used in sauces, salads, noodles, and dips. Like fresh peanut or almond butter, it splits as it sits, so you need to give it a good stir before using (and if you let it sit *too* long, you'll really have to work at scraping up the bottom of the jar). Tahini is a very similar Middle Eastern/Western Mediterranean condiment that is typically made with fresh, not roasted, sesame seeds. The Chinese stuff has a stronger, nuttier aroma and flavor, but tahini works just fine if it's all you can find (especially if you fry the tahini first; see page 320)

- → **How important is it?** Intermediate
- → **Substitutes:** Tah**ini or** fried tahini
- → **Brand Recommendation:** Huy Fong

Tamarind

Tamarind is an intensely sour tropical fruit that is cultivated around the world. If you've ever tasted the sweet-sour brown chutney commonly found at the Indian lunch buffet, you know it. It's one of the essential flavors of Pad Thai (page 378) and is used in drinks and sauces throughout Latin America.

You'll find tamarind sold in whole fruit, fruit pulp, paste, and concentrate. Any of those forms will work. (Follow instructions on jars of concentrate for dilution before using.) Whole fruits should have their hard, dry outer husk removed before the sticky, pulpy interior is used. Tamarind paste is easy to make at home by placing tamarind fruit pulp in a bowl with a roughly equal volume of warm water and working it with your fingers until it forms a thick paste. Push this paste through a fine-mesh strainer with a spatula and it's recipe-ready. (See page 381 for step-by-step instructions.)

- → **How important is it?** Intermediate
- → **Substitute:** None
- → **Brand Recommendation:** Me Chua

Shrimp Paste

Fermented shrimp paste is commonly used in curries, sauces, soups, marinades, and dips like nam prik or sambal. Like fish sauce, it has a pungent, fishy aroma. Unlike in fish sauce, the fermented shrimp are ground, not strained, which gives the finished paste a grainy texture and very powerful aroma that sticks around even in finished dishes. It's what gives Malaysian fried chicken its distinct flavor and aroma. It adds layers of flavor to some versions of satay.

In the markets I've seen in the United States, it's generally sold labeled *belacan* or *kapi*, the Malay and Thai words for shrimp paste, respectively.

- → **How important is it?** Advanced
- → **Substitute:** None
- → **Brand Recommendations:** Tra Chang and Old Man make powerful versions. Lee Kum Kee makes a milder version that is better if you have an aversion to strong fishy aromas.

VINEGARS

Acid! Where would we be without acid! Nine out of ten chemists and chefs agree: acid is essential. Like salt, sugar, umami, bitterness, and spiciness, acid is sensed directly in your mouth and on your tongue. But it's also unique: most acidic foods give off vapors that tickle our noses, perking them up and helping boost our reception of other aromas. Ever notice how that vinegary whiff of buffalo sauce or the swirl of vinegar in your hot and sour soup immediately gets your saliva flowing? Even thinking about a bag of salt and vinegar potato chips will do it (your mouth is watering right now, isn't it?). Acid helps to balance out richness, making dishes taste lighter and more palatable. And of course most culinary acids, whether made from fruits, wine, or grains, also bring a host of flavors with them. Finishing vinegars made with infusions or by aging in wooden barrels can add more layers of complexity.

Next to salt, acid is the most important element when seasoning food. But seasoning with acid works in a fundamentally different way. The right amount of salt to add to a dish generally fits within a pretty narrow window. Most people find around 1 to 1.5 percent by weight to be the most palatable range (in restaurants, especially those that want to sell you more beverages, you're more likely getting food pushing into the 2 percent salt range). Acidity, on the other hand, can vary wildly. Some foods taste great with a ton of acid—the vinegar in Hot and Sour Soup (page 546) or that Chinese American staple, General Tso's Chicken (page 485). Some dishes just need a splash—traditional Kung Pao Chicken (page 61) or the corner of a dumpling (page 405) dipped in black vinegar. Some need no additional acid at all: fried rice (page 268) and Beef Chow Fun (page 368) contain no extra acid other than what comes with the other ingredients.

Acids play an important role in Asian foods in

particular, where all sorts of grains, fruits, and vegetables are fermented into vinegar or other condiments. Properly closed bottles of vinegar can be stored in a cool, dark pantry nearly indefinitely.

Distilled White Vinegar

Distilled white vinegar is typically made from ethanol and is designed to be neutral in flavor. Its main use is to add sharp acidity for preservation or flavor in dishes where a strong aroma or other flavors might compete. It typically has an acidity level of around 5 percent acetic acid.

- → **How important is it?** Intermediate
- → **Substitutes:** White wine or rice vinegar
- → **Brand recommendation:** They're all identical

Rice Vinegar

Many vinegars are made from rice, but when I say "rice vinegar," I'm typically talking about the clear-to-pale-yellow stuff. Like most Asian vinegars, it's not as powerfully acidic-tasting as most Western vinegars and is diluted to a lower overall acetic acid content than most Western vinegars (about 3.5 percent versus 5 percent). I typically use Marukan, an inexpensive Japanese brand with decent flavor. Several Chinese brands are also widely available in the states.

One thing: be careful what you pick up. "Seasoned rice vinegar" is an entirely different product, which has had sugar, salt, and seasonings added to it. It's intended to be used as is for seasoning rice for sushi, but it's not really useful in other cooking applications.

- → **How important is it?** Essential
- → **Substitute:** In a big pinch, you can use apple cider vinegar, which has a similarly low-acid, slightly sweet flavor.
- → **Brand recommendation:** Marukan

Black Vinegar

This is hands down my favorite vinegar. Black vinegar is a class of vinegars made in China that are mildly acidic, highly aromatic and fruity, and very dark in color (like soy sauce). My favorite type of black vinegar is

The pH Scale

Acidity is measured on the pH scale, which typically ranges from 1 (most acidic) to 14 (most alkaline).* A pH of 7 is considered neutral. pH is measured on a logarithmic rather than linear scale. That is, a liquid with a pH of 4 will be 10 times more acidic than a liquid with a pH of 5. When experimenting in the kitchen, check the pH of your added liquids, especially if you plan to use them in a marinade. If it's anywhere below about 4 to 4.5, it's a good idea to dilute it well or to not let your meat marinate for more than half an hour or so.

INGREDIENT	Average pH (lower pH = higher acidity)
Lime juice	2.1
Lemon juice	2.2
Distilled white vinegar*	2.4
Rice vinegar*	2.6
Verjus	2.6
White wine vinegar*	2.7
Red wine vinegar*	2.7
Cider vinegar*	3.4
Honey	3.9
Balsamic vinegar	4
Chinese black vinegar	4
Chinkiang vinegar	4
Whiskey	4
Dry sherry	4
Shaoxing wine	4.2
Sake	4.2
Beer	4.3
Molasses	5
Water	7

* For a 5% acetic acid solution, which is the typical bottling dilution level of these vinegars

---

* If you *really* want to nerd out, pH is approximately the negative of the base 10 logarithm of hydronium ions (H_3O+) in a liquid. Technically, this value can range from about 10 moles per liter (a mole is a number equivalent to roughly 6×10^{23}, or 600,000,000,000,000,000,000,000) down to 10^{-15} moles, which means that on the extreme edge cases, the pH scale actually ranges from –1 to about 15. Hydrochloric (muriatic) acid, for instance, can have a pH of below zero, while that gel you pour into clogged drains to clear them can have a pH of 14 or above. Hydrochloric acid is about a quadrillion times more acidic than Drano!

Chinkiang vinegar, which originated in coastal Jiangsu province just north of Shanghai. It makes a wonderful dipping sauce for all manner of dim sum, it's the sour in your Hot and Sour Soup (page 546), and it brightens up countless stir-fries, soups, and stews. Because of its long aging process and the flavor from the gradual addition of rice hulls, it achieves a complex, almost balsamic-like flavor.

You can easily find it at Chinese grocers or on online retailers.

→ **How important is it?** Intermediate, but once you taste it you'll want it on everything
→ **Substitute:** Equal parts balsamic vinegar, red wine vinegar, and water
→ **Brand recommendations:** Soeos or Gold Plum

FATS AND OILS

As with most foods, heat, light, and air are the enemies of oil and can cause it to turn rancid. A general rule of thumb is that the more flavorful the oil, the more easily it will go bad and the more precaution you should take while storing it. To cut down on costs and improve shelf life, I buy most of my oils in large tins or tinted plastic bottles and store them in a cool, dark cabinet. For use, I use a funnel to fill (and refill) a set of dark tinted glass bottles of varying sizes fitted with pour spouts. The oils I use most go in emptied and cleaned green wine bottles, while the oils I use less frequently go in the smaller bottles I bought online.

After that I do something shocking: I store the bottles I use most on the countertop next to my stove. I know I shouldn't. I'm pretty sure I've even told people not to. But hear me out. While it's true that the heat from the stove can prematurely cause oil stored nearby to turn rancid, it still takes weeks for this to happen, which is typically more than enough time for me to finish and replenish a stock. In the five years I've been doing this regularly, I've only once had to throw out some canola oil that had become rancid. It's a small price to pay for years of convenience. Just don't put them straight *on* the burner or in the path of rising heat and vapors, OK?

Stir-Fry/Deep-Fry Oil

Stir-fries require oil that can be heated to a high temperature without breaking down too much. Canola, grapeseed, rice bran, and safflower are widely available and work great for stir-fries. Deep frying works better with an oil with a relatively high saturated fat content (which improves crisping). I use peanut or soybean oil, though sometimes I'll use more inexpensive canola oil for deep frying. See "The Best Oil for Stir-Frying," page 45, for more details on exactly why.

→ **How important is it?** Essential.
→ **Substitutes:** Any neutral high-temperature frying oil, such as vegetable or avocado
→ **Brand Recommendation:** Any

Roasted Sesame Oil

This oil, made from roasted sesame seeds, is an essential flavoring in many Chinese, Korean, and Japanese dishes. It can be used to add aroma to finished soups and sauces, it can flavor dumpling fillings, it's used to season stir-fries or marinate meats, and it can be used in dressings. Roasted sesame oil tends to be very prone to rancidity, so I keep a sealed tin in the pantry and use it to refill a small plastic squeeze bottle that I keep in the fridge.

→ **How important is it?** Essential
→ **Substitute:** None
→ **Brand Recommendation:** Kadoya

Caiziyou (Roasted Rapeseed Oil)

Caiziyou is an oil expressed from cultivars of the same plant (rapeseed) used to produce canola oil. Unlike canola oil, which has a neutral flavor, caiziyou has a rich, nutty, toasted aroma that reminds me of roasted barley with a hint of mustard. It's the cooking oil of choice in Sichuan, and, if you've ever thought that your chile oil or mapo tofu is lacking a certain flavor you get only at your favorite Sichuanese restaurant, caiziyou is most likely the answer. Unfortunately, it's also very difficult to find in the United States. I've discovered it at one Chinese mega-mart in Seattle (Asian Family Market), but nowhere else, including in New York and San Francisco. You can order it online via Mala Market, though it can be a little pricey.

The other problem is it can be tough to identify, as it's typically simply labeled "canola oil" or "rapeseed oil." Visually, caiziyou will have a much darker brownish yellow color than standard canola oil, which is how I identify it at the market.

If you cannot find caiziyou, peanut oil will work in its place, but it will not have quite the same flavor properties.

→ **How important is it?** Intermediate
→ **Substitutes:** A combination of canola and Indian mustard seed oil, or peanut oil
→ **Brand Recommendation:** Your selection will be limited, so whatever you can find!

Rayu or Other Simple/Clear Chile Oils

Chile oil is made by infusing a neutral oil with dried chiles. They can range in heat but are typically not insanely spicy. Instead they're more about adding a dash of that sweet roasted chile flavor to noodles, soups, and dipping sauce. *Rayu* is the Japanese version, and it comes in small bottles with a push-top designed for dispensing drops of oil over ramen. You can also find Chinese brands in larger bottles, with or without chile sediment.

Clear chile oil can be stored in a cool, dark pantry if you use it within about a year, or in the fridge otherwise. Chile oil with sediment should be stored in the fridge after being opened.

→ **How important is it?** Intermediate
→ **Substitute:** The clear oil from the top of a batch of Sichuan Málà Chile Oil (page 310).
→ **Brand Recommendation:** S&B La-Yu

Crispy Chile Oils

There is a wide range of crispy chile oils—that is, unstrained chile oil with a large volume of chile and other aromatic debris left in the bottle—from mild Japanese varieties to hotter Chinese oils.

Remember when people were putting Huy Fong sriracha on everything? I sure remember. Thankfully those days are over and we've now started spooning

Sichuan spicy chile crisp—specifically Lao Gan Ma brand—on everything. I'm appreciative of the upgrade (though I still question why we collectively must have *one sauce* to rule them all). Lao Gan Ma has a few more ingredients than typical crispy chile oils, including peanuts and citrusy Sichuan peppercorns.

At the table I use it in noodle dishes and soups, on dumplings and other dim sum, and on fried rice and other stir-fries. It's even great on vanilla ice cream (really).

The one big drawback of some of the prebottled stuff is shelf life. On more than one occasion I've opened brand-new bottles of Lao Gan Ma to reveal fishy-smelling rancid oil inside. After opening, it should be stored sealed in the refrigerator between uses.

→ **How important is it?** Intermediate
→ **Substitutes:** Sichuan Málà Chile Oil (page 310)
→ **Brand recommendations:** Momoya Chili Oil with Fried Garlic for mild, Lao Gan Ma Spicy Chili Crisp for hot, and Mom's Málà for Sichuan-style hot and numbing flavors.

Sichuan Pepper Oil

Sichuan peppercorns are the hull of the fruit of the prickly ash. It lends its citrusy aroma and mouth-numbing properties to many northern Chinese dishes. While Sichuan pepper oil is not a substitute for actual seeds, it does a nice job of adding a quick hit of aroma and numbingness to a stir-fry or dip without the need to pick through and grind fresh Sichuan peppercorn. Think of it as a cheaty route to *málà* (hot and numbing) dishes. You can buy it in most Asian supermarkets as well as online. Store the bottle in the fridge or a dark, cool pantry between uses.

→ **How important is it?** Advanced
→ **Brand recommendations:** Soeos or Li Hong

BOOZE

As in many European cuisines, various types of wine and other alcoholic fermented products are widely used in marinades, sauces, braises, and soups. When added to dishes during cooking, booze can add an extra layer of flavor and a bit of acidity that enhances the existing flavors in a dish. Alcohol is also useful for drawing out flavors from fat-soluble compounds that wouldn't otherwise be drawn out by water and water-based liquids like stock. (See the sidebar "Alcohol, Fat, and Water" on page 21 for some high school chemistry.)

Shaoxing Wine

Shaoxing wine is an amber-colored type of *huang-jiu*—fermented rice wine—that comes from the city of Shaoxing in eastern China. With a light amber color and a sweet, mildly oxidized aroma, it's been mentioned in recorded history for over two thousand years and is nearly ubiquitous in meat-based Chinese dishes. I haven't counted, but I'd take even odds that it's in at least 75 percent of the recipes in this book. It's typically used in small quantities for marinating meat or for adding its fragrant aroma to sauces, but some dishes call for lots of it. Red braised dishes like Taiwanese Braised Short Rib Noodle Soup (page 608) use cups of it. It's readily available in any Asian market, but if you can't find it, a dry sherry, with its oxidized aroma, is what most closely resembles it.

I avoid bottles labeled "cooking wine," as those typically have about 1.5 percent salt added to them, which makes it difficult to manage seasoning in finished dishes, especially if you're going to be reducing the wine (as you often do) and combining it with salty ingredients like soy sauce (as you often do). If it's unavoidable (as it often is), just be aware during final seasoning.

Shaoxing wine can be stored in a cool, dark pantry for six months or longer.

- → **How important is it?** Essential
- → **Substitute**: Dry sherry
- → **Brand recommendations:** Soeos or Li Hong

Sake

Japanese sake is brewed in a manner similar to beer. Soaked grains are heated and converted to sugars, then yeast takes over and converts those sugars to alcohol.

For cooking, as with wine in European cuisine, try to pick a sake that is not too rich, not too sweet, and not too expensive. An inexpensive bottle of Junmai-shu should run you under $10 or so. Ozeki, Sho Chiku Bai, and Gekkeikan are three brands of inexpensive sake that are widely available in the United States and are great for cooking.

Sake should be refrigerated after opening.

- → **How important is it?** Intermediate
- → **Substitutes:** If called for in quantities under a few tablespoons, a dry white wine can be used. In larger quantities, it's harder to duplicate its unique flavor.
- → **Brand recommendations:** Ozeki, Sho Chiku Bai, and Gekkeikan

Mirin

True mirin is a type of rice wine that is higher proof than sake and made with glutinous rice (also known as "sweet rice" or "sticky rice") that has a sweet, almost honey-like flavor. It's also very difficult to find in the United States. But that's OK. Even in Japan, many households use aji-mirin, a product made with sake, corn syrup (or other sweetener), and additional alcohol. Mirin is used extensively in glazes and barbecue sauces. It's what provides sweetness in dishes like teriyaki, grilled eel, or *yakiniku* (grilled meat).

Mirin can be stored in a cool, dark pantry for at least six months. I've had large bottles that have lasted a year or more and are still perfectly fine for cooking.

- → **How important is it?** Intermediate
- → **Substitute:** Place 2 cups of sake and 1 cup of sugar in a small saucepan and heat until the sugar is completely dissolved. Use the same way you'd use mirin.
- → **Brand recommendations:** Kikkoman for aji-mirin, Takara for true mirin if you can find it.

PICKLED AND DRIED INGREDIENTS

Like jarred condiments and sauces, pickled and dried ingredients play an important role in adding quick complexity and flavor to stir-fries, soups, and noodle dishes. Most of these products can easily be ordered online.

Pickles

Zha cai: *Zha cai* are Chinese pickled vegetables, the most famous of which is "Sichuan vegetable," the bulbous root of a mustardy brassica that has been fermented with salt and chiles. It comes from Chongqing (i.e., Chungking), a municipality that, until 1997, was part of neighboring Sichuan province. It's served sliced into thin slivers in dishes like Sichuan Pork and Pickle Soup (page 551), or to top noodle dishes like Dan Dan Noodles (page 317).

In the States, you'll find it sold by weight at better-stocked Chinese supermarkets. It's also sold in markets or online in its whole form in cans or preslivered in foil pouches. The latter format is the most convenient,

Alcohol, Fat, and Water

If you've ever made a salad dressing, seen the sheen of motor oil floating on a puddle, or are familiar with very common metaphors, you know that oil and water don't mix. But what about alcohol? And what does the ability of various liquids to mix have to do with flavor?

To understand this, you first need to understand a few basic principles. Miscibility is the ability of two liquids to mix together and form an even solution. Alcohol and water, for instance, are miscible. Oil and water are not. Shake up a jar of oil and water, let it sit, and eventually the oil and water will separate, forming distinct layers.

But what about alcohol? If alcohol and water weren't miscible, every bottle of 80-proof booze would end up with all the alcohol at the top and all the water at the bottom. But alcohol and fat can *also* be miscible, depending on the concentration of alcohol and the temperature of the solution. In general, the higher the alcohol content, the more easily oil will mix with it and the longer it will take for that oil to separate.

This all has to do with the polarity of a molecule, that is, the relative charge at either end of it. Molecules that are strongly polar tend to mix well with other molecules that are strongly polar, while those that are neutral mix well with other neutral molecules. Water molecules are highly polar, while oil is nonpolar. Ethanol is an amphipathic molecule, which means that it has a section that's polar and a section that's nonpolar. This allows it to mix to some degree with both water and fat.

If you're water, and that kid in college you never saw eye to eye with is fat (no, not that kind of fat), then alcohol is the stuff that might bridge the gap between you. And, just like in college, the exact degree to which fat will mix into a water/alcohol mixture is related to the alcohol content. The more alcohol, the better things mix.

So what does all this mean for cooking? It's true that the vast majority of alcohol will evaporate during the cooking process. There is always going to be at least a small amount left in the mix (assuming you don't cook it until all the water is also driven off), but this tiny amount is not really enough to help fat mix in. However, because ethanol (the type of alcohol in your wine or whiskey*) is less polar than water, some aromatic compounds that are fat-soluble can also be dissolved in alcohol. Adding alcohol to a marinade or to the liquid in a pot as a dish simmers can help draw out more of these fat-soluble compounds, making them more readily available for your nose and tongue to smell and taste.

All this stuff is only mildly applicable to day-to-day cooking, but it sure is fun to know. And if I learned anything from G.I. Joe, it's that most problems end with a fight, and that knowing is half the battle.

---

* But maybe not in your moonshine. Poorly made moonshine will contain some methanol, the stuff that can make you go blind. I once spent an evening drinking moonshine with some locals in northern Bali, which they gave to me on the condition that I play "Hotel California" on their guitar. Apparently that's the first song they associate with Americans. I did, and we drank. It was only the next day that I read about the British tourist who had gone blind doing the exact same thing (the booze, not the Eagles) a few months earlier. I can still see, and I hope that those guys still remember the lyrics, because nobody in the United States *ever* remembers all the lyrics. Try it right now. See what I mean?

Sidebar

as the packets last forever while sealed and are small enough to easily use up after opening. I buy them online ten packets at a time.

- → **How important is it?** Intermediate
- → **Substitutes:** Hot marinated olives from the bulk olive section at the supermarket or mild olives like pitted Cerignola or even canned black olives seasoned with a little chile oil.
- → **Brand recommendation:** Chongqing Fulin Zha Cai

Ya cai: Ya cai is the pickled stem of a mustard plant from Sichuan. It's similar to zha cai but has a stronger aroma. If you've had it in the States, it was most likely as an ingredient in Sichuan dry-fried string beans (page 181), where it adds a pleasant crunchy texture and pungent flavor. It's also commonly used as a noodle topping.

- → **How important is it?** Advanced
- → **Substitutes:** Zha cai or oil-cured olives from the bulk olive section at the supermarket, or a mix of finely minced sauerkraut or kimchi and finely minced capers
- → **Brand recommendation:** Yi Bin Sui Mi Ya Cai

Pickled Chiles, with or without Garlic: Hot pickled Thai bird or Sichuan heaven-facing chiles in vinegar are great for adding a quick, bright punch of heat to soups, stir-fries, and noodles. I use them in my Sichuan-Style Fish-Fragrant Eggplant (page 191) or to add heat at the table to Pad See Ew (Thai-style stir-fried wide rice noodles, page 372) and Chicken and Ginger Soup with Rice Cakes (page 544). You can find them on Chinese and Thai supermarket shelves, but they're very easy to make yourself if you have access to fresh hot chiles (even serrano or jalapeño will work). It takes all of five minutes.

- → **How important is it?** Intermediate
- → **Substitute:** Homemade pickled chiles (page 84)
- → **Brand recommendation:** Cock Brand

Dry Aromatics

Although there are plenty of dishes you can make without any dried spices or other dry pantry goods, they do make their way into many recipes, particularly noodles, soups, curries, and northern Chinese dishes. I buy my dried spices in bulk either online or from local spice shops, where you can get better deals (and fresher spices) than the little bottles you find at the supermarket. With few exceptions, I buy all my spices whole rather than ground. Whole spices retain their flavor much longer. Toasting spices whole also develops more complex

Do I Really Need to Toast My Spices?

Short answer: no. Even without toasting, so long as your spices are fresh, have been stored properly, and are ground just before use, they're going to pack plenty of flavor. On the other hand, if you want to really maximize complexity and aroma, toasting spices whole before grinding will do that for you. To toast spices, place them in a dry skillet over moderate heat and cook them, stirring and shaking the pan frequently, until you can start to smell them. This should take a minute or two. Once they're aromatic, keep going for 30 seconds or so, then transfer them from the skillet to your mortar and pestle and grind away.

In some dishes, like Stir-Fried New Potatoes with Hot and Numbing Spices (page 184), ground spices are added directly to the dish just before finishing. In others, like Kung Pao Chicken (page 61), spices and aromatics are bloomed in hot oil before the remaining stir-fry ingredients are added. In still others, such as Mapo Tofu (page 598) or Chongqing-Style Dry-Fried Chicken (page 441), you'll toast whole spices in oil, strain and discard them after they've given their flavor to the oil, then reinforce that flavor with more ground spices added during the final stages of cooking.

and varied flavor than trying to toast ground spices, which, due to their high surface-area-to-volume ratio, can quickly lose their aroma. Whole spices also have a much longer shelf life than ground spices. Properly stored in sealed containers in a cool, dark pantry, most spices will retain their flavor for a year or more.

Not sure if your spices are too old? Just use your nose. If they don't smell like anything in the bottle, they aren't going to add anything to your food.

Q *What spices and nuts do I need?*

A Dry spices play an important role in a wide variety of Asian cuisines, particularly those of northern Thailand and Laos, and in northern Chinese dishes, many of which were heavily influenced by Indian and Middle Eastern cuisines through their position at the end of the Silk Road trade route. Most spices and dried goods I use in this book are easy to find. Here are some of the basics that you can easily find at Western supermarkets or spice vendors:

→ Bay Leaves
→ Cardamom
→ Coriander seeds
→ Cumin
→ Cloves
→ Cinnamon
→ Fennel
→ Roasted Peanuts
→ White peppercorns
→ Black peppercorns
→ Pine nuts
→ Roasted or raw sesame seeds
→ Ground turmeric

Some other dried goods can be a little harder to source. Here are some of the more esoteric dried spices and seeds I'll frequently call for in this book.

Sichuan Science: What Makes Sichuan Peppercorns Tingle?

Unlike other types of pepper, Sichuan peppercorns have no real heat to speak of. Rather, they produce a numbing sensation known as *paresthesia*. How does this work? Well, Sichuan peppercorns are high in a chemical called *hydroxy-alpha-sanshool*, which seems to stimulate the Meissner receptors in our lips, mouths, and tongues. Meissner receptors are not taste buds. They are actually nerve endings found all over the body that are responsible for perceiving light touches. A study at the University of London had subjects tasting Sichuan peppercorns, then holding a vibrating rod against their lips, adjusting the frequency of vibrations until it felt the same as Sichuan peppercorns. They found that subjects consistently set the vibrations at around 50 Hertz (50 cycles per second).

In other words, tasting a Sichuan peppercorn has the same effect as rapidly vibrating your lips and tongue at a frequency roughly the same as an A-flat three octaves below middle C.

So why does that produce a numbing sensation? For the same reason that the sting of a hard slap can reduce the itchiness of a mosquito bite: when powerfully stimulated, or stimulated for a long period of time, our nerves tend to ignore weaker stimulations.

Sichuan Peppercorns

For many years, Sichuan peppercorns were banned for import to the United States due to the fear of citrus canker, a bacterial infestation that can harm the foliage of many trees and crops. Although officially banned since 1968, it was only loosely enforced in its later years and completely lifted in 2005. I remember the first time I tasted a dish made with them. It was mid-1999 at New Taste of Sichuan, and the dish was mapo tofu. A dish I grew up loving but didn't truly understand until I tasted the Sichuan-peppercorn-laced version. It was revelatory. As I ate the tofu, my mouth was hit with an initial wave of heat, something I expected from the fiery red stew. As I ate more, my lips and tongue slowly started tingling, with a unique numbing sensation that tamed some of the spiciness. The alternating feelings of intense heat and total numbness was invigorating and exciting, and I've been addicted ever since.

Sichuan peppercorns are the seeds of the prickly ash tree and have a warm, citrusy aroma. They are not spicy at all but produce the unique numbing, tingling effect on your mouth known as *ma* in Chinese. They are most commonly combined with hot chiles to produce a flavor combination called *málà* ("numbing hot") associated with Sichuan cuisine (see "Málà: Sichuan's Most Famous Flavor Export," page 313, for more details on that). Sichuan peppercorns come in both red and green varieties, with the former being milder and typically used for stir-fries or noodles and the latter being stronger in flavor and used more for soups and braises. The best place to get Sichuan peppercorns I've found is online through sources like the Mala Market (though I've had good luck with pretty much any brand that comes in sealed pouches).

If you're going to stock only one type of Sichuan peppercorn, make it red. Bags of Sichuan peppercorns can vary in quality. The useful part of the peppercorn is the outer husk (the red or green bit). Bags with lots of shiny black seeds or twiggy stems are harder to use—you'll have to carefully pick out those seeds and stems before grinding or blooming; the seeds have an unpleasantly crunchy, almost plastic-like texture.

Japanese cuisine uses a similar prickly ash berry, but Japanese sansho, a common condiment for grilled eel or noodle soups, is far less numbing than its Chinese counterpart.

Star Anise

Star anise is a spice originating from China shaped like an eight-pointed star. It has a licorice-like aroma similar to regular anise but is only distantly related. It's delicious ground and blended with other warm spices like cinnamon, clove, and nutmeg in Western desserts like apple or pumpkin pie. It's one of the essential spices in Chinese five-spice powder, and also flavors red-braised dishes in which hunks of meat are simmered in a spiced mixture of rice wine, sugar, and soy sauce. Outside of the wok, you'll see it used to season fatty Cantonese-style roasted meats like duck or char siu (the red-tinged

roasted pork shoulder you'll find in your steamed buns or sometimes added to soups, vegetables, and other dishes.)

Whole Dried Chiles

There are far too many varieties of dried chiles used throughout Asia to ever hope to remember, and you can easily get away with not being too picky if you don't want to be. As a general rule of thumb, when shopping for dried chiles, the smaller they are, the hotter they'll be. If you want to get more in-depth on chiles, see pages 313–15 for a guide to Sichuan chiles, where to get them, and when to use them.

Whole dried chiles should have a pliant texture. If they crack or split when you bend or poke them, they're past their prime and won't offer your food much more than heat and dusty flavor. The best way to keep dried chiles fresh is to keep them in an airtight freezer bag in the freezer. Stored that way, they'll last for years. Alternatively, store them in tightly sealed glass mason jars in a dark, cool pantry for up to around a year.

Ground Thai Chiles

Ground chiles are an essential ingredient in many Thai dishes. They are powerfully hot and have a flavor that balances bright fruitiness with an almost smoky aroma. They're commonly served as a table condiment for diners to add heat to suit their own taste; in my own house, we keep a small bowl of Thai chile flakes on the dining room table (next to the flaky sea salt and soy sauce) at all times. They're great on pizza, pasta, and soups, too.

Some recipes claim that red pepper flakes are a suitable substitute. They are not. Thai chiles are far fruitier and more fragrant. Ground Thai chiles also tend to be very unevenly ground. This is a good thing. You end up with the powdery bits distributed all around the food, with the larger pieces offering little bursts of heat as you eat. Frankly, I can't think of any decent substitute for Thai ground chile. Luckily, it's readily available online, inexpensive, and lasts a long time when stored in an airtight bag in a dark pantry. Raitip-brand chiles are my go-to.

Palm Sugar

If total authenticity is your goal, you'll need a half dozen different varieties of sugar to make all the dishes in this book. At home I keep only four types: granulated white sugar, brown sugar, Colombian panela (which my Colombian wife would be lost without), and palm sugar. The latter is a staple of Thai, Indonesian, and Malaysian cooking and comes either as a thick, granular paste in tubs or as 1- to 2-inch hemisphere-shaped nuggets in jars. I prefer the hard nuggets, as the paste tends to get firmer and firmer over time, making it hard to scoop out (a quick trip to the microwave helps if paste is all you can find).

Palm sugar is an unrefined raw sugar made by boiling down the sap of various species of palm. Most often it is cut with some amount of cane sugar to reduce production cost. Its flavor is distinctly nutty, with a caramelized aroma similar to dulce de leche or condensed milk. It's the sweet in the sweet-sour-hot flavor combo so popular in Thai cuisine and an essential ingredient in sweet chile sauce (the good stuff, not the stuff you get with your McNuggets or egg rolls) and numerous northern Thai salads, as well as a counterpoint to the heat of Thai curries.

Incidentally, the mortar and pestle is the best way to reduce those disks of palm sugar to a usable soft, moist crumble.

Sesame Seeds

Raw sesame seeds are pale white and bland. Toasted sesame seeds, on the other hand, have a complex peanutty aroma tinged with vanilla that pairs well with a host of other flavors, either whole, lightly crushed in a mortar and pestle or in paste form (which I buy prepasted). I'm a fan of convenience when it doesn't sacrifice quality (who isn't?), so I prefer to buy pretoasted sesame seeds rather than toasting raw seeds myself. (Especially because I've easily forgotten about and burnt more sesame seeds than I've successfully toasted.)

Black sesame seeds have a milder flavor than their white counterpart but make for a gorgeous garnish on finished dishes. I typically keep both black and toasted white sesame seeds on hand. If you can only find raw sesame seeds, you can toast them by stirring them constantly over medium-low heat in a dry wok until they are golden in color. Immediately transfer them to a rimmed baking sheet and spread them out to cool completely before storing in a sealed container in the pantry.

Lily Buds

Lily buds, also sold as "daylilies," "tiger lilies," or "golden needles," are the young, unopened blossoms of the daylily. They're about the thickness and length of a vanilla bean with a golden yellow color. When rehydrated and cooked, they have a mild flavor and pleasantly musky floral aroma (they are, after all, flowers) with a slightly crunchy texture. They're widely available at any Chinese grocer, sold dried in plastic pouches. Look for them near the dried mushrooms and plants. Look for lily buds that are pale yellow in texture and still quite pliable. Pass on dry, cracked, or dark buds. Stored in a sealed pouch in a dark pantry, the flowers should last several years.

Paired with wood ear mushrooms, lily buds are an essential part of both moo shu dishes (page 104) and Hot and Sour Soup (page 546).

Wood Ear Mushrooms

Also known as "Jew's ear" (a corruption of *Judas' ear*), wood ear mushrooms are typically sold dried and need to be rehydrated before use. They have very little flavor or aroma but have a wonderful texture that's simultaneously jellyish and crunchy. They're an essential ingredient in Moo Shu Pork (page 104) and Hot and Sour Soup (page 546), but can also be a great addition to simple stir-fries. The dried mushrooms can be stored in the pantry virtually indefinitely. See page 110 for instructions on how to clean wood ear mushrooms.

Dried Shrimp, Flounder, and Scallops

Dried seafood plays an important role in many coastal and island Asian cuisines. Dried shrimp are a star ingredient of Thai som tam (green papaya salad, page 619). Soaked and chopped, they can be added to soups, stir-fries, or rice.

Dried fish and scallops are rich sources of inosinate and guanosine, two proteins that are found in abundance in seafood, particularly dried seafood, where it gets concentrated. On their own, inosinate and guanosine have no real flavor; they merely act to increase our own perception of savoriness, much like sprinkling your meat with salt will not just make it taste salty but will actually make it taste more like itself.

(There's a reason disodium guanylate—a salt form of guanosine—is used regularly as a flavor enhancer in instant noodles and chips.)

They also enhance the effects of glutamic acid, the amino acid found in things like Parmesan cheese, mushrooms, and ham that give us the saliva-inducing sensation of umami, or savoriness. They're what separate a great

wonton soup from the thin, salty stuff you get at the strip mall (or at least the *bad* strip malls).

Combined with dried ham, garlic, ginger, chiles, and a handful of other glutamate-rich ingredients, they make XO sauce, an insanely savory condiment created in Hong Kong in the 1980s and so-named to capture the cachet of cognac, though it contains none. (See page 303 for more details and a recipe.)

Dried flounder, scallops, and shrimp are available at Asian grocers or online. In some recipes they're difficult to replace, but in brothier settings Japanese kombu (dried sea kelp) will add the umami depth (but not the stronger seafood aromas).

Why Are There So Many Chiles?

Perhaps you've been to a Sichuanese restaurant and ordered dishes packed with fistfuls of crimson red dried chiles. I know when I was younger my thought process in these situations went something like this:

Am I supposed to eat these? Will I out myself as a noob if I ask? Or will I out myself as a noob if I don't ask and do the wrong thing? They seem kinda papery. I don't like eating paper. Will I like eating these? Oh crap, here comes the server, and he already saw me poking at them. Better make a decision fast. Hmm. It is papery. Just look straight ahead and keep chewing. OK. That skin is finally breaking down and … oh man that's hot. Should I ask for water? Will I out myself as a noob if I ask for water? Why didn't I just order the wonton soup, egg rolls, and General Tso's again? At least those dishes won't out me as a noob.

Here's the answer: don't eat those chiles. They are not meant to be eaten. So what's the point of stir-frying an ingredient that nobody is going to eat? The answer is aroma and visual aesthetics. Typically those chiles are toasted lightly in the oil before other ingredients are added, lending the finished dish a sweet, fragrant scent. That scent is important! Our tongues and soft palates detect a range of different flavors, but the vast majority of what

makes a certain food taste of itself lies in its aroma—the molecules of stuff that jump off the food and into our noses.

You can easily test this at home by eating various foods while pinching your nose. Without the help of olfactory sensors, apples and pears taste virtually the same. Heck, even an *onion* and an apple taste remarkably similar when your nose is pinched. In other words, you don't need to eat those chiles to be able to taste them.

The visual appearance of food is also important in our perception. The phrase "you eat with your eyes" is more than just a folksy saying. Foods that look better taste better. This is because taste is not something that is perceived by our mouths and noses alone. It's something that is created in our brain. A whole confluence of sensory input affects it. Foods that are supposed to be crunchy don't taste as good when they're mushy, even if the flavor is exactly the same. Green ketchup tastes worse than red ketchup (do you remember when green and blue ketchup were a thing?). Very few people recognize that green Haribo gummi bears are actually raspberry flavored. (It's true! Take a green gummi bear, close your eyes, and taste it.) Those piles of red chiles may not significantly affect the flavor of our food as perceived on the tongue, but they definitely affect the way our brain interprets those flavors.

Kombu (Giant Sea Kelp)

Kombu, or giant sea kelp, is an essential ingredient in the Japanese stock dashi (page 519), and is the natural product from which pure MSG was first derived. It's sold in sheets typically a few inches wide and several inches long, ranging from dark moss green to pale beige or yellow. It comes in a wide range of qualities, at least if you look hard enough. (If you have good neighbors, you may even get by with a little kelp from your friends.) Most folks will have access to at most a few different quality levels and price points, representing different subspecies of kelp and different levels of retained glutamates. Unless you're after a pristine, subtle, crystal-clear, oceany broth (which, unless you happen to be the chef at a fancy *kaiseki* restaurant, you probably aren't), there's no need to spring for the fancy stuff. Even the cheapest grade of kombu will make great dashi.

I generally recommend looking for kombu that has more of the powdery white mineral deposits dried onto its surface, as my grandmother showed me. This frequently leads me to the cheaper stuff. While subtle broths are favored by many fancy restaurants, my tastes tend to run cheap when it comes to dashi, and those powdery crystallized minerals correlate to more robust umami flavor. (I'm not sure whether my grandmother bought it for the flavor or because she was thrifty, but either way, I follow the same path.)

1

THE SCIENCE OF STIR-FRIES
—

Many things can be called fast, versatile, and fun. My old Kodak Pocket Instamatic. Transformers. Bo Jackson. But add *delicious* to that mix and suddenly your list gets a whole lot shorter.

Stir-frying is fast. Most stir-fry recipes take under half an hour start to finish, and that's including prep time. The actual cook time of most stir-fries is just a few minutes.

Stir-frying is versatile. You can stir-fry meat. You can stir-fry seafood. You can stir-fry Asian vegetables or Western vegetables or tofu or rice or corn or mushrooms or lettuce or nuts or noodles or virtually anything that's at least semisolid and edible.

Stir-frying is fun. I mean, *I* think it's fun. If you enjoy activities that are simple enough for a first-timer to get good results, but also reward you greatly as you

practice and improve your skills, you may think it's fun as well.

Stir-frying is delicious. You know it, I know it, anyone who's eaten at even a mediocre Chinese chain restaurant knows it. Stir-fried vegetables retain their bright, fresh crispness and color. Properly marinated, massaged, and stir-fried meats are tender and packed with flavor. (We'll talk more about the importance of massaging meat later.) Stir-fried noodles and rice pick up a flavorful char and, when you get *really* good, some of that elusive *wok hei*—the smoky aroma you find at good Chinese restaurants. (You're gonna learn how to get it right at home, no matter what kind of stove you've got.) Stir-fries incorporate sauces, condiments, spices, pickles, and aromatics that pack flavor into foods quickly and easily, which means you can build complexity and depth into a dish even on a busy weeknight.

Of all the techniques I've learned over the years from all over the world, stir-frying is the one I'd take with me to the desert island. It's how the plurality of meals in my life have been cooked, and I imagine it'll stay that way until I die.[*]

The Anatomy of a Stir-Fry

More than anything, stir-frying is about technique. In a November 2018 study led by David Hu, a professor of fluid dynamics at the Georgia Institute of Technology, Hu used computer software to track and model the motion of fried rice in a wok as it was tossed by professional Taiwanese chefs. What they found was that the motion of a stir-fry could be broken down into oscillations that last about a third of a second. Within each of these oscillations, there are four distinct phases, each composed of translation motion (pushing and pulling the wok farther and closer) and rotational "seesaw" motion (pushing the handle up and down so that the wok pivots where it makes contact with the burner ring) that are slightly out of phase with each other, resulting in a back-and-forth rocking that causes food in the wok to leap toward the chef in a cascade, effectively mixing it. Here's what those phases look like in slow motion:

PHASE 1. With their hand firmly on the handle or the side of the wok closest to them, the cook pushes the wok forward while it is tilted downward away from them.

PHASE 2. As the wok gets close to its maximum distance away from the cook, the cook will begin to push down on the handle, causing the back edge of the wok to begin tilting back upward.

PHASE 3. While the back edge of the wok is still rising, the cook will begin pulling the wok back toward them. During this phase, the rotational motion and the rapid

translational acceleration cause the food to leap. The food near the top lip of the wok will feel the greatest acceleration, while the food closer to the base of the wok will feel less. This is what causes the cascading waterfall effect.

PHASE 4. The cook continues to pull the wok toward them, catching the food. Just as the wok reaches its point closest to the cook, the cook lifts up the handle, tilting the wok downward again and getting ready to push the wok forward to repeat Phase 1.

So, in effect, each rocking motion occurs in slight anticipation of each translational motion.

It is, in many ways, similar to the way I try to teach my daughter to pump her legs on the swing: To do it effectively, you need to straighten your legs and lean back just before you reach the apex of your back swing, and you need to lean forward and bend your knees just before reaching the apex of your front swing.

What Happens When You Toss?

As Grace Young explains in her book *Stir-Frying to the Sky's Edge*, the term *stir-fry* is misleading. Stirring, in the Western sense of moving things around the bottom of a pan using a spoon or spatula, is not what you want to do in a wok. "Tumble-fry" or "toss-fry" would be more accurate. Central to the technique of stir-frying is tossing food through the air. Why is this so vital?

The steam that evaporates off food and into your kitchen actually contains a huge amount of energy. Stir-frying takes advantage of this by recapturing some of that energy, which in turn speeds along cooking and helps develop intense flavors. In *Modernist Cuisine: The Art and Science of Cooking* the authors demonstrate how a column of hot air and steam will rise up around the back of a wok. As you stir-fry, you toss the food through this steamy air. The steam condenses on the surface

---

[*] Or at least until I get one of those awesome live-fire grills they have at fancy restaurants with the pulleys on the sides that let you lift the grates up and down. Those things are so cool.

of the food, depositing "formidable amounts of latent energy," which rapidly heats it. As it falls back into the wok, which has now had a chance to recover some of its heat energy, that surface moisture is revaporized and the cycle continues.

This is why stir-frying is such a quick cooking process and why the shape of a wok is so important: it allows for dramatic tossing.

So You Want to Practice Stir-Frying

Does your food more often end up in your stove grates or on the floor when you try to toss it? Does it seem like no matter how vigorously you stir the contents of your wok, nothing seems to cook evenly? Don't worry; you're not alone! Like riding a bike or trying to plug in a USB cable, stir-frying is one of those things where you have to keep at it until it suddenly just clicks. If you stir-fry a few times per week, it should come quickly enough, but if you want to speed up the process (and perhaps save yourself from a few hot or greasy spills), the best way I know how is to fill your wok with a cup of dry lentils, beans, or rice.

Here's the basic process, though images and words can only get you so far—practice is the only way you're going to get it.

MOVE 1 • Holding the handle of the wok, tilt the wok slightly away from you.

MOVE 2 • Push the wok forward in a smooth, relatively gentle motion, keeping it tilted away from you the whole time.

MOVE 3 • Just before you start pulling the wok back toward you, tilt it upward by pushing down on the handle. You should begin pulling it back toward you with a quick jerk about halfway through its upward rotation. This should send the food flying up into the air, with a parabolic trajectory that sends it back toward you.

MOVE 4 • Catch the food in the wok as you continue to pull it backward, then start to tilt it back down by lifting the handle just before you start pushing the wok forward again to repeat the cycle. As you practice, you'll find a natural rhythm of tossing and catching that varies slightly depending on how much food is in your wok, but it's typically two to three cycles per second.

How to Stir-Fry, Step by Step

To try to distill stir-fries down to a basic outline like this does a disservice to the vast array of flavors and textures you'll find in stir-fries throughout East Asia and the food courts of America, but we're gonna do it anyway.

Before we even get to the ingredients, the most important element in a stir-fry is the setup. It's typically a lightning-fast cooking process, which means no time to go digging through the fridge for that soy sauce you forgot to pull out. No waiting for that thick oyster sauce to dribble out of the jar. All of your ingredients need to be measured, chopped, mixed, and ready to go. Moreover, you should have all your tools on hand. Your mission is a delicious dinner, and this is your battle station. Make sure you're prepared.

Here is an equipment list for a basic stir-fry. All of these should be within arm's reach before starting:

- Your **wok**, on your stove's hottest burner

- A **wok spatula** with an appropriate resting place (like a spoon rest, a folded towel, or a stable crock)

- **Clean bowls** for holding cooked ingredients before returning them to the wok

- A **serving platter** for immediately transferring the food after cooking

- **Diners** ready to eat

Additionally, depending on the recipe, you might also consider:

- Some recipes in this book require you to cook certain ingredients in simmering water before stir-frying them (velveted meat, green vegetables, silken tofu, and noodles, for instance). Keeping a **saucepan of simmering water** on a separate burner, along with a **spider**, makes these steps much more streamlined, especially if you reuse the same water for multiple recipes cooked in series.

- A **pot with a fine-mesh strainer** set in it for collecting the excess oil some stir-fry recipes have you drain off, especially if using the oil-velveting technique

- A **butane or propane torch** is good for dishes that feature *wok hei* flavor (see page 42) when you don't have a very powerful gas burner or are working with electric or induction cooktops

- If your range does not have great ventilation, I would suggest some **powerful fans** to direct smoke out of an open window as well as temporarily **disabling your smoke detectors**. Stir-frying is often a smoky process. There's no way around that.

Now that we've covered the battle station, let's talk about ingredients, which should also be within arm's reach, preferably in individual small bowls (feel free to combine ingredients that hit the wok at the same time), or at the very least in neat piles on a big cutting board with a bench scraper handy for picking those piles up.

I'm going to simplify a multifaceted and diverse cooking technique into a very simple set of ingredients. Please don't get upset yet; we'll get to the more complicated stuff later. For now, just know that *most* stir-fries consist of a subset of the same basic ingredients:

OIL. Oil is needed to cook foods evenly and, more importantly, to help fat-soluble flavor compounds from aromatics coat everything in the pan. Neutral, high-heat-friendly oils like peanut, soybean, and rapeseed are best. Oil is also essential for dishes that achieve wok hei, as it's the oil singeing that lends some of that smoky flavor to the food.

OIL FLAVORINGS. These are aromatics that are bloomed in the oil before cooking begins in order to flavor it. Ginger, garlic, chiles, and dried spices (such as Sichuan peppercorns) are all common oil flavorings.

PROTEINS. If your stir-fry is a suit, either the protein or the vegetables are the jacket and slacks, while the other is the tie. And just as with a suit, the tie is often optional. When the protein is the main element, it is usually marinated, brined, and/or velveted (see page 72) before cooking to add flavor, moisture, and tenderness. When used as a flavoring, it's most often ground or finely chopped. Proteins should be cut to uniform size and shape so they cook evenly.

VEGETABLES. Like proteins, vegetables should be cut into uniform pieces to promote even cooking. Unless you are following a recipe that specifically calls for more vegetables, try to limit your vegetable selection to one or two carefully paired choices—otherwise you end up with what I call "food court syndrome," where there's so much junk inside that it's impossible to cook any one ingredient perfectly. (Avoid canned baby corn at all costs.*)

AROMATICS. Aromatics are intensely flavored ingredients that are chopped, sliced, or slivered finely enough that they readily give up their flavor and distribute themselves evenly throughout the dish. Common aromatics in this book are fresh chiles, herbs, garlic, ginger, scallions, lemongrass, and preserved and pickled vegetables.

SAUCE. Asian American restaurants tend to serve their stir-fries with a ton of glossy (or, in some unfortunate cases, gloopy) sauce, a practice I always imagine developed when restaurant owners realized their customers wanted extra sauce for their bland rice.† While saucy stir-fries do exist in Asia (not to mention dishes like curry, which are soupier than even Chinese American stir-fries), Asian stir-fries tend to be far drier than their Asian American counterparts, with just enough sauce to add flavor and a glossy sheen to meat or vegetables. Both styles of saucing can be delicious if done right. Stir-fry sauces often include ingredients like broth, soy sauce, rice wine, vinegar, sugar, oyster sauce, or any number of prepared chile pastes, fermented bean pastes, curry pastes, coconut milk, and citrus juices.

THICKENER. Stir-fry sauces are sometimes thickened with a starch, such as cornstarch or arrowroot, which allows it to coat and cling to ingredients rather than pooling off into the serving platter. A thickener will also help fat emulsify into the sauce instead of collecting into greasy puddles. This thickener is incorporated by stirring it with a bit of water to form a slurry before adding it to the wok. The key here is subtlety. Add it a little bit at a time. You can always thicken your sauce more, but you can't unthicken it without diluting it.

GARNISHES. These are kind of like the sprinkles on the ice cream cone—ingredients that don't require

much actual cooking but can simply be stirred or sprinkled in at the right time. This can be roasted nuts like peanuts or cashews (although if authenticity is your goal, they should be fried from raw); crunchy garnishes like fried shallots or fried garlic; fresh herbs or other vegetables like basil, cilantro, or scallions; or ground spices like Sichuan peppercorns or cumin.

Now that we've got that simplified outline under our belts, let's talk about the actual cooking process.

Restaurant-Style Stir-Fry at Home: Chasing the Flame

Want to know why your at-home stir-fries taste fundamentally different from those from a restaurant? It's not better ingredients, it's not ancient Chinese secrets, it's not even MSG (although all of those things can help). It's this: ridiculously high heat. And we're not talking Atlanta-on-a-hot-day high heat; we're talking campfire-set-by-a-Red-Dragon-who-came-straight-

---

* Unless you really enjoy it, in which case go for it! Rule number one of cooking is: don't let anyone else tell you what you enjoy.

† In many Asian cuisines, the rice is *supposed* to be bland, or at least subtle. It's used as a counterpoint to intensely flavored dishes or toppings. When I cook rice to go with stir-fries, I don't even add salt to it, although nothing stops you from doing so if you like.

The Right Amount of Thickener

The quantity of starch called for in any given recipe is at best a rough estimate. Adding just the right amount of starch to thicken a sauce is like trying to shoot a moving target; any sauce in a hot wok will continue to lose moisture through evaporation, which can cause the thickener to concentrate, turning the sauce from glossy and light to gloppy and thick. Moreover, a starch-thickened sauce doesn't fully thicken until it reaches a hard simmer. For this reason, it's important to add thickener a small quantity at a time and to wait until the very end of cooking before adding it to ensure that you've got the right texture before the dish comes out of the wok.

If you're familiar with the Italian technique of adding a few splashes of starchy pasta cooking water to pasta dishes at the last moment to lightly thicken the sauce and get it to cling to the pasta, the process of thickening a stir-fry sauce is very similar. As a stir-fry nears completion, I'll splash in a little bit of a starchy slurry (cornstarch or arrowroot mixed in a small amount of cold water), then let the sauce come to a hard simmer before deciding whether or not to add more. If the sauce is too thin, another splash goes in. If it's just right, I'll immediately transfer it to a serving platter. If, on the other hand, I find I've accidentally overthickened it, I'll add a splash of water or stock back into the wok to loosen it up again.

Professional Chinese chefs will frequently incorporate a cornstarch slurry in three distinct additions, fine-tuning the thickness of the dish with each addition.

Clean Your Vents!

Ranges with a vent hood will have filters that need to be cleaned regularly in order to operate efficiently and avoid the risk of fires. Stir-fries with their vaporized oil can be especially rough on these filters. I remove and wash mine (many are dishwasher-safe) at least once a month and recommend you do the same.

twenty to twenty-five times more powerful than a run-of-the-mill home burner.

These days, in the West there seems to be this idea that it's impossible to make a great stir-fry without one of those high-powered restaurant-style burners. (I'm probably partially responsible for this misconception.) Fortunately, that's not true.

For one thing, it's not like every apartment kitchen in China is outfitted like a restaurant. Most homes are equipped with gear not that different from your own home kitchen, and those work perfectly fine for most stir-fries, especially home-style dishes (you'll find plenty of those dishes in this book). But our cravings are colored by our experiences, and as a kid who grew up in the Cantonese-influenced Chinese American food landscape of New York City in the 1980s, when I crave a stir-fry, more often than not it's going to be a re-creation of a restaurant-style dish, with those distinct flavors that come from a high-octane wok setup. (See page 42 for more details on *wok hei*, the smoky flavor you find in many Cantonese-style restaurant dishes.)

Take a look at a Chinese restaurant kitchen and you'll see the wok chef tossing the contents of the wok with one hand while scooping up bits of sauce and seasonings with the wide flat ladle held in the other, all the while using a knee to adjust the gas flow to the burner. It's a beautiful dance.

These high-output burners allow a skilled cook to sear meat rapidly without overcooking it, to give a hint of smokiness to the vegetables while keeping them bright, fresh, and crisp, or to rapidly reduce added sauces, creating complex new flavors. High heat seems *essential* to pull off this restaurant style of cooking. If you use the exact same steps with a home burner, you end up with meat that steams in its own juices and vegetables that are drab and dreary rather than bright and crisp.

So the question is, is it possible to cook restaurant-style dishes with a home burner?

The answer is an emphatic yes! Let's wok through some of the science.

from-the-depths-of-Mount-Doom-if-Mount-Doom-were-on-the-sun hot. A Chinese restaurant range puts out about 200k BTU/hour* of heat energy, a good

---

* A British Thermal Unit (BTU) is a unit of energy equivalent to around one kilojoule.

Stored Heat vs. Heat Input

When talking about stir-fries, there's one important distinction to learn: the difference between stored heat energy and heat flux.

Stored heat energy is precisely what it sounds like: the energy that is stored in the pan itself. We measure this energy in degrees. When people ask you what the temperature of a given object is, they are really asking how much energy that object has stored up inside its molecules. Most cooking vessels we use are made of metal, and the amount of heat energy it can store is based on its specific heat capacity (the amount of energy a specific weight of the material contains per degree of temperature), and its mass (that is, functionally, its weight). You can review these concepts in the introduction on page 4.

Now, with Western cooking vessels, the stored energy in a pan is of vital importance. Most of the highest-quality Western cookware is thick and made of dense metals like cast iron or steel. The idea is that with proper preheating a Western pan will have enough energy stored in it that even when you add food to it—a big fat steak, for example—it won't drop much in temperature, allowing you to cook your food in an even, predictable manner. If we go back to the bucket metaphor from page 4, a heavy Western skillet is like a big, fat bucket of energy. It takes a long time to fill that bucket (which translates to lengthy preheating), but once full, it's got energy to spare—adding food to it will displace relatively little of its overall stored energy.

With a thick enough skillet and enough preheating—say to around 650°F or so—you could completely remove a pan from the heat, throw a steak in it, and still get a good sear from the stored energy. Once you've got your pan ripping hot, relatively little additional energy input is required to get good results.

A wok, on the other hand, relies on a different principle. Woks are thin, relatively lightweight vessels. The average wok is about a third the thickness of a standard Western pan. This means that at a given temperature, it's got relatively little stored heat. It's a small bucket that will quickly lose its energy stores as soon as you add food to it.

Thus, for good wok cooking, high heat energy input is required. Not only must the pan be ripping hot to start, but with most recipes you need to keep it above a high flame the entire time you cook in order to replenish the energy being pumped into the food.

Stir-Frying in Woks vs. Skillets

So why this distinction between stored heat and heat input/output? How are the two styles functionally different?

It's because with Western cooking vessels, even heating is of utmost importance. You want the pan to be of a consistent temperature from the edge to the center. Thick-gauge metals with an aluminum core help achieve this, maintaining a relatively high cooking temperature from start to finish. Indeed, if you graph the average temperature in a Western skillet versus a wok over a home range, you'lli find that this is the case:

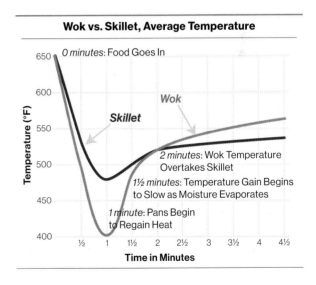

The leftmost edge represents the maximum preheat temperature of 650°F. When you add food to the pan, both a wok and a skillet show a rapid drop in temperature as heat gets transferred to the food. A Western skillet will drop to around 480°F, while a wok, because of its lower amount of stored heat energy, will drop all the way down to nearly 400°F. As the cooking continues, a Western skillet will slowly regain some of the energy that was lost when the food was added. Remember, a Western skillet is designed to heat and cool very slowly and evenly.

The wok, on the other hand, will regain that lost heat at a faster rate, but it's beginning with a lower initial temperature—it takes nearly a full two minutes before it makes up for lost time and overtakes the Western skillet.

Aha!, you may be thinking. *So a Western skillet is superior to a wok after all for cooking on a low-output burner!*

Well, let's take a look at a different graph, this time focusing only on the temperature of the bottom of the wok—the high-heat searing zone. For these readings, I added food, stir-fried it until it developed a reasonable sear, then pushed it to the sides of the skillet or wok.

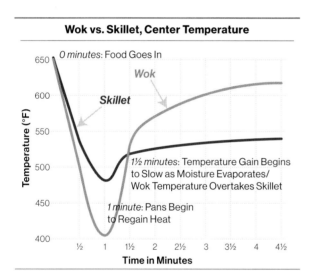

Wok vs. Skillet, Center Temperature

0 minutes: Food Goes In

Wok

Skillet

1½ minutes: Temperature Gain Begins to Slow as Moisture Evaporates/Wok Temperature Overtakes Skillet

1 minute: Pans Begin to Regain Heat

Now we see that in fact, in the area where it matters most—the very bottom of the wok where searing is taking place—a wok actually regains its heat significantly faster than a Western skillet does. Again, this is because a Western skillet is designed for *even* heat, while a wok is designed for *reactive* heat.

With wok cooking, you *want* different temperature zones inside the pan. You want a screaming-hot part at the very bottom. You want slightly cooler regions around the edges. You want heat rising up the sides of the wok and curling over the edge so that when you fling food up in the traditional stir-fry method, it hits a column of hot, steamy air. When food is pushed up the sides, the bottom very rapidly comes back up to

hard-searing temperatures, priming it for the next ingredients.

To demonstrate this difference, I used a thermal imaging camera to show the heat patterns in a Western skillet vs. in a wok.

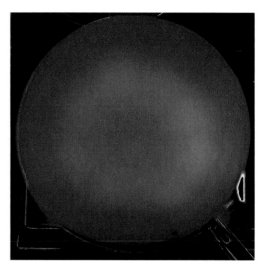

A preheated Western skillet has even heat all across its surface.

A preheated wok has a high-temperature zone in the very bottom and gets progressively cooler toward the edges.

So the key to good stir-frying on a home burner is to cook in small enough batches to allow this bottom section of the wok to remain hot throughout cooking. In a traditional Chinese-style meal with multiple small courses, this occurs naturally, as you are only cooking small batches of each dish. If you want to cook fewer dishes but larger portions, this means **cooking in batches.**

Whether I'm using a skillet or a wok for my stir-fry, I divide my meat and vegetables into one-pound portions (or even half-pound portions if I'm working on an especially slow burner) and add them to the wok one at a time, allowing them to sear and begin cooking before transferring them to a bowl on the side. Once the wok has regained some energy and starts smoking again, I cook the next batch, and so on. I can then mix everything back together at the very end just before adding my aromatics and sauce.

Will a Hot Wok and Cold Oil Really Prevent Sticking?

There's a basic rule of thumb in wok cooking that goes like this: a hot wok and cold oil will prevent your food from sticking. The idea is that you preheat your wok over high heat until it is ready to cook, then add your oil immediately before adding other ingredients.

But does this technique really work, and is it really the best way?

Let's quickly take a look at exactly what makes food stick in the first place. You may have heard that food sticks to pans by getting stuck in microscopic pores in the metal and that oil prevents this by filling those pores and creating a smooth surface. This is not true. Raw proteins interact with metal on a submicroscopic level, forming actual molecular bonds. Even on a perfectly smooth, polished surface with no cracks or imperfections whatsoever, meat will stick to hot metal.[*]

How does preheating prevent this? The thing is, only raw proteins will form this bond. Heat causes proteins to fold in on themselves, or even to break down and form all new compounds. Once in their folded or rearranged form, they no longer stick. So the goal is to get surface proteins to cook before they even come into contact with the metal by heating a film of oil hot enough that it can cook the meat in the time it takes for it to pass from the air, through the film of oil, and into the pan.

With Western-style cooking, I almost *always* add oil to the pan before I start to preheat it. It's a useful method of telling how hot your pan is. When the oil becomes very loose and starts shimmering (around 300° to 400°F), you're in sauté territory. When it starts to smoke lightly (400° to 500°F, depending on oil type), you're ready to sear, and when it starts to smoke heavily or you see flames licking across the surface, it's a sign that you should probably stop reading your social media feeds and focus on cooking.

So what about this hot pan, cold oil thing? It never really made sense to me; when you add a relatively small amount of oil to a really hot pan, it nearly instantly heats up to the same temperature as the pan—precisely the same temperature it would hit if you heated it up with the pan in the first place. Naturally, I thought that preheating the oil with the wok would work just as well for stir-frying. So I tried it side by side.

I found that whether I heated up the oil with the wok or added oil to an already preheated wok, my food was equally unlikely to stick. But there was one big difference: flavor. With stir-fries, you typically preheat the wok even hotter than you would heat a Western skillet for searing. If you start with oil in a cold wok, by the time it's hot enough to start cooking, the oil will have already broken down a great deal, producing free radicals and acrolein, which gives stir-fries a burnt, acrid flavor.

It turns out that as with much accepted wisdom, this one is right, but for the wrong reasons.[†]

---

[*] Nonstick coatings like Teflon are specially engineered to be smooth and virtually nonreactive, meaning that these types of molecular bonds will not form even if you start cooking in a cold pan. The problem with nonstick is that most nonstick coatings can't be heated hot enough to sear properly, nor are they robust enough for the vigorous scraping and tossing required for a good stir-fry.

[†] Incidentally, if you've watched any episode of Sichuan chef Wang Gang or Guizhou-based couple Stephanie Li and Christopher Thomas's excellent instructional videos on YouTube, you'll be familiar with the concept of *longyau*. It's a technique restaurant chefs use to season their woks to prepare them to accept food. The idea is that rather than adding a measured amount of oil to the preheated wok before cooking, you add a large amount of oil, swirl it around to coat, then dump the excess oil out, leaving the wok slicked and ready to go.

To successfully practice longyau, you need to have a separate saucepan or other heatproof container on your stovetop filled with oil, which you can ladle into your wok, then dump back in after swirling. If you stir-fry frequently enough to have a permanent longyau oil pot on your stove, this is a useful technique to keep in your arsenal.

Smoke Signals: How to Tell When Your Wok Is Hot Enough

But wait a minute. Without the visual cues that preheating oil provides, how can you tell if your wok is hot enough? Easy. The wok does this all by itself. A well-maintained and seasoned cast iron or carbon steel surface should always have a very thin layer of oil coating its surface, which means that even without added oil, you'll still see light smoking when it hits stir-fry temperatures. Just to make sure, I'll often rub a small amount of oil into the surface of the wok with a paper towel before preheating. This small amount of oil is not enough to produce off flavors in your stir-fries, but it's enough to indicate the surface temperature of the wok. Once it starts smoking, I add the remainder of my cooking oil, immediately adding my first stir-fry ingredients, which lowers the temperature of the wok and oil enough that the oil will not burn.

I recommend a carbon steel wok (see page 6), but if you happen to be using one made of stainless steel, aluminum, or some other nonseasoned surface, you won't be able to see any smoke coming off it. In these situations, I rely on the Leidenfrost effect. The Leidenfrost effect is named after Johann Gottlob Leidenfrost, the eighteenth-century German scientist whose epic discovery is only outdone by his epic hairdo. It occurs when a droplet of liquid is dropped onto a surface that is significantly hotter than its boiling point. As the liquid rapidly boils, it produces a cushion of vapors underneath it that will completely lift it from the surface, like a hovercraft. You'll see it when your science teacher spills liquid nitrogen across the table and it spreads out, nearly frictionless.

You also see it when you add a small amount of water to a sufficiently heated pan surface. Below a certain threshold—around 350°F (175°C)—water dropped onto a hot pan will make full contact with it, evaporating efficiently and rapidly. Above that point, the Leidenfrost effect takes place, lifting the drop off the pan and causing it to dance around inside, nearly frictionless. This in turn slows the rate of energy transfer to the water, effectively increasing the time it takes to evaporate. It's also a useful way to measure the surface temperature of your pan without a thermometer or oil. If it's hot enough to make water dance, it's hot enough to stir-fry.

And what if you don't *want* smoke in your kitchen while cooking? Unfortunately smoke and stir-frying (or even proper searing) go hand in hand. If you don't have a great hood that vents outside, there are two things you should do. First: get a couple of powerful fans to blow as much smoke as possible out an open window. Second: place a shower cap over the smoke detectors[*] near your kitchen (just don't forget to remove them when the smoke has cleared). Or better yet, if you have access to outdoor space and weather permits, take your wok cooking outside.

Stir-Frying Outdoors

A standard charcoal grill or, better yet, a dedicated propane-powered wok burner, will achieve heat output levels that far outstrip any home kitchen burner. The cheapest and most straightforward way to get the heat where you need it is to use a charcoal chimney starter as a makeshift burner. It's simple: just fill up your chimney starter with coals, light the sucker up, and once the coals are completely covered in gray ash and hot, put the wok on top, and let 'er rip.

---

[*]   Or, as Dave Arnold, author of *Liquid Intelligence* and the genius behind the *Cooking Issues* blog, calls them, "cooking detectors."

There are a couple difficulties to look out for here. The first is stability. A wok full of food can be a little precarious resting on top of a tall chimney, so make sure you have plenty of clearance around the grill just in case you accidentally knock the chimney over.

The second is that your wok will disrupt air flow in the chimney, which means that the coals inside will stop combusting while you are cooking. Make sure those coals are glowing hot before you place your wok on top, make sure to lift the wok occasionally to give the coals a breath of fresh oxygen, and leave the wok off the chimney while you aren't actively cooking with it. Alternatively, after your coals are glowing, you can dump them out, flip the chimney over, use a pair of long tongs to place the coals into the part of the chimney where the newspaper generally goes, and cook like that. The vent holes your chimney already has to provide fuel to kindling during normal use should be ample for ventilation during stir-fries.

There are also grill grates with a center hole removed designed to hold a wok in place available for the standard Weber kettle grill. This works alright, but it's difficult to manage the flame level, and without a flame guard, your hands get *hot*.

If you want to buy a more specialized piece of equipment, consider investing in a restaurant-grade wok burner. My favorite can be found at outdoorstirfry.com. It connects to a standard propane tank fitted with a 20-psi regulator and has a heat output of up to 160k BTU/hour—more than enough to cook big batches of restaurant-grade dishes for your family and friends. The Kahuna Burner made by Eastman Outdoor is a little more budget-friendly and still produces an ample 65k BTU/hour of heat, which is sufficient to cook four-serving batches of any recipe in this book.

BEFORE YOU STIR-FRY OUTDOORS

A few notes before you jump in and start grill-wokking or cooking on a dedicated restaurant-grade wok burner: This is not the world's safest cooking method. Things are hot, fast, and furious. Before you begin, I suggest the following (lest you learn the hard way):

- **Make sure you have plenty of clearance.** Things can and will get very hot, and the last thing you want to do is find out that the flowers two feet away from the grill are wilting from the heat or that the stairwell is about to catch fire.

- **Have on hand a stack of clean, dry dish towels or heatproof gloves.** To move the wok around, you're going to need hand protection. I use dry dish towels (wet towels will steam and burn your hands) for both the hand that shakes the wok around and the hand that wields the spatula. If you are using a heavy wok, you'll probably need both hands to lift it to get the food out at the end. It's a good idea to have another helper nearby to scrape the food out with the spatula while you tilt the wok over a serving platter.

- **Have a heatproof area nearby to place the wok.** In the midst of cooking, there may be times when you find that your wok is getting too hot. During these times, you'll want a safe place to rest it while it cools a bit. I use a small galvanized steel trash can and rest the wok right on top (it's the same can I use to store my spent ashes before discarding). This is also a good place to rest the wok while you clean it between dishes (I use water and a soft scrubby held with a long pair of tongs).

- **If using a restaurant-style wok burner, check that the ring you rest the wok on is oriented correctly.** Frequently, the rings will be open on three sides but have a heat shield on the fourth. That heat shield should be facing toward you in order to protect your hands and body from the flames that will lick up the other three sides of the wok.

- **Bring friends.** Nothing sadder than letting a good stir-fry go to waste. (That is, nothing sadder except for reheated stir-fries.)

Wok Hei (The Breath of a Wok)

Q *I've heard about this thing called* wok hei, *the "Breath of a Wok." What's that all about?*

A Growing up, my dad would take us out for beef chow fun at Sun Lok Kee, our favorite Cantonese restaurant in Chinatown. (In 2002, it, like several of my childhood favorite Chinese restaurants, burned down.) Their chow fun, cooked dry style, had incredibly tender beef and nice, chewy rice noodles, but the hallmark was what my dad referred to as "that nice smoky flavor."

What he was referring to was a flavor later coined *wok hei* by Grace Young in her book *The Wisdom of the Chinese Kitchen*. The literal translation is "wok energy" or "wok aroma." Some define it as the unique smokiness that dishes stir-fried over extremely high heat acquire, but that's by no means the agreed-upon definition.

Young identifies it as "when a wok breathes energy into a stir-fry, giving foods a unique concentrated flavor and aroma." In *The Chinese Kitchen*, Eileen Yin-Fei Lo says it's when "the proper amount of fire is made to curl up around the bowl of the wok to cook foods precisely to that point of optimum flavor."

Watch a Cantonese chef cook a batch of chow fun and you'll see this in action. As food gets tossed through the hot zone behind the wok, tiny droplets of aerosolized oil will ignite and flare up. With a big enough burner and enough stirring, that flame will actually leap down and dance across the inner surface of the wok itself. The burnt oil in turn leaves small, sooty deposits on the food as it gets tossed through the flames. It's the flavor of these sooty deposits—the same flavor that develops as a hamburger drips fat onto red hot coals below it—that I most strongly associate with *wok hei*.

Q *Does good Chinese food need wok hei?*

A My friends Steph Li and Chris Thomas, the Shenzhen-based couple behind the popular YouTube channel *Chinese Cooking Demystified*, describe *wok hei* as "that taste of the first bite of a hot restaurant stir-fry. It's got that taste of the restaurant oil, the slightly deeper restaurant browning, the heavier restaurant seasoning." Li added: "Seeing home cooks outside of China being obsessed about *wok hei* has always been kind of bewildering to me." In fact, until recently, the concept of *wok hei* was not widely known outside of the Cantonese regions of southeastern China, and virtually all home-style Chinese cooking gets along just fine without it.

This made me rethink my entire relationship with *wok hei* and why it plays such an outsized role in my perception of good Chinese food. I believe it all comes down to the fact that Americans largely experience Chinese food through the lens of restaurants, and specifically Cantonese restaurants. Chinese food in America has its earliest roots in Cantonese cuisine (according to Andrew Smith's *Eating History: 30 Turning Points in the Making of American Cuisine*, there were five Chinese restaurants in San Francisco by 1850, started by Cantonese immigrants who arrived during the Gold Rush).

Wok hei is a flavor I cherish and chase, but it's by no means necessary for great wok cooking, and that's reflected in the recipes in this book: Plenty of dishes require no *wok hei* at all, and plenty more dishes that typically *do* have *wok hei* will still be plenty delicious even without it. That's good news. It means even as a complete stir-fry noob, your dry-fried beef chow fun is gonna start out delicious and only get more so from there.

Q *But what is the flavor? Where does it come from? What's so different about cooking in a restaurant?*

A Some have claimed that good *wok hei* comes from rapid Maillard browning and caramelization. If this were the case, cooking in a heavy Western-style skillet, which is wonderful at browning foods, should produce more *wok hei* than a wok. To test this, I did a number of blind taste tests, stir-frying noodles, beef, and vegetables in three different ways:

→ The first I cooked in a Western-style skillet.

→ The second I cooked in a nonstick wok, gently stirring and tossing the food.

→ The third I cooked in my own well-seasoned carbon steel wok, more vigorously stirring and tossing.

As expected, of the three finished stir-fries, the one cooked in the Western skillet had the most browning and caramelization. However, neither the stir-fry cooked in the Western skillet nor the one gently tossed in a wok had any *wok hei* to speak of. Only the stir-fry cooked in a wok with vigorous tossing and stirring and direct exposure to flames came out tasting the way it should. I subsequently tested the nonstick wok and carbon steel wok again, this time vigorously stirring and tossing with both of them and allowing the flames of the burner to leap into the food.

This time, the nonstick wok achieved a small amount of *wok hei*, but nowhere near the level of the carbon steel wok.

The testing indicated that both the technique of rapidly tossing and allowing the flame of the burner to enter the wok and the material of the wok itself play an important role in *wok hei* flavor.

Q *Are there any other elements involved in* wok hei?

A On his YouTube channel, Sichuan-based chef Wang Gang emphasizes the importance of adding soy sauce around the perimeter of the wok, rather than directly onto the food. In her 2010 book, *Stir-Frying to the Sky's Edge*, Grace Young says the same. According to Young, adding sauces to the center of the wok decreases the temperature of the searing zone in the center, which can cause meat and vegetables to steam rather than sizzle. This is true, but there's something else at play here.

When you splash soy sauce around the perimeter of a wok, it immediately sizzles and sputters. Watching this happen, I was reminded of a Mexican cooking technique I learned from the late chef David Sterling at his home in the Yucatán: as he tipped fresh salsa into a ripping-hot preheated saucepan, it immediately superheated and erupted in a steamy sputter, giving it a richer color and smoky undertones. Could this concept of a seared sauce also be a factor in *wok hei* flavor?

To test this, I made two identical batches of lo mein, changing only the manner in which I finished them. For the first, I finished by splashing two tablespoons of soy sauce around the perimeter of the wok, while simultaneously splashing two tablespoons of water into the center of the wok. For the second, I swapped the water and soy sauce. (Adding water to the test ensured that both batches would experience the same cool-down effect of liquid added directly to the center, while only one would develop seared soy sauce flavors.) The difference was stark. Adding soy sauce to the center of the wok left the noodles with a raw soy sauce flavor, while drizzling it around the hot edges of the wok created smoky flavors reminiscent of grilled meat.

This was the final key to unlocking true *wok hei* flavor, and my beef chow fun has never tasted better.

Q *Give it to me straight. Where does* **wok hei** *come from?*

A In my testing, I've narrowed it down to three elements:

1 The intense flavors you get through high-heat cooking, specifically the flavors imparted by the layer of polymerized oils in a well-seasoned wok, and the rapid cooking that the action of constantly tossing food through a cloud of its own steam allows for (see "What Happens When You Toss?" on page 32)

2 The singeing of aerosolized fats that occurs as flames lick up over the back of the wok and into the food

3 The searing of soy sauce and other liquids added around the perimeter of the wok during the last stages of a stir-fry

Q *OK, that's all well and good, but it sounds to me that, without a gas burner, and a powerful one at that, achieving* **wok hei** *is simply not possible for the home cook. Is there a work-around?*

A For the longest time, I thought that *wok hei* was possible only with a powerful gas burner and a lot of practice. But I've discovered a reasonable work-around: If you can't bring your food to the flame, just bring the flame to the food by using a propane or butane torch (see "The Best Kitchen Torch?" on page 45). A camping-style fuel tank along with a brazing head that you point directly at the food inside a wok for a few brief moments as you toss and stir it can lend that vaporized oil flavor. You'll want to hold the torch far enough away that it doesn't immediately singe or char the food, but close enough that the little droplets of oil that fly up as you toss food catch on fire and make tiny little crackles and pops. Four to six inches is about right for my Iwatani Pro butane torch.

If you've got trouble tossing with one hand while aiming the torch with the other, enlisting the help of a friend to hold the torch while you stir-fry can be a good idea. Alternatively, I've found that transferring the stir-fried food to a rimmed baking sheet, spreading it in a single layer, and giving it a few leisurely passes with the torch before returning it to the wok for final saucing and garnishing is a simple and effective alternative.

Got an Electric Burner? You Can Still Stir-Fry!

There is no question I get asked more frequently about stir-frying than whether it's possible with an electric or induction cooktop. Good news: it is definitely possible. Not-as-good-but-not-as-bad-as-it-sounds news: it's more difficult than with a gas burner.

What makes stir-frying on an electric burner so difficult? Two factors.

First: electric burners are not as responsive as

gas burners. When stir-frying, you'll find that you frequently switch between high heat and low heat or even no heat. This is easy on a gas burner: more or less gas = instantly higher or lower heat. An electric burner, on the other hand, takes a long time to heat up and cool down (induction burners are more responsive than electric burners, but not as responsive as gas). The work-around for this is making sure that your burner and wok are well preheated before cooking and making sure that there's an empty burner set to low heat to move your wok to during cooking so you can make quick adjustments in heat input.

Second, and more important: electric and induction burners heat only the part of the pan in direct contact with the burner. This means that with a flat-bottomed wok, only the flat part of the wok will get heated. While it's true that in a stir-fry you *want* heat to be concentrated on this area, a gas flame will still spread some of its energy to the sides of the wok. This is particularly important for achieving *wok hei*, as that heat around the edges is (a) what allows you to sear sauces when adding them around the lip of the wok and (b) creates the column of hot air and steam along the back of the wok that promotes rapid cooking and singeing of fats.

There's no great work-around for this issue, but using a wok with a relatively large flat area along the bottom can help, as does using a kitchen torch for dishes that are improved with *wok hei* (see pages 42 and 44).

The easiest work-around for all of this is to buy a portable gas burner that runs on butane cartridges. Iwatani's ZA-3HP portable butane stove puts out an impressive 15k BTU/hour, which is more powerful than many regular home burners.

The Best Oil for Stir-Frying

If you enjoy jumping down rabbit holes, choosing the proper oil for stir-frying is a deep one. In Cantonese cuisine peanut oil is favored, while in Sichuan cuisine the oil of choice is caiziyou (see page 18), a roasted rapeseed oil that has a deep amber color and pungent aroma quite different from the mild rapeseed-based canola oil we can find in the United States. In Japan

The Best Kitchen Torch?

Kitchen torches aimed at home cooks are tiny, dinky little things barely stronger than your average lighter. What is this? A kitchen torch for ants?

Instead, go for a utility torch. Many folks will recommend propane over butane. I had always thought that propane burns hotter than butane, but in fact they burn at almost exactly the same temperature. Propane burns at 3,623°F (1,995°C), while butane burns at 3,578°F (1,970°C). The issue is that butane tanks and heads tend to be lower capacity, which means less fuel is burned at once, which means less heat is generated over a given period of time when compared to propane tanks and heads. That said, the best butane heads are more than adequate for most home cooking needs, and I find the form factor and price of butane canisters and accessories to be a strong selling point.

For the casual fire-slinger, I'd recommend getting an Iwatani Pro torch head. They cost around $40 online and fit on top of standard butane canisters, which you can find at most Asian supermarkets or camping supply stores. If you happen to already have a supply of propane canisters around the house for other purposes, I'd recommend the Bernzomatic TS4000 head, which is high output and has a trigger start.

you'll find centuries-old tempura restaurants that fry in nothing but sesame oil, or stir-fries that start and end with pork lard.

At home I do almost all of my stir-frying and deep frying in rice bran, peanut, or soybean oil, though virtually any heat-tolerant, neutral-flavored oil will work for most recipes.

There are two important factors when considering an oil to stir-fry with: smoke point and saturated fat content.

Cooking fats can be of animal or plant origin, but when we refer to oils—that is, fats that are liquid at room temperature—almost all of them are plant based. Virgin oils are made by crushing and pressing nuts, seeds, or other plant matter to extract oil that is then very minimally treated; typically filtering is the only treatment a virgin oil will receive. Virgin oils are packed with proteins, enzymes, minerals, and other teeny tiny bits of stuff that add flavor but make them unsuitable for cooking with even moderately high heat. All that is easily transformed by heat, turning what was once a wonderfully bright and grassy olive oil into something acrid and bitter.

Refined oils, on the other hand, are further filtered, purified, and treated to remove these contaminants. This process gives oils a longer shelf life, a higher smoke point, and a more neutral flavor. Refined oils are what you want for high-heat cooking like searing and stir-frying.

The ratio of saturated to unsaturated fat in a given oil can also affect its cooking performance. For those of you who need a quick brush-up on your seventh-grade biology, fat molecules consist of three fatty acid chains attached to a glycerol molecule. It looks sort of like the letter E, with extra-long arms. These fatty acid chains are composed of a long chain of carbon atoms, each with the ability to grab on to two hydrogen atoms. In a fully saturated fat, every carbon atom in the chain will have two hydrogen atoms attached to it (i.e., it is *saturated* with hydrogen atoms), which causes the arms of the E to stick out straight and stiff. In unsaturated fats, two or more carbon atoms may be missing a hydrogen atom. This causes the arms of the E to kink and bend.

This is why highly saturated fats tend to be more solid than unsaturated fats: those straightedge fat molecules are easier to pack together and stack than the kinky ones.

The saturation level of a fat is also closely linked to how crisp deep- or shallow-fried foods get. The higher the saturated fat content in your oil, the crisper your food will get.

Here's a chart showing some common culinary oils along with their smoke points and saturated fat content.

TYPE OF FAT	SMOKE POINT	SATURATED FAT
Safflower Oil	510°F (265°C)	6%
Rice Bran Oil	490°F (260°C)	20%
Corn Oil	450°F (230°C)	13%
Soybean Oil	450°F (230°C)	15%
Clarified Butter	450°F (230°C)	60%
Peanut Oil	450°F (230°C)	18%
Sunflower Oil	440°F (225°C)	11%
Canola Oil	400°F (205°C)	7%
Beef Tallow	400°F (205°C)	52%
Grapeseed	390°F (195°C)	10%
Chicken Fat	375°F (190°C)	31%
Lard (pork fat)	370°F (185°C)	41%
Vegetable Shortening	360°F (180°C)	23%
Sesame Oil	350°–410°F (175°–210°C)	15%
Butter	350°F (175°C)	65%
Coconut Oil	350°F (175°C)	92%
Extra Virgin Olive Oil	325°–375°F (165°–190°C)	14%

For stir-frying we want a fat that at the very minimum has a smoke point of around 400°F. Within that range, we also want a fat that has a relatively high level of saturated fat. Clarified butter and beef tallow fit that bill nicely, but neither is inexpensive or easy to attain (and neither is vegetarian, which limits their versatility).

This leaves us with **rice bran oil** and **peanut oil** as our next best options, and these are the fats I typically use at home for both stir-frying and deep frying. The only problem is that they can get a little pricey. Soybean oil is your next best bet, and it's available widely and cheaply. Most bottles of "vegetable oil" are a blend of soybean and corn. They will do just fine for stir-fries and deep frying.

Cutting Meat and Vegetables for Stir-Fries

There are three reasons meats and vegetables are sliced or chopped before stir-frying.

- **First,** stir-fried foods are typically eaten with chopsticks. Without a knife for cutting, foods must be served in bite-sized pieces.

- **Second,** cutting meat and vegetables into pieces allows for more rapid and even cooking.

- **Finally,** slicing, dicing, or julienning increases the surface-area-to-volume ratio of meats and vegetables, providing more surfaces for marinades and sauces to cling, giving the finished dish more flavor.

Depending on the particular dish, meat can be sliced into thin strips, diced into small chunks, slivered into fine julienne, or ground into mince. The latter is done with a meat grinder,* while the former three are done by hand. In each section of this chapter I'll show you exactly how to cut various proteins, but the basics are all the same: start with a very sharp knife, dry the meat well so that it doesn't slip, and make sure that it is very cold and firm before starting. Placing meat in the freezer for about 15 minutes can help firm it up and make it easier to slice.

Marinating for Stir-Fries 101

Many people believe that the purpose of marinating is to add flavor. But contrary to what you may think, marinades do not actually penetrate very far into meat, even with massaging or prolonged contact (see "No Room on the Meat Train," page 48, and "Experiment: How Deeply Does a Marinade Penetrate?" on page 48). And while a marinade packed with aromatic ingredients (like garlic, ginger, or spices) *can* add some flavor to meat, most of the time you'll find that adding flavorful ingredients directly to the stir-fry or sauce is a more effective way to get flavor into a dish.

The primary purpose of a marinade is to enhance texture, and most ingredients in a stir-fry marinade are designed to do just this. Here are the basics of most marinades.

COMMON MARINADE INGREDIENTS

- **Salt.** Just as it does in your Thanksgiving turkey brine, salt will tenderize meat by breaking down muscle proteins (mainly the protein myosin) while also causing the meat to retain more moisture during cooking. Salt also enhances the natural flavor of foods by activating ion pathways into certain taste receptors, giving our brains a wider range of stimulation. Salted chicken doesn't just taste saltier; it actually tastes *more like chicken.*

- **A Salty, Flavorful Liquid.** Typically this will be some form of soy sauce or fish sauce. Both of these liquids are high in salt (and we already know how that helps), but they are also rich in glutamates and inosinates, compounds that trigger our sense of umami, or savoriness.

---

* OK, traditionally ground meats for stir-fries are chopped by hand using a large cleaver or chef's knife. This process produces a mince that is more varied in texture, which is great for dishes where ground meat is the star, such as Lao/Thai *lap* salads. But for most purposes, preground mince from the supermarket will do. Unless you're *really* trying to use up an excess of elbow grease.

No Room on the Meat Train!

We know that large organic molecules don't penetrate too far into meat because of their large size, but there's another effect in action when talking about marinades that contain both salt and aromatic compounds: salting out, the tendency of salt to penetrate meats to the exclusion of other marinade ingredients.

It helps to think of your meat as a train, where each car is a cell, and your marinade as the platform. Waiting on that platform are molecules of various shapes and sizes. We've got quick, small, and zippy salt molecules and big, slow, lumbering aroma molecules. When that meat train pulls into the station, the pushy little salt molecules make a beeline for the doorways, elbowing everyone else out of the way and packing up the cars before anyone else has a shot. (If you've ever tried to get on a New York subway during rush hour, you know this feeling.) In fact, many of those larger molecules are so big that they couldn't fit through the doors even if they wanted to. You end up with a car full of salt and very little else (at least nothing that wasn't there to begin with).

Just as with a chunk of meat in a marinade, some of those larger molecules may grab on and hitch a ride on the exterior, but very few make it past the doorways.

How Deeply Does a Marinade Penetrate?

Most marinades don't penetrate particularly far into a meat. Here's an easy way to test it for yourself.

Materials

2 chicken breast halves of similar shape and size (preferably two breast halves split from a single whole breast)

½ cup soy sauce

4 medium garlic cloves, minced

Procedures

Place a single chicken breast half into a zipper-lock bag with ¼ cup of the soy sauce and half of the garlic. Squeeze out as much excess air as possible, then seal the bag, squishing it around a bit to ensure that the chicken is completely coated on all sides with the soy sauce. Place the bag in the refrigerator overnight.

The next day, place the second chicken breast half in a zipper-lock bag with the remaining ¼ cup soy sauce and remaining garlic, squeeze out the air, and seal it, turning to make sure the second chicken breast is also coated in soy sauce. Place the second chicken breast in the refrigerator and let it sit for 30 minutes to an hour.

Remove both chicken breasts, pat them dry on paper towels, then cook them by poaching them in simmering water or roasting them in a 400°F oven until they reach an internal temperature of at least 150°F. Let the chicken breasts cool, then slice them in half.

Results and Analysis

You'll notice that whether marinated overnight or for only 30 minutes, the soy sauce has barely penetrated the meat, coloring only the very outer layer. If you carefully trim away this outer layer (making sure the inner parts of the chicken breast don't come into contact with excess juices on the cutting board) and taste the two chicken breasts side by side, you'll find that neither one will have any discernible soy sauce or garlic flavor in the interior.

The chicken marinated overnight *should* taste saltier and juicier, however. What's going on here? Unlike large aromatic molecules, salt will readily pass through cell walls and travel into the meat. As it penetrates, it dissolves some muscle proteins, which in turn loosens the structure of the meat, helping it to retain more moisture as it cooks. This is the principle behind brining or curing meat and the reason that brined or cured meats stay juicier during cooking than unsalted meats.

- **Sugar.** Sugar can help balance out saltiness, heat, and acidity in a stir-fry. It can also help enhance the Maillard reaction, the browning reaction responsible for giving roasted or seared meats their dark color and complex flavor.

- **Oil.** Frequently oil will be added to marinades, especially marinades containing aromatics like spices or chiles. These aromatics have fat-soluble flavor compounds. Oil helps distribute those flavors evenly over the surface of the meat. Oil can also make it easier to separate pieces of meat when they hit the wok.

- **Cornstarch.** The role of cornstarch in a marinade is twofold. First, a light starchy coating can help protect muscle fibers from coming into direct contact with the hot surface of a wok, allowing you to cook and brown pieces of meat without their overcooking on the surface and becoming stringy. More importantly, cornstarch is absorptive. A light coat of cornstarch can help soak up meat juices that are exuded during cooking or sauces that are added toward the end. Think of it as a coat or primer for your meat just waiting for a new, flavorful paint job.

- **Acid.** Acid is frequently added in the form of wine or, occasionally, citrus juices or vinegars. It can balance out sweetness, fat, and heat. Note that with strong acids like vinegar or citrus juice (see "Experiment: Acid Test," page 77), you have to be extremely careful not to overmarinate the meat. Letting meat sit in a strongly acidic environment for any extended period of time will cause its proteins to coagulate, resulting in a dry, chalky texture no matter how carefully you cook it.

- **Baking Soda.** The secret ingredient in many meat and shrimp stir-fries. When added to a marinade it alkalizes the surface of the meat or seafood, which in turn makes it more difficult for proteins to bond and tighten when cooked. The result is extra-tender meat and shrimp with a snappy bite. (For more, see "Experiment: Alkalized Beef," page 123.)

- **Egg Whites.** Like baking soda, egg whites are quite alkaline and thus help meat stay tender during a stir-fry. Egg whites are also included in marinades when the meat is going to undergo the velveting process before being subsequently stir-fried. (See page 72 for more on velveting.)

Aside from these functional ingredients, marinades will often contain flavorings like white or black pepper, chiles, and other spices, pickles, and pastes.

Sidebar

Washing Meat for Stir-Fries: More Important Than You Think

Most Western recipes for stir-fries that I've seen recommend cutting meat, tossing it with marinade, and setting it aside. Chinese instructors, on the other hand, will often recommend washing sliced meat in cold water before squeezing out excess moisture and marinating, purportedly to tenderize meat and give it a cleaner flavor that absorbs sauce more readily.

I tested this side by side with two batches of sliced pork. The first I washed thoroughly in cold water before squeezing dry in a fine-mesh strainer and stirring with a basic marinade. The second I sliced and immediately stirred with the marinade. There was an immediate visual difference between the two batches: The washed pork had a distinctly paler color.

After letting both batches rest for half an hour, I stir-fried them and tasted them side by side. The differences were subtle but noticeable. The pork that had been washed vigorously had a more tender, almost slippery texture (a good quality in most stir-fried meats) and was more thoroughly seasoned—the mechanical action of washing and squeezing loosens up the muscle fibers of the meat, improving their ability to absorb and retain marinade. Given it's such an easy process, I've taken to doing it for all my stir-fries.

BASIC STIR-FRY MARINADE FOR ANY MEAT

INGREDIENTS

For every pound of meat:

½ teaspoon (1.5 g) kosher salt

1 teaspoon (5 ml) light soy sauce or shoyu

1 teaspoon (5 ml) Shaoxing wine or dry
  sherry

½ teaspoon (2 g) sugar

½ teaspoon (1.5 g) cornstarch

Small pinch of freshly ground white pepper
  (optional)

Small pinch of MSG (optional; see page 50)

½ teaspoon (2 g) baking soda (optional; see
  headnote)

1 teaspoon (5 ml) peanut, rice bran, or other
  neutral oil

This simple marinade is a good starting point for any simple stir-fry, as it will blend into most sauces. This is the mixture I turn to when I want to stir-fry without a specific recipe in mind. Tougher red meat like lamb or beef benefits the most from the baking soda treatment, but lean cuts of chicken breast or pork loin will also stay softer and more tender with the addition of baking soda. With chicken thigh or fattier cuts of pork, it's not really necessary.

DIRECTIONS

Place the meat in a medium bowl, cover with cold water, and vigorously agitate it. Drain through a fine-mesh strainer set in the sink and press on the meat with your hands to remove excess water, then return it to the bowl. Add the remaining marinade ingredients and stir vigorously with your fingertips or chopsticks for 30 seconds. Set aside at room temperature for 15 to 30 minutes or in the fridge up to overnight before stir-frying.

1.1 HOW TO STIR-FRY CHICKEN

I *love* chicken. Strike that. I love *good* chicken, and I admit, good chicken is a rarity. Chicken breast in particular lacks the flavor-enhancing properties of connective tissue and the moistening powers of fat. Unless you are *very* careful about how you cook and season it, *you're in big trouble, mister;* dry, bland results are on the horizon.

There are two techniques to master that will change your stir-fried chicken game forever. The first, **washing and marinating**, requires very little effort and will improve both juiciness and flavor (see page 49). It's a standard step in every stir-fry recipe. The second, **velveting**, is not always essential (it can't, for instance, be combined with dishes that require browning meat), but it will produce incredibly tender and juicy meat (see page 72).

Shopping for and Breaking Down a Whole Chicken, Step by Step

Considering the markup on prebutchered chicken, knowing how to quickly and efficiently break one down is a useful skill. At my supermarket, for the cost of a pound or so of boneless, skinless breast meat, you can buy an entire chicken, which comes with the same two breasts, plus two thighs, two legs, two wings, a carcass, and frequently a gizzard, liver, and heart thrown in as a bonus prize (I love chicken liver or heart sautéed in a bit of butter, but if you're not into that, dogs love them as well).

When shopping for whole chickens, I prefer to buy air-chilled chicken, which was cooled after slaughter with cold air as opposed to a dunk in an ice bath. Water-chilled chicken absorbs liquid into its meat, which then comes out during cooking and makes stir-frying or roasting difficult. It's also more slippery to the touch and can leave messy pools of pink juices on your cutting board. Air-chilled chicken is a little pricier, but it's worth it in my opinion. Chicken that is air-chilled will invariably be marked as such. If the labeling doesn't indicate one way or another, it's a good bet the chicken was water-chilled.

As for free range, organic, and the like, much of that comes down to the environmental impact and humane standards more than it does flavor, but typically the better-raised the chicken, the better the flavor, and the better it is for the environment (and, unfortunately, the pricier). Go with the highest quality of life that your budget allows. (See my book *The Food Lab* for a more detailed guide to chicken labeling.)

There are many ways to break down a chicken, but usually I'll remove the wings for making stock or frying, take the breasts off the bone to use in stir-fries (or leave them on the bone for poaching), and remove the legs to use in soups and stocks (or bone out the thigh and cut it up for stir-fries). You'll need a sharp chef's knife or cleaver, a heavy knife or cleaver you don't mind banging up a little (you'll be cutting through small chicken bones), and a nice big cutting board for the process. Here's how:

Step 1 • Spread the Legs

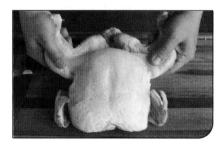

With the chicken on its back, grab the chicken by the drumstick and pull the leg out from the body until the skin is stretched taut.

Step 2 • Cut through the Skin

Start the operation by cutting through the skin between the leg and the body. Don't cut too deep—just through the skin. No matter what Cat Stevens says, the first cut should be the shallowest. Repeat this cut on the other side.

Step 3 • Pop Out the Joint

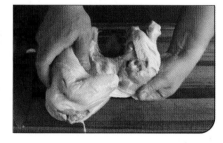

Grab both legs and fold them downward, using the two legs as a sort of lever that lifts the carcass of the chicken up toward you. Keep going until you see the ball joint from each leg pop out of its socket. This will require only minimal force.

Step 4 • Cut Off the Legs

Slip the blade of your knife into the joint you just exposed and cut away the leg. Try to push your knife blade as close to the chicken's backbone and hips as possible, following the contour of the bones to get the little nugget of dark meat that rests in there (this is called the *oyster*). If you don't get it, no worries; once you simmer the carcass for stock you can pull out the cooked oyster with your fingers. Repeat this process on the other leg.

Step 5 • Remove the Wings

With the chicken resting on its side, pull on its wing to stretch it out. This should allow you to estimate where the bone inside the drumette attaches to the carcass. Use the heel of your knife to cut through the breast from the side, aiming for that joint socket. (Once you get there, wiggle your knife to get through it and remove the wing. If you feel like your knife is hitting solid bone rather than getting through the ligaments around the joint, reposition and try again.) Repeat with the other wing.

At this point you can either remove the breast meat from the carcass for slicing or cubing for use in stir-fries (see below) or leave it on the carcass and further split the chicken for bone-in breast pieces for poaching or simmering.

HOW TO REMOVE CHICKEN BREAST MEAT FOR STIR-FRIES

Step 1 • Cut Along the Sternum

Cut along one side of the chicken's breastbone (sternum), using the tip of your knife and keeping it pressed against the bone as much as possible.

Step 2 • Free the Breast

Continue cutting along the chicken's sternum and rib cage, peeling the breast meat back with your free hand as you go to expose the carcass until the boneless breast is completely freed from the chicken carcass. Repeat on the other side.

Step 3 • Chop the Carcass

Use a heavy chef's knife or cleaver (one you don't mind beating up a little) to hack the carcass into smaller pieces for more efficient stock making. You can also peel the skin off the chicken breast pieces and add them to the stock ingredients for more body.

HOW TO SPLIT A WHOLE BONE-IN CHICKEN BREAST FOR POACHING OR SIMMERING

Step 1 • Split the Back

Hold the chicken by the back and position it vertically on your cutting board, with the butt end pointing up. Use your knife to cut through the skin and cartilage between the breast and the back until you get through the first or second rib. Switch over to your cleaver or a knife you don't mind beating up a little and continue cutting through the ribs, using short, firm strokes. Alternatively, use poultry shears to cut through the ribs on both sides. The backbone should now be completely separated from the whole breast. Hack it into smaller pieces and save it for stock.

Step 2 • Split the Breasts

To split the breast, cut through the center of the breastbone with firm, downward pressure until your knife cracks through the bone and splits the breast in half. These breast halves are now ready for poaching or simmering.

HOW TO CUT BONELESS CHICKEN BREAST FOR STIR-FRIES

Depending on the dish, chicken breast meat can be thinly sliced, cut into cubes, or cut into thin slivers. Here's how to do it. Start by carefully patting the chicken dry, then placing it on a plate and putting it in the freezer for 15 minutes.

Step 1 • Identify the Grain

All muscle matter has a grain to it. The muscle fibers align in the direction that they contract. The orientation of your knife to this grain will determine the length of the muscle fibers in an individual slice of meat, which in turn will have a profound effect on how tender or tough that meat is. (See "The Trigonometry of Slicing Against the Grain," page 57.)

A chicken breast consists of two sets of muscle grains—one large, one small—whose angles mirror each other across a seam in the center.

Step 2 • Cut the Chicken

For slices: When slicing chicken for stir-fries, set your knife perpendicular to this seam so that the knife ends up cutting at around a 45-degree angle to both muscle grains.

Hold the chicken breast with your nonknife hand, curling your fingertips under your knuckles (so you don't slice them off!), and slice the chicken with long, even strokes into slices about ¼ inch thick.

For slivers: Take those slices, stack a few at a time, and slice them lengthwise into matchsticks.

For dice: Start by slicing the chicken breast lengthwise into strips. The width of these strips should be the same as the dimensions of your final dice (i.e., for ½-inch dice, start by cutting the chicken into ½-inch strips).

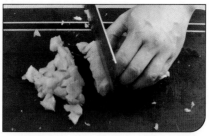

Next, cut each strip crosswise into dice.

NOTE: Chicken breasts are about ½ inch thick to start, so for fine, ¼-inch dice for recipes such as *san choi bao* (lettuce cups with hoisin and pine nuts), you'll need to start by cutting ¼-inch strips, turning each of those strips onto their wide side, then further splitting each one in half, yielding ¼-by-¼-inch strips that can then be cross-cut into ¼-inch dice.

HOW TO BONE OUT A CHICKEN THIGH FOR STIR-FRIES

Step 1 • Locate the Joint

If you're starting with whole chicken legs, you'll have to remove the drumstick from the thigh. Place your thumb over the joint and move the thigh bone back and forth with your other hand to find the articulation point. This is where you'll cut.

Step 2 • Divide the Leg

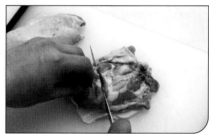

Insert a sharp boning or paring knife into the joint. It should slide right through. If there is resistance, move the blade around until you find the space between the joints. Set aside the drumstick for another use (such as simmering for stock or in place of wings in Extra-Crispy Korean Fried Chicken, page 460). Peel the skin off the chicken thigh using your hands and trim off any excessive bits of opaque yellow or white fat (a little is OK; just clean up the edges).

Step 3 • Find the Bone and Make the First Incision

Flip over the thigh so that the rough side is up and locate the single bone that runs through it. Your goal is to remove this bone with minimal damage to the meat. Keeping the fingers of your nonknife hand curled for protection (raw chicken can be slippery) and using the tip of the knife, score a line through the meat along the length of the bone.

Step 4 • Expose Bone

Expose the top of the bone by using the tip of your knife in short, flicking motions, making sure to keep your fingers well away from the blade. A clean paper towel can help you get a better grip.

Step 5 • Scrape the Bone

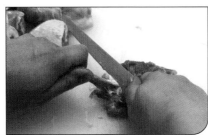

Grasp one end of the bone with your nonknife hand (a little piece of paper towel can help if it's very slippery), then, using the base of your knife, scrape the meat off of the bone in short, firm flicks. A boning knife should have a curved bolster designed for this task. If using a paring knife, chef's knife, or cleaver, just use the section of the knife closest to the handle.

Step 6 • Separate Meat from Bone

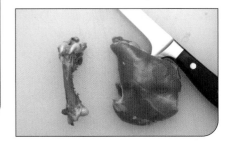

When the meat has been mostly scraped off the bone, separate the end of the bone completely from the meat. Trim away any gristle or bits of bone or cartilage that may have remained on the meat. Save the bones for stock and use the meat for recipes as desired.

HOW TO CUT CHICKEN THIGHS FOR STIR-FRIES

Chicken thighs, with their uneven musculature and ample connective tissue and fat, fare better diced than sliced or slivered. It's easiest to start with boneless, skinless chicken thighs, but you can also start with whole thighs and debone them yourself

Step 1 • Trim Fat

Trim off any large deposits of excess fat with your knife and discard.

Step 2 • Cut Strips

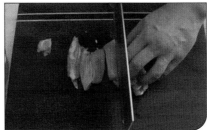

Cut both halves of the chicken thighs lengthwise into ½-inch strips.

Step 3 • Cut Dice

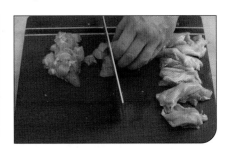

Rotate the strips 90 degrees and cut them crosswise into ½-inch dice.

The Trigonometry of Slicing against the Grain

It's all well and good to say that slicing against the grain leads to shorter muscle fibers, but how much difference does it actually make? Let's turn to a bit of eighth-grade trigonometry to find out.

Some definitions

→ First, let's define the angle between the knife blade and the meat fibers as *θ*.

→ Now, let's call the distance you move your knife between slices (i.e., the width of each slice) *w*.

→ With these two definitions, let's set up an equation to calculate the length of the muscle fibers in the resulting slices, *m*.

With these definitions, we arrive at the equation $w/\sin(\theta)=m$.

So if our goal is to minimize the length of muscle fibers, we can achieve that either by minimizing *w* (i.e., making thinner slices) or by maximizing *sin(θ)* (i.e., cutting perfectly perpendicular to the grain).

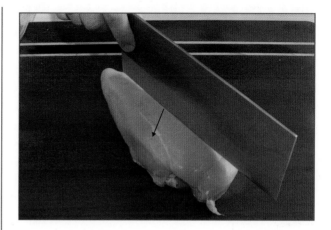

If, on the other hand, we cut with the knife held at a 45-degree angle to the meat fibers, while the width of the slice is still ½ inch, the length of the muscle fibers has reached a little over $7/10$ inch (that's $.5^{1/2}$), an increase of over 40%!

How much does that angle really make a difference? When the knife is held perpendicular to the direction of the meat fibers, *sin(θ)* is equal to 1 and the meat fibers are exactly as long as the slice is wide. If our knife strokes are ½ inch apart from each other, then the muscle fibers end up ½ inch long. This is as short as we can get them for a given cut width.

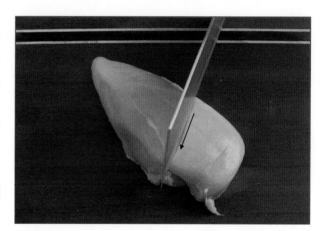

So what if we take it to the extreme: as the angle of the blade approaches the angle of the muscle fibers, *sin(θ)* will approach 0, while *m* will approach infinity. Thus, according to the unbreakable laws of mathematics, your meat fibers would stretch all the way out to the edges of the universe. Now that's a big, tough chicken!

TAKEOUT-STYLE DICED CHICKEN WITH HOT PEPPERS AND PEANUTS

Growing up, I spent my Saturdays at the Manhattan School of Music, just a few blocks away from the Morningside Heights location of Ollie's, a minichain of New York restaurants that specializes in Chinese American cuisine, in all its extra-saucy, moderately gloppy glory. My standard order there was the Diced Chicken with Hot Peppers and Peanuts. It's not too hot, not too powerfully flavored, and has a pretty good balance of meat and vegetables designed to be eaten as a meal (or in my case, a $6.95 lunch special) unto itself with a side of white rice.

The dish has its roots in *gong bao ji ding*, or kung pao chicken, the Sichuan classic made with hot dried chiles, Sichuan peppercorns, and peanuts in a mild sauce (you can find my recipe on page 61). Just trade out most of the dried chiles for diced bell peppers and celery and you're basically there. (If you're partial to the version served at the Chinese-owned takeout chain Panda Express, you can use zucchini in place of celery.) All you need is a bottomless pot of tea, some steamed white rice, perhaps a side of egg drop or hot and sour soup, and a fortune cookie or two and you've hit lunch-special nirvana.

It follows the basic stir-fry formula to a T, and it's a Chinese American staple, making it the perfect recipe to start honing your stir-fry chops. Let's go step by step for this one.

Before You Begin • Mise en Place

Mise en place is the French term for the things you should have in place before you begin cooking. It can include things like trimmed meat, chopped vegetables, minced herbs, ground spices, cooking vessels and tools. The idea is that at no point during the cooking process should you ever have to scramble to search for something while your food overcooks.

For a stir-fry, that means chopping your vegetables, cutting and marinating your meats, collecting your additional ingredients, mincing your aromatics, and measuring out and combining your sauce ingredients.

Before I begin, I always take a look at the complete recipe so that I can consolidate ingredients. In this case I can go ahead and put my marinated chicken in one bowl, my diced zucchini or celery and bell peppers together in another (they get added to the wok at the same time), peanuts and scallion segments in a third, combine all of my aromatics (smashed garlic, ginger, and whole dried hot chiles) in a fourth, combine my sauce ingredients in a fifth, and make a cornstarch slurry in the last.

Finally, I'll also keep a large bowl on hand for combining ingredients as they're cooked and a serving platter for when everything is done.

With my mise en place ready, it's time to cook.

Step 1 • Preheat the Wok

As with all large stir-fries on a home range, I cook meats and vegetables in batches to ensure that the wok doesn't lose too much heat during the cooking process, before combining them all at the end.

I start by heating a thin film of oil that I wipe into the wok with a paper towel. When it's literally smoking hot, I add a bit more cooking oil (see "Does a Hot Wok and Cold Oil Really Prevent Sticking?" on page 39). At this stage many recipes would call for adding some aromatics to the oil, like a slice of ginger, a smashed garlic clove, or spices, to add flavor to the oil before stir-frying. With the batch-cooking technique, however, I first par-cook all my ingredients, then add the aromatics to bloom in oil just before the last phase, where everything is recombined. This is done to ensure that the aromatics don't burn and that their volatile aromas are at their peak potency when eaten.

Step 2 • Stir-Fry the Chicken

In goes the chicken. With a rip-roaring, smoking-hot wok, the chicken should take on color in just a matter of minutes. Lightly browned but still raw in the center is what we're going for here. Don't worry about that raw center: The chicken will continue to cook via residual heat once it gets transferred to a bowl and set aside, and it'll get heated up once more in the sauce later on.

I usually stir-fry my meat first because meat is able to handle residual heat much better than most vegetables can. Vegetables will overcook and turn mushy if you let them sit for too long after cooking.

Step 3 • Infuse the Oil

The next step is to infuse the oil with some aromatics. In a traditional stir-fry, you'd do this right at the start, but when working in batches like this, I wait until the final batch of ingredients. Oil can be infused with a variety of aromatics. In this case I'm using whole dried chiles, smashed garlic, and ginger slices.

If you've ever eaten this dish at a Chinese restaurant, you'll know that it's typically hot in name only. There's not much heat to warrant the one red chile that gets printed on the menu next to the title. In this case the chiles are really more for their roasty aroma than for actual capsicum heat. (Although if you'd like, you can slit them open or snip them into segments with kitchen shears so that their seeds and ribs make it into the dish, adding significant heat.)

Step 4 • Stir-Fry the Vegetables

For this recipe I use red and green bell peppers cut into large dice, along with celery or zucchini that's cut into equal-size chunks.

If you have a pretty powerful burner, you'll probably be able to cook the vegetables together. Otherwise, you'll want to cook them in batches, transferring each batch to the bowl with the chicken as it cooks and letting the wok come to a light smoke in between batches. The goal is to get some charring and color on them before they soften too much—this shouldn't take more than a minute or two.

Step 5 • Add Peanuts and Scallions

Once the vegetables are done, in go the peanuts and scallion segments. Traditional Chinese recipes will have you par-cook raw peanuts by roasting, simmering, or frying before you subsequently stir-fry them. Thankfully, this is not a traditional Chinese recipe, and roasted peanuts straight off the supermarket shelf do just fine.

Step 6 • Return Everything to the Wok

Drop the chicken back into the wok (along with the vegetables if you cooked them in batches).

Step 7 • Sauce It Up!

Next, add the sauce, which you've thoughtfully pre-mixed and had ready to go from the start (right?). It's a simple blend of soy sauce, chicken broth, vinegar, sesame oil, and sugar. Like many Chinese American dishes, it has a distinctly sweet and sour flavor profile.

Step 8 • The Sauce Thickens

Last step: Splash in some of the cornstarch slurry and give it all a quick toss over the heat to thicken the sauce. If the sauce is too thin, add a little more slurry. If it's too thick, splash in a little water. The sauce should thicken enough to coat each piece in a glossy sheen without getting too gloppy.

OK, a little gloppiness is OK. It's an essential part of the totally authentic inauthentic experience.

I get a little giddy when I see food like this. Don't get me wrong, I get giddy when I see real Chinese food, with thousands of years of development and tradition poured into it, but there's a reason those Upper West Side Cantonese restaurants all do so well, and it's got something to do with food like this.

CHINESE AMERICAN KUNG PAO CHICKEN

Yield
Serves 4

Active Time
30 minutes

Total Time
30 minutes

NOTE
For the most efficient process, get your chicken in the marinade first, chopping your vegetables, mincing aromatics, and mixing your sauce while it marinates.

INGREDIENTS

For the Chicken:

1 pound (450 g) boneless, skinless chicken thighs, cut into ½- to ¾-inch chunks

½ teaspoon (1.5 g) kosher salt

1 teaspoon (5 ml) light soy sauce

1 teaspoon (5 ml) Shaoxing wine or dry sherry

½ teaspoon (2 g) sugar

½ teaspoon (3 ml) roasted sesame oil

½ teaspoon (1.5 g) cornstarch

For the Sauce:

1 tablespoon (15 ml) light soy sauce or shoyu

2 teaspoons (10 ml) dark soy sauce

1 tablespoon (12 g) sugar

2 teaspoons (10 ml) rice vinegar

1 tablespoon (15 ml) Shaoxing wine

1 teaspoon (5 ml) roasted sesame oil

For the Cornstarch Slurry:

2 teaspoons (6 g) cornstarch

1 tablespoon (15 ml) water

For the Stir-Fry:

3 tablespoons (45 ml) peanut, rice bran, or other neutral oil

2 coin-sized slices (10 g) fresh ginger

2 medium garlic cloves (5 g), smashed

8 small dried red Chinese or árbol chiles, snipped into ½-inch segments, or ¼ teaspoon hot red pepper flakes

1 small zucchini (about 5 ounces/145 g), cut into ½-inch dice

1 medium red bell pepper (about 5 ounces/145 g), cut into ½-inch dice

2 scallions, sliced ½ inch thick

½ cup (about 3 ounces/90 g) roasted peanuts

DIRECTIONS

(1) **For the Chicken:** Place the chicken in a medium bowl, cover with cold water, and vigorously agitate it. Drain through a fine-mesh strainer set in the sink and press on the chicken with your hands to remove excess water. Return the chicken to the bowl and add the salt, soy sauce, wine, sugar, sesame oil, and cornstarch. Stir vigorously with your fingertips or chopsticks for 30 seconds. Set aside while you prepare the remaining stir-fry ingredients (at least 15 minutes).

(2) **For the Sauce:** Combine the soy sauce, sugar, vinegar, wine, and sesame oil in a small bowl and stir together until homogenous. Set aside. Combine the cornstarch and water in a separate small bowl and stir with a fork until the cornstarch is dissolved.

(3) **BEFORE YOU STIR-FRY, GET YOUR BOWLS READY:**

a. Marinated chicken	f. Cornstarch slurry
b. Ginger, garlic, and dry chiles	g. Empty bowl for cooked ingredients
c. Zucchini and bell peppers	
d. Scallions and peanuts	h. Serving platter
e. Sauce	

(4) **For the Stir-Fry:** Using a paper towel, rub a thin film of oil into a wok and set it over high heat until smoking. Add 1 tablespoon of the oil and swirl to coat. Immediately add the chicken, spread into a single layer, and cook without moving until lightly browned, about 1 minute. Continue cooking, tossing and stirring frequently, until the exterior is opaque but the chicken is still slightly raw in the center, about 2 minutes longer. Transfer to a clean bowl and set aside.

(5) Wipe out the wok and reheat over high heat until lightly smoking. Add the remaining 2 tablespoons oil and swirl to coat. Immediately add the ginger, garlic, and chiles and stir-fry until the chiles darken in color, about 10 seconds. Immediately add the zucchini and peppers and stir-fry until the vegetables are tender-crisp, about 1 minute. Add the scallions and peanuts and toss to combine.

(6) Return the chicken to the wok and toss everything to combine. Stir the sauce and add to the wok by pouring it around the edges. Stir the cornstarch slurry and add a splash. Cook, tossing, until the sauce thickens and the chicken is cooked through, about 30 seconds longer. Adjust the sauce consistency with more cornstarch slurry if it is too thin or a splash of water if it is too thick. Transfer to a serving platter and serve immediately with steamed rice.

How to Cut Bell Peppers for Stir-Fries

Step 1 • Slice Down a Valley

Hold the pepper upright on your cutting board. Notice that the pepper has multiple deep valleys that run from top to bottom. These valleys are an indication of where the spongy interior pith (the stuff we want to remove) is attached to the outer walls (the stuff we want to keep).

Using a very sharp chef's knife or paring knife, slice downward, following the contour of one of these valleys to remove a section of the pepper's wall.

Step 2 • Work Around

Continue making similar slices, working your way around the pepper until every section of pepper wall has been removed and you are left with the stem, seeds, and pith all in one piece that can now be discarded or composted.

Step 3 • Cut into Spears or Dice

For spears or julienne: Slice each section lengthwise into pieces as thick or thin as the recipe calls for.

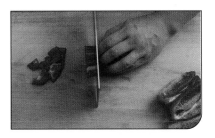

For dice: Start by cutting sections into spears, then rotate 90 degrees and cut crosswise to create dice.

How to Cut Celery for Stir-Fries

Step 1 • Peel the Outer Layers

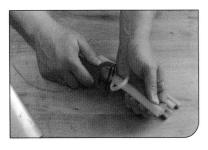

Peeling celery is not entirely necessary, but it removes the stringy fibers around the outside of each rib, which have a tendency to stick between your teeth. Using a vegetable peeler, peel this stringy outer layer off the celery rib.

Step 2 • Cut the Celery

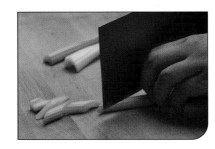

For crescents: Cut the celery rib crosswise either directly perpendicular to its length or on a bias into ¼-inch crescents. Use for dishes where meat is cut into wider slices, such as Cumin Lamb (page 134).

For batons: Cut the celery rib crosswise into 2- to 3-inch segments, then cut each segment lengthwise into thin batons. Use in dishes where meat is cut into thin julienne strips, such as Dry-Fried Beef (page 436).

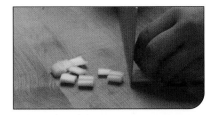

For dice: Split the celery rib lengthwise in half for large dice or into quarters for fine dice. Rotate and cut each strip crosswise into evenly sized dice. Use in dishes with diced meat, such as Kung Pao Chicken (page 61).

GONG BAO JI DING (SICHUAN CHICKEN WITH PEANUTS)

This one is the real deal. The Sichuan original that has been served in the mountainous regions of southwestern China since at least the nineteenth century. Unlike the Chinese American version, which is composed of nearly equal parts chicken and vegetables, the Sichuan original is mainly chicken with peanuts and scallions added in for textural variety. With a cooking time of mere minutes and prep that can be done while your rice is cooking, it's a near-perfect weeknight dish when paired with some simple stir-fried greens (see page 201).

The food in Sichuan can be explosively flavored with tons of hot chiles and fermented beans (see, for example, Mapo Tofu on page 598), but gong bao ji ding is decidedly more subtle. Its main aroma is citrusy and mouth-numbing Sichuan peppercorns, and rather than fatty nuggets of chicken thigh, it's made with cubes of tender, moist chicken breast coated in a sweet, hot, and numbing glaze.

When I started working to re-create this dish back at home, I didn't have to go much further than Fuchsia Dunlop's version in her book *Every Grain of Rice*. My recipe is adapted from hers, along with some notes I took in Chengdu. It starts with a handful of dried hot red chiles bloomed in oil along with some Sichuan peppercorns. This step allows the flavor of the chiles and the peppercorns to add a gentle fragrance to every bite without giving you the overwhelming metallic hit that powdered peppercorns can.

The easiest way to prepare the chiles is to snip them into short segments (about ⅓ inch/1 cm) with some kitchen shears, then shake out the excess seeds, which can make the dish too spicy. Sichuan peppercorns are not spicy at all, but rather have a curious mouth-numbing sensation that complements the heat of chiles very well (a combination of flavors unique to Sichuan cuisine known as *mmálà*, or "numbing hot," which I discuss in more detail on page 313). You can find Sichuan peppercorns in both green and red varieties at most Asian markets these days, or you can easily order them online. Green peppercorns tend to be a little stronger in flavor than red, though either variety will do in most recipes. The flavor in Sichuan peppercorns is all in the husks, so any small twigs or dark, shiny seeds you find should be picked out and discarded.

Once the oil has been infused, you stir-fry cubes of chicken breast that have been marinated with soy sauce, Shaoxing wine, cornstarch, and salt.

Recipes for *gong bao ji ding* vary in how garlic and ginger are incorporated. I first tried adding them in minced form but found it overpowered the mild chicken breast. Instead, I add the garlic in thin slices and the ginger in fine matchsticks (julienne).

In my recipe, my sauce is a simple mixture of soy sauce, Shaoxing wine, Chinkiang vinegar, and honey (I find even the smallest amount of sesame oil, a common ingredient in this dish, to be distracting, but you can add a few drops if you'd like), bound together with just a touch of cornstarch. Not all recipes include vinegar, but I enjoy the lightness it brings to the dish.

The whole dish cooks in about half the time it took you to read these notes. It's hard to think of an easier weeknight meal.

GONG BAO JI DING

Yield
Serves 4

Active Time
15 minutes

Total Time
15 minutes

INGREDIENTS

For the Chicken:

1 pound boneless, skinless chicken breast, cut into ½-inch cubes
1 teaspoon (5 ml) Shaoxing wine or dry sherry
1 teaspoon (5 ml) light soy sauce or shoyu
1 teaspoon (about 3 g) cornstarch
Large pinch of kosher salt

For the Sauce:

1 tablespoon (15 ml) honey
1 tablespoon (15 ml) Chinkiang vinegar
1 tablespoon (15 ml) Shaoxing wine or dry sherry
1 tablespoon (15 ml) light soy sauce or shoyu

For the Cornstarch Slurry:

1 teaspoon (3 g) cornstarch
1 tablespoon (15 ml) water

For the Stir-Fry:

3 tablespoons (45 ml) peanut, rice bran, or other neutral oil
6 to 12 small dried hot red chiles (such as Sichuan, jing tiao, or árbol), stems removed, cut into ½-inch pieces with scissors, and seeds discarded
1 teaspoon (about 2 g) Sichuan peppercorns, reddish husks only (stems and black seeds discarded)
4 medium garlic cloves (10 g), thinly sliced
One 1-inch knob fresh ginger (20 g), preferably young ginger, peeled and cut into fine matchsticks (see page 67)
6 scallions, white and pale green parts only, cut into ½-inch pieces
¾ cup (about 4 ounces/120 g) roasted peanuts

DIRECTIONS

(1) **For the Chicken:** Place the chicken in a medium bowl, cover with cold water, and vigorously agitate it. Drain through a fine-mesh strainer set in the sink and press on the chicken with your hands to remove excess water. Combine the chicken, wine, soy sauce, cornstarch, and salt in a small bowl and stir vigorously with your fingertips or chopsticks for 30 seconds. Set aside.

(2) **For the Sauce:** Combine the honey, vinegar, wine, and soy sauce in a small bowl and stir together until homogenous. Set aside. Combine the cornstarch and water in a separate small bowl and stir with a fork until the cornstarch is dissolved.

(3) **BEFORE YOU STIR-FRY, GET YOUR BOWLS READY:**

a. Dried chiles and Sichuan peppercorn
b. Marinated chicken
c. Garlic and ginger
d. Scallions and peanuts
e. Sauce
f. Cornstarch slurry
g. Empty bowl for cooked ingredients
h. Serving platter

(4) **To Stir-Fry:** Pour a small amount of oil into the bottom of a large wok or skillet and rub around with a paper towel. Place over high heat and pre-heat until smoking. Add 1 tablespoon oil and immediately add the chiles and Sichuan peppercorns. Stir-fry until fragrant but not burnt, about 5 seconds. Immediately add the chicken and stir-fry constantly until there are no pink spots on the exterior (chicken will still be raw in center at this stage), 2 to 2 ½ minutes. Transfer to an empty bowl.

(5) Wipe out the wok and add the remaining 2 tablespoons oil. Heat over high heat until shimmering. Add the garlic and ginger and stir-fry until fragrant, about 10 seconds. Add the scallions and peanuts and stir-fry for 30 seconds.

(6) Return the chicken to the wok and toss everything to combine. Stir the sauce and add to the wok by pouring it around the edges. Stir the cornstarch slurry and add a splash. Cook, tossing, until the sauce thickens and the chicken is cooked through, about 30 seconds longer. Adjust the sauce consistency with more cornstarch slurry if it is too thin or a splash of water if it is too thick. Transfer to a serving platter and serve immediately with steamed rice.

How to Cut Scallions for Stir-Fries

Scallions (also known as "green onions" or "spring onions") are used as an aromatic or as a sweet-savory vegetable in countless stir-fries and other Asian dishes.

SHOPPING AND STORAGE

Look for scallions that are firm and fresh looking with greens that stand up straight and don't show any signs of dryness around the upper edges where they've been cut. The outer layers of the scallions should also be firm and juicy, not papery or yellow-brown.

Fresh scallions can be stored in a loosely closed paper or plastic bag in the refrigerator for several days or longer.

Cut scallions can be stored in a container filled with cold water for up to a day. To use scallions that have been stored in water, pick them up with a fine-mesh strainer or your finger and give them a hard toss down onto a plate lined with paper towels to knock off extra moisture or drain them in a fine-mesh strainer and blot them on a clean kitchen towel or paper towels to dry them.

I've seen some folks recommend putting scallion whites in a cup of water on a windowsill to regrow greens that can then be reharvested for use and repeated multiple times. This is an OK method if you never want to use the scallion whites (the best part of the scallion!) and you don't mind scallion greens that are increasingly flavorless.

TO CLEAN SCALLIONS

If your scallions are ultrafresh, you can skip this step. But most scallions from the supermarket will have outer green and white layers that are a little limp or discolored. Remove those outer layers, then wash the root end of the scallion in cold water, rubbing with your fingers until the thin slippery membrane left behind by the layer you just removed is also completely gone.

Trim off the hairy roots at the base of the scallion.

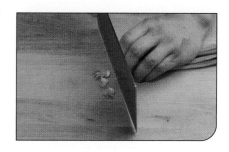

FOR SEGMENTS

Cut the white and pale green parts of the scallion crosswise into ½- to ¾-inch segments. Save the greens for another use.

FOR FINE SLICES

Scallions, like other delicate vegetables and herbs, should be cut using a slicing motion as opposed to chopping. When you chop, you move your knife up and down with very little horizontal motion. This can cause crushing or bruising. Slicing using the full length of the blade and minimal downward pressure creates the cleanest cuts. Here's a good rule of thumb: the more you can hear yourself slicing, the more you're crushing those poor scallions. A good, clean slice with a sharp knife should be nearly silent.

I like to employ a method called the **back-slice**, where you pull your knife blade toward you as you slice, rather than pushing forward away from you.

Hold the scallions with your nonknife hand, curling your fingertips back under your knuckles to keep them protected. Rest the flat part of your knife against the knuckles of your nonknife hand and place the tip of the knife on the cutting board. Slowly pull back the knife, using your knuckles as a guide to thinly slice the scallions. Continue cutting in this manner—slicing as you pull the knife backward—while guiding the scallions to the knife with your nonknife hand.

KNIFE SKILLS

FOR MINCE

Cut the scallions into 3- to 4-inch segments. Cut each segment lengthwise in half, then each half lengthwise again into quarters.

Collect the quartered segments and slice them crosswise into mince. You can further reduce this mince by rocking back and forth over it with your knife.

SCALLION HAIRS FOR GARNISH

Scallion hairs make a pretty garnish for salads, noodle soups, and other dishes. The process is the same as with the back-slice, but instead of cutting crosswise, slice the scallions nearly parallel to the blade. You may have to crush them a bit with your steadying hand to get them to slice cleanly.

Store the sliced scallions in a container of ice water in the fridge for at least 30 minutes and up to overnight and they'll absorb liquid, firming up and curling into pretty little threads.

(An added benefit of storing the sliced scallions in cold water, at least for those who are sensitive to raw onion flavor, is that it will temper their potency a little, resulting in crisp, fresh, and milder-tasting scallions.)

SCALLION BRUSHES

You ever order Peking duck at a Chinese restaurant and get served a bowl of hoisin sauce with some cute little scallion brushes to paint the sauce onto your pancakes? Those little brushes are supereasy to make at home.

Start by trimming down your scallion to about 2½ inches long and trim off the root end as close as you can to the base. Holding the scallion steady with your nonknife hand, align your knife parallel to the scallion and place the tip of your blade about an inch up from the cut side. Cut through to split the end of the scallion in half.

Repeat the process, rotating the scallion a few times so that you've made a total of four cuts, dividing the scallion-end into eight individual sections.

Transfer the brushes to a bowl of ice water in the fridge and let them soak for at least 30 minutes and up to overnight to get them to firm up and curl.

How to Cut Ginger for Stir-Fries

Ginger can be cut for stir-fries in a number of ways. For a very mild ginger flavor, thick coin-shaped slices with the skin on can be used to infuse oil before adding your main ingredients. Ginger can be minced for ginger flavor that permeates a dish (such as Ginger Beef on page 120), or it can be cut into fine julienne and treated more like a vegetable than an aromatic for bursts of flavor (like in Gong Bao Ji Ding on page 64).

SHOPPING AND STORAGE

Ginger is the edible rhizome of a perennial flowering plant.* **Young ginger** has pale yellow, relatively smooth and thin skin. It has a milder flavor and juicier, smoother texture, which makes it ideal for julienne. **Mature ginger** has thicker, darker skin and a more fibrous texture with stronger flavor. In most Western supermarkets, all you're going to find is mature ginger. This is OK. Most dishes will work just fine with older ginger. If you have access to a good Asian market, look for the younger stuff, which is usually sorted separately from the mature ginger.

When buying ginger, look for hands that are plump and smooth looking with a firm texture that doesn't bend or yield under pressure. Avoid soft or wrinkly roots. For ease of cutting and better yield, I look for hands of ginger with larger sections and as few smaller branches as possible.

Mature ginger can be stored on the counter at room temperature for several days or even weeks. Young ginger should be stored in a partially sealed container or loosely closed plastic bag in the refrigerator.

As with garlic, I find the mortar and pestle to be the best tool for mincing and crushing ginger. For a finer puree to use in things like dressings and marinades, you might consider investing in a Japanese-style ginger grater, which comes in either ceramic or metal. It's a small plate or paddle with tiny teeth for grinding and a well for collection. These graters can also be used for grating other vegetables like carrots (for Japanese Side Salad, page 622), garlic, daikon radish, wasabi or horseradish root, or onions. A rasp like a Microplane will also work for these purposes.

Unlike cut garlic, grated or chopped ginger can be stored for several days in a sealed container in the refrigerator.

TO PREPARE GINGER

Separate the fingers: Break sections off the main hand of ginger with your hands. Break off only as much as you need to use for a given recipe.

Peel: There are two easy ways to peel ginger. Neither involves a peeler. If you're comfortable with a knife, you can peel ginger by cutting it crosswise to create a stable plane, then using the tip of your knife to cut downward and remove the peel in sections.

The easier but slightly more time-consuming way to peel ginger is with a regular soupspoon. Scrape the spoon against the skin and it should come right off, leaving the interior intact.

continues

---

* Although the edible portion of ginger is often called "ginger root," it is in fact a rhizome: a modified underground plant stem from which roots shoot out downward and plant stems can shoot out upward. Tubers like potatoes are also not roots! They are, in fact, enlarged portions of rhizomes.

KNIFE SKILLS

With either method I recommend saving the peels and placing them in a container with some soy sauce in the fridge. The ginger-flavored soy sauce is great for dressings, marinades, and sauces. You can continuously add fresh soy sauce and ginger to the container to keep it topped up and flavorful. (Discard old ginger occasionally if the container starts to get too full of ginger skins.)

FOR SLICES OR COINS

For slices you plan on using to flavor oil, simply cut the peeled ginger crosswise into coin-shaped disks about ¼ inch thick.

FOR MATCHSTICKS

Start with a peeled 1½- to 2-inch section of ginger. Cut off one side of the section, cutting lengthwise to create a flat, stable surface for the ginger to rest on.

With the ginger resting on its newly cut surface, use a sharp chef's knife to cut the ginger into planks that are ⅟₁₆ to ⅛ inch thick. Alternatively, use a Japanese-style mandoline to slice the ginger into ⅟₁₆- to ⅛-inch planks.

Stack a few of the planks together and slice them lengthwise with your chef's knife to create fine matchsticks.

TO MINCE WITH A MORTAR AND PESTLE

Peel and slice ginger across the grain into rough ⅛- to ¼-inch slices. Place them in the bowl of a mortar and pestle and crush to the desired consistency. Ginger and garlic can be crushed together in this fashion if a recipe calls for both of them to be added at the same time.

TO MINCE WITH A KNIFE

Cut the ginger into ¼-inch coins, then smash each one firmly with the side of a knife or a cleaver.

Rock your knife over the smashed ginger to reduce it to a mince.

CHICKEN WITH BASIL, CHILES, AND FISH SAUCE

Yield
Serves 4

Active Time
30 minutes

Total Time
30 minutes

NOTE
Sliced pork loin or tenderloin can be used in place of the chicken. Thai or holy basil can be used in place of the sweet Italian.

INGREDIENTS

For the Chicken:
1 pound (450 g) boneless, skinless chicken breasts, cut into ⅛-inch slices
½ teaspoon (1.5 g) kosher salt
1 teaspoon (5 ml) fish sauce
¼ teaspoon freshly ground white pepper
1 teaspoon (2 g) sugar
½ teaspoon (2 g) baking soda
½ teaspoon (1.5 g) cornstarch

For the Sauce:
1 tablespoon (15 ml) fish sauce, plus more to taste
1 tablespoon (12 g) sugar, plus more to taste
⅛ teaspoon freshly ground white pepper
Hot red pepper flakes or Thai chile flakes to taste, plus more to taste

For the Stir-Fry:
2 tablespoons (30 ml) peanut, rice bran, or other neutral oil
4 medium garlic cloves, 2 gently smashed, 2 minced (about 2 teaspoons/5 g minced)
1 teaspoon (4 g) minced fresh ginger
1 medium shallot, sliced (about 1½ ounces/45 g)
2 cups loosely packed fresh basil or Thai basil leaves (about 2 ounces/60 g)

This recipe combines a few classic Thai flavors (basil, chiles, and fish sauce) in a supersimple weeknight stir-fry that is not particularly authentic to any specific dish found in Thailand. This is the dish for the kind of weeknight where you don't even want to bother mixing together a sauce. When I make dishes like this, I completely forgo the measuring spoons and scales. Eyeballing it and adjusting as you go is good enough.

DIRECTIONS

(1) **For the Chicken:** Place chicken in a medium bowl, cover with cold water, and vigorously agitate it. Drain through a fine-mesh strainer set in the sink and press on the chicken with your hands to remove excess water. Return the chicken to the bowl and add the fish sauce, white pepper, sugar, baking soda, and cornstarch. Stir vigorously with your fingertips or chopsticks for 30 seconds. Set aside while you prepare the remaining stir-fry ingredients (at least 15 minutes).

(2) **For the Sauce:** Combine the fish sauce, sugar, white pepper, and chile flakes.

(3) **BEFORE YOU STIR-FRY, GET YOUR BOWLS READY:**

a. Smashed garlic cloves	d. Sauce	
b. Marinated chicken	e. Basil leaves	
c. Minced garlic, ginger, and shallots	f. Serving platter	

(4) **To Stir-Fry:** Heat 1 tablespoon oil and the smashed garlic cloves in a wok over high heat until the garlic is sizzling and starts to brown. Add the chicken, spread it into a single layer, and cook without moving until lightly browned, about 1 minute. Continue cooking, tossing and stirring frequently, until the exterior is opaque, about 1 minute longer. Transfer to a bowl.

recipe continues

(5) Wipe out the wok, and the remaining tablespoon of oil, and heat over high heat until shimmering. Add the minced garlic, ginger, and shallots and stir-fry until fragrant, about 30 seconds.

(6) Return the chicken to the wok and stir-fry until the chicken is just cooked through and the shallots are softened, about 2 minutes longer.

(7) Add the sauce and toss to coat. Add the basil leaves and toss a couple times until they're wilted. Taste and adjust seasoning with more fish sauce, sugar, and chiles as desired, then transfer to a plate and serve immediately with jasmine or other rice and sliced cucumbers, if desired.

Rotten Anchovies, or How I Learned to Stop Worrying and Love Umami Bombs

Barrels and barrels of months-old anchovies. That's what I smelled that time I dropped an entire 750 ml bottle of fish sauce onto the hard tile floor of the kitchen at Clio, Ken Oringer's former Boston restaurant where I had just started on the *garde-manger* station. To be honest, it wasn't just me that smelled it. It was every cook, server, bartender, and guest in the restaurant. I watched as it dropped in slow motion, exploding like a grenade as the corner of the glass bottle hit the hard tile floor. The kitchen was immediately filled with a ripe stench that steadily wafted into the dining room over the course of the night. It took several days to dissipate completely.

While it's true that in large quantities fish sauce smells *terrible*, when used properly, it adds an incomparable depth of flavor and a big serving of umami to boot. Fermented fish-based condiments are old. In both China and the Mediterranean, fermented condiments made from salting and fermenting fish, meat, and soybeans date back to the third or fourth century B.C. Fish-based condiments dwindled in China when soy sauce became the condiment of choice around the first century A.D., but fish sauce maintained its popularity throughout Southeast Asia, where it remains the primary seasoning ingredient throughout Vietnam, Thailand, Indonesia, Laos, Cambodia, Burma, and the Philippines. A form of Malaysian fish sauce called *kecap* (see page 13) is thought to be the precursor to modern ketchup.

In Ancient Greece and Rome, a form of fish sauce called *garum* was produced originally by salting and fermenting fish guts. Garum of different qualities could be produced from the same batch of fish: after placing the fermented fish in a woven basket, the *liquamen* that dripped through the basket would be reserved for the upper classes, while the *allec* that remained—the muddy bits of fermented fish guts—were sold cheaply as seasoning. Eventually, rather than a by-product of fish guts, garum was produced primarily through the fermentation of mackerel, anchovies, and other oily fish.

In modern times, the Neapolitan condiment *colatura di alici* is garum's descendant, as is Worcestershire sauce, which gets some of its umami punch from fermented anchovies.

Modern Asian fish sauce is produced by cleaning and draining small fish and shellfish, drying it, salting it, packing it into large wooden containers, and keeping it submerged in brine while bacterial fermentation takes place over the course of nine months to a year. This process breaks down fish proteins into individual amino acids, as well as other organic compounds and minerals. It's these amino acids that give fish sauce its flavor-enhancing qualities. During fermentation, the fish liquefies, ending up as a sludgy mixture that is then strained and aged in the sun for a period of two or more weeks. It is clarified once more, then bottled.

Q: How does fish sauce work? What does it add to dishes?

A: As a condiment, fish sauce brings three distinct elements to the table: Saltiness, savoriness (or umami), and sweetness. Gram for gram, most fish sauces have nearly double the salt content of soy sauce (which means that you should use about half as much of it as you would soy sauce when seasoning a dish). Salt is vital in our perception of our flavor, as it opens up chemical pathways that allow us to perceive other flavors more easily. Properly salted food will taste more strongly of itself than unsalted food.

Perhaps more important than salt, though, is fish sauce's concentration of amino acids. In a 2010 study in the *Journal of Animal and Veterinary Advances*, researchers found that while the concentration of most amino acids would diminish in anchovies fermented for two months, the levels of three specific ones—glutamic acid, aspartic acid, and histadine—would skyrocket. The first two, glutamic acid and aspartic acid, are known to trigger our sensation of umami when it binds to receptors on our tongues. Histadine, on the other hand, has a sweet flavor, and indeed, many fish sauces have a distinctly sweet, almost caramel-like flavor to them.

It's these three flavors—salty, savory, and sweet—that give fish sauce its reputation as a potent flavor booster in all manner of dishes.

Q: When should I use fish sauce?

A: There are some obvious occasions. Fish sauce is an essential condiment in many Southeast Asian dishes, including Vietnamese pho and Pad Thai from Thailand (see page 378). But don't stop there! I use a few drops of fish sauce as a finishing condiment in nearly every meat-based stew I make, whether it's Asian or Western. Used sparingly, it melds into the background while doing its salty-savory-sweet magic to dishes ranging from Texas chili con carne to Italian ragù Bolognese to Hungarian goulash. I'll add a splash to my *michelada* or Bloody Mary or even to my summer pesto. Once you start seasoning with fish sauce, you'll never look at boring old salt the same way again.

Q: What is the best brand of fish sauce?

A: The flavor of fish sauce, like soy sauce, can vary from country to country. There's a slow-aged Vietnamese fish sauce brand called Red Boat that's all the rage today because it, like many Vietnamese fish sauces, has a milder, smoother flavor than, say Tiparos, a more pungent sauce you'll find throughout Thailand. In taste tests, the milder fish sauces typically come out on top, but nearly every taste test I've seen suffers the same

basic experimental design flaw: one of the tests is tasting the stuff on its own, which is not a useful taste test for anyone who doesn't take shots of straight fish sauce with their dinner.

In my own tests I've found that the only time a milder, more expensive fish sauce really makes a difference is in dipping sauces like Vietnamese nước chấm or Thai nam pla prik, and even then, most folks will notice a difference only when tasted directly side by side. When used as a seasoning, even the most one-dimensional fish sauces (such as, say, the inexpensive Squid or Three Crabs brand sauces) will work just fine.

Bottom line: I keep a bottle of fancy-yet-widely-available Red Boat for dipping sauces (and appearances—god forbid my foodie friends see me cooking with Three Crabs!), and a bottle of whatever was available at the Asian supermarket or the international aisle of the Western supermarket for everything else.

Q: How should I store fish sauce, and how long does it last?

A: An unopened bottle of fish sauce stored in the pantry will last for years, if not decades. Once you've opened up the bottle, however, it will start to change in flavor. According to a 2013 study from the Bangladesh Agricultural University, fish sauce still contains active bacterial cultures, including *Bacillus, Micrococcus, Lactobacillus,* and *Pseudomonas,* even after bottling, and they will continue to digest and ferment the fish sauce in aerobic conditions. Even so, as long as its tightly sealed after each use (and your nose will tell you if it's not), fish sauce should last at least six months in the pantry before it starts to seriously change in flavor, becoming a little more pungent and, well, fishier (but not in a good way) with time. With the cheaper stuff, you probably won't even notice the difference. With subtler sauces like Red Boat, storing it in the fridge after opening will minimize bacterial activity and help it retain its original flavor for a year or more.

In a bottle that is not perfectly sealed, water will also evaporate out of the fish sauce with time. Eventually this could lead to hypersalinity, which manifests as solid salt crystals that form on the bottom of the bottle or around the lid. Higher concentrations of protein can also lead to protein precipitation, which looks like cloudiness or crystals floating on the surface of the sauce. Neither the salt nor the protein crystals affect the palatability of fish sauce, and there's no need to worry about it.

Velveting: The Secret to the Juiciest, Tenderest White Meat

One of the problems with stir-frying is that the intense heat necessary to keep vegetables crisp and keep meats from steaming can also cause lean cuts of meat like chicken, fish, or pork loin to dry out and turn tough or stringy. To prevent this, you need to create some sort of insulative buffer to protect your meat as it cooks, much in the same way that you might bread a chicken breast or batter a piece of lean fish before frying it.

Enter velveting, a technique that solves this problem and starts with marinating meat using a few specific ingredients:

- **Egg whites** provide a loose protein matrix that sets up around the meat, protecting it from coming in direct contact with the pan.

- **Cornstarch** simultaneously prevents the egg white proteins from setting up too firmly while also absorbing excess liquid from both inside (meat juices expelled during cooking) and out (sauces added to the stir-fry).

- **A water-based liquid** such as Shaoxing wine, stock, or soy sauce further dilutes the egg proteins while also adding flavor and color.

Once the meat has been coated in this mixture, you can simply stir-fry it, but it's difficult to get the coating to actually stick evenly if you go straight into a hot wok. For the best results, it's best to par-cook velveted meat so that the coating sets into a soft, ultrathin halo of gel that coats the meat. You can subsequently stir-fry it along with aromatics, vegetables, and sauces to finish cooking.

Traditionally this is done in hot oil, a process called "passing through." If you peek into a Chinese restaurant kitchen that velvets its meat, you may see the cooks dunking their proteins into a deep fryer or a wok with a good pool of oil in it very briefly—just a matter of seconds—before subsequently stir-frying it. At home, you can accomplish this with an inch or so of oil in the bottom of your wok. When I oil-velvet, I pass the meat through the hot oil in batches, using a wire-mesh strainer to take the meat out as it cooks. I can then pour the oil off through a fine-mesh strainer into a pot that I keep on the stove. The oil can be used for stir-frying in the future.

If the prospect of heating up a cup or so of oil before stir-frying frightens you (there are so many people frightened of oil!), a friendlier process is water-velveting, a technique I learned from Shao Zhi Zhong, who was a contributor when I edited *Serious Eats*. The process is identical, but instead of passing velveted meat through a pool of oil, you simply blanch it for a few moments in boiling water. Tasted side by side, the two processes are distinguishable in a finished stir-fry, but both taste just fine, and both will produce meat that is significantly more tender and juicy than if it were stir-fried naked.

HOW TO VELVET MEAT

Velveting is most useful for lean cuts of meat such as sliced or slivered chicken breast or pork loin or sliced firm fish. Before velveting meat, it is important to very carefully dry your washed meat by firmly squeezing out excess moisture. Too much moisture will dilute the velveting mixture, preventing it from effectively coating the meat. Similarly, make sure you use large eggs for this technique. Too much or too little egg white will render it ineffective.

In a well-prepared Chinese kitchen, the chef may have a separate wok full of simmering water or hot oil to pass the meat through before adding it to the main wok for stir-frying. You can do something similar at home by having a pot of simmering water set on a side burner next to your main wok, along with a spider to move

meat and a fine-mesh strainer set in an empty bowl to transfer the meat to after velveting, allowing it to drain and steam-dry before stir-frying. This technique is also useful whenever you need to blanch ingredients before stir-frying, such as noodles, tofu, or green vegetables.

If you're not going to be blanching multiple ingredients as you cook, an easier method is to bring a few cups of water to a simmer in your wok, pass the velveted meat through the simmering water for 30 to 60 seconds to par-cook it, then use a spider to transfer the velveted meat to a large sheet tray to steam-dry while you empty and wipe out the wok. By the time the wok is cleaned and ready to go, the meat should be relatively dry and ready for the rest of the stir-fry.

BASIC VELVETING

INGREDIENTS

For every pound of sliced or slivered meat, you will need:

1 teaspoon (3 to 4 g) kosher salt (omit if using soy sauce or another salty liquid)

4 teaspoons (20 ml) water-based liquid such as Shaoxing wine, sake, soy sauce, or broth

½ teaspoon (2 g) baking soda

1 large egg white

2 teaspoons (6 g) cornstarch

This basic velveting technique will work for any lean poultry, pork, or firm-fleshed fish as the first step in a wide range of stir-fries where a tender, slippery texture is desired.

DIRECTIONS

(1) Combine the ingredients in a medium bowl and mix with a fork until no lumps remain.

(2) Place the meat in a medium bowl, cover with cold water, and vigorously agitate it. Drain through a fine-mesh strainer set in the sink and press with your hands to remove excess water. Transfer to the bowl with the marinade and stir vigorously with your fingertips or chopsticks for 30 seconds. Transfer to the refrigerator and let marinate for at least 15 minutes and up to 4 hours.

(3) **To Oil-Velvet:** Heat 1 to 2 cups of oil in a wok over high heat until it reaches 325°F. Add ½ pound of marinated meat and gently agitate with a spider to separate the pieces. Cook until they just start to hold their shape, about 30 seconds after they've been separated. Using the spider, transfer the velveted meat to a wire-mesh strainer set over a bowl to drain. The meat is now ready to add to a stir-fry. Par-cooked velveted meat can also be stored in the refrigerator for up to 2 days before stir-frying. Strain used oil through a fine-mesh strainer. The oil can be reused for stir-frying or deep frying.

To Water-Velvet: Bring 1 quart (1 liter) of water seasoned with a big pinch of salt to a boil over high heat in a wok. Drop the coated pieces of meat into the water one piece at a time to ensure that they don't clump together. Cook for 30 seconds after all the meat has been added. Using the wire-mesh strainer, transfer the velveted meat to a rimmed baking sheet and spread into a single layer to steam dry for at least 3 minutes before stir-frying. Velveted meat can be stored in the refrigerator for up to 2 days before stir-frying.

NOTE: In this book, the recipes are written using the water-velveting technique. You can always substitute oil-velveting with no other changes to the recipe.

SWEET AND SOUR CHICKEN OR PORK

Yield
Serves 4

Active Time
30 minutes

Total Time
30 minutes

NOTE
For the most efficient process, get your chicken in the marinade first, chopping your vegetables, mincing aromatics, and mixing your sauce while it marinates. For this recipe canned pineapple with its juice works better than fresh.

Depending on exactly what part of the United States you live in, you may know sweet and sour chicken in various forms. In a puffy batter with neon red sauce, perhaps. Or deep-fried until crisp and served with a sweet and vinegary glaze. The version I make is based on a recipe my old colleague Chris Chung used to make for staff meals when we worked together at Uni, a sashimi bar in Boston. Chris, a Honolulu-born Chinese chef, got his chops in various kitchens around Oahu, where he picked up this particular recipe. It's got canned pineapples (and ketchup!) on the ingredients list. I think I can safely say that this is the only recipe I've ever written that includes canned pineapple.

INGREDIENTS

1 pound (450 g) boneless, skinless chicken breasts or thighs or pork loin, cut into ⅛-inch slices
1 teaspoon (3 g) kosher salt
2 teaspoons (10 ml) light soy sauce or shoyu
2 teaspoons (10 ml) Shaoxing wine or dry sherry
½ teaspoon (2 g) sugar
½ teaspoon (2 g) baking soda
1 large egg white
2 teaspoons (6 g) cornstarch

For the Sauce:
Juice from one 8- or 10-ounce (225 to 290 g) can pineapple chunks or rings
3 tablespoons (45 ml) ketchup
2 tablespoons (30 ml) distilled white or apple cider vinegar
1 teaspoon (5 ml) light soy sauce or shoyu
2 tablespoons (25 g) sugar

For the Cornstarch Slurry:
2 teaspoons (6 g) cornstarch
1 tablespoon (15 ml) water

For the Stir-Fry:
3 tablespoons (45 ml) peanut, rice bran, or other neutral oil
1 large red bell pepper, cut into ¾-inch dice
1 large green bell pepper, cut into ¾-inch dice
1 small white or yellow onion, cut into ¾-inch dice
4 medium garlic cloves, minced (about 4 teaspoons/10 g)
2 teaspoons (5 g) minced fresh ginger (about ½-inch segment)
Chunks from one 8- or 10-ounce can (225 to 290 g) pineapple or pineapple rings cut into chunks
1 cup cashews (optional)

recipe continues

(1) **For the Chicken:** Place the chicken in a medium bowl, cover with cold water, and vigorously agitate it. Drain through a fine-mesh strainer set in the sink and press on the chicken with your hands to remove excess water. Combine the chicken, salt, soy sauce, wine, sugar, baking soda, egg white, and cornstarch in a medium bowl and stir vigorously with fingertips or chopsticks. Set aside for at least 15 minutes.

(2) **For the Sauce:** Combine the pineapple juice, ketchup, soy sauce, and sugar in a small bowl and stir together until homogenous. Set aside. Combine the cornstarch and water in a separate small bowl and stir with a fork until the cornstarch is dissolved.

(3) **To Velvet the Chicken:** Bring 1 quart (1 liter) water to a boil in a wok over high heat. Add the chicken, dropping it in a piece at a time to prevent sticking. Cook, stirring occasionally, until the water returns to a brief simmer and chicken is mostly cooked through, 30 to 60 seconds. Transfer the chicken to a rimmed baking sheet using a spider and spread it into a single layer to dry. Set aside. Dump out the contents of the wok and wipe clean.

(4) **BEFORE YOU STIR-FRY, GET YOUR BOWLS READY:**

a.	Bell peppers and onions	**d.**	Pineapple chunks and cashews
b.	Garlic and ginger		(if using)
c.	Velveted chicken on a rimmed	**e.**	Sauce
	baking sheet	**f.**	Cornstarch slurry
		g.	Serving platter

(5) **For the Stir-Fry:** Rub a thin film of oil into a wok and set it over high heat until smoking. Add 2 tablespoons of the oil and swirl to coat. Add the bell peppers and onion and cook, stirring and tossing occasionally, until brightly colored and browned in spots, about 1 minute. Make a space in the center of the wok, add the remaining tablespoon of oil, then add the garlic and ginger and cook, stirring, until fragrant, about 30 seconds.

(6) Return the chicken to the wok. Add the pineapple chunks and cashews (if using). Stir the sauce and add to the wok by pouring it around the edges. Stir the cornstarch slurry and add a splash. Cook, tossing, until the sauce thickens and the chicken is cooked through, about 30 seconds longer. Adjust the sauce consistency with more cornstarch slurry if it is too thin or a splash of water if it is too thick. Transfer to a serving platter and serve immediately with steamed rice.

Acid Test

Pop quiz: which is more acidic, white wine or supermarket balsamic vinegar?

We typically associate higher acidity with a more sour flavor, but interestingly, sourness and actual pH are only loosely related. This is important to know when designing marinades for stir-fries and other cooking projects, where too much time in a too-acidic marinade can lead to tough meat (even if the marinade doesn't taste very sour on our tongues).

Here's a quick and easy experiment to demonstrate.

Materials

Dry white wine (such as Sauvignon Blanc)

Water

Supermarket balsamic vinegar

Sugar

Lemon juice

Red or white wine vinegar

Procedures

Taste a little sip of white wine, rinse your mouth with water, then taste some balsamic vinegar (the thin, standard supermarket kind, not the fancy syrupy stuff). Which one is more sour?

Now add a teaspoon of sugar to a tablespoon of lemon juice, stirring it until it mostly dissolves. Taste it side by side with the distilled white vinegar, rinsing with water in between tastes. Which one is more sour?

Results and Analysis

Most likely the balsamic vinegar tasted more sour to you than the white wine, while the wine vinegar tasted more sour than the sugary lemon juice. Yet white wine is typically quite a bit more acidic than balsamic vinegar and lemon juice is more acidic than wine vinegars. So why doesn't it *taste* that way?

It's because sourness and acidity are only loosely linked. Sourness is a sensation we fabricate in our brain based not just on acidity but on a variety of stimuli. Sweetness—like the sugar we added to the lemon juice—can distract our brains from acidity, as can powerful aromatics like those found in balsamic vinegar. Spiciness, bitterness, temperature—heck, even our mood—can change the way in which we perceive acidity.

Knowing the relative pH of various acids is good information when designing marinades, but as far as flavor goes, the most reliable sensor for how good food is going to taste is still the three holes—your mouth and two nostrils—in the middle of your face.

VELVET CHICKEN WITH SNAP PEAS AND LEMON-GINGER SAUCE

Yield
Serves 4

Active Time
15 minutes

Total Time
40 minutes

INGREDIENTS

For the Velvet Chicken and Blanched Snap Peas:

1 pound (450 g) boneless, skinless chicken breasts, cut into ¼-inch slices

1 teaspoon (3 g) kosher salt

4 teaspoons (20 ml) Shaoxing wine or dry sherry

½ teaspoon (2 g) baking soda

1 large egg white

2 teaspoons (6 g) cornstarch

1 pound (450 g) sugar snap or snow peas, trimmed

For the Sauce:

1 tablespoon (15 ml) light soy sauce or shoyu

2 tablespoons (30 ml) Shaoxing wine or dry sherry

¼ cup (60 ml) low-sodium homemade or store-bought chicken stock or water

1 tablespoon (15 ml) fresh lemon juice

1 teaspoon (5 ml) roasted sesame oil

2 teaspoons (8 g) sugar

For the Cornstarch Slurry:

2 teaspoons (6 g) cornstarch

1 tablespoon (15 ml) water

For the Stir-Fry:

3 tablespoons (30 ml) peanut, rice bran, or other neutral oil

4 strips lemon zest removed with a vegetable peeler, about 2 inches long and 1 inch wide

2 teaspoons (5 g) minced garlic (about 2 medium cloves)

2 teaspoons (5 g) minced fresh ginger (about ½-inch segment)

3 scallions, cut into ½-inch segments

Kosher salt to taste

This simple stir-fry showcases the effects of velveting on chicken, which comes out moist and tender with minimal fuss. Unlike some meatier stir-fries, the chicken should get no color at all from Maillard browning; the flavor in this dish is light and bright with an acidic hit from lemon juice and a little heat from both stir-fried ginger and a little fresh ginger added directly with the sauce.

I like the sweet crunch of snap peas, but really any green vegetable of similar size and shape would do. Snow peas, asparagus cut into segments, broccolini or broccoli spears, and cabbage are all prime candidates. You can stir-fry green vegetables straight from raw, but for the brighter green color and better texture, blanch them in some salted water first.

DIRECTIONS

(1) **For the Velvet Chicken and Blanched Snap Peas:** Place the chicken in a medium bowl, cover with cold water, and vigorously agitate it. Drain through a fine-mesh strainer set in the sink and press on the chicken with your hands to remove excess water. Return the chicken to the bowl and add the salt, wine, baking soda, egg white, and cornstarch. Stir vigorously with your fingertips or chopsticks for 30 seconds. Let marinate in the fridge for at least 15 minutes and up to 8 hours.

(2) Bring 2 quarts of salted water to a hard boil in a small saucepan or wok. Add the snap peas and simmer until bright green but still crisp, about 45 seconds. Using a spider, transfer the peas to a wide plate in a single layer and set them aside to cool.

(3) Let the water return to a hard boil. Add the chicken, dropping it in a piece at a time to prevent sticking. Cook, stirring occasionally, until the water returns to a brief simmer and the chicken is mostly cooked through, 30 to 60 seconds. Transfer the chicken to a rimmed baking sheet using a spider and spread it into a single layer to dry. Set aside. Dump out the contents of the wok and wipe clean.

(4) **Make the Sauce:** Combine soy sauce, wine, chicken stock, lemon juice, sesame oil, and sugar in a small bowl and stir together until homogenous. Set aside. Combine the cornstarch and water in a separate small bowl and stir with a fork until the cornstarch is dissolved.

(5) **BEFORE YOU STIR-FRY, GET YOUR BOWLS READY:**

a. Lemon zest, garlic, and ginger
b. Scallions
c. Blanched snap peas on their plate
d. Velveted chicken on its baking sheet
e. Sauce
f. Cornstarch slurry
g. Serving platter

(6) **To Stir-Fry:** Heat a wok over high heat until lightly smoking. Add the oil and swirl to coat. Add the lemon zest, garlic, and ginger and stir-fry until fragrant, about 10 seconds. Immediately add the scallions, snap peas, and chicken and toss thoroughly to combine. Stir-fry until the chicken is just cooked through and the snap peas are tender-crisp, about 30 seconds.

(7) Stir the sauce and add to the wok by pouring it around the edges. Stir the cornstarch slurry and add a splash. Cook, tossing, until the sauce thickens and the chicken is cooked through, about 30 seconds longer. Adjust the sauce consistency with more cornstarch slurry if it is too thin or a splash of water if it is too thick. Transfer to a serving platter and serve immediately with steamed rice.

PICO'S NOT-SO-BLAND CHICKEN

Yield
Serves 4

Active Time
15 minutes

Total Time
30 minutes

INGREDIENTS

For the Chicken:

1 pound (450 g) boneless, skinless chicken breasts, cut into ¼-inch slices
1 teaspoon (3 g) kosher salt
4 teaspoons (20 ml) Shaoxing wine or dry sherry
½ teaspoon (2 g) baking soda
1 large egg white
2 teaspoons (6 g) cornstarch

For the Sauce:

1 tablespoon (15 ml) light soy sauce or shoyu
2 tablespoons (30 ml) Shaoxing wine or dry sherry
¼ cup (60 ml) low-sodium homemade or store-bought chicken stock or water
2 teaspoons (8 g) sugar
¼ teaspoon freshly ground white pepper

For the Cornstarch Slurry:

2 teaspoons (6 g) cornstarch
1 tablespoon (15 ml) water

For the Stir-Fry:

3 tablespoons (15 ml) peanut, rice bran, or other neutral oil
2 medium garlic cloves (5 g), smashed
2 coin-sized slices fresh ginger
½ pound button, cremini, or shiitake mushrooms, cut into ¼-inch slices
One 8-ounce can sliced water chestnuts, drained (about 5 ounces dry sliced water chestnuts)
Kosher salt to taste

My kid sister, Pico, is quite the accomplished home cook. I know, because she's cooked for me and sends me photos of meals she cooks on a regular basis. But it wasn't always that way. When my sister was younger, not only was she uninterested in cooking; she was also a picky eater.

This didn't jibe well with my dad's occasional stir-fry nights. The beef with ginger and basil he loved to cook was simply too powerfully flavored for her (you can find my own take on that recipe on page 120). My mother was an old school can't-leave-the-table-until-your-plate-is-clean kind of mom. The result was my parents nearly calling an ambulance when a whole slice of water chestnut my sister was trying to wash down with a glass of water got lodged in her throat.

My dad, in an effort to appease both of them, created a dish he called "Pico's Bland Chicken." It was simple slices of chicken breast stir-fried with a touch of soy sauce, with no other accompaniments to speak of.

It was bland, but she loved it.

Pico is grown up now, so it's time for her bland chicken to grow up too. This recipe upgrades her chicken with a bit of velveting for texture, a more complex (but still subtle) sauce, some mushrooms, and, oh, some water chestnuts too. My advice is to chew them and appreciate their distinct crunch rather than swallowing them whole.

Pico, I expect you to send me a photo of this dish within a week after this book is released.

DIRECTIONS

(1) For the Velvet Chicken: Place the chicken in a medium bowl, cover with cold water, and vigorously agitate it. Drain through a fine-mesh strainer set in the sink and press on the chicken with your hands to remove excess water. Return the chicken to the bowl and add the salt, wine, baking soda, egg white, and cornstarch. Stir vigorously with your fingertips or chopsticks for 30 seconds. Let marinate in the fridge for at least 15 minutes and up to 8 hours.

(2) For the Sauce: Combine the soy sauce, wine, chicken stock, sugar, and white pepper in a small bowl and stir together until homogenous. Set aside. Combine the cornstarch and water in a separate small bowl and stir with a fork until the cornstarch is dissolved.

(3) To Velvet the Chicken: Bring 1 quart (1 liter) of water to a boil in a wok over high heat. Add the chicken, dropping it in a piece at a time to prevent sticking. Cook, stirring occasionally, until the water returns to a brief simmer and the chicken is mostly cooked through, 30 to 60 seconds. Transfer the chicken to a rimmed baking sheet using a spider and spread it into a single layer to dry. Set aside. Dump out the contents of the wok and wipe clean.

(4) BEFORE YOU STIR-FRY, GET YOUR BOWLS READY:

a. Smashed garlic and ginger
b. Mushrooms
c. Velveted chicken on its baking sheet
d. Water chestnuts
e. Sauce
f. Cornstarch slurry
g. Empty bowl for cooked ingredients
h. Serving platter

(5) **To Stir-Fry:** Heat the wok over high heat until lightly smoking. Add the oil and swirl to coat. Add the garlic and ginger and let sizzle for 15 seconds. Add the mushrooms and stir-fry until most of their moisture has evaporated and they are starting to brown, about 4 minutes.

(6) Return the chicken to the wok, add the water chestnuts, and toss everything to combine. Stir the sauce and add to the wok by pouring it around the edges. Stir the cornstarch slurry and add a splash. Cook, tossing, until the sauce thickens and the chicken is cooked through, about 30 seconds longer. Adjust the sauce consistency with more cornstarch slurry if it is too thin or a splash of water if it is too thick. Transfer to a serving platter and serve immediately with steamed rice.

SHREDDED CHICKEN WITH PICKLED CHILES AND CARROTS

Yield
Serves 4

Active Time
30 minutes

Total Time
45 minutes

NOTES

Adjust the heat level in this dish by adjusting the number of pickled chiles you add. You can also make this dish with fresh chiles by replacing the pickled chile liquid with 1 tablespoon (15 ml) distilled white or rice vinegar along with one to six minced fresh red Thai bird chiles. The recipe as written is quite hot! You can adjust the heat by reducing (or even eliminating) the amount of pickled chiles, replacing them with an equal quantity of white or rice vinegar. You can use an inexpensive balsamic vinegar in place of the Chinkiang. Cowhorn or long green chiles are thin green chiles with moderate spice available at most Asian grocers. You can use Anaheim, poblano, or even jalapeño in their place. For milder heat, use a green bell pepper. Bamboo shoots can be found whole in the refrigerated section of a good Asian supermarket or canned whole or slivered in the international section of most well-stocked Western supermarkets.

Pico's Not-So-Bland Chicken (page 80) is not so bland, but it's hardly what I'd call a flavor punch to the mouth. This dish, on the other hand, is. It's based on *yuxiang rousi*—fish-fragrant pork. It's so named not because it contains or smells like fish but because it utilizes a combination of hot, sour, and sweet flavors that are typically served with fish in its native Sichuan. In Sichuan you'll commonly find fish-fragrant pork (and indeed, this recipe works just as well with slivers of pork in place of slivers of chicken breast), as well as fish-fragrant eggplant (see page 191). To make it, I start by velveting thin strips of chicken breast, then stir-frying them in a quick sauce flavored with pickled chiles, black vinegar, sugar, ginger, and garlic for a hearty, flavor-packed dish that comes together in one wok with minimal effort.

You can use fresh chiles for this, but traditionally the dish is made with pickled chiles, which work much better: the chiles spread their flavor throughout the dish instead of in discrete bursts. Pickled chiles are available at many Chinese grocers, but they aren't common in a standard supermarket. One solution is to simply pickle your own. It's easy, and pickled chiles last essentially forever in the refrigerator. Small Thai bird chiles are the best choice among fresh chile varieties available in the West, but any hot red chile will do, such as Fresno, red jalapeño, or red serrano.

This is the first recipe in the book to incorporate doubanjiang, a Sichuan-style condiment made with fermented broad beans and chiles (see page 13 for more information). When adding it to stir-fries, it's important to bloom it in the hot oil in much the same way a Thai curry paste or Indian curry powder would be bloomed, letting it sizzle and fry until the oil breaks out and takes on a deep red color. This not only adds complexity to the stir-fry but also ensures that the flavor of the paste will coat every morsel of food.

To maximize efficiency, marinate the chicken before you start gathering and preparing the other ingredients.

Properly bloomed *doubanjiang* will form a deep crimson-red oil in the wok.

INGREDIENTS

For the Chicken:

1 pound (450 g) boneless, skinless chicken breast or pork loin, cut into ¼-inch slivers

1 teaspoon (3 g) kosher salt

4 teaspoons (20 ml) Shaoxing wine or dry sherry

½ teaspoon (2 g) baking soda

1 large egg white

2 teaspoons (6 g) cornstarch

For the Sauce:

1 to 6 store-bought or homemade pickled chiles (page 84), plus 1 tablespoon (15 ml) pickling liquid (see Notes)

2 tablespoons (30 ml) Shaoxing wine or dry sherry

1 tablespoon (12 g) sugar

2 teaspoons (10 ml) light soy sauce or shoyu

1 tablespoon (15 ml) Chinkiang vinegar (see Notes)

For the Cornstarch Slurry:

2 teaspoons (6 g) cornstarch

1 tablespoon (15 ml) water

For the Stir-Fry:

3 tablespoons (45 ml) peanut, rice bran, or other neutral oil

1 medium carrot (about 4 ounces/120 g), peeled and cut into fine matchsticks

1 long green chile such as cowhorn or Anaheim (about 4 ounces/120 g), cut on a sharp bias into long, thin slices (see Notes)

4 ounces (120 g) bamboo shoots, cut into fine matchsticks (see Notes)

2 teaspoons (5 g) minced garlic (about 2 medium cloves)

2 teaspoons (5 g) minced fresh ginger (about ½-inch segment)

2 scallions, cut into 2-inch segments and quartered lengthwise to form fine slivers

2 tablespoons (20 g) Sichuan broad bean chile paste (doubanjiang)

Handful of roughly chopped fresh cilantro leaves, for garnish

DIRECTIONS

1. **For the Velvet Chicken:** Place the chicken in a medium bowl, cover with cold water, and vigorously agitate it. Drain through a fine-mesh strainer set in the sink and press on the chicken with your hands to remove excess water. Return the chicken to the bowl and add the salt, wine, baking soda, egg white, and cornstarch. Stir vigorously with your fingertips or chopsticks for 30 seconds. Let marinate in the fridge for at least 15 minutes and up to 8 hours.

2. **Meanwhile, Make the Sauce:** Combine the pickled chiles, wine, sugar, soy sauce, and vinegar in a small bowl and stir together until homogenous. Set aside. Combine the cornstarch and water in a separate small bowl and stir with a fork until the cornstarch is dissolved.

3. **To Velvet the Chicken:** Bring 1 quart (1 liter) water to a boil in a wok over high heat. Add the chicken, dropping it in a piece at a time to prevent sticking. Cook, stirring occasionally, until the water returns to a brief simmer and the chicken is mostly cooked through, 30 to 60 seconds. Transfer the chicken to a rimmed baking sheet using a spider and spread it into a single layer to dry. Set aside. Dump out the contents of the wok and wipe clean.

4. **BEFORE YOU STIR-FRY, GET YOUR BOWLS READY:**

   a. Carrots, chiles, and bamboo shoots
   b. Ginger, garlic, and scallions
   c. Broad bean chile paste
   d. Velveted chicken on its baking sheet
   e. Sauce
   f. Cornstarch slurry
   g. Serving platter

5. **For the Stir-Fry:** Heat the wok over high heat until lightly smoking. Add 2 tablespoons (30 ml) of the oil and swirl to coat. Add the carrots, chiles, and bamboo shoots and cook, stirring and tossing constantly until the vegetables are tender-crisp, about 1 minute. Transfer to the baking sheet with the velveted chicken.

6. Wipe out the wok and return to high heat until lightly smoking. Add the remaining 1 tablespoon (15 ml) oil and swirl to coat. Add the ginger, garlic, and scallions and stir-fry until fragrant, about 10 seconds. Add the broad bean chili paste and cook, stirring constantly, until the oil breaks out and turns deep red, about 30 seconds. Return the chicken and vegetables to the wok and toss to coat thoroughly in the red oil.

7. Stir the sauce and add to the wok by pouring it around the edges. Stir the cornstarch slurry and add a splash. Cook, tossing, until the sauce thickens and the chicken is cooked through, about 30 seconds longer. Adjust the sauce consistency with more cornstarch slurry if it is too thin or a splash of water if it is too thick. Transfer to a serving platter and serve immediately with steamed rice.

PICKLED CHILES

Yield
Makes
about
¾ cup

Active Time
5 minutes

Total Time
10 minutes

INGREDIENTS

3 ounces hot red chiles, such as Thai bird,
    Fresno, or cayenne, tops cut off and
    discarded to expose their centers
2 medium garlic cloves (5 g), roughly
    smashed
½ cup (120 ml) distilled white vinegar
2 teaspoons (12 g) kosher salt

Quick-pickling chiles is a really fast process: Just heat up some seasoned vinegar and chiles on the stove, then let them sit for about 5 minutes. That's it. To ensure that the chiles are thoroughly preserved, I cut off the tops with a knife, allowing the pickled brine to get to them inside and out. Chiles tend to float, which can be a problem: the tops of the chiles will stick up above the brine as they cool. To keep them submerged, I place a folded paper towel over the top of the liquid.

Make sure to wash and scrub your hands and work surfaces thoroughly after working with hot chiles. Use disposable plastic gloves if you are especially sensitive to capsaicin.

DIRECTIONS

Combine all the ingredients in a small saucepan and bring to a brief simmer over high heat. Transfer to a heatproof container and place a folded paper towel over the top, soaking it to keep the chiles submerged. (The chiles may bump up above the surface of the liquid, but so long as the paper towel is soaked in brine and covers them, you're good.) The chiles will be ready to use in about 5 minutes, or they can be transferred to a sealed container and stored in the refrigerator indefinitely.

PACKING HEAT: Understanding Chiles and the Scoville Scale

Heat in chiles comes from a chemical called *capsaicin*, and the level of capsaicin in chiles can range from none (bell peppers, for instance) to melt-your-face-off levels of infernal heat, especially these days, when our modern understanding of capsaicin production has allowed chile-heads to produce cultivars of pepper that contain capsaicin levels several times more potent than ever naturally occurs.

In chiles, capsaicin is most concentrated in the placenta—the white pith surrounding the seeds—though it also occurs in the flesh and seeds. Scientists believe that capsaicin has developed in chiles to ward off mammalian predators that fully digest chile seeds. Birds and reptiles, on the other hand, are not as affected by chile heat, nor do they fully digest seeds, allowing them to spread chile seeds far and wide. Capsaicin is also an effective fungicide and pesticide, protecting delicate chiles from mold, rot, and insects.[*]

Our bodies detect chile heat through a mechanism that is quite different from the way we detect other flavors like sweetness or sourness. Capsaicin triggers our pain receptors in the same way that physical heat does. Our body is actually fooled into thinking that it is being literally burned, although thankfully capsaicin does not cause permanent damage to nerves the way actual burns can.

Chile heat is measured in Scoville units. These days Scoville units are measured chemically, but the scale, as developed by Wilbur Scoville in 1912, was based on human perception. A fixed weight of dehydrated chile was fully dissolved in alcohol, then that solution was diluted with sugar water until tasters could no longer discern any heat. This dilution level is known as a *Scoville Heat Unit*.

---

[*]   Chile growers use this fact to their advantage. By feeding chile plants with feed rich in insect-based fertilizer, they can fool the plants into believing that they are being attacked by insects. In response, they produce higher levels of capsaicin.

This table shows the Scoville Heat Units of common dried and fresh chiles. If you want to go even deeper into chile varietals, I recommend checking out chilipeppermadness.com, which provides charts and tasting notes that go far beyond the scope of this book.

PEPPER	FORM TYPICALLY SOLD	SCOVILLE HEAT UNITS
Bell Pepper	Fresh	0
Banana Pepper	Fresh	0–500
Nora Chile	Dried	0–500
Shishito Pepper	Fresh	50–1,000
Padrón Pepper	Fresh	0–2,500
Peperoncino	Pickled	100–500
Red Anaheim Chile	Fresh	500–1,500
Poblano Chile	Fresh (sold dried as Ancho chiles)	500–2,500
Mulato Chile	Dried	500–2,500
Peppadew Chile	Pickled	1,000
Green Anaheim Chile (aka Hatch or New Mexico chile)	Fresh	1,000–1,500
Ancho Chile	Dried	1,000–1,500
Pasilla Negro Chile	Dried	1,000–2,000
Cascabel Chile	Dried	1,000–3,000
Cowhorn Chile (green capsicum, Chinese long chile)	Fresh	2,500–5,000
Guajillo Chile	Dried	2,500–5,000
Jalapeño Chile	Fresh	2,500–8,000
Chipotle Chile (smoked red jalapeño)	Dried or Canned	2,5000–8,000
Gochugaru (Korean chile flakes)	Dried, usually ground	5,000–8,000
Red Fresno Chile	Fresh	2,500–10,000
Puya Chile	Dried	5,000–8,000
Hungarian Wax Chile	Fresh	5,000–15,000
Aji Amarillo Chile	Fresh	5,000–25,000
Urfa Biber Chile	Dried	7,500
Cascabel Chile	Dried	8,000–12,000
Er Jing Tiao (mild Sichuan chile)	Fresh or Dried	10,000–20,000
Serrano Chile	Fresh	10,000–23,000
Chile de Árbol	Dried	15,000–30,000
Chile Japones	Dried	15,000–36,000
Tabasco Chile	Tabasco sauce	30,000–50,000
Cayenne Chile	Fresh or Dried	30,000–50,000
Chile Pequín	Dried	40,000–50,000
Facing Heaven Chile (chao tian jiao)	Dried	50,000–75,000
Thai Bird Chile	Fresh or Dried	-50,000–100,000
Habanero Chile	Fresh or Dried	100,000–200,000
Scotch Bonnet Pepper	Fresh or Dried	75,000–325,000
Ghost Pepper	Fresh or Dried	300,000–400,000
Carolina Reaper	Fresh or Dried	2,200,000
Pure Capsaicin	N/A	16,000,000

* Both shishito and padrón peppers are interesting in that the majority of them have little to no heat, but occasionally you'll get one that is quite hot. There is no real way to tell without eating them, making them the Russian roulette of the chile world.

How to Cut Carrots, Potatoes, and Other Firm Vegetables for Stir-Fries

In my high school cafeteria and college dining hall, when carrots were stir-fried they were invariably of the frozen crinkle-cut variety, usually prepackaged with broccoli, sliced mushrooms, bell peppers, and the occasional ear of baby corn in a bag labeled "Oriental Mix." We can do better than that.

Firm vegetables like carrots, potatoes, and bamboo shoots work well in stir-fries when they're finely shredded into thin, long matchsticks (zucchini also works well sliced and diced). Here's how to do it.

Step 1 • Peel and Trim

Peel your carrots, then cut them into 2- to 3-inch segments.

Step 3 • Cut into Planks

With the carrot resting on its newly cut surface, use a sharp chef's knife to cut the carrots into ⅛-inch planks. Alternatively, use a Japanese-style mandoline to slice the carrots into ⅛-inch planks.

Step 4 • Cut Matchsticks

Stack a few of the planks together and slice them lengthwise with your chef's knife to create even matchsticks.

Step 2 • Create a Stable Surface

Cut one thin slice lengthwise off the side of each segment with a sharp chef's knife to create a stable surface for the carrot to rest on.

If you don't have the knife skills (or patience) to cut carrots into matchsticks, just split the carrot in half lengthwise, then cut it on a sharp bias into thin slices. They won't be quite as pretty, but they'll cook up just fine.

Sidebar

How to Beat Chile Heat

We've all been there. For my uncle, "there" was running away from an ambulance ride he couldn't afford after waking up on the floor of a Chinese restaurant where he had just requested the chef make him the spiciest dish he could. The heat, coupled with undoubtedly a few too many Tsingtao beers, had knocked him right out. The sirens woke him back up.

For me, "there" was sitting in a friend's backyard in Colombia—a country where the food is typically quite mild—with a garden hose firmly planted in my mouth after I nonchalantly plucked and bit into a chile I couldn't identify.

Garden hoses and ambulance sirens are all well and good, but what's actually the best remedy for beating the heat when it comes to chiles? You've undoubtedly heard that milk is better than water, but is it? And why?

Capsaicin, the chemical responsible for chile heat, is hydrophobic. That is, it doesn't dissolve in water. Fighting fat-soluble capsaicin by drinking plain water is like trying to wash Vaseline off your hands without soap. It just doesn't work. Milk, especially full-fat milk, will work better (don't try it with skim!). Cream, even better. In my own personal testing (the sacrifices I make for science!), I found that creamy Greek yogurt was the most pleasant way to fight off too-much chile heat, while swishing a bit of olive oil in my mouth—while not altogether pleasant—was the most effective.

1.2 HOW TO STIR-FRY PORK

Depending on what part of the pig it comes from, pork can vary hugely in terms of toughness, fat content, connective tissue content, and flavor and thus must be cooked using different methods. For quick stir-fries using slices or strips of meat, you're looking for cuts that are naturally tender. Tougher cuts like pork butt (aka *pork shoulder*),* fresh ham, or rib meat won't cook for long enough to tenderize, giving you stringy, tough results. These cuts are typically better for techniques that reduce either the length of these connective tissues (such as grinding or mincing) or for slow-cooked dishes where tough connective tissue is tenderized.

For stir-fries, this leaves a few options:

- **Pork loin** is a relatively pale, lean, tender cut typically used for roasts. It is widely available, easy to prep, and great for most recipes (as long as you are careful not to overcook it!).

- **Pork sirloin** is a little darker with more fat and connective tissue. Still quite tender and easy to work with, it's my preferred cut for most recipes.

- **Country-style ribs** are not actually ribs. They're cutlets cut from the blade end of the loin that typically contain some shoulder meat and some loin meat. Country-style ribs can be quite flavorful and juicy but will have quite a bit more fat and connective tissue. They can be treated just like pork loin if you don't mind the occasional bit of chewy fat or connective tissue (I don't) but should be trimmed if you're worried about how your guests will judge you on such things.

- **Tenderloin** comes from the inside of the spine and is the most tender and the leanest cut on the hog. It's fine for stir-fries, but typically more expensive than other cuts, as well as more prone to drying out, so I would avoid it.

- **Ground pork** is in a category of its own, typically used to flavor vegetables, noodles, or tofu, or for meatballs, as a filling in dumplings, or in other dim sum. Ground pork with a very high fat content (like ground pork belly or extra-fatty pork butt/shoulder) is best for dumplings and other fillings. Leaner ground shoulder or ground sirloin is my preference for stir-fries.

As with chicken, lean pork does best with either marinating (page 47) or velveting (page 72) before cooking. In addition to standard marinade ingredients, pork can be treated with baking soda to tenderize it (see "Baking Soda and Deep Tissue Massage" on page 117 for some more on the science).

---

* Despite the confusing name, *pork butt* is actually just another term for pork shoulder. It got its name from the style of barrel it was packed into for shipment back when New England used to be a pork production powerhouse. Actually pork rear ends are sold as fresh pork ham.

How to Cut Pork Loin for Stir-Fries

Like chicken, pork meat can be thinly sliced, cut into cubes, or cut into thin slivers. Here's how to do it. The basic process is the same regardless of the cut of pork. If starting with a cut high in connective tissue like country-style ribs, trim out some of the wider swaths of fat before starting.

Step 1 • Identify the Grain

With pork loin, tenderloin, and sirloin there is a distinct grain that runs lengthwise down the muscle. Country-style ribs are typically cut against the grain already, so identification is not quite as essential—its grain tends to be cut pretty short already.

Step 2 • Cut the Pork

For slices: Split the pork lengthwise into strips about 1½ inches wide.

Slice each strip thinly against the grain into slices about ¼ inch thick.

For slivers: Take the same slices, stack a few at a time, and slice them lengthwise into matchsticks that are roughly ¼ by ¼ by 1½ inches.

For dice: Start by slicing the pork into ½-inch wide chops against the grain.

Working with one or two chops at a time, cut into ½-inch strips, then rotate and cut into ½-inch dice.

SLICED PORK WTH CHIVES: IN DEFENSE OF SUBTLE STIR-FRIES

We typically think of stir-fries as anything but subtle. Most food court fare is covered in bold sauces that pack hot, tart, and sweet flavors. And it's not just stir-fries! These days food media seems *obsessed* with EXTREME FLAVOR. Every recipe, every ingredient, every restaurant dish is designed to punch you in the mouth with flavor as hard as it can. I'm all for packing in the flavor for dishes that call for it, but there's a time and a place for subtlety. You'll taste (and feel) that bite of deep-fried Chongqing-style Dry-Fried Chicken (page 441) for days, but chicken simply poached (page 565) and served with rice can be a culinary triumph. Sometimes I like blue cheese or horseradish with my steak, but usually I opt for simple salt and pepper. Sometimes

you're in the mood for the layered sound of *Abbey Road*, sometimes you just want the raw genius of *A Hard Day's Night* to get lost in the feeling.

Similarly, not all stir-fries have to pack in the flavor, and this one—sliced pork with chives—demonstrates that perfectly. It starts with thin strips of lean pork in a standard marinade to which I add a little white pepper for seasoning and a pinch of baking soda for tenderization. You stir-fry it with two different types of chives—Chinese yellow chives and regular Chinese blossoming chives (you can find both pretty easily at an Asian market, or just substitute sliced scallions, leeks, or onions)—a few aromatics, and a touch more soy sauce and wine. That's it.

SLICED PORK WITH CHIVES

Yield
Serves 4

Active Time
20 minutes

Total Time
30 minutes

NOTE

Chinese yellow chives and green blossoming chives can be found at most Asian supermarkets. If unavailable, you can use leeks or regular yellow onions or shallots. For leeks, trim off the bases and green tops, then cut the whites lengthwise into ¼-inch strips. For yellow onions or shallots, remove the tops and bottoms, peel, split in half from pole to pole, and cut into ¼-inch slices from pole to pole.

INGREDIENTS

For the Pork:
1 pound boneless pork loin, cut into 2-inch matchsticks
¼ teaspoon (2 g) sugar
¼ teaspoon (1 g) freshly ground white pepper
1 teaspoon (5 ml) Shaoxing wine or dry sherry
1 teaspoon (5 ml) light soy sauce or shoyu
1 teaspoon (5 ml) roasted sesame oil
½ teaspoon (2 g) baking soda
1 teaspoon (3 g) cornstarch

For the Sauce:
½ teaspoon (2 g) freshly ground white pepper
1½ tablespoons (about 25 ml) Shaoxing wine
1½ tablespoons (about 25 ml) light soy sauce or shoyu

For the Stir-Fry:
3 tablespoons (45 ml) peanut, rice bran, or other neutral oil
4 ounces (100 g) yellow chives, cut into 2-inch segments (see Note)
4 ounces (100 g) Chinese chives, cut into 2-inch segments (see Note)
Kosher salt
2 teaspoons (5 g) minced garlic (about 2 medium cloves)
2 teaspoons (5 g) minced fresh ginger (about ½-inch segment)

DIRECTIONS

(1) **For the Pork:** Place the pork in a medium bowl, cover with cold water, and vigorously agitate it. Drain through a fine-mesh strainer set in the sink and press on the pork with your hands to remove excess water. Return the pork to the bowl and add the sugar, white pepper, wine, soy sauce, sesame oil, baking soda, and cornstarch. Stir vigorously with your fingertips or chopsticks for 30 seconds. Set aside for 15 minutes at room temperature.

(2) **Meanwhile, Make the Sauce:** Combine the white pepper, wine, and soy sauce in a small bowl. Set aside.

(3) **BEFORE YOU STIR-FRY, GET YOUR BOWLS READY:**

a. Yellow chives and Chinese chives
b. Marinated pork
c. Garlic and ginger
d. Sauce
e. Empty bowl for cooked ingredients
f. Serving platter

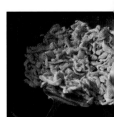

(4) **For the Stir-Fry:** Heat a wok over high heat until lightly smoking. Add 1 tablespoon (15 ml) of the oil and swirl to coat. Add the yellow chives and Chinese chives and cook, tossing and stirring occasionally, until brightly colored and barely tender, about 1 minute. Season with salt. Transfer to a large bowl and set aside.

(5) Wipe out the wok and return it to high heat until lightly smoking. Add 1 tablespoon (15 ml) of the remaining oil and swirl to coat. Add half of the pork, spread into a single layer, and cook without moving until lightly browned, about 45 seconds. Cook, tossing and stirring frequently until barely cooked through, about 30 seconds longer. Transfer to the bowl with chives.

(6) Wipe out the wok and return it to high heat until lightly smoking. Add the remaining tablespoon (15 ml) oil and swirl to coat. Add the remaining pork, spread into a single layer, and cook without moving until lightly browned, about 45 seconds. Cook, tossing and stirring frequently until barely cooked through, about 30 seconds longer. Return the other half of the pork and chives to the wok and clear a small space in the center. Add the garlic and ginger and cook, tossing constantly, until fragrant, about 30 seconds. Add the sauce mixture and toss to combine. Season to taste with more salt if necessary. Transfer to a serving platter and serve immediately.

STIR-FRIED KIMCHI PORK

Yield
Serves 4

Active Time
20 minutes

Total Time
30 minutes

NOTES

You can use practically any Asian chile sauce, such as sambal oelek or sriracha in place of gochujang and end up with something tasty, or even omit it—the kimchi provides plenty of heat. In Korea, this stir-fry is typically made with thinly sliced fresh pork belly, which you can find at most Asian markets. It's essential that it be quite thinly sliced, as pork belly is too tough to eat when sliced thick. Many well-stocked Western supermarkets will carry pork belly that the butcher counter can slice for you if you ask nicely. Sliced pork loin will work just fine if you can't get the belly.

INGREDIENTS

For the Pork:

1 pound (450 g) thinly sliced pork belly, cut into 1- to 2-inch pieces (see Notes)
1 tablespoon (15 ml) gochujang (see Notes)
1 teaspoon (5 ml) light soy sauce or shoyu
1 teaspoon (5 ml) roasted sesame oil
1 teaspoon (4 g) sugar
¼ teaspoon (1 g) baking soda
½ teaspoon (1.5 g) cornstarch

For the Stir-Fry

8 ounces (225 g) kimchi with its juices
3 tablespoons (45 ml) peanut, rice bran, or other neutral oil
1 medium onion (about 6 ounces/180 g), cut into ¼-inch slices
1 jalapeño, serrano, or Chinese cowhorn chile, cut into ¼-inch slices on a bias
1 teaspoon toasted sesame seeds (optional)
Kosher salt and freshly ground black pepper

Clocking in at the opposite end of the subtlety spectrum from my Sliced Pork with Chives is Stir-Fried Kimchi Pork, a classic Korean dish known as *jaeyook bokkeum*. This is one of those magical recipes that rely on one uber-flavorful ingredient (kimchi!) to provide most of the flavor in the dish, requiring very few other aromatics. Traditional recipes for jaeyook bokkeum use pureed Asian pear or pear juice in the pork marinade. This provides not only sweetness but tenderizing enzymes as well. However, my goal when developing this recipe was to make it as simple as possible.

The marinade is nothing more than a little soy sauce blended with a dab of gochujang (a Korean fermented chile paste; see page 14). Rather than Asian pear, I just use a touch of sugar for sweetness, and I use the baking soda tenderization technique in place of those pear enzymes. Roasted sesame oil and black pepper—a classic Korean flavor pairing—also make an appearance.

Because this dish relies so much on the flavor provided by the kimchi, it's important to use store-bought kimchi that actually tastes great right out of the jar or to make your own. The key step here is to drain the kimchi *very* well before you begin stir-frying. Wet kimchi will steam in the wok, causing your meat to overcook and your vegetables to turn mushy before any flavor development can occur. I put my kimchi in a fine-mesh strainer set over a bowl, then press on it and squeeze it as hard as I can with my bare hands. I then save that juice to add back to the stir-fry at the end.

DIRECTIONS

(1) **For the Pork:** Place the pork in a medium bowl, cover with cold water, and vigorously agitate it. Drain through a fine-mesh strainer set in the sink and press on the pork with your hands to remove excess water. Return the pork to the bowl and add the gochujang, soy sauce, sesame oil, sugar, baking soda, and cornstarch. Toss roughly with your fingertips or chopsticks until thoroughly combined. Set aside for 15 minutes at room temperature or refrigerate for up to 8 hours.

(2) **Meanwhile, Drain the Kimchi:** Place the kimchi in a wire-mesh strainer set over a bowl. Squeeze the kimchi firmly, pressing it against the strainer to remove as much liquid as you can. Reserve the drained kimchi and kimchi juice separately. You should have about ½ cup (120 ml) liquid. Less is OK. If you have too much, discard excess over ½ cup.

recipe continues

(3) **BEFORE YOU STIR-FRY, GET YOUR BOWLS READY:**

a. **Marinated pork**

b. **Drained kimchi and onions**

c. **Sliced chiles**

d. **Kimchi juice**

e. **Sesame seeds**

f. **Empty bowl for cooked ingredients**

g. **Serving platter**

(4) **For the Stir-Fry:** Heat a wok over high heat until lightly smoking. Add 1 tablespoon (15 ml) of the oil and swirl to coat. Add half of the pork, spread into a single layer, and cook without moving until lightly browned, about 45 seconds. Cook, tossing and stirring frequently until barely cooked through, about 30 seconds longer. Transfer the cooked pork to a clean bowl or plate. Wipe out the wok and repeat with more oil and the remaining pork, adding the cooked pork to the first batch.

(5) Wipe out the wok and return to high heat until lightly smoking. Add the remaining 1 tablespoon (15 ml) oil and swirl to coat. Add the drained kimchi and sliced onions and cook, tossing and stirring frequently, until the onions are lightly softened and the vegetables begin to take on a little color, about 1 minute. Add the sliced chiles and cook, stirring, until fragrant, about 30 seconds.

(6) Return the pork to the wok and add the kimchi juice. Cook, tossing and stirring constantly, until the kimchi juice is reduced and the mixture is relatively dry but glossy. Stir in the sesame seeds, if using. Season to taste with lots of black pepper and a little salt (you may not need salt, depending on how salty your kimchi is). Transfer to a serving platter and serve immediately.

JOYCE CHEN: The Godmother of Chinese American Cuisine

Opened in 1958, the Joyce Chen Restaurant in Cambridge, Massachusetts, was one of the first northern Chinese restaurants in the country (the Chinese restaurant landscape up to then was mostly dominated by the Cantonese cuisine made popular by a number of Chinese chefs in New York City and San Francisco, a city that has been home to Cantonese restaurants since at least the 1850s). Cantabrigians at her restaurant at 617 Concord Avenue were among the first in the United States to taste now-ubiquitous dishes like Peking duck, moo shu pork, hot and sour soup, panfried dumplings (for which Joyce coined the term "Peking ravioli"), and wonton soup. My parents, who were living in Cambridge at the time, picked up a taste for this stuff and a copy of the *Joyce Chen Cook Book* that lived in our kitchen, becoming increasingly tattered and oil-stained with each delicious meal my parents cooked from it. I'm too young to have any memories of eating at any of Joyce Chen's restaurants, but I know her food intimately.

I recently leafed through a copy of the book (now long out of print) and instantly recognized dishes we had at the family dinner table. The velveted chicken my dad made for my little sister (See Pico's Not-So-Bland Chicken, page 80). The flank steak stir-fried with snow peas in a light soy-based sauce my mom made (my version appears on page 120). Beef shreds dry-fried until crisp and chewy, soaked in an MSG-packed sauce (page 436). And then there was the Chungking pork.

I did a double take as I stumbled onto that last one. My mom's Chungking pork is a dish that has stuck in my memory as firmly as the dry, lean piece of pork she made it with used to stick in my throat. I dreaded those nights. I'd always figured that the use of lean pork loin in the dish was my mom's own attempt at trying to keep us healthy, but there it was, right on page 132: "1 pound lean pork." What was even more shocking to me was that this dish is actually meant to be Sichuan-style twice-cooked pork, a dish more commonly made with fatty pork belly or shoulder! (You can find my own hybrid version on page 95.)

This is one of the many charming anachronisms you'll find in the book, which contains a foreword by famed Boston-area cardiologist Paul Dudley White. At the time, fat was the enemy, and in what was presumably an attempt to entice a Western audience to try a cuisine that already had a reputation for being mostly gluey stews, Joyce Chen decided to use health as a selling point. This is why we end up with dishes like twice-cooked pork belly made with lean pork loin, but flavored with MSG, a seasoning against which Western audiences had yet to develop prejudices (see page 50).

I've found that you can greatly improve every recipe in the book by simply omitting the word *lean* (the MSG can stay).

Some may claim that these types of changes and concessions to Western palates render the recipes inauthentic. This is true, and Joyce Chen says as much herself. Her recipes and restaurants were created for an audience that was interested in learning about Chinese food but had no frame of reference and very little access to specialty Chinese ingredients. One of her greatest talents was in walking that fine tightrope between authenticity and accessibility. That's a talent I greatly admire as I frequently try to wobble my way along that line myself.

This was far from Joyce's only contribution to the culinary world. Maybe you own a company that sells chafing dishes, or perhaps you're the landlord of a suburban strip mall. Well, Joyce Chen invented the Chinese lunch buffets that are the bread and butter of your business. You know those flat-bottomed woks I wax poetic about? Joyce Chen is the original patent owner for the very first flat-bottomed wok. I still recommend hers for home cooks.

Do you like watching chefs cook on television? Joyce Chen was one of the pioneers of that medium as well. Her show *Joyce Chen Cooks* ran for two seasons, from 1966 to 1967. It was the first nationally syndicated cooking show to be hosted by a woman of color. Perhaps you're one of those patrons of the 41,000 Chinese restaurants in the United States who has an awkward time pronouncing some of the Chinese words and prefer to order your dishes by number. Thank Joyce Chen once again for the innovation of the numbered menu.

You can also add the introduction of bottled stir-fry sauces and polyethylene cutting boards to her list of American contributions.

Many of the recipes in this chapter and others owe a huge debt to the love of Chinese American food instilled in me by my parents, both Joyce Chen disciples, from a young age. Fortunately for my generation, getting those formerly hard-to-find ingredients is as simple as a trip to Chinatown or the Internet.

CHUNGKING PORK, TWO WAYS

Chungking pork is named after the city of Chong Qing, which until recently was part of Sichuan province but since 1997 has been its own separate municipality. The traditional Sichuan version of this dish is made with pork belly that is first boiled in water seasoned with spices until it becomes firm. It's then chilled, sliced, and subsequently stir-fried, which gives it a sort of tender-chewy texture with a bit of cartilaginous crispness to it, if you know what I mean.

I wondered how necessary this double-cooking process actually is, so I tested making it with pork boiled and sliced the traditional way versus fresh pork belly that I bought presliced. Turns out that there is not a huge difference. The traditional version gains a little flavor from the aromatics in the simmering step, but those flavors get nearly obliterated by the powerful flavor of fermented soybeans and sweet bean sauce in the finished dish. My (totally unconfirmed) hypothesis is that the boiling and chilling process was introduced to make thinly slicing soft and slippery pork belly easier. These days mechanical meat slicers at the supermarket do that job just fine, and if you can find pre-sliced pork belly, it's an easy time saver.

It is, in fact, quite possible to make the dish from leaner cuts of pork like loin or sirloin with deliciously juicy and tender results (so long as you skip the 30-minute boil, my mom's—OK, Joyce Chen's—version included). In Sichuan the pork is typically stir-fried with a type of tender leek that you can't really get in the States. I use a combination of leek whites and scallions instead. In Western versions from the Joyce Chen school, you're more likely to find sautéed green cabbage. Both versions are delicious and relatively easy.

Although Sichuan is famous for its fiery food, the flavors in Chungking pork are relatively mild on the heat scale, instead hitting you with a combination of three different types of fermented beans: doubanjiang (chile bean paste), tianmianjiang (sweet fermented wheat and soybean paste), and douchi (fermented black beans, which are actually fermented black soybeans). This hot-sweet-funky combo is a classic Sichuanese flavor combination, and it's what my traditional recipe calls for.

My mom's version of the Joyce Chen recipe omitted both of the bean pastes, using only fermented black beans. But for my take on my mom's version of the Joyce Chen recipe (do you follow?), I like to add a dab of hoisin sauce for sweetness and flavor.

BETTER-THAN-MY-MOM'S CHUNGKING PORK

Yield
Serves 4

Active Time
15 minutes

Total Time
30 minutes

NOTE
Thinly sliced fresh pork belly can be used in place of the pork loin or sirloin.

INGREDIENTS

For the Pork:

1 pound (450 g) boneless pork loin or sirloin, cut into ¼- by 1- by 2-inch pieces (see Note)

1 teaspoon (5 ml) dark soy sauce

1 teaspoon (5 ml) Shaoxing wine or dry sherry

¼ teaspoon (1 g) baking soda

1 teaspoon (3 g) cornstarch

¼ teaspoon (0.5 g) MSG (optional)

For the Sauce:

2 tablespoons (about 12 g) dried fermented black beans (douchi), roughly chopped

2 tablespoons (30 ml) hoisin sauce

2 teaspoons (10 ml) dark soy sauce

2 tablespoons (30 ml) homemade or store-bought low-sodium chicken stock or water

½ teaspoon (1.5 g) hot red pepper flakes or ground Chinese hot chiles

For the Stir-Fry:

3 tablespoons (45 ml) peanut, rice bran, or other neutral oil

3 slices fresh ginger (15 g)

3 medium garlic cloves (8 g), peeled and lightly smashed with the side of a knife or cleaver

6 ounces (170 g) green cabbage, cut into 1½-inch squares (about 3 cups)

DIRECTIONS

(1) For the Pork: Place the pork in a medium bowl, cover with cold water, and vigorously agitate it. Drain through a fine-mesh strainer set in the sink and press on the chicken with your hands to remove excess water. Return the pork to the bowl and add the soy sauce, wine, baking soda, and cornstarch. Stir vigorously with your fingertips or chopsticks for 30 seconds. Set aside for 15 minutes at room temperature or refrigerate for up to 8 hours.

(2) For the Sauce: Combine the fermented black beans, hoisin sauce, soy sauce, stock, and pepper flakes in a small bowl and mix with a fork until homogenous.

(3) BEFORE YOU STIR-FRY, GET YOUR BOWLS READY:

a. Marinated pork

b. Ginger and garlic

c. Cabbage

d. Sauce

e. Empty bowl for cooked ingredients

f. Serving platter

recipe continues

4 **For the Stir-Fry:** Heat a wok over high heat until lightly smoking. Add 1 tablespoon (15 ml) of the oil and swirl to coat. Add one slice of the ginger and one garlic clove and let sizzle for 5 seconds. Immediately add the cabbage and stir-fry until lightly translucent and browned in spots, 1 to 2 minutes. Transfer to a large bowl.

5 Wipe out the wok and return to high heat until lightly smoking. Add 1 tablespoon (15 ml) of the remaining oil and swirl to coat. Add one more slice of ginger and one more garlic clove and let sizzle for 5 seconds. Immediately add half of the pork and stir-fry until the pork is no longer pink and is mostly cooked through, about 1 minute. If using belly, cook until the belly begins to crisp lightly around the edges, about 2 minutes. Transfer the cooked pork to the bowl with the cabbage, wipe out the wok, and repeat with the remaining oil, ginger, garlic, and pork.

6 Return all the pork and cabbage to the wok. Add the sauce mixture and toss until the cabbage and pork are coated evenly. Transfer to a serving platter and serve immediately with steamed rice. (You can pick out the ginger slices and garlic cloves before serving if desired.)

How to Cut Leeks for Stir-Fries

Leeks available in China tend to be younger and more tender than the leeks we get in the West, which makes them more suitable for stir-frying. Typically, even Chinese leek greens are tender enough to include in a stir-fry. But that doesn't mean we can't stir-fry Western leeks as well! You just have to trim them properly, using only the white and pale green portions and discarding the tough greens (or saving them for stock).

To prepare leeks for a stir-fry, I do what's called a *diamond cut*. You start by trimming off the root end and the green tops. Next you split the leek in half lengthwise. Leeks grow in sandy soil, and oftentimes some of that soil gets caught between its layers, so I give leeks a good rinse under the tap after splitting them.

Finally, I cut each half crosswise at a 45-degree angle to form diamond-shaped segments that are easy to stir-fry and easy to pick up with chopsticks.

SICHUAN DOUBLE-COOKED PORK BELLY

Yield	Active Time
Serves 4	20 minutes
	Total Time
	1 hour

NOTE

You can skip the traditional simmering and slicing process (steps 1 and 2) and use thinly sliced fresh pork belly instead. If using store-bought sliced pork belly, omit all of the aromatics from step 1. It's nearly impossible to overcook pork belly, so there is no need to batch stir-fry the pork in this recipe—you can do it all in one go.

INGREDIENTS

For the Pork:

2 tablespoons (20 g) kosher salt
1 star anise pod
2 whole cloves
2 to 3 slices unpeeled fresh ginger
3 medium garlic cloves (8 g), peeled and lightly smashed with the side of a knife
¼ cup (60 ml) Shaoxing wine or dry sherry
2 quarts (2 l) water
1 pound (450 g) slab fresh pork belly, rind removed

For the Sauce:

2 teaspoons (10 ml) tianmianjiang (Chinese sweet bean paste)
1 tablespoon (about 6 g) dried fermented black beans (douchi), roughly chopped
1 teaspoon (5 ml) dark soy sauce

For the Stir-Fry:

3 tablespoons (45 ml) peanut, rice bran, or other neutral oil
3 scallions, cut into 2-inch segments
1 medium leek, white part only, quartered lengthwise and cut into 2-inch segments (about 1½ cups)
1 tablespoon (15 ml) doubanjiang (Chinese chile bean paste)

DIRECTIONS

① **For the Pork:** Combine the salt, star anise, cloves, ginger, garlic, wine, and water in a medium saucepan and stir until the salt is dissolved. Add the pork and bring to a simmer over high heat. Adjust the heat to maintain a gentle simmer until the pork is just cooked through, about 15 minutes. Reserve ¼ cup (60 ml) of the cooking liquid and discard the rest.

② Transfer the pork to a plate and refrigerate until firm, about 30 minutes. Cut the pork into slices between ¼ and ⅛ inch thick and about 2 inches square.

③ **Meanwhile, Make the Sauce:** Combine the reserved cooking liquid, sweet bean paste, fermented black beans, and soy sauce in a small bowl and stir with a fork until homogenous.

④ **BEFORE YOU STIR-FRY, GET YOUR BOWLS READY:**

a. Leeks and scallions
b. Sliced pork belly
c. Fermented chile bean paste (*doubanjiang*)
d. Sauce
e. Empty bowl for cooked ingredients
f. Serving platter

⑤ **For the Stir-Fry:** Heat a wok over high heat until lightly smoking. Add 1 tablespoon (15 ml) of the oil and swirl to coat. Add the scallions and leeks and stir-fry until tender-crisp, about 1 minute. Transfer to a plate.

⑥ Wipe out the wok and return it to high heat until lightly smoking. Add 1 tablespoon (15 ml) of the remaining oil and swirl to coat. Add all of the pork belly and cook, stirring and tossing occasionally until the pork is lightly browned and crisp around the edges, about 3 minutes. Transfer the pork to the plate with the leeks and scallions.

⑦ Add the remaining tablespoon of oil and the chile bean paste to the wok, stir-frying until the oil is dark red, about 15 seconds. Return the pork and leeks/scallions to the wok and add the sauce. Stir-fry until the sauce has reduced and coats the pork. Transfer to a serving platter and serve immediately.

SLICED PORK AND CUCUMBER

Yield
Serves 4

Active Time
15 minutes

Total Time
30 minutes

INGREDIENTS

For the Pork:
1 pound boneless pork loin, cut into 2-inch matchsticks
¼ teaspoon (2 g) sugar
¼ teaspoon (1 g) freshly ground white pepper
1 teaspoon (5 ml) Shaoxing wine or dry sherry
1 teaspoon (5 ml) light soy sauce or shoyu
1 teaspoon (5 ml) roasted sesame oil
½ teaspoon (2 g) baking soda
1 teaspoon (3 g) cornstarch

For the Sauce:
½ teaspoon (2 g) freshly ground white pepper
1½ tablespoons (about 25 ml) water
1½ tablespoons (about 25 ml) light soy sauce or shoyu

For the Cornstarch Slurry:
1 teaspoon (3 g) cornstarch
1 tablespoon (15 ml) water

For the Stir-Fry
3 tablespoons (45 ml) peanut, rice bran, or other neutral oil
2 medium garlic cloves (5 g), smashed
2 slices (10 g) fresh ginger
1 teaspoon chopped homemade (see page 84) or store-bought pickled chiles (optional)
2 scallions, white and pale green parts only, cut into 1-inch segments
One 8-ounce American or English cucumber, peeled, halved lengthwise, seeds removed, and cut on a bias into ¼-inch-thick half-moons

Cucumbers are an oft-forgotten vegetable when it comes to stir-fries. We tend to think of them as vegetables to be eaten raw or marinated in salads, but with a brief stir-fry they retain their bright crunch while picking up flavor from the wok. Paired with pork and pickled chiles, they make for a great stir-fry that tastes light and refreshing.

DIRECTIONS

(1) **For the Pork:** Place the pork in a medium bowl, cover with cold water, and vigorously agitate it. Drain through a fine-mesh strainer set in the sink and press on the pork with your hands to remove excess water. Return the pork to the bowl and add the sugar, white pepper, wine, soy sauce, sesame oil, baking soda, and cornstarch. Stir vigorously with your fingertips or chopsticks for 30 seconds. Set aside for 15 minutes at room temperature or refrigerate for up to 8 hours.

(2) **Meanwhile, Make the Sauce:** Combine the white pepper, water, and soy sauce in a small bowl and stir together until homogenous. Set aside. Combine the cornstarch and water in a separate small bowl and stir with a fork until the cornstarch is dissolved.

(3) **BEFORE YOU STIR-FRY, GET YOUR BOWLS READY:**

a. Marinated pork
b. Ginger, garlic, and pickled chiles
c. Cucumber and scallions
d. Sauce
e. Cornstarch slurry
f. Empty bowl for cooked ingredients
g. Serving platter

(4) **For the Stir-Fry:** Heat a wok over high heat until lightly smoking. Add 1 tablespoon (15 ml) of the oil and swirl to coat. Add half of the pork, spread into a single layer, and cook without moving until lightly browned, about 45 seconds. Cook, tossing and stirring frequently until barely cooked through, about 30 seconds longer. Transfer to a clean bowl and set aside.

(5) Wipe out the wok and return it to high heat until lightly smoking. Add 1 tablespoon (15 ml) of the remaining oil and swirl to coat. Stir-fry the remaining pork in the same manner and add it to the same bowl.

(6) Wipe out the wok and return it to high heat until lightly smoking. Add the remaining tablespoon (15 ml) oil and swirl to coat. Add the garlic, ginger, pickled chiles (if using), and scallions and cook, tossing and stirring constantly, until fragrant, about 30 seconds. Add the cucumber and scallions and stir-fry until just heated through, about 1 minute. Return the pork to the wok. Stir the sauce and add to the wok by pouring it around the edges. Stir the cornstarch slurry and add a splash. Cook, tossing, until the sauce thickens and the pork is cooked through, about 30 seconds longer. Adjust the sauce consistency with more cornstarch slurry if it is too thin or a splash of water if it is too thick. Transfer to a serving platter and serve immediately with steamed white rice.

How to Prepare Cucumbers for Stir-Fries

Cucumbers are one of the oldest cultivated vegetables, and a favorite for my daughter, Alicia, and me. They're great smashed with garlic Sichuan style (page 615) or paired with a sweet-and-savory Honey Mustard–Miso Dip (page 618), but they're also fantastic in stir-fries. While you can certainly simply slice whole cukes into salads, I typically peel and seed them, especially if I'm planning on stir-frying them, a process that can make the skins a little tougher and that doesn't benefit from the watery seeds hitting the wok.

These days, even at my Western supermarket, I can find English, American, Kirby, Persian, and Japanese cucumbers. For stir-fries I typically stick with English or American. Persian and Japanese I reserve for salads or eating raw, while Kirbys are for pickling.

Step 1 • Peel the Cucumber

Use a vegetable peeler to peel the cucumber.

Step 2 • Halve Lengthwise

Trim the tops and bottoms off the cucumber, then halve the cucumber lengthwise.

Step 3 • Remove the Seeds

Cucumber seeds can make your stir-fry watery, so they should be scraped out with a spoon and discarded.

Step 4 • Slice

Slice the seeded cucumber halves into slivers on a bias.

The Truth about MSG

Chances are you've eaten some monosodium glutamate (MSG) within the last twenty-four hours. It's in nearly all prepared foods, and the glutamate present in MSG is chemically identical to the glutamate naturally found in all kinds of foods ranging from Parmesan cheese to green peas to tomatoes. There's no denying its transformative culinary power. In its pure crystalline form, MSG can be added to soups, stews, sauces, and stocks to add a rounded, savory flavor. Like regular table salt, MSG can also help boost our perception of other existing flavors. Tomato soup with a pinch of MSG tastes a little more tomatoey. Add a dash to beef stew to make it taste beefier. I, like my mother, and her mother before her, keep a small jar of it right next to the salt in my kitchen.

For some readers this may come as a surprise. I can hear you now: *But Kenji, MSG is terrible for you! You'll get migraines and asthma and numbness and seventeen other symptoms, each more horrid than the last!*

For others, you may have the opposite reaction: *Yesssssss, validation at last! MSG reactions are all in your head and all those studies have proven it. MSG headaches are imaginary!*

Hold up. Because both of those reactions are out of line with reality. First let's take a brief look at the history of MSG use, then let's take a look at what those studies *really* have to say.

What Is MSG?

MSG is a sodium salt of glutamic acid (alpha-amino acid). It was first isolated in 1908 by Japanese biochemist Kikunae Ikeda, who was trying to discover exactly what gave dashi—the Japanese broth flavored with kombu (giant sea kelp)—its strong, savory character. Turns out that kombu is *packed* with glutamic acid. It was Ikeda who coined the term *umami*, which roughly translates as "savory," to describe the taste of glutamic acid (and other, similar amino acids). Until that point, scientists

had only discovered four flavors sensed by the tongue and soft palate: salty, sweet, sour, and bitter.

By 1909, pure crystalline MSG extracted from the abundant kelp in the sea around Japan was being sold under the brand name Aji-no-moto (roughly "element of flavor"). The company exists to this day, though with the current high demand for MSG, the chemical is synthesized rather than extracted. Pure MSG powder is available under a number of brand names (like Ac'cent), and glutamic-acid-rich ingredients are used extensively in packaged foods, typically in the form of autolyzed yeast extract or hydrolyzed soy protein. If the ingredients label lists either of those ingredients, there's MSG in there. This was all well and good until the late 1960s.

The Myth of "Chinese Restaurant Syndrome"

The term *Chinese Restaurant syndrome* started getting thrown around in 1968 when a letter, written by a reader named Dr. Robert Ho Man Kwok, was published in the *New England Journal of Medicine*. In it, he speculated that the numbness and palpitations he experienced after eating in Chinese restaurants may be linked to the liberal use of powdered monosodium glutamate (MSG) in Chinese food. Though no actual evidence was presented, the idea took off and went viral (even before the Internet!), and for decades MSG was blamed for everything from migraines and numbness to bloat and heart palpitations. MSG phobia was born, and it exists to this day, though the racially tinged pejorative "Chinese restaurant syndrome" has since been swapped out for "MSG symptom complex."

More recently, there's been a wave of anti-anti-MSG backlash. Article after article claims that science has proven that MSG has no ill effects. These articles are as guilty of misrepresenting scientific data as those who spread the idea of Chinese restaurant syndrome in the first place. Let's take a look at the actual science.

The Studies

A 1970 study by Dr. John Olney published in *Nature* found that injecting high doses of MSG under the skin of infant mice caused retinal damage, brain damage, and obesity as adults. We're talking huge doses of MSG injected directly into babies here, a far cry from the small amounts ingested orally by humans. An April 2000 meta-study in the *Journal of Nutrition* found that in twenty-one studies of MSG conducted on primates, only two found links between oral consumption and neurotoxicity. Both of these studies were done by Olney's laboratory, and nobody has been able to repeat those results since. Moreover, even in mice (the experimental species most sensitive to MSG), the oral dose of MSG required to produce brain lesions was 1 gram per kilogram of body weight, an absolutely massive amount the equivalent of a 170-pound person eating a third of a cup of pure MSG in a single sitting, with no food, on an empty stomach. This is about the amount of added MSG an average adult consumes in half a year.

Both the Federal Drug Administration (FDA) and the Federation of American Societies for Experimental Biology (FASEB) have done meta-studies on available experimental data. The conclusion was that while very large doses of MSG can both cause degenerative nerve cell damage and disrupt hormonal function in animal tests, there is no evidence to suggest any kind of long-term damage to humans in ordinary doses.

So far so good. Seems like the anti-anti-MSG folks are right. But what about short-term effects, i.e., MSG symptom complex? Surely not everyone who feels the short-term symptoms of consuming MSG can be hallucinating, can they? A 1993 study from the *Journal of Food and Chemical Toxicology* found that in a normal cross section of the healthy population there was little to no correspondence between MSG consumption and *MSG Symptom Complex*, especially when MSG consumption was paired with food. In fact, the effects were no greater than that of a placebo.

Doesn't sound so good for the MSG haters.

But how about in people who *specifically* self-identify as being sensitive to MSG? Here the results are a little different. In a November 2000 study from the *Journal of Allergy and Clinical Immunology*, scientists administered increasing doses of MSG and a placebo to 130 adults who self-identified as MSG-sensitive. While responses to MSG were not completely consistent with repeated testing, testing subjects generally showed more reactions to actual MSG (38% of respondents) versus a placebo (13% of respondents).

The conclusion of the study was that MSG does, in fact, elicit adverse responses from a particularly sensitive subgroup of the population when administered in large doses (more than 3 g) on a mostly empty stomach. The existence of MSG symptom complex is concrete scientific fact.

Anecdotally, some members of my family and I experience MSG symptom complex effects, but not regularly. I cook with MSG several times a week, but experience adverse reactions only a few times per year. Most MSG-sensitive people experience similar rates of reaction, and it is, as yet, unclear what exact circumstances will elicit a reaction or whether those reactions are in fact attributable to MSG, MSG in concert with other ingredients, or an as-yet unidentified trigger. Human metabolism is extraordinarily complex. More studies are needed.

What about Glutamic Acid in Other Foods?

Kombu isn't the only food rich in glutamic acid, though it may be the richest. Many commonly eaten foods are loaded with the stuff:

FOOD	GLUTAMIC ACID CONTENT (mg/100 g)
Kombu (giant sea kelp)	22,000
Parmigiano-Reggiano	12,000
Bonito	2,850
Sardines/Anchovies	2,800
Tomato Juice	2,600
Tomatoes	1,400
Pork	1,220
Beef	1,070
Chicken	760
Mushrooms	670
Soybeans	660
Carrots	330

According to the FDA, the average adult consumes about 13 grams of glutamate each day from natural sources, plus an additional .55 gram of added glutamate from MSG or other sources. This leads to an obvious question: Chemicals don't really care what source they come from. Glutamate is glutamate, whether extracted from seaweed, synthesized in a lab, produced by the body, or consumed in your Parmesan cheese. So why aren't folks sensitive to MSG also sensitive to glutamic-acid-rich foods? Why can my sister eat as much Parmesan cheese and as many anchovies as she wants?

It's important to remember that in virtually every study, it was only when glutamic acid was consumed on a nearly empty stomach that adverse reactions manifested. When paired with enough food, symptoms virtually vanished.

My friend Jeffrey Steingarten, *Vogue* magazine's longtime food correspondent, has suggested that the rash of people claiming MSG sensitivity in the seventies and eighties might be due to the fact that in those days many Chinese American restaurant meals started with a bowl of MSG-rich wonton soup consumed on an empty stomach before the rest of the meal. This hypothesis seems to fall in line with scientific data. Even though Parmesan cheese is packed with glutamic acid, it's got plenty of other "stuff" in it too, and most likely you're pairing that cheese with pasta or pizza.

Steingarten also rhetorically asked, why, if MSG is so bad, does everyone in China not walk around with a headache? This has become a popular refrain among Internet chat rooms and social media. However, it ignores several important factors: not everyone in China cooks with MSG, we don't actually have data specific to China on self-reported MSG sensitivity, and most importantly, different populations have different reactions to foods. Lactose intolerance runs much higher in China than in the United States, so when someone in China claims to get a stomachache when drinking milk, "Is everyone in the U.S. walking around with a stomachache?" is not a relevant response.

If our relatively recent acceptance of gluten intolerance as a real problem that affects a good chunk of the population is any indication, we, as a species, are not very good at judging the varying ways in which ingredients interact with our systems.

Some have hypothesized that when it comes to Chinese restaurants specifically, MSG-rich broths consumed on an empty stomach may be part of the culprit, but there's also a good possibility that some folks who claim sensitivity to MSG may in fact be experiencing reactions to other ingredients common in Chinese food but not so common in other restaurant cuisines, such as the peanut oil frequently used for stir-frying, the shellfish extracts used for flavoring, or herbs like cilantro. As far as I am aware, there is currently no scientific data that would elevate this hypothesis to theory.

One final note: whether you believe MSG sensitivity may exist or you believe that it is purely a placebo effect, there is never a legitimate reason to invalidate somebody's reaction. If someone claims to be experiencing a negative reaction or feeling a certain way, believe it. At best, this may well be another piece of evidence to suggest that MSG sensitivity is a legitimate concern, and at worst, this person is experiencing a placebo effect. In either case, the feelings of discomfort are equally real and should be met with empathy.

So Should I Cook with It?

So where does that leave us in terms of using it for cooking? In the end, it seems that the subgroup sensitive to MSG is small enough and the adverse reaction rare enough that in all likelihood you're gonna be just fine using it in your own food, especially if you make sure to eat a little MSG-free stuff to lay down a bed in your belly before getting to the goods. Moreover, all evidence suggests that the effects are at worst a short-term discomfort with no long-lasting consequences.

If you do, however, feel that you have a sensitivity to MSG, by all means avoid it! And you can tell those people who say "You're just imagining it!" to buzz off. Your ally is science, and a powerful ally it is.

REVISITING MOO SHU PORK

Moo shu pork is a northern Chinese dish from Shandong, popularized in the United States by Joyce Chen. The name stems from *mùxī*, the Chinese name for sweet osmanthus flowers, which the scrambled eggs in this classic stir-fry are said to resemble.* The version in her book (and at her restaurant) tracks closely with the traditional Shandong version: lightly marinated pork is stir-fried with scrambled eggs, wood ear mushroom, and daylily buds. In Beijing you may find the dish made with sliced cucumbers in place of daylily buds, whereas in the United States, variants of the dish with mung bean sprouts and green cabbage are not uncommon. The stir-fry itself is relatively mild, flavored only with soy sauce and wine, roasted sesame oil, a little white pepper, and a hint of ginger. A paper-thin Mandarin pancake brushed with sweet hoisin sauce folded around the filling like a little burrito gives it an adjustable punch of flavor.

I've been eating and making the Joyce Chen version for years. It's extraordinarily easy to make and, aside from the pork, uses ingredients I pretty much always have in my pantry (even the smallest packages of dried wood ears and daylily buds will last you *years*). Recently I found myself with a glut of mushrooms (this sometimes happens when I'm left unsupervised at the farmers' market) and thought to myself that in addition to the fantastic alliteration, moo shu mushrooms would make a tasty variant.

I cut back on the amount of pork that a typical moo shu recipe calls for and replaced it with a big pile of mixed mushrooms that I stir-fried until browned and slightly crispy around the edges (we're after moo shi mushrooms, not mushy mushrooms). As I was eating I quickly came to realize that, more than flavor, the little bit of pork that remains offers texture, which means that it can very easily be replaced with slivered chicken or even slivered extra-firm pressed tofu. The latter choice would make this a 100 percent vegan dish. This mushroom-heavy version has now become my standard.

As for the pancakes, they are quite simple and fast to make at home, though you can also do what many strip-mall Chinese restaurants do: serve the stir-fry with warm flour tortillas. Even the best-quality flour tortilla is going to be thicker than a Mandarin pancake, but it'll still work just fine.

---

* This seems to be the general consensus, at least. In the original Joyce Chen book, the dish is transliterated as *moo shi*, but many Chinese restaurants and cookbooks these days (including this one!) transliterate it as *moo shu*, which translates to "wood whiskers," a supposed reference to the appearance of daylily and wood ear fungus. This latter explanation is most likely incorrect, stemming from misspellings on early Chinese American restaurant menus. Yet the name has stuck and is now widely accepted.

MOO SHU (MOO SHI) MUSHROOMS OR MOO SHU PORK

Yield
Serves 4

Active Time
20 minutes

Total Time
40 minutes

NOTE
If you prefer to make moo shu pork, omit the mushrooms, increase the pork to 12 ounces, and double all of the pork marinade ingredients. Proceed as instructed, stir-frying the pork in two separate batches, adding the scallions, wood ears, and daylilies to the second batch of pork as instructed in Step 7.

INGREDIENTS

The Dry Ingredients:
¼ cup (½ ounce/about 15 g) dried Chinese wood ear mushrooms
¼ cup (½ ounce/about 15 g) dried daylily buds

For the Pork:
4 ounces (120 g) pork loin, pork sirloin, chicken breast, or extra-firm tofu, cut into thin slivers
1 teaspoon (5 ml) Shaoxing wine or dry sherry
1 teaspoon (5 ml) light soy sauce or shoyu
¼ teaspoon (0.5 g) freshly ground white pepper
Pinch of kosher salt
Pinch of MSG (optional)
1 teaspoon (3 g) cornstarch

For the Sauce:
1 tablespoon (15 ml) Shaoxing wine or dry sherry
1 tablespoon (15 ml) light soy sauce or shoyu
½ teaspoon (1 g) freshly ground white pepper

For the Stir-Fry:
¼ cup (60 ml) roasted sesame oil
3 large eggs, thoroughly beaten with a pinch of kosher salt
2 slices fresh ginger
8 ounces (225 g) mixed sliced mushrooms (see page 109)
2 scallions, thinly sliced on a sharp bias
¼ teaspoon (about .5 g) MSG (optional)
Kosher salt and freshly ground white pepper

To Serve:
Mandarin Pancakes (page 106) or warm flour tortillas
Hoisin sauce or sweet bean sauce

DIRECTIONS

(1) **Rehydrate the Dried Ingredients:** Place the wood ears and daylily buds in a large bowl or measuring cup large enough to allow for them to expand about fourfold. Cover with very hot water and set aside until rehydrated, about 15 minutes. Drain thoroughly. Remove tough centers from the wood ears, then thinly slice them. Cut the daylilies into 2-inch pieces.

(2) **While the Wood Ears and Daylilies Rehydrate, Marinate the Pork:** Place the pork in a medium bowl, cover with cold water, and vigorously agitate it. Drain through a fine-mesh strainer set in the sink and press on the pork with your hands to remove excess water. Return the pork to the bowl and add the wine, soy sauce, white pepper, a pinch of kosher salt, a pinch of MSG, and the cornstarch. Stir vigorously with your fingertips or chopsticks for 30 seconds. Set aside for 15 minutes at room temperature.

(3) **Meanwhile, Make the Sauce:** Combine the wine, soy sauce, and white pepper in a small bowl and whisk with a fork until no lumps remain.

(4) **BEFORE YOU STIR-FRY, GET YOUR BOWLS READY:**

a.	Beaten eggs	f.	Sauce
b.	Ginger slices	g.	Empty bowl for cooked
c.	Marinated pork		ingredients
d.	Mushrooms	h.	Serving platter
e.	Sliced scallions, wood ears, and daylilies		

(5) **Cook the Eggs:** Heat a wok over high heat until lightly smoking. Add 2 tablespoon (15 ml) of the sesame oil and swirl to coat. Pour the beaten eggs into the center and cook without moving them for 10 seconds. Continue to cook, stirring and breaking up the eggs with a spatula until they are barely set, 30 to 45 seconds. Transfer the eggs to a large bowl.

(6) Wipe out the wok and return it to high heat until lightly smoking. Add 1 tablespoon (15 ml) of the remaining sesame oil and swirl to coat. Add one slice of the ginger and let sizzle for 5 seconds. Immediately add the pork and stir-fry until the pork is no longer pink and is mostly cooked through, about 1 minute (if making Moo Shu Pork instead of Moo Shu Mushrooms, cook the pork in two batches—see Note). Transfer to the bowl with the eggs.

(7) Wipe out the wok and return to high heat until lightly smoking. Add the remaining 1 tablespoon (15 ml) oil and swirl to coat. Add the remaining ginger slice and let sizzle for 5 seconds. Immediately add the mixed mushrooms and stir-fry until the mushrooms are lightly browned around the edges, 2 to 3 minutes. Add the scallions, wood ears, and daylilies and stir-fry until softened and fragrant, about 30 seconds.

(8) Add the pork and eggs back to the wok and toss everything to combine. Stir the sauce and add to the wok by pouring it around the edges. Stir-fry everything together to combine and season to taste with salt and more white pepper. Transfer to a serving platter and serve immediately with Mandarin pancakes and hoisin sauce.

MANDARIN PANCAKES

Yield
Makes
12 large
pancakes
or up to
36 smaller
pancakes

Active Time
15 minutes

Total Time
45 minutes

INGREDIENTS

10 ounces (280 g) all-purpose flour, plus
    more for dusting
3½ ounces (100 ml) boiling water
3½ ounces (100 ml) cold water
Vegetable or roasted sesame oil for
    brushing

Mandarin pancakes* are those ultrathin pancakes you use to wrap up moo shu pork or Peking duck. They're really magical. And I don't mean that in the way that, say, eating crab by the moonlight on a beach in Thailand is magical or the way drinking an ice-cold beer in a steaming hot shower on a Sunday afternoon with no plans for the rest of the day is magical. I mean it in the way that a neat card trick is magical. You can pick up one of those lightly blistered pancakes with their pliant elasticity and think to yourself *How in the heck did they get these so translucently thin?*—but as with all magic tricks, once you see how it's done, it all seems so simple.

These pancakes are one of the first things I ever remember cooking. I watched as my dad made a dough out of flour and boiling water (which results in dough that is as supple and easy to roll as play dough), then helped him knead it into a smooth ball, which we cut up into smaller balls that we lightly flattened out. The next step is the real trick. Rather than rolling out the pancakes one at a time, he brushed one pancake with a thin layer of oil before stacking another on top of it and rolling them out *together*. As the stacked disks of dough cooked in a hot, dry skillet, they started to puff and steam. Once they were blistered on both sides, my dad would take them out, then it was my job to peel the two pancakes apart—an easy task thanks to the oil and steam.

What you wind up with is two pancakes that are half as thick as the thinnest single pancake you can roll out.

The purpose of the hot water is to speed up starch hydration and to break down some of the proteins responsible for gluten formation. This makes hot water doughs very easy to roll out and shape as well as quite tender once cooked. Reducing gluten formation also means the finished pancakes are a little less stretchy and elastic than they would be with a cold-water dough. I've found that to get the best of both worlds it's best to start the dough with boiling water (to deactivate some protein), then finish it with cold water (for more elasticity). Resting the dough after kneading allows gluten to relax and starch to finish hydrating, which is essential for achieving a smooth, pliable dough that's easy to roll.

If you want very thin, small pancakes, you can also use a pasta roller in place of a rolling pin to roll out the stacked dough balls. (Make the dough balls about a third of the size recommended in the recipe, and don't go thinner than setting 3 or 4 or the pancakes will become too delicate to peel apart!)

---

* These pancakes are known variously as *chun bing, dan bing,* or *bao bing,* depending on what they're being served with or where you are.

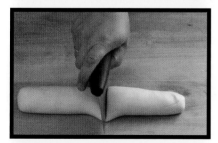

DIRECTIONS

(1) Place the flour in a medium bowl. Add the boiling water in a thin stream while stirring with chopsticks or a wooden spoon. It helps to have a friend stabilize the bowl while you do this or to set the bowl in a heavy saucepan lined with a dish towel to keep it stable. Add the cold water in a thin stream, continuing to mix the whole time. Stir the mixture until it turns into a shaggy ball, then dump the ball out onto a lightly floured work surface.

(2) Knead the dough with your hands until it forms a smooth ball, about 5 minutes. Cover the dough ball with a damp dish towel and let rest for at least 30 minutes and up to a couple hours.

(3) Roll the dough into a long log, then cut it in half. Line up the two half-logs, then further split them to form 12 to 36 evenly sized pieces (12 pieces for approximate 8-inch pancakes, 16 pieces for approximate 7-inch pancakes, 20 pieces for approximate 6-inch pancakes, or 36 pieces for approximate 4-inch pancakes).

recipe continues

(4) Working two pieces at a time, roll each piece into a smooth ball between your hands, then, using a rolling pin or wine bottle, gently roll them into circular disks about ¼ inch thick.

(5) Brush the top of one disk with a thin, even layer of oil, then stack the second disk on top. Using a rolling pin, roll the stacked disks into a circle; the size of the circle depends on the number of balls you made (see step 3).

(6) Preheat a cast iron, carbon steel, or nonstick skillet over medium heat, then add the rolled, stacked disk. Let cook on one side until blistered and browned in spots, about 1 minute. Flip and cook until the second side is blistered and browned. Sometimes the pancakes will bubble up with steam as they cook, preventing the second side from making good contact with the pan. You can gently press down on them with a flat spatula if this happens.

(7) Remove the cooked disks, then carefully peel them apart into two thin pancakes while still hot. Transfer to a plate and cover with a clean dish towel.

(8) Repeat steps 4 through 7 for the remaining dough balls. Finished pancakes should be served immediately. To store leftovers, place the pancakes on large squares of plastic wrap or aluminum foil, then roll them up like a jelly roll and refrigerate. Reheat covered in the microwave or by briefly heating one at a time in a hot, dry skillet.

Common Asian Mushrooms

Mushrooms are a staple in Asian cookery. While Western varieties of mushroom work well in many stir-fries and other dishes, it's good to get familiar with common Asian varieties to expand your repertoire. Mushrooms are grown or harvested in dirt or straw, so you can expect them to have a bit of dirt on them when you buy them. You can wipe off excess dirt with a paper towel, a pastry brush, or a quick rinse under the tap (contrary to popular belief, mushrooms don't really absorb much liquid when you wash them).

No matter what type of mushroom you are shopping for, look for specimens that are smooth and blemish-free with a dry (not slimy or wet) appearance.

→ **Oyster mushrooms** come in white, brown, or even grayish blue varieties. They have tender, gilled flesh and a mild flavor with hints of bitter almond (thanks to the chemical benzaldehyde) and anise. They're great stir-fried or sautéed. Trim off the tough bottom stem of oyster mushrooms before cooking.

→ **Shiitake mushrooms** can be found fresh or dried. When young and fresh their flavor is quite mild but packs a nice umami punch. More mature shiitake, and especially dried and rehydrated shiitake, have a powerful earthy, savory aroma with a hint of smokiness. They're excellent multipurpose mushrooms that work stir-fried and sautéed, simmered in soups and broth, or grilled. Shiitake stems are tough and leathery and should be removed by pinching the stem between your fingertips right where it meets the cap and pulling it out before cooking.

→ **Shimeji mushrooms** come in a few varieties, either white or brown. They're also sold as beech or clamshell mushrooms. Their texture is pleasantly crunchy and tender, and they have a nutty flavor with a fresh, grassy undertone. Shimeji mushrooms have to be cooked before being eaten as they're unpleasantly bitter when eaten raw. They're best quickly sautéed or stir-fried but are also commonly used in soups. Shimeji mushrooms require minimal trimming—just remove the dirty nub at the bottom of the stem. You can separate them into individual mushrooms by breaking them apart with your hands.

- → **Wood ear mushrooms.** See page 25 for more details on shopping or "Working with Dried Wood Ears" on this page for details on preparing.

- → **Enoki mushrooms** have a similar aroma to that of oyster mushrooms, albeit much milder. Their texture is mildly crunchy. They're best stir-fried or in thin soups where they can sop up broth like a bundle of noodles. The individual stems merge into one large stem at the bottom. Cut the mushrooms off just above where the stems merge before cooking.

- → **King oyster mushrooms**, also known as **trumpet royale**, **king trumpet**, or **eryngii**, are large, extrameaty mushrooms with a round cross section that can span up to a couple inches. Like oyster and enoki mushrooms, they have a very mild flavor, especially when raw. When cooked, especially when browned, they develop a strong umami flavor with a tender, meaty texture similar to abalone. They're best split lengthwise and sautéed or stir-fried until well browned. As for oyster or shimeji mushrooms, only the very bottoms of the stems need to be trimmed off before cooking.

- → **Maitake mushrooms**, also called **hen-of-the-woods** or **ram's head**, are sold in frilly, voluminous tufts. They have a very intensely nutty, savory flavor that's best when enhanced by some browning by a good, long, hot sauté or stir-fry or by tossing them with a little oil and roasting them whole until the edges become nice and crispy. Like a good piece of meat, maitake mushrooms don't need much more than a pinch of salt and pepper to bring out their flavor, though they do just fine with sauces and other aromatics. These guys are definitely my favorite. Trim off any woody bits from the base of the stem. You can leave them whole for roasting or separate them into frilly fronds with your fingers for sautéing.

- → **Matsutake mushrooms** (not pictured) are one of the most highly prized mushrooms in Japan, fetching prices of up to $500 a pound for the highest-quality specimens. They have a uniquely spicy, citrusy aroma. Lower-quality mushrooms can be grilled or sautéed, while the best are typically treated more like truffles: raw and thinly shaved, particularly into hot clear broths, where the heat from the broth releases and aerosolizes the mushroom's aroma. Trim the very end of the base off the mushroom before using.

Working with Dried Wood Ears

Remember those little rubber dinosaurs you had as a kid that you'd place in a cup of water, then over the course of a few days, they'd grow and grow and grow until they were the size of a mop bucket? Wood ear mushrooms are the Magic Grow Dinosaurs of the culinary world. They start as hard, plastic-like, shriveled nubs, but place them in a bowl of hot water and over the course of 15 to 20 minutes they gradually absorb water and unfurl until they achieve their final large, smooth, ear-shaped form.

Once rehydrated, the little nub where the mushroom formerly attached itself to a tree needs to be removed, as it's typically too tough to eat. (If you are anatomically inclined, it's the bit that's the equivalent of the tragus—the little nub in front of your ear hole—on the human ear.) You can do this by pinching it off with your finger and thumb.

Once that nub is gone, you can slice the wood ear into fine shreds.

GROUND PORK WITH HOLY BASIL (PAD KA-PRAO) IS THE EASIEST STIR-FRY FOR BREAKFAST, LUNCH, DINNER, OR ANY TIME IN BETWEEN

Pad ka-prao is a ubiquitous street dish in Thailand, where cooks wielding woks will rapidly stir-fry sliced or minced meat flavored with garlic, shallots, fish sauce, and fiery Thai bird chiles, finish it off with a big handful of holy basil, and serve it with rice and perhaps a fried egg on top. Unless there's running water nearby, you'll probably eat it from plates wrapped in the world's thinnest plastic bags (designed to be slipped off and discarded after use, like a plate condom), knees bent and back hunched, over a small plastic table. The only things thinner than those plastic bags are the napkins that disintegrate as you try to wipe the sweat from your brow.

In the United States, on the other hand, it's simultaneously one of the most commonly ordered Thai dishes and the least consumed. Let me explain. Order pad ka-prao from a typical American Thai restaurant and instead of the spicy, almost medicinal flavor of jagged-edged, fuzzy-leafed holy basil (ka-prao), you're going to taste the sweet, anise-like flavor of Thai purple basil (bai horapa), or perhaps even sweet Italian basil (the horror!). Holy basil is difficult to come by 'round these parts, you see.

Now, I could let this unfortunate state of affairs drive me to great lengths—literally—in search of the few leaves of holy basil that make their way within my shopping radius so that I might be able to recapture some of that Thai flavor. Instead, I generally choose to accept the fact that pad bai horapa is not pad ka-prao, but it's still darned delicious in its own right. Even in Thailand, stir-fries with purple basil are commonly served, so we don't have to lose out on the authenticity points.*

It's really an issue only if you're a stickler for proper nomenclature or *really* want that authentic holy basil flavor. (Unless you've been to Thailand, there's a good chance you've never tasted it anyway.) As my friend and Thai food expert Leela Punyaratabandhu explains, just call your ground meat stir-fry made with purple or sweet basil pad bai horapa instead, and everyone should

be happy, especially when invited for lunch. (See the sidebar "Common Culinary Basils" on page 130 for more on basil types.)

Unlike many Chinese-stir-fries that rely on intense heat for flavor development with aromatics added toward the end to prevent burning, Thai stir-fries frequently use more moderate heat, instead building flavors by frying aromatics in oil at the start before adding the remaining ingredients. This stir-fry starts with one of the Holy Trinities of Thai stir-fries: chiles, shallots, and garlic. A big granite mortar and pestle is by far the best tool for releasing the flavor of these aromatics (see page 576 for more on the science of mortars and pestles), though you can also chop them by hand or use a minichopper.

As for the meat, preground stuff from the supermarket is an easy option and works just fine. With store-bought meat you can have this dish on the table in about 15 minutes start to finish. But if you want to go that extra mile, I would recommend chopping meat by hand or in the food processor, as I do when I want the best hamburgers.

Purists will insist that this dish be seasoned with nothing but fish sauce and perhaps a little palm sugar, but most versions you'll find in the United States—and even frequently in Thailand—will also be seasoned with dark soy sauce and perhaps a dash of oyster sauce. I generally prefer the fish-sauce-only version, which has a brighter, fresher flavor, but it really depends on my mood.

If you want to make this into an easy, slightly more balanced meal, you can add some green beans or long beans that have been sliced into short segments. They cook in about the same time as the meat does, so you can go ahead and add them to the wok together with the meat.

No matter which version I make, a fried egg—and I mean a *really* fried egg that's crispy and lacy around the edges (see page 114)—has a home right on top of it.

---

* Everyone is keeping track of their authenticity points, yes?

THAI-STYLE STIR-FRIED GROUND PORK WITH BASIL (PAD BAI HORAPA OR PAD KA-PRAO)

Yield
Serves 4

Active Time
15 minutes

Total Time
15 minutes

NOTES

For best results, start with a whole piece of pork sirloin (or chicken breast, or firm tofu, or fish, or beef sirloin, or any lean meat really) and chop by hand. For easiest results, use ground meat from the supermarket.

Two Thai bird chiles will be quite hot. Eight chiles will be blazing hot (have that cool, sweet, milky Thai iced tea handy!). For milder heat, replace the Thai bird chiles with half of a jalapeño or serrano chile.

Beans are not a traditional addition to the stir-fry, but they can be delicious and are a nice way to break up the meatiness.

If you want a more traditional version of the dish, omit the dark soy sauce and oyster sauce and season with more fish sauce to taste. For the most authentic results, look for holy basil at an Asian supermarket (bai ka-prao). Thai purple basil or plain old sweet Italian basil can be used in its place.

A mortar and pestle will produce the most flavorful results, but you can easily make the dish without one.

INGREDIENTS

6 medium garlic cloves, peeled (about 2 tablespoons/16 g)

1 medium shallot (about 1½ ounces/45 g), peeled

2 to 8 Thai bird chiles, stems removed (⅛ to ½ ounce/4 to 15 g; see Notes)

2 tablespoons (30 ml) peanut, rice bran, or other neutral oil

1 pound (450 g) lean ground pork, chicken, or beef or crumbled firm tofu (see Notes)

⅓ pound (150 g) green beans or long beans, cut into ½-inch pieces (optional; see Notes)

2 tablespoons (30 ml) fish sauce, plus more to taste

1 teaspoon (4 g) granulated sugar or palm sugar, more or less to taste

1 tablespoon (15 ml) dark soy sauce (optional; see Notes)

1 tablespoon (15 ml) oyster sauce (optional; see Notes)

1½ ounces (45 g) fresh basil leaves (about 1½ cups packed; see Notes)

To Serve:

Steamed jasmine or short-grain rice
Nam Pla Prik (optional; page 257)
Extra-Crispy Fried Eggs (optional; page 114)

DIRECTIONS

(1) **If Using a Mortar and Pestle:** Roughly chop the garlic, shallots, and chiles and place in the mortar. Add a small pinch of kosher salt. Pound with the pestle until roughly mashed (no need to form a paste here).

If Not Using a Mortar and Pestle: Mince the garlic, shallots, and chiles by hand or in a minichopper.

(2) Combine the oil and garlic/shallot/chile mixture in a wok or skillet and place over medium-high heat. Cook, stirring frequently, until the aromatics are lightly softened and the oil is fragrant, about 30 seconds after it starts sizzling.

(3) Add the meat or tofu and cook, stirring and tossing while breaking it up with a spatula until no longer pink, about 2 minutes. Add the fish sauce, sugar, soy sauce (if using), and oyster sauce (if using). Continue to cook until most of the liquid is evaporated but the mixture is still nice and moist, about 1 minute.

(4) Remove the wok or skillet from the heat. Add the basil and toss to combine until wilted. Serve immediately with rice, nam pla prik, and extra-crispy fried eggs.

Most Fried Eggs Are a Lie. These Aren't.

Most of the fried eggs we eat are not really fried. I mean, they're fried, but they're not fried.

The first time I tasted eggs that were truly fried was in the streets of Thailand, where a lady with a mobile wok burner served me a plate of rice topped with pad ka-prao. She handed the plate over but held her hand up, indicating I should wait. As I held the plate, she added more oil to the empty wok, heating it up until it looked like it was just about to start smoking, before slipping an egg into it. The egg immediately started sputtering and spitting as she used her spatula to help the hot oil flow in waves over the top of the egg. Thirty seconds later, it was deposited on my plate with crisp, lacy edges, a tender center, and a runny yolk to mix in with my rice.

It was a revelation.

Fancy French-style fried eggs with their tender texture and pure-white whites are all well and good, but for topping my rice or ka-prao, a fried egg should taste *fried*, with cratered, bubbly whites, crispy brown edges, and all. It's the built-in texture and flavor contrasts that really make it. Here's how I cook mine.

I start by breaking a couple eggs into a bowl and having it handy while I preheat my bare wok until it starts to smoke. I then reduce the heat to medium and swirl in a few tablespoons of oil. Next I add my eggs, making sure to tip them into the pan gently from just above the surface of the oil. You don't want that oil splashing up onto you! The eggs should immediately start sputtering and spitting when they reach the pan. (I hit them with salt and pepper at this stage.)

When the eggs are in the wok, I tilt it upward, using a dish towel to protect my hand from any oil splatter. This causes the hot oil to pool, allowing me to use a spatula to lift that oil and baste the egg with it, aiming it wherever the egg whites seem loosest.

Once the eggs are puffy and crisp around the edges—about 45 seconds or so—I transfer them to a serving platter.

They aren't the prettiest eggs around, but boy have they got a great personality.

EXTRA-CRISPY FRIED EGGS

Yield
Makes 2

Active Time
2 minutes

Total Time
2 minutes

INGREDIENTS

3 tablespoons (45 ml) vegetable or
    olive oil
2 large eggs
Kosher salt and freshly ground black
    pepper

DIRECTIONS

(1) Heat the oil in a 10-inch cast iron, carbon steel, or nonstick skillet or a wok over medium-high heat until shimmering. (A small drop of water dropped into it should immediately sizzle.) Carefully break the eggs into hot oil, dropping them from right above the surface to prevent hot oil from splashing. Season with salt and pepper.

(2) Tilt the pan toward you so that oil pools against the side of the pan. Using a spoon, baste the eggs with hot oil, aiming at the uncooked portions of the egg whites and avoiding the yolk. Continue basting until the eggs are puffy and cooked, 45 to 60 seconds. Transfer to a plate and serve.

1.3 HOW TO STIR-FRY BEEF AND LAMB

When it comes to stir-fries, the best cuts of beef are ones that are loose-textured enough to absorb the flavorings but beefy enough to stand up on their own. Because you're slicing them so thin, expensive, super-tender cuts like strip or tenderloin are overkill. Much better are the so-called butcher's cuts. These are my favorites, in order:

- **Skirt steak**, also labeled "fajita meat," is a cut from the plate, the region near the belly, just behind the front leg of the steer. It comes in a thin strip about 18 inches long and 5 inches wide, with the grain running the short way. It's my favorite cut for stir-fries.

- **Flap meat**, also sold as "sirloin tip" in the New England area, or *bavette* at fancy butchers, comes from the sirloin (that's top side of the steer, right in front of its butt). It's tough to track down, but if you can, jump on it, particularly if you can get it as

a whole cut rather than the cubes or strips it often comes in. Its texture and flavor are similar to those of hanger (a little milder), but its large, uniform size makes it much easier to butcher.

- **Hanger steak**, known in French as the *onglet*, used to be strictly the domain of chefs and butchers but is becoming more and more widely available these days. Cut from the diaphragm, it is extraordinarily beefy and, when cut right, is as tender as you'd like. It's got a slightly odd prism shape that can make the grain a little tough to identify. It also tends to command higher prices than the alternatives.

- **Flank steak** used to be one of the cheapest cuts at the butcher, until it saw a huge boom in popularity in the late nineties and aughts. Nowadays it commands prices nearly as high as loin cuts. Its advantage? You can find it pretty much anywhere. Unlike skirt steak, its grain runs the long way. The flavor is lightly metallic and not quite as robust as that of skirt.

Other cuts of beef that will do well in stir-fries are sirloin, boneless chuck, and bottom or top round. With these cuts you'll need to take some additional care to make sure that all large swaths of fat and connective tissue are trimmed out and discarded and that your final slices are made against the grain of the beef.

Like all meats, beef should be kept well wrapped and used within a few days of purchase. Don't slice the meat into strips until you are ready to marinate it. Preslicing will increase its surface area, increasing oxidation, which can cause the meat to discolor or develop livery off-flavors.

How to Cut Beef for Stir-Fries

As with chicken and pork, cutting beef for stir-fries is all about shortening muscle fibers to improve tenderness.

Step 1 • Identify the Grain

Identify which direction the grain runs. For instance, in a flank steak (left) the grain runs lengthwise. In a skirt steak (right) the grain runs crosswise.

Step 2 • Cut into Strips with the Grain

Cut the meat into 2-inch-wide strips with the grain. With a flank steak (left) this results in about three long strips. In a skirt steak (right), you should wind up with around ten shorter strips.

Step 3 • Partially Freeze (optional)

If your knife isn't perfectly sharp or you just haven't quite got the hang of working with slippery meat, place the strips in the freezer for about 10 minutes.

Step 4 • Slice against the Grain

Hold a sharp chef's knife or santoku knife at a shallow angle against the cutting board. Slice the meat at this angle into very thin strips. This will increase its surface area, allowing for better sauce adhesion and faster cooking.

Step 5 • Cut into Matchsticks

For dishes where beef is cooked in thin matchsticks, stack a few slices on top of each other and slice them lengthwise into matchsticks.

Baking Soda and Deep Tissue Massage: The Secrets to Meltingly Tender Beef

You ever notice how even the crummiest, dingiest take-out joint in the city still manages to serve beef that is meltingly tender? How do they do it? Do they have access to beef cuts we can't get?

Nope. There are two secrets. The first is vigorous massage. If you watch Chinese chefs at work in a restaurant (or on a YouTube channel, as the case may be), they do not handle their meat gently. If you've spent time working in Western kitchens where cuts of meat are

frequently served whole, you are trained to handle it gingerly. In nearly every professional kitchen I've worked in, tongs were forbidden on the line because they could bruise the product. Spatulas and calloused fingers were the only tools that could touch the meat.

With meat that is going to be stir-fried, on the other hand, the more abuse it gets, the better. Vigorously washing the meat in water, squeezing it out as hard as you can, then marinating it through massaging, slapping, lifting, throwing, and general manhandling will only make for meat that has better flavor penetration and a more tender texture.

The second, more important secret to tender stir-fried beef is something you've already got in your pantry: baking soda.

The scientific data on exactly how baking soda manages to keep red meat tender is not completely understood, but at least part of the reason it works is that it prevents proteins from bonding; the cross-linking and tightening that proteins do when cooked require a pretty narrow pH range to effectively take place. Just as sitting too long in an acidic marinade can

cause meat to tighten up, essentially "cooking" before it has even hit the pan, an alkaline marinade can have the opposite effect, effectively protecting the exterior of the meat from overcooking.

Moreover, alkaline environments expedite the Maillard browning reactions, which means that your meat can develop more flavor in less time while retaining more moisture. It's a win all around.

The most effective way to use baking soda is to give your meat a bath in alkalized water: for every pound of sliced meat, add a teaspoon of baking soda and 2 cups of water, then vigorously swish it around in a bowl and refrigerate the mixture for a couple hours before rinsing the meat under fresh running water (too much baking soda can introduce off-flavors to the dish). Squeeze it dry in a fine-mesh strainer, then roughly massage it in whatever marinade the recipe calls for.

The other method is to just add a small amount of baking soda directly to your meat and massage it in before adding the rest of the marinade. In small enough quantities, you don't really taste it (especially in dishes with plenty of other powerful flavors), and your meat comes out noticeably more tender, with a hint of slipperiness (this is a good thing in stir-fries).

BEEF WITH BROCCOLI

Yield
Serves 4

Active Time
15 minutes

Total Time
30 minutes

INGREDIENTS

For the Beef:
1 pound (450 g) beef skirt, flank, hanger, or flap, sliced for stir-fries
½ teaspoon (2 g) baking soda
½ teaspoon (1.5 g) kosher salt
1 teaspoon (5 ml) light soy sauce or shoyu
1 teaspoon (5 ml) Shaoxing wine or dry sherry
½ teaspoon (2 g) sugar
1 teaspoon (5 ml) roasted sesame oil
½ teaspoon (1.5 g) cornstarch

For the Sauce:
1 tablespoon (15 ml) light soy sauce or shoyu
1 tablespoon (15 ml) dark soy sauce
3 tablespoons (45 ml) oyster sauce
1 tablespoon (12 g) sugar
2 tablespoons (30 ml) Shaoxing wine

For the Cornstarch Slurry:
2 teaspoons (6 g) cornstarch
1 tablespoon (15 ml) water

For the Broccoli:
12 ounces broccoli or broccolini, heads cut into bite-sized florets, stems peeled and cut on a bias into 1½- to 2-inch segments

For the Stir-Fry:
¼ cup (60 ml) peanut, rice bran, or other neutral oil
2 medium garlic cloves, minced (about 2 teaspoons/5 g)
2 teaspoons minced fresh ginger (5 g/ about ½-inch segment)

Although it's a staple of food courts, beef stir-fried with broccoli in a garlicky oyster sauce has its roots in China, where it is made with gai lan, a leafy Chinese variety of broccoli.

There's really nothing to this recipe once you have the basics of stir-frying down. I wanted the flavors of garlic, ginger, and scallions to be pretty prominent, so I incorporated them minced. If you prefer milder garlic and ginger flavor, you can start the stir-fry by frying a slice of ginger and a couple of smashed garlic cloves in the stir-fry oil before adding the meat (pick out the ginger slice and whole garlic before serving).

DIRECTIONS

(1) **For the Beef:** Place the beef in a medium bowl, cover with cold water, and vigorously agitate it. Drain through a fine-mesh strainer set in the sink and press on the beef with your hands to remove excess water. Return the beef to the bowl, add the baking soda, and vigorously massage the baking soda into the meat, lifting the meat, throwing it down, and squeezing it

about for 30 seconds to a minute. Add the salt, soy sauce, Shaoxing wine, sugar, sesame oil, and cornstarch and roughly work the marinade into the meat for at least 30 seconds. Set aside to marinate for at least 15 minutes and up to overnight.

(2) **For the Sauce:** Combine the soy sauces, oyster sauce, sugar, and wine in a small bowl. Stir with a fork until the sugar is dissolved and no lumps remain. Combine the cornstarch and water in a separate small bowl and stir with a fork until the cornstarch is dissolved.

(3) **For the Broccoli:** Bring 1 quart of lightly salted water to a boil in your wok. Add the broccoli, stir well, cover, and boil, shaking the pan occasionally, until bright green but still quite firm, about 1 minute. Drain the broccoli and spread into a single layer on a sheet tray or large plate.

(4) **BEFORE YOU STIR-FRY, GET YOUR BOWLS READY:**

a. Marinated beef
b. Blanched broccoli
c. Garlic and ginger
d. Sauce

e. Cornstarch slurry
f. Empty bowl for cooked ingredients
g. Serving platter

(5) **For the Stir-Fry:** Rub a thin film of oil into a wok and set it over high heat until smoking. Add 1 tablespoon (15 ml) of the oil and swirl to coat. Add half of the beef and stir-fry until mostly cooked through and lightly browned in spots, about 1 minute. Transfer to a large bowl. Wipe out the wok and repeat with another tablespoon (15 ml) of oil and the remaining beef. (You may need a quick rinse under the sink if any excess beef marinade threatens to burn on the wok.)

(6) Wipe out the wok and return it to high heat until lightly smoking. Add 1 tablespoon (15 ml) of the remaining oil and swirl to coat. Add half of the broccoli and stir-fry until tender-crisp, about 1 minute. Transfer to the bowl with the beef.

(7) Wipe out the wok and return it to high heat until lightly smoking. Add the remaining tablespoon (15 ml) of oil and swirl to coat. Add the remaining half of the broccoli and stir-fry until tender-crisp, about 1 minute. Return all the beef and broccoli to the wok along with the garlic and ginger. Stir-fry until fragrant, about 30 seconds.

(8) Stir the sauce and add to the wok, pouring it in around the edges. Stir the cornstarch slurry and add a splash. Cook, tossing, until the sauce thickens and the chicken is cooked through, about 30 seconds longer. Adjust the sauce consistency with more cornstarch slurry if it is too thin or a splash of water if it is too thick. Transfer to a serving platter and serve immediately with steamed white rice.

GINGER BEEF (WITH OR WITHOUT SNOW PEAS)

Yield
Serves 4

Active Time
15 minutes

Total Time
30 minutes

NOTE
The snow peas can be omitted or replaced with any other crunchy green vegetable such as snap peas, asparagus, or green beans. For best results, look for young, thin-skinned ginger that is juicy and fresh. Older, stringy ginger with tough skins will not work as well.

This is another recipe based on a classic from the Joyce Chen book that my father made frequently while I was growing up (he still makes it). I distinctly remember that when my mother got a Braun handheld immersion blender with a mini-chopper, my parents christened it by trying to mince some old, dry ginger. It didn't work particularly well. Instead of mince, the ginger ended up as a pulpy, stringy mess. At least the meal came with its own dental floss.

The key here is to use tender, young ginger, which is thankfully easier to find now than it was back then (look for smooth, taut skins when shopping). Joyce's recipe calls for cilantro, but I also like to make it with basil. You can serve it Chinese style with some vegetables prepared separately on the side, or, for a quick one-wok meal, add some green vegetables. Snow peas are great.

INGREDIENTS

For the Beef:
1 pound (450 g) beef skirt, flank, hanger, or flap, sliced for stir-fries
½ teaspoon (2 g) baking soda
½ teaspoon (1.5 g) kosher salt
1 teaspoon (5 ml) light soy sauce or shoyu
1 teaspoon (5 ml) Shaoxing wine or dry sherry
½ teaspoon (2 g) sugar
½ teaspoon (1.5 g) cornstarch

For the Sauce:
1 tablespoon (15 ml) dark soy sauce
1 tablespoon (15 ml) light soy sauce
2 tablespoons (30 ml) Shaoxing wine
2 teaspoons (4 g) sugar
Small pinch of freshly ground white pepper (optional)
Small pinch of MSG (optional)

For the Cornstarch Slurry:
2 teaspoons (6 g) cornstarch
1 tablespoon (15 ml) water

For the Snow Peas (optional; see Note):
8 ounces (225 g) snow peas or snap peas, strings and ends removed

For the Stir-Fry:
¼ cup (60 ml) peanut, rice bran, or other neutral oil
2 ounces (55 g) fresh young ginger, peeled and minced in a food processor or by hand (about 6 tablespoons; see Notes)
2 ounces fresh cilantro or basil leaves (about 2 packed cups), very roughly chopped

DIRECTIONS

(1) **For the Beef:** Place the beef in a medium bowl, cover with cold water, and vigorously agitate it. Drain through a fine-mesh strainer set in the sink and press on the beef with your hands to remove excess water. Return the beef to the bowl, add the baking soda, and vigorously massage the baking soda into the meat, lifting the meat, throwing it down, and squeezing it for 30 to 60 seconds. Add the salt, soy sauce, wine, sugar, and cornstarch, roughly work the marinade into the meat for at least 30 seconds. Set aside to marinate for at least 15 minutes and up to overnight.

(2) **For the Sauce:** Combine the soy sauces, wine, sugar, white pepper, and MSG in a small bowl and stir together until homogenous. Set aside. Combine the cornstarch and water in a separate small bowl and stir with a fork until the cornstarch is dissolved.

(3) **For the Snow Peas (optional step, see Note):** Bring 1 quart of lightly salted water to a boil in your wok. Add the snow peas, stir well, cover, and boil, shaking the pan occasionally, until the peas are bright green but still quite firm, about 1 minute. Drain and spread into a single layer on a sheet tray or large plate.

(4) **BEFORE YOU STIR-FRY, GET YOUR BOWLS READY:**

a. Marinated beef

b. Blanched snow peas

c. Ginger

d. Cilantro or basil

e. Sauce

f. Empty bowl for cooked ingredients

g. Serving platter

(5) **For the Stir-Fry:** Heat a wok over high heat until lightly smoking. Add 1 tablespoon (15 ml) of the oil and swirl to coat. Add half of the beef and stir-fry until no longer red, about 45 seconds. Transfer to a large bowl. Wipe out the wok and repeat with another tablespoon (15 ml) of oil and the remaining beef. (You may need a quick rinse under the sink if any excess beef marinade threatens to burn on the wok.)

(6) Wipe out the wok and return it to high heat until lightly smoking. Add 1 tablespoon (15 ml) of the remaining oil and swirl to coat. Add the snow peas (if using) and stir-fry until tender-crisp, about 30 seconds. Transfer to the bowl with the beef.

(7) Wipe out the wok and return it to high heat until lightly smoking. Add the remaining tablespoon (15 ml) oil and swirl to coat. Add the ginger

recipe continues

and stir-fry until very fragrant, about 15 seconds. Return all the beef and snow peas to the wok and stir-fry to combine.

(8) Stir the sauce and add to the wok by pouring it around the edges. Stir the cornstarch slurry and add a splash. Cook, tossing, until the sauce thickens and the beef is cooked through, about 30 seconds longer. Adjust the sauce consistency with more cornstarch slurry if it is too thin or a splash of water if it is too thick. Add the cilantro or basil leaves and toss to combine. Transfer to a serving platter and serve immediately with steamed rice.

How to Trim Snap Peas and Snow Peas

Sweet snap peas and crunchy snow peas are two of my favorite green vegetables to add to stir-fries, and they're easy to prep. All you've got to do is remove the fibrous tips and strings. Once cleaned, store snap peas or snow peas in a zipper-lock bag or a sealed reusable container with a damp paper towel in the refrigerator. They should keep fresh for several days, though farm-fresh peas will lose sweetness rather dramatically with any storage.

Step 1 • Pinch Off the Stem End

Use your fingers to pinch off the stem end, bending it backward toward one of the seams of the pod.

Step 2 • Pull the String

Pull the pinched bit downward, taking along the string that's attached to it. If no string comes along with it, you're all good—it just means the string is already tender enough to eat.

Step 3 • Repeat on the Other End

Pinch off the flower end by bending it toward the seam that you have not cleaned yet. Pull it downward to take the string along with it.

Alkalized Beef

Don't believe in the magic of baking soda? Try it out yourself.

Materials

12 ounces (340 g) beef flank or skirt steak, cut into strips as for a stir-fry (see page 116)

½ teaspoon (2 g) baking soda

1 recipe Basic Stir-Fry Marinade (page 50), baking soda omitted

3 tablespoons (45 ml) peanut, rice bran, or other neutral oil

Procedures

Divide the meat into three bowls. Add the baking soda and a cup of water to the first bowl, vigorously stirring the meat to loosen up its grain and ensure that the alkalized water fully penetrates each piece. Add a cup of water (no baking soda) to the second bowl and repeat. Set aside all three bowls in the refrigerator for 1 hour.

Drain the baking-soda-treated beef and carefully rinse under running water. Drain through a fine-mesh strainer set in the sink and press on the beef with your hands to remove excess water. Return it to the bowl and add a third of the Basic Marinade and massage it into the meat.

Drain the second bowl of meat through a fine-mesh strainer set in the sink and press on the beef with your hands to remove excess water. Return it to the bowl and add another third of the Basic Marinade and massage it into the meat.

Add the remaining third of the Basic Marinade to the final bowl of beef and massage it into the meat.

Heat a wok over high heat until lightly smoking. Add a tablespoon of oil, swirl to coat the wok, then add the first batch of beef. Stir-fry until just cooked through, about 1 minute. Transfer to a plate and set aside. Wipe out the wok. Cook the other two batches in the same manner.

Taste all samples side by side.

Results and Analysis

The batch of beef marinated with baking soda should be noticeably softer, juicier, and more tender than the other two batches. You may also notice that the beef with baking soda exuded less moisture while you were stir-frying. Both of these effects are caused by the alkalinity of the baking soda interfering with the meat protein's ability to coagulate and tighten. Less tightening means less juice is squeezed out and the meat remains juicier and more tender as it cooks.

The beef simply washed in water may also taste a little juicier and more tender than the meat that was marinated without any massaging or water treatment.

SHREDDED BEEF WITH HOT PEPPERS AND CHILES

Yield
Serves 4

Active Time
15 minutes

Total Time
30 minutes

NOTE
You can replace the carrot and leek with 7 to 8 ounces of any vegetable you can find that can be cut into thin matchsticks. Some good options are celery, bell pepper, sliced shiitake mushrooms, or potatoes soaked in cold water for 15 minutes.

When I was a kid, ordering delivery from Hunan Balcony was like miniature Christmas. The plastic bags would be delivered with their tops tied shut in a bow, my mom would get dishes, and we would unload the stacks of expertly packed aluminum foil trays onto the dining room table. I remember them feeling unreasonably heavy for their size, like ripe fruit. We'd peel back the lids and the puff of steam that escaped would announce what was inside each one before we could even see it. Frequently that was a dish of their Shredded Beef with Four Flavors: slivers of beef stir-fried with slivered carrots, leeks, and hot peppers in a hot and vinegary sauce. At least that's how I remembered it. When I asked my sister, she remembered it as a dish of sliced beef stir-fried and served on top of a pile of spinach. Who was right? Hunan Balcony has been closed for a number of years, so I turned to the Internet for some help.

It turns out that in the New York Public Library's database of NYC menus, the dish makes only a single appearance, and it's in a 1984 takeout menu from Hunan Balcony. We were both partially right: shredded beef stir-fried and served over a bed of stir-fried watercress. I'm not sure exactly what the four flavors were, as there are at least five listed on that menu: red pepper, watercress, scallion, garlic, and ginger. I'm not even certain what the origins of the dish are, though it bears a passing resemblance to what is called "Hunan beef" on Chinese American menus. According to the Chinese cooking website The Woks of Life, the authentic Hunan version of the dish is typically made with smoked, partially dried beef, which would give it a similar texture to Sichuan-style dry-fried beef (page 436), but with more fresh chile heat, rather than the fermented chile used in the Sichuan dish.

Whatever its source, I cook my own version of the dish these days, taking a Hunan approach with plenty of fresh chiles and fermented black beans in a relatively dry sauce. I love it because the technique of stir-frying several shredded ingredients together makes the dish easily adaptable to a host of vegetables. Hot peppers are a must (I like using Anaheim chiles or Chinese green cowhorn peppers), but beyond that, it works with slivered scallions, leeks, carrots, zucchini, bell peppers, shiitake mushrooms, bamboo shoot, celery, cucumber, or even potato. Just keep the basic ratio of meat to veggies the same and feel free to substitute as you or your fridge sees fit. You can serve it on top of briefly stir-fried watercress if you'd like, or just serve it with rice.

INGREDIENTS

For the Beef:

12 ounces (340 g) beef skirt, flank, hanger, or flap, cut into slivers (see page 116)

½ teaspoon (2 g) baking soda

½ teaspoon (1.5 g) kosher salt

1 teaspoon (5 ml) light soy sauce or shoyu

1 teaspoon (5 ml) dark soy sauce

1 teaspoon (5 ml) Shaoxing wine or dry sherry

½ teaspoon (2 g) sugar

½ teaspoon (1.5 g) cornstarch

For the Sauce:

1 tablespoon (15 ml) dark soy sauce

1 tablespoon (15 ml) light soy sauce

1 tablespoon (15 ml) distilled white vinegar

1 tablespoon (15 ml) Shaoxing wine

1 tablespoon (4 g) sugar

6 to 8 small red pickled chiles (homemade, page 84, or store-bought), finely minced, or 1 tablespoon (15 g) fermented chile sauce such as sambal oelek

Small pinch of MSG (optional)

For the Cornstarch Slurry:

1 teaspoon (6 g) cornstarch

1 tablespoon (15 ml) water

For the Stir-Fry:

3 tablespoons (45 ml) peanut, rice bran, or other neutral oil

2 long green chiles such as Chinese cowhorn or Anaheim, cut into 2-inch matchsticks (about 6 ounces/180 g)

1 small hot chile, such as Fresno, jalapeño, or serrano, cut into 2-inch matchsticks (about 1 ounce/30 g)

1 leek, white and pale green parts only, cut into 2-inch matchsticks (about 3 ounces/90 g)

1 medium carrot, peeled and cut into 2-inch matchsticks (about 4 ounces/120 g)

2 teaspoons (5 g) minced fresh garlic (about 2 medium cloves)

2 teaspoons (5 g) minced fresh ginger (about ½-inch segment)

2 tablespoons (about 12 g) dried fermented black beans (douchi), roughly chopped

24 to 30 small dried chiles such as er jing tiao or chao tian jiao

Toasted sesame seeds, for garnish

DIRECTIONS

(1) **For the Beef:** Place the beef in a medium bowl, cover with cold water, and vigorously agitate it. Drain through a fine-mesh strainer set in the sink and press on the beef with your hands to remove excess water. Return the beef to the bowl, add the baking soda, and vigorously massage the baking soda into the meat, lifting the meat, throwing it down, and squeezing it for 30 to 60 seconds. Add the salt, soy sauces, wine, sugar, and cornstarch, roughly work the marinade into the meat for at least 30 seconds, and set aside to marinate for at least 15 minutes and up to overnight.

(2) **For the Sauce:** Combine the soy sauces, vinegar, wine, sugar, pickled chiles or chile sauce, and MSG in a small bowl and stir together until homogenous. Set aside. Combine the cornstarch and water in a separate small bowl and stir with a fork until the cornstarch is dissolved.

recipe continues

③ BEFORE YOU STIR-FRY, GET YOUR BOWLS READY:

a. Marinated beef

b. Fresh chiles, leeks, and carrots

c. Garlic, ginger, fermented black beans, and dried chiles

d. Sauce

e. Cornstarch slurry

f. Empty bowl for cooked ingredients

g. Serving platter

④ For the Stir-Fry: Heat a wok over high heat until lightly smoking. Add 1 tablespoon (15 ml) of the oil and swirl to coat. Add the beef and stir-fry until no longer red, about 1 minute. Transfer to a large bowl.

⑤ Wipe out the wok and return it to high heat until lightly smoking. Add 1 tablespoon (15 ml) of the remaining oil and swirl to coat. Add the fresh chiles, leeks, and carrots and stir-fry until tender-crisp, about 1 minute. Transfer to the bowl with the beef.

⑥ Wipe out the wok and return it to high heat until lightly smoking. Add the remaining tablespoon (15 ml) oil and swirl to coat. Add the garlic, ginger, black beans, and dried chiles and stir-fry until very fragrant, about 15 seconds. Return all the beef and toss until evenly mixed.

⑦ Stir the sauce and add to the wok by pouring it around the edges. Stir the cornstarch slurry and add. Cook, tossing, until the sauce has nearly dried up, about 1 minute. Stir in a small handful of sesame seeds. Transfer to a serving platter, sprinkle with more sesame seeds, and serve immediately with steamed rice.

THAI-STYLE BEEF WITH BASIL AND FISH SAUCE

This Thai stir-fry starts, as do most of my kitchen projects, with my favorite tool, the mortar and pestle, which I use to pound garlic, chiles, and palm sugar into a fine paste, which I loosen up with some fish sauce. This mixture (essentially a garlic-heavy Nam Pla Prik, page 257) is the sauce for the stir-fry.

Next I marinate sliced beef in a modified basic beef marinade—baking soda, fish sauce, soy sauce, and a bit of sugar—before stir-frying it in two batches in a hot wok. Once both batches of beef are browned, I wipe out the wok and reheat it for the final steps of the stir-fry. The beef goes back in, along with sliced

aromatics—shallots, more garlic, and more chiles. (Yep, we're doubling up on chile and garlic flavor here—the sliced version of each has a different flavor from the pounded version.) Traditional versions of this dish don't typically contain makrut* lime leaf, but I love the aroma of citrus leaves, so I often add some. You can find makrut lime leaf frozen at some well-stocked Asian supermarkets, but if you can't find it, head to a good greengrocer during citrus season and pluck some citrus leaves out of the display bins. I've found the most success with tangerine or clementine leaves.

---

* For a long time, *Citrus hystrix*, the wrinkly green lime whose leaves and zest lend their flavor to many dishes in Southeast Asia, was known as "kaffir lime," a term I write out now only for the sake of clarity. Unfortunately, that K-word is used as a racial slur against black South Africans, the equivalent of the N-word in America. The etymology of the two words—the racial epithet and the fruit—is different, but nonetheless I see no good reason to continue using the term when *makrut*, its name in Thai, will work just as well.

As soon as my aromatics are, well, aromatic, and my beef is as browned as I'd like it to be, I add in the chile/garlic sauce. It should very rapidly reduce to a thin glaze (we're going for moist-but-not-saucy here). A big ol' handful of Thai purple basil goes into the wok, and a couple of tosses later we've got dinner on the table in about 15 minutes. This is just one of the many reasons I love my wok.

THAI-STYLE BEEF WITH BASIL AND FISH SAUCE

Yield
Serves 4

Active Time
15 minutes

Total Time
30 minutes

NOTES

You can adjust the heat by adjusting the number of chiles in the dish. One chile will be moderately hot, while five will be scorching. Makrut lime leaves are available fresh or frozen at Thai or Southeast Asian grocery stores. If you can't find it, any very thinly sliced citrus leaves can be used in its place, or substitute the zest of 1 lime. You can use any type of basil for this recipe (see my basil guide on page 130). Fried shallots can be found in plastic tubs at most Asian supermarkets, or follow my recipe for Fried Shallots (page 255).

INGREDIENTS

For the Beef:

1 pound (450 g) beef flank, skirt, hanger, or flap, cut into ¼-inch-thick strips

½ teaspoon (2 g) baking soda

1 teaspoon (5 ml) soy sauce

2 teaspoons (10 ml) fish sauce

1 teaspoon (4 g) granulated sugar

½ teaspoon (1.5 g) kosher salt

For the Sauce and Stir-Fry:

1 to 5 red or green Thai bird chiles, thinly sliced (see Notes)

6 medium garlic cloves (15 to 20 g), thinly sliced

1 medium shallot (1½ ounces/45 g), thinly sliced

1½ tablespoons (20 g) palm sugar

2 teaspoons (10 ml) light soy sauce or shoyu

1 tablespoon (15 ml) fish sauce

4 makrut lime leaves, very thinly sliced into hairs (central veins discarded), plus more for garnish (see Notes)

2 tablespoons (30 ml) peanut, rice bran, or other neutral oil

2 cups packed Thai purple basil (about 2 ounces/55 g) (see Notes)

Thai chile flakes or hot red pepper flakes to taste (optional)

Large handful of store-bought or homemade fried shallots (see Notes)

DIRECTIONS

1) **For the Beef:** Place the beef in a medium bowl, cover with cold water, and vigorously agitate it. Drain through a fine-mesh strainer set in the sink and press on the beef with your hands to remove excess water. Return the beef to the bowl, add the baking soda, and vigorously massage the baking soda into the meat, lifting the meat, throwing it down, and squeezing it for 30 to 60 seconds. Add the soy sauce, fish sauce, sugar, and salt and roughly work the marinade into the meat for at least 30 seconds.

2) **For the Sauce and Stir-Fry:** Place half of the chiles, half of the garlic, half of the shallot, and the palm sugar in a mortar. Grind with a pestle until a mostly smooth paste has formed. Add the soy sauce and fish sauce and mash in the mortar to form a sauce. Set aside. Toss the remaining chiles, garlic, shallot, and the makrut lime leaves in a small bowl to combine.

3) **BEFORE YOU STIR-FRY, GET YOUR BOWLS READY:**

   a. Marinated beef

   b. Chiles, garlic, shallot, lime leaves

   c. Sauce (which you can leave in the mortar)

   d. Basil

   e. Empty bowl for cooked ingredients

   f. Serving platter

4) **For the Stir-Fry:** Heat a wok over high heat until lightly smoking. Add 1 tablespoon (15 ml) of the oil and swirl to coat. Add half of the beef and cook, without moving it, until well seared, about 1 minute. Continue cooking, while stirring and tossing, until the beef is lightly cooked but still pink in spots, about 1 minute longer. Transfer to a large bowl. Repeat with the remaining tablespoon (15 ml) oil and the remaining beef.

5) Return all the beef to the wok, along with sliced garlic/shallot/chile/makrut lime mixture. Continue to cook, tossing and stirring constantly, until the stir-fry is aromatic and the shallots have completely softened, about 1 minute.

6) Stir the sauce mixture, add it to the wok, and cook, tossing and stirring constantly, until completely reduced. (The beef should look moist, but there should be no liquid in the bottom of the wok.) Immediately add the basil and toss to combine. Season to taste with more fish sauce and the Thai chile flakes (if using). Transfer to a serving platter. Top with more makrut lime threads and the fried shallots. Serve immediately with steamed rice.

Common Culinary Basils

Basil is one of the most diverse herbs in the world with well over a hundred separate species (all true basils are of the genus *Ocimum*). The vast majority of the time we're using different cultivars of the same species,' *Ocimum basilicum*.

Sweet basil is the most common in the supermarket. It has mid-sized, somewhat shiny leaves that are relatively round and cupped and a sweet, clove-like aroma. *Genovese basil* has a slightly stronger aroma with flatter, pointier leaves. *Neapolitan basil* is the strongest flavored of the three common Italian varieties. It has slightly wrinkled-looking leaves and a distinctly spicy aroma.

All three of these basil varieties have delicate leaves that don't hold up particularly well to cooking. They do best added as a last-second aromatic, whether in Western-style dishes or in stir-fries (the exceptions are in simmered sauces, where basil leaves and stems may be removed before serving, or on top of Neapolitan pizza, where the basil perfumes the oven and the pie while cooking away to almost nothing.)

Purple (or opal) basil has a dramatic dark purple color and smooth or frilly leaves. You can grow it yourself, find it at farmers' markets, or occasionally at fancy grocery stores. Its flavor is milder and its leaves even more delicate than sweet or Genovese basil, and it's best used in totally uncooked settings as an ingredient in salads or as a last-second garnish.

While Italian varieties of basil will work alright for most dishes that call for Thai or holy basil— especially Neapolitan basil with its stronger flavor and slightly sturdier structure—if you have access to an Asian market, you're better off seeking out those other varieties when called for.

The Best Basil for Stir-Fries

Thai purple basil is another cultivar of *Ocimum basilicum* with smooth green leaves that turn purplish as they meet the dark purple stems. Their flavor has a distinctly spicy anise-like scent, and the leaves have a hardier structure that can hold up better to stir-frying, allowing them to spread their aroma throughout a dish without turning mushy or unpleasant. They're also excellent for Thai- or Vietnamese-style salads and spring rolls, where their spicier flavor can stand up to punchier accompaniments.

Holy basil is the only basil I call for in this book that is of a different species: *Ocimum sanctum* (aka *Ocimum tenuiflorum*). It has soft, almost velvety leaves with saw-toothed edges and a flavor that is more clovey than other basil varieties. I find that it also has a sort of licorice-like sweetness not dissimilar to *stevia* (both are rich in sugar-based molecules called *glycosides*). Holy basil has no true substitute, so if you stumble upon some (for me that's either at the farmer's market or on rare occasions at the Asian grocery store), pounce on it and plan your meal around it!

* Every dog from a chihuahua to an Italian mastiff is of the same species: *Canis familiaris*. You can think of cultivars as breeds of dogs. A cultivar is a plant variety that has been created through selective breeding. Often many cultivars can exist within a single species. For instance, there are over seven thousand cultivars of apple, all within the species *Malus pumila*.

PEPPER STEAK

Yield
Serves 4

Active Time
15 minutes

Total Time
30 minutes

INGREDIENTS

For the Beef:
1 pound (450 g) beef flank, skirt, hanger, or
  flap, cut into ¼-inch-thick strips
½ teaspoon (2 g) baking soda
2 teaspoons (10 ml) light soy sauce or
  shoyu
2 teaspoons (10 ml) Shaoxing wine
½ teaspoon (2 g) sugar
½ teaspoon (1.5 g) cornstarch

For the Sauce:
⅓ cup low-sodium homemade or store-
  bought chicken stock or water
1 tablespoon (15 ml) light soy sauce or
  shoyu
2 teaspoons (10 ml) dark soy sauce
2 tablespoons (30 ml) Shaoxing wine
1 tablespoon (15 ml) roasted sesame oil
1 tablespoon (12 g) sugar
1 tablespoon (about 8 g) freshly ground
  black pepper

For the Cornstarch Slurry:
2 teaspoons (6 g) cornstarch
1 tablespoon (15 ml) water

For the Stir-Fry:
3 tablespoons (45 ml) peanut, rice bran, or
  other neutral oil
1 medium green bell pepper, cored and
  cut into 1-inch squares (about 5
  ounces/150 g)
1 medium red bell pepper, cored and cut into
  1-inch squares (about 5 ounces/150 g)
1 medium onion, cut into 1-inch strips from
  pole to pole (about 6 ounces; 180 g)
2 medium garlic cloves, minced (about 2
  teaspoons/5 g)
2 teaspoons (5 g) minced fresh ginger
  (about ½-inch segment)
3 scallions, whites only, minced
Kosher salt to taste

There was no Yelp or *Serious Eats* or even a Zagat guide when Lawton Mackall published *Knife and Fork in New York*, but if the Internet had existed, the book would most likely have been a series of blog posts rather than a single volume. The seventeenth chapter, "Pagoda Provender," mentions "green-pepper steak with tomatoes and onions" right in between "steamed fish prepared with soy beans and ginger sauce" and "*egg rolls served with slices of roast pork and a secret sauce.*"

I've always known "Green-Pepper Steak" as simply Pepper Steak or Black Pepper Beef, and I've never seen it cooked with tomatoes, but a quick Internet search of recipes turns up a good number of recipes that do in fact add tomatoes to the basic stir fry of sliced beef, bell peppers, and onions. If you do choose to make it with tomatoes, I find that cherry tomatoes cut in half or small Roma tomatoes split into quarters work better than larger beefsteak tomatoes, which turn watery when stir-fried (this is a good thing for a moist dish like Home-Style Tomato and Scrambled Eggs, page 165, but not for a dryer stir-fry like this one).

recipe continues

DIRECTIONS

(1) **For the Beef:** Place the beef in a medium bowl, cover with cold water, and vigorously agitate it. Drain through a fine-mesh strainer set in the sink and press on the beef with your hands to remove excess water. Return the beef to the bowl, add the baking soda, and vigorously massage the baking soda into the meat, lifting the meat, throwing it down, and squeezing it for 30 to 60 seconds. Add the soy sauce, wine, sugar, and cornstarch and roughly work the marinade into the meat for at least 30 seconds. Set aside to marinate for at least 15 minutes and up to overnight.

(2) **For the Sauce:** Combine the chicken stock or water, soy sauces, wine, sesame oil, sugar, and pepper in a small bowl and stir together until homogenous. Set aside. Combine the cornstarch and water in a separate small bowl and stir with a fork until the cornstarch is dissolved.

(3) **BEFORE YOU STIR-FRY, GET YOUR BOWLS READY:**

a. **Beef**

b. **Bell peppers and onions**

c. **Garlic, ginger, and scallions**

d. **Sauce**

e. **Cornstarch slurry**

f. **Empty bowl for cooked ingredients**

g. **Serving platter**

(4) **For the Stir-Fry:** Heat a wok over high heat until lightly smoking. Add 1 tablespoon (15 ml) of the oil and swirl to coat. Add half of the beef and cook without moving it until well seared, about 1 minute. Continue cooking while stirring and tossing until lightly cooked but still pink in spots, about 1 minute. Transfer to a large bowl. Wipe out the wok and repeat with 1 more tablespoon (15 ml) of the oil and the remaining beef, adding the beef to the same bowl.

(5) Wipe out the wok and return it to high heat until lightly smoking. Add the remaining tablespoon (15 ml) oil and swirl to coat. Add the peppers and onions and stir-fry until lightly charred in spots and the vegetables are tender-crisp, about 1 minute.

(6) Return the beef to the wok and add the garlic/ginger/scallion mixture. Cook, tossing and stirring until fragrant, about 30 seconds. Stir the sauce and add to the wok by pouring it around the edges. Stir the cornstarch slurry and add a splash. Cook, tossing, until the sauce thickens and the beef is cooked through, about 30 seconds longer. Adjust the sauce consistency with more cornstarch slurry if it is too thin or a splash of water if it is too thick. Transfer to a serving platter and serve immediately with steamed rice.

CUMIN LAMB

I remember the first time I had lamb with cumin. It was at New Taste of Asia, a now long-gone Sichuan restaurant in Brookline, Massachusetts. Tender strips of thinly sliced lamb coated in a lightly crunchy, intensely flavored crust, fried until it was almost dry on the exterior, yet still housing a juicy core.

The aroma had the distinct musky scent of cumin but was bound together with other, more complex flavors. A hint of Sichuan peppercorns was there—my mouth became ever so slightly numb after the first few bites—as were a handful of dried chiles, though you'd be hard pressed to call the dish spicy. *Aromatic* is a better term. Garlic, soy, and a big, fat bed of cilantro.

I soon started seeing it pop up in one form or another on menus all over Boston and New York, usually in Sichuan restaurants, quite often under a separate part of the menu titled "Northern Specialties" or the like.

Turns out that the dish is not exactly a Sichuan staple, at least not until recently. As *northern* implies, it's a dish that originates in Xinjiang, China's vast northwestern landlocked province that borders Mongolia, Russia, Kazakhstan, Pakistan, and Kyrgyzstan, among other places. One of the most ethnically diverse regions in the country, until the latter half of this century, its dominant group was the now-persecuted Turkic Uyghurs, and it is from their Muslim cuisine that the dish originates. Since then, it's been brought deeper into China, becoming a staple of street cart vendors throughout northern China, and even to Muslim restaurants in major cities in the South and East. I even spied it on a menu in Hong Kong a couple years ago.

Its cultural background explains its unique flavor profile, but what about cooking technique? It's clearly not a standard stir-fry. The pieces of lamb come out far drier, with a sort of crust around them. It seems to me to be more closely tied to the Sichuan method of dry-frying, a technique in which meat is par-cooked in oil until the exterior is crunchy, chewy, and dry before being reincorporated into the dish. At least it must be somewhere between dry-frying and standard stir-frying.

In Jeffrey Alford and Naomi Duguid's *Beyond the Great Wall*, a beautiful book about the cuisines of northern China and Mongolia, they offer a version they were served in a stall near the ancient Silk Road. They start by toasting cumin and garlic, adding sliced lamb, then cooking the whole thing down with bean sprouts and greens. Mark Bittman published a similar recipe in the 2008 *New York Times Diner's Journal* using cubed lamb and scallions. Neither one achieved quite the level of crusty flavor I was looking for in my lamb, but both offered the good advice to use whole cumin seed and to take the time to toast them beforehand.

Toasting whole spices not only volatilizes some of their aromas, making your kitchen smell great, but it actually physically transforms some of them, effecting chemical reactions that trigger the formation of hundreds of new, aromatic compounds. Tasted side by side, the difference is undeniable. Using whole cumin (and, in my version, Sichuan peppercorn) is essential—cumin powder can't be toasted properly, and it doesn't give you the nice little crunchy bits that make the dish interesting to eat.

I tried cooking it using several methods, and the one that I found worked best was to stir-fry it with just a bit more oil than I'd typically use so that rather than simply searing, the meat was essentially shallow-frying.

To get the cumin flavor into the lamb, I toast the spices first, then combine them along with some garlic and a touch of soy sauce—not much—into a paste, which I then rub all over the lamb. As the lamb cooks, this paste dehydrates and chars, forming the crunchy, flavorful crust I was looking for.

The only thing left was to add a bit of heat and aroma in the form of dried roasted chiles and a couple of carefully chosen vegetables. While the sprouts and greens that Alford/Duguid use are nice, I prefer the sweetness of onions—another vegetable brought to China from Eurasia via the Silk Road—and a few stalks of crunchy celery.

And unless your family really, really loves cumin and garlic—and my wife, Adri, doesn't—I suggest you make this dish while they are out of the house and not expected to return for the several days it takes for the awesome aromas to clear out.

CUMIN LAMB

Yield
Serves 4

Active Time
20 minutes

Total Time
20 minutes

NOTE
This recipe also works well with beef (use any stir-fry-friendly cut, such as skirt, flank, or flap meat).

INGREDIENTS

For the Lamb:
1 pound (450 g) lamb leg (or beef; see Note), trimmed of gristle and sliced into ¼-inch-thick slices
½ teaspoon (2 g) baking soda

For the Marinade:
3 tablespoons (about 15 g) cumin seeds
2 teaspoons (about 4 g) whole Sichuan peppercorn
12 small dried red Chinese or árbol chiles
3 medium garlic cloves, minced (about 1 tablespoon/8 g)
1 tablespoon (15 ml) light soy sauce or shoyu

For the Stir-Fry:
5 tablespoons (75 ml) peanut, rice bran, or other neutral oil
1 medium onion, cut pole to pole into ½-inch slices
3 celery stalks, sliced lengthwise into thirds and crosswise into 2-inch segments
Kosher salt
1 bunch cilantro, leaves and tender stems only

DIRECTIONS

1. **For the Lamb:** Place the lamb in a medium bowl, cover with cold water, and vigorously agitate it. Drain through a fine-mesh strainer set in the sink and press on the lamb with your hands to remove excess water. Return the lamb to the bowl, add the baking soda, and vigorously massage the baking soda into the meat, lifting the meat, throwing it down, and squeezing it for 30 to 60 seconds.

2. **For the Marinade:** Heat the cumin seeds, peppercorns, and chiles in a large skillet over medium-high heat, tossing constantly until fragrant, about 2 minutes. Transfer to a mortar and pestle. Pick out the chiles and set them aside. Grind the cumin and peppercorns until roughly crushed but large pieces still remain. Add the garlic and smash until a rough paste is formed. Stir in the soy sauce and scrape the mixture into the bowl with the lamb. Roughly work the marinade into the meat for at least 30 seconds.

3. **BEFORE YOU STIR-FRY, GET YOUR BOWLS READY:**

   a. **Marinated lamb**
   b. **Onion and celery**
   c. **Chiles**
   d. **Cilantro**
   e. **Empty bowl for cooked ingredients**
   f. **Serving platter**

4. **For the Stir-Fry:** Heat a wok over high heat until lightly smoking. Add 1 tablespoon (15 ml) of the oil and swirl to coat. Add the onion and celery and cook, stirring and tossing occasionally until lightly charred and tender, about 2 minutes. Transfer to a bowl.

5. Wipe out the wok and return it to high heat until lightly smoking. Add 2 more tablespoons (30 ml) of the oil and swirl to coat. Add half of the lamb and cook without moving for 1 minute. Continue cooking while stirring and tossing until lightly cooked but still pink in spots, about 1 minute. Transfer to the bowl with the onions and celery. Repeat with the remaining 2 tablespoons (30 ml) oil and the remaining lamb, adding the cooked lamb to the same bowl.

6. Return the wok to high heat until lightly smoking. Add the chiles and immediately return the cooked lamb and vegetables. Cook, stirring and tossing occasionally until the lamb develops a mild crust, about 2 minutes longer. Season to taste with salt. Add the cilantro and give it one final toss to combine. Transfer to a serving platter and serve immediately with steamed rice.

1.4 HOW TO STIR-FRY SEAFOOD

While I was a teenager growing up in New York, my father worked and lived in Boston during the week. On most weekends he'd come back down to New York, but several times a year we'd drive up to Boston instead. Those trips to Boston inevitably included two things: a trip to the Bertucci's in Harvard Square (I was, and still am, a sucker for street performers and family-friendly pizza restaurants), and a visit to East Ocean City in Boston's Chinatown. Aside from being home to the finest dry-style beef chow fun in the world (at least according to my little sister, Pico), they also sold pristine seafood that you selected from the banks of giant saltwater tanks at the front of the restaurant. Whatever we picked—fresh tautogs, spider crabs with 5-foot leg spans, or, in the summertime, lobsters—would get scuttled off into the kitchen to meet its maker while we

sat at our table picking at razor clams with black bean sauce, shrimp-paste-stuffed hot green chiles, and live Maine shrimp stir-fried plain in the shell with a dish of mild soy sauce for dipping the bodies into as you sucked the juices out of the heads.

I now live on the opposite coast from Boston (and my dad), but I still have access to fresh seafood, and there are few better ways to showcase it than by giving it a spin in the wok.

Fish can be tricky to stir-fry, as it tends to be far more delicate than meat or poultry, and if you're not careful with it, it will fall apart in the wok. There are two keys to ensuring that your fish stays intact during a stir-fry.

The first is to pick the right kind of fish. Firm-fleshed white fish, such as sea bass, striped bass, grouper, mullet, blackfish (wrasse), mahimahi, and halibut, are all excellent choices. Avoid fish that flake excessively when cooked, such as cod and pollock, or flat delicate fish like fluke, flounder, or sole. Just as with meat, fish should be sliced against the grain into bite-sized pieces, though these slices should be a little bit thicker.

The second is technique, and when I stir-fry fish, I precook it using the same water-velveting technique that works so well on chicken and pork.

To water-velvet fish, I start by marinating it with a mixture of Shaoxing wine, white pepper, light soy sauce, oil, egg whites, and cornstarch. Because fish has such delicate flesh, I skip the washing and squeezing steps I typically include with poultry or meat. It's important that the fish be coated in the cornstarch mixture and be neither too wet nor too dry. There should be no liquid pooled in the bowl, and there should be no dry cornstarch on the surface of the fish. Depending on the fish, sometimes I have to adjust the consistency by either draining off excess liquid or adding a small splash or water to the bowl, as the case demands.

Once marinated, the fish takes a quick swim in simmering water until it's barely cooked through. The starchy layer on the surface of the fish should be slick and translucent.

Fish velveted in this way can then be stir-fried just like velveted chicken or pork.

STIR-FRIED FISH WITH WOOD EAR, CELERY, AND OYSTER SAUCE

Yield
Serves 4

Active Time
15 minutes

Total Time
40 minutes

NOTE

Dried wood ear mushrooms, also called *black fungus*, can be found at any Asian supermarket or online. You can use 4 ounces (120 g) of fresh shiitake mushrooms in their place. Remove the stems and cut the shiitakes into quarters, then proceed as instructed, omitting step 1.

INGREDIENTS

For the Wood Ears:
¼ cup (½ ounce/about 15 g) dried Chinese wood ear mushrooms (see Note)

For the Fish:
1 pound (450 g) firm white fish, such as sea bass, striped bass, mahimahi, or halibut, cut into ¼- to ½-inch slices
1 tablespoon (15 ml) Shaoxing wine
1 teaspoon (5 ml) light soy sauce or shoyu
Pinch of kosher salt
Pinch of freshly ground white pepper
1 large egg white
2 teaspoons (6 g) cornstarch
1 teaspoon (5 ml) peanut, rice bran, or other neutral oil

For the Sauce:
¼ cup (60 ml) homemade or store-bought low-sodium chicken stock or water

1 tablespoon (15 ml) oyster sauce
1 teaspoon (5 ml) light soy sauce of shoyu
½ teaspoon (2 g) sugar
Pinch of freshly ground white pepper
Pinch of kosher salt

For the Cornstarch Slurry:
2 teaspoons (6 g) cornstarch
1 tablespoon (15 ml) water

For the Stir-Fry:
2 tablespoons (30 ml) peanut, rice bran, or other neutral oil
2 celery stalks, peeled and cut on a bias into ½-inch segments
2 teaspoons (5 g) minced garlic (about 2 medium cloves)
2 teaspoons (5 g) minced fresh ginger (about ½-inch segment)
1 scallion, white and pale green parts only, thinly sliced on a sharp bias

recipe continues

DIRECTIONS

(1) Place the wood ears in a large bowl or measuring cup large enough to allow for them to expand about fourfold. Cover with very hot water and set aside until rehydrated, about 15 minutes. Drain thoroughly. Remove the tough centers from the wood ears, then cut them into ½-inch ribbons.

(2) **Velvet the Fish:** Combine the fish, wine, soy sauce, salt, pepper, egg white, cornstarch, and vegetable oil in a small bowl and toss with your fingers until the fish is thoroughly coated in the marinade. There should be no extra moisture in the bowl, and there should be no dry cornstarch on the fish. If there is any pooled liquid, drain it off. If there is any dry cornstarch, add a few drops of wine until no dry starch remains.

(3) Bring 2 quarts of lightly salted water to a boil in a wok over high heat. Lower the coated pieces of fish into the water one piece at a time to ensure that they don't clump together. Cook for 1 minute after all the fish has been added. Using a spider, transfer the velveted fish to a rimmed baking sheet and spread into a single layer to steam dry. Set aside.

(4) **For the Sauce:** Combine the chicken stock or water, oyster sauce, soy sauce, sugar, white pepper, and salt in a small bowl and stir together until homogenous. Set aside. Combine the cornstarch and water in a separate small bowl and stir with a fork until the cornstarch is dissolved.

(5) **BEFORE YOU STIR-FRY, GET YOUR BOWLS READY:**

a. Velveted fish
b. Celery and wood ears
c. Garlic, ginger, and scallions
d. Sauce
e. Cornstarch slurry
f. Serving platter

(6) **For the Stir-Fry:** Heat a wok over high heat until lightly smoking. Add 1 tablespoon (15 ml) of the oil and swirl to coat. Add the celery and wood ears and stir-fry until the celery is tender-crisp, about 1 minute. Return the vegetables to their bowl.

(7) Wipe out the wok and return it to high heat until lightly smoking. Add the remaining tablespoon (15 ml) of oil and swirl to coat. Add the garlic, ginger, and scallions and stir-fry until fragrant, about 15 seconds. Return the vegetables to the wok and add the fish. Toss to combine. Stir the sauce and add to the wok. Stir the cornstarch slurry and add a splash. Cook, tossing, until the sauce thickens, about 15 seconds. Adjust the sauce consistency with more cornstarch slurry if it is too thin or a splash of water if it is too thick. Transfer to a serving platter and serve immediately with steamed rice.

STIR-FRIED FISH WITH GINGER AND SCALLIONS

Yield
Serves 4

Active Time
15 minutes

Total Time
30 minutes

INGREDIENTS

For the Fish:

1 pound (450 g) firm white fish, such as sea
    bass, striped bass, mahimahi, or halibut,
    cut into ¼- to ½-inch slices
1 tablespoon (15 ml) Shaoxing wine
1 teaspoon (5 ml) light soy sauce or shoyu
Pinch of kosher salt
Pinch of freshly ground white pepper
2 teaspoons (6 g) cornstarch
1 teaspoon (5 ml) peanut, rice bran, or other
    neutral oil

For the Sauce:

¼ cup (60 ml) homemade or store-bought
    low-sodium chicken stock or water
1 tablespoon (15 ml) Shaoxing wine
1 teaspoon (5 ml) light soy sauce or shoyu
½ teaspoon (2 g) sugar
½ teaspoon (2.5 ml) roasted sesame oil
Pinch of freshly ground white pepper
Pinch of kosher salt

For the Cornstarch Slurry:

2 teaspoons (6 g) cornstarch
1 tablespoon (15 ml) water

For the Stir-Fry:

2 tablespoons (30 ml) peanut, rice bran, or
    other neutral oil
One 2-inch knob fresh ginger, peeled and
    thinly sliced
2 scallions, cut on a bias into 1-inch
    segments

DIRECTIONS

(1) **Velvet the Fish:** Combine the fish, wine, soy sauce, salt, pepper, corn-starch, and vegetable oil in a small bowl and toss with your fingers until the fish is thoroughly coated in the marinade. There should be no extra moisture in the bowl, and there should be no dry cornstarch on the fish. If there is any pooled liquid, drain it off. If there is any dry cornstarch, add a few drops of wine until no dry starch remains.

(2) Bring 2 quarts of lightly salted water to a boil in a wok over high heat. Lower the coated pieces of fish into the water one piece at a time to ensure that they don't clump together. Cook for 1 minute after all the fish has been added. Using a spider, transfer the velveted fish to a rimmed baking sheet and spread into a single layer to steam dry. Set aside.

(3) **For the Sauce:** Combine the chicken stock or water, wine, soy sauce, sugar, sesame oil, white pepper, and salt in a small bowl and stir together until homogenous. Set aside. Combine the cornstarch and water in a sep-arate small bowl and stir with a fork until cornstarch is dissolved.

(4) **BEFORE YOU STIR-FRY, GET YOUR BOWLS READY:**

a. Velveted fish
b. Ginger and scallions
c. Sauce
d. Cornstarch slurry
e. Serving platter

(5) **For the Stir-Fry:** Heat a wok over high heat until lightly smoking. Add the oil and swirl to coat. Add the ginger and scallions and stir-fry until fragrant, about 30 seconds. Add the fish and toss to combine. Stir the sauce and add to the wok. Stir the cornstarch slurry and add a splash. Cook, tossing, until the sauce thickens, about 15 seconds. Adjust the sauce consistency with more cornstarch slurry if it is too thin or a splash of water if it is too thick. Transfer to a serving platter and serve immediately with steamed rice.

Stir-Fried Shrimp

Americans love their shrimp. We eat more shrimp than any other kind of seafood, and it is by far the most commonly ordered seafood at Chinese, Thai, and Vietnamese restaurants across the country. Shrimp are excellent for stir-fries. While most other proteins require some knifework to cut them to bite size, shrimp don't, and if God didn't intend for us to stir-fry shrimp, why would they come to us in perfectly chopstick-friendly portions?

HOW TO SHOP FOR SHRIMP

Even at a standard Western supermarket, there are a lot of options when it comes to shrimp—size, level of processing, species, etc. Here's a quick guide to what to look for when shopping.

Q *Is there ever a good time to buy precooked shrimp?*

A Unless you're already 15 minutes late to the potluck and you happened to win a quart of cocktail sauce in the office raffle, there's no reason to buy precooked shrimp. Precooked shrimp should really be advertised as pre-*over*cooked shrimp.

Q *I have access to a Chinese market where they sell live shrimp from tanks. Are those a good choice?*

A Yes! Lucky you! Live shrimp have firmer flesh and a sweeter, fresher flavor than any kind of processed shrimp. If you can get shrimp from a live tank, or if you are lucky enough to live near a shrimp fishery where shrimp are delivered to the store alive and kicking, that should always be your first choice for cooking.

The easiest and most humane way to kill live shrimp is to lay them in a single layer on a rimmed baking sheet, refrigerate them for at least 15 minutes (the cold temperature of a refrigerator slows down their metabolism and brain activity to a crawl), then transfer the whole tray to the freezer for another 15 minutes. Thaw them at room temperature for about 5 minutes before proceeding with a recipe.

Q *I can't get live shrimp, but I can find head-on shrimp. That's gotta be better than the headless kind, right?*

A I avoid buying head-on shrimp unless they're live. The reason for this is that shrimp and other crustaceans have an enzyme in their head that, shortly after the animal dies, will slowly work its way into the shrimp's body, breaking down tissues and causing them to turn mushy. Even within a day or two the difference can be striking. (This is the same reason lobster is generally sold either alive or as already-separated tails and claws.)

Deheading the shrimp before freezing at the farm or at sea prevents this enzyme from spreading into the meat. As a result, headless shrimp are almost invariably plumper and firmer than head-on shrimp.

Q *What about shell-on vs. shell-off?*

A Completely shelled shrimp I find can sometimes be a little mangled—the people or machines that shell the shrimp are a little rougher on them than I like to be. Moreover, in many preparations, shrimp can and should be cooked in their shells, as that shell not only adds flavor to the meat underneath but also acts as a temperature buffer, protecting the shrimp from overcooking. In certain dishes, such as Cantonese Pepper and Salty Shrimp (page 447), I eat the shrimp shell and all.

A good choice is so-called EZ-peel shrimp, which come with the shell on but the back split open and the dark vein removed. With a bag of EZ-peels in the freezer, I can pull out as many as I need, place them in a bowl of brine (see Brined Shrimp for Stir-Fries, page 144), and they're ready to go in just about 15 minutes.

Q *I've seen shrimp that are frozen individually as well as shrimp that come in a big block of ice. Which is better?*

A IQF stands for *individually quick frozen*, and the term means that each shrimp was frozen on its own and typically glazed in ice before being bagged. Block shrimp come frozen together in a large block of ice. As a general rule, the faster you freeze something, the smaller the loss in textural quality, so go with the IQF. They also have the advantage that they are much quicker to defrost.

Q *What size shrimp should I buy?*

A You'll probably see terms like *medium*, *large*, and *jumbo* printed on bags of shrimp, but you should ignore those descriptors: those terms are unregulated, which means that they can change from producer to producer or supermarket to supermarket.

Instead, look for a set of two numbers, such as 26–30 or 16–20. These numbers indicate the number of individual shrimp that it takes to make up a pound. So in a package labeled *26–30*, it will take between 26 and 30 shrimp to make up a pound, placing them on average at a little over half an ounce each. Thus, the smaller the number, the larger the shrimp. Once you get to around 15 shrimp or fewer per pound, you may seem them listed as U15 or U10, which means that it takes that many or fewer shrimp to make up a pound. U15 shrimp, for instance, would weigh a little over an ounce apiece.

For most of the recipes in this book, I use 26–40 count shrimp (usually marketed in the large to extra-large range), which thaw, brine, and cook fast in a stir-fry or when deep-fried.

Q *Once I get the shrimp home, how should I store it?*

A Frozen shrimp should be stored in the freezer until the day you are going to prepare them. Live shrimp or freshly killed head-on shrimp should be cooked as soon as possible. Thawed shrimp can be stored in the refrigerator. If you are planning on storing them for more than a day, I would suggest placing them on a plate or a rimmed baking sheet, wrapping them with plastic wrap, then putting a bag of ice cubes or an ice pack on top of the wrap to ensure that they stay chilled below fridge temps. Stored this way, thawed shrimp should stay fresh for about three days (change the ice every day).

HOW TO CLEAN SHRIMP

The most difficult step in cleaning shrimp is removing the digestive tract that runs down their back (often euphemistically referred to as the "vein"). If you plan on shelling or butterflying the shrimp, this is simple: just slit the back open with a sharp knife or some slender kitchen shears all the way down to the second-to-last segment.

To remove the shell of the shrimp, squeeze the shrimp from the second to last segment, pinching it upward so that the tail is pushed away from the meat inside the body. The back half of the shell should come right off.

Finally, peel the rest of the shell (including the legs) off the top portion of the shrimp and rinse out the vein under cool running water.

If serving shrimp with the head on and the shell intact, it's a little bit trickier. I find that the best method is to bend the head of the shrimp forward and down until you can slip the tip of a wooden skewer between the back of the head and the first shell segment on the body. Use the skewer to carefully pull the start of the vein out, then gently pull it out with the skewer or tweezers. The goal is to pull out the whole vein in one go without damaging the shrimp shell. It can be frustrating. For several months at one of my jobs as a line cook, it was my task to do this daily to a few dozen shrimp, and even after months, my success rate was not at 100%.

You can, of course, just choose to leave the vein in place or to butterfly the shrimp (see page 449). It doesn't really make a difference in flavor, and you don't really notice it's there unless you're specifically looking for it (and if you have dinner guests who are specifically checking your deveining work, might I suggest finding new dinner guests, or perhaps not serving them shrimp anymore?).

BAKING SODA: THE SECRET TO PLUMPER, SNAPPIER SHRIMP

Have you ever bitten into a perfect, crystal-skinned har gow dumpling at a dim sum restaurant and marveled at how plump and almost crunchy the shrimp inside tastes? I have. In Chinese, the term is *shuang cui*, which translates roughly to "crisp-clear." For a long time I thought it was simply a matter of perfectly cooking them. It wasn't until I came across a post on the excellent website Rasa Malaysia that I discovered there was more to it than that. In that article, recipe writer Bee Yinn Low spoke with chefs from Hong Kong to California and along the way discovered that the key to extra-plump shrimp is to soak it in alkaline water.

I tested this by trying shrimp soaked in plain water (my tap comes out slightly alkaline at a pH of 7.5), shrimp soaked in salt water, shrimp soaked in baking-soda-spiked water (between pH 8 and 9), and completely unsoaked shrimp.

The saltwater shrimp came out a little bit juicier—brining can help meat retain moisture—while the baking soda water showed a clear improvement in texture; the shrimp nearly popped in my mouth. Combining baking soda and salt was the best option, delivering shrimp that were both crunchy and juicy.

There is surprisingly little writing and research I can find that explains why this technique works, but some further research led me to an article in the August 2011 issue of *Food Science and Technology International* in which Malaysian researchers found that shrimp soaked in solutions with a higher pH level would retain more moisture during cooking, while also solubilizing some muscle proteins, a combination that explains the increased tenderness and plumper texture of baking-soda-treated shrimp. In that study, soaking shrimp in a brine solution with 2.5 percent salt and 2 percent baking soda by weight yielded the optimum results, and my own testing at home gave similar results.

Furthermore, the alkaline environment serves to break down the layer of slick proteins in between the shrimp's shell and the meat. Left intact, this protein layer gives the surface of the shrimp a softer, mushier texture. In fact, some chefs recommend washing shrimp under cold running water for extended periods of time—anywhere from 15 minutes to an hour— to remove this slime layer, a process that ends up delivering similar results to a shorter alkaline water soak.

Given the large quantity of water it takes to use the washing method, I stick with the alkaline soak. It's a technique I use nearly every time I prepare shrimp, whether for stir-fries or a plain old shrimp cocktail.

Q *Frozen shrimp? Not a problem.*

A Typically I let frozen shrimp defrost in a bowl of water. At room temperature that takes all of 15 minutes. But then I thought to myself, *Can I combine the defrosting and brining steps?*

The answer is yes, which is good news for folks like me, who work with frozen shrimp the majority of the time. All you have to do is make your brine solution, then add your shrimp to it straight from the freezer. If using frozen shrimp, don't add any ice cubes to the brine while they're soaking—the shrimp themselves will keep it plenty cold.

BRINED SHRIMP FOR STIR-FRIES

NOTE

12.5 grams is about 1⅓ tablespoons Diamond Crystal kosher salt, 1 tablespoon Morton's kosher salt, or 2½ teaspoons table salt. Note that the same brine ingredient quantities can be used for any amount of shrimp, so long as they are completely submerged in brine. This recipe is listed in metric units first, as metric units make calculating ratios and scaling quantities simple.

INGREDIENTS

For the Brine:
½ liter (500 g/about 2 cups) very cold water
12.5 g salt (see Note)
10 g (about 2 teaspoons) baking soda

For the Shrimp:
Up to 2 pounds (900 g) shrimp, shell on
or off
A cup or so of ice cubes

DIRECTIONS

Combine the water, salt, and baking soda in a bowl and stir until the salt and baking soda are dissolved. Add the shrimp and stir to separate them and ensure the brine flows all around. Add the ice cubes and let the shrimp brine for at least 15 minutes and up to 30.

PEEL-AND-EAT SHRIMP WITH GARLIC, SCALLIONS, AND CHILES

Yield
Serves 4

Active Time
10 minutes

Total Time
25 minutes

NOTES

12.5 grams is about 1⅓ tablespoons Diamond Crystal kosher salt, 1 tablespoon Morton's kosher salt, or 2½ teaspoons table salt. This recipe is especially good with small live shrimp, such as *amaebi* (a variety of pink shrimp) or Royal Red shrimp, which are caught wild off the Gulf Coast and have an extrasweet, rich flavor.

INGREDIENTS

For the Shrimp:

2 cups (500 ml) very cold water
12.5 g salt (see Notes)
2 teaspoons (10 g) baking soda
1 pound (450 g) shell-on shrimp (see Notes)
A cup or so of ice cubes

For the Stir-Fry:

3 tablespoons (45 ml) peanut, rice bran, or other neutral oil
8 medium garlic cloves (20 to 25 g), cut into ⅛-inch slices
1 fresh hot green chile, such as serrano, jalapeño, or Thai bird, thinly sliced
2 scallions, thinly sliced on a bias
Kosher salt and freshly ground white pepper
1 recipe Soy and Fragrant Oil Dipping Sauce (optional; page 146)

There are few things my wife, Adri, loves more than sitting at a table (or on the beach) and slowly and steadily turning a pile of shrimp into a pile of shrimp shells with nothing but her bare hands (and perhaps a bib). Good shrimp are so flavorful that even a quick stir-fry in olive oil or caiziyou and no seasoning beyond some salt can yield delicious results, but I *love* the combination of sweet slices of fried garlic and shrimp. The garlic picks up the shrimp flavor, and the shrimp in turn get some of the garlic. I don't know who gets the better end of that deal, but I do know that everyone comes out a winner.

DIRECTIONS

(1) **For the Shrimp:** Combine the water, salt, and baking soda in a bowl and stir until the salt and baking soda are dissolved. Add the shrimp and stir to separate them and ensure the brine flows all around. Add the ice cubes and let the shrimp brine for at least 15 minutes and up to 30. Drain thoroughly and pat dry on paper towels or spin in a paper-towel-lined salad spinner.

(2) **For the Stir-Fry:** Heat a wok over high heat until lightly smoking. Add the oil and swirl to coat. Immediately add the garlic and chiles and stir-fry until the garlic is turning pale golden brown around the edges, 15 to 30 seconds. Add the drained shrimp and stir-fry until barely cooked through, about 1 minute. Add the scallions and season with a big pinch of salt and white pepper. Transfer to a serving platter and serve immediately with dipping sauce, if desired.

SOY AND FRAGRANT OIL DIPPING SAUCE

Yield
Makes ½ cup

Active Time
5 minutes

Total Time
5 minutes

This light and fragrant sauce is an excellent dipping sauce for stir-fried or simply boiled or steamed shrimp, boiled or steamed crab or lobster, or steamed fish. It's also great as a sauce for dumplings, poached chicken, or cold noodles. The chiles and warm spices are optional.

INGREDIENTS

1 medium garlic clove, roughly chopped
One ¼-inch segment fresh ginger, peeled
Kosher salt
1 scallion, thinly sliced
1 teaspoon (3 g) dried hot chile, such as Sichuan er jing tiao or Thai bird (optional)
¼ teaspoon (0.5 g) ground Sichuan peppercorns (optional)
1 star anise pod (optional)
2 tablespoons peanut, rice bran, or other neutral oil
3 tablespoons (45 ml) light soy sauce
2 tablespoons (15 ml) Chinkiang, black, or rice vinegar
1 tablespoon (15 ml) water
1 tablespoon (12 g) sugar

DIRECTIONS

(1) Combine the garlic, ginger, and a pinch of kosher salt in the bowl of a mortar and pestle and pound into a paste. Scrape the mixture into a small heatproof bowl. Add the scallions and optional chile, Sichuan peppercorns, and star anise to the bowl and stir with a fork or chopsticks to combine.

(2) Heat the oil in a wok or small skillet until smoking hot, then pour directly on top of the garlic/ginger/scallion mixture. Stir immediately with chopsticks or a fork. It should sizzle rapidly and release a very nice aroma. Stir in the soy sauce, vinegar, water, and sugar until dissolved. The flavored dipping sauce can be stored in a sealed container in the refrigerator for several weeks.

KUNG PAO SHRIMP

Yield
Serves 4

Active Time
25 minutes

Total Time
40 minutes

NOTE
12.5 grams is about 1⅓ tablespoons Diamond Crystal kosher salt, 1 tablespoon Morton's kosher salt, or 2½ teaspoons table salt

You can replace the chicken in either classic Sichuan gong bao ji ding or Chinese American kung pao chicken with small, plump peeled shrimp or larger shrimp cut into bite-sized pieces. The only minor adjustment that I make is adding a baking soda brine to the shrimp for plumpness. Instead of peanuts, I like to use cashews in this dish. Their shape and size resembles the shrimp, and their sweeter, milder flavor pairs well with the sweetness of shrimp.

INGREDIENTS

For the Shrimp:
2 cups (500 ml) very cold water
12.5 g salt (see Note)
2 teaspoons (10 g) baking soda
1 pound (450 g) large shrimp (around 31–40 count), peeled
A cup or so of ice cubes
1 teaspoon (5 ml) Shaoxing wine or dry sherry
1 teaspoon (5 ml) light soy sauce or shoyu
1 teaspoon (about 3 g) cornstarch

For the Sauce:
4 teaspoons (20 ml) honey
1 tablespoon (15 ml) Chinkiang vinegar
1 tablespoon (15 ml) Shaoxing wine or dry sherry
4 teaspoons (20 ml) light soy sauce or shoyu

For the Cornstarch Slurry:
1 teaspoon (3 g) cornstarch
1 tablespoon (15 ml) water

For the Stir-Fry:
3 tablespoons (45 ml) peanut, rice bran, or other neutral oil
6 to 12 small dried red chiles (such as árbol), stems removed, cut into ½-inch pieces with scissors, and seeds discarded
1 teaspoon (about 2 g) Sichuan peppercorns, reddish husks only (stems and black seeds discarded)

4 medium garlic cloves (12 g), thinly sliced
One 1-inch knob fresh ginger, preferably young ginger, peeled and cut into fine matchsticks (about 20 g; see page 67)
6 scallions, white and pale green parts only, cut into ½-inch pieces
¾ cup cashews or roasted peanuts (about 4 ounces/120 g)

recipe continues

DIRECTIONS

1. **For the Shrimp:** Combine the water, salt, and baking soda in a bowl and stir until the salt and baking soda are dissolved. Add the shrimp and stir to separate them and ensure the brine flows all around. Add the ice cubes and let the shrimp brine for at least 15 minutes and up to 30. Drain thoroughly and pat dry on paper towels or spin in a paper-towel-lined salad spinner.

2. Transfer to a bowl and add the wine, soy sauce, and cornstarch. Toss to combine.

3. **For the Sauce:** Combine the honey, vinegar, wine, and soy sauce in a small bowl and stir together until homogenous. Set aside. Combine the cornstarch and water in a separate small bowl and stir with a fork until the cornstarch is dissolved.

4. **BEFORE YOU STIR-FRY, GET YOUR BOWLS READY:**

   a. Dried chiles and Sichuan peppercorns
   b. Marinated shrimp
   c. Garlic and ginger
   d. Scallions and cashews
   e. Sauce
   f. Cornstarch slurry
   g. Empty bowl for cooked ingredients
   h. Serving platter

5. **For the Stir-Fry:** Heat a wok over high heat until lightly smoking. Add 1 tablespoon (15 ml) of the oil and swirl to coat. Immediately add the chiles and Sichuan peppercorns. Stir-fry until fragrant but not burnt, about 5 seconds. Immediately add the shrimp and stir-fry constantly until the shrimp is nearly cooked through, about 3 minutes. Transfer to a bowl and set aside.

6. Wipe out the wok (there may be a film on the bottom, which you can scrub out in the sink; there is no rush to continue). Heat the remaining 2 tablespoons (30 ml) oil over high heat until shimmering. Add the garlic and ginger and stir-fry until fragrant, about 10 seconds. Add the scallions and cashews and stir-fry for 30 seconds.

7. Return the shrimp to the wok and toss everything to combine. Stir the sauce and add to the wok by pouring it around the edges. Stir the cornstarch slurry and add a splash. Cook, tossing, until the sauce thickens and the shrimp is cooked through, about 30 seconds longer. Adjust the sauce consistency with more cornstarch slurry if it is too thin or a splash of water if it is too thick. Transfer to a serving platter and serve immediately with steamed rice.

SHRIMP- OR FISH-STUFFED CHILES IN BLACK BEAN SAUCE

I grew up eating seafood-stuffed chiles in New York's Chinatown. Long green chiles (I've seen them sold as "Green Capsicum" or "cowhorn" at Asian markets in the United States) would get split in half, filled with a seasoned emulsion of carp and shrimp, and panfried until golden brown. You could get it served dry with a little soy-based dipping sauce on the side (the Soy and Fragrant Oil Dipping Sauce on page 146 would work well) or, as we preferred it, in a glossy, salty, fermented black bean sauce. Eating them was like a game of Russian roulette, as hiding among the generally mild chiles would be one or two bites with a fiery burn.

The dish originates from Shunde, at the cradle of the Pearl River Delta, in Guangdong province. Along with Chengdu, it's one of two cities in China with a UNESCO City of Gastronomy designation. In the streets of Hong Kong, you can find it deep-fried and served by the piece on wooden skewers, along with eggplant and bitter melon stuffed with the same mixture (a combination known as "Three Stuffed Treasures").

If you want to be very traditional, you'll have to seek out fresh dace (a type of white-fleshed carp that you'll have to carefully rid of its thin bones) and those long green peppers. At home, I typically make it with white-fleshed ocean fish like sea bass or hake or, more frequently, shrimp, which is inexpensive and produces a cohesive mixture that's easy to work with. If you

can't find those long green peppers, any slender pepper will do—cubanelle if you want it mild or jalapeño if you like it hot (or a mix if you're dining in mixed company).

The filling is made by finely mincing the shrimp or fish with a cleaver. I start by dicing it, then just go to town chopping the mixture on a cutting board, using the flat of the cleaver to fold it over itself until it forms a fine paste (a food processor makes short work of this as well). It's then mixed with Shaoxing wine, cornstarch (which makes the mixture more tender), scallions, salt, sugar, and white pepper. The mixing step is really key here. Just like kneading dough or making sausage, the goal is to encourage proteins—mainly myosin—to cross-link, giving the mixture its characteristic bouncy, springy texture.

As you mix, you'll see the mixture get stickier and stickier, eventually leaving a thin film of protein on the sides of the bowl. If you pick up a handful and hold it upside down in your open palm, it should stick to your hand.

To stuff the chiles, you start by splitting them in half lengthwise and rinsing them out under cool running water, removing all of the seeds and ribs. You then toss them in cornstarch (this ensures that the filling will stick to the moist surface and gives the outer surface a slick texture that helps sauce cling to it) and fill their cavity with the stuffing before panfrying them in a well-oiled wok. I start with the filling side down to brown and set it, then flip the chiles over and cook until the second side is brown and tender.

SHRIMP- OR FISH-STUFFED CHILES IN BLACK BEAN SAUCE

Yield
Serves 4

Active Time
25 minutes

Total Time
35 minutes

NOTES

If you can't find Chinese long green chiles (also sold as "green horn chile" or "cowhorn chile"), you can use 4 cubanelles, 3 green bell peppers, or 10 to 12 jalapeños in their place. If using bell peppers, split into quarters lengthwise instead of halves. I like serving these chiles in black bean sauce, but you can also serve them with Soy and Fragrant Oil Dipping Sauce (page 146). If using dipping sauce, omit all the black bean sauce ingredients and step 7.

INGREDIENTS

For the Filling:
12 ounces (340 g) peeled shrimp or mild flaky white fish such as sea bass or hake
1 tablespoon (15 ml) Shaoxing wine
1 tablespoon (15 ml) water
2 tablespoons (about 18 g) cornstarch
1 teaspoon (3 g) kosher salt
½ teaspoon (2 g) sugar
½ teaspoon (1 g) freshly ground white pepper
1 scallion, thinly sliced

For the Peppers:
6 long green peppers (see Notes)
1 tablespoon (about 9 g) cornstarch
¼ cup (60 ml) peanut, rice bran, or other neutral oil

For the Black Bean Sauce (optional; see Notes):
1 tablespoon (15 ml) peanut, rice bran, or other neutral oil
2 teaspoons (5 g) minced fresh garlic (about 2 medium cloves)
2 teaspoons (5 g) minced fresh ginger (about ½-inch segment)
2 tablespoons (about 12 g) dried fermented black beans (douchi), roughly chopped
1 tablespoon (15 ml) Shaoxing wine
1 tablespoon (15 ml) oyster sauce
1 teaspoon (5 ml) dark soy sauce
1 teaspoon (4 g) sugar
⅔ cup (160 ml) homemade or store-bought low-sodium chicken stock or water
2 teaspoons (6 g) cornstarch mixed with 1 tablespoon (15 ml) cold water
1 scallion, thinly sliced

DIRECTIONS

(1) **For the Filling:** Using a cleaver or heavy chef's knife, finely mince the shrimp or fish. Continue chopping, folding it over itself on the cutting board until a fine paste is formed, about 5 minutes. Alternatively, chop the mixture in a food processor, pulsing and scraping down the sides as necessary until a fine paste is formed.

(2) Transfer the mixture to a medium bowl. Add the wine, water, corn-starch, salt, sugar, white pepper, and scallion. Roughly knead the mixture with clean hands or a fork, working it until it feels tacky, it leaves a thin film along the walls of the bowl, and a small handful of it sticks to your open hand when you hold it upside down. This process should take about 3 minutes.

(3) **For the Peppers:** Split each pepper in half lengthwise. Remove the tops, then rinse out the seeds and ribs under running water. Drain well, then cut crosswise into 3-inch segments (if using jalapeños, you can leave each half as is). In a large bowl, toss the rinsed pepper pieces with the cornstarch until they are lightly coated on all sides (you may need a little more cornstarch).

④ Using a knife, chopsticks, or a spoon, fill each pepper piece with filling, smoothing out the exposed surface of the filling as you go. Transfer each pepper piece to a large plate face up.

⑤ **BEFORE YOU STIR-FRY, GET YOUR BOWLS AND PLATES READY:**

a. Stuffed peppers
b. Garlic, ginger, and black beans for sauce
c. Shaoxing wine, oyster sauce, dark soy sauce, sugar, and chicken stock for sauce
d. Cornstarch slurry
e. Sliced scallions for sauce
f. Serving platter

⑥ Heat half of the oil in a wok over medium heat until shimmering but not smoking hot. Remove from the heat, then carefully place half of the stuffed chiles face down into the oil. Return the wok to medium-high heat and cook, swirling the wok occasionally to ensure even browning, until the fish paste is well browned and cooked through, about 3 minutes. Using chopsticks or tongs, carefully flip each chile. Cook the second side until the chiles are lightly browned and have a wrinkled appearance, about 1 minute longer. Transfer the cooked chiles to a serving platter. Repeat with the remaining oil and stuffed chiles. Serve immediately with Soy and Fragrant Oil Dipping Sauce (page 146), or continue to step 7 to make black bean sauce.

⑦ **For the Black Bean Sauce:** Heat the oil in a wok over medium-high heat until shimmering. Add the garlic, ginger, and black beans and cook, stirring, until fragrant, about 15 seconds. Add the wine, oyster sauce, soy sauce, sugar, and stock and bring to a simmer. Stir the cornstarch slurry and drizzle it in. Cook until the sauce is thick enough to coat the back of a spoon, about 1 minute. Stir in the scallion, then spoon over the chiles and serve.

CANTONESE-STYLE CLAMS IN BLACK BEAN SAUCE

Yield
Serves (see Note)

Active Time
10 minutes

Total Time
15 minutes, plus 30 to 60 minutes for purging the clams

NOTE

Depending on size, season, and provenance, clams can vary widely in their ratio of weight to edible meat. Use your judgment or ask the fishmonger when shopping for clams to ensure four full portions. To purge clams, submerge them in a bowl of cold, salty water (about 3 tablespoons Diamond Crystal kosher salt or 2 tablespoons Morton's kosher salt per liter of water; a 2½ percent brine solution) for half an hour, then drain. Repeat until there is no grit left in the water.

INGREDIENTS

2 tablespoons (30 ml) peanut, rice bran, or other neutral oil

3 teaspoons (7 g) minced garlic (about 3 medium cloves)

2 teaspoons (5 g) minced fresh ginger (about ½-inch segment)

1 small fresh hot chile, such as Thai bird, serrano, or Fresno, minced (optional)

2 tablespoons (about 12 g) dried fermented black beans (douchi), roughly chopped

1 tablespoon (15 ml) Shaoxing wine

1 tablespoon (15 ml) oyster sauce

1 teaspoon (5 ml) dark soy sauce

1 teaspoon (4 g) sugar

1½ to 2½ pounds (680 to 1,100 g) live Littleneck clams, Manila clams, or cockles, purged (see Note)

⅓ cup (80 ml) water

1 scallion, cut on a bias into ½-inch segments

1 tablespoon (9 g) cornstarch mixed with 2 tablespoons (30 ml) cold water

Clams steamed in a garlicky broth is a flavor combination that crosses international boundaries, from Italian *linguine alle vongole in bianco* to Portuguese *porco à alentejana* to Cantonese clams in black bean sauce, and a wok is the ideal vessel for steaming clams or mussels. Unlike, say, a Dutch oven with its angled corners that make it hard to stir hard shells, the gently sloped sides of a wok make it simple to move the clams around, letting them tumble in the sauce and cook quickly and evenly.

Clams in black bean sauce is a Cantonese classic that combines the sweet, slightly bitter flavor of clams with a spicy, salty, umami-heavy black bean sauce. When people talk about flavor-packed food, this is the kind of stuff they're talking about. When we eat clams at home, we encourage our daughter, Alicia, to pluck the plump meat out from inside the shell, then suck on the shell itself, which will inevitably have caught plenty of the rich, glossy sauce.

DIRECTIONS

(1) Heat the oil in a wok over medium-high heat until shimmering. Add the garlic, ginger, chile, and black beans and stir-fry until fragrant, about 30 seconds. Add the wine, oyster sauce, soy sauce, sugar, clams, and water and stir to combine. Bring to a simmer. Cover and cook, shaking the wok occasionally and adjusting the heat to maintain a steady simmer, until all the clams are open, about 3 minutes.

(2) Increase the heat to high and stir in the scallion. Stir the cornstarch slurry and add. Cook, tossing, until the sauce thickens enough to coat the back of a spoon. Transfer to a serving platter and serve immediately.

How to Buy and Store Clams

 What are the best clams for stir-fries?

A Whether farmed or wild, clams are among the most sustainable (and delicious!) forms of seafood you can eat. When shopping for clams for stir-fries, the most important quality is freshness. You should be buying only live clams. Once dead, their slightly bitter flavor tends to go south extremely fast. Live clams will either be stored in running saltwater tanks (what you'll find at a larger Chinese fish market), or in mesh bags on ice (as is common in Western supermarkets). Depending on what part of the country you're in, you are likely to find a few different types of clams. Here are my recommendations for stir-fries:

→ **Littlenecks, topnecks, or cherrystones:** These are all species of the same hard-shelled clam, known as *quahogs* (pronounced ko-hog, from the Narraganset word *poquahock*) in New England. Littlenecks are the smallest, followed by topnecks and cherrystones. They have very hard, pale gray to beige shells and a clean, briny, sweet flavor.

→ **Manila clams** resemble quahogs but have shells that are a bit thinner and range in color from beige to reddish brown. Their flavor is a little sweeter and less salty than that of quahogs.

→ **Cockles** are small bivalves that range across the entire globe. You'll find cockles on both coasts, as well as farmed cockles imported from New Zealand. They are generally smaller than quahogs or Manila clams and cook about 30 percent faster than either.

→ **Atlantic razor clams,** so called because of their resemblance to a folded barber's razor blade, have long, thin, brittle shells and long siphons that extend past their bodies, which never fully close. You can find them live at fish markets in the Northeast, though it's rare to find them outside of that region. They have deliciously tender, sweet flesh without the bitterness that quahogs and Manilas can have. If you have access to them, snatch them up; they're a real treat. Do not confuse them with Pacific razor clams, which are much larger and are not particularly well suited for stir-fries (though they are delicious breaded and fried).

 How should I store clams when I bring them home?

A The best thing to do with live clams is to cook them the day you buy them! If you must store them, keep them in an open container in the refrigerator. Do not wrap them tightly or put them in a plastic bag, which can suffocate them and lead to an early demise. In the fridge, healthy clams should last for a couple of days.

Q **How can I tell if my clams are still good to eat?**

A Live quahogs, Manila clams, and cockles will typically gape slightly in the fridge or be very gently closed. The easiest way to check if they're still alive is to give them a little squeeze and see if they, well, clam up. They should close fully and tightly. Razor clams, which never close, should react when you touch their siphons, retracting away from your finger.

If your clams are already tightly shut, they are most likely perfectly fine to eat. So long as they smell fresh and briny, go ahead and cook them (dead clams will give off more distinctly fishy aromas). Even clams that don't open when cooked are fine to eat, provided they smell alright.

Q *Do I need to purge clams?*

A While not strictly necessary, purging clams by letting them soak in cold salty water before cooking them is typically a good idea. First, it gives them a chance to spit out any grit that might be contained within their shells (sometimes a significant amount). Second, it ensures that they have plenty of moisture in them to expel during cooking, which helps them steam and cook evenly.

To purge clams, first make a 2½ percent brine: for every liter of water, add 25 grams of salt (that's 3 tablespoons Diamond Crystal kosher, 2 tablespoons Morton's kosher, or 1½ tablespoons table salt per liter). Submerge the clams in this brine and refrigerate them for half an hour. Check the bottom of the bowl for any grit. Drain and repeat the process until the bowl is clean.

CLAMS WITH GARLIC, SAKE, AND BUTTER

Yield
Serves 4

Active Time
10 minutes

Total Time
15 minutes, plus 30 to 60 minutes for purging the clams

NOTE
To purge clams, submerge them in a bowl of cold salty water (about 3 tablespoons of Diamond Crystal kosher salt or 2 tablespoons of Morton's kosher salt per liter of water; a 2½% brine solution) for half an hour, then drain. Repeat until there is no grit left in the water.

This recipe combines classic Western flavors—garlic, butter, and clams—with a dash of sake and soy sauce. It's equally at home with noodles, rice, or a good loaf of crusty bread to sop up the juices.

INGREDIENTS

1 tablespoon (15 g) unsalted butter
3 medium garlic cloves (8 g), thinly sliced
1 medium shallot (1½ ounces/45 g), thinly sliced
Pinch of hot red pepper flakes or Thai chile flakes
½ cup (120 ml) dry sake
1 teaspoon (5 ml) light soy sauce or shoyu

1½ pounds (675 g) live Littleneck clams, Manila clams, or cockles, purged (see Note)
Handful of roughly chopped fresh cilantro leaves
1 scallion, thinly sliced
1 teaspoon (3 g) cornstarch mixed with 1 tablespoon (15 ml) cold water

DIRECTIONS

(1) Heat the butter in a wok over medium heat until melted. Add the garlic, shallot, and chile flakes and cook until the garlic is softened but not browned, about 30 seconds. Add the sake and soy sauce. Increase the heat to high and bring to a boil. Add the clams and stir. Cover and cook, shaking the wok occasionally and adjusting the heat to maintain a steady simmer, until all the clams or mussels are open, about 6 minutes.

(2) Stir in the cilantro and scallions. Stir the cornstarch slurry and add half. Cook, tossing, until the sauce thickens very lightly and emulsifies. Adjust the sauce consistency with more cornstarch slurry if it is too thin or more water if it is too thick. Transfer to a serving platter and serve immediately.

1.5 HOW TO STIR-FRY EGGS, TOFU, AND VEGETABLES

The irony of those old wok infomercials is that every one of them pushed woks as the ideal vessel for cooking vegetables, while simultaneously demonstrating the worst possible way to stir-fry vegetables in them. *Watch as I fill this wok to the brim with broccoli, celery, onions, carrots, and bell peppers! Watch as ten minutes later they all emerge, a veritable rainbow of brownish green, brownish orange, and greenish brown!*

The wok *is* a wonderful vessel for cooking vegetables—stir-fried vegetables can range in texture and flavor from bright and crisp to charred and chewy to smoky and tender. But you're going to have to do at least a modicum of study and practice to get them there. In this section, we'll cover the basics of how to stir-fry eggs, tofu, and vegetables. Note that as is common in Asian dishes, many of the vegetable dishes are vegetable based but lean on nonvegetarian ingredients—bits of meat or seafood-based sauces—to add texture and boost flavor. In most cases there are simple vegetarian or vegan substitutes for those.

Scrambled Eggs in the Wok

Depending on how you cook them, Western-style scrambled eggs can range from firm and fluffy to soft and creamy or moist and sauce-like. Scrambled egg dishes cooked in a wok are, if anything, even more diverse than their Western counterparts.

In their softest, most extreme form, you'll find dishes like Slippery Egg with Beef (page 156) and Shrimp with Lobster Sauce (a dish that contains no lobster) in which the eggs wind up somewhere in between a sauce and a soup. A little bit firmer and you're in

the territory of *fanqie chow dan*—Home-Style Tomato and Scrambled Eggs (page 165). At the far end of the spectrum are puffy, browned scrambled egg dishes like Khai Jiao (Thai-Style Omelet, page 168) or classic egg foo young.

It's this incredible diversity that makes eggs one of my favorite ingredients to work with.

SLIPPERY EGG WITH BEEF

Yield
Serves 4

Active Time
15 minutes

Total Time
30 minutes

NOTE
I like using thinly shaved beef for this dish. Thinly sliced beef chuck roll, rib eye, or short rib intended for shabu, sukiyaki, or Korean BBQ can be found at many Asian supermarkets. You can also use skirt or flank steak thinly sliced against the grain by hand (see page 116 for tips on cutting beef for stir-fries). For an even faster, easier, and more inexpensive dish, you can use ground meat in place of the sliced meat. If using ground meat, omit the baking soda and the rinsing process in step 1. This dish works well with plant-based ground meats like Impossible or Beyond.

This beef and egg stir-fry is not a dish I was familiar with growing up, but as soon as I saw a version of it on the wonderful Chinese-cooking website The Woks of Life, I knew it would become a staple for me. In its ingredients and preparation, it resembles Japanese rice dishes like Gyudon (page 235) or Oyakodon (page 233), with the key difference being that Slippery Egg with Beef starts with stir-frying the beef rather than simmering it, and the broth gets thickened into a viscous sauce, the gently scrambled egg suspended in it.

My own recipe is a hybridized version of the Cantonese original with the Japanese flavors of sake and mirin. The technique is very versatile: It works with sliced beef, shaved beef, or any type of ground meat (even plant-based ground meat substitutes). It's also easy to add vegetables to. Even frozen peas come out bright and flavorful when coated in the slippery egg mixture. I love the way you can scoop up a clump of rice with chopsticks and the eggs and beef will just barely cling together as they make the trip to your mouth.

The only real trick to getting this dish right is to pay careful attention to the thickness of the sauce you make in the wok as you drizzle in the egg. It should be quite viscous, to the point that it coats the back of a spoon and bubbles of steam slowly burst rather than vigorously boil, but not so thick that it's gloppy or pasty. The good news is it's easy to adjust that texture: let it simmer and reduce if it's too thin and add a little extra water if it becomes too thick.

INGREDIENTS

For the Beef:

12 ounces (340 g) thinly sliced beef (see Note)
¼ teaspoon (1 g) baking soda (optional; see Note)
1 teaspoon (5 ml) light soy sauce or shoyu
½ teaspoon (2 g) kosher salt
½ teaspoon (1.5 g) cornstarch

For the Sauce:

2 tablespoon (30 ml) sake
1 tablespoon (15 ml) mirin
1 tablespoon (15 ml) light soy sauce or shoyu
Pinch of freshly ground white pepper
Pinch of kosher salt
2 cups (500 ml) homemade or store-bought low-sodium chicken stock, dashi, or water

For the Cornstarch Slurry:

2 tablespoons (18 g) cornstarch
¼ cup (120 ml) water

For the Stir-Fry:

1 tablespoon (15 ml) peanut, rice bran, or other neutral oil
2 coin-sized slices fresh ginger (optional)
2 scallions, cut on a bias into ½-inch segments
2 medium garlic cloves, minced or crushed in a mortar and pestle (about 2 teaspoons/10 g)
Kosher salt and freshly ground white pepper
½ cup (100 g) frozen peas, thawed (optional)
4 large eggs, lightly beaten with a pinch of kosher salt

4 bowls steamed rice

DIRECTIONS

(1) **For the Beef:** Place the beef in a medium bowl, cover with cold water, and vigorously agitate it. Drain through a fine-mesh strainer and press on the beef with your hands to remove excess water. Return the beef to the bowl, add the baking soda, and vigorously massage the baking soda into the meat, lifting the meat, throwing it down, and squeezing it for 30 to 60 seconds. Add the soy sauce, salt, and cornstarch. Roughly work the marinade into the meat for at least 30 seconds. Set aside to marinate for at least 15 minutes and up to overnight.

(2) **For the Sauce:** Combine the sake, mirin, soy sauce, white pepper, salt, and stock or water in a medium bowl and stir together until homogenous. Set aside. Combine the cornstarch and water in a separate small bowl and stir with a fork until the cornstarch is dissolved.

(3) **For the Stir-Fry:** Rub a thin film of oil into a wok and set it over high heat until smoking. Add the tablespoon of oil and swirl to coat. Add the ginger and let it sizzle for 15 seconds. Add the beef and stir-fry until mostly cooked through and lightly browned in spots, about 1 minute. Add the scallions and garlic and stir-fry until fragrant, about 30 seconds.

(4) Add the sauce mixture and peas (if using) and bring to a boil. Stir the cornstarch slurry and add it to the wok. Simmer until the sauce is thick enough to coat the back of a spoon, 2 to 3 minutes. Adjust the seasoning with salt and white pepper to taste. If there's a lot of foamy scum floating on top of the broth, you can skim it off with a ladle and discard if desired.

(5) Reduce the heat to a bare simmer. Drizzle the egg mixture into the sauce, then very slowly stir it with a ladle or wok spatula until the eggs form tender ribbons, about 30 seconds. Divide the mixture evenly over individual bowls of steamed rice and serve.

SLIPPERY EGG WITH MUSHROOMS

Yield
Serves 4

Active Time
15 minutes

Total Time
30 minutes

INGREDIENTS

For the Sauce:

2 tablespoons (30 ml) sake
1 tablespoon (15 ml) mirin
1 tablespoon (15 ml) light soy sauce or shoyu
Pinch of freshly ground white pepper
Pinch of kosher salt
2 cups (500 ml) homemade or store-bought low-sodium chicken stock, dashi, or water

For the Cornstarch Slurry:

2 tablespoons (18 g) cornstarch
¼ cup (120 ml) water

For the Stir-Fry:

1 tablespoon (15 ml) peanut, rice bran, or other neutral oil
2 coin-sized slices fresh ginger (optional)
8 ounces (225 g) mixed mushrooms, such as sliced shiitake caps or button, whole trimmed beech mushrooms, or roughly sliced oyster or maitake mushrooms
2 scallions, cut on a bias into ½-inch segments
2 medium garlic cloves, minced or crushed in a mortar and pestle (about 2 teaspoons/10 g)
Kosher salt and freshly ground white pepper
½ cup frozen peas, thawed (optional)
4 large eggs, lightly beaten with a pinch of kosher salt

4 bowls steamed rice

Mushrooms and eggs are a natural pair in all kinds of cuisine, and mushrooms work especially well with slippery eggs. I like to use a mix of Asian mushrooms for this, but you can use any mushrooms you'd like.

DIRECTIONS

(1) **For the Sauce:** Combine the sake, mirin, soy sauce, white pepper, salt, and stock or water in a medium bowl and stir together until homogenous. Set aside. Combine the cornstarch and water in a separate small bowl and stir with a fork until the cornstarch is dissolved.

(2) **For the Stir-Fry:** Rub a thin film of oil into a wok and set it over high heat until smoking. Add the tablespoon of oil and swirl to coat. Add the ginger and let it sizzle for 15 seconds. Immediately add the mixed mushrooms and stir-fry until the mushrooms are lightly browned around the edges, 2 to 3 minutes. Add the scallions and garlic and stir-fry until fragrant, about 30 seconds.

(3) Add the sauce mixture and peas (if using) and bring to a boil. Stir the cornstarch slurry and add it to the wok. Simmer until the sauce is thick enough to coat the back of a spoon, 2 to 3 minutes. Adjust the seasoning with salt and white pepper to taste. If there's a lot of foamy scum floating on top of the broth, you can skim it off with a ladle and discard if desired.

(4) Reduce the heat to a bare simmer. Drizzle the egg mixture into the sauce, then very slowly stir it with a ladle or wok spatula until the eggs form tender ribbons, about 30 seconds. Divide the mixture evenly over bowls of steamed rice and serve.

SHRIMP OR TOFU WITH LOBSTER SAUCE

Yield
Serves 4

Active Time
15 minutes

Total Time
30 minutes

NOTES
You can use tofu in place of shrimp for this dish (instructions follow). For the salt, 12.5 grams is about 1⅓ tablespoons Diamond Crystal kosher salt, 1 tablespoon Morton's kosher salt, or 2½ teaspoons table salt. You can omit the pork.

This is the first of two dishes in this book in which a sea creature in the name of the dish does not appear in the ingredients (bonus points if you can figure out what the second one is). Shrimp with lobster sauce contains no lobster. Rather, it's shrimp served in a sauce that was originally paired with lobster by Cantonese immigrants in the northeastern United States, according to a *Toronto Life* interview with Chinese historians Leo and Arlene Chan. In menus at restaurants like New York's Shun Lee Palace, that sauce was a translucent mixture of Shaoxing wine and chicken stock, thickened with cornstarch and semi-scrambled egg whites, studded with bits of ground pork, scallions, ginger, and garlic.

As North Americans gained a taste for the sauce and lobster prices rose, the lobster was eventually replaced with cheaper shrimp (and often a handful of peas), and the dish "shrimp with lobster sauce" was born. As it traveled throughout the country, it evolved into a number of regional variations that still exist today. North, in Boston and Toronto, the same basic sauce was transformed into a brown gravy with the addition of dark soy sauce and sometimes fermented black beans. On the West Coast, the pork is often omitted in lieu of vegetables like carrots, corn, and mushrooms.

I prefer my shrimp with lobster sauce without the dark soy and fermented black beans, but I do enjoy including some vegetables in the mix. Stir-frying some beech or shiitake mushrooms with the shrimp is easy, because they both have the same cook time and can be stir-fried together before making the sauce.

Store-bought or homemade chicken stock works just fine for this dish, but since you're peeling shrimp anyway, we might as well eke out as much flavor as possible from them, and that means using the shells to fortify the stock with some shrimpiness. Another variation of the dish is to omit the shrimp and pork entirely and instead serve the sauce over quickly stir-fried greens (see Snow Pea Shoots with Lobster Sauce, page 207).

recipe continues

INGREDIENTS

For the Shrimp (see Notes):
2 cups (500 ml) very cold water
12.5 g salt (see Notes)
2 teaspoons (10 g) baking soda
12 ounces (340 g) large shrimp, peeled,
    shells reserved
A cup or so of ice cubes

For the Sauce:
2 tablespoons (30 ml) Shaoxing wine
1 cup (240 ml) homemade or store-bought
    low-sodium chicken stock or water
Reserved shrimp shells
½ teaspoon (2 g) sugar
Dash of freshly ground white pepper
Pinch of kosher salt

For the Cornstarch Slurry:
1 tablespoon (3 g) cornstarch
1 tablespoon (15 ml) water

For the Stir-Fry:
2 tablespoons (30 ml) peanut, rice bran, or
    other neutral oil
6 ounces (175 g) beech mushrooms, ends
    trimmed and discarded, or shiitake
    mushrooms, stems discarded and caps
    sliced
2 teaspoons (5 g) minced garlic (about 2
    medium cloves)
2 teaspoons (5 g) minced fresh ginger
    (about ½-inch segment)
2 scallions, chopped, white and green parts
    reserved separately
4 ounces (120 g) ground pork
Kosher salt and freshly ground white
    pepper
½ cup (70 g) frozen peas, thawed (optional)
2 large egg whites, lightly beaten with a
    pinch of kosher salt

DIRECTIONS

1 **For the Shrimp:** Combine the water, salt, and baking soda in a bowl and stir until the salt and baking soda are dissolved. Add the shrimp and stir to separate them and ensure the brine flows all around. Add the ice cubes and let the shrimp brine for at least 15 minutes and up to 30. Drain thoroughly and pat dry on paper towels or spin in a paper-towel-lined salad spinner.

2 **For the Sauce:** Combine the wine, stock or water, shrimp shells, sugar, white pepper, and salt in a small saucepan or in your wok. Bring to a simmer and cook for 10 minutes. Drain and reserve the shrimp stock (discard the shells). Combine the cornstarch and water in a separate small bowl and stir with a fork until the cornstarch is dissolved.

3 **BEFORE YOU STIR-FRY, GET YOUR BOWLS READY:**

a. **Brined shrimp and mushrooms**
b. **Garlic, ginger, and scallion whites**
c. **Ground pork**
d. **Sauce**
e. **Cornstarch slurry**

f. **Beaten egg whites**
g. **Empty bowl for cooked ingredients**
h. **Serving platter**

(4) **For the Stir-Fry:** Heat a wok over high heat until lightly smoking. Add 1 tablespoon (15 ml) of the oil and swirl to coat. Add the shrimp and mushrooms and stir-fry until the shrimp are pink all over but not quite cooked through (you can cut one open to check—the center should still be translucent) and the mushrooms are tender, about 2 minutes total. Transfer the shrimp and mushrooms to a bowl and set aside.

(5) Wipe out the wok and return it to high heat until smoking. Add the remaining tablespoon of oil and swirl to coat. Add the garlic, ginger, and scallion whites and stir-fry until fragrant, about 15 seconds. Immediately add the pork and stir-fry, breaking the pork up with a spatula until it is no longer pink, about 1 minute.

(6) Stir the sauce and add to the wok. Bring to a boil. Stir the cornstarch slurry and add it to the wok. Simmer until the sauce is thick enough to coat the back of a spoon, about 1 minute. Adjust the seasoning with salt and white pepper to taste and stir in the peas (if using).

(7) Drizzle the egg mixture into the sauce, then gently stir it with a ladle or wok spatula until the eggs form tender ribbons, about 30 seconds. Return the shrimp and mushrooms to the sauce and simmer until the shrimp are cooked through, about 30 seconds. Transfer to a serving platter and sprinkle with scallion greens.

Tofu and Peas with Lobster Sauce

Prepare Shrimp with Lobster Sauce, omitting the ingredients listed under "For the Shrimp," and using vegetable stock in place of chicken stock. In step 4, stir-fry the mushrooms on their own. Fold one 12-ounce block of silken tofu, diced, and 1 cup thawed frozen peas into the simmering sauce along with the mushrooms in step 6, then finish the dish and serve as directed.

CREAMY LAYERED SCRAMBLED EGGS (WHAMPOA EGGS)

My friends Steph Li and Christopher Thomas from the YouTube channel *Chinese Cooking Demystified* posted a video for what they called "Cantonese scrambled eggs" in September of 2020. It quickly became one of their most popular videos, and for a good reason: the eggs are spectacular. To make their version, they beat eggs with a cornstarch slurry and a drizzle of sesame oil, then pour them into a hot wok greased with lard. By repeatedly shifting the wok on and off the heat, they control how fast the eggs cook. As each layer of egg set on the bottom, they lift it with a spatula, letting more raw egg run off the top and into the bottom of the hot wok. By never actually stirring or flipping the eggs, you wind up with scrambled eggs that have layers of softly set curds, the tops of which are still moist and glistening, cooked only by the heat rising from the eggs below them.

Theirs is just one of many techniques for making Whampoa-style scrambled eggs.

The origins of the dish are not clear. Apocryphally, it was created by the boat-dwelling Tanka in Guandong's Whampoa anchorage, the main anchorage of the Pearl River Delta (a region that has been inhabited since the Neolithic era) and a necessary stop along maritime trade routes to Canton. In cheffy versions, the scrambled eggs are seasoned with a dash of fish sauce and lard, then cooked in a thin layer on the bottom of a wok and skillfully folded into glistening waves with a spatula before being arranged radially on a plate, the tops of the eggs resembling folds of golden silk. Street vendors make rapid-fire versions, the eggs never sitting still in the pan during their 15- second cook time before they're deposited in moist folds on disposable plates. (I've tried making both of these versions on numerous occasions, with varying degrees of failure.)

Other chefs insist that the egg whites be beaten separately into a soft foam before the yolks and seasonings are whisked in. This frothy scramble is then cooked extremely rapidly over high heat, folding and shaking the wok to prevent any browning of the eggs and pulling them out onto a plate while still semiraw, letting the residual heat finish them as they rest at the table.*

Sho Spaeth at *Serious Eats* offers a version his family made where paper-thin half-cooked omelets are stacked one of top of the other, the liquid eggs on the top of each one warming through with the residual heat of the next omelet stacked on top. (This version I can handle.)

Of the half dozen techniques I've tried, my favorite is inspired by Steph and Chris's recipe. The technique of whisking a cornstarch slurry into the eggs goes a long way toward foolproofing the dish. Plain eggs can go from tender to tough with just a few seconds of overcooking—part of what makes the cheffier recipes so difficult to master. This is because as scrambled eggs are heated, their proteins form a three-dimensional matrix that tightens up as it's heated. Eventually, it tightens enough that moisture will get squeezed out.

---

* There is a similar modern dish popular in Japan, Korea, and Taiwan called "tornado omelet." It starts as a thin layer of well-beaten egg ladled into a hot pan. As soon as the eggs are beginning to set and bubble around the edges, the cook gathers two sides and pulls them to the center of the pan with a pair of chopsticks and begins slowly rotating the pan so that the set curd forms an inverted vortex, its folds coated in a moist sheen of barely set egg. This tornado omelet is served on top of fried rice. (I can't make this one either, and not for lack of trying.)

Yield
Serves 2
to 3 (see
Notes)

Active Time
10 minutes

Total Time
10 minutes

NOTES

This recipe is easy to make for any number of people by scaling up all the ingredients and repeating step 4 as needed. You can omit the fish sauce and use ½ teaspoon salt and an optional ¼ teaspoon MSG in its place. Alternatively, season the eggs with only a bare pinch of salt and serve them with a drizzle of soy sauce on top. In place of the butter you can use lard or rendered bacon fat. Heat the fat in the wok or in the microwave until it is just barely melted before whisking it into the eggs in step 1.

The cornstarch slurry mitigates this effect by interfering with that protein matrix and preventing proteins from bonding together too tightly. Even slightly overcooked eggs stay moist and tender that way. Recipe writer Mandy Lee of the blog *Lady and Pups* uses this technique for extra-moist scrambled eggs. Many recipes I've seen from Guangdong also recommend adding clarified lard to the eggs. This adds richness while also helping to keep the eggs tender as they cook. I don't typically keep lard at home, and less-saturated oils don't really offer the same richness, so I wondered how butter would work. I incorporated it into the scrambled eggs in the same way I do for soft French omelets: dicing the butter into fine cubes and beating them into the eggs. The butter melts as the eggs cook, serving the dual purpose of enriching them while slowing down the cooking process to a manageable speed.

(If you keep a container of strained bacon fat in your kitchen, it's a wonderful variation on the dish. Heat it until it's just barely liquefied, then whisk it into the scrambled eggs in place of the butter or lard in my recipe.)

Aside from overcooking, there's only one other way to mess this dish up: not properly preheating your wok. If your wok is too cold when the eggs go in, they will stick to the bottom. The eggs should begin to sputter and bubble as soon as they hit the hot fat in the bottom of the wok. On Western burners with very wide rings, I find that sometimes the center of the wok will fail to preheat properly, so for egg dishes, I like to move the wok around as it preheats, making sure that the center of the wok spends some time directly over the flames.

If you're feeling decadent or happen to have a few spare egg yolks lying around because you used up the whites in a marinade or lobster sauce, make this dish with a combination of whole eggs and egg yolks for extra-creamy richness.

recipe continues

INGREDIENTS

6 large eggs (or 4 eggs plus 4 egg yolks)
2 teaspoons (10 ml) fish sauce (optional; see Notes)
1 teaspoon (3 g) cornstarch whisked together with 1 tablespoon (15 ml) water
2 tablespoons (about 30 g) unsalted butter, cut into small cubes (see Notes)
2 tablespoons (30 ml) peanut, rice bran, or other neutral oil or lard or bacon fat
Handful of sliced scallions or chives (optional)

DIRECTIONS

(1) In a large bowl, beat the eggs very thoroughly with a whisk, a fork, or a pair of chopsticks. This process should take at least 1 minute, and when you are done, the egg should be completely smooth. Test this by lifting your utensil up out of the eggs, letting them drizzle back down. There should be no visible strands or lumps. If there are, keep beating.

(2) Add the fish sauce (if using), cornstarch slurry, and butter to the eggs and beat to incorporate (the butter will stay solid at this stage).

(3) Heat a wok over high heat until lightly smoking, moving it around the burner so that the entire bottom surface heats evenly. Reduce the heat to medium-low. Add 1 tablespoon (15 ml) of the oil and swirl to coat. Immediately add half of the egg mixture. It should immediately start to bubble and puff. Swirl the wok around to make the omelet as wide as possible. Continue swirling until the liquid egg no longer forms deep pools, 15 to 30 seconds total. Remove the wok from the heat, then, using a wok spatula, carefully push the omelet from one side of the wok to the other, lifting and layering it as you go. Make sure not to fold the omelet; the goal is to leave a layer of liquid egg on top. When the omelet is gathered to one side, lift it out and place it on a plate. (It's OK if it breaks and you lift it in sections.)

(4) Wipe out the wok with a paper towel, return it to high heat until lightly smoking, reduce the heat to medium-low, and repeat the process with the second batch of eggs, shingling them over the first batch on the plate as they are finished. Sprinkle with scallions or chives (if desired), let the eggs rest for 20 to 30 seconds, and serve.

HOME-STYLE TOMATO AND SCRAMBLED EGGS

My wife, Adri, grew up in Colombia, and until she moved to the United States her exposure to Chinese food was relatively limited. So I was surprised when one morning I woke up to find her cooking scrambled eggs with tomatoes and scallions. It was a dish I was familiar with from my own childhood, when my mother would occasionally cook it for a quick lunch on Saturday afternoons between my Japanese school and music school classes. She, in turn, learned the dish from her mother, my grandmother, Yasuko, who would serve it to her when she was a toddler. Yasuko called it *to-tama*, a play on the word *tomato* and the Japanese word for egg, *tamago*.

In China, it's called *fanqie chao dan* (literally "tomato fried egg"), and it's a dish that is simultaneously ubiquitous—all children are familiar with their own home-cooked version—but also hidden to casual visitors. It won't appear on restaurant menus, as it isn't a restaurant dish. It's unlikely to appear in a Chinese cookbook just as it would be unlikely to find a recipe for buttered toast in an American cookbook. Francis Lam wrote an article for the *New York Times* about it, in which he described it as "like air, present and invisible [in Chinese cooking]."

As it turns out, the Colombian version of the dish, called *huevos pericos*, shares no heritage with the Chinese, but it's telling that people in both countries independently discovered the sweet-tart-savory-tender magic of tomatoes and eggs cooked together. It doesn't stop there. It's in Italy in Roman *uova all'Amatriciana* and Neapolitan *ova' 'mpriatorio* (eggs in purgatory).

recipe continues

In France you find *oeufs Provençal*. It's the same flavors you'll find in the Arab dish *shakshuka*, the related Turkish dish *menemen* (though in the case of menemen, the addition of onions is a hotly contested subject), the Parsi *tomato per eedu*, or Mexican *huevos rancheros*. There's even a strong vocal minority of folks who will die on the hill that ketchup belongs on a fried egg breakfast sandwich.* The combination of eggs and tomatoes is one that crosses cultural lines and enters the realm of the universally delicious.

As a home-style Chinese dish, there's a huge amount of variation in technique (and don't let anyone tell you there's a right or wrong way to do it—the right way is the way you like it). My favorite way to make it is to think of it almost as a tomato-and-egg sauce for rice, rather than scrambled eggs with tomatoes. As such, the technique I use is somewhere in between the Creamy Layered Scrambled Eggs (page 162) and Slippery Eggs (pages 156 and 158).

I start by gently stir-frying the whites of a couple scallions in the wok before adding sliced tomatoes. Roma or small cherry tomatoes work best here, as they have a higher pectin content than larger beefsteak tomatoes. More pectin results in a thicker, more concentrated sauce (the same reason Roma-style tomatoes like San Marzano are so revered for Italian pasta sauces), which keeps the dish from being watery.

Once the tomatoes have broken down and started to concentrate, it's time to transform them into a sauce. For this, I first add a cornstarch slurry, which thickens up the juices and suspends the chunky bits of tomato. While it's perfectly fine to stop right there, if you want to really boost tomato, use a trick I learned from KP Kwan of the YouTube channel *Taste of Asian Food*: add a dash of ketchup. Yes, ketchup! My old friend and colleague Chichi Wang suggests the same in her recipe on *Serious Eats*. As she says, "We could go back and forth all day about whether or not ketchup oughta be a legitimate condiment in Chinese cuisine. My feeling . . . is that ketchup makes the tomatoes taste more like themselves," and she's right. A small dab of ketchup adds concentrated tomato flavor while also adding some sweetness and tartness to balance out the dish.

At this point, many recipes will have you remove the tomato sauce from the wok to cook the eggs before stirring the sauce back in. I prefer to drizzle my eggs—seasoned with a dash of fish sauce and moistened with cubes of butter and a cornstarch slurry—directly into the simmering tomato mixture, gently folding them until the entire thing is silky and tender.

---

* They are wrong.

Yield
Serves 2 to
3 with rice

Active Time
15 minutes

Total Time
15 minutes

INGREDIENTS

For the Eggs:

6 large eggs
2 teaspoons (10 ml) fish sauce (optional; see Notes)
2 tablespoons (about 30 g) unsalted butter, cut into small cubes (see Notes)

For the Cornstarch Slurry:

2 teaspoons (6 g) cornstarch
¼ cup (60 ml) water

For the Stir-Fry:

2 tablespoons (30 ml) peanut, rice bran, or other neutral oil
4 scallions, chopped, dark green parts reserved separately
8 to 12 ounces (230 to 340 g) ripe Roma or large cherry tomatoes, cut into bite-sized chunks (about 5 Roma tomatoes or 1 pint cherry tomatoes)
Kosher salt and freshly ground white pepper
1 tablespoon (15 ml) ketchup
1 teaspoon (4 g) sugar

DIRECTIONS

(1) **For the Eggs:** In a large bowl, beat the eggs very thoroughly with a whisk, a fork, or a pair of chopsticks. This process should take at least 1 minute, and when you are done, the egg should be completely smooth. Test this by lifting your utensil up out of the eggs, letting them drizzle back down. There should be no visible strands or lumps. If there are, keep beating.

(2) **For the Cornstarch Slurry:** Combine the cornstarch and water in a separate small bowl and stir with a fork until the cornstarch is dissolved.

(3) Add half of the cornstarch slurry (set aside the other half for now), the fish sauce, and the butter to the eggs and beat to incorporate (the butter will stay solid at this stage).

(4) **For the Stir-Fry:** Heat the oil in a wok over high heat until shimmering. Add the scallion whites and pale greens and cook, stirring, until aromatic, about 15 seconds. Add the tomatoes, a pinch of salt, a pinch of white pepper, the ketchup, and the sugar and cook, stirring, until the tomatoes break down and release their juices but still have some of their shape, about 2 minutes. Stir the remaining cornstarch slurry and add it to the wok.

(5) As soon as the sauce has thickened, add the beaten egg mixture and cook, folding and occasionally stirring gently, until the eggs are barely set and the sauce is silky, rich, and no longer watery, about 1 minute. Fold in the scallion greens, season to taste with salt and white pepper, transfer to a serving bowl, and serve immediately with steamed rice.

KHAI JIAO (THAI-STYLE OMELET)

If a sliding omelet scale based on how violently they are cooked existed, all the way on the left side would be French omelets, with their pale golden color and tender, custardy curd. Slide that to the right a little bit and you'd arrive at American-style diner omelets: a little bit firmer, with a pale golden-brown exterior. Push that slider all the way to the right and you get Thai-style *khai jiao*. Rather than custardy and dense, Thai omelets are fluffy and light, with deeply browned crispy edges and layers of texture. Imagine a deep-fried cloud—a deep-fried cloud that you'd want to serve on top of rice with a drizzle of Sriracha or nam pla prik—and you're on the right track.

These omelets are a ubiquitous street food across Thailand, where an omelet on top of a pile of warm jasmine rice makes a quick lunch on the go. The simplest versions are nothing but eggs beaten with a touch of fish sauce and white pepper before being poured into a hot wok with just enough hot oil to shallow-fry the eggs. As the eggs go in, their water content is rapidly converted to steam, which causes the omelet to puff dramatically around the edges (and in the best omelets, there are a lot of these jagged, crispy, puffy edges). After around 20 seconds of cooking, the bottom side is golden brown and ready for a flip (I use two spatulas when flipping these types of omelets to keep from accidentally splashing hot oil onto myself). After another 20 seconds, it's done.

There are only three things to be aware of when cooking Thai omelets. The first is oil temperature. Your oil needs to be piping hot before you pour in the eggs for the eggs to puff properly. I heat around a cup of oil over high heat until it registers 375°F (190°C) before adding the eggs and slightly reducing the heat. (If you don't want to use a thermometer, just heat the oil until the very first wisp of smoke appears). Second, the eggs needs to be thoroughly beaten. There should be no lumpy bits of white or yolk, and there should be plenty of frothy bubbles in the raw egg mixture before you pour it into the oil (pouring the eggs from a height will create a more irregular shape, which increases the amount of crispy edges the omelet will have). Third, you should have a plate of steamed rice ready and waiting for the omelet before you start cooking. These omelets are fluffy, crispy, and light when they come out of the wok, but they will turn limp and greasy after a few minutes, so eat up fast!

Yield
Serves 1

Active Time
6 minutes

Total Time
7 minutes

NOTE

This recipe serves only one person, but it's incredibly fast. To cook more than one omelet, have the egg mixture for subsequent omelets already beaten and ready to go in bowls. After cooking and serving the first omelet, there's no need to empty the wok or strain the leftover oil. Just add enough fresh oil to bring the total amount up to around ½ cup and let the oil reheat before cooking the next omelet. Any errant bits of egg left from the first omelet will become part of the second.

INGREDIENTS

8 large eggs
1 teaspoon (5 ml) fish sauce
Small pinch of sugar (optional)
Small pinch of freshly ground white pepper (optional)
½ cup (120 ml) peanut, rice bran, or other neutral oil

To Serve:

1 cup steamed rice, ready and waiting on a plate
Sriracha or Nam Pla Prik (page 257)

If you want a heartier meal, Thai omelets are infinitely variable, and I've included some of my favorite variations after the recipe. So long as you cut your add-ins into small pieces (think about how you'd prepare ingredients for a Western-style omelet or a frittata) and keep the total amount of add-ins to around 3 ounces or less for every two-egg omelet, you can let your creativity run wild. This is an especially good way to use up leftovers from the fridge. These omelets are also a fun way to let guests or family members customize their meals by picking and choosing exactly which ingredients go into their eggs.

DIRECTIONS

(1) Break the eggs into a medium bowl. Add the fish sauce, sugar (if using), and white pepper (if using). Beat very thoroughly with a whisk, a fork, or a pair of chopsticks. This process should take at least 1 minute, and when you are done, the egg should be completely smooth. Test this by lifting your utensil up out of the eggs, letting them drizzle back down. There should be no visible strands or lumps. If there are, keep beating. The eggs should be frothy and bubbly.

(2) Heat the oil in a wok over high heat until it registers 375°F (190°C) on an instant-read thermometer or until you see the very first faint wisps of smoke. Immediately pour the egg mixture into the center of the wok and reduce the heat to medium (if using an outdoor wok burner, you'll need to reduce the heat down to very low) in a steady stream over the course of 3 to 5 seconds. The eggs should immediately puff and sputter.

(3) Cook, swirling the wok gently and pushing the eggs around with the back of a spatula until the edges are golden brown and the bottom is golden brown, about 30 seconds. Using 2 spatulas (see step-by-step photos on page 170), carefully flip the omelet.

(4) Cook the second side, swirling gently, until the eggs are cooked through and the second side is golden brown, about 20 seconds longer. Lift the eggs with a wide spatula and allow the excess fat to drain off them, then place them on top of the rice and serve immediately with sriracha or nam pla prik.

recipe continues

Making a Thai Omelet, Step by Step

Step 1 • Beat the Eggs

Beating the eggs until frothy will make the omelet puff more.

Step 2 • Pour the Eggs into Hot Oil

Pouring the eggs into hot oil in a steady stream from a height will increase the amount of crispy bits.

Step 3 • Carefully Flip the Omelet

Use two spatulas when flipping the omelet, using one to flip it onto the other before lowering it back into the oil to reduce the risk of splashing.

Step 4 • Serve Immediately

Your plate of rice should be ready and waiting so that you can dig straight in (after adding a dash of sriracha or nam pla prik).

Thai-Style Omelet with Ground Pork and Shallots

Follow the recipe, but in step 1, add 2 ounces of raw ground pork and 1 small shallot, thinly sliced, to the eggs as you beat them. Proceed as directed. (Don't worry, the pork will cook through!)

Thai-Style Omelet with Green Beans, Chiles, and Herbs

Follow the recipe but in step 1, add a small handful of green beans cut into ½-inch pieces, a finely chopped hot chile (such as Thai bird, jalapeño, or serrano), a chopped scallion, and a small handful of roughly chopped basil or cilantro leaves to the eggs as you beat them. Proceed as directed.

Thai-Style Omelet with Crab, Shrimp, or Oyster

Follow the recipe but in step 1, add 2 ounces picked lump crabmeat, roughly chopped raw shrimp, or a few raw shucked oysters (canned or smoked oysters work fine for this), along with a chopped scallion and a small handful of roughly chopped cilantro leaves to the eggs as you beat them. Proceed as directed.

Vegetables in the Wok

I remember walking into the kitchen of my college fraternity house one afternoon as our cook, Clint, was making dinner. On the menu were beef and broccoli and a vegetarian stir-fry with broccoli, carrots, green beans, and red bell peppers. We chatted as he stirred the contents of the large rondeau with a wooden spoon, raw vegetables coming halfway up the sides of the pan and a big cloud of steam emanating from within. When the vegetables had cooked for a good ten minutes, some of them still raw, some softened to a drab brown, he glugged in a few cups of food-service all-purpose teriyaki marinade and sauce.

By the time dinnertime rolled around half an hour later, the "stir-fry" was a drab vegetable stew. I distinctly remember eating those sauce-saturated broccoli florets and thinking that Clint was a much better conversationalist than cook (at least when it came to Asian food; his chicken soup and pan pizzas were fantastic).

Ever since their introduction to Western cooks, woks have had a cozy-but-troubled relationship with vegetables and health-conscious cookery. On the one hand, the idea is enticing. We've all had perfectly cooked vegetables from good Chinese restaurants that retain their brightness and crunch while simultaneously developing complex flavors layered with aromatics, sauces, and smoky *wok hei*. On the other hand, we've also experienced a Clint-style motley mix of vegetables, cooked together until it's tough to distinguish the green beans from the bell peppers.

So what's the trick? How do you stir-fry vegetables *right*?

The rules for cooking vegetables in a wok are similar to the rules for cooking meat. Here is my basic advice (and of course, there are some recipes in this book that will flatly ignore some of these rules, but we'll get to those).

VEGETABLE STIR-FRY RULE #1:
Cut vegetables into uniform, bite-sized pieces.

In most stir-fries, your vegetables should spend no more than a minute or two inside the wok, and in that time they need to cook through and pick up flavor. Greens like bok choy or romaine lettuce should be roughly chopped, green vegetables like green beans or broccoli should be sliced on a bias into 1- to 2-inch pieces, root vegetables like carrots or radishes should be cut thin enough to heat through rapidly.

VEGETABLE STIR-FRY RULE #2:
Dry vegetables thoroughly after washing.

Remember: it takes about five times more energy to evaporate a single drop of water than it does to raise the temperature of that water all the way from freezing to boiling. Any moisture left clinging to vegetables will significantly lower the temperature of your wok, leading to less-than-optimal flavor development. It's a good idea to spin any washed vegetables through a salad spinner before stir-frying, unless they're going to be blanched first (see the next rule).

VEGETABLE STIR-FRY RULE #3:
Blanch (or microwave) green vegetables.

Green vegetables such as asparagus, broccoli, green beans, and baby bok choy are especially sensitive to heat. It's possible to stir-fry them from raw, but it's very difficult to get them to cook evenly this way. The bit in direct contact with the wok will cook much faster than the bits just above the wok, while the bits at the very top will absorb very little energy at all. Even with constant stirring and tossing, even cooking is not an easy accomplishment. Blanching green vegetables will ensure that the vegetables cook through evenly while simultaneously enhancing their color. (See "Blanching Green Vegetables for Stir-Fries" on page 173 for more details.)

VEGETABLE STIR-FRY RULE #4:
Don't cook the whole garden.

The more vegetables you add to your wok, the more difficult it becomes to nail the perfect cook on every one. If you are planning on making up your own stir-fried vegetable recipe (and you should!), try to stick to a manageable number of options. Three different vegetables is about as complex as I'd get.

VEGETABLE STIR-FRY RULE #5:
Don't crowd the wok.

With their high water content and propensity for softening rather than searing, vegetables suffer from a crowded wok even more than meat. Do not cook more than around a half pound of raw vegetables or a pound of blanched vegetables at a time. If you're using more than this, cook the vegetables in batches, transferring them to a separate bowl as you cook each successive batch before adding them all back to the wok to toss with the sauce at the end.

VEGETABLE STIR-FRY RULE #6:
Don't overcook.

As vegetables cook, the pectin glue that holds together their cells will begin to break down. Simultaneously, cells themselves will lose moisture, causing vegetables to turn limp and lose their bright color and fresh flavor. The most crucial step when stir-frying vegetables is getting them out of the wok right when they are done, and not a moment later.

Sidebar

Blanching Green Vegetables for Stir-Fries

I've always taken it as a given that green vegetables should be blanched in hot water then shocked in ice water before stir-frying. But is it really necessary? To test this, I stir-fried two batches of Chinese Broccoli with Oyster Sauce (page 205):

1. Broccoli blanched in boiling water for 45 seconds, then shocked in cold water, drained, then added to the stir-fry

2. Stir-fried directly from raw

Immediately there were noticeable differences between the batches. Vegetables stir-fried from raw take longer in the pan, and because the heat in a wok is so strongly directional and fierce, it's difficult to get them to soften evenly. You wind up with vegetables that are charred and soft in some spots but still raw and fibrous in others. Moreover, the blanched broccoli came out with a much more vibrant green color than the broccoli stir-fried from raw.

This was the case whether I was cooking broccoli, snap peas, or string beans. The results of vegetables cooked from raw aren't *bad*—I might consider skipping blanching on nights when I'm in a rush—but if you've got a few extra minutes, blanching is worth the trouble.

So how about shocking in ice water? Do we really need to dunk our vegetables in ice water after boiling them if we're going to be reheating them again so soon?

I cooked up another two batches, blanching the broccoli in both batches, but shocking only one in cold water. The other I simply fished out with a spider and transferred it to a sheet tray and spread it into a single layer, where I let it sit on the kitchen counter while I prepped the remaining ingredients for the stir-fry.

Surprisingly, it turned out that the unshocked broccoli was better than the broccoli that was shocked! The reason? Shocking chills your vegetables fast, but it also leaves them wet, and even a salad spinner can't completely rid them of that cold water. Wet vegetables means rapid cool-down when you add them to the wok (remember: evaporating water takes far more energy than simply heating water), which in turn means more time in the wok, which translates to overcooked broccoli.

Blanching and setting them aside while still steaming hot, on the other hand, allows your vegetables to cool rapidly enough to retain color while simultaneously coming out nice and dry as the hot water clinging to them readily evaporates. By the time they hit the wok, they're bright green and perfectly dry, ready for a toss through the oil and sauce.

Cooking Multiple Vegetable Dishes for One Meal

When stir-frying a dish that requires blanching vegetables, I always start by boiling salted water in my wok while I prepare my ingredients so that the water is hot and ready as soon as I'm ready to cook. I blanch my vegetables, drain them and dump the water, then start my stir-fry. But what if I wanted to cook a couple vegetable dishes that both require blanching for the same meal?

Let's say, I'm making Beef with Broccoli (page 118) as well as Spring Vegetables with Olives and Sichuan Peppercorns (page 176). One method is to do all the blanching at the beginning: Boil the water, blanch the broccoli, fish it out using a spider and transfer it to a rimmed baking sheet to cool and dry, then blanch the asparagus, followed by the snap peas, and so on.

In fact, blanching green vegetables is something you can do well ahead of time. If I know I have a few stir-fries that I'm going to be cooking over the next couple of days, I'll blanch all of my green vegetables in a single batch of boiling water (blanching them in succession), let them steam dry, then store them in the fridge until I'm ready to stir-fry.

Another solution I turn to from time to time is the microwave.

If one were to ask the Internet to vote on the Most

Depressing Cookbook Ever, a 1999 volume called *Microwave Cooking for One* would be a top-seeded contender. This is a malignment only slightly less unfair than the disdain microwave ovens themselves receive.

Would you believe me if I told you that some of the greatest restaurants in the world rely on microwaves to cook green vegetables? It's true! (I mentioned the process, as it applies to Western cooking, in my first book, *The Food Lab*, under the section "Micro-steaming.")

Why are microwaves so great at blanching green vegetables? Let's quickly take a look at how they work. Microwaves are a form of electromagnetic radiation. Sounds scary, but don't be afraid. Not all forms of EM radiation (as we'll refer to it from now on) are dangerous. We'd be in a lot of trouble if it weren't around. It's literally everywhere. The ultraviolet rays that are blocked by your carefully applied sunblock are EM radiation. The gamma rays that transform Bruce Banner into the Hulk are EM radiation. The X-rays the doctor used to image the hairline fracture in my daughter's elbow were EM radiation. The cell towers and WiFi routers that beam music to your iPhone (or the waves that beam your shopping, browsing, and travel habits to EvilMegaCorp.com) use EM radiation. The warm glow of a fire is EM radiation. The heat emitted from your space heater is EM radiation. The very light that we see is EM radiation.

Some wavelengths are inherently dangerous, some are safe, and some are only dangerous if you jam the door open and stick your head inside the metal box while it's operating. Microwave ovens work through a process called *dielectric heating*. Essentially, dipoles—that is, molecules that have an imbalance of positive and negative charges from one end to the other—will align themselves in an electromagnetic field. If that field is rapidly shifting, as it is when microwaves are beamed at them from the magnetron housed in the side of your microwave oven, those molecules will oscillate rapidly—billions of times per second—creating heat.

Water is one such molecule, with the oxygen side holding a negative charge and the hydrogen sides holding a positive charge. (Both fat and sugars are also dipoles, but much weaker than water.) Because vegetables are composed largely of water, they heat up extremely efficiently in a microwave oven.

This is good news for stir-fries, as it means you can par-cook your green vegetables and get them stir-fry ready in a matter of minutes, no big pot of boiling water necessary.

The only downsides? Microwaves tend to cook unevenly, which means you either have to be OK with slightly unevenly cooked vegetables or be very diligent in stopping the microwave to stir and toss every 15- to 20 seconds. Some very strongly flavored brassicas, such as mustard greens or particularly hot Chinese broccoli, also benefit from an actual dunk in boiling water to help dilute some of their bitterness.

Here's how I micro-steam vegetables:

Step 1 • Prep

Prep vegetables by peeling, trimming, and cutting as needed. Place vegetables in a microwave-safe bowl* and add a couple tablespoons of water.

Step 2 • Cover

Cover with a lid, plastic wrap, or a second, slightly smaller microwave-safe bowl inverted over the first.

Step 3 • Cook

Microwave on high power at 15-second intervals, stirring and repeating until the vegetables are tender-crisp, usually around 1 minute total.

---

* Believe it or not, that includes metal bowls. Modern microwaves can handle metal bowls without issue. However, avoid putting sharp or crinkly metallic objects, such as forks or aluminum foil in a microwave. With irregular shapes, electrons that freely move about in metal tend to aggregate at points, creating a heavy charge differential that can lead to arcing – the electric discharge created as air converts to a plasma – either within the metallic object itself or between the object and the microwave wall. It's the same principle by which a lightning rod attracts lightning, except rather than safely leading the current into the ground, an arcing microwave can damage the microwave and whatever happens to be inside it at the moment.

HOW TO PREPARE ANY VEGETABLE FOR A STIR-FRY

VEGETABLE	HOW TO PREPARE
Broccoli (Western)	Separate florets into bite-sized pieces. Peel thick stems, split in half or quarters lengthwise, and cut on a sharp bias into 1- to 2-inch pieces. Blanch in boiling salted water for 1 minute, drain, and spread on a baking sheet to cool and air-dry.
Broccolini or gai lan (Chinese broccoli)	Cut on a bias into 1- to 2-inch pieces. Blanch in boiling salted water for 1 minute, drain, and spread on a baking sheet to cool and air-dry.
Cabbages such as Napa, bok choy, and green	Discard core. Cut into 1½- to 2-inch squares.
Carrots	Peel and cut into fine matchsticks or split in half or into quarters lengthwise and slice on a sharp bias.
Cauliflower	Discard core. Separate florets into bite-sized pieces. Blanch in boiling salted water for 1 minute, drain, and spread on a baking sheet to cool and air-dry.
Celery	Cut on a sharp bias into 1- to 2-inch pieces or dice.
Fresh corn	Cut kernels off of cob.
Eggplant	Cut into pieces, soak in a 6 percent brine solution (60 g salt per liter of water, about ⅓ cup kosher salt per quart of water) for 10 to 20 minutes, drain, and spin in salad spinner or pat dry with paper towels.
Green vegetables such as snap peas, snow peas, green beans, and asparagus	Trim and slice on a bias into bite-sized pieces. Blanch in boiling salted water for 1 minute, drain, and spread on a baking sheet to cool and air-dry.
Hearty greens such as kale, mustard, or collard greens	Remove and discard tough stems. Roughly chop leaves. Blanch in boiling salted water for 1 minute, drain, and spread on a baking sheet to cool and air-dry.
Leafy greens such as spinach, mizuna, or tatsoi	Wash and spin dry in a salad spinner.
Lettuces such as romaine or iceberg	Roughly chop, wash, and spin dry in a salad spinner.
Mushrooms	Trim stems. Small mushrooms like beech and enoki can be cooked whole. Slice larger mushrooms.
Onion	Cut into slivers or dice.
Peppers, such as bell, shishito, or Anaheim	Cut into slivers or dice.
Potatoes (russet or Yukon gold)	Peel and cut into fine matchsticks and wash in several changes of water until no starch can be seen.
Potatoes (new or fingerling)	Boil in heavily salted water until tender, then drain.
Radishes and small turnips	Scrub clean, trim greens, and cut into bite-sized sections.
Shoots, such as pea shoots or fava bean shoots	Wash and spin dry in a salad spinner.
Scallions	Cut on a bias into 1- to 2-inch segments.

SPRING VEGETABLES WITH OLIVES AND SICHUAN PEPPERCORNS

Yield
Serves 4

Active Time
15 minutes

Total Time
30 minutes

INGREDIENTS

For the Green Vegetables:
Kosher salt

8 ounces (225 g) asparagus, cut on a bias into 2-inch pieces

4 ounces (about 1 cup/120 g) shelled English peas or frozen peas, thawed

8 ounces (about 2 cups/225 g) sugar snap peas, split in half on a sharp bias

For the Stir Fry:
3 tablespoons (45 ml) peanut, rice bran, or other neutral oil

4 ounces (120 g) shiitake mushrooms, stems discarded, caps cut into ¼-inch slices

4 small hot dried chiles (such as árbol or Japones), stems removed, snipped into ½-inch pieces with kitchen shears

1 teaspoon (2 g) Sichuan peppercorns

¼ cup (about 3 ounces/80 g) pitted kalamata or other black olives, minced

1 tablespoon (7.5 g) minced garlic (about 3 medium cloves)

1 tablespoon (7.5 g) minced fresh ginger (about ¾-inch segment)

1 tablespoon (15 ml) light soy sauce or shoyu

1 tablespoon (15 ml) Chinkiang or balsamic vinegar

This recipe started as a dinner party where I planned on stir-frying some green beans to serve alongside a batch of Mapo Tofu (this is the format for many of my dinner parties). But seeing as it was early spring, I decided to alter the recipe and pair it with my favorite springtime activity: raiding the vegetable section.

Asparagus, peas, and snap peas might not be typical ingredients at your average Chengdu greasy spoon—but hey, we've managed to transform Western broccoli, something almost entirely unheard of in China, into the most common vegetable on the takeout menu, so why not branch out even farther? In fact, I ended up taking it an extra step farther from China by adding a handful of olives I found languishing in the back of my fridge. The end result is a sort of play on the traditional Sichuan combination of long green beans stir-fried with preserved mustard root (ya cai, which has a pungent, salty flavor similar to that of olives).

And because I happened to spot some morel mushrooms at the farmers' market and they have such an affinity for green vegetables, I ended up adding some of those to the stir-fry as well. It was lip-smackingly delicious.

Since that initial accidental dinner, I've made similar dishes using different vegetables (fiddleheads, snow peas, and, yes, green beans all work well) as well as different mushrooms (the written recipe calls for shiitake, which are more widely available than morels, but use any mushroom you'd like—maitake are especially tasty) while keeping the same base flavor and the same technique. I haven't run into a single failure yet, which leads me to believe that in the future maybe I'll just stir-fry ALL THE VEGETABLES.

DIRECTIONS

(1) **For the Green Vegetables:** Bring a couple quarts of heavily salted water to a boil in a wok. Add the asparagus, peas, and sugar snap peas and cook for 1 minute. Drain the vegetables and transfer to a couple of large plates or a rimmed baking sheet. Spread into a single layer and let the vegetables air-dry and cool while you prepare the remaining ingredients.

(2) **For the Stir-Fry:** Heat a wok over high heat until lightly smoking. Add 1 tablespoon (15 ml) of the oil and swirl to coat. Add the mushrooms and stir-fry until spotty brown and crisp in spots, about 1 minute. Transfer to the tray with the green vegetables.

(3) Return the wok to high heat until smoking. Add the remaining 2 tablespoons (30 ml) oil and swirl to coat. Immediately add the dried chiles and Sichuan peppercorns and cook until aromatic, about 10 seconds. Immediately add the olives, garlic, and ginger and cook, stirring frequently, until fragrant, about 30 seconds. Return the mushrooms and vegetables to the wok and toss to combine. Swirl in the soy sauce and vinegar around the edge of the wok and toss to combine. Transfer to a serving platter and serve immediately.

STIR-FRIED CORN AND MUSHROOMS WITH HOT PEPPERS AND SOY BUTTER

Yield
Serves 4

Active Time
15 minutes

Total Time
15 minutes

NOTE
You can use frozen corn for this recipe. Thaw the corn and spin it in a paper-towel-lined salad spinner to remove excess moisture.

INGREDIENTS

2 tablespoons (30 ml) peanut, rice bran, or other neutral oil
2 coin-sized slices fresh ginger (10 g)
6 ounces (175 g) shiitake mushrooms, stems discarded and caps thinly sliced
4 medium garlic cloves (12 g), thinly sliced
12 fresh hot chiles, such as Chinese cowhorn, Anaheim, jalapeño, or serrano (or fewer to taste), split in half, stem, seeds, and ribs removed, thinly sliced on a bias
1½ cups (about 9 ounces/260 g) fresh corn kernels, cut from 4 ears fresh corn (see Note)
2 tablespoons (30 g) unsalted butter
1 tablespoon (15 ml) light soy sauce or shoyu
Kosher salt

Grilled corn drizzled with soy sauce and melted butter is a common street snack in Japan (and my backyard during the summer). In this dish I decided to combine the same flavors—butter and soy sauce and corn—in a simple stir-fry.

Corn is a unique vegetable because, well, it's not really a vegetable. It's a grain, and as for all grains, each kernel is covered in a hard layer called the *pericarp*. This layer is very good at standing up to prolonged cooking, making it nearly impossible to overcook corn. This is particularly useful when stir-frying, as it means you can easily let the corn in the wok develop a nice nutty char without worrying about it turning mushy.

Corn works well with hot peppers, so I add some long green peppers thinly sliced on a bias to this stir-fry (any hot pepper like serrano or jalapeño would do), as well as some shiitake mushrooms for texture and some umami depth. It's delicious as a side dish for pork or chicken or simply on its own over a bowl of rice.

recipe continues

DIRECTIONS

(1) Heat a wok over high heat until lightly smoking. Add 1 tablespoon (15 ml) of the oil and swirl to coat. Add 1 slice of the ginger and let it sizzle for 10 seconds. Immediately add the mushrooms and stir-fry until spotty brown and crisp in spots, about 1 minute. Add the garlic and hot peppers and stir-fry until fragrant and the garlic is lightly browned, about 30 seconds. Transfer to a bowl and set aside.

(2) Return the wok to high heat until lightly smoking. Add the remaining tablespoon (15 ml) of oil and swirl to coat. Add the remaining ginger and let it sizzle for 10 seconds. Add the corn and cook, stirring and tossing occasionally, until the corn is blistered and lightly blackened in spots, about 5 minutes.

(3) Return the mushrooms, garlic, and chiles to the wok. Add the butter. Swirl in the soy sauce around the edges of the wok. Toss to combine until the butter is melted. Season to taste with salt, transfer to a serving platter, and serve immediately.

TIGER-SKIN PEPPERS

I remember driving through Hatch, New Mexico, during chile-roasting season one summer on a cross-country road trip. The smell that permeated the air was intoxicating. Smoky, charred, sweet, grassy, and hot.

A few summers later, on the opposite side of the planet, I smelled the same aroma at a restaurant in Chongqing, where I'd asked the chef to prepare their specialties. As the server deposited a plate at my table and I inhaled its scent, I was transported back to that summer driving through New Mexico. I guess charred, blackened chiles are a universally appealing aroma.

The dish was *hupi qingjiao*, or "tiger-skin peppers," so called because of the way pepper skins will split as they char, forming stripes like a tiger's coat. It's a simple, chile-forward dish with only a few auxiliary ingredients to complement the pepper flavor. In Chongqing, the dish was made with small, moderately hot Hunan peppers called *xiao qingjiao* (literally "small green pepper"), but back here in the United States I use whatever I can get my hands on. When Hatch chile season rolls around and I can find them, I snatch them up. Otherwise, regular old Anaheims (a milder California cultivar of the same New Mexico chiles) or long green peppers from the Asian supermarket work well.

There are many techniques for roasting the chiles, but my favorite is the one that produces the most char: cooking the chiles in a dry wok, pressing on them firmly with the bottom of my wok spatula to get really good contact between the chiles and the metal. When the wok is the right temperature, you should be able to feel the vibrations in your spatula as the chiles bubble and split under the heat and pressure.

Once the chiles are tender and charred, the rest is a quick stir-fry of garlic seasoned with soy sauce. The recipe includes directions for adding pork to the stir-fry, but the pork is completely optional. I leave it out most of the time. The chiles are the real star here.

recipe continues

Yield
Serves 4

Active Time
10 minutes

Total Time
10 minutes

NOTES

This recipe will work with any green, moderately hot to hot chile, such as Chinese cowhorn chiles, padrón, or even serranos or jalapeños (if you like it real hot). The pork is optional. If you prefer to leave it out, just skip the bit where you stir-fry it in step 2, jumping straight to adding the garlic instead.

INGREDIENTS

12 ounces (350 g) fresh long green hot chiles such as Hatch or Anaheim (see Notes), stems removed

2 tablespoons (30 ml) peanut, rice bran, or other neutral oil

2 ounces (60 g) ground pork (optional; see Notes)

2 tablespoons (15 g) minced garlic (about 6 medium cloves)

1 tablespoon (15 ml) light soy sauce or shoyu

Pinch of kosher salt

Pinch of sugar

DIRECTIONS

(1) Heat a dry wok over medium-high heat until lightly smoking. Add the chiles, spread them into a single layer, and cook, tossing occasionally and pressing firmly on the chiles with a spatula to make good contact between the chiles and the wok. Cook until the chiles are blistered and browned on all sides, about 6 minutes total. Transfer the chiles to a bowl and set aside.

(2) Return the wok to medium-high heat until lightly smoking. Add the oil, swirl to coat, and immediately add pork (if using). Stir-fry until the pork is no longer pink, about 30 seconds then immediately add the garlic. Stir-fry until fragrant, about 15 seconds. Return the chiles to the wok and toss to combine. Splash in the soy sauce around the edges of the wok and season with a pinch of salt and sugar. Toss to combine, transfer to a serving platter, and serve with steamed rice.

Sichuan-Style Blistered Green Beans

SICHUAN-STYLE BLISTERED GREEN BEANS

Gan bian si ji dou—Sichuan-style dry-fried green beans with chiles and pickles—is one of my favorite vegetable dishes in the world. It's a bright and flavorful dish, featuring beans with blistered skins and snappy interiors, plenty of mouth-tingling Sichuan peppercorns, and the funky aroma of ya cai—preserved mustard root—along with plenty of garlic and ginger.

While many restaurants will start the dish off by deep frying green beans or long beans to get them to blister and shrivel, doing this prevents the beans from charring in spots, an essential step if you want to maximize flavor. The better method is to dry-fry them (see page 436 for more on dry-frying). For this process, you use a wok with a moderate amount of very hot oil—not enough to completely submerge the beans, but just enough that the beans can shallow-fry while also charring in spots. Once the beans are cooked, they're drained of excess oil, then briefly stir-fried in fresh oil laced with aromatics.

The method is quite easy to do at home, and I'm including instructions for the process in this recipe, but it does leave you with a cup of slightly used oil to deal with after your meal. This drained oil is perfectly fine to reuse, but I understand the hesitation some people show when they realize they're going to have to strain hot oil. Wouldn't it be great if there were a method that gave you similar results without the need for all that excess fat?

To this end, I tried a half dozen different techniques, starting with the most common: blanching in water and shallow-frying. The former method, touted by the always-incredible Fuchsia Dunlop, produces a dish that's very tasty, with bright, fresh flavors and nice snappy beans. In fact, if you're the kind of person who likes green beans bright and snappy, I highly recommend skipping the dry-fry step in my recipe and blanching your green beans instead.

But for my own recipe, I turned my attention to the oven. I figured that if I were to preheat my oven enough, I might be able to get a similar effect by tossing my beans in a little oil and throwing them in for a few moments. The regular oven, even when heated to its maximum temperature of 550°F, didn't cook quite fast enough—the beans still turned soft by the time they were blistered—but the *broiled* beans were fantastic. By letting the broiler heat up to inferno-levels, then placing the beans as close as possible underneath, I was able to get them to blister and brown in record time.

The rest of the recipe is very straightforward: you stir-fry some minced pork (or omit it) with garlic, ginger, Sichuan peppercorn, and ya cai (see Note), add some snipped dried chiles, then add the beans, season, and serve.

recipe continues

Yield
Serves 4

Active Time
20 minutes

Total Time
20 minutes

NOTES

If broiling the green beans instead of dry-frying, reduce the amount of oil for the green beans to 1 tablespoon (15 ml). This dish is quite numbing from the green Sichuan peppercorns. For a milder effect, use red peppercorns and reduce the amount to 1 or ½ teaspoon. Ya cai can be ordered online or found at most Asian supermarkets. If unavailable, you can use a mix of finely chopped sauerkraut or kimchi mixed with finely chopped capers. The pork is optional. If you prefer to leave it out, just skip the bit where you stir-fry it in step 3, jumping straight to adding the Sichuan peppercorns, garlic, and ginger instead.

INGREDIENTS

For the Green Beans:

½ cup (120 ml) peanut, rice bran, or other neutral oil (see Notes)

1 pound (450 g) green beans or long beans, trimmed and cut into 2-inch segments

Kosher salt

For the Stir-Fry:

1 tablespoon (15 ml) peanut, rice bran, or other neutral oil (this can be the same oil you shallow-fried the beans with if using the wok method)

2 ounces (60 g) ground pork (optional; see Notes)

2 teaspoons (4 g) whole Sichuan peppercorns, preferably green

1 tablespoon (7.5 g) minced garlic (about 3 medium cloves)

1 tablespoon (7.5 g) minced fresh ginger (about ¾-inch segment)

2 tablespoons (about 20 g) finely minced ya cai (see Notes)

6 whole dried small hot chiles (such as árbol), stems removed, snipped into 1-inch segments

2 teaspoons (10 ml) light soy sauce or shoyu

2 teaspoons (10 ml) Chinkiang or balsamic vinegar

1 teaspoon (4 g) sugar

DIRECTIONS

(1) **To Blister Beans in a Wok (if using the broiler method, skip to step 2):** Heat the oil in a wok over high heat until very lightly smoking. Add half of the green beans and cook, stirring and tossing occasionally, until the beans are cooked through, blistered, and spotty dark brown, about 4 minutes. Using a spider, transfer them to a rimmed baking sheet and set aside. Return the oil to the heat until lightly smoking and repeat with remaining green beans, adding them to the same tray with the first. Sprinkle all the beans with a little kosher salt. Drain off all the oil, reserve 1 tablespoon for the stir-fry, and save the rest for another use. Skip to step 3.

(2) **To Blister Beans under a Broiler:** Position the rack as close as possible to the broiler and preheat the broiler to high. In a large bowl, toss the green beans with 1 tablespoon (15 ml) oil and season with salt. Arrange in a single layer on a foil-lined rimmed baking sheet or broiler pan. Broil until the beans are blistered and very lightly charred, 2 to 5 minutes depending on the strength of your broiler. Return the beans to the bowl.

(3) **For the Stir-Fry:** Heat the wok over high heat until lightly smoking. Add 1 tablespoon (15 ml) oil and swirl to coat. Immediately add the pork (if using). Stir-fry until the pork is no longer pink, about 45 seconds, then immediately add the Sichuan peppercorns, garlic, ginger, and ya cai and stir-fry until aromatic, about 15 seconds. Add the snipped chiles and stir-fry until aromatic, another 15 seconds.

(4) Add the blistered green beans to the wok and toss to coat in the aromatics. Add the soy sauce and vinegar around the edge of the wok. Add the sugar. Toss thoroughly, season to taste with more salt, transfer to a serving platter, and serve immediately.

SOY-GLAZED MUSHROOMS

Yield
Serves 4

Active Time
10 minutes

Total Time
10 minutes

NOTE
This recipe also works very well with maitake mushrooms. Cut the tough base off the maitakes, then separate the frond-like caps into bite-sized clusters.

INGREDIENTS

2 tablespoons (30 ml) peanut, rice bran, or other neutral oil

12 ounces (340 g) shiitake, button, or cremini mushrooms, trimmed (remove and discard stems from shiitake entirely), caps cut into quarters (see Note)

2 teaspoons (5 g) minced garlic (about 2 medium cloves)

2 teaspoons (5 g) minced fresh ginger (about ½-inch segment)

1 tablespoon (15 ml) light soy sauce or shoyu

2 teaspoons (8 g) sugar

1 teaspoon (5 ml) roasted sesame oil

2 scallions, thinly sliced on a bias

2 teaspoons toasted sesame seeds

Kosher salt and freshly ground black pepper

These simple stir-fried mushrooms are meaty and tender with crispy browned bits and an intensely savory flavor. They work well on their own as a side dish, but they're almost better as leftovers added straight to a salad, tossed into another stir-fry for the last minute, dropped into a bowl of instant ramen, or eaten straight from the container at midnight by the harsh light of the refrigerator door.

The recipe will work well with most mushrooms, but I find shiitake or maitake will give you the meatiest bite and the most crispy bits.

DIRECTIONS

Heat a wok over high heat until lightly smoking. Add the oil and swirl to coat. Add the mushrooms and stir-fry until the mushrooms are deeply browned and crisp in spots, but still juicy and tender, about 5 minutes, reducing the heat if the mushrooms threaten to burn. Add the garlic and ginger and stir-fry until fragrant, about 15 seconds. Splash the soy sauce around the edges of the wok and toss to combine. Add the sugar, sesame oil, scallions, and sesame seeds and toss until the mushrooms are thoroughly coated in the mixture. Season to taste with salt and pepper. Transfer to a serving platter and serve immediately or let them cool, transfer to a sealed container, and store them in the refrigerator for up to a week. Add them to salads, soups, or as a last-minute addition to other stir-fries.

STIR-FRIED NEW POTATOES WITH HOT AND NUMBING SPICES

Yield
Serves 4
to 6

Active Time
20 minutes

Total Time
40 minutes

NOTE

This recipe will work with a wide range of spice blends. Replace the Hot and Numbing Spice Blend one to one with any spice blend you enjoy, including Blistered Cumin and Mustard Curry Spice Blend (page 186).

INGREDIENTS

For the Potatoes:

2 pounds (900 g) small yellow new potatoes, scrubbed and rinsed

Kosher salt

For the Stir-Fry:

¼ cup (60 ml) peanut, rice bran, or other neutral oil

4 medium garlic cloves, minced (about 4 teaspoons/20 g)

2 scallions, chopped

2 to 3 tablespoons (about 20 g) Hot and Numbing Spice Blend (page 185)

This is a dish I first tasted from a street vendor in Xi'an, the capital of central China's Shaanxi province at the eastern end of the Silk Road. In my head I had romantic notions that it was a product of that geography, like so many of the Muslim-influenced, warm-spiced dishes you find in the city. However, when I reached out to Fuchsia Dunlop and Steph Li about the origins of the dish, I discovered that they are by all accounts a modern creation, a product of the city's burgeoning tourism industry. This doesn't make them any less delicious.

The vendors have mobile carts with two cooking stations. One is a wide, flat pan in which small yellow new potatoes shallow-fry in a single layer. When a customer places an order, the vendor scoops out some of those potatoes and transfers them to a wok, where they're stir-fried with ground chiles, garlic, scallions, chile oil, and a spice blend heavy on warm spices like cumin, fennel, and anise, as well as some mouth-numbing Sichuan peppercorns. Li also helped me identify a mystery powder as a specific Chinese brand of chicken bouillon. At home I use Knorr powdered bouillon, though replacing it with a little extra salt and a pinch of MSG will keep the dish fully vegetarian. (The same spice blend is wonderful on fried chicken wings—see my recipe for Málà Salt and Pepper Chicken Wings on page 452—or even frozen French fries.)

I've also found that boiling the potatoes in heavily salted water is a good alternative to the shallow-fry method the street vendors use. This basic technique—boiling, stir-frying, and tossing with spices—works for a wide range of spice blends (see Note).

DIRECTIONS

(1) **For the Potatoes:** Place the potatoes in a large pot. Cover with cool water by 2 inches. Season heavily with salt (it should taste like very salty sea water when dissolved). Place over high heat, bring to a boil, and cook until the potatoes show no resistance when a knife or cake tester is poked through the largest one, about 10 minutes after they come to a boil. Drain the potatoes and spread into a single layer on a rimmed baking sheet to air-dry.

(2) **For the Stir-Fry:** When the potatoes are dry, heat 3 tablespoons (45 ml) of the oil in the wok over high heat until shimmering. Add the potatoes and cook, stirring and tossing frequently, until browned and crisped in spots, about 4 minutes.

3) Clear a small space in the center of the wok and add the remaining oil to it. Immediately add the garlic, scallions, and spice mixture to the oil and stir it around briefly until aromatic, about 15 seconds. Toss everything until the potatoes are thoroughly coated in spices, about 15 seconds. Season to taste with more salt as desired. Transfer to a serving bowl and serve.

HOT AND NUMBING SPICE BLEND

Yield
Makes about ¼ cup

Active Time
10 minutes

Total Time
10 minutes

NOTES

You can double or triple this recipe and save it for future use. It's great on all kinds of vegetables, as the base for a chile oil, or sprinkled on any fried food. To keep this blend vegetarian or vegan, omit the chicken bouillon. Replace with an additional ½ teaspoon salt and ¼ teaspoon MSG powder (optional)

INGREDIENTS

1 star anise pod
1 teaspoon (2 g) fennel seeds
2 teaspoons (4 g) red Sichuan peppercorns (red husks only, twigs and black seeds removed)
1 teaspoon (2 g) whole white peppercorns or ½ teaspoon freshly ground white pepper
2 teaspoons (5 g) cumin seeds
2 whole dried hot chiles (such as árbol or Japones)
1 teaspoon (4 g) kosher salt
1 teaspoon (4 g) sugar
1 teaspoon (3 g) powdered chicken bouillon (optional; see Notes)

DIRECTIONS

1) Combine the star anise pod, fennel seeds, Sichuan peppercorns, white peppercorns, and half of the cumin seeds in a dry wok. Toast over medium heat, stirring and tossing frequently, until you can start to smell their aroma, about 1 minute. Add the dried chiles and continue to toast the spices and chiles until very aromatic, about 1 minute longer. Transfer the mixture to a small bowl to cool slightly. Return the wok to the heat and add the remaining cumin seeds. Toss and stir until very aromatic, about 1 minute. Transfer to a second bowl.

2) When cool, transfer the spice mixture in the first bowl to the bowl of an electric spice grinder or a mortar and pestle. Add the salt, sugar, and chicken bouillon (if using). Grind to a fine powder and return to the bowl.

3) Add the whole cumin seeds to the spice grinder or the mortar (no need to clean it out) and pound or pulse until very coarsely ground (there should be distinct large pieces of cumin seed). Add these half-ground cumin seeds and the sesame seeds to the rest of the spice mixture and stir to incorporate. Store at room temperature in a sealed container in a dark pantry for up to a year (smell it before using—as long as it smells good, it will taste good).

BLISTERED CUMIN AND MUSTARD CURRY SPICE BLEND

Yield
Makes about ¼ cup

Active Time
10 minutes

Total Time
10 minutes

INGREDIENTS

2 tablespoons (30 ml) peanut, rice bran, or other neutral oil

1 tablespoon (6 g) cumin seeds

1 tablespoon (6 g) black mustard seeds

2 tablespoons (18 g) curry powder, such as Sun Brand Madras Curry Powder or S&B Oriental Curry Powder

1 teaspoon (4 g) kosher salt

DIRECTIONS

1. Heat the oil, cumin seeds, and mustard seeds in a wok over medium-high heat, stirring constantly until the seeds start to sizzle and pop, 1 to 2 minutes. Continue stir-frying until the popping starts to subside, then strain through a fine-mesh strainer set in a small heatproof bowl (you can save this oil for stir-frying or to use in dressings or drizzle on noodle soups). Transfer the seeds to a plate lined with a few layers of paper towels and blot out the excess oil.

2. Combine the blistered cumin and mustard seeds with the curry powder and salt in a small bowl. Store at room temperature in a sealed container in a dark pantry for up to a year (smell it before using—as long as it smells good, it will taste good).

STIR-FRYING SHREDDED POTATOES

Potatoes cut into thin matchsticks, rinsed of excess starch, then stir-fried with aromatics is a dish found in both Sichuan cuisine (where it is called *tudou si)* and in Korean cuisine (where it is called *gamjachae bokkeum*).

The key lies in finely shredding and then soaking the potato in several changes of water until all of the starch is leached out. This process accomplishes two distinct goals. The first is more obvious: removing starch ensures that the potato strands don't stick together or become gummy as they are stir-fried.

The second goal is less obvious. As it turns out, there are enzymes in potato cells that when released through shredding will interact with the pectin glue holding potatoes cells together, strengthening their structure with the help of calcium ions present in the potatoes and in your tap water. This interaction helps the potatoes stay firm and crunchy even when fully cooked, and that's what gives these stir-fried potatoes their uniquely crisp texture. (Read more about this in "The Science of Rinsing Potatoes," page 189.)

Korean shredded potatoes are a common *banchan* (side dish) and are wonderful served hot from the wok, at room temperature, or even straight from the fridge. It's about as simple as stir-fries get: rinsed shredded potatoes quickly stir-fried in oil with some sliced onions and sometimes shredded carrots, finished with black pepper, roasted sesame oil, and sesame seeds. The Sichuan version is a little more complex with the addition of aromatics like Sichuan peppercorns, garlic, and dried chiles, along with a splash of soy sauce and vinegar for seasoning. Both dishes clock in at around 5 minutes once you've shredded and rinsed your potatoes (something that can be done by hand—see "How to Shred Potatoes for Stir-Fries" on page 187—but is much faster and easier with a mandoline), which makes stir-frying easily the fastest way I know to cook potatoes.

How to Shred Potatoes for Stir-Fries

The easiest way to shred potatoes for stir-fries is to use a mandoline or a food processor with a julienne attachment. For stir-frying, you're looking for shreds around ⅛ inch wide. I use an inexpensive Japanese Benriner mandoline, the same exact model I've seen in every professional kitchen I've ever worked in. If your mandoline does not have a julienne attachment or if you've lost it (I *always* lose mine), you can still use your mandoline to make the first slices and get your potatoes into nice, even, ⅛-inch planks, at which point you can just go straight to step 4 below.

If you have neither a mandoline nor a food processor, don't worry. A little practice and patience will get you there.

Step 1 • Peel and Trim

Peel your potatoes and rinse them so that the excess surface starch doesn't make them slippery.

Step 2 • Create a Stable Surface

Cut one thin slice lengthwise off the side of the potato with a sharp chef's knife to create a stable surface for the potato to rest on.

Step 3 • Cut into Planks

With the potato resting on its newly cut surface, use a sharp chef's knife to cut the potato into ⅛-inch planks. (Alternatively, use a Japanese-style mandoline to slice the potatoes into ⅛-inch planks.)

Step 4 • Cut Matchsticks

Stack a few of the planks together and slice them lengthwise with your knife to create even matchsticks.

KNIFE SKILLS

KOREAN STIR-FRIED SHREDDED POTATOES (GAMJACHAE BOKKEUM)

Yield
Serves 4 as a small side dish

Active Time
10 minutes

Total Time
10 minutes

NOTES
You can easily scale this recipe up by 50 or 100 percent. Increase the cooking time after adding the potato by a minute or two to account for the increased volume. If your tap water is particularly soft (low mineral content), you might find that the potatoes soften or turn mushy during cooking. You can fix this issue by boiling your potatoes in acidic water. Add 2 tablespoons (30 ml) distilled white vinegar to 2 quarts (2 l) water and bring it to a boil in your wok. Add the shredded, rinsed potatoes and cook for 30 to 45 seconds (it's OK if the water loses its boil during this process), drain, spread on a rimmed baking sheet to steam-dry, and proceed with the recipe as directed.

INGREDIENTS

1 large white or Yukon Gold potato (about 8 ounces/225 g)
2 tablespoons (30 ml) peanut, rice bran, or other neutral oil
½ small yellow onion (about 2 ounces/60 g), thinly sliced
½ medium carrot (about 2 ounces/60 g), peeled and cut into fine matchsticks
2 teaspoons (10 ml) roasted sesame oil
Sprinkle of toasted sesame seeds (optional)
Kosher salt and freshly ground black pepper

DIRECTIONS

(1) Peel the potato and cut into fine matchsticks (see "How to Shred Potatoes for Stir-Fries, page 187). Rinse in several changes of cold water until the water is completely clear. Spin the potatoes dry in a salad spinner or blot dry with a clean kitchen towel or paper towels.

(2) Heat a wok over high heat until lightly smoking. Add the oil and swirl to coat. Add the potatoes and stir-fry until translucent and just beginning to turn pale golden brown in spots, 2 to 3 minutes. Add the onions and carrots and continue to stir-fry until the onions and carrots are lightly softened, about 30 seconds. Add the sesame oil and sesame seeds (if using) and season with salt and pepper to taste. Toss to combine, transfer to a serving platter, and serve.

The Science of Rinsing Potatoes

So what exactly is going on that causes shredded potatoes to retain their structure when cooked better than, say, whole or cubed potatoes?

It has to do with the pectin methylesterase (PME) released from inside potato cells and calcium ions present both inside the potato and in the tap water you rinse them in. PME is an enzyme produced by vegetables and microorganisms that can alter pectin, the carbohydrate glue that gives vegetable cell walls their structure. It's used in food production to help frozen or otherwise processed fruits and vegetables retain their structure—according to a 2014 paper in *Applied Biochemistry and Biotechnology*,[*] pectin treated with PME can then interact with calcium ions to form strong networks that are less affected by freezing and cooking than non-PME-treated pectin.

When cutting the potatoes, you end up releasing both PME and calcium ions. With chunky potato cuts, the effect of PME and calcium will be limited to the surface. Dave Arnold of the website *Cooking Issues* uses commercial PME to his advantage by treating French fries with it before frying, which helps accentuate the difference between the fluffy interior and firm, crisp exterior of a good fry. With finely shredded potatoes, on the other hand, their surface area to volume ratio is so large that they're effectively *all* surface, which means that PME and calcium will very rapidly affect the texture of the entire strand. In tests I've done, julienned or finely sliced potatoes soaked in hard tap water and then boiled will stay completely intact and firm even when boiled for a full 45 minutes!

The water used to soak and rinse the potatoes can also have an impact on finished texture. Most tap water contains a lot of calcium ions, which have the effect of firming up shredded potatoes. This explains why the hash browns my friends and I make at the hunting cabin in Michigan where all we have is extremely hard well water always come out crispier and firmer than the same hash browns I make at home with relatively soft water. Conversely, if your tap water is extremely soft or if you use distilled water for cooking, the shredded potatoes may come out soft or mushy.

If you are in this situation and find that your potatoes fall apart or get soft rather than remaining crunchy during the stir-fry,

there's an easy solution: par-boil them in acidulated water. A 1975 study in the *Journal of the Science of Food and Agriculture*[†] found that cooking potatoes in low pH (acidic) environments can have an even greater strengthening effect on pectin than calcium ions. The potato chip recipe in my book *The Food Lab* uses this fact to its advantage: par-cooking thinly sliced potatoes in water with a dash of vinegar will give them a firmer, crisper structure when you boil and subsequently fry them, and it works just as well for stir-fried potatoes.

If you have very soft water or find that your potatoes are softening during the stir-fry, start the recipe by bringing a couple quarts of water with a couple tablespoons of distilled vinegar to a vigorous boil, add the rinsed shredded potatoes, and let them blanch for 30 to 45 seconds before draining and continuing the recipes as directed.

---

[*] "Large-Scale Single Step Partial Purification of Potato Pectin Methylesterase That Enables the Use in Major Food Applications," Robin Eric Jacobus Spelbrink and Marco Luigi Federico Giuseppin.

[†] "Texture of Cooked Potatoes: The Effect of Ions and pH on the Compressive Strength of Cooked Potatoes," J. Carey Hughes, Alex Grant, and Richard M. Faulks.

SICHUAN-STYLE HOT AND SOUR STIR-FRIED SHREDDED POTATOES

Yield
Serves 4 as
a small side
dish

Active Time
10 minutes

Total Time
10 minutes

NOTES

You can easily scale this recipe up by 50 or 100 percent. Increase the cooking time after adding the potato by a minute or two to account for the increased volume. If your tap water is particularly soft (low mineral content), you might find that the potatoes soften or turn mushy during cooking. You can fix this issue by boiling your potatoes in acidic water. Add 2 tablespoons (30 ml) distilled white vinegar to 2 quarts (2 l) water and bring it to a boil in your wok. Add the shredded, rinsed potatoes and cook for 30 to 45 seconds (it's OK if the water loses its boil during this process), drain, spread on a rimmed baking sheet to steam-dry, and proceed with the recipe as directed.

INGREDIENTS

1 large white or Yukon Gold potato
(about 8 ounces/225 g)
2 tablespoons (30 ml) peanut, rice bran,
or other neutral oil
2 teaspoons (4 g) red Sichuan
peppercorns (red husks only, twigs
and black seeds removed)
1 tablespoon (7.5 g) minced garlic (about
3 medium cloves)

1 small dried hot chile (such as árbol or
Japones), stems removed, snipped
into ½-inch pieces with kitchen
shears (squeeze out and discard the
seeds if you want it less spicy)
1 teaspoon (5 ml) light soy sauce or
shoyu
2 teaspoons (10 ml) Chinkiang or
balsamic vinegar
1 teaspoon (4 g) sugar
Kosher salt

DIRECTIONS

1 Peel the potato and cut into fine matchsticks (see "How to Shred Potatoes for Stir-Fries," page 187). Rinse in several changes of cold water until the water is completely clear. Spin the potatoes dry in a salad spinner or blot dry with a clean kitchen towel or paper towels.

2 Heat a wok over high heat until lightly smoking. Add the oil and swirl to coat. Add the Sichuan peppercorns, garlic, and chiles and stir-fry until fragrant, about 10 seconds. Immediately add the potatoes and start stir-frying (do not let the garlic and chiles burn at the bottom of the wok). Stir-fry until the potatoes are translucent but still pale in color, 1½ to 2 minutes. Splash in the soy sauce and vinegar around the edge of the wok and toss to combine. Add the sugar and season with salt to taste. Transfer to a serving platter and serve.

SICHUAN-STYLE FISH-FRAGRANT EGGPLANT

Yield
Serves 4

Active Time
25 minutes

Total Time
25 minutes

NOTES
For homemade pickled chiles, see page 84. If you prefer a milder version of the dish, omit the pickled chiles and use distilled white vinegar in place of the pickling liquid in the sauce. The ground pork is optional. If you omit it, the dish is entirely vegan.

This is another *yuxiang* (fish-fragrant) dish that, like Shredded Chicken with Pickled Chiles and Carrots (page 82), contains no seafood. You stir-fry eggplant until smoky and tender, then toss it with a quick sauce flavored with chiles, garlic, ginger, vinegar, and sometimes minced pork, for a flavor-packed dish that comes together in one wok with minimal effort.

Cooking the dish at home is pretty straightforward, and the effort-to-flavor ratio is off the charts. The only tricky part is handling the eggplant. It needs to be steamed, salted, or brined before being stir-fried to break down its structure a bit and allow it to cook without absorbing excess moisture. (See "Buying and Salting Eggplants for Stir-Fries," page 194.)

Eggplant really benefits from a nice deep browning. Plain eggplant is bland. Mushy, watery, insipid—it's no wonder so many people dislike it. Many versions of this dish call for deep frying the eggplant to uniformly brown it before stir-frying. I prefer to shallow-fry it in the wok, taking a rather orderly approach by arranging the eggplant in a single layer and turning the pieces individually until they are well browned on all sides. It makes for a lighter dish (not to mention you don't have a couple cups of slightly used strained oil on your hands, as you do with the deep-fry method).

So: eggplant gets brined, eggplant gets browned, aromatics are added, sauce is stirred in, everybody inside the pan gets happy for a minute or two, then everyone outside the pan gets even happier as they down it.

INGREDIENTS

For the Eggplant:
Kosher salt
1 pound (450 g/3 to 4 medium) Chinese or Japanese eggplants, cut for stir-fries (see page 193)
2 teaspoons (6 g) cornstarch

For the Sauce:
2 teaspoons (10 ml) Chinkiang or balsamic vinegar
2 teaspoons (10 ml) pickling liquid from homemade or store-bought pickled chiles (see Notes)
2 teaspoons (10 ml) light soy sauce or shoyu
1 teaspoon (5 ml) dark soy sauce
1 tablespoon (12 g) sugar
2 tablespoons (30 ml) homemade or store-bought low-sodium chicken stock or water
Pinch of kosher salt
Pinch of MSG (optional)
1 teaspoon (3 g) cornstarch

For the Stir-Fry:
6 tablespoons (90 ml) peanut, rice bran, or other neutral oil
2 ounces (60 g) ground pork (optional)
2 tablespoons (15 g) minced garlic (about 6 medium cloves)
2 teaspoons (5 g) minced fresh ginger (about ½-inch segment)
1 tablespoon (12 g) Sichuan chile broad bean paste (doubanjiang)
1 teaspoon (4 g) minced homemade or store-bought pickled chiles (optional; see Notes)
2 scallions, whites and pale green parts cut into 1-inch segments, dark green parts thinly sliced, for garnish
Small handful of chopped fresh cilantro, for garnish (optional)

recipe continues

DIRECTIONS

(1) **For the Eggplant:** Combine ½ cup (120 g) kosher salt with 2 quarts (2 l) water in a medium bowl. Add the eggplant pieces, cover with a clean paper towel, press down to soak the paper towel in brine, and set aside to soak for at least 10 and up to 20 minutes. Drain the eggplant and spin in a salad spinner or blot dry with paper towels or a clean kitchen towel. Transfer to a bowl, sprinkle with the cornstarch, and toss with your fingertips until lightly coated. Set aside.

(2) **While the Eggplant Soaks, Make the Sauce:** Combine the vinegar, pickled chile liquid, soy sauces, sugar, stock or water, salt, MSG, and cornstarch in a small bowl and mix with a fork until no lumps remain. Set aside.

(3) **BEFORE YOU STIR-FRY, GET YOUR BOWLS READY:**

a. Brined eggplant
b. Ground pork (if using)
c. Garlic, ginger, chile broad bean paste, scallions, and pickled chiles (if using)
d. Sauce
e. Empty bowl for cooked ingredients
f. Serving platter

(4) **For the Stir-Fry:** Heat a wok over high heat until lightly smoking. Add ¼ cup (60 ml) of the oil and swirl to coat. Reduce the heat to medium-high. Add the eggplant and spread into a single layer. Cook, turning the eggplant occasionally, until softened and well browned on all sides, about 4 minutes. Transfer the eggplant to an empty bowl and set aside.

(5) Return the wok to high heat until lightly smoking. Add the remaining 2 tablespoons (30 ml) oil and swirl to coat. Add the garlic, ginger, chile paste, scallion whites and pale greens, and pickled chiles and stir-fry until fragrant and the oil has become dark red from the bean paste, about 30 seconds. Stir the sauce and add it to the wok by swirling it around the sides. Stir-fry until the sauce is thickened and glossy, about 15 seconds.

(6) Return the eggplant to the wok and toss to coat in the sauce (if the sauce overthickens and becomes gloppy, thin it out with a splash or water). Transfer to a serving bowl, garnish with the scallion greens and chopped fresh cilantro leaves, and serve.

How to Cut Eggplants for Stir-Fries

There are two ways to cut a Chinese or Japanese eggplant for stir-fries. Which method you choose is up to your own personal taste; both will work equally well.

METHOD 1 • THE ROLL CUT

Roll-cut eggplants form bite-sized wedges.

Step 1 • Trim Off the Stem

Start by trimming the stem end. I like to pull back the edges of the stem that hang down over the eggplant flesh to maximize the amount of edible eggplant I get from each plant.

Step 2 • Make the First Cut

Cut a bite-sized wedge off of the top, holding your knife at a 45-degree angle to the eggplant.

Step 3 • Roll and Cut Again

Roll the eggplant away from you by a quarter turn and make another cut at the same angle.

Step 4 • Roll and Repeat

Continue cutting, rolling the eggplant a quarter turn each time you cut until you reach the end.

METHOD 2 • BATONS

Eggplant batons are small bite-sized segments. Start by trimming the stem off the eggplant in the same manner as for a roll cut.

Step 1 • Split Lengthwise

Split the eggplant lengthwise.

Step 2 • Split Again

Lay each eggplant half cut side down on a cutting board and split them again. For particularly large eggplants, you may want to split each half lengthwise into thirds or even quarters.

Step 3 • Cut Segments

Cut the eggplant crosswise into 2- to 3-inch batons.

Buying and Salting Eggplants for Stir-Fries

If you're used to big ol' globe eggplants—the kind you slice and fry for eggplant Parmesan—the wide range of Asian eggplants available at the Asian supermarket may be baffling to you. If you have access to a well-stocked Southeast Asian market, you'll find an even wider range, from pure white egg-shaped eggplants (the variety the plant gets its name from) to tiny green eggplants no larger than a pea. But there are really only three varieties you need to know about for most recipes.

→ **Japanese eggplants** are deep purple to black in color and look sort of like miniaturized versions of globe eggplants. They are dense and mildly flavored and work well in both Western and Asian recipes. The best should feel quite heavy for their size.

→ **Chinese eggplants** are longer and skinnier and range from dark to pale purple. They soften and become sweet and dense in stir-fries and are great at absorbing the flavor from sauces. Look for eggplants that have pure white skin underneath their stems and are shiny and blemish-free for the best flavor.

→ **Thai eggplants** are round and the size of golf balls. Green are the ones you'll typically find in Southeast Asian supermarkets in the West, but they also come in purple and white varieties. They are commonly used in green and red curries or sliced raw and used in salads.

For stir-fries I typically reach for Chinese or Japanese eggplants. Either way, simply cutting them and stir-frying them does not work. The eggplants absorb all the oil in the wok, which in turn causes the eggplant to stick and burn. Raw, untreated eggplants also take a long time to cook through, exacerbating the burning problem.

Why is this? It's because eggplants contain a lot of excess air distributed within a spongy cell network. Air acts as an insulator, which means that heat travels through an eggplant very slowly. This is one of the reasons you always want to buy an eggplant that feels nice and heavy for its size: denser eggplants have less air and will cook more evenly, with better flavor and texture.

So how do you solve this problem? There are a few suggested techniques, and I tested all of them.

Almost all of the methods you hear about involve an attempt to break down the internal cellular structure of the eggplant either through heating or with the application of salt. In the past I've used the steaming method for dishes in which the eggplant is going to be braised until fall-apart tender. It's simple: put the eggplant slices in a bamboo steamer set over a wok of simmering water and steam them for about 10 minutes until tender.

Steaming works great if you've got a steamer. Just be aware that it comes out *extremely* tender when you treat it this way and can only handle a few very brief stirs in the wok without turning to a homogenous mush.

Microwaving the eggplant until cooked through is a technique I use when I'm breading eggplant for American-style eggplant Parmesan, but it's not ideal for stir-fries. The eggplant pieces end up a little shriveled and lack the velvety texture I'm looking for.

That leaves salting. Typically, salting takes place on dry land. You sprinkle the eggplants with a bit of salt, then let them sit until the salt pulls out excess moisture through osmosis, causing the cell structure to collapse. But I've also seen recipes that call for brining eggplant: soaking them in a saltwater solution. This seems counterintuitive to me. Aren't we trying to get rid of excess moisture? I decided to compare the two

methods side by side, also testing them against eggplant soaked in unsalted water and plain, untreated eggplant as a control.

After their brief 10-minute soak in salt water the eggplant pieces did not look all that different, but after drying them with paper towels and weighing them, I found that they actually lost a little weight during their soak. Osmosis would explain this: so long as the concentration of salt outside the eggplant is higher than the concentration of other solutes inside the eggplant's cell, water from the cells should be forced outward in an attempt to reach equilibrium. Sixty grams of salt for each liter of water—about ¼ cup kosher salt per quart—worked well.

I cooked all four batches of eggplant using the same method in a hot wok with oil, cooking them until lightly charred on the exterior and tender throughout. Both the salted and brined eggplants cooked faster and browned better than their water-soaked or untreated counterparts.

And whaddaya know? The brined eggplant was actually the best of the bunch. It managed to brown and soften while still retaining a nice meaty bite. The salted eggplant came in a close second, but was not quite as easy to cook. Brining eggplant is also easier than salting: salting eggplant requires a big rack to lay the slices out. Brined eggplant is good to go with just a single bowl.

All about Garlic

The aromatic compounds we associate with alliums like garlic and onions are collectively known as *lachrymators* (from the Latin root for tears), and the one responsible for garlicky aroma is called *allicin*. Interestingly, they don't actually exist in raw, unblemished garlic and onions. Those compounds are created only after cells are burst open and precursor chemicals combine and react to form new, pungent molecules. The more active precursor in each cell and the more cells that get ruptured, the more of those compounds are created, so the method by which you cut or mince your garlic can have a profound impact on its flavor, as does the form in which you buy your garlic.

Let's start with shopping.

At the supermarket, there are really only two forms of garlic you should be considering: whole heads or prepeeled raw cloves.*

As for fresh garlic, because garlic flavor is created as soon as garlic cells are ruptured and increases steadily with time, any form of garlic that comes precut—such as minced garlic, garlic paste, or garlic extract—either will be lacking in fresh garlic flavor or will have a flavor that is far too pungent as the *allicin*-forming reactions have been allowed to progress for too long. Garlic is one of those ingredients that *must* be chopped right before use.

In side-by-side tests, I've found that in dishes where garlic is the primary flavor or where garlic is served mostly raw, fresh cloves removed from a whole head and peeled just before use have a cleaner, more garlicky flavor than prepeeled raw cloves of garlic, though the latter do just fine the vast majority of the time.

Here are some common methods along with when you may want to employ them:

→ **Crushing in a mortar and pestle** is the method I use most of the time. With a heavy granite mortar and pestle, you can get your garlic any texture ranging from lightly crushed to a fine mince, or even a smooth paste in a matter of seconds. If a recipe calls for chopped garlic, this is the way I'm going to do it. (Bonus: for recipes that call for both minced garlic and ginger, you can peel and slice your ginger, then pound it in the mortar and pestle together with the garlic.)

The only downside of this method is that it crushes plenty of cells, so the garlic has a tendency to get pungent unless used within 10 to 15 minutes of crushing. Just make sure you leave the garlic until just before you start cooking and it'll be just fine.

→ **Mincing with a knife** by smashing a clove and then rocking a chef's knife back and forth or chopping up and down with a cleaver or santoku knife lets you mince as fine as you'd like. Because a sharp knife ruptures fewer cells than a blunt pestle, this method is best for when you intend to use the garlic raw, such as for topping Dan Dan Noodles (page 317) or incorporating into a smashed cucumber salad (see page 615). It can also be used for garlic that you are going to stir-fry if you don't have a mortar and pestle.

→ **Using a garlic press or Microplane** squeezes out a ton of garlic juice, which can turn quite pungent and hot just a few moments after pressing. I would not recommend a garlic press or Microplane for any garlic intended to be eaten raw, and if you plan on using it for a stir-fry, your best option is to press or plane it immediately before you start the cooking process to minimize the time between when it's crushed and when it's cooked.

→ **Slicing with a knife** will give you mildly flavored pieces of garlic that are distinct in the final dish and can be eaten and enjoyed for their flavor and texture like other vegetables. In a dish like Pepper and Salty Shrimp (page 447), sweet, mild slices of garlic that you can pick up with your chopsticks and eat are almost as essential a part of the dish as the shrimp.

→ **Smashing whole cloves with the side of a knife or cleaver** is a good technique for exposing the interior of a garlic clove just enough to allow you to use it to infuse oil for stir-frying. This allows you to impart a sweet garlic flavor without adding excess pungency.

---

* The other exception is granulated or powdered garlic, which, like powdered ginger, tastes nothing like its fresh form, but it has a flavor all its own and can be useful in spice blends (or for sprinkling on pizza).

How to Cut Garlic for Stir-Fries

Step 1 • Separate Cloves

Start by separating a head of garlic into individual cloves by pressing it down and slightly forward against your cutting board with the palm of your hand.

Step 2 • Trim

Trim the bottoms off each clove of garlic you intend to use (the rest can be stored at room temperature for a few days or in the fridge for a few weeks).

Step 3 • Gently Smash and Peel

Place the flat side of your knife over a clove and give it a gentle but sharp rap. This will loosen the skin, allowing you to remove it with your fingers.

TO SLICE

Step 1 • Stabilize . . .

Cut a thin sliver off the widest side of the garlic clove to create a flat surface. Place that surface against the cutting board to stabilize the garlic clove.

Step 2 • . . . and Slice

Holding the garlic steady with your non knife hand (remember to keep thumb and fingertips tucked in!), slice it to the desired thickness. Typically this is around ⅛ inch.

TO MINCE WITH A MORTAR AND PESTLE

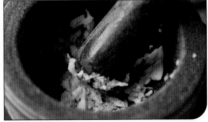

Place the peeled garlic in a mortar with a pinch of salt (this will add friction and keep the garlic from sliding around the bowl too much), then crush it as coarse or as fine as you'd like using the pestle.

TO MINCE WITH A KNIFE

Step 1 • Smash it . . .

Place the flat side of a chef's knife or a Chinese cleaver over the garlic and give it a firm rap to crush the cloves and separate the fibers.

Step 2 • . . . and Mince

Rock your chef's knife back and forth or your santoku or Chinese cleaver straight up and down to reduce the smashed clove to as fine a mince as you'd like. Minced garlic should be used immediately.

STIR-FRIED EGGPLANT WITH SAKE AND MISO

Yield
Serves 4

Active Time
30 minutes

Total Time
30 minutes

INGREDIENTS

For the Eggplant:
Kosher salt
1 pound (450 g/3 to 4 medium) Chinese or Japanese eggplants, cut for stir-fries (see page 193)

For the Sauce:
1 tablespoon (about 115 g) white, yellow, or brown miso paste
1 tablespoon (15 ml) shoyu or tamari
3 tablespoons (45 ml) sake
2 teaspoons (8 g) sugar

For the Stir-Fry:
¼ cup (60 ml) peanut, rice bran, or other neutral oil
1 teaspoon (2.5 g) minced garlic (about 1 medium clove)
2 teaspoons (5 g) minced fresh ginger (about ½-inch segment)
2 scallions, thinly sliced on a bias, greens reserved separately for garnish
Pinch of shichimi togarashi or hot red pepper flakes (optional)

This classic Japanese dish starts with the same basic eggplant treatment as Fish-Fragrant Eggplant (page 191), but where that dish is a punch-you-in-the-mouth flavor fest, this one is much more subtle, instead relying on sake, miso, soy sauce, and sugar for a classic sweet-and-savory Japanese flavor profile. Serve the eggplant on top of a bowl of rice with some cucumber with Honey Mustard–Miso Dip (page 618) or cold spinach with Soy-Dashi (page 231) on the side, and you've got Japanese home-style comfort food at its best.

DIRECTIONS

1 **For the Eggplant:** Combine ½ cup (120 g) kosher salt with 2 quarts (2 l) water in a medium bowl. Add the eggplant pieces, cover with a clean paper towel, press down to soak the paper towel in brine, and set aside to soak for at least 10 and up to 20 minutes. Drain the eggplant and spin in a salad spinner or blot dry with paper towels or a clean kitchen towel.

2 **While the Eggplant Soaks, Make the Sauce:** Put the miso paste and shoyu in a small bowl and mix with a fork until homogenous, then add the sake and sugar and stir to combine.

3 **For the Stir-Fry:** Heat a wok over high heat until lightly smoking. Add 3 tablespoons (45 ml) of the oil and swirl to coat. Reduce the heat to medium-high. Add the eggplant and stir-fry until the eggplant is starting to soften and is lightly browned, 3 to 4 minutes.

4 Push the eggplant to the side of the wok and add the remaining tablespoon (15 ml) of oil to the center of the wok. Add the garlic, ginger, and scallion whites and cook until fragrant, about 15 seconds. Add the sauce mixture and stir-fry the entire contents of the wok until the eggplant is very tender and the sauce has reduced to a light coating on each piece, about 3 minutes longer. Transfer to a serving plate and sprinkle with scallion greens and shichimi togarashi (if using). Serve with steamed rice.

STIR-FRIED KABOCHA SQUASH WITH SAKE AND MISO

Yield
Serves 4

Active Time
25 minutes

Total Time
25 minutes

INGREDIENTS

½ small kabocha squash (about 1 pound/450 g), seeds and guts discarded

1 tablespoon (15 ml) peanut, rice bran, or other neutral oil

½ cup (120 ml) dry sake

3 tablespoons (45 g) white or yellow miso paste

2 teaspoons (10 ml) shoyu or tamari

1 teaspoon (4 g) sugar

Pinch of shichimi togarashi or hot red pepper flakes (optional)

Another vegetable that is delicious with a similar sake-miso coating is pumpkin. Kabocha is a Japanese pumpkin with deep orange flesh, dark green skin, and a flavor and texture that resemble sweet potato when cooked. It's easily my favorite squash for one simple reason: you don't need to peel it. Once cooked, the skin becomes as soft and tender as the flesh, making it a snap to prepare. All you've got to do is split it in half, scoop out the seeds and guts, trim off the stem, then cut it up for simmering or stir-frying.

This pumpkin is delicious as a side dish, on top of a bowl of rice, at room temperature the next day, or tossed into a salad straight from the fridge.

DIRECTIONS

(1) Cut the squash into 1-inch wide wedges, then cut crosswise into ¼-inch slices.

(2) Heat the oil in a wok over medium heat until shimmering. Add the squash and cook, stirring and tossing occasionally, until beginning to soften, about 5 minutes. Increase the heat to high and add ¼ cup (60 ml) of the sake. Stir-fry until the sake is mostly dry, about 2 minutes longer.

(3) Add the remaining sake and the miso paste, shoyu, and sugar. Cook, tossing and folding gently so as not to break the squash pieces, until the squash is fork-tender and the miso mixture lightly coats each piece, about 4 minutes longer. Transfer to a serving platter, sprinkle with hot pepper flakes (if using), and serve.

How to Prepare Kabocha Squash

Kabocha squash is not as firm as winter squashes like butternut or acorn, but it can, nevertheless, be a little tough to cut without a very hefty knife and a bit of weight. If you find that your squash is too difficult to cut into, try microwaving it on a plate for 2 minutes to lightly soften the outer layers.

Step 1 • Cut the Squash in Half

With the stem side facing up, cut the squash in half straight down the middle through the stem.

Step 2 • Remove the Seeds

Use a spoon to remove the seeds and the stringy flesh from inside the squash.

Step 3 • Remove the Stem

Holding one squash half stem side down and using the tip of your knife, cut out the stem.

FOR SIMMERING OR STIR-FRYING

Step 1 • Cut into Wedges

Cut the squash into wedges.

Step 2 • Cut into Pieces

Cut each wedge into pieces (thin slices for stir-fries, thicker chunks for simmering).

FOR TEMPURA

Hold one half of the squash with the cut side down, then cut into 1/6- to ¼-inch slices.

STIR-FRYING LEAFY GREEN VEGETABLES

Though meat consumption in Asia has been steadily increasing in recent years, vegetables still play a huge role in the regular diet of nearly every Asian country, and frequently that vegetable is some sort of simple stir-fried green, leafy vegetable. There is a wide range of flavor profiles and sauces that pair well with greens, but I'll cover four of my favorite methods in the next section. If you've got these four techniques under your belt, you're ready to tackle just about any greens the farmers' market or supermarket can throw at you.

With each technique I'll lay out the basics, tell you what types of greens it works best for from the table on the right, and give you a sample recipe to start with.

TYPE OF GREENS	COMMON EXAMPLES
Pale Green and Crunchy	Napa cabbage, green cabbage, iceberg lettuce, escarole, romaine lettuce
Leafy and Sweet	Pea greens, fava bean greens, snow pea leaves, Chinese spinach (amaranth), spinach, Malabar spinach
Leafy and Strong	Mustard greens, watercress, AA choy, tatsoi, chrysanthemum greens, turnip greens, mizuna
Stalky and Crunchy	Broccolini, Chinese broccoli (gai lan), morning glory or water spinach (ong choy), bok choy and baby bok choy, yu choy, Chinese celery (kun choy), chard

**Stir-Fried Greens Technique 1:
With Wok Hei, Garlic, and Ginger**

What it works best with: Stalky and crunchy greens (such as gai lan, yu choy, or baby bok choy) or leafy and strong greens (such as tatsoi, watercress, or mustard greens)

SMOKY BOK CHOY WITH GARLIC SAUCE

Yield	Active Time
Serves 4	15 minutes
	Total Time
	15 minutes

NOTES

This recipe will work with any vegetables from the stalky and crunchy or the leafy and sweet categories in the chart on page 201. Vegetables should be trimmed of hard stems and cut into 2- to 3-inch segments. Wide vegetables like bok choy should be split lengthwise into halves or quarters. If you are not comfortable holding the torch while stir-frying, have a partner hold the torch for you or return the bok choy to the rimmed baking sheet after stir-frying for 30 seconds in step 4, spread into a single layer, place on a heatproof surface (like your range top), and sweep the torch back and forth over the bok choy until a smoky aroma reaches your nose, about 15 seconds. Return the bok choy to the wok and continue with step 5.

Wok hei, that smoky "breath of a wok" (see page 42) can go a long way toward livening up mildly flavored greens, and a simple garlicky glaze seasoned only with salt and white pepper accentuates the natural flavor of stalky greens or sweet leafy greens. If I'm not using my outdoor wok burner, I use my kitchen blowtorch to get smokiness into the greens. Transferring them to a tray to apply the torch makes it a simple and (relatively) safe operation that's still fun to watch.

When blanching greens for stir-frying, add the tougher stalks to the water first to give them a jump start on cooking before adding the greens.

DIRECTIONS

(1) **For the Greens:** Bring 1½ quarts lightly salted water to a boil in a wok. Add the bok choy stalks, stir well, cover, and boil, shaking the pan occasionally, for 30 seconds. Add the greens and boil, using a spider to move the greens around, until bright green but still crisp, about 15 seconds. Drain the bok choy and spread into a single layer on a sheet tray or large plate.

(2) **For the Cornstarch Slurry:** Combine the cornstarch and water in a separate small bowl and stir with a fork until the cornstarch is dissolved.

(3) **For the Stir-Fry:** Heat the wok over high heat until lightly smoking. Add the oil and swirl to coat. Add the garlic and ginger and stir-fry until fragrant but not browned, about 10 seconds.

INGREDIENTS

For the Greens:
Kosher salt

12 ounces (340 g) bok choy, trimmed, each
    stalk split lengthwise, and cut into 2- to
    3-inch pieces, leafy greens and white
    stalks washed and reserved separately
    (see Notes)

For the Cornstarch Slurry:
½ teaspoon (1.5 g) cornstarch

1 tablespoon (15 ml) water

For the Stir-Fry:
1 tablespoon (15 ml) peanut, rice bran, or
    other neutral oil

3 medium garlic cloves, minced (about 1
    tablespoon/8 g)

2 teaspoons (10 g) minced fresh ginger
    (about ½-inch segment)

½ teaspoon (2 g) sugar

Pinch of freshly ground white pepper

(4) Immediately add the bok choy and stir-fry for 30 seconds. Working quickly, ignite your blowtorch and, holding the flame 2 to 3 inches above the vegetables, sweep across the surface while shaking the pan, until a smoky aroma reaches your nose, about 15 seconds. (You should hear a distinct crackle and see small bursts of orange flame as the oil on the vegetables jumps and combusts. See Notes.)

(5) Continue stir-frying until the vegetables are tender-crisp, about 30 seconds longer. Add the sugar and season with salt and white pepper to taste. Stir the cornstarch slurry and add it to the wok. Cook, tossing vigorously, until the vegetables are coated in a glossy glaze, about 15 seconds. Transfer to a serving platter and serve immediately with steamed white rice.

**Stir-Fried Greens Technique 2:
With Chiles and Vinegar**

What it works best with: Pale green and crunchy greens (such as Napa or white cabbage or romaine or iceberg lettuce)

STIR-FRIED NAPA CABBAGE WITH VINEGAR AND CHILES

Yield
Serves 4

Active Time
10 minutes

Total Time
10 minutes

NOTE
For the best results, separate the tender tips of the cabbage leaves from the heartier bottoms. Start the stir-fry with just the bottoms and let them cook for 15 to 30 seconds before adding the tops so that everything finishes cooking at the same time.

INGREDIENTS

For the Sauce:

1 teaspoon (4 g) sugar
2 tablespoons (30 ml) black, Chinkiang, or balsamic vinegar
1 tablespoon (15 ml) light soy sauce

For the Stir-Fry:

2 tablespoons (30 ml) peanut, rice bran, or other neutral oil
3 medium garlic cloves (8 g), minced
2 small dried hot chiles (such as árbol or Japones), stems removed, snipped into ½-inch pieces with kitchen shears (squeeze out and discard the seeds if you want it less spicy)
1 small head Napa cabbage (about 1 pound/450 g), cored, leaves cut into 1½- to 2-inch squares
Kosher salt

If you're anything like me, you'll occasionally find yourself with three-quarters of a head of iceberg lettuce left over after you had to buy a whole head to shred just a bit of for burger night or hard-shell taco night. What can you do with the rest of that head of lettuce? Why, stir-fry it of course. Even lettuce that is slightly past its prime and starting to soften a bit is wonderful when stir-fried. Greens with vinegar and dried chiles is a classic Sichuan preparation you'll most frequently see with Napa cabbage, but it works well with any pale green crisp greens (including that hamburger iceberg).

DIRECTIONS

1 **For the Sauce:** Combine sugar, vinegar, and soy sauce in a small bowl and set aside.

2 **For the Stir-Fry:** Heat a wok over high heat until lightly smoking. Add the oil and swirl to coat. Add the garlic and dried chiles and stir-fry until aromatic, about 10 seconds. Immediately add the cabbage and stir-fry until the cabbage is starting to wilt but still quite crisp, 1 to 2 minutes. Swirl the sauce in around the edges of the wok and stir-fry until the sauce is almost dry and the greens are tender-crisp, about 1 minute longer. Season with salt to taste, transfer to a serving platter, and serve immediately.

What it works best with: Stalky and crunchy greens (such as bok choy, yu choy, or water spinach)

CHINESE BROCCOLI WITH OYSTER SAUCE

Yield
Serves 4

Active Time
20 minutes

Total Time
20 minutes

NOTE
I love adding some fried garlic or shallots to this dish right before serving. You can use store-bought fried garlic or shallots, or homemade fried shallots (page 255), or just leave them off if you prefer.

Chinese broccoli with oyster sauce is a classic dim sum side dish, but it's so good that variations have managed to travel throughout Asia in various forms (not to mention to the United States), and it doesn't always have to come with dumplings. It's also great as a side dish with meat- or tofu-based stir-fries or simmered dishes. As with all oyster-sauce-based dishes, the quality of the finished dish will depend on the quality of the oyster sauce, so look for bottles that list oysters as the very first ingredient.

Chinese broccoli (gai lan) is widely available at Asian supermarkets. It's got crunchy stems and tender leaves that resemble mature spinach. Older gai lan can tend to get a little stringy and strongly flavored, so look for slender bright green stalks. If there are any flowers on the stalks (they look like very small broccoli florets), they should be dark or pale green. Yellow florets are an indication that the gai lan is probably past its prime. If you're shopping in a Western supermarket, broccolini works wonderfully in this dish.

INGREDIENTS

For the Broccoli:
1 pound (450 g) Chinese broccoli (gai lan) or broccolini, tough stems trimmed off and discarded
Kosher salt

For the Sauce:
3 tablespoons (45 ml) oyster sauce
1 teaspoon (3 g) cornstarch
3 tablespoons (45 ml) homemade or store-bought low-sodium chicken stock or water
1 tablespoon (15 ml) Shaoxing wine
1 tablespoon (15 ml) light soy sauce or shoyu
½ teaspoon (2 g) sugar

For the Stir-Fry:
1 tablespoon (15 ml) peanut, rice bran, or other neutral oil
3 medium garlic cloves (8 g), smashed and very roughly chopped
2 teaspoons (5 g) minced fresh ginger (about ½-inch segment)
A few tablespoons fried garlic or shallots (optional; see Note)

DIRECTIONS

1. **For the Broccoli:** Bring 1½ quarts lightly salted water to a boil in a wok. Add the broccoli, stir well, cover, and boil, shaking the pan occasionally, until bright green but still quite firm, about 30 seconds. Drain the broccoli and spread into a single layer on a sheet tray or large plate.

recipe continues

(2) **For the Sauce:** Combine the oyster sauce and cornstarch in a small bowl and stir to dissolve. Add the stock or water, wine, soy sauce, and sugar and stir until the sugar is dissolved.

(3) **For the Stir-Fry:** Heat the wok over high heat until lightly smoking. Add the oil and swirl to coat. Add the garlic and ginger and stir-fry until fragrant and garlic is starting to brown around the edges, about 30 seconds. Add the broccoli and toss to coat in the garlic and ginger oil. Transfer to a serving platter.

(4) Return the wok to high heat (no need to wipe it out) and immediately add the sauce ingredients. Bring to a boil and reduce until lightly thickened, about 45 seconds. Pour the sauce over the broccoli on the serving platter. Sprinkle with fried garlic (if using) and serve immediately.

PAD KHANA BACON KROP (THAI-STYLE STIR-FRIED CHINESE BROCCOLI WITH OYSTER SAUCE AND BACON)

Yield
Serves 3
to 4

Active Time
10 minutes

Total Time
10 minutes

NOTE
For a more traditional version of this dish, replace the pancetta with 8 ounces (225 g) Crispy Fried Pork Belly (page 434), cut into ½-inch chunks.

INGREDIENTS

1 teaspoon (5 ml) peanut, rice bran, or other neutral oil
4 ounces (120 g) thick-cut pancetta or bacon, cut into ½-inch dice
5 medium garlic cloves, finely minced (about 5 teaspoons/15 g)
Fresh or pickled hot chiles, thinly sliced
12 ounces (340 g) Chinese broccoli (gai lan), washed and drained, leaves roughly chopped, stems cut on a sharp bias into 1- to 2-inch pieces
1½ tablespoons (25 ml) oyster sauce
1 tablespoon (15 ml) dark soy sauce or shoyu
1 tablespoon (12.5 g) sugar

Pad khana moo krop is a Thai reinterpretation of Chinese broccoli with oyster sauce. The classic dish combines chunks of crispy pork belly with briefly stir-fried Chinese broccoli flavored with chiles, garlic, and oyster sauce. I rarely go through the trouble of deep frying my own pork belly just for the sake of this dish (though if I have leftovers of the fried pork belly from page 434, I use it!). Instead, I use thick-sliced bacon or pancetta, which, while by no means traditional, is undeniably delicious, and it cuts the total time from fridge to table down to around 10 minutes. Perfect for a harried weeknight.

Unlike Chinese-style Chinese broccoli with oyster sauce, in this version the broccoli is thinly sliced and very briefly stir-fried to retain a nearly raw crunch when served.

DIRECTIONS

Heat the oil in a wok over high heat until shimmering. Add the pancetta or bacon and cook, stirring, until well rendered and crisp, 1 to 2 minutes. Add the garlic and chiles to taste and stir-fry until fragrant, about 15 seconds. Add the Chinese broccoli and stir-fry for 15 seconds. Add the oyster sauce, soy sauce, and sugar and stir-fry until lightly wilted, about 30 seconds. Transfer to a serving platter, and serve.

What it works best with: Leafy and sweet greens (such as snow pea or fava greens or spinach) and leafy and strong greens (such as tatsoi, chrysanthemum, and watercress)

SNOW PEA SHOOTS WITH LOBSTER SAUCE (WITH OR WITHOUT CRABMEAT)

Yield
Serves 4

Active Time
30 minutes

Total Time
30 minutes

NOTE

This dish is delicious even without the crabmeat, but if you are feeling extra decadent, the combination of sweet crabmeat with sweet greens is unbeatable. On the West Coast, I use picked Dungeness crab, but you should use whatever freshly picked crab is available to you. Chunky king or snow crabmeat is a real treat. If your wallet is feeling a little slim, imitation crabmeat (surimi) can be a perfectly tasty alternative. Snow pea leaves are also called "snow pea shoots" and can be found during the springtime at the farmers' market or Asian produce market. If you can't find them, you can use regular pea shoots, watercress, or any other stir-fry green in this book.

Pea shoots with lobster sauce is another one of those dishes I grew up eating at Cantonese seafood restaurants in New York and New England, not realizing how difficult it is to find the dish outside of that region (or knowing anything about its origins). Like Shrimp with Lobster Sauce (page 159), the dish contains no lobster. Instead, it's a plate of simple stir-fried greens that is ladled with the same translucent sauce with its deliciously silky (OK, slimy) ribbons of egg white. In fancier restaurants, you could order the dish with chunks of crabmeat cooked into the sauce.*

The combination of seafood and pea shoots exists in other Chinese dishes—crab roe on pea shoots or dried scallops with eggs on pea shoots, for instance—but I have not been able to trace this particular dish back to any specific origins in Asia. I'm fairly certain it's another brilliant adaptation of Cantonese American chefs.

recipe continues

---

* With a premium price to boot—a single side dish order would regularly cost upward of $20 in restaurants that offered $5.99 lunch specials. This was a dish I enjoyed only when I went out with my parents and they were footing the bill.

INGREDIENTS

For the Sauce:

2 tablespoons (30 ml) Shaoxing wine

1 tablespoon (8 g) cornstarch

¾ cup (180 ml) homemade or store-bought low-sodium chicken stock or water

½ teaspoon (2 g) sugar

Dash of freshly ground white pepper

Kosher salt

For the Stir-Fry:

1 tablespoon (15 ml) peanut, rice bran, or other neutral oil

2 teaspoons (5 g) minced garlic (about 2 medium cloves)

2 teaspoons (5 g) minced fresh ginger (about ½-inch segment)

8 ounces (225 g) snow pea leaves, stems torn into 1- to 2-inch pieces (see Note)

2 large egg whites, lightly beaten with a pinch of kosher salt

3 to 4 ounces (90 to 120 g) picked crabmeat (optional)

DIRECTIONS

(1) **For the Sauce:** Combine the wine and cornstarch in a small bowl and stir until the cornstarch is dissolved. Add the chicken stock, sugar, white pepper, and a pinch of salt. Set aside.

(2) **BEFORE YOU STIR-FRY, GET YOUR BOWLS READY:**

a. Garlic and ginger

b. Greens

c. Sauce

d. Cornstarch slurry

e. Beaten egg whites and crabmeat (if using)

f. Serving platter

(3) **For the Stir-Fry:** Heat a wok over high heat until lightly smoking. Add the oil and swirl to coat. Add the garlic and ginger and stir-fry until fragrant, about 15 seconds. Immediately add the snow pea leaves and stir-fry until the leaves are wilted but still bright green, 1 to 2 minutes (if the greens are having trouble wilting, add a small splash of water). Transfer to a serving platter.

(4) Return the wok to high heat. Stir the sauce and add to the wok. Bring to a boil. Simmer until the sauce is thick enough to coat the back of a spoon, about 1 minute. Adjust the seasoning with salt and white pepper to taste.

(5) Drizzle the egg whites and crabmeat (if using) into the sauce, then gently stir it with a ladle or wok spatula until the eggs form tender ribbons, about 30 seconds. Pour the sauce over the top of the greens. Serve immediately.

TOFU LETTUCE CUPS WITH PINE NUTS AND HOISIN SAUCE (SAN CHOI BAO)

If you've ever been to a P. F. Chang's (which serves food that is honestly much better than any massive shopping mall chain has any right to be), you're familiar with a version of *san choi bao*—lettuce wraps. I grew up eating a variation of the dish at the original Phoenix Garden in New York's Chinatown, a now-shuttered Cantonese restaurant that burned down twice during its decades of service. As opposed to the sort of gloopy version served at P. F. Chang's, Phoenix Garden's featured minced squab stir-fried with pine nuts and finely diced water chestnuts and vegetables in a way that allowed each piece to remain distinct. You spread a little hoisin sauce in the bottom of a piece of ice-cold iceberg lettuce, pile some of the loose mixture into it, and eat it with your hands like a taco. This thing is all about texture as the mix of crunchy, crisp, and tender bits comes together in your mouth.

Despite the fact that it says "squab" on the menu, and I trust that they were, in fact, using squab (the price certainly justified it), I never actually get much squab flavor out of the mix. You could tell me it's chicken or pork or tofu, and I wouldn't think to contest it. As in many Chinese dishes, the meat isn't the star; it's just a bit player, there to add texture that complements the vegetables. That's good news: it means you can use diced chicken, pork, or even firm or extra-firm tofu without any real sacrifice.

Nearly every recipe in this book starts with a marinade, but this one doesn't. The small dice cook quickly and are small enough that the flavor of the sauce nicely coats them, even without a flavorful marinade.

Typically san choi bao uses water chestnuts for crunch. I love water chestnuts—they have a satisfyingly crisp texture that stays crisp even after cooking. Fresh water chestnuts are difficult to find (and mildly annoying to prepare), but the canned water chestnuts my mom threw into our stir-fries growing up work just fine. That said, I prefer working with fresh ingredients whenever I can. One afternoon, as I was wandering the aisles of my local Latin produce shop, I saw a pile of jícama and realized that the texture of jícama is actually very similar to that of water chestnut. Diced into a stir-fry, it has the same watery crunch and mild flavor and has become my go-to vegetable for dishes that call for water chestnuts. (I still keep a couple cans of water chestnuts around in case I can't find jícama.)

The remaining ingredients are straightforward: diced celery for more crunch and flavor, pine nuts toasted slowly in oil until deep golden brown, some diced shiitake mushrooms, some garlic, ginger, and scallions for aroma, and fresh cilantro leaves to finish it off. For the sauce, I use a sweet-and-savory mix of Shaoxing wine, soy sauce, hoisin sauce, black or Chinkiang vinegar (balsamic works, too), and a very light touch of cornstarch.

The finished dish is a powerhouse of textures and flavors, with a great mix of crisp, tender, fresh, and nutty. I serve it with chilled iceberg lettuce—you can also use green leaf if you're one of those folks who, for whatever reason, can't abide iceberg—which I spread with a little extra hoisin sauce before spooning in the mixture. Inevitably I overstuff, which makes eating it a messy affair, but getting messy is half the fun, isn't it?

SAN CHOI BAO

Yield
Serves 4

Active Time
30 minutes

Total Time
30 minutes

NOTES
You can use finely diced chicken breast or lean pork in place of the firm tofu if desired. Canned or fresh peeled water chestnuts can be used in place of jicama.

INGREDIENTS

For the Tofu:
14 ounces (400 g) firm tofu

For the Sauce:
1 tablespoon (15 ml) Shaoxing wine or dry sherry
1 tablespoon (15 ml) dark soy sauce
2 teaspoons (10 ml) Chinese black vinegar or cider vinegar
¼ cup (60 ml) hoisin sauce
2 teaspoons (10 ml) chile sauce, such as sriracha or sambal oelek (optional)

For the Cornstarch Slurry:
1 teaspoon (3 g) cornstarch
1 tablespoon (15 ml) water

For the Stir-Fry:
1½ ounces (40 g/about ¼ cup) pine nuts
¼ cup (60 ml) peanut, rice bran, or other neutral oil
2½ ounces (70 g) shiitake mushrooms, stems removed, cut into ¼-inch dice (about 1 cup)
1 tablespoon (7.5 g) minced garlic (about 3 medium cloves)
1 tablespoon (7.5 g) minced fresh ginger (about ¾-inch segment)
3 scallions, white and pale green parts only, thinly sliced
4 ounces (120 g) jicama, peeled and cut into ¼-inch dice (about ½ apple-sized jicama; see Notes)
2 ounces (60 g) celery, cut into ¼-inch dice (about 1 large stalk)
Handful of chopped fresh cilantro leaves
Kosher salt
Freshly ground white pepper

To Serve:
1 head iceberg or green leaf lettuce, picked into individual leaves and stored in ice water until ready to use
Hoisin sauce

(1) Cut the tofu into ¼-inch slabs. Press firmly between paper towels to remove excess moisture, then cut into ¼-inch dice. Set aside.

(2) **For the Sauce:** Combine the wine, soy sauce, vinegar, hoisin sauce, and chile sauce (if using) in a small bowl and stir together until homogenous. Set aside. Combine the cornstarch and water in a separate small bowl and stir with a fork until the cornstarch is dissolved.

(3) **BEFORE YOU STIR-FRY, GET YOUR BOWLS READY:**

a. **Diced tofu**

b. **Pine nuts**

c. **Shiitakes**

d. **Garlic, ginger, and scallions**

e. **Jícama and celery**

f. **Sauce**

g. **Cornstarch slurry**

h. **Cilantro**

i. **Empty bowl for cooked ingredients**

j. **Serving platter**

(4) **For the Stir-Fry:** Combine the pine nuts and 1 tablespoon (15 ml) of the oil in a wok and place over medium heat. Cook, stirring frequently, until the nuts are well toasted, about 5 minutes. Transfer to an empty bowl and set aside.

(5) Return the wok to high heat and heat until lightly smoking. Add 1 tablespoon (15 ml) of the remaining oil and swirl. Add the tofu or chicken and cook, stirring frequently, until the tofu is browned all over, 6 to 8 minutes. Transfer to the bowl with the pine nuts.

(6) Wipe out the wok and return it to high heat until lightly smoking. Add 1 tablespoon (15 ml) of the remaining oil and swirl. Add the shiitakes and cook, stirring occasionally, until well browned all over, about 3 minutes. Transfer to the bowl with the tofu and pine nuts.

(7) Wipe out the wok and return it to high heat until lightly smoking. Add the remaining tablespoon (15 ml) oil and swirl. Add the garlic, ginger, and scallions and cook, stirring and tossing constantly, until fragrant, about 15 seconds. Add the jícama and celery and toss to combine.

(8) Return the tofu, mushrooms, and pine nuts to the wok and toss everything to combine. Stir the sauce and add to the wok by pouring it around the edges. Stir the cornstarch slurry and add it to the wok. Cook, tossing, until the sauce thickens and the mixture is glossy and dry, about 30 seconds. Stir in the cilantro (reserve a little for garnish) and season with salt and white pepper to taste. Transfer to a warm serving platter and sprinkle with the reserved cilantro.

(9) Serve immediately with lettuce leaves and hoisin sauce. To eat, spread a little hoisin sauce on the bottom of a lettuce leaf and spoon the filling into the lettuce. Eat with your hands.

GIREUM TTEOKBOKKI (STIR-FRIED KOREAN RICE CAKES AND KOREAN CHILE PASTE)

Garae-tteok are dense, chewy rice cakes made by pounding steamed rice into a dough similar to Japanese mochi but denser and even chewier (if you can imagine). In China, they are called *nian gao* and take on a variety of shapes and textures (many of them sweet).

While not technically noodles, they bear a resemblance in their use as popular ingredients in both stir-fries and brothy soups and stews. When stir-fried, they're called *tteokbokki* (pronounced like "duck Bucky," with particularly hard consonants), a dish I was introduced to by my friend Soohyun Chang. As undergrad architecture students we'd split our time between the all-nighters at the studio and cheap restaurants like Color near Packard's Corner in Boston's Allston neighborhood, where the hearty $7 plates of shareable Korean home cooking and street food fit our appetites and our budget. Soohyun has gone on to become a renowned architect, while I ended up focusing on those rice cakes (Color has closed).

Her career may be more beautiful and functional, but I'm pretty sure mine is more delicious. You may be familiar with *gungmul tteokbokki*, which are rice cakes stewed in a spicy red broth or sauce (see my recipe on page 540), but *gireum tteokbokki* are its more modern, street-friendly cousins. The flavors—lots of Korean chile flakes, sesame oil, scallions, soy sauce, and a sweetener to balance out the heat—are similar, but rather than being simmered in broth, the rice sticks are slowly fried until all the liquid evaporates and the spicy-sweet seasonings form a sticky, lightly caramelized layer on the exterior of each rice cake.

Unlike most stir-fries in this book, this one works best at a leisurely pace, which allows the seasonings to reduce and concentrate to really coat the sticks as they soften. I like to add a little butter to the wok—the nutty toasted milk solids add flavor and help the rice cakes caramelize and brown a little better—but you can omit it to keep the dish vegan.

Yield	**Active Time**
Serves 4	15 minutes
	Total Time
	30 minutes

NOTES

This recipe is traditionally made with rod-shaped Korean-style rice cakes, but disk-shaped cakes will work as well. If using frozen rice cakes, allow an additional 10 minutes of soaking time in step 1 so they thaw. This quantity of gochujang and gochugaru will make a moderately hot dish. Add more or less to taste.

INGREDIENTS

1 pound (450 g) Korean or Chinese rice cakes

1 tablespoon (15 ml) peanut, rice bran, or other neutral oil

4 to 5 scallions, thinly sliced

1 tablespoon (7 to 8 g) minced garlic (about 3 medium cloves)

1 tablespoon (15 g) unsalted butter

2 tablespoons (30 ml) gochujang, more or less to taste (see Notes)

2 tablespoon (10 g) gochugaru, more or less to taste

2 tablespoons (24 g) sugar

2 tablespoons (30 ml) light soy sauce

1 tablespoon (30 ml) roasted sesame oil

1 tablespoon (8 g) toasted sesame seeds

DIRECTIONS

(1) Place the rice cakes in a large bowl and cover with water. Heat the oil in a wok over medium heat until simmering. Add the scallions and garlic and cook, stirring, until softened but not browned, about 2 minutes. Add the butter and stir until melted. Add the gochujang, gochugaru, sugar, soy sauce, and sesame oil. Drain the rice cakes and add to the wok with whatever water is clinging to them.

(2) Cook, stirring frequently, until the sauce is completely reduced, the oil breaks out, and the rice cakes and scallions start to sizzle and brown in spots, about 10 minutes. Take your time here; the goal is a gentle, even cook so that the rice cakes are very soft and fully coated in the chile and oil as they tenderize—reduce the heat if they are sizzled very hard or the sauce seems like it'll reduce down before the 10-minute mark. When the rice cakes are soft and caramelized, season to taste with more chile flakes, stir in the sesame seeds, transfer to a plate, and serve, preferably with toothpicks.

RICE CAKES WITH PORK, SHRIMP, PINE NUTS, AND VEGETABLES

Tteokbokki might be most famous in its chile-laced forms, but its history dates back only to the middle of the twentieth century, while stir-fried rice cakes predate even the introduction of chiles to Korean cuisine. *Gungjung tteokbokki*, or "royal tteokbokki," for instance, features rice cakes stir-fried with beef, vegetables, and pine nuts and seasoned with soy sauce and sesame oil. The idea of using pine nuts in a stir-fry intrigued me, as did the idea of cooking down rice cakes in soy sauce until their edges crisp and the soy sauce forms a lightly charred glaze, similar to how it coats rice noodles in Beef Chow Fun (page 365) or Pad See Ew (page 372). You see stir-fries similar to this one in southern China, particularly in and around Shanghai.

Like many recipes in this book, I think of this one as more a blueprint than a recipe. You can use any green vegetable in place of the snap peas and any meat or tofu in place of the pork and shrimp. You could replace the shredded cabbage with Brussels sprouts leaves or shaved fennel or bok choy, or you could use a mix of mushrooms instead of the shiitake. Read through the recipe before hitting the supermarket and let your brain guide you once you're there. Or just follow the recipe exactly as written and save your brain for something more important. Like architecture.

Yield
Serves 4

Active Time
15 minutes

Total Time
30 minutes

NOTES

If using frozen rice cakes, allow an additional 10 minutes of soaking time in step 1 so they thaw. For even more flavor, instead of ground pork and chopped shrimp, you can use 8 ounces of "The Mix" (page 280) if you have any around. You can also omit the shrimp and pork and increase the ratio of vegetables by 2 ounces each to keep this dish vegetarian.

INGREDIENTS

1 pound (450 g) Korean or Chinese rice cakes (see Notes)

Kosher salt

4 ounces (120 g/about 1 cup) snap peas, green beans, or other crunchy green vegetables cut into 1½-inch pieces

¼ cup (40 g) pine nuts

¼ cup (60 ml) peanut, rice bran, or other neutral oil

4 ounces (120 g/about 1 cup) shredded green cabbage

4 scallions, cut on a bias into 1½- to 2-inch pieces

4 ounces (120 g/about 1 cup) shiitake mushrooms, stems discarded, caps cut into quarters

4 ounces (120 g) ground pork

4 ounces (120 g) shrimp, peeled and cut into ½-inch pieces

2 teaspoons (5 g) minced garlic (about 2 medium cloves)

2 tablespoons (30 ml) light soy sauce

1 tablespoon (12 g) sugar

2 teaspoons (10 ml) roasted sesame oil

DIRECTIONS

1. Place rice cakes in a large bowl and cover with water. Set aside while you cook the other ingredients.

2. Heat a quart (1l) of lightly salted water in a wok over high heat until boiling. Add the green vegetables and cook until bright green but still crisp, about 1 minute. Drain and spread the vegetables out on a large plate to cool and air-dry. Drain the rice cakes.

3. Wipe out the wok, add the pine nuts, and toast over medium heat, tossing and stirring frequently, until golden brown and a toasty aroma hits your nose, about 3 minutes. Transfer to a large bowl and set aside.

4. **For the Stir-Fry:** Heat the wok over high heat until lightly smoking. Add 1 tablespoon (15 ml) of the oil and swirl to coat. Add the cabbage and scallions and stir-fry, letting them sit undisturbed for 10 to 15 seconds at a time between tosses, until the cabbage is charred in spots, about 2 minutes. Transfer to the bowl with the pine nuts.

5. Wipe out the wok and reheat over high heat until lightly smoking. Add a tablespoon (15 ml) of the remaining oil and swirl to coat. Add the mushrooms and stir-fry until lightly browned in spots, about 2 minutes. Transfer to the bowl with the cabbage mixture.

6. Wipe out the wok and reheat over high heat until lightly smoking. Add a tablespoon (15 ml) of the remaining oil and swirl to coat. Add the drained green vegetables and stir-fry until lightly browned in spots, about 1 minute. Transfer to the bowl with the cabbage mixture.

7. Wipe out the wok and reheat over high heat until lightly smoking. Add the remaining tablespoon (15 ml) of oil and swirl to coat. Add the pork and shrimp and stir-fry until the pork is no longer pink and the shrimp are no longer translucent, about 1 minute. Add the rice cakes, garlic, soy sauce, sugar, sesame oil, and the vegetable mixture from the bowl. Stir-fry until the sauce has evaporated and the rice cakes begin to char lightly in spots, about 2 minutes. Transfer to a serving platter and serve immediately.

2

RICE

As the child of a Japanese American household, I grew up eating rice. A lot of rice. We ate it with our mapo tofu (page 598) and our Japanese curry. We stirred a raw egg into leftover rice to make *tamago-kake gohan* (page 230). On road trips my grandmother would pack a plastic container full of *onigiri*—Japanese rice balls that she seasoned with salt and MSG. We ate them wrapped in nori with a side of salty pickled plums—*umeboshi* or on their own. White rice with a sprinkle of *furikake* (a seasoned Japanese rice topping; see page 521) was a reliable side dish at any meal. Indeed, the Japanese word for meal—*gohan*—is the same as the word for rice.

Similarly, my wife, as a Colombiana, also grew up eating rice. A lot of rice. Consequently, our daughter is also growing up eating rice. A lot of rice.

We're going to be learning a lot about rice in this chapter. As you read it, you may notice that not every recipe uses the wok. Despite the conceit of this book, it seemed a shame not to share some of my favorite ways to enjoy rice. I apologize in advance for any extra deliciousness that may ensue.

We've Got Rice. You've Got Questions.

Rice in Asia is as much a cultural cornerstone as bread in Europe or corn in Mexico. But what makes it unique? Well, it starts with the quantity of it consumed.

Q *How much rice do we really eat in the world?*

A As the staple grain throughout Asia and the Middle East, as well as much of Africa and Central and South America, rice is the main nutrition source for over 60 percent of the world's population. Though corn is the most widely produced grain in the world (around 850 million metric tons annually, compared to rice's 725), rice is the most popular grain for human consumption (much of the corn grown in the world is used for animal feed, or further processing into other ingredients).

This is surprising, given that rice is more labor- and resource-extensive to produce than other grains. Not only does it generally take more water to grow and more labor to harvest (travel to Asia and you'll still find fields and fields of rice paddies tended to by human hands), but it's also more tedious to process. This is not so much because of its makeup or shape, but because while wheat and corn are typically ground into flour or meal, rice is unique among grains in that humans have developed a taste for eating it whole.

Q *I don't get it. Why does grinding other grains into flour make them less labor-intensive? Isn't grinding an extra step?*

A Grains have three key parts: the bran, the germ, and the endosperm. In refined flours (like the white flour you use to bake biscuits), the bran and germ are completely removed. Whole-grain flours still contain those bits. With flours and meals, the process for removing the bran and germ is industrialized and efficient. Grains are ground or rolled whole, then sieved to remove the undesirable bits. Rice, on the other hand, is generally consumed in grain form, not as a flour, which means that the outer layers must be carefully removed from each grain during processing.

Q *Ah, I got it. So how about . . .*

A But wait! There's more. Not only does rice have the same bran layer that wheat and corn have; it also has a husk on top of that. Think of it like undressing a toddler. It's hard enough to keep them still while you pull off their jacket and pants. By the time you get to the shirt and underwear, they've had it, and sometimes, no amount of Tumbleleaf can help. Rice is like wheat that's wearing an extra jacket. Like wheat and corn, rice has a bran and germ that needs to be removed. But it's also got an extra layer of husk. Even the healthy "whole-grain" stuff—brown rice—has had that husk layer removed before drying and packaging.

Q *Wow, that is a lot of extra work! Here's my next que . . .*

A That's not all! After the husk, bran, and germ have all been removed, rice is further polished to remove aleurone, the layer of fats and proteins that form the outer coat of the endosperm. This is the bit that turns rancid when brown rice is stored too long. Removing it is essential to extending the storage life for rice.

Q *Are you finished? Can I speak o . . .*

A It gets worse! Corn and wheat are grown in huge quantities with relatively few varieties—they are monocrops—while rice is extraordinarily varied. Just think about trying to make sushi with fragrant Indian basmati rice or serving sticky glutinous Thai rice with your beans and enchiladas. For a worldwide staple, rice is still a fiercely regional food. In larger Asian markets, the varieties of rice you'll find on the shelves are as numerous as, well, grains of rice.

Q *Alright, alright. I get it. So why do we bother with all that processing? Why don't people in Asia just eat wheat and corn?*

A There's not a simple answer to that question, but the most obvious is that humans have developed a taste for the stuff. We *like* it whole. Sure, some people *pretend* to like whole-grain wheatberries, and that fancy restaurant down the street might be serving farro risotto to folks who'd secretly rather be eating the real stuff, but rice? We like rice, we like it in grain-sized bits, and we're willing to go through great lengths to get it. Indeed, though these days we mainly eat one species of rice, *Oryza sativa* (albeit in a wide range of cultivars), rice was actually domesticated as a staple independently on three separate continents, South America, Africa, and Asia. (The South American variety was replaced with Asian rice when the Spaniards came to the New World, while the African variety is rarely seen outside of Africa.)

Q *I've noticed that the Chinese restaurant down the street serves rice that's different from the sushi place, and **really** different from the Indian restaurant. What gives?*

A Broadly, rice falls into two categories: *indica* and *japonica*.
  Japonica rice is grown in temperate or high-altitude locations, like the more mountainous regions of northern China, Japan, and Korea. Much of the *japonica* rice sold and consumed in the United States is grown in California.

Japonica typically has shorter grains than *indica*. Most medium- or short-grain rices are *japonica*, including the Arborio used for risotto, the Bomba used for paella, sushi rice, and the steamed rice at your local Chinese restaurant.

Japonica rice is notable for its texture. It sticks together in moist clumps, or, in the case of risotto or paella, offers up extra starch to make its own creamy sauce.

Indica rice is grown in tropical and subtropical lowland areas, like India, much of Southeast Asia, and the American South. Unlike *japonica* rice, *indica* varieties cook up with individual grains, giving it a loose, fluffier texture. Carolina rice is *indica*. So are basmati and jasmine or the rice you get at the Persian restaurant. The rice you'll find in Louisiana Creole red beans and rice is *indica*.

Interestingly, you'll find that in countries where stickier varieties of rice prevail—Japan and China, for instance—rice is typically consumed with chopsticks. In places that favor Indica—India, much of Southeast Asia, the Southern United States, and the Middle East, for instance—rice is typically eaten with forks, spoons, or fingers.

For more details on different types of rice, see the chart on page 224.

Q *What's this "converted rice" all about?*

A Converted rice is rice, typically long- or medium-grain *indica* varieties, that have been par-cooked and dried *before* the husk, bran, and germ are removed. The par-cooking not only let's the rice cook faster at home, but it also imparts some of the nutrients from the outer layers to the central germ. Uncle Ben's is the most well-known converted rice.

Q *Occasionally I see bags labeled "New Crop" at the Asian grocery store. What does that mean?*

A "New Crop" rice is exactly what it sounds like: rice from the first, or newest, harvest of the year. Like beans and other dried goods, *japonica* rice has a long but not indefinite shelf life, and as time goes on, starch granules will tighten and surface proteins start to form a hardened layer on the surface of each grain. Thus, New Crop *japonica* rice typically releases its aroma better and cooks up a little more tender and sticky than non-new-crop rice. In many countries, new-crop rice is an annual luxury people will indulge in. I try to pick up a bag of it whenever I see it on the shelf, usually around early December.

Because it is fresher and absorbs water more easily, I never rinse new-crop rice before cooking.

Indica rices that are prized for the firm, individual grains, on the other hand, are frequently aged—basmati rice in particular, where the best stuff can be aged for a year or more to improve grain texture and develop its fragrant aroma.

Q *But what rice is best? I need to know, because I'm having a debate on the Internet and I NEED to be right.*

A Whatever your position is, if you've picked a *best* rice, you're wrong. I'm sorry.

It all depends on the situation and your personal preference. Some folks love brown rice for its nutty flavor, chewy texture, or health benefits. Other prefer the moist clumps of medium-grain rice or the floral aroma of Thai jasmine rice.

Most of the rice I cook at home is *japonica* rice grown in California. Growing up, my family ate mostly *japonica*, and it's what I stock most frequently in my own pantry. Koshihikari is a widely available variety that seems to clump in perfectly bite-sized nuggets that are easy to pick up with chopsticks. It has a delicate floral aroma and a pleasantly firm chew when properly cooked. (Think: al dente pasta.) I like Tamaki Gold brand, a premium brand from California that is available in both white (hulled) and brown (whole grain) varieties.

But when it comes to rice, I'm a firm believer in free love. If I'm making an Indian meal, I'll cook basmati. If I'm making Thai food, I may break out the jasmine or even the glutinous sticky rice.

Calrose, a *japonica* variety also grown in California, is the most popular medium-grain rice in the world for a reason. It is mildly fragrant and cooks up very tender and moderately sticky. It's most likely what you're getting at the Chinese restaurant and is especially ideal for fried rice (page 268). Kokuho Rose is a popular brand of Calrose that I enjoy with lots of Chinese stir-fries.

Q *So . . . should I rinse my rice or not? I have an Asian mother-in-law, if that makes any difference.*

A Rinsing rice removes some of the powdered starch that is clinging to its surface, resulting in looser, more separate grains than unrinsed rice. But whether you rinse or not comes down to personal preference and the exact brand of rice you're using. Broadly, if you're using an *indica* variety where individual grains are expected, it's useful to rinse them to reduce excess starch. However, with these varieties, since the starch and trace vitamins and minerals on the surface are removed during rinsing anyway, you can accomplish the same goal (and eliminate the difficulty of nailing that perfect water-to-rice ratio) by just boiling them in way too much water, like pasta.

I know. Blasphemy. Delicious, foolproof blasphemy.

With *japonica* varieties, rinsing can be useful if your rice often comes out gummy or too sticky,

but personally, I rarely bother other than in very specific circumstances (if I'm making sushi, for instance, I'd rather not have my rice be too sticky).

Rinsing relatively unprocessed brown rice accomplishes very little. (I can't help you with the mother-in-law situation.)

The one time you'll always want to rinse rice is if you plan on cooking it and immediately using it for fried rice (see page 270). The excess starch can cause it to clump in the wok, which will require you to add more oil, leading to heavy, greasy results. Rinsing the rice prevents this issue.

Q *OK, I get that* japonica *rice is stickier than* indica *rice, but what is* sticky *rice? Is that the same as sushi rice? And is it OK to eat it if I'm on a gluten-free diet?*

A "Sticky rice" does not mean simply "rice that is sticky"! Although sushi rice or even the steamed rice at Chinese restaurants is sometimes referred to as "sticky rice," it should really be called "stickier than *indica* rice" rice. Actual sticky rice is a few specific varieties (of both *indica* and *japonica*) that are exceptionally low in amylose and high in amylopectin, making them glue-like and sticky. The dry grains are easily distinguishable from standard rice by their opaque white appearance. They look chalky, as opposed to translucent.

Sticky rice is famously served with sweet mangoes and coconut syrup in Thai mango sticky rice and in many types of Chinese dim sum, where it can be steamed in bamboo leaves, formed into a paste and wrapped around sesame paste, deep-fried into dumplings, or made into rice cakes for stir-fry. Glutinous rice is also very popular in Burma.

Glutinous rice also has uses outside of cooking. One of my favorite ways to use it (and the main reason I keep a bag of it around) is to toast it dry, crush it in a mortar and pestle, and use it to flavor dipping sauces like *Jaew* (page 440) or sprinkle it over Lao or Isan Thai *larp* salads.

Glutinous should not be confused with *glutenous*. The former refers to the glue-like texture of glutinous rice, while the latter refers to gluten, the protein matrix formed when flour and water are combined. Glutinous rice contains no gluten and is perfectly fine for folks on a gluten-free diet.

Q *And "broken" rice? Why would I want to buy something that's broken?*

A Broken rice is exactly what it sounds like: rice grains that have been broken into smaller pieces. It is typically used for dishes like congee (page 249), a thick rice porridge in which you *want* extra starch released and the rice grains to break down. You can make congee just fine with unbroken rice, but broken rice is cheaper and cooks faster, making it a popular choice in Asian households.

Q *Why do they call it "steamed rice" anyway, when it's not really steamed?*

A You got me. I guess it sounds better than "simmered rice," or, if frequently when I'm trying to cook it, "rice that's steamed in the middle, raw on the top, and burnt on the bottom." There are some rices that are truly steamed, notably Thai sticky rice, which is traditionally steamed in bamboo baskets over simmering water.

Q *How do you feel about those microwavable single-serving bowls of white or brown rice that have been popping up at my supermarket or Asian market?*

A As a convenience food, they're great. They cook in about 90 seconds in the microwave, and they taste pretty decent, though occasionally a bit mushier than I prefer. I use them when I'm in a pinch and my daughter needs a quick snack (or it's late night and I'm feeling peckish and lazy). The major downside is the packaging and price. Good brands, like Tamaki, cost about $1.75 apiece for a single serving of rice, and of course, that's one plastic bowl to recycle for each serving you use. A much better option is to just cook more rice than you need each time you cook a batch and save the extra for the future.

Q *OK, so if I cook more rice than I need, what's the best way to store and reheat it? Does it come out as good after reheating?*

A I store cooked rice in sealed deli containers in the fridge, or, if I know I'm not going to eat it within the next week or so, in zipper-lock freezer bags. I put the rice in the bag, squeeze the air out as I seal it, then press the rice down into a flat, even layer for rapid freezing and defrosting.

But rice, like any starch-based food, gets stale as it cools and sits, which means that its starches revert from a loose, gel-like structure to a more rigid crystalline structure, making the individual grains taste dry and unpleasantly firm. Staleness is a separate phenomenon from dryness—breads and rice can get stale without losing moisture and can lose moisture without getting stale. This means that even in a perfectly airtight container, rice will get stale as it cools in the refrigerator.

Fortunately, cold rice is very easy to revive. There are a couple ways to do it. The simplest is in the microwave, where it revives to pretty much as good as fresh, whether from the fridge or the freezer. Crack the lid of your storage container a little bit to allow steam to escape or transfer the rice to a microwave-safe bowl with a microwave-safe plate placed on top of it and microwave on high power. Start with 60 seconds of heating time per cup of rice (or 90 seconds per cup if it's coming from the freezer), then heat in 15-second intervals until it's as hot as you'd like it.

If you don't have a microwave, you can reheat rice by placing it in a bowl on top of a steamer insert set in a pot with a couple inches of simmering water. Place the lid on the pot and let the rice steam until it's fully heated.

The other alternative is to not bother trying to reheat it to its original form at all. Stale, refrigerated rice works great in dishes like fried rice (268) and congee (249).

Q *Oh—one more question! I've noticed that the rice served on the side at Chinese or Japanese restaurants can* **smell** *great but sometimes taste kinda bland. What gives?*

A Most likely it's because you are used to eating rice from parts of the Western world that typically salt their rice while cooking, whereas in Asia, rice is frequently cooked in plain, unsalted water. Having grown up in a Japanese American household, I find that Japanese rice cooked with salt tastes . . . wrong to me. As wrong as Carolina rice cooked without it.

The reason for this is not entirely clear, but the fact that rice in those Asian countries is frequently served alongside highly seasoned dishes is the most likely answer. It acts sort of as a palate cleanser—a neutral base to give your mouth a break from the assault of flavor in a typical stir-fry.

In many countries, in fact, it's typical to have plain, unsalted steamed rice when it's served as a side dish, but in dishes where the rice is the star, it'll be seasoned. Fried rice is seasoned with salt, soy sauce, or oyster sauce. Sushi rice is seasoned with vinegar, salt, and sugar. The rice balls my grandmother packed for our road trips would be seasoned with salt and MSG before being shaped. Tamago-Kake Gohan (page 230) is rice mixed with an egg and salty soy sauce. I also love putting salty-sweet furikake on top of it.

Rice Varieties

There is a huge variety of rice available worldwide, so I'm not even going to attempt to cover them all. These are the ones I see most frequently in American markets and the ones I'm likely to buy.

Japonica

TYPE	DESCRIPTION	WHERE YOU'D EAT IT	POPULAR BRANDS
Calrose	A medium-grain rice grown in California that has won multiple awards from various international rice organizations, including "World's Best Rice" from the World Rice Conference	As a side for Chinese stir-fries. It's what you'd get at the local Chinese restaurant	Nishiki, Kokuho Rose, and Botan
Koshihikari	A short-grain rice from Japan that is stickier than Calrose	Formed into sushi or served at a Japanese restaurant. This is my go-to variety, even when I serve it with stir-fries.	Tamaki Gold, Kagayaki, and Sekka
Arborio	A short-grain Italian rice	It's the primary rice used in risotto, though Carnaroli and Vialone Nano are also excellent for risotto.	Riceselect is widely available in the United States, but I typically look for Italian brands at import stores.
Bomba	A short-grain Spanish rice	It's what gives traditional Spanish paella its creamy, risotto-like texture.	Look for any imported brand with the "D.O.P. Calasparra" designation on the packaging.

Indica

TYPE	DESCRIPTION	WHERE YOU'D EAT IT	POPULAR BRANDS
Basmati	A very long-grained, fragrant rice with distinct, fluffy grains. Basmati rice is typically aged for a year or more to help it develop its unique flavor.	Indian, Pakistani, and Middle Eastern restaurants	Daawat, Royal, and Tilda
Jasmine	A highly fragrant, floral rice with medium-long grains native to Thailand, where it's known as Hom Mali rice	It's the rice of choice in Thai restaurants and some Chinese restaurants.	Asian Best ("Red Elephant") and Dynasty
Black Rice	Also known as "forbidden rice," it's a whole-grain rice with a deep black outer bran layer left intact. Once cooked, it turns purplish.	In some Chinese restaurants	Lotus and Lundberg
American Long-Grain	A long-grain rice that cooks into individual grains with a mild flavor and aroma.	In the American South or at the school cafeteria	Carolina, Lundberg, and Canilla

Rice Tools

You don't need any special tools for cooking or serving rice, but here are some that I find particularly useful.

A RICE COOKER OR COUNTERTOP PRESSURE COOKER

You can cook rice in a saucepan or in a wok (see "How to Cook Rice without a Rice Cooker or Pressure Cooker," page 226), but I almost never bother when a rice cooker (or, these days, a countertop electric pressure cooker) does the job so much more consistently and effortlessly. No need to set the timer or adjust the flame of a burner; just add your rice and water, put on the lid, hit the button, and focus on preparing the rest of your meal.

A BAMBOO RICE PADDLE

A regular metal or wooden serving spoon works alright for rice, but a short-handled, wide-bowled bamboo spoon specifically designed for rice works much better, especially for stickier rice varieties like Calrose or Japanese sushi rice. The short handle offers more leverage to scoop up sticky rice, and the naturally breathable bamboo surface releases that rice onto a plate or serving bowl much more easily than metal or hardwood spoons. You can find bamboo rice paddles for around $5 online or at any Asian supermarket or kitchen supply store.

A WOODEN WOK LID

If you want to use a wok to cook your rice, a tight-fitting wooden lid will help it cook more evenly. I bought mine online from a Chinese manufacturer called Zhen San Huan, which offers well-crafted, lightweight lids custom-sized for your own wok. (See page 9 for more on lids.)

Rice Ratios

The method for cooking most any type of rice is similar, but the amount of water you need to cook the rice varies by grain size and variety. When I buy rice, I transfer it to clear, sealable containers in my pantry (OXO POP containers and mason jars are my containers of choice), onto which I affix a label printed with the variety of rice as well as the ratio of water to rice. My koshihikari rice, for example, says "Koshihikari, 1.1:1" indicating a ratio of 1.1 parts of water to 1 part of rice by volume. Here are more water ratios for common rice varieties. Note that because a pressure cooker releases less moisture through evaporation than a lidded pot or a rice cooker, it requires a little less water.

RICE VARIETY	WATER-TO-RICE RATIO, by volume (stovetop or rice cooker)	WATER-TO-RICE RATIO, by volume (pressure cooker)
Japanese sushi rice (Koshihikari)	1.2 to 1	1.1 to 1
Jasmine rice	1.5 to 1	1.4 to 1
Medium-grain American Rice	1.5 to 1	1.4 to 1
Long-grain American Rice	2 to 1	1.8 to 1
Calrose	1.3 to 1	1.2 to 1
Basmati	1.75 to 1	1.7 to 1
Black or Red Rice	1.5 to 1	1.4 to 1

The Best Way to Cook Rice, or, How I Learned to Stop Worrying and Love the Rice Cooker

I can't cook rice. It's just one of my many deficiencies, but the one that gave me the most embarrassment in the kitchen. We've heard about those sushi masters who make their apprentices cook nothing but rice for decades before being allowed to even begin to think about starting to glance in the direction of a fish or a knife. This is a reasonable approach if instilling honor and discipline with a healthy bit of hazing is your goal. But as it turns out, there is zero correlation between one's ability to *cook* great rice and one's ability to *serve* great rice.

Just do what virtually every modern Japanese household does: get a rice cooker. You don't need a fancy one. Even the simplest will cook rice more evenly and consistently at the touch of a button than you'll ever achieve on the stovetop. They work via a simple but ingenious sensor mechanism that mechanically disengages the electronic circuit powering a heating element as soon as the temperature at the base of the pot rises above the boiling temperature of water, an indication that the liquid has been absorbed by the rice.

Fancier models from brands like Zojirushi will have different settings for different grains, will monitor the contents of the pot and make adjustments on the fly using fuzzy logic circuits, will have timers to deliver hot rice first thing in the morning or when you get home from work, and will be better at keeping your rice warm. It's the best way to produce flawless rice over and over and what's more, there's no fiddling with the heat, setting timers, or doing that thing where you worry the rice isn't cooking right so you crack the lid to check and the steam escapes and then your rice *actually* doesn't cook right.

Personally, I use an electric countertop multicooker on the pressure cooker setting, which cooks rice faster and as well as most dedicated rice cookers, and does whole slew of other useful things. InstantPot makes a number of models with different sizes and features at a price that fits most budgets. The Breville Fast-Slow Pro is my top pick for electric multi-cookers

if you've got a little more money to invest in features and performance.

To cook rice in a pressure cooker, add the rice and the volume of water listed on the package, then set the pressure cooker to low (7.5 psi) and cook white rice for 5 minutes after the pressure has been achieved, or brown rice for 10 minutes. Release the pressure with a series of short bursts, or if you're not in a hurry, allow for a natural release.

I can't cook rice, but my multicooker sure can.

HOW TO COOK RICE WITHOUT A RICE COOKER OR PRESSURE COOKER

Alright, I do *actually* know how to cook rice without a pressure cooker or rice cooker. It's not too difficult. Here are the basic steps:

Step 1 • Measure and Rinse the Rice (Rinsing Optional)

Rinsing rice will remove excess starch and make it less clumpy and sticky. Whether this is a good thing is up to personal preference and your intended use. I typically do not rinse my rice unless I'm going to use it immediately for fried rice (see page 270).

If not rinsing, this step is straightforward. Just measure the rice and water using the chart on page 225, then transfer it to a saucepan large enough that the combined rice and water comes no higher than three-quarters of the way up the pan. If you have a tight-fitting wooden lid for your wok, you can use that in place of the saucepan.

The one snag that rinsing introduces is that the water that clings to the rice after rinsing throws the ratio of water to rice off. To solve this problem, I first measure my rice and water by volume, then combine them in a liquid measuring cup, noting the level of the top of the water on the side of the cup.

Next, I drain the rice in a fine-mesh strainer and run it under cool running water, agitating it until the water runs clear—an indication that the excess surface starch has been removed. I then transfer it back to the liquid measuring cup and refill it with water up to the level I had noted earlier.

Finally, I transfer the perfectly measured rice and water to my cooking vessel.

Step 2 • Season as Desired

Typically, rice served alongside stir-fries or other Asian dishes is unseasoned. It is meant as a mild counterpart to intensely flavored dishes. But if you like salt in your rice, go ahead and add a pinch or two to the water before cooking. You can also season your rice with aromatics like bay leaves, cinnamon sticks, star anise, and other whole spices at this stage if desired.

Step 3 • Bring to a Boil

Bring the rice and water to a boil over high heat, stirring once or twice as it heats up to ensure that the rice is not stuck to the bottom of the pot.

Step 4 • Simmer

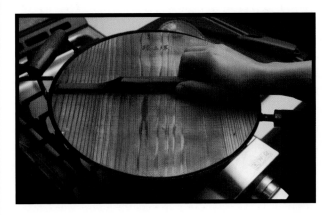

As soon as the rice boils, cover the pot or wok with a tight-fitting lid (if your lid is a little loose, you can wrap it in a damp kitchen towel before placing it on the pot or wok to form a tighter seal), reduce the heat to the minimum your stovetop can handle, and let the rice cook undisturbed for 10 minutes. Peeking during cooking can release steam and heat, so don't do it, even if you're tempted to, and definitely *do not stir!*

Step 5 • Rest

After 10 minutes, completely shut off the heat and let the rice rest for another 5 to 10 minutes to finish absorbing water. At this point you can hold the rice off the heat in the lidded pot until ready to serve.

2.1 RICE BOWLS

This is a bowl of rice. It is delicious, but it is boring. It is boring in the way that monster-truck shows and movies about aliens aren't. It's so boring that the term *white rice* is used to describe other things that are as boring as it. I could go on about how boring it is, but I'm afraid that this paragraph would then become a little too white rice.

How do you stop having a boring bowl of rice? Top it. A bowl of rice topped with simple simmered, stir-fried, broiled, or pickled ingredients is a staple meal in Japan and other parts of Asia. Growing up, we ate *donburi*—the Japanese name for both the vessel that topped rice is served in and the dish itself—of one form

or another at least once a week. In the following section, I'll show you how to make a few of the classics. Any of the cooked dishes can be made in your flat-bottomed wok (a 14-inch wok is the perfect size for feeding four) or in smaller skillets for single or double portions. All of the recipes scale easily.

TAMAGO-KAKE GOHAN

"I want egg and rice and soy sauce" is what my daughter, Alicia, says to me every morning when I ask her what she wants for breakfast. It used to be pancakes. Now it's *tamago-kake gohan*.

Other than maybe pouring milk over cereal, *tamago-kake gohan* ("Tah-MAH-go KAH-keh GOH-hahn," literally "egg-covered rice"), was the very first recipe I learned, and it's Japanese comfort food at its simplest. When I was growing up in New York, my Japanese grandparents lived in the apartment one floor below us. On weekends, my mom would occasionally shoo us off to spend the night downstairs. My sisters

and I would sleep on a thick futon rolled out on the floor, drinking barley tea and Calpis, a Japanese yogurt-flavored soft drink. In the morning, we'd head into my grandmother's sitting room for more tea and *tamago-kake gohan*.

We'd each get a bowl of hot rice (or, in my older sister's case, room-temperature rice, which she preferred) and an egg to break into it. Then we'd season it with a little bit of soy sauce, a pinch of salt, and a shake of Aji-No-Moto, a Japanese brand of pure powdered MSG. We'd whip up the rice with a pair of chopsticks, the egg turning pale yellow and foamy, holding the rice in a light, frothy suspension somewhere between a custard and a meringue. The Japanese have a thing for this kind of slippery, tender texture. If we were feeling extra bold, we'd top it up with a bit of shredded dried nori or a shake of furikake, the mixed seasoning that's typically eaten on plain rice but works particularly well here.

It's been a staple meal for me my entire life (and it mildly grossed out my wife the first time she saw me eat it). It's something hearty and delicious to throw together in minutes for breakfast or a late-night snack—I'll microwave leftover rice to get it hot again for tamago-kake gohan. It's such a simple, common food for me that it wasn't until I posted a picture of it on

Instagram (where it quickly became my most liked post) that I realized that tamago-kake gohan, or—as the kids are calling it these days—"TKG," is now a *thing*. It's been primped and primed and is ready for the spotlight. I would frankly not be surprised if food trucks selling eggy rice already exist in Austin or if fancy chefs in Brooklyn are serving bowls of seasoned rice topped with sous-vide eggs.

Tamago-kake gohan, your time has come.

The good news is, you don't really need to go anywhere to get it. It's a two-minute recipe (three, tops, if you're real slow), and you probably already have most of the ingredients you need to make it. Start with a bowl of rice—about a cup of cooked rice per egg is right. So long as it's not stale, it can be cold, lukewarm, hot, or anywhere in between. If you've got leftover rice in the fridge, put some in a bowl, cover it with a saucer, and microwave it for a minute, and it'll be good to go. I keep those little plastic trays of shelf-stable, precooked, microwave-ready rice in my pantry specifically for tamago-kake gohan (you can find them at most Asian markets near the dry rice).

Next, you need an egg. You do want to use a good, clean egg and break it cleanly, as you're going to be eating it raw. If you are squeamish about such things, buy pasteurized eggs (or pasteurize them yourself, using a sous-vide circulator at 135°F for 2 hours), or gently coddle your eggs in simmering water for a couple of minutes before adding them. Coddled eggs won't have quite the same lightness after they're added to the rice, but you'll get the general effect.

Some people like to be fussy, perhaps separating the egg and mixing the white into the rice before folding in the yolk. Others will whip together the soy sauce and the egg before stirring it into the rice. I've tried all these techniques, and honestly, I can find absolutely no reason to use them when the easiest method works just as well: Dump the egg into the rice, season it, and stir.

My grandmother always used extremely simple seasonings. Some people like to add a dash of dashi (or, more frequently, some granules of Hondashi), which can give it an appealingly savory and smoky flavor. Some people drizzle in mirin for sweetness. I generally don't bother, although, when I've got some on hand, I've been known to use bottled, concentrated soba noodle *tsuyu*, which contains all of those ingredients in a conveniently premixed form.

The real trick is in the beating. You need to beat thoroughly, and you need to beat vigorously. It'll take a little effort to get all the clumps out of the rice, but you want to continue beating even after that's happened. Just like creaming butter and sugar for a cookie dough, as you beat the rice and egg mixture, it will incorporate more and more air. Meanwhile, egg proteins will also stretch and tangle, giving the dish more cohesion. By the time you're done, the mixture should flow and settle very, very slowly in the bowl—just slightly thicker than an Italian-style risotto, but far lighter.

It's ready to eat as is, but if you want to get extra fancy with it, do what I like to do: Top it off with an extra egg yolk. Your grandmother isn't here to stop you right now.

TAMAGO-KAKE GOHAN

Yield
Serves 1

Active Time
2 minutes

Total Time
2 minutes

NOTES

Hondashi is powdered dashi that can be found at any Japanese market and most well-stocked supermarkets. Furikake is a seasoning mixture typically made with seaweed, dried sweetened bonito, and sesame seeds, among other ingredients. It can be found at any Japanese market.

INGREDIENTS

1 to 1½ cups hot cooked white rice

1 large egg, plus 1 large egg yolk (optional)

Light soy sauce, preferably Japanese usukuchi shoyu

Kosher salt

MSG powder, such as Aji-No-Moto or Ac'cent (optional)

Mirin (optional)

Hondashi (optional; see Notes)

Furikake (optional; see Notes)

Thinly sliced or torn nori (optional)

DIRECTIONS

Place the rice in a bowl and make a shallow indentation in the center. Break the whole egg into the center. Season with ½ teaspoon soy sauce, a pinch of salt, a pinch of MSG (if using), ½ teaspoon mirin (if using), and a pinch of Hondashi (if using). Stir vigorously with chopsticks to incorporate the egg; it should become pale yellow, frothy, and fluffy in texture. Taste and adjust the seasonings as desired. Sprinkle with furikake and nori (if using), make a small indentation in the top, and add the extra egg yolk (if using). Serve immediately.

Soy Sauce, Dashi, and Mirin: The Heart of Japanese Cooking

The combination of savory soy sauce, smoky dashi stock, and sweet mirin is the heart of Japanese cooking. Where France has its chicken stock and butter and Mexico has its dried chiles, Japan has soy-dashi-mirin. It's used in countless savory dishes. It's what you dip cold soba or somen noodles into. It's the basic broth for a bowl of udon. Thinly sliced beef is simmered in it to make sukiyaki. It's what you dip your tempura into. It's *everywhere*.

In Japanese supermarkets you're likely to see bottles of concentrated soy-dashi-mirin labeled *mentsuyu* (noodle dipping sauce), or simply *tsuyu*, with dilution levels listed for various dishes. You can buy that stuff—most brands are good to great—or you can easily make it yourself at home. It takes about 10 minutes to make, and once finished, it will last indefinitely in the fridge, ready to dispense at a moment's notice without the need to pull out each of the individual ingredients every time.

How to Shred Nori for Rice Bowls

Nori is thinly pressed sheets of dried laver, a type of seaweed. At a Japanese supermarket you're likely to find it in a few different forms: large sheets intended to be used to wrap sushi, seasoned bite-sized snack strips, and finely shredded as a topping for rice bowls. Don't bother buying the preshredded stuff—the full sheets are typically cheaper, and it's simple to shred nori at home.

You can use a knife, but I find that the most effective method is to fold the nori over onto itself a few times into a tight bundle, then snip it into fine shreds with a pair of sharp kitchen shears. Nori should be stored as whole sheets in an airtight pouch (usually it's sold in resealable packaging).

HOMEMADE CONCENTRATED MENTSUYU (SOY-DASHI-MIRIN MIX)

NOTE
You can use an additional ¾ cup (180 g) of sake mixed with ½ cup (5 ounces/150 g) of sugar in place of the mirin. Katsuobushi is dried smoked bonito flakes, available anywhere Japanese groceries are sold (see page 516).

INGREDIENTS

½ cup (120 ml) sake
1 cup (240 ml) mirin (see Note)
1 cup (240 ml) shoyu
½ ounce (15 g/about 1½ cups) katsuobushi
  (see Note)
½ ounce (15 g/about two 3-inch square
  pieces) kombu

DIRECTIONS

Bring the sake and mirin to a boil in a small saucepan and cook until there are no strong alcohol aromas left, about 2 minutes. Add the soy sauce, katsuobushi, and kombu. Simmer for 2 more minutes. Let cool, strain through a fine-mesh strainer, and transfer to an airtight container. Store in the refrigerator indefinitely.

Tsuyu Dilution

Now that you have concentrated tsuyu, here's a rough guide to how to dilute it for various common Japanese dishes.

DISH	TSUYU TO WATER RATIO	INSTRUCTIONS
Cold soba or somen noodles	1 to 3	Combine the tsuyu with cold water. Dip chilled noodles in the sauce as you eat.
Hot udon or soba noodles	1 to 6	Combine the tsuyu with boiling water and pour over cooked noodles.
For donburi (rice bowls)	1 to 4	Simmer donburi ingredients in diluted tsuyu (see donburi recipes starting on page 230)
For oden (hot pot)	1 to 8	Simmer the tsuyu and water in a hot pot at the table. Serve with fresh green vegetables, mushrooms, sliced meats, tofu, and noodles for cooking tableside.
For tempura (see page 471)	1 to 3	Combine the tsuyu with cold water. Add grated daikon radish if desired. Dip hot tempura in the sauce as you eat.
For hiyayakko (silken tofu with sauce; page 621)	1 to 1	Dilute the tsuyu with cold water and drizzle over silken tofu. Top with bonito flakes and scallions.
For agedashi tofu (fried tofu with soy-dashi; page 446)	1 to 3	Dilute the tsuyu with boiling water and pour over fried tofu. Top with bonito flakes, grated daikon radish, and scallions.

Chart

OYAKODON

This is Japanese soul food.

In Japanese, *oya* means "parent" and *ko* means "child." In this case, the oya and the ko are chicken and egg. To make it, I start with the classic Japanese sweet and savory combination of dashi, soy sauce, sake, and mirin or sugar (you can use diluted tsuyu, page 231, in place of all of these ingredients). After bringing the mixture to a simmer, I add a thinly sliced yellow onion. If you want to get all fancy or plan on making this a lot, you can spring for a donburi pan, a small, saucer-like skillet designed specifically for simmering ingredients destined for rice topping. Otherwise, an 8-inch skillet works well for two portions, or a wok will do the job for four.

I like to use a little bit more broth than is typical—I start with about a cup for every three eggs—because I like to simmer it down to tenderize the onion and to concentrate the flavor of the stock. I find that cooking the onions for a full 5 minutes at a hard simmer before adding some thinly sliced chicken gives them plenty of time to tenderize.

I also like to use boneless, skinless chicken thighs, which stay juicy as they simmer, though you can easily use chicken breast if you prefer. Just be sure to slice the chicken thin so that it cooks rapidly, and don't let it overcook! Five to 7 minutes is plenty of time for thighs, and 3 to 4 minutes should do for breasts.

Once the chicken is cooked through, I add some sliced scallions. If you can get your hands on *mitsuba*, this is the place to use it. It's a Japanese herb that looks and tastes a bit like parsley, but the flavor is much milder. The aroma reminds me a little of watercress, but without any of the pepperiness. It won't make or break the dish, but it's nice to have if you can find it.

Next, I add eggs. The key here is to not overbeat them. I like to see distinct sections of egg white and yolk. Chopsticks are my favorite tool for beating eggs like this, and the chopsticks can then be used to scatter the eggs as you drizzle them into the broth, just as you would do for egg drop soup (page 545). Traditionally, the eggs are cooked until just *barely* set, though you can cook them as hard or soft as you'd like. Just remember: eggs always continue cooking a bit on their way to the table, so stop cooking when they are a little bit underdone.

Once the eggs are cooked, I pour the contents of the pan over rice. There will be quite a bit of extra juice. This is fine. It should soak into the rice and flavor the entire bowl.

If you want to get extra fancy, you can separate one of the egg yolks and reserve it to add back to the top of the bowl before serving.

OYAKODON

Yield
Serves 2

Active Time
15 minutes

Total Time
15 minutes

NOTES

This recipe can be doubled. If doubling, prepare it in a wok instead of a saucepan. Hondashi is powdered dashi that can be found at any Japanese market and most well-stocked supermarkets. You can use ½ cup of concentrated tsuyu (page 231) diluted with a cup of water in place of the dashi, soy sauce, sake, mirin, and sugar. Chicken breast can be used in place of chicken thigh if you prefer. Mitsuba is a Japanese herb similar to parsley. It can be found at Japanese grocery stores; omit it if unavailable. Togarashi is Japanese chile powder, which comes in both ichimi (chiles only) and shichimi (chiles blended with other dried aromatics) versions. Either will work in this dish. For a richer finished dish, use four eggs, reserving two of the yolks. Beat the extra egg whites together with the remaining eggs in step 2, then add the reserved egg yolks to the finished bowls just before serving.

INGREDIENTS

1 cup (240 ml) homemade dashi (pages 519–21) or the equivalent in Hondashi (see Notes)

1 tablespoon (15 ml) shoyu, plus more to taste

2 tablespoons (30 ml) dry sake

2 tablespoons (30 ml) mirin

1 tablespoon (15 g) sugar, plus more to taste

1 large onion, slivered (about 6 ounces/170 g)

12 ounces (340 g) boneless, skinless chicken thighs, thinly sliced (see Notes)

3 scallions, thinly sliced

2 stems mitsuba (optional; see Notes)

3 to 4 large eggs (see Notes)

To Serve:

2 to 3 cups hot rice in a large serving bowl or individual bowls

Togarashi (see Notes)

DIRECTIONS

(1) Combine the dashi, soy sauce, sake, mirin, and sugar in a medium skillet and bring to a simmer over medium heat. Add the onion and simmer until half tender, about 5 minutes.

(2) Add the chicken pieces and cook, stirring and turning the chicken occasionally, until the chicken is cooked through and the broth has reduced by about half, 5 to 7 minutes. Stir in half of the scallions and all of the mitsuba (if using), then season the broth to taste with more soy sauce or sugar as desired. The sauce should have a balanced sweet-and-salty flavor.

(3) Reduce the heat to a bare simmer. Beat the eggs lightly with chopsticks in a medium bowl. Pour the eggs into the pot in a thin, steady stream (see Notes), holding your chopsticks over the edge of the bowl to help distribute the eggs evenly. Stir gently, then cover and cook until the eggs are cooked to the desired doneness, about 1 minute for runny eggs or 3 minutes for medium-firm.

(4) **To Serve:** Transfer the hot rice to a single large bowl or 2 individual serving bowls. Top with the egg and chicken mixture, pouring out any excess broth from the saucepan over the rice. Add an extra egg yolk to the center of each bowl, if desired (see Notes). Garnish with the remaining scallions and togarashi to taste. Serve immediately.

GYUDON

You know that scene at the beginning of *Saturday Night Fever* where John Travolta orders a couple of slices of pizza from a sidewalk window, stacks them on top of each other, gives them the New York fold, and struts down the street, meal in hand? That is a scene you are unlikely to see in Japan, and it's not because disco wasn't popular (it was) or because Japanese people have a thing against John Travolta (they don't) or even because they don't love pizza (they do).

The issue is the whole walking-while-eating thing. It just doesn't happen in Japan. Going to the 7-Eleven to pick up some pizza-flavored steamed buns? You're taking them home before you dig in. Hitting up Starbucks for a coffee? You're standing there and finishing the coffee before you step back out on the street.

Because of this, traditional fast-food culture in Japan is quite different from that of the United States. Fewer sandwiches and handheld snacks; more hastily slurped or shoveled bowls of food. All this is changing as cultural exchange with the West increases, of course, but ramen, curry, and rice bowls still remain staples of the quick-dining scene.

Gyudon was popularized by Yoshinoya, a chain of fast-food rice bowl restaurants that now have an international presence. They've been serving the dish since 1899, making gyudon one of the oldest continuously served fast-food menu items still available today, if not *the* oldest, predating the hamburger by several decades. Head into any Japanese shopping-mall food court and I guarantee gyudon will be on the menu.

What's fantastic is that it's also incredibly easy to make at home, requiring only a single pan and virtually no experience or skill whatsoever. If you can boil water, you can make gyudon.

There are a couple of keys to good gyudon. First is getting the beef. It's typically made with rib eye or chuck that's been shaved extra thin on a meat slicer. You'll be able to find good meat for gyudon at Japanese supermarkets, but if you don't have access to that, any beef intended for Philly cheesesteaks will work (even the frozen stuff!).

If your local supermarket has a butcher department that will slice rare roast beef to order, ask them to slice it as thin as they possibly can and use that for your gyudon (it's OK that it's already partially cooked).

Alternatively, you can buy a chuck steak, place it in the freezer until it's very firm but not frozen solid, then slice it as thin as you can with a knife. It's OK if the meat ends up shredding a bit. Perfection is not what we're going for here.

The rest of the dish is very similar to oyakodon. Simmer the onions in a soy-dashi-sake-mirin broth, add the meat, and simmer a bit more. If you like daikon radish, a few slices of daikon added with the onions are also excellent.

Because the beef is so thinly sliced, it will cook very quickly, losing its red color almost instantly. The goal is to cook it all down until the broth reduces to an intensely flavored sauce that penetrates the meat. With a typical braise, this can take hours. With the thinly shaved beef in gyudon, it takes just a couple of minutes. I like to stir in some grated ginger during the last minute or so of simmering, which preserves some of the ginger's fresh heat.

At Yoshinoya, they top their gyudon with a little pile of bright red *beni-shoga* (red-pickled ginger) and a sprinkle of togarashi. I've never met a bowl of gyudon that couldn't be improved with a runny poached egg and a handful of sliced scallions either.

If you want to go all in, do it the Japanese way, with a raw egg broken on top and stirred in, tamago-kake gohan style. It's not for everyone, so I'll understand if you want to pass on it. I'll judge you only about as much as I judge people who don't like sauerkraut on their hot dogs.

GYUDON

Yield	Active Time
Serves 2	15 minutes
	Total Time
	15 minutes

NOTES

This recipe can be doubled. If doubling, prepare it in a wok instead of a saucepan. Hondashi is powdered dashi that can be found at any Japanese market and most well-stocked supermarkets. You can use ½ cup concentrated tsuyu (page 231) diluted with a cup of water in place of the dashi, soy sauce, sake, mirin, and sugar. Look for thinly shaved beef at Japanese markets, ask your butcher to shave it for you, or use frozen shaved steak intended for Philly cheesesteaks. The beef can be cooked directly from the freezer if using frozen; just add a few minutes to the cooking time and make sure to carefully stir the beef and break it apart as it thaws. Beni-shoga is bright red pickled hot ginger. Togarashi is Japanese chile powder, which comes in both ichimi (chiles only) and shichimi (chiles blended with other dried aromatics) versions. Either will work in this dish. All of these ingredients can be found at any Japanese market or well-stocked Western supermarket.

Instead of topping the bowls with poached eggs, you can also use fried eggs or drizzle the eggs into the simmering beef as in oyakodon (see step 2 in the oyakodon recipe on page 233).

INGREDIENTS

¾ cup (180 ml) homemade dashi (pages 519–21) or the equivalent in Hondashi (see Notes)
1 tablespoon (15 ml) shoyu plus more to taste
2 tablespoons (30 ml) dry sake
2 tablespoons (30 ml) mirin
1 tablespoon (15 g) sugar, plus more to taste
1 large onion, slivered (about 6 ounces/170 g)
12 ounces (340 g) thinly shaved beef rib eye or chuck steak (see Notes)
1 teaspoon (5 ml) grated fresh ginger
Kosher salt

To Serve:

2 to 3 cups hot rice in individual serving bowls
2 poached large eggs (optional; see Notes)
Sliced scallions
Beni-shoga (see Notes)
Togarashi (see Notes)

DIRECTIONS

1 Combine the dashi, soy sauce, sake, mirin, and sugar in a medium skillet and bring to a simmer over medium heat. Add the onion and simmer until half tender, about 5 minutes.

2 Add the beef and cook, stirring, until the beef is cooked through and the liquid has reduced to an intensely flavored broth, about 5 minutes. Stir in the ginger and simmer for 1 minute longer. Adjust the seasoning with salt and sugar to taste.

3 Top the rice bowls with the beef and sauce mixture. Garnish each bowl with a poached egg (if using), sliced scallions, beni-shoga, and togarashi. Serve immediately.

KATSUDON

In the United States we're obsessed with keeping our crisply fried foods as crisp as possible. What's the point of frying a chicken cutlet or battering an onion ring if it's just gonna get soggy again, right?

This is not the case in Japan, where there are tons of dishes that start with crisply frying food, only to then douse it in a soup or sauce that kills its crispness: dishes like agedashi tofu (tofu that's fried until crackling like an eggshell, then coated in dashi stock so it turns slippery and tender, page 446), or tempura udon (crisply fried tempura shrimp, served all soggy-like in udon broth), or *chazuke* (hot tea poured over crisply fried seafood and vegetables until they're limp and saturated).

I admit, the idea doesn't sound so great when you describe it like that, but these dishes all end up with

really unique textures and flavors. Frying drives off excess moisture from batters and breadings, which leaves behind plenty of open spaces to absorb flavorful liquids. Mexican chiles rellenos use a similar concept. Not sold? Well, an easy way to dip your feet into the world of fried-then-soaked foods is katsudon (page 446), a dish made with leftover chicken katsu or pork tonkatsu simmered with eggs in a soy-dashi broth, then served over a bowl of rice.

There's no easy way to reheat katsu so it comes out crisp and juicy, so what harm can it do to give this version, which embraces the sogginess of leftovers, a shot?

My advice: embrace the sogginess, and let the flavor wash over you.

KATSUDON

Yield	Active Time
Serves 2	15 minutes
	Total Time
	15 minutes

NOTES

This recipe can be doubled. If doubling, prepare it in a wok instead of a saucepan. Hondashi is powdered dashi that can be found at any Japanese market and most well-stocked supermarkets. You can use ½ cup concentrated tsuyu (page 231) diluted with a cup of water in place of the dashi, soy sauce, sake, mirin, and sugar.

INGREDIENTS

1 cup (240 ml) homemade dashi (pages 519–21) or the equivalent in Hondashi (see Notes)

1 tablespoon (15 ml) shoyu, plus more to taste

2 tablespoons (30 ml) dry sake

2 tablespoons (30 ml) mirin

1 tablespoon (15 g) sugar, plus more to taste

1 large onion, slivered (about 6 ounces/170 g)

8 to 12 ounces (225 to 340 g) leftover Japanese fried chicken or pork cutlet (page 465), cut crosswise into ½-inch strips

4 large eggs

2 scallions, white and light green parts only, thinly sliced, plus more for garnish

To Serve:

2 bowls steamed rice

DIRECTIONS

(1) Combine the dashi, soy sauce, sake, mirin, and sugar in a medium skillet and bring to a simmer over medium heat. Add the onion and simmer until half tender, about 5 minutes.

(2) Add the sliced fried cutlet and let simmer for 1 minute. Meanwhile, beat together the eggs and scallions in a small bowl. Pour the egg mixture on top of the cutlets and around the broth. Cover and cook until the eggs are as set as you'd like them, about 1 minute for very soft or 2 minutes for medium. Slide the broth, egg, and chicken out on top of each bowl of rice. Sprinkle with scallions and serve.

SANSHOKU DON (THREE-COLOR RICE BOWLS)

Yield
Serves 2

Active Time
15 minutes

Total Time
15 minutes

NOTES

Pork and chicken are the most common choices for the ground meat topping, but it will work with any ground meat you have, including vegan ground meat alternatives. You can use a cup of thinly sliced snap peas or two cups of tightly packed spinach leaves in place of the thawed frozen peas. Blanch snap peas or spinach in lightly salted boiling water for 1 minute, drain, and chill under cool running water, then dry carefully in a salad spinner or by pressing with paper towels.

Another staple from my childhood, *sanshoku don* translates as "three-color rice bowl." It's made with sweet stir-fried ground meat, scrambled eggs, and a green vegetable, typically peas or snow peas (though my mother frequently made it with spinach), all arranged like a pie chart on top of a bowl of rice. It's great eaten warm, but equally good packed into a lunch box.

I find that if I cook the individual components—the meat, the egg, and the green vegetable—in advance and store them in the fridge, all I need to do is heat up a bowl of rice and top it, letting the heat of the of the rice warm up the toppings. *Sanshoku don* is typically garnished with *beni-shoga* or *tsukemono* (salty chopped Japanese pickles).

INGREDIENTS

For the Meat:

1 tablespoon (15 ml) peanut, rice bran, or
    other neutral oil
1 tablespoon (7.5 g) minced fresh ginger
    (about ¾-inch segment)
12 ounces (340 g) ground meat (see Notes)
2 tablespoons (30 ml) shoyu
2 tablespoons (30 ml) sake
2 tablespoons (30 ml) mirin
1 tablespoon (12.5 g) sugar

For the Eggs:

3 to 4 large eggs
2 tablespoons (30 ml) mirin
Kosher salt
1 teaspoon (5 ml) peanut, rice bran, or other
    neutral oil

To Serve:

4 bowls hot rice
1 cup frozen peas (see Notes), thawed
Beni-shoga or tsukemono, for garnish
    (optional)

DIRECTIONS

(1) For the Meat: Heat the oil in a wok or skillet over medium heat until shimmering. Add the ginger and cook until fragrant, about 30 seconds. Immediately add the ground meat and cook, breaking it up with a wooden spoon or spatula, until it is mostly cooked through, about 2 minutes. Add the soy sauce, sake, mirin, and sugar and cook until all excess moisture evaporates and the mixture looks dry, a couple minutes longer. Transfer to a bowl and set aside.

(2) For the Eggs: Scramble the eggs with mirin and a pinch of salt. Rub a thin film of oil into a wok or skillet and heat over high heat until lightly smoking. Turn off the heat, add the remaining oil, swirl to coat, then immediately add the eggs. Return the wok to medium heat and cook, scrambling vigorously until the eggs are completely cooked through and broken into very fine pieces, but not browned, about 1 minute. Transfer to a separate bowl and set aside. At this stage, the meat and eggs can be stored in sealed containers in the refrigerator for up to 3 days.

(3) To Serve: Top bowls of hot rice with the meat mixture, egg, and green vegetables, dividing them into colored sections like a pie chart. Garnish with beni-shoga or tsukemono if desired.

Miso-Broiling

Broiling fish and vegetables glazed in a mixture of *Saikyo* miso (a type of sweet white miso paste), sake, and mirin is a surefire way to add intense umami flavor. It's most commonly used for fish and eggplant, but the technique also works well on pumpkin, sweet potatoes, scallions, broccoli, corn, or even Western foods like bacon and hamburgers (seriously: coat a beef patty in the same miso mixture used in the following black cod recipe, broil that burger, and then send out that handwritten thank-you note to me).

SAIKYO-MISO-MARINATED BLACK COD OR SALMON RICE BOWLS

These days, miso-marinated black cod is almost synonymous with Nobu Matsuhisa's eponymous New York restaurant, though he by no means invented the dish. It stems from a traditional Japanese preparation called *kasuzuke*, in which fish and vegetables are marinated in the leftover lees from sake production before being broiled or grilled (kasu = sake lees, and zuke = to apply). You can still buy black cod premarinated in lees at Japanese markets, ready to broil and serve.

But Nobu's version, made with miso and sake, is a little bit easier in terms of finding ingredients at your standard supermarket. It's also every bit as delicious (perhaps even more). This is the fish dish to pull out when you're ready to blow away your spouse or dinner guests but don't want to put more than five minutes of effort into making dinner. Five minutes. Really.

The dish can be made with any high-fat fish with thick filets, but I find it works best with black cod (also known as *sablefish*), Chilean sea bass (aka. Patagonian toothfish—it's heavily overfished, so be careful about buying this one), or salmon. The same qualities that make sablefish and salmon great for smoking—a very rich, buttery texture and high fat content with flesh that turns tender when cooked rather than flaky or tough—makes them ideal for broiling. In the case of sablefish, it's nearly impossible to overcook it. Seriously. Try. I dare you.

Nobu's recipe calls for marinating the fish for a full 3 days in a mixture of miso, sake, and mirin, but I've actually found that a one-day marinade produces a superior end product—it's just as flavorful (marinades don't penetrate particularly far into meat) and comes out more tender. If I'm pressed for time, I'll even go with a 15- to 30-minute marinade. Here's how to do it:

Step 1 • Marinate the Fish

The marinade is a simple mix of miso, sake, sugar, soy sauce, and a bit of oil. The miso and soy are both quite salty, and it's this salty liquid that acts as a brine, weakening proteins and allowing the fillet to retain more moisture as it cooks. Both are also high in glutamates, the chemical class responsible for our sensation of umami, or meatiness. Sugar speeds up the browning process, while oil acts as a medium of heat transfer, causing the surface to char and sizzle evenly.

I whisk up the marinade, add the fish fillets, turn them to coat, then let them rest at least 15 minutes and up to a few days (I transfer them to a zipper-lock bag in the refrigerator if marinating longer than half an hour or so).

Step 2 • Broil

Once marinated, cooking it is as simple as transferring it to a foil-lined rimmed baking sheet, then setting it under a preheated broiler in the oven or toaster oven. If I want to make a full meal out of it, I'll add some vegetables like scallions or broccoli or sliced kabocha squash to the tray, drizzling them with extra marinade before broiling everything together.

Why bother lining the tray with foil? Well, not only does it make for simple cleanup; it also acts as a built-in protector. If you notice your fish browning in one section faster than the other, just fold the edge of the foil up and over the darker sections to serve as a shield while the fish continues cooking.

Broil until the top surface is deeply caramelized and the fish is just barely cooked through. How do you know it's done? Easy: use the bones to tell you. When the fish is barely cooked through to the center, its pin-bones should come out with no effort when you gently tug them with a pair of tweezers (pull them in the direction they are facing to prevent tearing the flesh). If your fish doesn't have any bones, poke it with a thin metal skewer or cake tester. When cooked through, the tester should meet no resistance. If the fish is still underdone, you'll feel it poking through the membrane between layers of flesh.

Step 3 • . . .

There . . . is no step 3. By the time your fish is lightly charred on the surface, the center should be at just about 115° to 125°F (aka a perfect rare to medium-rare), and it's ready to eat.

MISO-GLAZED BROILED BLACK COD OR SALMON

Yield
Serves 4

Active Time
15 minutes

Total Time
45 minutes

NOTE
If your fish comes with skin, leave the skin on during cooking. It'll slide off easily once the fish is done.

INGREDIENTS

¼ cup (75 g) white miso paste, preferably saikyo miso

¼ cup (60 ml) dry sake

2 tablespoons (30 ml) mirin

2 teaspoons (10 ml) shoyu

1 tablespoon (15 ml) peanut, rice bran, or other neutral oil

¼ cup (50 g) sugar

4 black cod or salmon fillets, 5 to 7 ounces (150 to 200 g) each

8 scallions, cut into 4-inch lengths, plus 1 scallion, thinly sliced, for garnish

To Serve:

4 cups steamed white rice

Sliced cucumber

Pickled ginger

Sesame seeds

DIRECTIONS

1   Whisk together the miso, sake, mirin, soy sauce, oil, and sugar. Rub the mixture over every surface of the fish. Proceed immediately to the next step or, for the best results, marinate for at least 30 minutes or up to 2 days. (If marinating for longer than 30 minutes, transfer to a zipper-lock bag and store the fish in the fridge.)

2   Adjust the broiler rack to 3 to 4 inches from the heat source and pre-heat the broiler or toaster oven broiler to high. Line a rimmed baking sheet with aluminum foil. Place the fish fillets skin side down on the pan. Add the scallions to the marinade and turn to coat, then scatter them around the fish. Broil until the top surface of the fish is well charred and a thin skewer inserted into the center shows no resistance at all when piercing through layers of flesh, and bones pull out easily, about 10 minutes for black cod or 5 minutes for salmon. If any areas of fish threaten to burn, fold up the aluminum foil and use it to shield the darker areas.

3   When the fish is cooked, carefully remove the pinbones with a pair of tweezers (there should be no resistance). If the fish had skin, slide a thin metal spatula between the fish and the skin and lift. The skin should be left behind on the foil. Serve the fish and scallions on top of individual rice bowls. Garnish with cucumber, ginger, sliced raw scallion, and sesame seeds.

NASU DENGAKU (BROILED MISO EGGPLANT)

Deep, rich red miso is a natural partner for the smoky flavor of grilled or broiled eggplant. This classic Japanese vegetable dish is delicious on its own or in a bowl of rice. It can be done in the broiler or with a combination of the grill and the broiler. You can pre-cook the eggplant through the end of step 4 and store it in the refrigerator for up to 3 days before proceeding with step 5.

Yield
Serves 4

Active Time
30 minutes

Total Time
30 minutes

INGREDIENTS

2 tablespoons (30 ml) mirin
2 tablespoons (20 ml) dry sake
¼ cup (75 g) red or brown miso
¼ cup (50 g) sugar
4 Japanese, Italian, or Chinese eggplants, stemmed and cut in half lengthwise (about 1 pound/450 g)
1 tablespoon (15 ml) peanut, rice bran, or other neutral oil

To Serve:

4 cups steamed white rice (optional)
Toasted sesame seeds, for garnish
2 scallions, thinly sliced

DIRECTIONS

(1) Combine the mirin, sake, miso, and sugar in a small bowl and stir with a fork until a homogenous paste is formed. Set aside.

(2) Rub all surfaces of the eggplants with vegetable oil.

(3) **To Start on the Grill:** Preheat a gas or charcoal grill to high heat. Grill the eggplant, cut-side down, until charred grill marks appear, about 1½ minutes. Rotate 45 degrees and cook until checkered hash marks appear, about 1½ minutes longer. Flip and continue cooking until nearly tender, about 4 minutes longer. Transfer the eggplant to a large plate and allow to cool slightly. Adjust the broiler rack to 4 to 6 inches from the heat source and preheat the broiler or toaster oven broiler to high. Proceed with step 5.

To Start in the Broiler: Adjust the broiler rack to 4 to 6 inches from the heat source and preheat the broiler or toaster oven broiler to high. Place on a rimmed baking sheet or foil-lined broiler pan, cut side up, and broil until lightly browned and fully tender, about 5 minutes. Remove from the oven and proceed with step 5.

(4) Spread the miso glaze on the cut surface of every eggplant. Place the glazed eggplant on a rimmed baking sheet or foil-lined broiler pan, cut side up. Broil until the glaze has begun to caramelize, about 4 minutes. Transfer to a platter or individual rice bowls, sprinkle with sesame seeds and scallions, and serve.

BIBIMBAP

If donburi is Japanese soul food, bibimbap is its Korean counterpart. It's existed since at least the sixteenth century and has never gone out of style. It's easy to see why: it's infinitely customizable, and it can be as simple or as elaborate as you'd like.

Bibim translates as "mixed," while *bap* is the Korean word for "rice," and as its name suggests, bibimbap is rice mixed with stuff. Typically that stuff is a mix of fresh and briefly stir-fried vegetables, pickled vegetables (such as kimchi), and a swirl of Korean-style sweet fermented chile paste or fermented soybean paste (gochujang or doenjang; see pages 14 and 15). Frequently, marinated cooked meat and a fried egg will be added to the top as well.

The best way to enjoy bibimbap is in a heavy stone bowl called a *dolsot*. The bowl is preheated in an oven or on the stove, then the inside is coated with a thin layer of sesame oil before the rice is added, which sizzles and forms a crispy brown crust. You mix the vegetables, meat, egg, and rice, eat your meal, then scrape the crust out with a spoon. Finally, hot water or barley tea can be added to the bowl to make a scorched rice infusion called *sungnyung* to finish the meal. Don't have a dolsot? Don't worry; you can crust up your rice in your wok just fine.

Bibimbap was originally developed centuries ago as a peasant dish intended to transform inexpensive scraps of vegetables and meat into a hearty meal, and I like to think of it the same way, using whatever ingredients I happen to find in my fridge to top it. So long as you have a mix of quickly stir-fried vegetables, raw fresh vegetables, and pickled vegetables, the dish will work (even without the meat).

Cooking bibimbap can seem a little daunting when you think about all the individual toppings, but it's actually a very streamlined, simple process. Virtually every topping is served in one of three ways: dressed raw, simply blanched in simmering water, or very briefly stir-fried. As far as work flow goes, you can prep all your ingredients first, bring a couple cups of salted water to a simmer in your wok or saucepan, simmer ingredients that need simmering in succession, then empty out the pan and set it back on the stove to briefly stir-fry those that need to be stir-fried. I never bother cleaning my wok between ingredients when stir-frying for bibimbap. Finally, if you'd like, you can crisp up the rice in the wok just before topping and serving.

Here are a few ideas for toppings:

INGREDIENTS	PREPARATION
Cucumbers, zucchini, daikon radish, summer squash	Slice and salt, then set aside for 10 minutes. Squeeze out excess moisture and season with sesame oil, minced garlic, and sesame seeds. Alternatively, stir-fry for 1 minute with a little sesame oil; season to taste with salt and sesame seeds.
Carrots, shiitake or button mushrooms, eggplant, bell peppers	Finely julienne or slice and stir-fry with sesame oil until tender-crisp. Season with salt and pepper.
Bean sprouts, spinach, and other tender greens	Blanch in boiling water for 1 minute for tender greens or 3 minutes for bean sprouts, rinse under cold water, squeeze out excess moisture, then dress with a little sesame oil and minced garlic.
Beef, chicken breast, or pork	Cut meat into thin slices or fine matchsticks. For every 4 ounces of meat, add 2 teaspoons (10 ml) soy sauce, 1 teaspoon (5 ml) sesame oil, 1 minced garlic clove, and 2 teaspoons (10 ml) honey or sugar. Stir-fry in vegetable oil over medium-high heat until just cooked through, about 1 minute. Sprinkle with sesame seeds

BIBIMBAP

Yield
Serves 4

Active Time
45 minutes

Total Time
45 minutes

INGREDIENTS

For the Toppings:
Roasted sesame oil

Toasted sesame seeds

Minced garlic (optional)

Thinly sliced scallions (optional)

Light soy sauce or shoyu

2 cups (about 5 ounces) soybean or
mung bean sprouts

2 cups (about 3 ounces) packed fresh
spinach leaves

1 medium carrot, peeled, cut in half
lengthwise, and thinly sliced on a bias

Kosher salt

1 Kirby or Japanese cucumber (or ½
American cucumber), peeled, split
lengthwise, and cut into half-moons

4 ounces (120 g) shiitake mushroom caps,
thinly sliced

4 ounces (120 g) ground beef or thinly
sliced beef (such as beef you'd find
for shabu or bulgogi at an Asian
supermarket or thinly sliced Philly
cheesesteak beef)

2 teaspoons (10 ml) honey

To Serve:
4 cups (800 g) cooked white short-grain
rice

Raw egg yolks or sunny-side-up fried eggs

1 recipe Bibimbap Sauce (page 247)

DIRECTIONS

(1) **For the Toppings:** Set up your topping station by putting out bottles and containers of sesame oil, sesame seeds, garlic (if using), scallions (if using), and soy sauce on the counter. Set a stack of 6 small bowls on the counter as well.

(2) In a wok or a small saucepan, bring 2 cups (500 ml) water to a simmer. Add the bean sprouts and cook for 3 minutes. Fish them out with a slotted spoon, run them under cold water until you can handle them easily, then squeeze out excess moisture or spin them dry in a salad spinner. Place them in one of the small bowls.

(3) Add the spinach to the simmering water and cook for 1 minute. Repeat the draining, cooling, and squeezing process and place the spinach in a second bowl.

(4) Empty out the wok and return it to medium-high heat, allowing it to dry fully. Add 2 teaspoons (10 ml) sesame oil and heat until shimmering, then add the carrots, season with a pinch of salt, and stir-fry until heated through and lightly softened, about 1 minute. Transfer to a third small bowl.

(5) Return the wok to medium-high heat. Add 2 teaspoons (10 ml) sesame oil and heat until shimmering, then add the cucumber, season with a pinch of salt, and stir-fry until heated through and lightly softened, about 1 minute. Transfer to a fourth small bowl.

(6) Return the wok to medium-high heat. Add 2 teaspoons (10 ml) sesame oil and heat until shimmering, then add the mushrooms, season with a pinch of salt, and stir-fry until lightly browned, about 3 minutes. Transfer to a fifth small bowl.

7 Season the beef with 2 teaspoons (10 ml) soy sauce, the honey, 1 teaspoon (5 ml) sesame oil, some minced garlic (if using), and a sprinkle of sesame seeds. Return the wok to medium-high heat. Add 2 teaspoons (10 ml) sesame oil and heat until shimmering, then add the beef and stir-fry until lightly browned, about 3 minutes. Transfer to a sixth small bowl.

8 Now season all of the vegetables to taste with about 1 teaspoon sesame oil, a sprinkle of sesame seeds, a dash of soy sauce, and some minced garlic and/or scallions. Make sure you taste as you go.

9 **To Serve with Plain Steamed Rice:** Serve steamed rice in individual bowls at the table, allowing diners to pick and choose their toppings and finishing off each bowl with a fried egg or a raw egg yolk (if desired) and a drizzle of as much or as little sauce as they'd like (even if that's none). Toss the bowl to mix the ingredients thoroughly before eating.

To Serve with Crispy Rice: Wipe out the wok and return it to high heat until lightly smoking. Add 1 tablespoon sesame oil and swirl to coat. Add the rice and press it down into an even layer. Cook over medium-low heat until the rice has a crispy coating on the bottom, about 1 minute (you can check by peeking underneath with a wok spatula). You can top the rice directly in the wok or transfer the rice to individual serving bowls, making sure to scoop out some of the crispy bottom for each serving.

BIBIMBAP SAUCE

Yield
Makes
¾ cup

Active Time
2 minutes

Total Time
2 minutes

This sweet and spicy sauce is great on bibimbap, but don't stop there! It's excellent on fried or grilled chicken wings or on grilled meats or vegetables of any kind.

DIRECTIONS

Combine all the ingredients in a bowl and whisk until homogenous. Store the sauce in a sealed container in the fridge indefinitely.

INGREDIENTS

½ cup (120 ml) gochujang

2 tablespoons (30 ml) roasted sesame oil

2 tablespoons (25 g) sugar

2 tablespoons (30 ml) cider vinegar or rice vinegar

3 medium garlic cloves, minced or smashed in a mortar and pestle (about 1 tablespoon/8 g)

2 tablespoons black or toasted white sesame seeds (or a mix)

¼ cup (60 ml) water

2.2 JOOK, CONGEE, AND OTHER NAMES FOR RICE PORRIDGE

Rice porridge. Gruel. Mush. Pap. These are all excellent words to use if you want to describe to someone what congee is without giving any hint of its deliciousness or its exciting possibilities. Silky, creamy, comforting, and intensely savory are how I'd describe it. There's a reason it's eaten all across Asia at all hours of the day, whether for breakfast in Thailand, at a dim sum house in Hong Kong, or at an all-night hawker center in Singapore after an evening of drinking.

Congee (known as *zhou* in mainland China, *juk* in Korea, *bubur* in Indonesia, *okayu* in Japan, etc.) on its own can be deliciously comforting, but it really shines when you spruce it up with mix-ins and condiments. Leftover roast chicken or turkey can be transformed into a meal by simmering it in a pot of congee with some fresh ginger, white pepper, and a sprinkle of scallions. The head of romaine that is not quite crisp and fresh enough for Caesar salad can find a new home wilted in a bowl of congee. The farmers' market haul of corn and kale makes a hearty congee lunch. You get the idea.

In Asia, congee is frequently made with an inexpensive bag of broken rice grains, but it's not easy to find broken rice in the States. That's OK. Congee can just as easily be made with regular rice. At home, I most frequently make it with short-grain Japanese rice or other varieties high in amylopectin, which gives the finished congee a velvety, tongue-coating texture (think: risotto taken to the extreme), though jasmine rice also makes great, fragrant congee.

The simplest way to make congee—by simmering rice in water or stock on the stove—is also the most time-consuming. It's largely hands-off time, but it still takes about an hour, start to finish.

Fortunately there are several ways to speed up the process. Here are some of my favorites:

THE PRESSURE COOKER METHOD: Combine rice and water in a pressure cooker (pressure cookers don't allow as much liquid to escape via evaporation as a saucepan on the stove, so cut water down by about 10 percent), seal the cooker, and cook at high pressure (12 to 15 psi) for 20 minutes. Allow the pressure to release naturally (do not attempt a quick release—the starchy water will come bubbling and shooting out of the release valve and make a huge mess), then open the cooker and bring to a vigorous simmer, stirring until the porridge is as thick as you like it.

THE OVERNIGHT SOAKING METHOD: This method was inspired by my favorite way to cook steel-cut oatmeal: toast it dry and soak it overnight to hasten cooking the next morning. It works the same way with rice: Combine water and rice in a saucepan (you can toast the rice beforehand if you like the aroma of toasty rice), cover, and let it sit overnight. The next morning, bring it to a simmer, stirring occasionally. It should be creamy and ready to eat in about half an hour.

THE MORTAR AND PESTLE METHOD: Grinding up the dry rice in a mortar and pestle to break it into smaller pieces and release more starch before simmering it on the stove can reduce overall cooking time by about 25 percent.

THE LEFTOVER RICE METHOD: Day-old leftover rice that's spent the night in the refrigerator can be cooked into congee in about 30 minutes using the basic congee method, but cutting the amount of liquid to just 4 cups per cup of cooked rice. If you have the foresight to freeze the cooked rice, this cooking time can be cut down even further (a technique I learned from the excellent blog *The Woks of Life*). The process of freezing and thawing causes the rice grains to crack, releasing their starch much faster. You can take a cup of frozen rice, add it to 4 cups of water or stock in a saucepan, heat it up, and stir as it melts and comes to a boil. You end up with perfectly creamy congee in 20 to 30 minutes.

BASIC CONGEE

Yield
Serves 4

Active Time
10 minutes

Total Time
1 hour

NOTE
This is the simplest way to make stovetop
congee. See page 248 for various methods to
speed up or otherwise alter the process. If rice
grains with slightly more bite are desired, sauté
the rice in 1 tablespoon of oil until the edges are
translucent, about 3 minutes, then add stock and
continue as directed.

INGREDIENTS

½ cup (about 3½ ounces/100 g) short-grain or jasmine rice
Water or low-sodium chicken or vegetable stock (6 cups for short-grain, 5 cups for
jasmine)

DIRECTIONS

Combine the rice and stock or water in a wok or large saucepan. Bring to
a simmer over high heat, stirring occasionally. Reduce to a bare simmer
and cook, stirring occasionally, until the rice is completely tender and the
water has thickened into a velvety porridge, about 1 hour total.

Basic Congee with "The Mix"
(Pork, Shrimp, Garlic, and Ginger)

Follow directions for basic congee. Once the rice is velvety, add 1 recipe of
"The Mix" (page 280), breaking it up with a whisk and stirring vigorously
so it gets distributed evenly throughout the congee. Cook until the shrimp
are cooked through, about 1 minute. Serve immediately, garnished with
scallions and cilantro. Pass chile oil or sambal oelek at the table.

How to Prepare Ingredients for Congee

When cooking a pot of congee, it's generally a good idea to stick to a few clean flavors. One or two alliums (such as onions and scallions or scallions and garlic), one to three types of vegetables, and one type of meat or other protein is a good blueprint for a successful pot.

The major exception? Springtime, with its short-lived but prolific gluts of sweet, bright, green produce. It's the easiest time of year to pull off amazing-looking and -tasting meals; it's almost unfair. Your guests will never know what hit them. Almost all green spring vegetables can be incorporated into congee with minimal prep, and they are all interchangeable in these settings, which means you can go for a big mix or just stick with what strikes your fancy at the market. I like to pair spring vegetables with mushrooms.

Here's how to prepare a whole variety of ingredients for the congee pot:

CATEGORY	INGREDIENT	METHOD
Meat/Protein	Cured meats such as ham, bacon, or spam	Cut into ¼-inch dice. Stir in for the last minute of cooking.
Meat/Protein	Cooked chicken	Shred into bite-sized pieces. Stir in for the last minute of cooking.
Meat/Protein	Ground meats, such as ground pork or chicken	Leave plain or marinate with a touch of soy sauce and ½ teaspoon cornstarch (1 g) per 4 ounces meat. Stir in, using a whisk to break it up and cook until no longer pink, 1 to 2 minutes.
Meat/Protein	Tofu	Use extra-firm, pressed, marinated, or fried tofu, cut into matchsticks or cubes. Add to congee for the last 2 minutes of cooking.
Seafood	Shrimp	Peel, devein, and cut into ½-inch pieces or leave whole if very small. Stir in for the last minute of cooking.
Seafood	Crabmeat	Pick over and discard any bits of shell. Stir in for the last minute of cooking.
Seafood	Cooked salmon or tuna	Flake gently with a fork. Stir in for the last minute of cooking.
Seafood	Salt cod	Soak in clean water overnight, changing the water a few times over the course of the night. Flake with a fork. Stir in for the last 20 minutes of cooking.
Seafood	Hot-smoked fish, such as salmon, sablefish, or marlin	Flake gently with a fork. Stir in for the last minute of cooking.
Vegetable	Asparagus	Peel stalks below the top 2 inches and cut or snap off the woody bottoms. Cut into ¼-inch lengths, either straight or on a bias, leaving the tips whole or splitting them lengthwise. Cook directly in the congee for the last 2 minutes before serving
Vegetable	Bell peppers and other chiles	Cut into ¼-inch dice. Sauté in oil at the start of cooking before adding the rice and stock.
Vegetable	Broccoli and cauliflower	Cut heads into ½-inch florets. Peel tougher bits of stem, then cut stems into ¼-inch dice. Add to the congee for the last 4 minutes before serving.
Vegetable	Cabbage and Brussels sprouts	Thinly slice. Sauté in oil at the start of cooking before adding the rice and stock or stir in for the last 2 minutes of cooking.

Chart

CATEGORY	INGREDIENT	METHOD
Vegetable	Celery	Peel any tough outer stalks. Split each rib lengthwise into 3 or 4 thin rods. Cut into ¼-inch dice. Sauté in oil at the start of cooking before adding rice and stock.
Vegetable	Corn	Cut from the cob. Add to the congee for the last 3 minutes before serving.
Vegetable	Cucumber	Peel, split lengthwise, remove seeds with a spoon, split again lengthwise into quarters, then cut into ¼-inch segments. Add to the congee for the last 5 minutes before serving.
Vegetable	English peas	Remove peas from pods. Cook directly in the congee for the last 3 minutes before serving
Vegetable	Fava beans	Remove peas from pods. Blanch in boiling salted water for 2 minutes, then drain and transfer to an ice bath to cool. Remove pale green skin from each bean and discard. Add to congee for the last minute before serving.
Vegetable	Firm, crisp root vegetables, such as carrots, parsnips, turnips, radish, rutabaga, jícama, or water chestnut	Cut into ¼-inch dice or finer. Sauté in oil at the start of cooking before adding rice and stock.
Vegetable	Green beans	Break off tops and bottoms with your fingers, pulling out any strings that come with them. Cut on a sharp bias into ¼-inch pieces. Cook directly in the congee for the last 3 minutes before serving
Vegetable	Kale	Remove tough central ribs. Cut leaves into ribbons, roughly tear, or cut into squares. Cook directly in the congee for the last 5 minutes before serving.
Vegetable	Leeks	Trim and discard roots and dark green tops. Split pale green and white parts lengthwise into quarters. Cut into ¼-inch dice. Sauté in oil at the start of cooking before adding the rice and stock.
Vegetable	Lettuce	Separate leaves and cut into ribbons or squares. Cook directly in the congee for the last minute before serving
Vegetable	Mushrooms	Slice thinly. Sauté in oil at start of cooking before adding rice and stock.
Vegetable	Onions and shallots	Cut into fine dice. Sauté in oil at the start of cooking before adding the rice and stock.
Vegetable	Scallions	Trim and discard roots. Slice thinly and add to the congee just before serving or as garnish at the table.
Vegetable	Snap peas	Break off the tops and bottoms with your fingers, pulling out any strings that come with them. Cut on a sharp bias into ¼-inch pieces. Cook directly in the congee for the last 2 minutes before serving.
Vegetable	Snow peas	Break off the tops and bottoms with your fingers, pulling out any strings that come with them. Cut on a sharp bias into ¼-inch pieces. Cook directly in the congee for the last 2 minutes before serving.
Vegetable	Zucchini and other tender squashes	Cut into ¼-inch dice. Sauté in oil at the start of cooking before adding the rice and stock.
Herbs	Fresh herbs, such as cilantro, mint, parsley, rosemary	Pick leaves from stems and mince. Stir in just before serving.

THAI-STYLE JOK WITH PORK MEATBALLS

Yield
Serves 4

Active Time
30 minutes

Total Time
1½ hours

This is a classic Thai-style rice porridge with little pork meatballs flavored with fish sauce and white pepper that cook directly in the porridge. A raw egg stirred into each bowl of congee at the table adds richness and flavor—my friend Leela Punyaratabandhu suggests adding a layer of congee to each bowl, topping it with an egg, and ladling more congee on top to gently cook the egg with the residual heat of the porridge. It's a wonderful method that gives you an egg surprise in the middle of each bowl as you stir. I also like adding some greens to the congee, like spinach, iceberg, or romaine lettuce, which become tender and sweet in the bowls. If you've got some sweet Thai preserved radish in your pantry, it makes a great addition to these bowls as well.

INGREDIENTS

1 lemongrass stalk

½ cup (about 3.5 ounces/100 g) grain or jasmine rice

Water or low-sodium chicken or vegetable stock (6 cups for short-grain, 5 cups for jasmine)

½ teaspoon freshly ground white pepper

Fish sauce

For the Meatballs:

8 ounces (225 g) ground pork

¼ teaspoon freshly ground white pepper

1 teaspoon (5 ml) fish sauce

½ teaspoon (2 g) kosher salt

1 tablespoon (15 ml) light soy sauce or shoyu

2 medium garlic cloves, minced (about 2 teaspoons/5 g)

1 tablespoon (12.5 g) sugar

To Serve (all additions are optional but recommended):

2 cups (about 3 ounces/90 g) greens such as kale (thick central stem discarded, leaves roughly chopped), spinach, chopped iceberg, or chopped romaine lettuce

4 eggs

Minced fresh cilantro

Thinly sliced scallions

Minced sweet Thai preserved radish

Fried Shallots (page 254)

Nam Pla Prik (page 257)

Prik Nam Som (page 256)

DIRECTIONS

(1) Using the back spine of a knife, bash the lemongrass a dozen or so times to bruise it and help release flavor. Combine the rice, lemongrass, and water or stock in a wok or large saucepan. Bring to a simmer over high heat, stirring occasionally. Reduce to a bare simmer and cook, stirring occasionally, until the rice is completely tender and the water has thickened into a velvety porridge, about 1 hour total. Discard the lemongrass when the congee is done. Season with white pepper and fish sauce to taste. Keep the congee at a bare simmer on the stove, stirring occasionally and thinning it with water if it starts to get too thick.

(2) **For the Meatballs:** Combine the pork, white pepper, fish sauce, salt, soy sauce, garlic, and sugar in a small bowl. Mix with your fingers until the mixture is homogenous and sticky, about 30 seconds. Wash your hands. Using wet hands, pinch off teaspoon-sized pieces of the pork mixture and form into small balls. Drop the balls directly into the simmering congee. Cover and continue to simmer until the meatballs are starting to firm up, about 1 minute.

(3) **To Serve:** Stir in the greens and continue cooking until greens are wilted and the meatballs are cooked through, about 3 minutes longer.

(4) Ladle some piping-hot congee into the bottom of each of 4 serving bowls, then crack a raw egg on top. Divide remaining congee among the bowls. Let them rest for a couple minutes before serving to allow the egg to cook slightly. Garnish each bowl with cilantro, scallions, preserved radish, and fried shallots. Serve, passing nam pla prik and prik nam som at the table to be added as desired.

FRIED SHALLOTS

Yield
Makes
about 1½
cups

Active Time
25 minutes

Total Time
25 minutes

NOTE
The cup and a half that
this recipe makes may
seem like a lot, but
it's not.

INGREDIENTS

1 pound (450 g) shallots, peeled
2 cups (500 ml) vegetable oil
Kosher salt

When I was a *garde-manger* cook at the now-shuttered Clio in Boston's Eliot Hotel, one of my daily tasks was to make fried shallots for the entire line. This was no easy feat. They made their way into a host of dishes— a crunchy garnish on salads or sashimi, as a flavoring garnish in soups and stews, in sauces, relishes, and condiments like spicy chile crisp—but that was only part of the issue. The real problem was that the things are *addictive* and everyone from the line cooks to the chef to the servers would sneak handfuls of them to crunch on throughout their shift. I still occasionally wake up with cold sweats as I relive the pain of accidentally leaving the fried shallots unattended for a quick trip to the walk-in only to find the container half empty by the time I get back.

I'm no longer a line cook, but that hasn't eased my suffering much: when I make fried shallots at home, I have to wait until Adri is out of the house all day with the hopes that she won't recognize the sweet, tell-tale aroma lingering in the air, because once she does, the jig is up, and no matter how many shallots I fry, they'll disappear within the day.

The point is: **they're that good.**

They're also really finicky to get just right. Undercooked fried shallots are limp and greasy, but overcook them even slightly and they develop a bitter aftertaste that makes them completely unpalatable. What's worse, they need to be sliced perfectly evenly so that they can cook perfectly evenly. Fortunately, in the thousands of batches of fried shallots I've had to make in my lifetime, I've picked up a few tricks that will help you pull them off correctly right out of the gate.

If you don't feel like subjecting yourself to the same torture that I do, you can always buy fried shallots from the Asian supermarket. (Jarred fried shallots are almost always criminally underseasoned, so make sure to salt them well before using them.) Incidentally: you can add some fresh lemongrass sliced the same thickness as the shallots while you fry for an even tastier mixture. Save the oil that you strain off. The delicious shallot-scented oil is great to use in stir-fries, as the base for Fragrant Scallion-Ginger Oil (page 566), or in salad dressings.

DIRECTIONS

(1) Using a mandoline, slice the shallots into ¹⁄₁₆-inch-thick rounds. Line a rimmed baking sheet with 6 layers of paper towels. Set a fine-mesh strainer over a large heatproof bowl or medium saucepan.

(2) Combine shallots and oil in a medium saucepan or wok. Place over medium-high heat and cook, stirring frequently, until the shallots begin to bubble, 2 to 3 minutes. Continue cooking, stirring constantly as the

shallots fry to ensure even cooking, until the shallots turn pale golden brown, 8 to 10 minutes longer. (The shallots will continue cooking for a brief period after draining, so do not allow them to get too dark.) Working quickly, pour the contents of the saucepan into the strainer.

(3) Immediately transfer the shallots to the prepared baking sheet, spread them out into an even layer, and season with salt. Allow the shallots to drain, then carefully lift the top layer of paper towels and roll the shallots onto the second layer, blotting gently with the first. Repeat until the shallots are on the last layer of paper towels and mostly grease-free. Allow the shallots and oil to cool to room temperature, then store separately in airtight containers.

Fried Shallots, Step by Step

Step 1 • Trim and Slice the Shallots on a Mandoline

Trim the ends of your shallots and peel them, then slice them into rings on a mandoline. You don't need a fancy one—a $25 plastic Benriner Japanese-style mandoline will do the job right. You want to adjust the thickness of the opening to $\frac{1}{16}$ inch—that's about the thickness of two credit cards stacked on top of each other.

Step 2 • Set up a Landing Pad

When the shallots are done, you need to *immediately* drain and blot them of excess oil before the residual heat of the oil causes them to overcook. Ready your station by placing a fine-mesh strainer into a heatproof bowl for draining, then line a rimmed baking sheet with six layers (yes, six) of paper towels or clean kitchen towels for blotting.

Step 3 • Heat Them Slowly

Combine the shallots with cold vegetable oil in a wok or saucepan; about 2 cups of oil per pound of shallots is the right ratio. Set the wok over medium-high heat and begin to cook them. Starting the shallots in cold oil helps them cook more evenly.

Step 4 • Stir Constantly

As the shallots and oil heat up, stir constantly to make sure that the shallots cook evenly (if you stop stirring, you'll probably notice that the shallots around the edges of the pan will be sizzling harder than those floating in the center. That's why you stir. Cook until the shallots turn a pale golden brown and the sizzling starts to slow, 10 to 12 minutes total.

continues

Step 5 • Drain Immediately

As soon as the shallots are uniformly pale golden with no white sections remaining, pour the content of the saucepan into the strainer set over the bowl. Shake the strainer, them immediately transfer the shallots to the paper-towel-lined baking sheet, spreading them into an even layer.

Step 6 • Blot and Season

Pick up one end of the top layer of paper towels and, shaking it gently, roll the shallots off the towel and onto the layer of towels below, then gently blot them with the first towel. Discard

the first towel, then immediately spread the shallots back into a single layer. Repeat this process until you get to the last towel. The shallots should be mostly cool and dry by this point.

Step 7 • Season and Store

Season the shallots with a generous sprinkle of salt. Let them rest at room temperature until completely cooled, about 30 minutes. Transfer to a sealable container and store in a cool, dark pantry for up to 3 months (or, if your home is like mine, more like the 3 hours it takes before your spouse discovers and devours them).

THAI TABLE CONDIMENTS

No Thai table is complete without a set of condiments to adjust the flavor of dishes to suit each diner's taste. At the very least, I like to provide Prik Nam Som and some form of Nam Pla Prik (see following recipes), as well as roasted ground Thai Chile flakes. In Bangkok, you'll often find a dish of white sugar served as well.

PRIK NAM SOM

Yield
Makes 1 cup

Active Time
3 minutes

Total Time
3 minutes

Prik nam som is an essential table condiment that pairs especially well with noodle dishes such as Pad See Ew (page 372), but it's also great with congee, soups, and egg dishes.

INGREDIENTS

½ cup (120 ml) distilled white vinegar
½ cup (120 ml) cup boiling water
1 tablespoon (12.5 g) sugar

A few garlic cloves
½ cup thinly sliced serrano or Thai bird chiles

DIRECTIONS

Combine all the ingredients in a jar. Allow to cool. Prik nam som can be stored indefinitely in a cool, dark pantry.

NAM PLA PRIK

Yield
About ½
cup

Active Time
2 minutes

Total Time
2 minutes

At its most basic, nam pla prik is simply fish sauce (nam pla) and thinly sliced Thai bird chiles (prik), and it can be as simple as combining those two ingredient, no recipe or special technique needed. Other versions of the sauce will include garlic, shallots, lime juice, and/or sugar. In my fridge I typically keep a fish-sauce-heavy version made with Thai bird chiles, garlic, and sugar that lasts for months, as well as a simple sliced chile and fish sauce version. Lime juice adds some nice refreshing acidity to the mix, but adding it will reduce its shelf life, so I prefer to squeeze in fresh lime juice at the table rather than mix it directly into my big batch of nam pla prik.

Make sure to wear gloves or *really* scrub your hands after working with this volume of chiles. Though it's not a common method, I like using the mortar and pestle for this—it draws more flavor out of the garlic and chiles, and keeps your cutting board from absorbing tough-to-remove chile and garlic aromas. You can also chop the chiles in a mini-chopper or food processor, pulsing the machine to roughly chop (rather than puree) the chiles (just be careful when opening the lid, as atomized chile juice can hurt your eyes and nose).

INGREDIENTS

10 to 30 fresh Thai bird chiles (red or a
    mix of red and green)
2 to 4 medium garlic cloves (optional)
2 tablespoons palm sugar (optional)
½ cup fish sauce

To Serve:
Lime wedges

DIRECTIONS

Trim the tops off the chiles and roughly chop. Trim and peel the garlic cloves (if using) and smash with the side of a knife. Place the chiles and garlic in a mortar and smash with a pestle to form a rough paste. Add the sugar (if using) and smash with the pestle until the sugar is dissolved and the mixture is a fine paste. Add the fish sauce and stir with the pestle until homogenous. Transfer to a sealed container. Nam pla prik can be stored at room temperature for several days or in the fridge for several months or more. If desired, stir in some fresh lime juice just before serving.

CHEESY CONGEE WITH BACON, CHARRED CORN, SCALLIONS, AND CILANTRO

Yield
Serves 4

Active Time
30 minutes

Total Time
1½ hours

Bacon, corn, scallions, and cheese work well together in a bowl of grits, so I figured, why not try it in a bowl of congee? Turns out it's fantastic, especially with a drizzle of chile oil at the table. This is breakfast congee, which makes the quick-cook overnight soak method on page 248 ideal.

INGREDIENTS

½ cup (about 3.5 ounces/100 g) short-grain or jasmine rice

Water or low-sodium chicken or vegetable stock (6 cups for short-grain, 5 cups for jasmine)

1 teaspoon (5 ml) vegetable oil

4 ounces (120 g) bacon, cut into ½-inch pieces

1 cup (about 175 g) raw corn kernels, cut from 2 ears

2 ounces (60 g) shredded or sliced cheese, such as Cheddar, Jack, or Swiss

A small handful of chopped fresh cilantro leaves and tender stems

3 scallions, thinly sliced

Kosher salt and freshly ground black pepper

DIRECTIONS

(1) Combine the rice and water or stock in a wok or large saucepan. Bring to a simmer over high heat, stirring occasionally. Reduce to a bare simmer and cook, stirring occasionally, until the rice is completely tender and the water has thickened into a velvety porridge, about 1 hour total. Keep the cooked congee warm. (Transfer to a saucepan if you cooked it in your wok; you'll need your wok for the next steps.)

(2) Heat the oil in a wok over medium heat until shimmering. Add the bacon and cook, stirring frequently, until well rendered and crisp, about 4 minutes. Transfer the bacon to a bowl and set aside, leaving the fat in the wok. Return the bacon fat to high heat until lightly smoking. Add the corn, shake to coat it in bacon fat, then let it cook without moving until the bottom layer is charred, about 45 seconds. Stir and toss and repeat, allowing the corn to char without moving between stirs until most of the corn is lightly charred in spots, about 3 minutes total.

(3) Add the corn to the congee. Stir in the cheese until melted. Add the bacon, cilantro, and scallions and stir, reserving some of each for garnish. Season with salt and pepper to taste. Garnish with the reserved bacon, cilantro, and scallions. Serve immediately.

CONGEE WITH WILTED LETTUCE AND MUSHROOMS

Yield
Serves 4

Active Time
15 minutes

Total Time
1¼ hours

NOTE
You can use rehydrated wood ears instead of shiitake or, if you have Soy-Glazed Mushrooms (page 183), just toss those straight into the congee (skip the stir-frying step if using them).

INGREDIENTS

½ cup (about 3.5 ounces/100 g) short-grain or jasmine rice

Water or low-sodium chicken or vegetable stock (6 cups for short-grain, 5 cups for jasmine)

1 tablespoon (15 ml) peanut, rice bran, or other neutral oil

4 ounces (120 g) shiitake mushroom caps, thinly sliced (see Note)

2 medium garlic cloves, smashed in a mortar
and pestle or finely minced (about 2 teaspoons/5 g)

1 tablespoon (15 ml) Shaoxing wine

1 teaspoon (5 ml) light soy sauce or shoyu

1 head romaine lettuce, cut crosswise into ½-inch ribbons

3 scallions, thinly sliced

Kosher salt and freshly ground white pepper

Working in Western kitchens, wilted lettuce is a sign of a vegetable past its prime that has only one home: the compost bin. But once you wrap your head around the idea that lettuce doesn't *have* to be crisp and firm, you'll find that wilted lettuce can be delicious. My favorite way to enjoy it is in a bowl of silky congee. Simple lettuces like iceberg and romaine achieve a unique moist yet crunchy texture with a more concentrated flavor than raw lettuce has.

DIRECTIONS

(1) Combine the rice and water or stock in a wok or large saucepan. Bring to a simmer over high heat, stirring occasionally. Reduce to a bare simmer and cook, stirring occasionally, until the rice is completely tender and the water has thickened into a velvety porridge, about 1 hour total. Keep the cooked congee warm. (Transfer to a saucepan if you cooked it in your wok; you'll need your wok for the next steps.)

(2) Heat the wok over high heat until lightly smoking. Add the oil and swirl to coat. Add the mushrooms and stir-fry until tender, about 1 minute. Add the garlic and stir-fry until fragrant, about 15 seconds. Add the wine and soy sauce and toss until reduced and the wok is mostly dry, about 30 seconds.

(3) Transfer the mushrooms to the congee. Bring the congee to a brisk simmer and add the romaine. Stir until wilted, about 1 minute. Stir in the scallions, reserving some for garnish. Season with salt and white pepper to taste. Sprinkle with the reserved scallions and serve.

DAKJUK (KOREAN-STYLE CONGEE WITH CHICKEN AND VEGETABLES)

Juk is the Korean version of congee. Unlike many other types of congee, where the rice is simply cooked in water or broth, Korean rice porridge typically starts by sautéing the rice in oil, just like an Italian-style risotto. And like risotto, this first toasting step results in a porridge that comes out creamy yet intact, with rice grains that have a little bite to them.

In addition to the rice, Korean juk typically features vegetables that are minced to nearly the same size as the rice grains (typically carrot, zucchini, and scallion, though celery, pumpkin, potato, sweet potato, and other vegetables are not uncommon) cooked along with the rice so that the porridge winds up studded with a rainbow of colors. *Dak* (chicken) juk features chicken meat that is simmered in water with a few aromatics, then shredded. Many recipes call for simmering a whole chicken, then using the broth to cook the rice. I find whole chickens to be a little unwieldy, not to mention it is difficult to cook the legs through without letting the breast meat dry out. Instead, I prefer to use a whole bone-in, skin-on chicken breast, which cooks quickly and evenly.

DAKJUK (KOREAN-STYLE CONGEE WITH CHICKEN AND VEGETABLES)

Yield
Serves 4
to 6

Active Time
45 minutes

Total Time
1¾ hours

NOTES

The chicken will be more tender and the broth more flavorful if you use bone-in, skin-on chicken, but it tastes just fine with boneless, skinless breasts if that's what you have. You can chop the vegetables in a food processor if you prefer. Roughly chop them with a knife, add them to the bowl of a food processor, and pulse until they are finely minced.

INGREDIENTS

For the Chicken and Broth:

1 pound (450 g) bone-in, skin-on chicken breast or 12 ounces (340 g) boneless, skinless chicken breast
4 coin-sized slices fresh ginger
3 whole scallions, roughly chopped
6 medium garlic cloves (15 to 20 g), smashed with the side of a knife

For the Congee:

¾ cup (about 5 ounces/150 g) short-grain rice
1 tablespoon (30 ml) vegetable oil
1 small carrot (about 4 ounces/120 g), peeled and finely diced (see Notes)
1 small zucchini (about 4 ounces/120 g), finely diced (see Notes)
2 celery stalks (about 3 ounces/90 g), peeled and finely diced (see Notes)
2 scallions, thinly sliced
Kosher salt and freshly ground white pepper
Toasted black or white sesame seeds (optional)
Drizzle of roasted sesame oil

DIRECTIONS

(1) **For the Chicken and Broth:** Combine the chicken, ginger, scallions, and garlic in a large saucepan or wok. Add 2 quarts (2 l) water and bring to a boil. Reduce to a bare simmer, cover, and cook, turning the chicken occasionally, until it registers 155°F on an instant-read thermometer, about 30 minutes. While the chicken cooks, soak the rice in a bowl of cold water.

(2) When the chicken is cooked, transfer it to a plate and allow it to rest until cool enough to handle. Meanwhile, strain and reserve the broth, discarding the solids. Wipe out the saucepan or wok.

(3) **For the Congee:** Drain the rice. Heat the oil in the saucepan or wok over medium heat until shimmering. Add the drained rice and cook, stirring, until the rice turns translucent, about 2 minutes. Add the carrot, zucchini, and celery and cook, stirring, until the vegetables are lightly softened but not browned, about 1 minute. Add the reserved broth, scraping up the rice from the bottom of the pot. Bring to a brisk simmer and cook, stirring occasionally, until the rice is fully tender and the juk is silky, 30 to 40 minutes.

(4) Meanwhile, shred the chicken meat by hand (discard the bones and skin if using skin-on, bone-in chicken). When the juk is cooked, add the shredded chicken meat and the scallions, reserving some scallions for garnish. Season with salt and white pepper to taste. Serve, sprinkling with the reserved scallions and the sesame seeds and drizzling with a little sesame oil.

How to Cut Zucchini, Summer Squash, Carrots, and Other Long, Thin Vegetables into Planks, Matchsticks, and Dice

Cutting zucchini, carrots, parsnips, slender eggplants, and other long, skinny, firm to semifirm vegetables into planks, matchsticks, and fine dice is essentially the same process, no matter which vegetable you're working with. Here I'll show you how to do it with zucchini.

Step 1 • Cut Crosswise into Segments

Using a sharp chef's or santoku knife, cut the vegetables crosswise into 2- to 3-inch segments. Shortening their length makes it easier to cut planks and matchsticks down the line.

Step 2 • Form a Stable Base

Holding a segment firmly against the cutting board, slice off one side to form a flat surface. Set the slice aside and turn the vegetable down so that the flat side is against the cutting board, giving it a stable base for your next cuts.

CUT INTO PLANKS

Hold the vegetable steady with your nonknife hand. Keep your fingers curled backward and your thumb tucked behind them to prevent accidental injuries. Hold your knife flush against the knuckles of your nonknife hand and cut into thin, even planks. Stack three or four of the cut planks.

CUT INTO MATCHSTICKS

Hold the vegetable steady with your nonknife hand. Keep your fingers curled backward and your thumb tucked behind them to prevent accidental injuries. Hold your knife flush against the knuckles of your nonknife hand and cut into thin, even matchsticks.

CUT INTO DICE

Rotate the matchsticks 90 degrees. Hold the vegetable steady with your nonknife hand. Keep your fingers curled backward and your thumb tucked behind them to prevent accidental injuries. Hold your knife flush against the knuckles of your nonknife hand and cut into fine dice.

CONGEE WITH PUMPKIN AND PINE NUTS

Yield
Serves 4

Active Time
30 minutes

Total Time
1½ hours

INGREDIENTS

1 tablespoon (15 ml) vegetable oil

1 small leek, white and pale green parts only, finely minced (about 3 ounces/90 g)

2 medium garlic cloves, minced (about 2 teaspoons/5 g)

½ cup (about 3.5 ounces/100 g) short-grain or jasmine rice

Water or low-sodium chicken or vegetable stock (6 cups for short-grain, 5 cups for jasmine)

8 ounces (225 g) peeled and seeded kabocha squash (about ½ small squash), cut into rough ½-inch dice

9 cups water, vegetable, or chicken broth

1 tablespoon (12 g) light or dark brown sugar or maple syrup

Kosher salt and freshly ground black pepper

3 tablespoons (45 g) unsalted butter

¼ cup (35 g) pine nuts

A few tablespoons chopped fresh cilantro

3 scallions, thinly sliced

Cooking rice and kabocha squash together results in a strikingly bright orange congee. Kabocha is one of the few squash varieties that doesn't require peeling before cooking (see my recipe for Simmered Kabocha Squash on page 530), but in this particular dish the squash needs to almost completely break down, so peeling is necessary. A little brown sugar or maple syrup accentuates the natural sweetness of the squash. I finish it off with a scattering of pine nuts that are slowly toasted in butter.

DIRECTIONS

(1) Heat the oil in a Dutch oven or wok over low heat until shimmering. Add the leek and cook, stirring frequently, until softened but not browned, about 4 minutes. Add the garlic and cook, stirring, until fragrant, about 30 seconds. Add the rice, squash, water or stock, and brown sugar or maple syrup. Bring to a boil, reduce to a bare simmer, and cook until the rice and squash are completely tender and the broth is silky and thick, about 1 hour.

(2) Using a potato masher or stiff whisk, mash the pumpkin until it is mostly incorporated into the rice and only a few small chunks remain. Season with salt and pepper to taste. Keep the congee warm.

(3) Heat the butter in a wok or small skillet over low heat until melted. Add the pine nuts and cook, stirring frequently, until the nuts are evenly browned all over and have a toasted, nutty aroma, about 5 minutes. Alternatively, toast nuts in the microwave (see page 264).

(4) Stir half of the nuts and the cilantro, and scallions into the congee, reserving some scallions and cilantro for garnish. Sprinkle the remaining nuts with the browned butter and the reserved cilantro and scallions on top of the congee. Serve immediately.

Toasting Nuts? The Microwave Is Your Best Friend

Like good music, a good cookbook should be rewarding every time you open it up. Take Harold McGee's *On Food and Cooking*. Every single time I browse through its pages I pick up on something that I totally glossed over the first time around. Case in point: on page 503 in the section on cooking nuts, he mentions that "They can also be roasted in the microwave oven."

The microwave heats quickly, efficiently, and evenly from all directions and, with small items like nuts, can actually cook them from the outside and the inside at basically the same rate.

After a bit of testing I came to realize one thing: toasting in the microwave works, but it's not quite as good as toasting in the oven. While the nuts do fill the kitchen with a nutty, toasted aroma, they just don't get as browned or develop as much flavor. The problem is that we're used to tasting nuts that have been more thoroughly toasted on the outside than on the inside, as both the oven and a skillet will cook the exteriors faster than the centers.

The solution? Just help the outsides along a bit by tossing the raw nuts in a bit of oil or melted butter before placing them on a plate. I add a teaspoon of neutral oil to a cup of nuts before spreading the nuts in a single layer on a microwave-safe plate.

Microwave the nuts at 1-minute intervals, stirring in between until evenly toasted and golden. Depending on the amount of nuts you're working with, this takes between 3 and 8 minutes or so, and the results are more even and better-flavored than anything you can get out of a skillet or toaster oven.

Paella, Risotto, and Congee: The Creamy Rice Continuum

At their core, congee and Italian-style risotto are not too different. Both use starchy strains of *japonica* rice for the creamy amylopectin it adds to broth. Both act as a blank, comforting canvas for whatever flavors you want to add in. The only real difference lies in the amount of liquid used and the length of cooking. For that matter, Spanish paella, made with Bomba rice—another *japonica* variety—is not all that different either. If we were to chart out a creamy rice continuum, we'd have paella on one end and congee on the other, like this:

DISH	AMOUNT OF LIQUID	COOKING TEMPERATURE	FINAL TEXTURE
Paella	Very little	Very high	Mostly dry, with light creaminess
Risotto	Moderate	Moderate	High moisture; it flows like lava
Congee	Very high	Very low	Soupy, with some intact rice grains

Given how similar the three dishes are, I wondered how classic risotto and paella flavors would work in a congee setting. The answer: very well. For the risotto-inspired version, I start with the springtime combo of mushrooms and green vegetables (asparagus, peas, snap peas, fava beans, and snow peas all work really well here), flavored with some white wine and Parmigiano-Reggiano (if you've ever questioned whether your wok's seasoning can handle the acidity, now is the time to find out—don't worry; I promise it's going to be OK). I lean a bit on Asian flavors with the addition of miso and soy sauce, but then I've been known to add that stuff to my Italian risotto as well. Meanwhile, the paella-inspired congee dives into deeper, heartier flavors with saffron, smoky Spanish chorizo, and stock that is reinforced with flavor from the shells of the shrimp that make their way back into the finished congee. The only question: what do I call these risotto- and paella-congee hybrids? Risongee? Paejook? Help me out here.

MUSHROOM AND SPRING VEGETABLE CONGEE

Yield
Serves 3
to 4

Active Time
30 minutes

Total Time
1½ hours

NOTE
This risotto-inspired congee works with any combination of spring vegetables, so long as they are prepared according to the chart on page 250.

INGREDIENTS

Water or low-sodium chicken or vegetable stock (6 cups for short-grain rice, 5 cups for jasmine)

1 ounce (30 g) dried porcini or shiitake mushrooms

½ cup (about 3.5 ounces/100 g) short-grain or jasmine rice

¼ cup (60 ml) extra virgin olive oil

¼ cup (50 g) unsalted butter

1½ pounds (700 g) mixed fresh mushrooms, such as shiitake, cremini, oyster, and chanterelle, trimmed and thinly sliced

Kosher salt and freshly ground black pepper

3 scallions, finely chopped

2 medium garlic cloves, minced (about 2 teaspoons/5 g)

2 teaspoons (10 ml) light soy sauce or shoyu

1 tablespoon (15 ml) light miso paste

½ cup (175 ml) dry white wine or Shaoxing wine

12 ounces (325 g) spring vegetables of your choice (see Note), prepped for congee

1 ounce (30 g) finely grated Parmigiano-Reggiano cheese, plus more for serving

Small handful of minced fresh parsley leaves

Small handful of minced fresh tarragon leaves

DIRECTIONS

1 Place the water or stock and dried mushrooms in a microwave-safe container and microwave on high power until simmering, about 5 minutes. Remove from the microwave. Using a slotted spoon, transfer the rehydrated mushrooms to a cutting board and cut into bite-sized pieces. Add the rice to the stock and set aside.

2 Heat the oil and butter in a wok over medium-high heat, swirling, until the foaming subsides. Add the fresh mushrooms, season with salt and pepper, and cook, stirring occasionally, until excess moisture has evaporated and the mushrooms are well browned, about 8 minutes.

3 Add the scallions, garlic, and chopped rehydrated mushrooms and cook, stirring frequently, until softened and aromatic, about 4 minutes. Stir in the soy sauce and miso paste until evenly incorporated.

4 Add the wine and cook, stirring, until the raw alcohol smell has cooked off and the wine has almost fully evaporated, about 2 minutes.

5 Add the stock and rice. Add a large pinch of salt, increase the heat to high, and bring to a simmer. Stir the rice once, making sure no stray grains are clinging to the side of the pan above the liquid. Cover the wok and reduce the heat to a bare simmer. Cook, stirring occasionally, until the rice is tender and the congee has thickened to a creamy porridge, about 1 hour.

6 Increase heat to high and add the prepared spring vegetables, simmering according to the timing on the chart. Remove from the heat, add the cheese, and stir rapidly to incorporate thoroughly. Season with salt and stir in the herbs. Serve.

CONGEE WITH SHRIMP, SAFFRON, AND SPANISH CHORIZO

Yield	Active Time
Serves 4	30 minutes
	Total Time
	90 minutes

NOTE

Smoked Spanish paprika is also sold as *pimentón de la vera* and comes in sweet (*dulce*), medium (*agridulce*), and spicy (*picante*) varieties. Any will work, though I typically keep agridulce on hand.

INGREDIENTS

1 pound (450 g) shell-on shrimp, peeled, shells reserved

¼ teaspoon (1 g) baking soda

1 teaspoon (5 g) paprika, preferably Spanish smoked paprika (see Note)

Kosher salt

3 tablespoons (45 ml) extra virgin olive oil

8 medium garlic cloves (20 to 25 g)

6 ounces (180 g) Spanish chorizo, split in half lengthwise, casing removed and discarded, cut into ¼- to ½-inch half-moons

Two coin-sized slices fresh ginger

8 scallions, cut into ¼-inch pieces

½ cup (about 3.5 ounces/100 g) short-grain or jasmine rice

8 small dried chiles, such as Sichuan or árbol (omit if you don't want it spicy)

Pinch of saffron threads

2 dried bay leaves

Water or low-sodium chicken or vegetable stock (6 cups for short-grain, 5 cups for jasmine)

½ cup (about 2 ounces/60 g) frozen peas, thawed

Handful of minced fresh cilantro leaves

This congee starts with a flavorful shrimp and chorizo stir-fry. The smoky red oil left behind forms the flavor base for the rice, though to be honest, you could skip the whole rice bit and simply serve the chorizo and shrimp stir-fry on its own with a side of regular-old steamed rice and nobody would complain.

DIRECTIONS

(1) Combine the peeled shrimp, baking soda, Spanish paprika, a big pinch of kosher salt, and 1 tablespoon (15 ml) of the olive oil in a medium bowl. Mince 4 cloves of the garlic and add to the bowl. Toss the shrimp thoroughly and set aside.

(2) Meanwhile, combine the remaining 2 tablespoons (30 ml) olive oil and the Spanish chorizo in a wok over medium-low heat. Cook, stirring and tossing frequently, until the chorizo has rendered most of its fat and is starting to crisp around the edges, about 8 minutes. Remove the chorizo from the wok using a slotted spoon and transfer it to a clean bowl.

(3) Smash the remaining 4 garlic cloves with the side of a knife. Add the shrimp shells, ginger, and smashed garlic to the chorizo oil in the wok and set over medium-low heat. Cook, stirring and tossing frequently, until the shrimp shells are bright red and the garlic is starting to brown, about 7 more minutes. Using a slotted spoon, remove the garlic, ginger, and shrimp shells from the wok and discard, pressing on them with a second spoon to release as much fat back into the wok as possible.

(4) Increase the heat to high and heat until the shrimp-infused chorizo fat is just starting to show wisps of smoke. Immediately add the marinated shrimp and stir-fry until mostly cooked through and starting to brown around the edges, about 2 minutes. Add the scallions and continue to stir-fry for 1 minute. Transfer the shrimp and scallions to the bowl with the chorizo and set aside in the refrigerator.

(5) Return the wok to the heat and reduce the heat to medium-low. Add the rice and dried chiles and cook, stirring and tossing frequently, until the chiles smell toasted and the rice is translucent around the edges, about 2 minutes. Add the saffron and bay leaves and stir-fry for 30 seconds.

(**6**) Add the water or stock, increase the heat to high, and bring to a simmer. Stir the rice once, making sure no stray grains are clinging to the side of the pan above the liquid. Cover the wok and reduce the heat to a bare simmer. Cook, stirring occasionally, until the rice is tender and the congee has thickened to a creamy porridge, about 1 hour.

(**7**) Stir in the thawed peas, cilantro, shrimp, scallions, and chorizo, reserving some of each for garnish. Top with the reserved frozen peas, cilantro, shrimp, scallions and chorizo, and serve immediately.

2.3 FRIED RICE

We eat a lot of rice at home, and a lot of rice means a lot of leftover rice, which means fried rice makes an appearance on our lunch or dinner table at least a couple times a month.

Virtually every country in East and Southeast Asia has its own version, all of which can be traced back to its origins in sixth- or seventh-century China, when it was first developed as a means of using up leftover rice. While fancy restaurant versions exist, fried rice is a peasant food with thriftiness at its core.

When making fried rice at home, I think of it more as a technique—a series of steps—than as a specific recipe. Thinking about it this way allows you to maximize fried rice's potential as the ultimate leftover-user-upper. Scraps of roasted chicken? Into the fried rice it goes. That slab of corned beef from St. Patrick's Day? Fry it up with rice! Four asparagus stalks and a handful of torn kale leaves? The perfect addition to a wokful of fried rice. Practically anything can make its way into the wok.

Myth-Busting Fried Rice

The number of rules that everyone says you simply *must* follow when making fried rice makes it the perfect subject for some hard-core testing and myth-busting.

Let's get started.

Fried rice comes in many styles. In China (and more authentic Chinese restaurants in the States), it's typically lightly seasoned with salt and perhaps a little soy sauce or another sauce, along with scant amounts of aromatics and meat. In the Chinese American tradition, you'll find it made with bigger chunks of meat and much more sauce. Thai-style fried rice made with jasmine rice is frequently flavored with fish sauce, while in Indonesia it may be sweet soy sauce and shrimp paste. No matter how you season it, most folks agree upon one thing: each grain of rice should remain individual. Nobody wants to eat sticky, clumpy fried rice. So how do we get there?

Myth # 1 • You Must Use Medium-Grain Rice

The Truth: The best rice is whatever you have left over to use up.

Perfect fried rice is all about texture. Strike that: perfect fried rice is all about using up leftover rice, followed by texture. In my testing I was looking for rice that had distinct grains, each with a slightly chewy fried exterior and a tender bite. I wanted grains that were separate enough from each other that you could taste and appreciate their texture, but still sticky enough that you could pick up small clumps with a pair of chopsticks or a spoon.

Fried rice recipes typically call for Chinese-style medium-grain rice, though Thai-style versions use fragrant jasmine and Japanese-style fried rice can even be made with short-grain sushi rice. I tried making fried rice with all of those, as well as with long-grain rice (standard Carolina and basmati rice) and par-boiled rice (like Uncle Ben's). (I have not done any testing on brown, wild, or black rice varieties.)

I was expecting disasters from at least a couple of batches, but surprisingly, they all produced decent results. Longer-grain rice varieties tended to be the most troublesome, as they fell apart a little bit during stir-frying and lacked the plumpness that gives fried rice its signature chewy-tender texture, but the results were still more than passable and an excellent way to use up leftover rice.

These are my favorite types of rice for frying:

- **Jasmine:** A medium-grain Thai variety that has the perfect balance of stickiness (for easy eating) and individual grains (for superior texture). Jasmine rice brings its own aroma to the game, so it should be used in very light stir-fries where its flavor can shine.

- **Medium-grain white rice:** The variety you'll most commonly see in Chinese restaurants. Like jasmine, medium-rice grains boast a great balance: They're strong individuals but also good team players. White rice has less of a floral aroma than jasmine, which makes it a little more versatile.

- **Sushi rice:** Japanese-style sushi rice has a very short grain and tends to be stickier/starchier than medium-grain rices. This makes it a little bit more difficult to stir-fry without clumping, but the resulting texture is the chewiest of the lot, which can be a good thing.

Myth # 2 • Use Day-Old Rice

The Truth: Day-old rice is best, but fresh rice is great too.

I'd always heard that fried rice is best made with day-old rice and that fresh rice will turn to mush if you try to fry it. But is this really true? And if so, what is it about the resting period that makes older rice superior to fresh rice?

As rice sits after cooking, a couple things happen. First, there's evaporation: the rice gets drier. Second, we've got starch retrogradation: gelatinized starches that have swollen up and softened during cooking will recrystallize as they cool, turning the rice firm and less sticky. The same things happen with bread; in the past, I've found that most recipes that call for "stale" bread are actually really more interested in "dry" bread (see the stuffing recipe in *The Food Lab*, for instance).

I wasn't sure what I was looking for with rice, stale or dry. So I tried it. Over and over and over again. To test dryness, I used batches of rice that I set under a table fan at room temperature, which I hoped would rapidly dry out the rice without giving it much of a chance to turn stale. To test staleness, I stored batches of rice for lengths of time varying from half an hour to 12 hours, very tightly covered on plates in the fridge, allowing their starches to recrystallize without drying out. I also stored rice the way most of us do: in not-well-sealed Chinese takeout containers. Presumably these batches would get both dry and stale.

I then stir-fried the batches, one after the other, in a little vegetable oil.

My results showed some very interesting twists. First off, all of the batches of rice that were under a fan (dried and not staled) worked out well. None of the very tightly wrapped batches worked, which indicates that dryness is an essential factor for fried rice. The batches that were stored loosely wrapped for times ranging between 1 hour and around 6 hours actually

became more difficult to fry properly. After that, they got easier and easier; by hour 12, they were ideal.

But here's the thing: Even freshly cooked rice worked great. In fact, it worked better than rice that had been stored loosely covered in the refrigerator for 1 to 6 hours. What gives? Most of my other tests indicated that dryness matters, but surely fresh rice is the moistest of the lot?

Well, not necessarily. Freshly cooked rice spread out on a plate will steam a great deal as its surface moisture is evaporated. That's the important part. It's the surface moisture that is going to cause your rice to rapidly suppress the temperature of the wok; it's the surface moisture that's going to cause your rice to stick together.

That explains why fresh rice and rice that's been placed underneath a fan work well. With rice placed in the refrigerator, on the other hand, you slow down the evaporation process. Meanwhile, internal moisture from the grains will start to move outward, adding moisture to the surface of each grain and making the rice more difficult to fry. Eventually that surface moisture will evaporate again and the rice will become easier to fry.

Here are my recommendations for rice treatment, in order of preference:

Fanned rice: Rice that has been cooked, spread onto a tray, then placed under a fan for about an hour comes out dry but not stale—exactly what you want.

Fresh-cooked rice: So long as you spread the rice out on a plate or tray while it's still hot and give it a few minutes to allow some surface moisture to evaporate, you can make excellent fried rice with fresh rice.

Day-old rice: Day-old rice tends to clump, so you'll need to break it up by hand before stir-frying. It's also

drier internally than fresh rice, so you have to be faster with the stir-fry to ensure that it doesn't become overly hard. That said, if you happen to have day-old rice, it'll make excellent fried rice.

Myth # 3 • You Must Rinse the Rice

The Truth: Even unrinsed rice works fine if it's used the next day.

Excess starchiness is what causes rice to clump or turn mushy. This can be pronounced when using freshly cooked unrinsed rice, even when you allow excess moisture to evaporate. With freshly cooked rice, it's best to rinse it before cooking. A quick dunk and shake in a bowl of cold water, or a 30-second rinse under a cold tap while agitating the rice, is plenty.

By the next day, however, the recrystallized starch is not nearly as sticky and clumpy, which means that day-old leftover rice will work fine, even it if wasn't rinsed. That takes us to our next myth:

Myth # 4 • You Must Break Up the Rice Before Cooking

The Truth: This one is true!

If you're using rice that has had a chance to clump or get stale, it works best to break it up with your fingertips before it goes into the wok or to break it up with the bottom of a wok ladle once it's in the wok. This will ensure that the rice separates into individual grains without breaking or getting crushed.

I did consider whether or not oiling the rice while it was still cold before it hit the wok was a good idea. It's not: cold oil doesn't spread as well as hot oil, so you end up using way more than you'd typically need. Best to break up the rice by hand and leave the oil for the wok.

Once the rice is broken up, you're ready to cook. Fried rice is more forgiving than most stir-fries (unlike meat or green vegetables, rice is not easy to overcook), but it's still a fast process. Make sure you have your other ingredients ready to go before putting the wok on the flame.

Myth # 5 • **Keep Things Hot. Very Hot.**

The Truth: Ding! It's true.

Here is where I've made the most fried rice mistakes in my life: not getting the wok hot enough and cooking too much rice at a time. Try it and see what happens. Then come back here after you've scraped out the solid clump of mushy rice from the center of your wok.

Cooking fried rice is not all that different from, say, searing chunks of beef for a beef stew: You want to make sure that the pan is ripping-hot before you add the rice, so that the exterior has a chance to sear and acquire some texture before the rice exudes too much internal moisture and ends up steaming instead of frying.

In a Chinese restaurant, with its jet-engine wok burners, this is pretty easy. Even a large batch of rice will sear just fine. Our Western burners typically have around one-tenth the heat output of wok burners. To compensate for this, I use two strategies.

First: preheat. I'm talking turn-on-the-fan-and-unplug-the-smoke-detectors hot. Second: cook in batches, adding no more than about a cup of rice at a time to the wok, stirring and tossing it as soon as it goes in to get it nicely coated in oil. You're looking for rice that is starting to take on a toasty golden brown color, with a tight skin around each grain. This will most likely take a little bit longer than you expect it to, so be patient and keep tossing and stirring.

As each batch of rice is cooked, I transfer it to a bowl and set it aside. Once all the rice is cooked, I add it all back to the wok together.

Fried rice often features smoky *wok hei* flavor. If you want to achieve it, either stir-fry with an outdoor high-output setup (such as a turkey fryer or a hot charcoal grill with a wok insert; see page 40) or by using a torch (see page 44).

Myth # 6 • **Go Easy with the Add-Ins**

The Truth: You can add as many add-ins as you'd like, provided you cook in batches.

Just as a plate of pasta is really about the pasta itself, not the sauce, fried rice is all about the rice. I'll often make the simplest fried rice, using just onion, carrot, garlic, and scallion, along with a bit of ham, shrimp, chicken, or egg. The basic rule is that mix-ins should all be flavor enhancers, not stars unto themselves.

But, of course, all rules are meant to be broken, so if you feel like throwing the entire kitchen sink into the wok (or at least the entire contents of your fridge), don't let me stop you. Just remember: as with all stir-fries, cook in small batches and consolidate ingredients as they cook before returning them to the wok. The chart on page 276 will show you how to prepare some of my favorite ingredients for fried rice.

I almost always try to add some bright green elements to fried rice, whether that's chopped green chiles; aromatics like cilantro, basil, or scallions; or fresh vegetables like peas or minced snap peas.

Myth # 7 • **Go Easy With the Sauce**

The Truth: Please, please go easy with the sauce.

Some fried rice recipes call for massive amounts of soy sauce, oyster sauce, or hoisin sauce. This has never made much sense to me. Why go through the trouble of making sure your rice grains are dry and individual if you're going to then turn around and sog them all up with extra sauce again? You end up with a clumpy, stodgy mess.

So long as you're using good technique and high-quality rice, you don't need a ton of sauce. For this batch, a small dash of soy sauce or a smidge of aromatic sesame oil can add fragrance without overpowering the smoky *wok hei* of perfectly fried rice. Oyster sauce, fish sauce, and other Asian sauces, like kecap manis (the Indonesian sweet soy sauce used in nasi goreng), will all work. Feel free to suit your own tastes. (Some poor misguided souls even like to stir-fry their rice with ketchup and Worcestershire sauce.)*

Rather than season fully with a sauce, I typically add a dash of kosher salt (and a touch of powdered MSG) to the wok. Dry salt will not add excess moisture, nor will it distract from other, more subtle flavors in the rice.

---

* I will not judge them, for their judgment shall come in the next life.

Adding Eggs to Fried Rice

There are three increasingly complex schools of thought when it comes to adding an egg to fried rice. None of them is the *right* way per se, and the method that requires the most effort is not necessarily better than the simplest. It's all a matter of what end results you're looking for.

Method 1 • Add the Egg Directly to the Rice

With this method, you crack a raw egg directly into the rice as it stir-fries. The egg ends up forming a thin coating over individual grains, melding into the finished dish and giving the rice a little bit more cohesion. This method is incredibly simple and foolproof.

Method 2 • Clear a Space for the Egg

After stir-frying the rice, you push it up the sides of the wok to reveal the bottom of the wok. You add a little oil, then crack the egg into it, scrambling it in the center of the wok and using your spatula or ladle to break it up into small pieces, eventually tossing them with the rice for even distribution.

This is the method I almost always use, as it is simple enough to do but gives you distinct bits of egg mixed together with the rice.

Method 3 • Cook the Egg Separately

This is the method favored by most restaurant-trained fried-rice chefs. You heat a good amount of oil in the bottom of the wok (enough to pool gently around the egg), then add very lightly beaten eggs directly to the hot oil, letting them puff, sputter, and brown, before removing it from the wok, adding your other ingredients, and continuing with the stir-fry. The egg goes back in at the end to get chopped up and incorporated. In some fancy restaurants, you'll even find fried rice with egg whites and yolks that have been cooked separately to give you more variation in flavor. When done correctly, the eggs come out poofy and light, leading to a dish that is much airier and lighter than with either of the other methods.

Fried Rice, Step by Step

Here's the basic blueprint for a wokful of fried rice.

Step 1 • Break Up the Rice

Break the rice up into individual grains if using day-old rice. If using fresh rice, cook it, then spread it on a rimmed baking sheet to cool near a drafty spot or under a desk fan for 1 hour before frying. If the rice is especially sticky, sprinkle it with up to a half teaspoon of cornstarch per cup of rice as you break it up (see the sidebar on the following page).

Step 2 • Gather Your Mise en Place

Your fried rice mise en place should consist of:

- Oil in a dispenser

- Eggs, precracked

- 2 to 3 ounces (60 to 90 g) meaty bits (if using)

- 4 to 5 ounces (120 to 150 g) vegetables (sorted into separate bowls according to cook time)

- A pound or so (450 g) of broken-up rice

- Aromatics like minced garlic, ginger, scallions, or chiles (if using)

- A few teaspoons (5 to 15 ml) sauces (premixed if using more than one sauce or seasoning)

- Dry seasonings and finishing garnishes (such as herbs and scallion greens)

Decide now whether you want to fry your egg at the start (Method 3 on page 273) or simply add it to the rice as its finishing (Method 1 or 2 on page 272)

Step 3 • Start Cooking

Heat up the wok, add some oil, and start stir-frying your ingredients until just cooked through. Start with meaty bits (or eggs, if you are planning on cooking them separately via Method 3 on page 273), then the vegetables. Cook as many batches as you need to ensure that the wok doesn't get crowded, transferring the cooked ingredients to a bowl on the side as you go.

Step 4 • Cook Your Rice

Once all the mix-ins have been precooked, reheat the wok, add a little more oil, and stir-fry your rice, using the bottom of a ladle to break up any remaining clumps and hitting it with a kitchen torch if you're after *wok hei*. As with all stir-fries, work in as many batches as your cooktop necessitates to keep the wok and rice piping hot as you go. Keep tossing and stirring until the rice starts to firm up and take on a touch of color. If adding an egg via Method 1 or 2 on page 272, do it now.

Step 5 • Add Aromatics

Add aromatics like garlic, ginger, scallions, and chiles to the rice in the wok and stir-fry until fragrant, then return everything to the wok and add your final seasonings and garnishes (such as soy sauce, fish sauce, salt and white pepper, or chopped herbs). Stir-fry to combine everything, transfer to a serving platter, and serve.

Sidebar

My Rice Is Too Wet!

Sometimes, depending on the specific rice, the weather, and storage conditions, even day-old rice can feel a little moist and sticky and resist breaking up by hand. If you find that your rice refuses to separate into individual grains as you're preparing for your stir-fry, you can use a trick I learned from Sichuanese chef Wang Gang (definitely check out his YouTube or Weibo channel): add some extra starch. A half teaspoon of rice flour or cornstarch sprinkled over each cup of rice and tossed with it will help capture excess moisture and allow the grains to separate. (Incidentally, the same concept is behind adding powdered cellulose to preshredded cheese, preventing it from reclumping in the bag.)

How to Prepare Ingredients for Fried Rice

The goal when preparing ingredients for fried rice is to cut and/or otherwise prep the ingredients to the point where they all take approximately the same amount of time to cook, which takes the guesswork out of properly cooking everything when stir-frying. Meaty bits should be cut small enough to cook through with only the briefest of stir-fries.

CATEGORY	INGREDIENT	METHOD
Meat	Cured meats such as ham, bacon, or Spam	Cut into ¼-inch dice.
Meat	Cured sausage, such as *lap cheong*, chorizo, pepperoni, or salami	Remove casing if necessary. Cut into ¼-inch dice or ¼-inch half- or quarter-moons.
Meat	Cooked chicken	Shred into bite-sized pieces or cut into ¼-inch dice.
Meat	Ground meats, such as ground pork or chicken	Marinate with a touch of soy sauce and a ½ teaspoon cornstarch per 4 ounces meat.
Meat	Leftover steaks or roasts	Cut into ¼-inch dice.
Seafood	Shrimp	Peel and cut into ½-inch pieces or leave whole if very small.
Seafood	Crabmeat	Pick over and discard any bits of shell.
Seafood	Cooked salmon or tuna	Flake gently with a fork.
Seafood	Salt cod	Soak in clean water overnight, changing the water a few times over the course of the night. Flake with a fork.

Chart

CATEGORY	INGREDIENT	METHOD
Seafood	Hot-smoked fish, such as salmon, sablefish, or marlin	Flake gently with a fork.
Vegetable	Asparagus	Peel the stalks below the top 2 inches and cut or snap off the woody bottoms. Cut into ¼-inch lengths, either straight or on a bias, leaving the tips whole or split lengthwise.
Vegetable	Snap peas	Break off the tops and bottoms with your fingers, pulling out any strings that come with them. Cut on a sharp bias into ¼-inch pieces.
Vegetable	Snow peas	Break off the tops and bottoms with your fingers, pulling out any strings that come with them. Cut on a sharp bias into ¼-inch pieces.
Vegetable	English peas	Remove peas from the pods. Blanch in boiling salted water for 2 minutes, then drain and transfer to an ice bath to cool. Dry well before stir-frying.
Vegetable	Green beans	Break off the tops and bottoms with your fingers, pulling out any strings that come with them. Cut longer beans into bite-sized pieces. Blanch in boiling salted water for 2 minutes, then drain and transfer to an ice bath to cool. Dry well before stir-frying.
Vegetable	Fava beans	Remove peas from the pods. Blanch in boiling salted water for 2 minutes, then drain and transfer to an ice bath to cool. Remove pale green skin from each bean and discard. Dry well before stir-frying.
Vegetable	Firm, crisp root vegetables, such as carrots, parsnips, turnips, radish, rutabaga, jícama, or water chestnut	Cut into ¼-inch dice.
Vegetable	Corn	Cut from the cob. When stir-frying, let the kernels sit without moving in the wok for a few moments to char lightly before tossing and repeating until charred all over.
Vegetable	Onions and shallots	Cut into fine dice.
Vegetable	Scallions	Trim and discard the roots. Cut white and pale green parts into ¼- to ½-inch segments. Reserve and slice the greens for garnish.
Vegetable	Leeks	Trim and discard the roots and dark green tops. Split pale green and white parts into quarters lengthwise. Cut into ¼-inch segments.
Vegetable	Celery	Peel any tough outer stalks. Split each rib lengthwise into 3 or 4 thin rods. Cut into ¼-inch segments.
Vegetable	Bell peppers and other chiles	Cut into ¼-inch dice.
Vegetable	Zucchini and other tender squashes	Cut into ¼-inch dice.
Vegetable	Cucumber	Peel, split lengthwise, remove seeds with a spoon, split again lengthwise into quarters, then cut into ¼-inch segments.
Vegetable	Cabbage and brussels sprouts	Thinly slice.
Vegetable	Broccoli and cauliflower	Cut heads into ½-inch florets. Peel tougher bits of stem, then cut the stems into ¼-inch dice.
Vegetable	Mushrooms	Thinly slice.

BASIC VEGETABLE AND EGG FRIED RICE

Yield
Serves 2
or 3

Active Time
15 minutes

Total Time
15 minutes

NOTES

This very simple fried rice is a blueprint for all of your future fried rice adventures. Feel free to omit or replace any of the vegetables and to add meat or seafood to the rice as you see fit, following the chart on page 276. If using fresh rice, rinse the rice well before cooking, and once cooked, transfer it to a rimmed baking sheet set by a breezy window or under a fan for 1 hour before continuing with step 2. You can use a blowtorch to add *wok hei* to the rice in step 3.

INGREDIENTS

2 cups cooked white rice (12 ounces/340 g; see Notes)
¼ cup (60 ml) peanut, rice bran, or other neutral oil
2 large eggs, lightly beaten
1 small onion, finely chopped (4 ounces/ 120 g)
1 medium carrot, peeled and cut into small dice (3 ounces/85 g)
2 scallions, thinly sliced (1 ounce/30 g)
2 medium garlic cloves, minced (about 2 teaspoons/5 g)
1 teaspoon (5 ml) light soy sauce or shoyu
1 teaspoon (5 ml) roasted sesame oil
4 ounces (120 g) frozen peas, thawed
Kosher salt and freshly ground white pepper

DIRECTIONS

(1) If using day-old rice (see Notes), transfer to a medium bowl and break the rice up with your hands into individual grains.

(2) Heat a wok over high heat until very lightly smoking. Add 3 table-spoons (45 ml) of the vegetable oil and swirl to coat. Reduce the heat to medium, pour the eggs into the center of the wok, and cook, swirling the wok, until the eggs are puffy and golden brown around the edges, about 30 seconds. Use a spatula to release the eggs from the bottom of the wok, carefully flip, cook for another 15 seconds, swirling, then transfer the eggs to a bowl and set aside.

(3) Return the empty wok to high heat until lightly smoking. Add the onion and carrot and cook, stirring and tossing constantly, until lightly softened and fragrant, about 1 minute. Transfer to the bowl with the cooked egg.

(4) Return the empty wok to high heat until lightly smoking. Add the remaining tablespoon (15 ml) oil and swirl to coat. Add the rice and cook, stirring and tossing, until the rice is pale brown and toasted and has a lightly chewy texture, about 3 minutes (see Notes). Add the scallions and garlic and stir-fry until fragrant, about 30 seconds.

(5) Return the vegetables and egg to the wok, using the spatula to break up the egg into small pieces as you toss everything together. Add the soy sauce, sesame oil, and peas.

(6) Season with salt and pepper to taste. Transfer to a serving platter and serve immediately.

BACON AND EGG FRIED RICE

This is fried rice that my mom used to make, with American bacon, egg, onion, and plenty of black pepper. I like to use Chinese bacon, which is typically cured a little longer and has a smokier flavor with warm spices like cinnamon and star anise. You can find it at most large Asian supermarkets in the meat section near the Chinese dried sausage. If using Chinese bacon, make sure to cut off the rind, as it will come out inedibly tough in a quick-cooking dish like this.

Yield
Serves 2 or 3

Active Time
15 minutes

Total Time
15 minutes

NOTES

If using fresh rice, rinse the rice well before cooking, and once cooked, transfer it to a rimmed baking sheet set by a breezy window or under a fan for 1 hour before continuing with step 2. You can also use *lapcheong* (Chinese sausage) in place of the bacon. You can use a blowtorch to add *wok hei* to the rice in step 3.

INGREDIENTS

2 cups cooked white rice (12 ounces/340 g; see Notes)
3 tablespoons (45 ml) peanut, rice bran, or other neutral oil
2 large eggs, lightly beaten
4 slices bacon or Chinese bacon, cut into ¼-inch pieces (see Notes)
1 small onion, finely chopped (4 ounces/120 g)
2 scallions, finely chopped
1 teaspoon (5 ml) light soy sauce or shoyu
1 teaspoon (5 ml) roasted sesame oil
Kosher salt and freshly ground black pepper

DIRECTIONS

(1) If using day-old rice (see Notes), transfer it to a medium bowl and break the rice up with your hands into individual grains.

(2) Heat a wok over high heat until very lightly smoking. Add the vegetable oil and swirl to coat. Reduce the heat to medium. Pour the eggs into the center of the wok and cook, swirling the wok, until the eggs are puffy and golden brown around the edges, about 30 seconds. Use a spatula to release the eggs from the bottom of the wok, carefully flip, cook for another 15 seconds, swirling, then transfer the eggs to a bowl and set aside.

(3) Add bacon to the empty wok and cook, stirring and tossing over medium heat until rendered and starting to crisp, about 2 minutes. Add the onion and cook, stirring and tossing constantly, until lightly softened and fragrant, about 1 minute. Transfer the bacon and onion to the bowl with the cooked egg.

(4) Return the wok with any rendered bacon fat to high heat until lightly smoking. Add the rice and cook, stirring and tossing, until the rice is pale brown and toasted and has a lightly chewy texture, about 3 minutes (see Notes). Add the scallions and stir-fry until fragrant, about 30 seconds.

(5) Return the bacon, onion, and egg to the wok, using the spatula to break up the egg into small pieces as you toss everything together. Add the soy sauce and sesame oil. Season with salt and pepper to taste. Transfer to a serving platter and serve immediately.

"THE MIX"

"The mix" is what my friend Brandon Jew of Mr. Jiu's, a modern Chinese restaurant in San Francisco, calls the all-purpose seasoned mixture of seasoned pork and shrimp that makes its way into several of his menu items. I loved the idea so much that I've taken to keeping a similar mixture in my freezer at home. You can use it as the filling for dumplings or wontons (page 414). You can use it to stuff scallion pancakes (page 396). You can stir-fry it as a topping for crispy panfried noodles (page 359). You can form it into balls and drop them into simmering broth. You can use it in place of the shrimp filling for stuffed peppers with black bean sauce (page 150). It's about as versatile as it gets.

Once made, you can transfer the mix to zipper-lock bags, squeeze the air out of them, press them flat, seal them, and store them in the freezer for months. Pressed flat this way, the mix will defrost overnight in the fridge, in an hour or so on an aluminum baking sheet on the counter, or in about 10 minutes in a bowl of water in the sink.

The flavorings in the mix are savory and a little sweet. White pepper adds heat; soy sauce, garlic, and ginger add aroma; sugar adds sweetness; cornstarch helps it retain moisture as it cooks; and finally, a dash of baking soda gives the pork a bouncier texture and the shrimp a firm, juicy crunch.

THE MIX (SEASONED PORK AND SHRIMP BASE)

Yield
Makes 12 ounces

Active Time
5 minutes

Total Time
5 minutes

INGREDIENTS

8 ounces (225 g) ground pork
4 ounces (120 g) raw shrimp, roughly chopped into ¼-inch pieces
¼ teaspoon (1 g) freshly ground white pepper
1 tablespoon (15 ml) light soy sauce
2 teaspoons (5 g) minced garlic (about 2 medium cloves)
2 teaspoons (5 g) minced fresh ginger (about ½-inch segment)
1 teaspoon (4 g) sugar
1 teaspoon (3 g) cornstarch
¼ teaspoon baking soda

DIRECTIONS

Combine all the ingredients in a bowl and mix vigorously with your fingertips until the mixture feels slightly tacky, about 1 minute. Store in a sealed container in the refrigerator for up to 3 days before using or transfer to zipper-lock bags, press flat, squeeze out the air, seal the bags, and freeze for up to 3 months.

EGG FRIED RICE WITH "THE MIX"

This fried rice is similar to classic Yangzhou-style fried rice, frequently called "house special fried rice" on Chinese American restaurant menus. For the pork and shrimp, I use "The Mix" (page 280), but if you like, you could also use shrimp combined with diced store-bought char siu pork, Chinese sausage, or bacon instead. I like the umami depth that oyster sauce adds to this particular fried rice variation.

Yield
Serves 2
or 3

Active Time
30 minutes

Total Time
30 minutes

NOTES

If using fresh rice, rinse the rice well before cooking, and once cooked, transfer it to a rimmed baking sheet set by a breezy window or under a fan for 1 hour before continuing with step 2. You can use a blowtorch to add *wok hei* to the rice in step 3.

INGREDIENTS

2 cups cooked white rice (12 ounces/340 g; see Notes)
¼ cup (60 ml) peanut, rice bran, or other neutral oil
2 large eggs, lightly beaten
6 ounces "The Mix" (page 280)
1 small onion, finely chopped (4 ounces/120 g)
1 medium carrot, peeled and cut into small dice (3 ounces/90 g)
2 scallions, chopped (1 ounce/30 g)
1 teaspoon (5 ml) oyster sauce
1 teaspoon (5 ml) light soy sauce or shoyu
1 teaspoon (5 ml) roasted sesame oil
4 ounces (120 g) frozen peas, thawed
Kosher salt and freshly ground white pepper

DIRECTIONS

(1) If using day-old rice (see Notes), transfer it to a medium bowl and break the rice up with your hands into individual grains.

(2) Heat a wok over high heat until very lightly smoking. Add 3 tablespoons (45 ml) of the vegetable oil and swirl to coat. Reduce the heat to medium. Pour the eggs into the center of the wok and cook, swirling the wok, until the eggs are puffy and golden brown around the edges, about 30 seconds. Use a spatula to release the eggs from the bottom of the wok, carefully flip, cook for another 15 seconds, swirling, then transfer the eggs to a bowl and set aside.

(3) Return the empty wok to high heat until smoking. Add the remaining tablespoon (15 ml) oil, swirl to coat, then immediately add "The Mix" and cook, stirring and tossing, until the shrimp and pork are barely cooked through, about 1 minute. Add the onion and carrot and cook, stirring and tossing constantly, until lightly softened and fragrant, about 1 minute. Transfer to the bowl with the cooked egg.

(4) Return the wok to high heat until lightly smoking. Add the rice and cook, stirring and tossing, until the rice is pale brown and toasted and has a lightly chewy texture, about 3 minutes (see Notes). Add the scallions and stir-fry until fragrant, about 30 seconds.

(5) Return the pork, shrimp, vegetables, and egg to the wok, using the spatula to break up the egg into small pieces as you toss everything together. Add the oyster sauce, soy sauce, sesame oil, and peas, and toss until well combined. Season with salt and pepper to taste. Transfer to a serving platter and serve immediately

BLISTERED GREEN BEAN FRIED RICE

Yield
Serves 2
or 3

Active Time
25 minutes

Total Time
25 minutes

NOTES

If using fresh rice, rinse the rice well before cooking, and once cooked, transfer it to a rimmed baking sheet set by a breezy window or under a fan for 1 hour before continuing with step 2. You can use a blowtorch to add *wok hei* to the rice in step 3.

INGREDIENTS

2 cups cooked white or jasmine rice (12 ounces/340 g) (see Notes)
5 tablespoons (75 ml) peanut, rice bran, or other neutral oil
2 large eggs, lightly beaten
8 ounces (225 g) yard-long or green beans, trimmed and cut into ¾-inch pieces
2 scallions, thinly sliced
2 medium garlic cloves, minced (about 2 teaspoons/5 g)
1 to 3 fresh Thai bird chiles (to taste), thinly sliced, plus more for serving
1 teaspoon (5 ml) light soy sauce or shoyu
1 teaspoon (5 ml) fish sauce, plus more for serving
1 ounce (30 g) Thai or sweet Italian basil leaves, roughly torn
Kosher salt and freshly ground white pepper
Sugar

To Serve:

1 lime, cut into 4 wedges
1 small cucumber, thinly sliced

In this recipe for fried rice I decided to take a slightly different approach, placing nearly equal focus on vegetables and rice. Charred, blistered green beans (or better, yard-long beans) are an excellent accompaniment to rice, and here the beans make up over 50 percent of the weight of the finished dish. The flavors are Thai, with garlic, scallions, Thai chiles, white pepper, fish sauce, and a whole lot of fresh Thai basil.

DIRECTIONS

(1) If using day-old rice (see Notes), transfer it to a medium bowl and break the rice up with your hands into individual grains.

(2) Heat a wok over high heat until very lightly smoking. Add 3 tablespoons (45 ml) of the oil and swirl to coat. Reduce the heat to medium. Pour the eggs into the center of the wok and cook, swirling the wok, until the eggs are puffy and golden brown around the edges, about 30 seconds. Use a spatula to release the eggs from the bottom of the wok, carefully flip, cook for another 15 seconds, swirling, then transfer the eggs to a paper-towel-lined bowl and set aside.

(3) Return the empty wok to high heat until smoking. Add 1 tablespoon (15 ml) of the remaining oil and swirl to coat. Add the green beans and cook, stirring and tossing occasionally, until deeply blistered and charred, about 3 minutes. Transfer to the bowl with the eggs.

(4) Return the wok to high heat until lightly smoking. Add the remaining tablespoon (15 ml) oil and swirl to coat. Add the rice and cook, stirring and tossing, until the rice is pale brown and toasted and has a lightly chewy texture, about 3 minutes). Add the scallions, garlic, and chiles and stir-fry until fragrant, about 30 seconds.

(5) Return the beans and egg to the wok, using the spatula to break up the egg into small pieces as you toss everything together. Add the soy sauce, fish sauce, and basil. Season with salt, white pepper, and sugar to taste. Transfer to a serving platter and serve immediately with lime and cucumber.

EASY PORK FRIED RICE WITH CORN AND SHISHITO PEPPERS

Yield
Serves 2
or 3

Active Time
15 minutes

Total Time
15 minutes

NOTES

If using fresh rice, rinse the rice well before cooking, and once cooked, transfer it to a rimmed baking sheet set by a breezy window or under a fan for 1 hour before continuing with step 2. Spanish-style raw cured chorizo comes in sticks, like salami or pepperoni. I like Palacios brand, which is available at many online retailers, such as LaTienda.com. Spanish chorizo should not be confused with Mexican-style raw chorizo or other Latin American chorizos. You can use a blowtorch to add *wok hei* to the rice in step 3.

INGREDIENTS

2 cups cooked white rice (12 ounces/340 g)
     (see Notes)
2 tablespoons (30 ml) peanut, rice bran, or
     other neutral oil
3 to 4 ounces (90 to 120 g) Spanish-style
     raw cured chorizo, skin removed, finely
     diced (see Notes)
6 ounces (170 g) fresh corn kernels, cut
     from 1 to 2 ears
2 scallions, sliced, whites and greens
     reserved separately
12 shishito peppers, thinly sliced, or 1
     medium green bell pepper, finely diced
     (about 6 ounces/170 g)
1 teaspoon (5 ml) light soy sauce or shoyu
1 teaspoon (5 ml) roasted sesame oil
Kosher salt
Small handful of chopped fresh cilantro
     leaves

This recipe was a product of an overstuffed fridge, as fried recipes often are. I happened to have some leftover pork tenderloin. It was also summer, which means that I have a near-endless supply of corn and shishito peppers in my fridge at all times (those two are fantastic partners in crime), and a stick of Spanish-style raw cured chorizo is never far from reach in my house. Put it all together, and what do you get? This simple pork fried rice with charred corn and peppers.

I start by stir-frying the diced chorizo until sizzling, then remove it and cook the corn directly in the rendered chorizo fat. When cooking the corn, I make sure to leave it in the wok long enough to get some nice dark charring on it. Unlike many other vegetables, corn doesn't get mushy if you overcook it, nor does it lose its flavor. If anything, its flavor intensifies as it gets darker. Shishito peppers, on the other hand, need to be cooked hot and fast to keep their fresh green crunch.

If you don't have chorizo, don't worry—this recipe is just as tasty with ham, bacon, or no meat at all.

Swap out shishitos for green bell peppers or omit them entirely. Got half an onion sitting around? Use that instead of the scallions. The whole point of a 15-minute recipe like this is to keep things simple, so just relax, OK?

DIRECTIONS

(1) If using day-old rice (see Notes), transfer it to a medium bowl and break the rice up into individual grains with your hands before proceeding.

(2) Heat the wok over high heat until very lightly smoking. Add 1½ teaspoons (8 ml) of the oil and swirl to coat. Add the chorizo and stir-fry until the fat is rendered and the chorizo is crisp around the edges, about 1 minute. Transfer the chorizo to a bowl, leaving the fat in the wok.

(3) Return the wok to high heat until lightly smoking. Add the corn and cook, stirring occasionally, until lightly charred on several surfaces, about 4 minutes. Transfer to the bowl with the chorizo.

(4) Return the wok to high heat until lightly smoking. Add another 1½ teaspoons of the oil and swirl to coat. Add the scallion whites and peppers, and stir-fry until lightly softened and fragrant, about 1 minute. Transfer to the bowl with the corn and chorizo.

recipe continues

(5) Return the wok to high heat until lightly smoking. Add the remaining tablespoon of oil and swirl to coat. Add the rice and cook, stirring and tossing, until the rice is pale brown and toasted and has a lightly chewy texture, about 3 minutes (see Notes).

(6) Return the corn, chorizo, and pepper mixture to the wok. Add the soy sauce and sesame oil and toss everything to combine. Season with salt to taste. Add the scallion greens and cilantro and toss to combine. Serve immediately.

THAI-STYLE CRAB FRIED RICE

My wife, Adri, is a crab fiend. I once watched her down a full pound of picked crabmeat in a covered market in Bangkok, pulling the crab—still warm from cooking—piece by piece out of a Styrofoam tray, dipping it into nam pla prik, and sucking the juices off her fingers as she went. That's just about a full 1 percent of her body weight!

Southeast Asia is a great place for crab lovers,* and there are worse ways to eat it than in Thai *khao pad pu*—fried rice with crab, made with fragrant jasmine rice that's gently seasoned with garlic and chiles, then tossed with scrambled egg, picked crabmeat, and scallions, finished with a little fish sauce, and served with cilantro and cucumbers.

Knowing how much Adri loves crab, I decided to treat her with this recipe. It's custom-made for crab lovers.

Now that I've set out my rules for fried rice, once again I'm going to go ahead and break them right from the get-go. Instead of adding my rice directly to hot oil, then subsequently adding aromatics, for this recipe I'm starting with the aromatics and letting them infuse the oil before adding the rice. This sequence—aromatics before main ingredient—is common in Thai stir-fries, which tend to use a little less heat and rely less on *wok hei* than Chinese stir-fries.

Next, in go some minced garlic and finely sliced Thai bird chiles. If you (or maybe a loved one you are serving this to) are particularly sensitive to heat, omit the chiles. They can always be added later on at the table.† To this infused oil, I add the rice and scrambled egg.

Don't you hate that feeling you get at amusement parks when, just as you start really getting into a ride, it's over and that spotty-faced teenager is forcing you to get out of the car? I get that feeling with cooking in a wok sometimes. We've only just begun this delicious fried rice trip, but unfortunately, it's also almost at a close.

The last two twists in the track: the crab and the scallions. I like to add the crab in large chunks. Around these parts, that means Dungeness crab claws, knuckles, and legs, roughly torn into bite-sized pieces by hand. Back on the East Coast, it's probably jumbo lump blue crab, in pieces as large as you can find.

Fresh-cooked crab or frozen crab is your best bet here, but canned crabmeat will do in a pinch if you can't find fresh. Canned crab tends to have a much stronger seafood aroma, which can be offputting to some people (like me). I add the crab along with some sliced scallions, cooking it only long enough to heat everything through. You don't want to overcook that crab!

Because jasmine rice is so fragrant, it requires very little in the way of sauce or extra seasoning. I add a couple of teaspoons of fish sauce, then season to taste with salt and white pepper. Stir in some cilantro, then serve the rice immediately with some sliced cucumber on the side, along with extra fish sauce and Thai chiles (for the brave). And, if your dining companion is anything like Adri, stand back, because you don't want to get caught in the cross fire as she sets her sights on the crab.

---

*   Though it might be a good idea to confirm what you're ordering. At a small beachside restaurant in the Vietnamese fishing and resort village of Phan Thiet, we perused a menu that offered both "crap soup" and "real crap soup." We opted for the former.

†   On second thought, think long and hard about the state of the relationship between you and that chile-sensitive loved one, then decide whether it's the chiles or the loved one that stays or goes.

CRAB FRIED RICE

Yield
Serves 2
or 3

Active Time
30 minutes

Total Time
30 minutes

NOTE

If using fresh rice, rinse the rice well before cooking, and once cooked, transfer it to a rimmed baking sheet set by a breezy window or under a fan for 1 hour before continuing with step 2.

INGREDIENTS

2 cups cooked jasmine rice (12 ounces/340 g) (see Note)
2 tablespoons (30 ml) peanut, rice bran, or other neutral oil
1 to 3 Thai bird chiles (according to your heat tolerance), finely sliced, plus more for serving
2 medium garlic cloves, minced (about 2 teaspoons/5 g)
1 large egg
Kosher salt
4 ounces (115 g) picked cooked crabmeat
2 scallions, thinly sliced
2 teaspoons (10 ml) Asian fish sauce, plus more for serving
Freshly ground white pepper
¼ cup (60 ml) minced fresh cilantro leaves

To Serve:

1 lime, cut into 4 wedges
1 small cucumber, thinly sliced

DIRECTIONS

(1) If using day-old rice (see Note), transfer it to a medium bowl and break the rice up with your hands into individual grains before proceeding.

(2) Heat a wok over high heat until lightly smoking. Add 1 tablespoon (15 ml) of the oil and swirl to coat. Add the chiles and garlic and cook, stirring, until fragrant, about 10 seconds. Add the rice and cook, stirring and tossing, until the rice is pale brown, toasted, and has a lightly chewy texture, about 4 minutes.

(3) Push the rice to the side of the wok and add the remaining tablespoon (15 ml) oil. Break the egg into the oil and season with a little salt. Use a spatula to scramble the egg, breaking it up into small bits. Toss the egg and rice together.

(4) Add the crabmeat, scallions, and fish sauce. Toss to combine and cook, tossing and stirring constantly, until the crab is heated through and the scallions are lightly softened, about 1 minute. Season with white pepper and salt to taste. Stir in the cilantro.

(5) Serve immediately with sliced cucumber, lime wedges, additional fish sauce, and sliced Thai chiles at the table.

KIMCHI AND SPAM FRIED RICE

The setting: The rice was left over from dinner a few days back. The kimchi had been resting in the back of the second shelf of my fridge for many months. (Actually, I'm pretty sure it had been sitting there for nearly a year, meaning it was extra sour and funky.) The Spam . . . I'm honestly not sure where the Spam came from. I can't remember buying Spam since that one time eight years ago, when I tasted every flavor of Spam on the market for an article on *Serious Eats* and took a brief lie-down to deal with the salt rush, immediately followed by a second lie-down to deal with the withdrawal symptoms.

Perhaps Spam spontaneously generates in dimly lit pantry closets, the way mice spontaneously appear when a piece of soiled linen is stored with the wheat.

Whatever the provenance, I knew its destination: Add to it an egg, an onion, and a few other aromatics, and I had everything on hand to make myself a big ol' plate of the ultimate Korean American late-night drunk food: kimchi and Spam fried rice. This is the kind of stuff you eat while swaying gently over the kitchen counter in your underwear.

To start, I drain away as much of the kimchi juice as possible into a bowl, pressing on the cabbage to really force it out. The reason is that we want to sauté the kimchi and give it a little flavor, and any excess moisture will inhibit that. Don't worry; we'll use it all again later on.

Next, I start stir-frying, beginning with diced Spam. Even though Spam is packed with fat, you need a little oil in the pan to get it started. I cook the Spam until it's crisp, then add chopped onions and the chopped kimchi, stir-frying it all together until the onions are softened and the kimchi is just starting to brown a bit around the edges. I then transfer everything to a bowl to empty out the wok.

After frying my rice in the now-empty wok, I add my aromatics: scallions, garlic, and thinly sliced hot chiles to double down on the heat from the kimchi. As soon as they're fragrant, I return the kimchi/Spam mixture to the wok and toss it all together.

Now we get to seasoning. The kimchi juice is the first step, and with high enough heat, it should sizzle and dry up pretty rapidly. I also use a big splash of fish sauce, a touch of toasted sesame oil, and a ton of ground black pepper. Sesame oil and ground black pepper go together like Bert and Ernie, if Bert and Ernie tasted way, way better than they do.

Here's the real trick for this particular dish: letting that rice sit in the wok without moving it. The idea is to create a crisp, charred fried-rice shell, like what you'd find in the bottom of a good paella or a dolsot bibimbap.

It's the textural element and toasty flavor that push this over the edge, from "this is pretty good" to "please don't talk to me while I'm eating this"–level stuff. Top it all off with a crisply fried egg and some hot sauce, and . . . I'm not even sure what territory we're in, but it's a good place to be.

Whether it's first thing in the morning or late at night, any time that you're typically in your underwear is the right time for kimchi and Spam fried rice. It's time to rock out with your wok out, or maybe chow down with your pants down. Or both. Or neither. I'm too tipsy and hungry to care, really.

KIMCHI AND SPAM FRIED RICE

Yield
Serves 4

Active Time
30 minutes

Total Time
30 minutes

NOTE
If using fresh rice, rinse the rice well before cooking, and once cooked, transfer it to a rimmed baking sheet set by a breezy window or under a fan for 1 hour before continuing with step 2.

INGREDIENTS

2 cups cooked white rice (12 ounces/340 g) (see Note)

12 ounces kimchi with juices (about 1 cup packed/340 g)

3 tablespoons (45 ml) peanut, rice bran, or other neutral oil

One 12-ounce (340 g) can Spam, cut into ¼- to ½-inch dice

1 large onion (12 ounces/340 g), finely diced (1½ cups)

4 scallions, white and pale green parts only, thinly sliced

2 medium garlic cloves, minced (about 2 teaspoons/5 g)

1 fresh red or green hot chile (such as jalapeño, serrano, or Thai bird), thinly sliced

Freshly ground black pepper

2 teaspoons (10 ml) fish sauce

1 teaspoon (5 ml) roasted sesame oil

½ cup chopped fresh cilantro leaves and fine stems (½ ounce/14 g)

Kosher salt

To Serve:

4 Extra-Crispy Fried Eggs (optional; page 114)

Hot sauce

DIRECTIONS

(1) If using day-old rice (see Note), transfer it to a medium bowl and break the rice up with your hands into individual grains before proceeding. Place the kimchi in a fine-mesh strainer set over a large bowl and squeeze out excess liquid. Reserve the liquid and finely chop the kimchi.

(2) Heat 1 tablespoon (15 ml) of the vegetable oil in a wok over medium-high heat until shimmering. Add the Spam and cook, tossing and stirring frequently, until well browned and starting to crisp. Add the chopped kimchi and onion and cook, stirring and tossing regularly, until the vegetables are softened, about 4 minutes. Transfer to a bowl and set aside.

(3) Heat the empty wok over high heat until lightly smoking. Add 1 tablespoon (15 ml) of the remaining oil and swirl to coat. Add the rice and cook, stirring and tossing, until the rice is pale brown, toasted, and has a slightly chewy texture, about 4 minutes.

(4) Press the rice up the sides of the wok, leaving a space in the middle. Add the remaining tablespoon (15 ml) oil to the space. Add the scallions (reserving some for garnish), garlic, and chile and cook, stirring gently, until lightly softened and fragrant, about 1 minute. Toss with the rice to combine. Add the onion, kimchi, and Spam mixture and toss to combine. Pour in the reserved kimchi juice and season generously with black pepper. Add the fish sauce, sesame oil, and cilantro (reserving some cilantro for garnish). Toss everything to combine. Season with salt to taste if necessary.

(5) When ready to serve, allow the rice to sit in the wok without tossing to create a crisp crust underneath, about 1 minute. Scoop the rice out onto a serving platter, trying to get as much of the crispy rice facing up as possible. Top with Really Fried Eggs (if using), sprinkle with the reserved scallions and cilantro, and serve immediately with hot sauce.

NASI GORENG: THE FUNKIEST OF FRIED RICES

Yield
Serves 4

Active Time
30 minutes

Total Time
30 minutes

NOTE
If using fresh rice, rinse the rice well before cooking, and once cooked, transfer it to a rimmed baking sheet set by a breezy window or under a fan for 1 hour before continuing with step 2.

INGREDIENTS

For the Spice Paste:
1 small shallot (about 1 ounce/30 g), roughly chopped

2 medium garlic cloves (5 g), smashed with the side of a knife

2 fresh red or green Thai bird chiles or 1 serrano chile, roughly chopped, more or less, according to your spice tolerance

Kosher salt

½ teaspoon terasi, belacan, or other Asian shrimp paste (optional)

For the Rice:
3 tablespoons (45 ml) peanut, rice bran, or other neutral oil

4 to 6 ounces (120 to 180 g) cooked shredded chicken breast or small whole shrimp (optional)

2 cups cooked jasmine rice (12 ounces/340 g) (see Note)

1½ tablespoons (22.5 ml) Kecap Manis (page 291)

2 scallions, sliced into ¼-inch pieces on a bias

Freshly ground white pepper

To Serve:
4 Extra-Crispy Fried Eggs (optional, page 114)

Fried shallots, store-bought or homemade (page 255)

1 small tomato, sliced

1 small cucumber, thinly sliced

Indonesia's version of fried rice, nasi goreng, has two unique flavorings. The first is kecap manis, a sweetened soy sauce (whose name comes from the same root word as Western ketchup), which adds sweetness and warm spice notes to the rice. The second is *terasi*, the Indonesian version of the Malaysian *belacan*, or shrimp paste. It's potent stuff. While fish sauce has the ability to meld into the background, providing umami oomph without overt fishy aromas, when you include shrimp paste in a dish, you're going to know it's there. It's not for everyone, but I strongly urge you to try it, because once you get a taste for it, it's addictive in all kinds of dishes.

Recipes for nasi goreng are all over the map, but the most delicious (and interesting) technique I've seen was from Indonesian *Serious Eats* contributor Pat Tanumihardja, who makes hers by first pounding some aromatics into a curry-like paste in a mortar and pestle. Any technique that uses the mortar and pestle is alright by me, so that's how I've made my nasi goreng ever since.

recipe continues

(1) For the Spice Paste: Combine the shallots, garlic, and chiles in the bowl of a mortar and pestle and add a pinch of kosher salt. Pound until a chunky paste is formed. Add the shrimp paste and grind in a circular motion until homogenous.

(2) If using day-old rice (see Note), transfer it to a medium bowl and break the rice up with your hands into individual grains before proceeding.

(3) For the Rice: Heat 2 tablespoons (30 ml) of the oil in a wok over medium heat until shimmering. Add the spice paste and cook, stirring constantly until the spice mixture breaks and starts to darken, about 2 minutes. Add the chicken or shrimp (if using) and stir-fry until the chicken is heated through or the shrimp are cooked. Transfer the contents of the wok to a separate bowl and wipe it out.

(4) Return the wok to high heat until lightly smoking. Add the remaining tablespoon (15 ml) oil and swirl to coat. Add the rice and cook, stirring and tossing, until the rice is pale brown, toasted, and has a slightly chewy texture, about 4 minutes. Return the chicken or shrimp to the rice and toss to incorporate.

(5) Add the kecap manis and scallions, reserving some scallions for garnish. Cook, stirring and tossing constantly until the scallions are lightly softened and everything is piping hot, about 1 minute.

(6) To Serve: Transfer to a serving platter and serve immediately with Really Fried Eggs, a sprinkle of fried shallots and the reserved sliced scallions, and tomato slices, cucumber slices, and extra kecap manis on the side.

HOMEMADE KECAP MANIS

Yield
Makes
about 1½
cups

Active Time
30 minutes

Total Time
30 minutes

INGREDIENTS

1 cup (240 ml) dark soy sauce

1 cup (about 8 ounces/225 g) packed dark
   brown sugar

2 tablespoons (30 ml) molasses

2 medium garlic cloves (5 g), smashed

Two ¼-inch-thick slices fresh ginger

1 cinnamon stick

1 whole star anise pod

1 teaspoon (3 g) black peppercorns

2 cloves

Kecap manis is Indonesian soy sauce made by combining fermented soybeans with palm sugar, giving it a thick, syrupy consistency and salty-sweet flavor that is similar to Chinese *tianmianjiang*, and indeed, the latter thinned out with a touch of water is a reasonable replacement for it in a pinch. The main difference is that kecap manis is very frequently flavored with a slew of warm spices that balance out the salty funk of the fermented soybeans. If you have trouble finding kecap manis or simply don't want to keep a whole bottle, you can make it yourself from pantry ingredients by infusing soy sauce with aromatics and sweetening it with brown sugar (or, if you can get your hands on it, palm sugar). The process takes about 15 minutes.

DIRECTIONS

Combine all the ingredients in a small saucepan. Bring to a bare simmer over medium heat, stirring frequently to avoid burning. Cook until very slightly reduced and thickened and all of the sugar is dissolved, about 15 minutes. Let cool to room temperature, then strain through a fine-mesh strainer. Store in a sealed container in the refrigerator for at least a few months or even years.

3

NOODLES

Know Your Noodles

My wife, Adri, and I started keeping track of all the different noodles we've eaten in Asia over the years. (OK, I keep track; she keeps busy trying to discover brand-new ways of telling me she's sick of noodles.) We've had long, thin, noodles in broth in Beijing. We've had wide, flat hand-stretched noodles in chile oil in Wuhan. We've had flat steamed rice noodles in Saigon and stir-fried rice sticks in Bangkok. We've had bright yellow alkalized wheat noodles doused in chiles and mouth-numbing Sichuan peppercorns in

Chengdu alongside noodles made by pouring a sweet potato starch batter through a potato ricer into a pot of simmering water. We've eaten stir-fried noodles with dark soy sauce for breakfast in Indonesia and vermicelli in spicy coconut broth for lunch in Malaysia.

We've had steamed bean starch noodles with cucumbers and cilantro in Xi'an and noodles tossed with ground pork and preserved mustard root in Chongqing. We've eaten buckwheat noodles on a snowy mountainside in Nagano and stir-fried yakisoba in Kyoto. We've eaten pale white wheat noodles doused with sesame paste and chile oil in Shanghai,* fried egg noodles in curry broth in Chiang Mai, and crispy pan-fried noodles in Singapore. We saw noodles that were pulled, peeled, extruded, twisted, kneaded, cut, sliced, steamed, rolled, tossed, flicked, and lovingly caressed before being firmly slapped down onto a steel table. Noodles for breakfast, noodles for lunch, noodles for dinner, noodles for elevensies, noodles for a midnight snack, noodles for a pre-midnight-snack snack. You'd have to be a true wet noodle to ever get bored of noodles (though I don't blame Adri).

Does all of this variety make you a little uncomfortable? Don't worry; me too. Despite having grown up in a Japanese household where noodles were a staple, I *still* get a little nervous when I head into the Asian supermarket to pick up some fresh noodles for dinner, knowing that I'm going to have to pick from dozens of different packages that all look sort of similar, marked in unfamiliar languages.

Well, here's the good news. Once you learn a few of the basics and get a general grasp of what you're looking at, you'll find that a lot of the choices really boil down to nothing more than brand loyalty. And just like your spaghetti carbonara is gonna work even if the supermarket was out of DeCecco and you had to pick up a box of Barilla, the odds of ruining your dinner (or midnight snack!) because you picked up some noodles that were not *exactly* right are pretty low.

Still, you can improve these odds by understanding the basic categories of noodles you'll find and what specific dishes and situations they're best used for. Rather than bother with the impossible task of being comprehensive, I'm just going to do my darnedest to be useful. In this guide you'll find a few common noodle-related terms that can help with identification, followed by a thorough guide to the Asian noodles you're most likely to come across in the United States and the noodles that I find most useful for home cooks.

And if you don't have access to Asian noodles at all, well don't worry—when cooked right, even Italian pasta can be delicious in many Asian noodle dishes (see "Turn Spaghetti into Ramen," page 300).

NOODLE TERMS

Before we get to specific types of noodles, here are a few basic noodle terms to be aware of when looking at packaging or recipes. In most recipes, unless you want to be a real stickler, any noodles within a broad category will work. Any type of wheat noodle (*mein, mien,* or *miàn*) can be substituted for another. Recipes that call for vermicelli-style noodles will work with any vermicelli, whether rice, mung bean, or sweet potato based.

Miàn, mien, or mein

The Chinese term for wheat noodles (think: lo mein or chow mein) or *mien.* Many Japanese noodles share this etymological root, ra**men** and so**men**, for instance.

Fěn or fun

Chinese noodles made from nonwheat starches, such as *hor fun* (the wide steamed rice noodles that Beef Chow Fun, page 365, is made from) or *mi fun* (thin dried rice noodles used in soups and stir-fries throughout Asia).

Chow

Chow is a stir-fry. The Chinese symbol for chow, 炒, is composed of 火 ("fire") and 少 ("little" or "less"), indicating a quick cooking method. Combine it with miàn or fěn and you've got chow mein and chow fun, a couple of classic noodle stir-fries. (This is also where we get the American English term "chow," as in, "chow down.")

Hand-pulled

Lā translates from Mandarin as "to pull." Hand-pulled noodles (*lāmiàn*) are made from wheat flour doughs that are stretched by hand to form noodles. The thinness of

---

* I'll be honest: only I ate that one; my wife had disappeared to one of the rare noodle-free corners of the city by that point, probably looking for *xiao long bao*—Shanghai-style soup dumplings—which are another story for another time.

the noodle depends on how long the dough is stretched. Master noodle-makers can start with a solid block of dough and transform it into a single noodle hundreds of meters long with the width of a strand of angel hair pasta as they repeatedly lift, twist, fold, and stretch the dough. Some hand-pulled noodles, on the other hand, are wide and stubby with a heartier texture. Think pappardelle vs. capellini.

Alkaline noodles

Some Asian noodles, most notably ramen and some types of Chinese noodles, are made with water that has alkalizing minerals added to it. This liquid, known as *kansui* in Japanese, gives ramen noodles their characteristic yellow color, extra-springy and slippery texture, and a flavor that is a bit hard to describe. I find alkaline noodles to be a little sulphurous, a touch soapy, and definitely eggy (all in a good way).

Vermicelli

Any extra-thin noodle. Commonly made from rice, but you'll also frequently find mung bean or sweet potato starch vermicelli.

HOW TO IDENTIFY NOODLES IN THE WILD

Italians may be known for their pasta, but for sheer variety of fresh and dried noodles, Asia's got them beat by a landslide.* To be fair, they've had a head start. While pasta as we know it was developed in Italy sometime around the twelfth or thirteenth century (most likely well before Marco Polo's famous trip to Asia), noodles have been consumed in China for several millennia. In 2005, a team of archaeologists led by Dr. Houyuan Lu of the Institute of Geology and Geophysics at Beijing's Chinese Academy of Sciences identified the husks of millet used to produce noodle dough in a 4,000-year-old sealed earthenware container in Lajia, a Neolithic site in northwestern China. Noodles made from millet dough, which lacks the gluten-forming proteins found

in wheat flour, would not have had the same elasticity and bite we expect in wheat-based Asian noodles today, but may have borne some resemblance to buckwheat soba or other nonwheat noodles.†

By the middle of the third century, during the Han Dynasty, noodles were already a staple part of the Han Chinese. By the end of the first millennium, wheat production was widespread in China and toothsome, elastic wheat noodles had become the norm. As noodles made their way across China and the rest of Asia, they've taken on countless forms and have been produced from a wide range of grains and vegetables. Today the range of diversity you'll find in China alone is truly staggering. Expand that to the rest of Asia and it becomes a mind-breakingly huge variety.

Attempting to write a fully comprehensive guide would take up an encyclopedia-sized volume, so I am not going to. Instead, I'll focus on the most common types of noodles you are likely to find at the supermarket, as well as a couple of the less common noodles that I happen to love.

Wheat Noodles

Lāmiàn

Appearance: Long and thin with an off-white to yellow color
Country of Origin: China
Main Ingredient: Wheat
Formation Method: Hand-stretched and sold fresh or dried
Uses: The best all-purpose noodles for stir-fries and noodle soups. If I had to pick one noodle to take to my desert island, these would be it. These are ideal as the base for fiery Dan Dan Noodles (page 317) or Zhajiang Miàn (page 326), served with Thai Basil and Peanut Pesto (page 324), and in Shanghai-Style Sesame Noodles (page 323).
Cooking and Storage: Fresh lāmiàn needs to be cooked in boiling water before it is used. Because Chinese noodles are typically salted before forming, you don't need to use salted water as you would for

---

* OK, having a hugely diverse population and land mass approximately 150 times greater and a population 71 times greater probably helps a bit with that diversity.

† Buckwheat, despite its name, is not in fact related to wheat and contains no gluten-forming proteins.

Italian pasta. Plain old boiling water is fine. Add the noodles to boiling water and cook al dente, then transfer immediately to hot soup or drain and dry well for a stir-fry or to serve cold.

Similar Alternatives: Fresh ramen or Italian spaghetti (or capellini) cooked in alkaline water (see "Turn Spaghetti into Ramen," page 300).

Lo Mein

Appearance: Long and thin with a deep yellow color. Typically a little thicker than lāmiàn

Country of Origin: China

Main Ingredients: Wheat and eggs

Formation Method: Hand-stretched or rolled and cut

Uses: *Lo mein* is actually the name of a preparation, not just the noodles themselves, but you'll often see noodles labeled "lo mein" or "for lo mein" in the United States. In Chinese cuisine, lo mein range from as thin as wonton noodles to slightly thicker and are typically served either stirred together with a sauce or braise or as a form of deconstructed wonton noodle soup: noodles, boiled wontons, and greens, with soup on the side. In the United States, lo mein noodles are thicker egg noodles and are almost always stir-fried in a soy-based sauce with vegetables and meat or seafood. These thicker noodles are what you want for my Chinese American Stir-Fried Lo Mein with Shiitake, Chives, and Charred Cabbage (page 348).

Cooking and Storage: Add the noodles to boiling water and cook al dente, then transfer immediately to hot soup or drain and dry well for a stir-fry or to serve cold.

Similar Alternatives: Fresh lāmiàn can be par-cooked in boiling water, drained, and stir-fried like lo mein, as can spaghetti cooked in alkaline water (see "Turn Spaghetti into Ramen with This One Easy Trick," page 300). *Cumian* are thick, rectangular noodles commonly used in Shanghai-style noodle dishes.

Chow Mein

Appearance: Long and thin with a deep yellow color, thinner than lo mein.

Country of Origin: China

Other Names: Hong Kong noodles or "panfried noodles"

Main Ingredients: Wheat and eggs

Formation Method: Hand-stretched or rolled and cut.

Uses: As with lo mein, *chow mein* is technically the name of the preparation, though you'll find fresh noodles labeled "chow mein" at the Asian market. Chow mein are typically served panfried.

Cooking and Storage: Fresh chow mein should be boiled before stir-frying. Frequently, chow mein will be sold par-cooked and ready to fry, in which case they only need to be loosened up before stir-frying with a sauce to soften them up slightly, or panfried plain in oil to crisp into a sort of cake before being topped with saucy ingredients or finished with a sauce in the wok.

Similar Alternatives: Wonton noodles are essentially raw chow mein noodles and can be boiled, drained, and used in the same manner for panfrying or stir-frying.

Wonton Noodles

Country of Origin: China

Other Names: *Wantan mee* (Malaysia), *bami kiao* (Thailand)

Main Ingredients: Wheat and eggs

Formation Method: Rolled and cut or machine-formed with rollers and dies

Classic Uses: You'll find these thin, springy noodles in Chinese-style wonton soups (add them to The Best Wonton Soup, page 554) or served lightly blanched topped with aromatic oil and other seasonings. They're also commonly used throughout Southeast Asia for soups and dry noodle dishes, such as *bami mu daeng* (Thai noodles with roast pork) and *mami* (Philippine noodle soup).

Similar Alternatives: In most cases you can use thin lāmiàn or ramen in place of wonton noodles, though they don't have quite the same eggy flavor or firm texture.

Biangbiang Miàn

Country of Origin: China

Other Names: *Youpo chemian*, hand-torn noodles

Main Ingredient: Wheat

Formation Method: Made by hand-stretching rectangles of dough into wide strips, then tearing them in half lengthwise. During the stretching process, the noodle-maker will whip the dough up and down, letting it whap against an oiled tabletop repeatedly as the noodles stretch out to arm's length.

Classic Uses: Biangbiang miàn are boiled and served in soups and savory salads.

Similar Alternatives: Dried Italian pappardelle or other very wide pasta cooked in alkaline water (see "Turn Spaghetti into Ramen with This One Easy Trick," page 300).

Liangpi

Country of Origin: China
Other name: Cold skin noodle
Main Ingredient: Wheat starch
Formation Method: Liangpi are made by rinsing a wheat dough in water to release its starch. The dough is then discarded and the starchy water is allowed to rest overnight, during which time the wheat starch settles to the bottom of the container. The clear water on top is poured off, then the starch slurry at the bottom is poured into flat sheets, steamed, and cut.

Classic Uses: Liangpi are most frequently served cold, dressed with chile oil, garlic, and a variety of other condiments and garnishes, such as sesame paste, vinegar, cucumber, mung bean sprouts, and cilantro.

Ramen (Fresh)

Country of Origin: Japan, by way of China (in Japan ramen is still thought of as a Chinese noodle dish, despite having its own unique identity)
Main Ingredient: Wheat flour
Formation Method: Ramen is made from alkalized dough. The noodles can be formed via hand-stretching, rolling, or extruding.

Classic Uses: Ramen noodles are most frequently consumed in the form of ramen soup, but they are also used for Hiyashi Chūka (cold ramen noodle salad, page 343) and for *tsukemen* (broth-free ramen noodles served with a dipping sauce on the side). Ramen are also stir-fried along with a Worcestershire-style sauce to make Yakisoba (page 352), a popular Japanese street food or bar food (which is made with ramen despite having the word *soba* in the name).

Similar Alternatives: Lāmiàn or Italian spaghetti or capellini cooked in alkaline water (see "Turn Spaghetti into Ramen with This One Easy Trick," page 300).

Ramen (Dried)

Country of Origin: Japan
Other Name: Instant noodles
Main Ingredients: Wheat flour and fat
Formation Method: Par-cooked ramen noodles are dehydrated and sold in ready-to-cook blocks with a long shelf life. Cheaper brands deep-fry the noodles to remove excess moisture, resulting in slightly faster cooking but an inferior texture. Better brands (my favorite is Myojo Chukazanmai, available online and at most Japanese supermarkets) naturally air-dry the noodles, leading to springier, more natural texture when cooked.

Classic Uses: Late night snack. College food. Drunk food. When properly customized, a bowl of instant ramen can form an extremely satisfactory (if not healthy) meal.

Similar Alternatives: None

Somen

Country of Origin: Japan
Main Ingredient: Wheat
Formation Method: Stretched or rolled and cut. Somen are thin, thin, thin. Thinner than Italian angel hair. Because of this, even in dried form they cook up in record time and are wonderful for mopping up delicate sauces.

Classic Uses: Frequently somen are served chilled on ice and dipped into cold soy-dashi broth as a summer snack. You'll find restaurants that serve cooked noodles that flow down an endless waterfall, allowing you to fish them out with your chopsticks and dip as you eat. Somen can also be served hot in delicate broths.

Similar Alternative: Very thin angel hair pasta

Udon

Country of Origin: Japan
Main Ingredient: Wheat
Formation Method: Usually rolled and cut, sometimes stretched. There is a wide variety of udon noodles in Japan, but most of them are wide, flat, and maintain a

nice bouncy chew after cooking. They are sold dried or frequently fresh-frozen.

Classic Uses: Udon are most frequently served hot or cold in simple dashi and soy-based broths or curry broth.

Similar Alternatives: Dried linguine or fettuccine cooked using the baking soda method (see "Turn Spaghetti into Ramen," page 300)

Soba

Country of Origin: Japan
Main Ingredients: Buckwheat or a mixture of buckwheat and regular wheat
Formation Method: Rolled and cut
Classic Uses: Soba is frequently served hot in a dashi-based broth or cold with a dashi-based condiment for dipping and slurping. Because buckwheat does not form gluten as easily as refined wheat flour, soba noodles have a more delicate texture and are known as a difficult style of noodle to master.
Similar Alternatives: None

Rice Noodles

Hor Fun

Country of Origin: China
Other Names: *Shahe fěn*, *chow fun* (*chow* means "fried," but in the West *hor fun* noodles will often be labeled "chow fun," as stir-frying is the most common way they are prepared); *kway teow* (Malaysia, Singapore), *sen yai* (Thailand), *pho* (Vietnam)
Main Ingredient: Rice
Formation Method: A rice starch slurry is poured onto a flat, wide surface, steamed, then cut.
Classic Uses: Wide, fresh hor fun are stir-fried with soy sauce for Beef Chow Fun (page 365), Pad See Ew (page 372), or *char kway teow* or served in brothy or saucy preparations. Narrower rice noodles are used for noodle soups throughout Southeast Asia. Pho noodles are similar to hor fun in preparation, but typically much more delicate.
Similar Alternatives: None

Rice Stick

Country of Origin: China
Other Names: *Banh pho* (Vietnam), pad Thai noodle, *jantaboon* or *chantaboon* (Thailand), or wide rice noodle
Main Ingredient: Rice
Formation Method: Same as for hor fun, but typically thinner and more delicate. Rice sticks are typically sold dried, while hor fun is sold fresh.
Classic Uses: Noodle soups such as pho or Thai boat noodles, in Vietnamese spring rolls and salads, stir-fried. Because rice noodles are so delicate, they are very easy to overcook in soups and are easy to break in stir-fries, so extra care must be taken when preparing them.
Similar Alternatives: Bean thread noodles can be used in place of thin rice sticks (vermicelli). Wheat-based noodles can be used in place of thicker rice sticks for soups and stir-fries.

Rice Cakes

Country of Origin: China
Other Names: *Tteok* or *dduk* (Korea), Shanghai-style *nian gao* (China), *mochi* (Japan)
Main Ingredient: Glutinous rice
Formation Method: Traditionally, glutinous rice is pounded into a sticky dough that is then shaped and steamed. Modern rice cakes are made by machine and extruded. Korean dduk is usually shaped into short cylinders, while Shanghai-style nian gao is shaped into bias-cut disks. In Japan, mochi is formed into square cakes or small balls called *dango*.
Classic Uses: There is a huge variety of rice cakes in Korea, China, and other Asian countries, which range from soft and sticky to firm and chewy. They are used in both savory and sweet applications and can be grilled, simmered, steamed, baked, or stir-fried. They are the main ingredient in Spicy Korean Rice Cake Stew (Gungmul Tteokbokki) with Kimchi (page 540) and in several other Korean and Chinese soups and stir-fries. In Japan, a softer form of rice cake called *mochi* is grilled, simmered, or baked (in modern times it is also formed around ice cream as a dessert). Rice cakes are a traditional food for New Year's Day in Korea, China, and Japan.
Similar Alternatives: None

Other Starch Noodles

Shirataki

Country of Origin: Japan
Main Ingredient: *Konnyaku* (yam starch)
Other Names: *Ito konnyaku* or Devil's tongue noodle
Formation Method: Shirataki noodles are made by extruding a yam starch (*glucomannan*) mixture into boiling water or by setting the yam starch mixture into solid sheets and cutting by hand or machine. They are typically sold in sealed packages containing starchy water. They should be rinsed in clean water before use.
Classic Uses: Shirataki are excellent served cold with simple dressings. They can also be panfried or roasted and served in soup.
Similar Alternatives: None

Bean Thread Noodles

Country of Origin: China
Other Names: *Fensi* (China), cellophane noodles, glass noodles, *dangmyeon* (Korea)
Main Ingredient: Mung bean, sweet potato, potato, or tapioca starch
Formation Method: They are made by extruding a starchy slurry into boiling water.
Classic Uses: Bean thread noodles have a huge number of uses. They can be stir-fried (see my recipe for Ants Climbing Trees, page 382), used in soups or hot pots, used to fill dumplings, or used in warm or cold noodle salads.
Similar Alternatives: Thin rice sticks (vermicelli)

Turn Spaghetti into Ramen with This One Easy Trick

It was a normal Thursday afternoon in 2014. I was testing pizza ovens on the balcony of our apartment in Harlem (as was my habit on your average Thursday back then) when my mom texted me: "I was reading this Japanese cooking blog that says to boil spaghetti with baking soda to make ramen. Have you ever heard of that?"

I hadn't, and given that I had a few fire-breathing pizza ovens in front of me and dough that wasn't going to wait, I filed it away in the back of my mind and didn't think much about it until a couple weeks later when my colleague at *Serious Eats*, Daniel Gritzer, texted me, asking if I had any recommendations for how to make ramen when one doesn't have access to ramen noodles. (These days, there are a ton of fresh ramen options in most major cities, but back then you had to find a specialty shop.) I remembered my mother's baking soda suggestion, and it seemed like it was worth a shot.

See, ramen (and other alkaline noodles) get their distinct yellow color, springy bite, and lightly sulfurous aroma from *kansui*, an alkaline mineral water used to make the noodles. In the West, recipes for alkaline noodles will frequently call for either adding baking soda directly to the dough or baking the baking soda first to convert sodium bicarbonate into sodium carbonate, a more intensely alkaline powder (see page 17). But the idea that you can take noodles that are already made and simply boil them in alkaline water to achieve similar results was enticing.

I set up two pots side by side, one with plain water and one to which I added a couple teaspoons of baking soda per liter of water. I salted both of them to the same degree, then cooked thin spaghetti noodles in them until they were just cooked through. Side by side, the difference in appearance was striking, with the alkaline noodles showing a deeper yellow color. A promising sign!

The aroma of the alkaline noodles was also more intense, and biting into one proved that the test was a success: the noodle was distinctly springier than the one cooked in plain water, with the slurpable, slippery texture of good alkaline noodles.

Are they as good as real-deal fresh alkaline noodles? No, but they're an excellent alternative for noodle soups and dressed noodles for anyone who doesn't have easy access to an alternative and doesn't feel like making noodles from scratch.

Q: Is It Worth Making Your Own Noodles?

A: Let me tell you something reassuring: It's *OK* to buy your noodles.

I'll be honest. I very rarely make my own noodles for the same reason that I don't make my own soap or my own sneakers: we live in the modern age of specialization, and there are people who make it their life's work to master these crafts so that I don't have to. The noodles I can buy at the Asian supermarket are excellent, inexpensive, and accessible. In fact, in most cases they are better than the noodles I can make myself at home.

That said, noodle accessibility can vary around the country and the world, and there are times when you simply feel like producing a meal 100 percent from scratch.* For times like these, I want to go over three different methods for making noodles yourself at home. The first, a technique for making

ramen-style alkaline noodles, is by far the most labor-intensive and most-likely-to-not-work-perfectly-the-first-time. The second two are hand-pulled noodles, which are much more forgiving and, frankly, more fun.

I'm fairly certain you will fall into one of three categories:

A. You are a glutton for noodles.

B. You are a glutton for punishment.

C. You enjoy noodles and trying new things with friends and family.

1. If you're type A, buy your noodles.

2. If you're type B, I refer you to Sho Spaeth's excellent guide to homemade alkaline noodles on *Serious Eats*, which is far more in-depth than the scope of this book would allow for (and to which I have personally very little to add). Search for "How to Make Ramen Noodles from Scratch."

3. If you're type C, then hand-pulled noodles are for you, and again, I refer you to a *Serious Eats* guide, this one by Tim Chin and titled "How to Pull Off Thin Hand-Pulled Lamian Noodles."

---

* Well, as from-scratch as is reasonable without first creating the universe.

3.1 HOT DRESSED NOODLES AND PASTA

The easiest way to enjoy good noodles is simply dressed with a variety of flavorful toppings and condiments. Unlike Italian pasta dishes, in which pasta is typically combined with a sauce in the pan before being served, some of the best noodle dishes are constructed the way we would think of salads in the West: Put everything together into a bowl, toss it a few times to incorporate, and serve it up. Street vendors and fast-food cooks will have an array of a dozen or so tall steel containers filled with prepared condiments and aromatics—chopped garlic, sugar, vinegar, soy sauce, crushed spices, crimson-red chile oil, sesame paste, bean pastes, minced herbs—that they will spoon on top of a bowl of freshly cooked noodles rapid-fire before handing it all over to you to toss before slurping it down.

It pays to take a note from these noodle vendors and devote at least part of your fridge to condiments and toppings. If you're me, that part of your fridge is an entire shelf and a half (most chefs I know have similar fridge situations). At any given moment I'll have a half dozen flavors of chile oil, various fermented bean pastes and prepared sauces, salad dressings, mustards, lots and lots of pickles from both the East and the West, dried and fermented meats, anchovies and shrimp pastes, a dozen hot sauces, concentrated stocks and soup bases, and plenty of flavored oils. These are my flavor bombs, ready to be deployed whenever a meal threatens to be bland. With the contents of my fridge and a package of fresh or dried noodles, I am never more than a boiling pot of water away from a simple, flavorful meal.

UMAMI OIL ("XO PEPPERONI SAUCE")

Yield
Makes
about 2
cups

Active Time
45 minutes

Total Time
45 minutes

NOTES

Mincing the pepperoni and bacon by hand is easy if you buy it presliced. You can make the job even easier by placing them in the freezer for 15 minutes before cutting. Alternatively, if you prefer the quality of stick pepperoni and slab bacon (I do), you can use a food processor: freeze the pepperoni and bacon solid, then push it through a food processor fitted with a large-holed grating disk.

If using chorizo, make sure to buy Spanish-style dry-cured chorizo, which will have a salami-like firm texture, not to be confused with fresh Mexican-style chorizo or other cooked Latin American sausages that may be labeled "chorizo."

If you don't have a food processor with a grating attachment, you can grate stick pepperoni and slab bacon by hand on a box grater (I strongly suggest wearing cut-resistant gloves if attempting this—slippery meat and a box grater can lead to accidents otherwise) or finely mince it with a knife.

I like using Korean chile flakes for this oil because they offer lots of flavor without an overwhelming amount of heat. For more heat, feel free to add ground Sichuan heaven-facing, er jing tao, or Thai chile flakes to taste.

XO sauce is a modern condiment created by Hong Kong chefs that combines a ton of ingredients rich in the glutamates and inosinic acids that trigger our sense of savoriness. It's named after XO cognac only because of its association with opulence. In the kitchen at Clio, I'd make a big batch of it a few times per month, carefully rehydrating and shredding dried scallops and shrimp, chopping up the rinds of Spanish Iberico ham (Hong Kong versions would use Chinese Jinhua ham), then cooking it all down in oil with a host of aromatics until it reduced into a sticky, oily, intensely flavored mixture.

At home where I've rarely got dried scallops but always have a stick of pepperoni on hand, I've adapted the same basic technique, giving it a distinctly smoky paprika-scented aroma that is killer on noodles. In addition, I add a few smashed anchovies for their salty umami kick, some dried porcini mushrooms, and a number of common XO sauce ingredients, like soy sauce, sugar, fish sauce, oyster sauce, and Shaoxing wine.

Making this sauce is pretty straightforward, though a little time consuming. The good news is that the recipe makes quite a bit of sauce, and stored in a sealed jar in the fridge, it keeps virtually forever. That is, if you don't do what I do and sneak a big heaping spoonful straight out of the jar at bedtime.

INGREDIENTS

- 1 cup (240 ml) homemade or store-bought low-sodium chicken stock or dashi
- ½ ounce (15 g) dried porcini, shiitake, or maitake mushrooms
- 6 medium garlic cloves (15 to 20 g), smashed with the flat side of a knife
- One 2-inch piece fresh ginger, cut into coin-sized disks
- 2 medium shallots (about 3 ounces/90 g), roughly chopped
- 4 ounces (120 g) pepperoni or Spanish dry-cured chorizo, very finely minced (see Notes)
- 4 ounces (120 g) bacon or pancetta, very finely minced (see Notes)

- ¾ cup (180 ml) vegetable or canola oil
- 6 oil-packed anchovy fillets, finely minced
- 1 tablespoon ground Korean chile flakes (gochugaru; see Notes)
- 2 dried bay leaves
- 1 whole star anise
- ½ cup (120 ml) Shaoxing wine
- 2 tablespoons (45 ml) oyster sauce
- 1 tablespoon (30 ml) fish sauce
- 2 tablespoons (30 ml) light soy sauce or shoyu
- 2 tablespoons (24 g) dark brown sugar

recipe continues

(1) Heat the stock in a small saucepan on the stove or in a microwave-safe container until steaming hot, then add the dried mushrooms, remove from the heat, and allow the mushrooms to rest for 5 minutes to rehydrate. Pick the mushrooms out of the chicken stock (reserve the stock) and roughly chop them.

(2) Place the mushrooms, garlic, ginger, and shallots in the bowl of a food processor or mini-chopper and pulse until finely chopped but not pureed, about 12 short pulses. (Alternatively, chop all those ingredients by hand on a cutting board until finely chopped.)

(3) Combine the pepperoni, bacon, and oil in a wok and heat over medium-high heat. Cook, stirring, as the bacon and pepperoni start to bubble. Continue cooking, stirring frequently, until the bacon and pepperoni are starting to turn crisp and golden brown, about 8 minutes total, maintaining a steady bubble throughout the cooking process. Add the anchovies, stir to combine, and continue to cook for 1 minute, until the bacon and pepperoni are mostly crisp.

(4) Add the garlic/ginger/shallot/mushroom mixture and cook, stirring constantly, until the vegetables turn light golden brown, about 2 minutes. Do not let them overbrown at this stage or they will turn bitter. Add the chile flakes, bay leaves, and star anise and cook, stirring, until aromatic, about 30 seconds.

(5) Immediately add the Shaoxing wine, stir thoroughly, and allow to simmer for 30 seconds. Add the reserved chicken stock, the oyster sauce, fish sauce, soy sauce, and brown sugar. Reduce the heat to medium and continue to cook, stirring occasionally to prevent stuff from burning on the bottom, until the liquid no longer looks watery or soupy and the sauce has a thick, jam-like texture with a layer of oil on top, about 15 minutes. Remove from the heat and allow to cool. Discard the bay leaves and star anise, transfer to sealable containers, and store in the refrigerator for up to several months.

Noodles with XO Pepperoni Sauce

Cook noodles according to package directions. As soon as they're done cooking, place each portion in an individual serving bowl. Top with a tablespoon of light soy sauce or shoyu and a dash of black or Chinkiang vinegar. Add a couple tablespoons XO Pepperoni Sauce, some chopped scallions, toss with chopsticks, and serve. If desired, add a handful of mung bean sprouts or shredded cabbage to the water as you boil the noodles and serve them in the same bowl.

Other Good Uses for XO Pepperoni Sauce

- As a table condiment for fried rice, or mixed right into the wok as the rice fries.

- Spooned over grilled, roasted, or steamed vegetables (it's especially nice over broccolini or Chinese broccoli, where it gets caught in the florets and leaves).

- A spoonful added when stir-frying clams, shrimp, or other shellfish.

- Added to any of the stir-fried eggplant recipes in this book.

- Drizzled over grilled corn on the cob.

- As a topping for tomato-based pasta dishes.

- As a topping for grilled fish, shellfish, or meats.

- A little added to salads, especially those with strong peppery or bitter greens.

BURNT GARLIC SESAME AND CHILE OIL

Yield
Makes
about 1 cup

Active Time
15 minutes

Total Time
15 minutes

NOTE
You can use Korean or Sichuan chile flakes in place of the Thai bird chiles for a milder sauce.

INGREDIENTS

¼ cup (60 ml) canola or vegetable oil

12 medium garlic cloves, minced (about ¼ cup/30 to 40 g)

¼ cup (60 ml) roasted sesame oil

2 fresh red Thai bird chiles, minced (see Note)

6 tablespoons (50 g) toasted sesame seeds

1 teaspoon (4 g) sugar

Kosher salt

The idea for this sauce originated when I was ever-so-briefly in Fukuoka in southern Japan a number of years ago. I stopped by the original Ippudo ramen branch, where I picked up a bottle of their spicy sesame oil condiment. Thick, creamy, and oily, the stuff in that little bottle was magical, transforming pots of mediocre store-bought broth into powerful flavor bombs and elevating simple bowls of plain noodles with its sweet-salty-savory aroma. I went through the whole thing in about a month and haven't been able to find more since.

I vowed to come up with my own version of that garlicky sesame sauce that I could keep around in my fridge. I started by deciding to use *mayu* as the oil base for my sauce.

Mayu is a condiment made by cooking grated garlic in oil until it is pitch black in color, then grinding it into an oily sludge.* On its own it has a strong bitter flavor, but when paired with savory and salty ingredients, it tastes wonderful and unique. Starting with this base, I experimented with a whole slew of different flavorings—sesame oil, tahini paste, chile bean pastes of various sorts—before coming up with my final recipe: After cooking down the garlic, I blitz it all in a blender with some sesame oil and then return it to a clean skillet. To this mixture, I add some fresh grated garlic—to layer that burnt garlic with a bit of a more pungent, fresh aroma—and some sliced Thai bird chiles, whose bright heat I preferred to any of the fermented pastes. I heat it up just until it starts bubbling, then let it all cool down so that the flavors can infuse.

Finally, I mix in some roasted sesame seeds that I've ground to a very rough paste in a mortar and pestle, adjusting the seasoning with a hint of sugar and salt. The resultant sauce is thick, creamy, and slightly oily, with a robust, noodle-clinging texture that adds flavor to every bite. It's really dreamy stuff.

---

*   Note that this burnt black garlic is not the same thing as "black garlic," which is garlic that is treated to a weeks-long low-temperature aging process.

(1) Combine the canola oil and 10 cloves of the minced garlic in a wok and cook over medium-low heat, stirring, until it starts to brown. Reduce the heat to low and continue to cook, stirring frequently, until the garlic turns completely black, about 10 minutes (the garlic will become very sticky).

(2) Transfer the mixture to a heatproof bowl and add the sesame oil. Transfer to a blender and blend on high speed until completely pulverized, about 30 seconds. Return the mixture to the wok and add the chiles and remaining garlic. Cook gently over low heat until the chiles and fresh garlic begin to bubble. Remove from the heat and set aside to cool.

(3) Grind the sesame seeds in a mortar and pestle or a food processor until roughly ground but some large pieces remain. Stir the sesame seeds and sugar into the oil mixture. Season with salt to taste. Transfer to a sealable container and store in the refrigerator for up to 2 months.

Noodles with Burnt Garlic Sesame and Chile Oil

Cook noodles according to package directions. As soon as they're done cooking, place each portion in an individual serving bowl. Top each with a tablespoon of light soy sauce or shoyu. Add a couple tablespoons of Burnt Garlic Sesame and Chile Oil and some chopped scallions and slivered cucumbers. Stir it all together and slurp it up.

Other Good Uses for Burnt Garlic Sesame and Chile Oil

- Drizzle over grilled or broiled green vegetables such as broccolini, green beans, or asparagus.

- Use to dress salads. It pairs especially nicely with cucumbers, tomatoes, corn, and peppers.

- Spoon into any bowl of noodle soup.

- Serve as a dip for grilled meats and seafood or as a sauce for steak, pork chops, or chicken.

- Drizzle on top of very gently poached eggs served on a bowl of rice.

- Use as the dressing for stir-fried mushrooms, onions, and peppers.

SHANGHAI-STYLE SCALLION OIL

Yield
Makes 2½
cups

Active Time
15 minutes

Total Time
15 minutes

NOTE
You can use Korean or Sichuan chile flakes in place of the Thai bird chiles for a milder sauce.

INGREDIENTS

- 2 cups (500 ml) peanut, rice bran, or other neutral oil
- 6 ounces (180 g about 8 whole) scallions, cut into 1-inch segments, white, pale green, and dark green sections reserved separately
- 2 medium shallots (about 3 ounces/90 g), thinly sliced (optional)
- 1 teaspoon (4 g) kosher salt

Scallion oil is a classic Shanghai condiment that's used in everything from simple bowls of noodles to marinades to dipping sauces. It's one of the easiest oils to make and extraordinarily versatile. Its flavor will meld with just about any savory dish.

Some recipes for scallion oil call for cooking the scallions until they are completely browned and crispy. I prefer stopping the cooking when the scallions are golden brown in spots, but still a little juicy and tender in others, though if you prefer the sweeter flavor and crisp texture of fully browned onions, don't let my preferences stop you from cooking them however you like. Just make sure to taste as you go and shut off the heat a little *before* you think they're done, as they'll continue cooking in the hot oil for a few moments after the heat is off.

DIRECTIONS

(1) Heat the oil, scallion whites and pale greens, and shallots (if using) in a wok over medium heat until the scallions start to bubble gently. Reduce the heat to maintain a very slow, lazy bubble. Cook, stirring frequently, until the scallions and shallots start to wrinkle and turn a little brown around the edges, about 8 minutes. The shallots should maintain a steady bubble throughout the cooking.

(2) Add the scallion dark green sections and the salt and continue to cook, stirring, until the scallions and shallots are wrinkled and pale brown all over, about 4 minutes longer. Remove from the heat, allow to cool, transfer to a sealable container, and store in the refrigerator for up to 2 months.

Shanghai-Style Noodles with Scallion Oil

Cook noodles according to package directions. Rinse the noodles briefly under cold water when they are done to stop cooking. For every 2 portions of noodles, heat ¼ cup (60 ml) scallion oil (along with some of the scallion pieces), 2 tablespoons (30 ml) light soy sauce or shoyu, 1 tablespoon (15 ml) dark soy sauce, and 2 teaspoons (8 g) sugar over high heat until the sugar dissolves and the sauce is simmering. Add the noodles, toss to coat in the sauce, cook until just heated through, then transfer to a serving platter and serve (you can top them with more of the fried scallions from the jar of scallion oil if you'd like).

Other Good Uses for Scallion Oil

- Splash a few teaspoons of scallion oil into the wok toward the end of a stir-fry to give it an extra boost of aroma.

- Use it to stir-fry eggs in any of the egg dishes on pages 156–168.

- Drizzle a few drops of it over any soup and allow the heat of the soup to bring out its aroma. (This is a quick and easy way to boost your favorite instant ramen.)

- Use it in place of sesame oil in meat marinades.

- Add a little drizzle to salad dressings.

- Drizzle it on top of pizza, French fries, or roasted potatoes.

- Use it in place of sesame oil to brush dough for Chinese-Style Scallion Pancakes (page 394) or Mandarin Pancakes (page 106).

- Add a splash to a dish of soy sauce and vinegar as a dip for your dumplings (or use it to flavor the dumpling filling itself).

- Use it to add flavor and fat to steamed or poached chicken or fish.

SICHUAN MÁLÀ (HOT AND NUMBING) CHILE OIL

Yield
2½ cups
(625 ml)

Active Time
20 minutes

Total Time
45 minutes

NOTES

For a more authentic flavor, use whole er jing tiao and chao tian jiao chiles in step 1. If authenticity is not your goal, you can use whatever chiles you like for this, or a mix of chiles, the more the merrier. (See the chart "Packing Heat" on page 84 for an indication of how hot you should expect your chile oil to be.) I like to use a minimum of two different types of whole chiles for this, but even one type will work just fine.

Caiziyou is roasted rapeseed oil and considered by some to be an essential flavor in Sichuan cooking. You can find it online at the Mala Market or at a well-stocked Chinese supermarket. The easiest way to identify it is to look for bottles labeled "rapeseed" with a significantly darker, more amber-yellow color.

When adding the chile flakes in step 4, note that Sichuan er jing tiao chile flakes will be significantly spicier than Korean chile flakes.

INGREDIENTS

2 ounces (60 g) mixed dried chiles, such as árbol, Japones, pasilla, California, negro, or ancho (see Notes)

3 tablespoons (15 g) Sichuan peppercorns

2 cups (500 ml) oil, preferably caiziyou (roasted rapeseed oil; see Notes)

4 medium garlic cloves (10 to 15 g), lightly smashed with the side of a knife

One ½-inch knob fresh ginger (about 30 g), smashed with the side of a knife

1 medium shallot (about 1½ ounces/45 g), roughly chopped

1 cinnamon stick

3 dried bay leaves

2 whole star anise pods

1 tablespoon (8 g) whole fennel seeds

One 2-inch piece orange zest removed from a fresh orange with a vegetable peeler

To Finish:

¾ cup (75 g) ground Sichuan er jing tiao or Korean chile flakes (see Notes)

2 tablespoons (16 g) white sesame seeds (optional)

½ teaspoon (2 g) MSG (optional)

1 teaspoon (4 g) kosher salt

There is a wide range of chile-infused oils used throughout Asia, from sweet-hot versions with nubs of crispy garlic spooned into Japanese ramen to savory soy-sauce-laced Chaozhou-style (Chiu Chow) chile oil, to trendy Lao Gan Ma spicy chile crisp, with its crunchy bits of chile and peanut. Sichuan málà chile oil is among the most complex and satisfying to make, and I can't remember the last time I didn't have a batch of it in my fridge.

Recipes you'll find in books and online vary wildly. Some recommend pouring the hot oil over a small mound of chile flakes to bloom their flavor. Others recommend toasting the chiles in a small amount of oil first, grinding them, then recombining them with the remaining oil. Most call for infusing the oil with a variety of warm spices like cinnamon, star anise, and ginger. Heck, if you check online, I probably have a half dozen different variations of homemade chile oil published on various sites, and when I make it at home, I rarely make it exactly the same way twice.

That said, I have refined my technique to the point where I believe it's optimal for my own uses. The exact ingredients I use still vary a little from batch to batch, depending on the chile selection I have at home and my mood when I raid the spice cabinet.

For the chile element, I'll typically include either ground Sichuan er jing tiao chile (see "Shopping for Sichuan Peppercorns and Sichuan Chiles," page 314) or—be ready for some blasphemy—ground Korean gochugaru. Both are flavor-first chiles with relatively mild heat, but the gochugaru are the milder of the two, which is good if you or a family member have low tolerance for spiciness but still love the flavor and aroma of chile oil. In addition to ground chile, I add about an equal amount of dried whole chiles. Traditional recipes would call for chao tian jiao

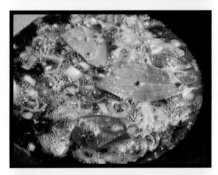

(heaven-facing chiles) or fiery *xiao mi la*, which are fine if you're after authenticity, but where I live, I can find a wide variety of high-quality dried Mexican chiles, so I often include a mix of those in my chile oil as well. Fruity guajillo or smoky, raisiny ancho make for a really tasty chile oil.

As for technique, I start by toasting the whole chiles in a dry wok to bring out their flavor, then grind them up in the food processor or in a mortar and pestle (the latter method offers better texture and is, in fact, easier—dried chiles have a tendency to ride around the blades of a food processor). Next I slowly infuse oil with a variety of aromatics—garlic, ginger, shallots, cinnamon, bay leaf, star anise, fennel, and a piece of fresh orange zest (an addition I tried on a whim one year during California's lengthy citrus season). There's a relatively small ideal temperature window for this infusion. Below 200°F and you will barely get any flavor transfer and transformation at all, but above 250°F and you'll start to burn your aromatics before they have a chance to fully give up their flavor. For this reason, I strongly recommend using an accurate digital instant-read or deep-fry thermometer while you make the infusion. Around 30 minutes at 225°F is what to aim for.

Once the oil is infused, I strain out and discard the aromatics, then reheat the infused oil with my toasted and pounded whole chiles, as well as the ground chile flakes. As with the aromatics, slowly heating up the chiles and making sure that they don't heat past 250°F is key to developing aroma and color without introducing any burnt off-flavors. I find that this technique offers much more control over the flavor of the finished oil than the admittedly more dramatic sizzling pour-over method. (Don't worry, if you want to be dramatic, Water-Boiled Beef on page 601 includes a sizzling pour-over that you can do right in front of your guests. They *will* find it awesome, I promise.)

I season the finished oil with some sesame seeds, MSG (which you don't have to add; see "The Truth About MSG" on page 100), and salt.

DIRECTIONS

(1) Using a pair of kitchen shears, cut all of the whole chiles into ½-inch pieces and discard the seeds. Toast the cut chiles and 1 tablespoon (5 g) of the Sichuan peppercorns in a dry wok or saucepan over medium heat, stirring and shaking constantly, until fragrant and lightly darkened in color, about 2 minutes. Transfer the toasted chiles to the bowl of a food processor or mortar and pestle and pulse or pound until the chiles break into ⅛- to ¼-inch pieces that resemble store-bought red-pepper flakes or flaky sea salt. (Be careful not to overprocess.) Set aside.

recipe continues

(2) Combine the remaining 2 tablespoons (10 g) Sichuan peppercorns, the oil, garlic, ginger, shallot, cinnamon stick, bay leaves, star anise, fennel seeds, and orange zest in your wok. Heat over medium-low heat until gently bubbling, then reduce the heat until the bubbling mostly subsides (the oil should register 200° to 225°F (95° to 105°C) on an instant-read thermometer). Cook until the garlic and shallots are pale golden brown and the oil is intensely aromatic, about 30 minutes.

(3) Strain the oil through a fine-mesh strainer and discard the spices and aromatics (you can save the lightly browned garlic and shallots to chop and add to eggs or noodle dishes, or just season with salt and eat them on their own; they are delicious).

(4) Return the oil to the wok and add the pounded chile/Sichuan peppercorn mixture as well as the ground chile flakes. Heat over medium-low heat, stirring constantly, until the chile flakes begin to bubble gently, then reduce the heat until the bubbling mostly subsides (the oil should register 200° to 225°F (95° to 105°C) on an instant-read thermometer). Cook stirring occasionally, until the oil is deep red and has a slightly nutty aroma, 5 to 7 minutes. Remove from heat and stir in the sesame seeds, MSG, and salt. Allow the oil to cool completely, then transfer to sealable containers. For best flavor, let the oil rest overnight in the refrigerator before using. The oil should last for several months or longer in sealed containers in the refrigerator.

How to Prepare Dried Chiles

Whether using Chinese or Central American dried chiles for chile oil, I recommend removing their stems and seeds to improve flavor and texture. The easiest way to do this is with a pair of kitchen shears. For small chiles like er jing tiao or árbol, simply snip off the tops, then turn them upside down to shake out the seeds. For larger chiles like chile California or chile ancho, cut off the stems with shears, snip down one side to open them up, then scrape out the seeds and any large bits of their inner ribs with your fingers, then snip the chiles into uniform pieces for toasting.

Málà: Sichuan's Most Famous Flavor Export

In Fuchsia Dunlop's classic cookbook *The Food of Sichuan*, she translates a Chinese saying, *shi zai zhongguo, wei zai sichuan*: China is the place for food, but Sichuan is the place for flavor. While Sichuan's reputation in the West may be for incendiary, fiery dishes, that's only part of the story. It's certainly true that Sichuan food tends to be spicy—dried, pickled, and fresh chiles, fermented chile pastes, and crimson-red chile oils permeate the cuisine—but that chile heat is always balanced with an array of other flavors. "Fish fragrant" (*yu xian wei*) dishes temper chile heat with pickled ingredients and lots of garlic (as in Fish-Fragrant Eggplant, page 191, or Shredded Chicken with Pickled Chiles and Carrots, page 82), for instance. "Strange flavor" (*guai wei*) combines chile oil with vinegar, soy sauce, sesame paste, garlic, Sichuan peppercorn, sugar, and more for a kitchen sink approach that allows you to identify each flavor on its own, while blending them all into a new flavor that is, well, strange (and delicious! See Bang Bang Chicken, page 568).

Málà, or "numbing hot," is Sichuan's most famous flavor export and also one of its simplest. It's the flavor of dishes like Mapo Tofu (page 598), or the ironically named Water-Boiled Beef (which should really be called chile-simmered beef, page 601). At its core, it's the combination of mouth-numbing Sichuan peppercorns and dried chiles. What makes it so enticing? For me it's the way that Sichuan peppercorns and dried chiles play off each other. You take a bite of mapo tofu and the first sensation you get is that complex aroma of fruity, roasted chiles mingling with the citrusy fragrance of the Sichuan peppercorns. Next you feel the heat on your tongue, as the capsaicin in chiles acts fast. Just when the heat might threaten to get overwhelming, the numbingness kicks in and you're distracted by the strange tingle as the fire starts to subside. It's a rush of feelings, each bite a roller coaster of sensation that leaves your mouth ready for the next crest.

Shopping for Sichuan Peppercorns and Sichuan Chiles

From 1968 to 2005, the United States had a loosely enforced ban on the import of Sichuan peppercorns due to fears of a bacterial infection that could affect citrus trees, and between 2005 and 2007 the only peppercorns available had to be pasteurized through heat treatment before sale, dramatically reducing their aroma and potency. So while it was still possible to find Sichuan peppercorns during that time, the majority of them were of very questionable quality. I remember sitting at my kitchen table in the mid-2000s, painstakingly sorting through bags of Sichuan peppercorns to pick out the piles of hard black seeds, dried leaves, and twigs to get at the good stuff: the flavorful seed husks.

These days, while it's still possible to run across some bad-quality spices, we are in a veritable golden era of ingredient availability. The quality of Sichuan peppercorns and variety of chiles imported from Sichuan and neighboring Guizhou can be stellar, whether from online retailers or at the Asian supermarket. Here's what you should be looking for.

Whole Sichuan Peppercorns

Sichuan peppercorns, known as *huajiao* in China and *sansho* in Japan, are not actually peppercorns; they're the husk of berries from Chinese prickly ash. The main flavor component they add to a dish is a light, citrusy, piney aroma, but equally important is their physiological effect. Sichuan peppercorns are not spicy in the traditional sense. Rather, they produce a numbing, tingling effect on your tongue and lips, similar to a light anesthetic.

The chemical responsible for this reaction is hydroxy-alpha sanshool, a compound that has been found to stimulate our light-touch receptors by inhibiting two-pore potassium channels. The phrase "tickle your taste buds" is especially apt when it comes to Sichuan peppercorns, because that is quite literally what they trick you into feeling (see "What Makes Sichuan Peppercorns Tingle" on page 23). There are several subspecies of prickly ash, but in general you'll find two categories of Sichuan peppercorn, red and green, the latter having a more powerful numbing effect and aroma.

The quality of Sichuan peppercorns can vary dramatically, with low-quality versions containing lots of twigs and black seeds (which must be picked out and discarded) and only mild flavor and the best being usable straight out the bag with a powerful numbing effect and aroma. Soeos and SNS are two brands that have consistently high standards. You can also get excellent Sichuan peppercorns from themalamarket.com, or from spicyelement.com.

Sichuan peppercorns should be stored in a sealed container in a cool, dark pantry, where they will last for about a year before you notice a significant deterioration in aroma or numbing ability.

Ground Sichuan Peppercorns

Ground Sichuan peppercorns and Sichuan pepper oil are also commonly found at Chinese markets, but I would avoid them, as their quality can be quite variable and spices lose their flavor much more rapidly in ground form. Instead, for recipes that call for ground Sichuan pepper, toast and grind the peppercorns yourself. Start by sorting through the peppercorns to remove any twigs and shiny dark seeds. Heat the husks in your wok over medium-low heat, stirring constantly, until an intense floral fragrance fills the room. This should take a couple of minutes. Transfer the peppercorns to a mortar and pestle and grind them with a circular motion until they're reduced to a mix of fine powder and white husks. You can use the mixture as is, or for better results, shake it through a fine-mesh strainer to remove the husks and discard them. (You can also grind toasted peppercorns in an electric spice grinder.) Store ground Sichuan pepper in an airtight container in a dark pantry where it will be fine to use for several weeks, after which it'll steadily start to lose flavor.

Dried Sichuan Chiles

To contrast this feeling of numbness, there is a wide variety of dried chiles used in Sichuan cuisine, the most important being *er jing tiao* and *chao tian jiao*.

Er jing tiao chiles are prized for their fragrant, floral aroma and moderate heat. They are an essential ingredient in true Sichuan-style chile oils, where they typically make up the bulk of the chile content. You'll find them online or at the Chinese supermarket labeled either "er jing tiao" or sometimes "mild Sichuan chile" (though mild is a relative term here). You'll recognize them by their distinct curved, lowercase j shape and deep red color. If there's only one type of chile that you're going to special order, I'd make it this one.

Chao tian jiao, or "heaven-facing chiles," are so called because they grow with their fruit pointed upward. Bullet head or *zidantou* are the most common cultivars of this chile, and you'll sometimes find them sold under those names. They are hotter than er jing tiao, though not unbearably so. They're noted for their deep red color, which in turn gives chile oil its dark hue. Their attractive appearance makes them good for dishes in which a ton of dried chiles add visual appeal and aroma, but not absurd levels of heat, such as Chongqing-style Dry-Fried Chicken (page 441) or Water-Boiled Beef (page 601). If you can't find chao tian jiao, árbol, Japones, or pequín all make decent substitutes. You can use dried Thai bird chiles as well; just be aware that they are often significantly hotter.

Other popular chiles in Sichuan are *xiao mi la*, which are small, fiery chiles similar to Thai Bird chiles, and *deng long jiao*, or lantern chiles, which are short and stubby with a similar flavor profile and heat level to those of heaven-facing.

As with Sichuan peppercorns, I find that online is the best place to get high-quality Sichuan chiles. I buy mine from themalamarket.com or spicyelement.com.

If shopping for chile peppers at a supermarket, look for peppers that have smooth, unblemished surfaces and that are pliable when you bend them. (Most peppers are sold in clear plastic bags, which makes it easy to feel how pliable and moist they are.) Peppers that crack, are browning, or crumble when bent or squeezed are no good. I store all of my dried chiles in zipper-lock bags in the freezer to preserve their freshness. In the freezer dried chiles should last a year or more.

DAN DAN NOODLES

In the short time I spent in Chengdu, I found that dan dan miàn are to Sichuan what the hamburger is to the United States: they're ubiquitous, there are certain expectations, but there are no hard and fast rules other than the basic ingredients (noodles, chile oil, pickled Sichuan vegetables, Sichuan peppercorns, and vinegar) and the manner in which they're served (fast and cheap). They get their name from *dan*, a heavy stick carried over the shoulders onto which noodle vendors would balance two loads, the noodles on one side and the toppings on the other. Known as "peddler's noodles," they are the prototypical street food and, according to Hong Kong–based food writer Man Wei Leung, have been enjoyed as a quick, inexpensive meal on the streets of Chengdu and Chongqing continuously since 1841.

Beyond that they can be soupy or dry. They may or may not have sesame seeds or peanuts. They might have greens or bean sprouts boiled together with the noodles or not. Sometimes they have a dollop of creamy roasted sesame paste. Oftentimes they are sprinkled with a shower of fatty stir-fried minced pork. Sometimes they have raw garlic or even a sprinkle of sugar on top. In other words, get the chile oil and Sichuan peppercorn bit right and the rest is really up to you.

If you've got a batch of Sichuan Málà Chile Oil already sitting in your fridge, congratulations; you are 95 percent of your way to a quick, delicious meal. If not, head over to page 310 and make it. I promise you will not regret it.

What's that? You're just not in the mood to babysit a wokful of aromatics for 45 minutes? That's OK, too.

I know a lot of writers will tell you that it's impossible to make great dan dan noodles with store-bought chile oil, and that may be true, but it's definitely possible to make really really good dan dan noodles with store-bought chile oil. My favorite is Mom's Málà, though I've also had good luck playing chile oil roulette in the Sichuan section of the Chinese supermarket. Lao Gan Ma Spicy Chile Crisp, with its heavy addition of fried shallots and soybeans, has a different flavor profile from a classic Sichuan málà chile oil, but it's still delicious in a bowl of dan dan noodles, as are a number of high-quality competitors that have sprung up on the market (such as Fly by Jing's Sichuan Chili Crisp or David Chang's Chili Crunch).

The only other ingredient that can truly elevate a bowl of dan dan noodles is *sui mi ya cai*, which are salty-savory semidry preserved mustard greens that come from Yibin, in southeastern Sichuan. It's hard stuff to find at the supermarket, where you are more likely to find its cousin zha cai, preserved mustard root. You can use zha cai in place of ya cai, but it doesn't have quite the same umami punch. I order my Yibin sui mi ya cai from a company called Yibin Sui Mi Yacai Co., which is sold through themalamarket.com (or Amazon) and comes delivered in small foil pouches that last indefinitely until you open them. I stir-fry the ya cai together with fatty ground pork, cooking it until it's completely dry to really concentrate its punchy flavor.

DAN DAN NOODLES

Yield	Active Time
Serves 4	15 minutes
	Total Time
	15 minutes

NOTES

For the best results, use homemade Sichuan Málà Chile Oil (page 310). If you can't find ya cai (preserved mustard greens), you can use zha cai (preserved mustard root) in its place or a combination of equal parts finely chopped sauerkraut and drained capers (really!). If you prefer a soupier version, you can add a ladle of the noodle-cooking liquid to the bowl before adding the drained noodles or a ladle of hot broth.

INGREDIENTS

2 teaspoons (4 to 5 g) red Sichuan peppercorns

For the Sauce:
2 tablespoons (30 ml) Chinese sesame paste, store-bought or homemade (page 321), or 4 teaspoons (20 ml) tahini or unsweetened peanut butter mixed with 2 teaspoons (10 ml) roasted sesame oil

2 tablespoons (30 ml) warm water

2 tablespoons (30 ml) light soy sauce or shoyu

2 tablespoons (30 ml) Chinkiang or balsamic vinegar

2 teaspoons (8 g) sugar

½ cup (120 ml) homemade or store-bought Sichuan chile oil with its sediment (see Notes)

2 teaspoons (5 g) minced fresh garlic (about 2 medium cloves)

For the Pork:
1 tablespoon (15 ml) peanut, rice bran, or other neutral oil

6 ounces (180 g) ground or finely chopped pork (preferably with plenty of fat)

2 ounces (about ¼ cup) minced preserved mustard root or stem (ya cai or zha cai; see Notes)

1 tablespoon (15 ml) Shaoxing wine

1 tablespoon (15 ml) light soy sauce or shoyu

To Serve:
Kosher salt

1 pound (450 g) fresh wheat noodles

4 ounces (120 g) greens, such as spinach or baby bok choy (optional)

2 ounces (60 g) mung bean sprouts (optional)

¼ cup (40 g) roasted peanuts or Fried Peanuts (page 319), gently crushed in a mortar and pestle

4 to 5 scallions, thinly sliced

DIRECTIONS

(1) Toast the Sichuan peppercorns in a dry wok over high heat until fragrant, about 1 minute. Transfer to a mortar and pestle or spice grinder and grind into a fine powder. Set aside.

(2) **For the Sauce:** Combine the sesame paste and water in a medium bowl and stir until completely smooth. Add the soy sauce, vinegar, sugar, chile oil, garlic, and half of the ground Sichuan peppercorns and stir until homogenous and the sugar is dissolved. Divide the sauce evenly among 4 individual bowls or pour it into one large serving bowl to share.

(3) **For the Pork:** Heat a wok over high heat until lightly smoking. Add 1 tablespoon (15 ml) of the oil and swirl to coat. Add the pork and cook, stirring and tossing and using a spatula to break up the pork until it is no longer pink, about 1 minute. Add the preserved mustard root and cook, stirring and tossing until all excess moisture has evaporated and the mixture starts to stick to the wok, about 1 minute longer. Add a big pinch of the ground Sichuan peppercorns and toss to combine. Swirl in the wine

recipe continues

and soy sauce around the edges of the wok and continue to cook, stirring and tossing, until the wine and soy sauce have completely evaporated. Transfer the pork mixture to a small bowl.

(4) **To Serve:** Bring 3 quarts of lightly salted water to a boil in the wok or in a large pot over high heat. When the water is boiling, add the noodles, greens, and bean sprouts (if using) and cook according to the noodle package directions until barely cooked through, just a couple minutes.

(5) Drain the noodles, reserving some of the cooking liquid, and divide evenly among the individual bowls or transfer them to the serving bowl. Add a few tablespoons of the cooking liquid to each bowl. Spoon the pork mixture on top. Sprinkle with the remaining ground Sichuan peppercorns and the sliced scallions. Serve immediately.

FRIED PEANUTS

Yield
Makes
1 cup

Active Time
5 minutes

Total Time
25 minutes

NOTE
The oil you use to fry the peanuts can be strained through a fine-mesh strainer lined with a coffee filter and used again for stir-frying or deep frying.

INGREDIENTS

1 cup (150 g) raw peanuts
1 cup peanut, rice bran, or other neutral oil

Peanuts make frequent appearances alongside noodles to add crunch and nutty flavor. The easiest way to incorporate them into your pantry is to just buy jars of roasted salted peanuts, which can be lightly crushed in a mortar and pestle or under a heavy skillet before sprinkling on your noodles, but for better flavor and texture, try frying your own raw peanuts. They get considerably crisper and have a deeper, nuttier aroma than regular roasted peanuts. They're also easy to do in bulk and last a long time in a cool, dark pantry. They are a classic topping for dan dan noodles and pad Thai, among other dishes.

DIRECTIONS

(1) Combine the peanuts and oil in a wok. Heat over medium-high heat, stirring occasionally, until the peanuts start to bubble gently. Reduce the heat to maintain a very gentle bubble around the peanuts (the oil should register around 250°F on an instant-read thermometer) and cook at this temperature, stirring occasionally, until the peanuts are a light, even golden brown and have a toasty aroma, about 20 minutes.

(2) Retrieve the peanuts with a fine-mesh strainer or metal spider and transfer to a rimmed baking sheet lined with a few layers of paper towels or a clean kitchen towel. Let the peanuts cool a little, then blot off excess oil with more paper towels or a kitchen towel. When completely cool, transfer the peanuts to a sealed container and store in a cool, dark pantry for 2 to 3 months. (The peanuts will start to smell a little fishy if they have turned rancid. They are still safe to eat; they just won't taste very good.)

Hot and Numbing Fried Peanuts

Hot and numbing fried peanuts are a great snack or bar food. To make them, toss a cup of freshly fried peanuts with a few tablespoons of the Hot and Numbing Spice Blend on page 185. Let the mixture cool completely and store in sealed containers in the pantry for several weeks.

Chinese Sesame Paste and Its Substitutes

If you compare ingredients, Chinese sesame paste may seem very much like Middle Eastern tahini, but take a quick glance at them side by side and you'll notice that they are quite different. Where tahini, made from raw, hulled sesame seeds, is a pale tan color and has a mild flavor, Chinese sesame paste is made from whole roasted sesame seeds. As a result, Chinese sesame paste has a much stronger, roastier aroma and darker color. Chinese sesame paste also tends to be a little thinner than tahini paste.

Chinese sesame paste is relatively easy to find at any decent Asian supermarket, and it lasts forever in the fridge, but if you're shopping from a Western supermarket, there are a few reasonable substitutions for the Chinese stuff. None of them are particularly difficult to do.

Easy Mode • Tahini or Peanut Butter with Sesame Oil

The easiest substitution is to simply combine tahini or unsweetened peanut butter (the natural stuff that you have to stir) with roasted sesame oil. Peanuts and sesame seeds have very similar flavor profiles, and adding a touch of roasted sesame oil will get you even closer to the right flavor.

For every tablespoon of Chinese sesame paste called for, substitute 2 teaspoons (10 ml) of tahini or unsweetened natural peanut butter stirred together with 1 teaspoon (5 ml) of roasted sesame oil. You can make this stuff in larger batches using the same two-to-one ratio. Store it in a sealed container in the fridge indefinitely.

Normal Difficulty • Fry Tahini Paste

For significantly better results, try this: Fry regular tahini until it darkens and takes on a roasted aroma. I got this idea after watching Chris Matthews and Steph Li from Chinese Cooking Demystified fry peanut butter in their recipe for Shaxian peanut noodle sauce to approximate the flavor of deeply roasted Chinese peanut paste.*

It's a brilliant idea that works just as well with tahini. To do it, start by heating up ¼ cup (60 ml) of roasted sesame oil in a wok over medium heat until shimmering, then add ½ cup (120 ml) of

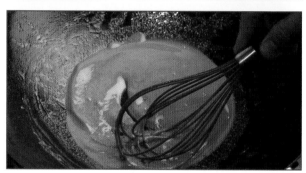

stirred tahini paste, reduce the heat, and cook until the sesame paste is a rich almond brown. This takes about 20 minutes on the lowest heat with some lazy stirs with a whisk every few minutes, or 5 to 7 minutes at medium-low with frequent stirring. It's very easy to overcook the tahini to the point where it turns bitter, so it's better to err on the side of caution and scrape it out of the wok to cool a little too soon rather than too late.

Expert Mode • Make It Yourself

The final method is to just make the stuff yourself (page 321) by roasting sesame seeds until golden brown, then grinding them with just enough sesame oil to thin them out into a smooth, silky paste. With a food processor it's very easy. With a mortar and pestle it's only slightly harder.

---

* You can find their recipe, a homemade clone of a popular Chinese fast food dish, for free on YouTube.

HOMEMADE SESAME PASTE

Yield
Serves 4

Active Time
15 minutes

Total Time
30 minutes

INGREDIENTS

1 cup (about 4 ounces/120 g) sesame
seeds
2 to 4 tablespoons (30 to 60 ml) roasted
sesame oil

DIRECTIONS

(1) Heat the sesame seeds in a dry wok over medium-low heat and cook, stirring constantly, until the seeds are golden brown and give off a pleasant nutty aroma, about 8 minutes. Transfer the roasted sesame seeds to a bowl to cool.

(2) **To Finish in a Food Processor:** When cool, transfer the sesame seeds to the bowl of a food processor. Add 2 tablespoons (30 ml) oil and process until the sesame seeds start to form a thick paste. With the machine running, drizzle in additional sesame oil until a smooth paste is formed that gently settles when you stop the machine (with some sesame seeds, you may need additional sesame oil to get to the right consistency). Transfer to a sealed container and store in the refrigerator for up to several months. Stir before using.

To Finish in a Mortar and Pestle: When cool, transfer the sesame seeds to a large mortar. Grind with the pestle using a circular motion until the seeds form a thick paste that starts to clump together. Scrape down the sides of the mortar and pestle with a spoon. Add 2 tablespoons (30 ml) of the sesame oil and continue grinding with a circular motion until the sesame paste is relatively smooth. Drizzle in additional sesame oil until the paste is thin enough to slowly settle when you lift the pestle out of it. Transfer to a sealed container and store in the refrigerator for up to several months. Stir before using.

SHANGHAI-STYLE SESAME NOODLES (MA JIANG MIÀN)

Ma jiang miàn—Shanghai-style wheat noodles served with a ladle of sesame sauce and chile oil—belongs in the pantheon of simple dishes whose short ingredient list and simple preparation belie their soul-satisfying flavor. Think pizza Margherita, cheesesteak, or a peanut butter and dill pickle sandwich. On the recommendation of Ken Phang, a Shanghai native and *Serious Eats* reader, I headed solo to Wei Xang Zhai on Yandong Road, a popular shop that has been slinging hot bowls of sesame noodles for the better part of a century.

The restaurant was a small, scruffy, no-frills type place, and the clientele—who were jammed shoulder to shoulder into tiny tables next to complete strangers—ranged from on-duty policemen to men in suits on lunch breaks to perfectly dressed young men and women laden with shopping bags (Shanghai has no shortage of high-end shopping outlets). I glanced at the menu, but there seemed to be no point. Nearly every item on it

was marked as "sold out," and judging by how worn and tattered they were, it seems they had been sold out for years if not decades. The only two things I saw anyone eating were noodles with a meat-based sauce and sesame noodles. It was the latter I was there for.

Despite getting elbowed out of the way a few times and more than a few snags securing a table and figuring out the convoluted ticket-based ordering system, none of it mattered once I started eating. The reason? Well, the noodles were pretty much perfect. Super-fresh and springy, served on top of a pool of soy-sauce-laced chile oil, with a ladle of sesame-peanut sauce on top, a one-two-three punch of spicy, savory, and creamy.

At the restaurant, part of that savoriness comes from the chile oil they use, which is fortified with rendered fat from their meat sauce. At home I capture that umami kick with a little smidge of Marmite, an intensely umami yeast extract that Brits like to spread on toast (Vegemite will also work), or, when I'm feeling like something extra, some Better Than Bouillon beef base will punch it up even more.

Quick word of advice: Eat fast, as the sesame sauce has a tendency to get thick and grainy if you let the noodles cool too much. Just follow the locals' lead: start slurping as soon as the plate is laid in front of you, and don't stop until they're all gone.

SHANGHAI-STYLE SESAME NOODLES (MA JIANG MIÀN)

Yield
Serves 2

Active Time
10 minutes

Total Time
10 minutes

NOTES

For the best results, use homemade chile oil (page 310). This recipe can easily be doubled or tripled. These noodles must be served as soon as they are ready, as the sauce will become thick and grainy if it cools too much.

INGREDIENTS

For the Sesame Sauce:

1 medium garlic clove, minced (about 4 g/1 teaspoon)

2 tablespoons (30 ml) Chinese sesame paste, store-bought or homemade (page 321), or 4 teaspoons (20 ml) tahini mixed with 2 teaspoons (10 ml) roasted sesame oil

2 tablespoons (30 ml) creamy peanut butter (preferably natural, the kind you have to stir)

1 teaspoon (4 g) sugar

1 tablespoon (15 ml) light soy sauce or shoyu

2 teaspoons (10 ml) rice vinegar

To Serve:

¼ cup (60 ml) homemade or store-bought chile oil with its sediment (see Notes)

1 tablespoon (15 ml) light soy sauce or shoyu

½ teaspoon Marmite, Vegemite, or Better Than Bouillon beef base (optional)

Kosher salt

8 ounces (225 g) fresh wheat noodles

Handful of sliced scallions

DIRECTIONS

1. **Make the Sauce:** Combine the garlic, sesame, peanut butter, sugar, soy sauce, and rice vinegar in a medium bowl. Stir with a fork to combine (it will be quite thick; that's Ok).

2. **To Serve:** Combine the chile oil, soy sauce, and Marmite (if using) in a small bowl and stir with a fork until the blob of Marmite is broken up. Divide the chile oil mixture between two individual serving bowls.

3. Bring 3 quarts of lightly salted water to a boil in a wok. Ladle a few tablespoons of boiling water into the bowl with the sesame sauce and stir until smooth. Continue adding hot water until the sauce is creamy and loose, 4 to 5 tablespoons total. Add the noodles to the wok and cook according to the package directions until barely cooked through, just a couple minutes.

4. Drain the noodles and divide between the serving bowls. Divide the sesame sauce on top of the noodles, sprinkle with scallions, and serve immediately, tossing the noodles to dress them in the bowl as you eat.

NOODLES WITH THAI BASIL AND PEANUT PESTO

Yield
Serves 4

Active Time
15 minutes

Total Time
15 minutes

NOTES

For best results, follow the recipe as written, using a heavy mortar and pestle. If you're in a hurry, you can also use the food processor. If using the food processor, freeze the garlic, ginger, chiles, basil leaves, and cilantro leaves on a rimmed baking sheet for 15 minutes to help rupture their cell structure, allow to thaw at room temperature for a few minutes, then grind in the food processor along with the peanuts, drizzling in olive oil with the machine running until a smooth sauce is formed. Instead of tofu, you can add a cup of shredded leftover roast chicken, rotisserie chicken, or poached chicken.

If you've been reading this book from the beginning, you should be aware by now that the mortar and pestle is my favorite tool in the kitchen. There's nothing better for crushing aromatics, grinding spices, or making flavorful pastes and sauces. I love it so much that it seemed almost a shame not to include a recipe for Ligurian pesto. Italian pesto made in a mortar and pestle has a creamy texture and intense flavor that simply cannot be matched by a food processor or blender (read more about why in "The Mortar and Pestle Is the Most Underrated Tool in Your Kitchen" on page 576).

This got me thinking: What would happen if I replaced standard Ligurian pesto ingredients—Italian sweet basil, garlic, pine nuts, Parmesan cheese, and olive oil—with some common Thai ingredients instead? It wouldn't be so different from a curry paste after all. I quickly discovered the answer to that question by pounding together Thai basil and cilantro, garlic and ginger, fried peanuts, fish sauce, olive oil, and some hot chiles. The answer was simple and delicious.

As with San Francisco–Style Vietnamese American Garlic Noodles (page 330), I prefer to use dry Italian pasta for this dish instead of Asian noodles (though they will work just fine). Unlike a typical Thai curry paste, which is fried to bloom its flavors before incorporating into a stir-fry or curry, this pesto works best when treated just like Italian pesto: don't cook it at all after pounding it. Instead, toss it straight in the serving bowl with hot pasta, adding just enough pasta water to form a smooth, creamy sauce. In Liguria, it's common to toss some blanched green beans and potatoes directly with the pasta and pesto. In my recipe, I keep the green beans and swap out the potatoes for panfried firm tofu. (Shredded chicken or nothing at all also works.)

INGREDIENTS

For the Pesto:

3 medium garlic cloves, roughly chopped (about 1 tablespoon/8 g)
One ¼-inch slice fresh ginger, peeled
1 fresh hot green chile, such as jalapeño, serrano, or Thai bird, roughly chopped
Kosher salt
¼ cup (40 g) roasted peanuts or Fried Peanuts (page 319), plus some extra crushed peanuts for garnish
2 ounces (about 2 cups) fresh Thai or sweet basil leaves
1 ounce (about 1 cup) fresh cilantro leaves and fine stems
1 tablespoon (15 ml) fish sauce, plus more to taste
1 tablespoon (15 ml) prepared chile sauce, such as sambal oelek or sriracha (optional)
½ cup (120 ml) extra virgin olive oil

For the Tofu (optional):

8 to 12 ounces (225 to 340 g) extra-firm tofu, cut into ½- by ½- by 2-inch strips, pressed firmly between paper towels to dry off surface moisture
1 tablespoon (15 ml) peanut, rice bran, or other neutral oil

For the Noodles:

Kosher salt
1 pound (450 g) dry spaghetti
8 ounces (340 g) green beans or yard-long beans, trimmed and cut into 1½-inch segments

DIRECTIONS

1. **For the Pesto (see Notes):** In the bowl of a heavy granite mortar and pestle, combine the garlic, ginger, and chile with a large pinch of kosher salt. Pound until a paste is formed. Add the peanuts and pound until a sticky, slightly chunky paste is formed. Add the basil leaves a handful at a time, pounding until they are completely broken down. Continue with the cilantro leaves. Add the fish sauce and chile sauce and incorporate by grinding with a firm circular motion. Drizzle in the oil a bit at a time, working it into the pesto with the pestle until a creamy, emulsified sauce is formed. Season with salt to taste and set aside.

2. **For the Tofu (optional):** Heat a wok over high heat until lightly smoking. Add the oil and swirl to coat. Reduce the heat to medium. Add the tofu, spread it into a single layer (work in batches if necessary), and cook, occasionally shaking pan gently, until crisp on first side, about 3 minutes. Flip the tofu and continue cooking until the second side is crisp, about 3 minutes longer. Transfer the tofu to a large serving bowl.

3. **For the Noodles:** Bring 1½ inches of lightly salted water in a 12-inch skillet or sauté pan to a boil over high heat. Add the pasta, stir a few times to make sure it's not clumping, and cook, stirring occasionally, until the noodles are perfectly al dente (taste one to make sure), about 1 minute less than the package directions instruct. Add the green beans during the last 3 minutes of cooking. Drain, reserving 1 cup of the cooking water.

4. Transfer the pasta and green beans to the bowl with the tofu. Scoop out the pesto and add it to the bowl along with a big splash of the reserved cooking water. Toss the noodles and the pesto, adding more water as necessary until a loose creamy sauce coats the noodles and beans. (The noodles should freely pull out of the bowl with chopsticks. If they come up in large clumps, add more cooking water.) Season with salt or more fish sauce to taste. Garnish with crushed peanuts and serve immediately.

ZHAJIANG MIÀN (BEIJING "FRIED SAUCE" NOODLES)

Yield
Serves 4

Active Time
15 minutes

Total Time
30 minutes

NOTES

Tianmianjiang is a wheat-based sweet fermented northern Chinese sauce. I use Koon Chun brand, which is widely available at Chinese markets in the United States. If you can't find it, you can use virtually any fermented bean sauce, such as doubanjiang, a combination of miso paste and hoisin sauce, or Korean doenjang. If you prefer, use 6 ounces of pork belly that you cut into ¼- to ⅛-inch dice in place of the ground pork. (Many classic versions of zhajiang miàn use chunks of fatty pork in place of the ground pork.)

One of the regulars in my mother's weeknight rotation was a dish she called "Peking noodles," which she adapted from a recipe she found in the 1962 *Joyce Chen Cook Book*. It was spaghetti tossed in a meat sauce that was flavored with miso paste, hoisin sauce, and soy sauce, along with julienned cucumbers and bean sprouts (the Joyce Chen recipe also calls for frozen spinach and radishes, but I don't remember ever coming across a radish until college). It wasn't until years later, when I looked back through that book, that I realized the dish was meant to be *zhajiang miàn*, Beijing's famous "fried sauce noodles." It all clicked together. In 1962, when Chen was writing her book, hoisin sauce and miso paste would have been exotic but available ingredients, while the *tianmianjiang* (sweet fermented wheat and soybean paste) used for the Shandong version of zhajiang miàn—widely regarded as the standard in China—would not.

Compared to the versions I've had in Beijing, Chen's 1962 America-Friendly version is not too far off as far as the vegetable toppings go. Cucumber, bean sprouts, and radish are all common. Frozen spinach, not so much—you're more likely to find fresh soybeans (edamame).

The only moderately difficult to find ingredient in this recipe is the tianmianjiang, but any decently stocked Asian supermarket should have it in the sauces and condiments aisle, and if not, it's available for order online. There's a huge amount of regional variation when making this dish—in Sichuan province it's more likely to be made with spicy doubanjiang, and Cantonese chefs will use hoisin sauce, for instance—so feel free to use whatever fermented bean sauce you happen to have at hand. Joyce Chen's recommendation of miso paste and hoisin sauce is something you can make out of most Western supermarkets these days.

While any wheat noodle will work for this dish, in Beijing you'll find zhajiang miàn frequently made with relatively thick, sturdy wheat noodles with a rectangular cross section. You may find these noodles sold as "cumian" at the Asian supermarket. If you can't find them, dry or fresh Japanese udon would also work.

INGREDIENTS

For the Sauce:

2 tablespoons (30 ml) peanut, rice bran, or other neutral oil

1 tablespoon (5 g) whole Sichuan peppercorns

1 star anise pod

6 ounces (175 g) ground pork (see Notes)

2 teaspoons (5 g) minced garlic (about 2 medium cloves)

2 teaspoons (5 g) minced fresh ginger (about ½-inch segment)

¼ cup (120 ml) sweet bean sauce (tianmianjiang; see Notes)

1 tablespoon (15 ml) dark soy sauce

½ cup (120 ml) water or homemade or store-bought low-sodium chicken stock

To Serve:

1 pound (450 g) fresh wheat noodles

Kosher salt

3 ounces (90 g) cucumber, cut into thin matchsticks

3 ounces (90 g) carrot, cut into thin matchsticks

2 ounces (60 g) radish or watermelon radish, cut into thin half-moons or fine matchsticks

2 ounces (60 g) fresh or frozen edamame, blanched in boiling water for 1 minute

2 ounces (60 g) mung bean sprouts, picked over and blanched in boiling water for 1 minute

DIRECTIONS

(1) **For the Sauce:** Heat the oil, Sichuan peppercorns, and star anise pod in a wok over medium-high heat until sizzling. Reduce the heat to low and cook, stirring, until the spices smell toasted and very fragrant, about 2 minutes. Remove the spices with a slotted spoon and discard, leaving the oil in the wok.

(2) Add the pork, garlic, and ginger, increase the heat to high, and cook, stirring and tossing frequently to break up the pork, until the pork and aromatics begin to turn crisp and golden in spots, about 3 minutes.

(3) Add the bean sauce and soy sauce and cook, stirring, until the oil separates out of the sauce and starts to sizzle, about 2 minutes. Add the water or stock and simmer until the sauce is reduced to a rich, thick paste and the oil has separated again and started to sizzle, about 15 minutes. Shut off the heat.

(4) Meanwhile, cook the noodles in a large pot of salted water according to the package directions. Drain and place the cooked noodles in a large serving bowl. Top with the sauce, cucumber, carrot, radish, edamame, and mung bean sprouts. Toss at the table before serving.

VIETNAMESE AMERICAN GARLIC NOODLES: A REAL SAN FRANCISCO TREAT

Garlic noodles are not *the* San Francisco treat. That would be Rice-a-Roni. But garlic noodles are *a* San Francisco treat and one worth making for yourself.

I do love Vietnamese food and have spent some time traveling in the country, but I'd never heard of garlic noodles before moving to the Bay Area, and that's because they are not Vietnamese: They are Vietnamese American, created right in San Francisco by Helene An at Thanh Long restaurant. Born to an aristocratic family outside Hanoi, Helene's family, the Trans, fled North Vietnam in 1955 and resettled in the South Vietnamese city of Dalat. In 1975, Helene was forced to flee once again, this time with her husband and three daughters. They eventually settled, penniless, in San Francisco, where they took up residence with An's mother-in-law, Diana, who ran a small deli she bought in the Outer Sunset neighborhood in 1968.

The exact history of Thanh Long is a little muddy. In interviews, Helene's daughter Elizabeth claims that her grandmother Diane's deli was Italian when Helene and her family arrived in 1975, but an old poster touting its opening as the "first authentic Vietnamese restaurant on the West Coast" advertises its opening date as July 1, 1971, four years before Helene's arrival. On that opening menu is baked crab—presumably the same baked Dungeness crab that is served today—but the garlic noodles are not there yet.

In any case, Helene, who had had experience with both Chinese and French cuisine, felt that the restaurant would find more success by eschewing authenticity in favor of dishes that were designed specifically to appeal to the local clientele. After a trip to a Nob Hill Italian restaurant where Helene was served a disappointingly bland bowl of garlic spaghetti, she created

Thanh Long's famous garlic noodles, a potent concoction flavored with fistfuls of garlic and a number of secret ingredients that my taste buds (and most copycat recipes) suggest are fish sauce, oyster sauce, soy sauce, lots of butter, and a smattering of Parmesan cheese. It's an umami party, and all of the big names are invited. Since then, the An family has built an empire of swanky restaurants in San Francisco and Los Angeles out of those noodles, and it's easy to taste why.

I had them for the first time in 2014, nearly 40 years after their creation. I had recently moved to San Francisco's Mission District and had been invited out for dinner by a friend. I, not understanding the intricacies of San Francisco weather, set out on a warm summer afternoon, riding my friend's little black Vespa from the Mission to the Outer Sunset, through San Francisco's winding streets and hills, in nothing but a T-shirt. By the time we had finished our fourth bowl of noodles, San Francisco's thick fog had set in and the temperature had dropped into the low fifties. By the time I made it home, soaking wet and shivering, the only thing I could think about was remembering my jacket the next time I went back.

BRINGING IT HOME

The Outer Sunset is a long way from where I live now, and the several trips I've made back there since have all been accompanied by long waits to snag a table. Fortunately, over the years I've worked out my own recipe, inspired by Helene An's original, suited to fit my own preferences. I start by smashing fresh garlic cloves in a mortar and pestle, then sweating them gently in butter in my wok. Once they've lost their sharp bite and start to develop some mellow sweetness, I add the umami triple-threat of soy sauce, fish sauce, and oyster sauce. Meanwhile, I cook my spaghetti in a large skillet on another burner.

I did say spaghetti, and I did say skillet. Though the noodles at Thanh Long are tender fresh wheat noodles, I actually prefer to use dried Italian spaghetti for this dish, cooking it just under al dente and finishing it in the pan with the garlic sauce, more of a nod to its Italian origins. While many books would have you believe that you need a vat of vigorously boiling water to cook pasta, I prefer to cook pasta in a much smaller volume. It makes no difference to the pasta's ability to retain a proper al dente bite (in blind taste tests, tasters, even expert tasters, cannot tell the difference between spaghetti cooked in a big pot vs. in a skillet with a couple inches of water), and it offers a few advantages. The first is that it's faster: you don't need to wait for a large pot of water to come to a boil. It also uses less water, something I am particularly conscious of when cooking in California. Finally, it actually improves the manner in which sauce clings to the pasta.

When I worked in an Italian restaurant, we had a fifteen-gallon gas-fired pasta machine that could boil six batches of fresh pasta at a time. To finish a plate of pasta, we'd add the cooked pasta to a pan with sauce, then splash some of the pasta water into the pan before vigorously heating it. The starchy pasta water would help the sauce emulsify. Sauce with pasta water comes out creamy, emulsified, and light. Sauce without pasta water comes out greasy and broken and has trouble sticking to the pasta. Over the course of the night, as the water in the machine got starchier and starchier, the dishes we sent out to customers would get progressively better—the starchier the pasta water, the better it is at getting sauce to cling.

At home, I don't use the same pasta water over and over for dozens of servings of pasta, but using a smaller volume of water to cook dried pasta has much the same effect, creating pasta water with a more concentrated starch content.

When my spaghetti is just shy of al dente (typically 2 minutes short of the recommended cook time on the package), I transfer it over to the wok with a pair of tongs, along with whatever starchy liquid is clinging to it, grate in my cheese, and toss everything vigorously over the highest heat my cooktop can muster until the noodles are fully cooked and the liquid has reduced to a creamy, emulsified, garlic-packed sauce that you will want to eat by the spoonful.

SAN FRANCISCO–STYLE VIETNAMESE AMERICAN GARLIC NOODLES

Yield
Serves 4

Active Time
15 minutes

Total Time
15 minutes

NOTE

The noodles on their own are extraordinarily simple and delicious, but that doesn't mean you can't fancy them up a bit. They go very well with seafood, and some raw, shell-on shrimp stir-fried along with the garlic right from the start would be an excellent addition. Recently I've taken to adding a few spoonfuls of *tarako* or *mentaiko*—Japanese salted pollock roe. Sushi-style flying fish roe (*tobiko*) or salmon roe (*ikura*) would also be a great addition, as would chunks of crab or lobster meat, or even Western-style caviar (if you're feeling flush).

INGREDIENTS

4 tablespoons (60 g) unsalted butter
20 medium garlic cloves (60 to 70 g), minced or smashed in a mortar and pestle
4 teaspoons (20 ml) oyster sauce
2 teaspoons (10 ml) light soy sauce or shoyu
2 teaspoons (10 ml) fish sauce
1 pound (450 g) dry spaghetti
1 ounce (30 g) grated Parmesan or Pecorino Romano cheese
Thinly sliced scallions (optional)

DIRECTIONS

(1) Melt the butter in a wok or saucepan over medium heat. Add the garlic and cook, stirring, until fragrant but not browned, about 2 minutes. Add the oyster sauce, soy sauce, and fish sauce and stir to combine. Remove from the heat.

(2) Meanwhile, bring 1½ inches of water to a boil in a 12-inch skillet or sauté pan over high heat. Add the pasta, stir a few times to make sure it's not clumping, and cook, stirring occasionally, until just shy of al dente (about 2 minutes short of the recommended cook time on the package). Using tongs, transfer the cooked pasta to the garlic sauce, along with whatever water clings to it. Increase the heat to high, add the cheese to the wok, and stir and toss vigorously until the sauce is creamy and emulsified, about 30 seconds. If the sauce looks too watery, let it keep reducing. If it looks greasy, splash some more cooking water into it and let it re-emulsify. Stir in the scallions (if using) and serve immediately.

3.2 COLD DRESSED NOODLES

I remember walking into a small ramen shop in Tokyo with my late grandmother, Yasuko, when I was much younger. When we sat down and I ordered the *kamo soba*—buckwheat noodles with hot duck broth—my grandmother started giggling at my choice, explaining that it was crazy to order hot noodles on such a muggy, sweltering summer day. She instead opted for the *hiyashi chūka*, a cold noodle salad made with chilled ramen noodles, a variety of fresh vegetable toppings, and a vinegary dressing that you toss together at the table.

She was right, of course, as grandmothers tend to be.

If the first thing that comes to mind when you think of cold pasta is the globs of glistening mayo that coat American-style pasta salads that compete with the barbecue as the biggest gut-bomb on the picnic table, prepare to have your world turned upside down, because cold noodle salads dressed in bright, tangy sauces with fresh flavors are about as light and refreshing as a meal can get. What's more, they make prep a breeze, as noodles can be precooked, dried, and stored in the fridge right until you're ready to dress them without any loss in quality, making them the ideal food for a picnic, a potluck, or a quick midday meal.

AIR-DRYING COLD NOODLES FOR SALADS

Chilling cooked noodles by running them under cold running water is fast and easy, and in general it works fine if you're in a hurry and perfection is not your goal, but it has a couple of downsides. First, it rinses away excess surface starch, which means that sauces will have a harder time clinging to them. Second, they end up wetter, as cold water doesn't evaporate very readily, which in turn will water down your dish.

For the best cold noodles, it's a good idea to cool your noodles naturally in the air. Here's how you do it.

Step 1 • Drain

Drain your noodles through a fine-mesh strainer or colander in the sink (reserve some cooking water if the recipe calls for it).

Step 2 • Toss with a Little Oil

Use a pair of chopsticks to toss the noodles directly in the strainer with a little bit of oil—a couple of teaspoons per pound—to prevent them from sticking together.

Step 3 • Spread Them Out

Spread the noodles out on a rimmed baking sheet large enough to hold them in a thin layer (use multiple trays if drying a large batch).

Step 4 • Cool Them

Let the noodles cool naturally, moving them around occasionally with a pair of chopsticks to make sure they are not sticking together. A desk fan or a manual fan can speed this process along, though even in still air it takes only 10 to 15 minutes.

Once the noodles are cooled, you can proceed with the recipe or transfer them to a sealed container and store them in the refrigerator for several days.

SICHUAN-STYLE COLD NOODLES

Yield
Serves 4

Active Time
15 minutes

Total Time
15 minutes

NOTES

The noodles and sauce can be prepared ahead and stored in separate sealed containers in the fridge for up to 3 days. If you plan on serving these noodles to folks with varying levels of heat tolerance, leave the chiles out of the aromatic oil and serve the noodles with a small bowl of homemade or store-bought chile oil on the side to adjust heat level to taste. You can add a couple of tablespoons of Chinese sesame paste (see pages 320 and 321) to the sauce if you'd like, which transforms it into a sauce known as *guai wei*, or "strange flavor."

INGREDIENTS

For the Noodles:

Kosher salt
1 pound (450 g) fresh wheat noodles
A little peanut, rice bran, or other neutral oil

For the Dressing:

2 teaspoons (3 g) Sichuan peppercorns
2 medium garlic cloves (5 g)
One ¼-inch segment fresh ginger, peeled
Kosher salt
4 scallions, thinly sliced
1 teaspoon (3 g) dried hot chile flakes,
    such as Sichuan er jing tiao or Korean
    gochugaru
1 star anise pod
¼ cup (60 ml) peanut, rice bran, or other
    neutral oil
3 tablespoons (45 ml) light soy sauce, plus
    more to taste
2 tablespoons (15 ml) Chinkiang, black, or
    rice vinegar, plus more to taste
1 tablespoon (15 ml) water
2 teaspoons (8 g) sugar
2 tablespoons Chinese sesame paste (see
    Notes)
Chile oil, for serving

Right around 2016 to 2018, it seemed like Adri and I would attend a potluck baby shower or toddler's birthday party every other weekend. I got excited every time I saw my friend Jimmy Sun would be there. Not because he's a swell guy who everyone should be excited to be around (he is), but because I knew he'd be bringing his cold noodle salad. That was Jimmy's move, and it was a good one. He'd bring the noodles (which he'd precooked and air-dried) in a covered bowl, along with two jars: one filled with chile oil (he used Lao Gan Ma Spicy Chili Crisp), and the other with a premixed dressing, dark with black vinegar with a slick of fragrant oil floating on top. Once at the party, he'd toss the noodles with the dressing and set it on the table, leaving the jar of chile sauce on the side for guests to add to taste. Those noodles would inevitably be the first thing to go. (At *really* good parties, he'd have a backup batch in a bag hidden under the table.)

These noodles, which Jimmy learned how to make from his mother, Lucia Huang, are his family's version of *liang miàn* (cold noodles), a dish that has as many variations as there are street vendors and home cooks in his parents' native Sichuan. The basics are typically the same: make a quick dressing by infusing either oil or water with aromatics like chiles, Sichuan peppercorn, star anise, garlic, ginger, and scallions, then toss cooked and chilled noodles with that aromatic liquid, black vinegar, and soy sauce.

When using the water-based approach, you'd heat the aromatics in boiling water and let them steep like tea before straining and using the infused water as the base for the dressing. With the oil-infusion approach, you follow a process identical to the Soy and Fragrant Oil Dipping Sauce on page 146: combine your aromatics in a heatproof bowl, then pour the hot oil over them before adding your remaining ingredients. I much prefer the hot oil approach, as the high temperature that the oil can achieve will toast the spices, giving the finished dish a more intense aroma.

If making this dish ahead of time, make sure to store the noodles and the dressing in *separate* sealed containers in the fridge to avoid a scandal.

DIRECTIONS

(1) Bring a large pot or wokful of salted water to a boil. Add the noodles, stir with chopsticks to separate them, and cook according to the package directions until the noodles are just cooked through and retain a springy bite (typically about 90 seconds). Drain the noodles through a fine-mesh strainer, chill with cold running water, and toss with a couple teaspoons of oil to prevent sticking—or for, better results, chill by using the air-drying method explained on page 331. Set aside.

(2) **For the Dressing:** Grind the Sichuan peppercorns to a powder in a mortar and pestle. Add the garlic, ginger, and a pinch of salt and pound into a paste. Add the scallions (reserving some for garnish) along with the chiles and star anise (if using; see Notes) and stir with a fork or chopsticks to combine.

(3) Heat the oil in a wok or small skillet until smoking-hot, then pour directly on top of the garlic/ginger/scallion mixture. Stir immediately with chopsticks or a fork. It should sizzle rapidly and release a very nice aroma. Stir in the soy sauce, vinegar, water, and sugar until dissolved.

(4) When ready to serve, combine the noodles and sauce in a serving bowl, toss to combine, and season with more soy sauce and vinegar to taste if desired. Garnish with the reserved scallions and serve immediately with chile oil on the side

Why My Fridge Is Never without Shirataki Noodles

I'm just about the furthest thing you'll find from a health nut. My general philosophy on healthy eating is this: we all know what crap is; don't eat too much of it. My doctor seems to think it's working alright for me thus far. I'm prefacing this sidebar this way because, for better or worse, shirataki noodles—those slick, slippery, yam starch noodles you find next to the tofu at your supermarket— have a reputation as a low-calorie health food. But that's not what this sidebar is about, and it's certainly not why I keep a few packages of shirataki in my fridge at all times.

I'd eaten shirataki or similar yam noodles before, but it wasn't until recently that I started noticing pouches of them suspended in water at American supermarkets. Admittedly, my first reaction to seeing them in the refrigerated display case was *Oh man, here we go. Another "health" food.* But despite garish packaging and large starbursts filled with "Zero Calorie!" and "Gluten-free!" claims, what's inside those bags is pretty much identical to the traditional Japanese preparation. Shirataki (or *ito konnyaku*) can vary in appearance and texture depending on where you are in Japan, but all are made with glucomannan starch extracted from devil's tongue yams. It's an indigestible dietary fiber that basically passes straight through you, giving you a noodle with zero net calories and zero net carbs.

Does that talk of carbs and dietary fiber and calories make your eyes glaze over? Yeah, I feel the same way. If you eat shirataki noodles as a diet food, more power to you. But the real reason I love them (and perhaps the reason you should too) is their texture, and that's really all we need to talk about when it comes to shirataki. They are virtually flavorless on their own, which means that they're superb for picking up the flavors of whatever sauce they're in. Texture-wise, they're slippery and slick, sort of like a cross between spaghetti and Jell-O, and it's this texture that makes them such a joy to eat.

Because shirataki are so mild in flavor and so light in texture, you can really gorge yourself on a bowl of them, sopping up all that flavorful sauce without feeling like you just ate an entire six-pack of hot pockets like you used to be able to in college. With wheat noodles, my body says "uncle" long before my mouth and my tongue do. With shirataki noodles, they're on relatively even footing.

Then, of course, there's the convenience aspect. Aside from a bit of draining and rinsing, shirataki noodles require no preparation at all. Drain, rinse, dress, and you're ready to eat. It takes longer for me just to heat up a pot of water to cook wheat noodles than it does for me to prepare a cold shirataki noodle salad from start to finish. For pure convenience-to-flavor ratio, that's pretty darn tough to beat.

Shirataki are equally delicious and convenient in hot preparations. Have you ever been tempted to cook, say, fresh ramen noodles directly in the pot of hot broth on your stove? There's a good reason not to do this: wheat noodles shed a ton of starch as they cook, severely altering the texture of your broth, which can turn it thick and gummy. With shirataki noodles, cooking directly in the hot soup you're going to serve them with is not just possible but actually better, infusing more flavor into the noodles and saving you from having to heat up a separate pot of water. Just pour your broth into a saucepan or wok, add your rinsed noodles, and heat everything up together on the stovetop.

I know that some of you aren't going to be convinced here. Slippery is a common texture in many East Asian foods, but not necessarily one that is familiar or comforting to the Western palate. For those of you who can't get past slippery noodles, I'm afraid I can't help you. But for the rest of you who, like me, have been vaguely wary of shirataki noodles and all that they imply, I strongly urge you to put those fears aside just long enough to try a bowl. This spicy shirataki noodle and cucumber salad is a pretty good place to start.

SPICY SHIRATAKI AND CUCUMBER SALAD

Yield
Serves 2
as an
appetizer

Active Time
15 minutes

Total Time
15 minutes

NOTES

For the best results, use homemade Málà Chile Oil (page 310). If using an American cucumber, peel and seed it before cutting into matchsticks.

INGREDIENTS

One 8-ounce package shirataki noodles

¼ cup (60 ml) homemade or store-bought Sichuan chile oil with its sediment (see Notes)

1 medium garlic clove, minced (about 4 g/1 teaspoon)

2 tablespoons (30 ml) Chinese sesame paste, store-bought or homemade (page 321), or 4 teaspoons (20 ml) tahini mixed with 2 teaspoons (10 ml) roasted sesame oil

1 tablespoon (15 ml) light soy sauce or shoyu

1 tablespoon (15 ml) Chinkiang or balsamic vinegar

2 teaspoons (8 g) sugar

½ large American or English cucumber or 1 Japanese or Persian cucumber (about 4 ounces/120 g), cut into fine matchsticks (see Notes)

¼ cup thinly sliced scallions, white and pale green parts only

Small handful chopped fresh cilantro leaves and tender stems

Big pinch of toasted sesame seeds

¼ cup (40 g) roasted peanuts or Fried Peanuts (page 319), gently crushed in a mortar and pestle

DIRECTIONS

① Pour the shirataki noodles into a colander or strainer. Rinse under cold running water for 30 seconds, then set over a bowl to drain while you make the sauce.

② Combine the chile oil, garlic, sesame paste, soy sauce, vinegar, and sugar in a large bowl and stir with a spoon to combine. Add the cucumbers, scallions, cilantro, sesame seeds, and drained noodles. Toss to coat, adjusting the seasoning with more chile oil, sesame paste, sugar, soy sauce, or vinegar to taste. Transfer to a serving platter, top with peanuts, and serve.

How to Julienne Cucumbers

A fine julienne of cucumbers is a classic addition to many noodle-based salads. Thin strips align with noodles much better than chunks or slices do, which makes them easier to pick up with chopsticks together with the noodles.

For noodle salads, I like using thin-skinned English or Persian cucumbers. If using American cucumbers, peel them first and discard any watery seed sections after cutting into strips.

Step 1 • Divide into Sections

Trim off the ends of the cucumber, then divide it crosswise into 2- to 3-inch segments.

Step 2 • Form a Base

Working one section at a time, cut a thin segment lengthwise off one side of the cucumber to form a stable base for it to rest on. Alternatively, use a mandoline slicer to cut the cucumber into even ⅛-inch planks and skip to step 4.

Step 3 • Cut into Planks

Hold the cucumber steady against its stable base, then with the tip of your knife planted against the cutting board and using the knuckles of your nonknife hand to guide you, cut the cucumber into ⅛-inch planks by pulling your knife backward through it in steady, even strokes. Pulling back through the cucumber like this instead of chopping up and down will prevent the planks from sticking to the side of your knife, making them easier to stack and align in the next step.

Step 4 • Cut into Strips

Stack the planks into piles 3- to 4-planks high, then cut the planks into 1⅛-inch strips.

FOOD TRUCK CHICKEN AND SESAME NOODLE SALAD

I was working in a biology lab in Kendall Square, Cambridge, during the summer of 1999, earning $8 an hour but lunching like a king from Goosebeary's, a popular food truck that, for a few bucks, handed over a heavy Styrofoam clamshell container full of inexpensive pan-Asian food to hungry biotech workers and students for over two decades. A good 75 percent of my calorie intake came in the form of Goosebeary's Sesame Chicken Salad that summer.

It closed in the early 2010s, right around the time that food trucks became *gourmet* food trucks and disposable Styrofoam trays were no longer in fashion, but I'm still reminded of that summer every time I make sesame noodle salads at home.

The noodles are clearly a riff on similar sesame noodle dishes from China, perhaps Sichuan-style liang miàn, or a cold adaptation of Shanghai-style ma jiang miàn (page 323), but the Chinese American version is a uniquely delicious dish unto itself. According to Chinese American chef Martin Yan and Sam Sifton at the *New York Times*, cold sesame noodle salad was invented at Hwa Yuan restaurant in New York's Chinatown during the 1970s by Sichuanese restaurateur Shorty Tang (a new incarnation of the restaurant opened in 2017). In his version, cold noodles are dressed with a simple concoction of peanut butter and Chinese sesame paste seasoned with soy sauce, vinegar, garlic, ginger, chile sauce, and sugar, then tossed with slivered cucumbers and topped with roasted crushed peanuts.

SESAME CHICKEN NOODLES MY WAY (OR YOUR WAY)

Yield
Serves 4

Active Time
30 minutes

Total Time
30 minutes

NOTES

For maximum efficiency, start poaching the chicken for this recipe before you start the knifework on the additional ingredients. You can also use leftover roasted chicken or rotisserie chicken instead of poaching a chicken breast. If using already-cooked chicken, omit the chicken ingredients, skip step 2, use water or store-bought chicken stock to thin out your sauce in step 5, and shred your chicken as directed in step 6. Save the broth strained in step 4 to use with any recipe that calls for chicken stock in this book. If using unsweetened natural peanut butter, add an extra teaspoon of sugar or honey when making the sauce in step 2. The noodles can be cooked ahead and stored in a sealed container in the fridge for up to 3 days.

My adaptation starts with poaching a chicken breast in water with a couple slices of ginger and scallion, cooking the chicken just until it hits 150°F (66°C) on an instant-read thermometer. This temperature is lower than the government-suggested temperature of 165°F (74°C), but don't worry; it's still perfectly safe to eat and a heck of a lot juicier than chicken cooked to 165°F. (See "Chicken and Food Safety" on page 561 for more info.) If you don't feel like poaching chicken, you can omit it or use leftover roast chicken or rotisserie chicken from the supermarket.

While that chicken is poaching, I julienne my cucumbers and scallions, then mix together a sauce that's mainly peanut butter (for this recipe regular old supermarket Skippy will do fine), seasoned with vinegar, soy sauce, chile garlic sauce, and sugar.

I've written down a recipe for the sauce here, but it's more useful to think of it as a set of guidelines, as I rarely make it the exact same way twice at home. You can use chunky or smooth peanut butter (or even almond or cashew butter). You can add sesame oil or not (or add a dollop of tahini or Chinese sesame paste if you're in the mood). The garlic and ginger are optional. Any kind of vinegar or even citrus juice will do, including cider vinegar, lime juice, or even balsamic. Don't want it hot at all? Leave out the hot sauce. Want it hotter? Add more. The amount of sweetener I add depends on my mood as well as whether or not my peanut butter was the sweetened kind or the natural kind.

At the end of the day, the balance you're looking for is creamy, acidic, salty, sweet, and hot, and so long as each of those elements is represented and works for your own palate, the details are irrelevant.

Aside from control over texture, the other advantage of poaching your own chicken is that you end up with a couple quarts of delicious chicken-scallion-ginger broth. The strained broth can be used in place of chicken stock for any recipe in this book.

INGREDIENTS

For the Noodles:

Kosher salt

2 teaspoons (6 g) baking soda

1 pound (450 g) dry spaghetti, linguine, or fettuccine

A little peanut, rice bran, or other neutral oil

For the Chicken (see Notes):

One 8-ounce (225 g) boneless, skinless chicken breast

2 coin-sized slices fresh ginger

2 whole scallions, cut into 2-inch segments

For the Sauce:

⅓ cup (80 ml) chunky peanut butter (see Notes)

2 tablespoons (30 ml) roasted sesame oil

1 tablespoon (8 g) minced garlic (about 3 medium cloves)

2 teaspoons (5 g) minced fresh ginger (about ½-inch segment)

2 tablespoons (30 ml) Chinkiang, black, or rice vinegar

3 tablespoons (45 ml) light soy sauce or shoyu

1 tablespoon (15 ml) prepared chile sauce, such as sambal oelek or sriracha (optional)

1 tablespoon (12 g) sugar or honey (see Notes)

To Serve:

1 medium American or English cucumber or 2 Japanese or Persian cucumbers (about 6 ounces/180 g total), cut into fine matchsticks

3 scallions, cut into fine hairs (see page 66)

Handful of fresh cilantro, roughly chopped

Big pinch of toasted sesame seeds

1 fresh hot green chile, such as jalapeño or serrano, cut in half lengthwise, seeds removed, thinly sliced on a sharp bias

¼ cup (40 g) roasted peanuts or Fried Peanuts (page 319), gently crushed in a mortar and pestle

DIRECTIONS

(1) Bring a large pot or wokful of salted water to a boil. Add the baking soda and pasta, stir with chopsticks to separate them, and cook according to the package directions until al dente (about 1 minute less than package time indicates). Drain the pasta in a colander set in the sink, toss with a few teaspoons of oil, then spread into a single layer on a large rimmed baking sheet to cool.

(2) **For the Chicken:** Add 2 quarts (2 l) of water to a wok or saucepan. Add the chicken, ginger, and scallions. Bring to a boil over high heat, reduce to a bare simmer, and cook until the chicken registers 150°F on an instant-read thermometer, 15 to 20 minutes.

(3) **Meanwhile, Make the Sauce:** Combine the peanut butter, sesame oil, garlic, ginger, vinegar, soy sauce, chile sauce, and sugar or honey in a large bowl and stir with a fork to combine. It will still be quite chunky and thick at this point.

(4) When the chicken is cooked, remove with a set of tongs and transfer to a cutting board. Skim off and discard any scum from the surface of the water with a ladle. Strain the broth through a fine-mesh strainer and reserve. Discard the ginger and scallions.

(5) Add a few tablespoons of chicken-poaching liquid to the bowl with the peanut sauce and stir until smooth. Continue adding poaching liquid until the sauce is creamy and loose, 4 to 5 tablespoons total. Allow any remaining broth to cool and reserve in a sealed container in the refrigerator for another use. Once cooled, the broth can be frozen for several months.

(6) Use 2 forks to shred the chicken into bite-sized shreds. Add the chicken to the bowl with the sauce.

(7) Add the noodles to the bowl with the chicken and sauce. Add the cucumber, scallions, cilantro, sesame seeds, and chile. Toss everything until thoroughly coated in the sauce. Adjust the seasoning with more soy sauce, vinegar, sugar, or chile sauce to taste. Top with the crushed peanuts and serve.

BÚN TRỘN TÔM (VIETNAMESE SHRIMP AND RICE NOODLE SALAD) WITH CITRUS AND HERBS

Vietnamese salads frequently combine ingredients with a wildly diverse range of textures and flavors with light, punchy dressings, making them wonderful for a quick, light meal. This one, made with cold rice noodles, poached shrimp, pomelo, peanuts, and tons of herbs, is inspired by one that Adri and I ate in Saigon as we hunkered down during one of the torrential flash storms that crop up during the summer monsoon season. It's simultaneously light and refreshing while being completely satisfying as a meal in itself.

I start by poaching shrimp very gently in water. To do this, I like to add shell-on shrimp directly to cold water, then heat it up in a wok over medium-high heat just until the water shows the very first hint of simmering. I shut off the water, let the shrimp sit for 2 minutes, then drain them and rinse under cold water to chill them. By slowly bringing them up to temperature, you cook them far more evenly than if you drop them into already-boiling water, which has a tendency to turn the exteriors rubbery and bouncy before the shrimp have a chance to cook all the way through. (See page 140 for tips on shopping for shrimp.)

Bún—the Vietnamese word for "rice vermicelli"—are very easy to prepare: just soak them in hot water for a couple minutes, then rinse them in cold water to chill. For this salad, I soak them right in the poaching liquid from the shrimp, to allow them to pick up some of that shrimp flavor.

With the shrimp and noodles done, I start constructing the salad in a large serving bowl, starting with crisp shredded lettuce or cabbage at the bottom, followed by the noodles. I then top the noodles with finely julienned carrots (or, if you happen to have them already made, đồ chua—lightly pickled carrots and daikon radish), fresh mung bean sprouts, slivered cucumbers, big handfuls of mint and cilantro (you could also use basil here), and some grapefruit that I've peeled and cut into bite-sized chunks (or, if I can find it, pomelo, grapefruit's larger, dryer, slightly less bitter cousin). Finally, for crunch, I sprinkle some crushed roasted or fried peanuts and fried shallots on top.

For the dressing, I use classic Vietnamese nước chấm, an all-purpose dipping sauce and dressing made with lime juice, garlic, sugar, and fish sauce.

BÚN TRỘN TÔM (VIETNAMESE SHRIMP AND RICE NOODLE SALAD) WITH CITRUS AND HERBS

Yield
Serves 4

Active Time
30 minutes

Total Time
30 minutes

NOTES

You can make a vegetarian version of this salad by replacing the shrimp with extra-firm tofu cut into ½- by ½- by 2-inch strips (poach it the exact same way) or simply omitting it (use vegetarian nước chấm in place of regular nước chấm). I like to make this salad with đồ chua (Vietnamese pickled carrot and daikon; page 342) in place of fresh carrots when I have some in the fridge. If using an American cucumber, peel and seed the cucumber before cutting into matchsticks. If you can find pomelo, use it in place of the grapefruit.

INGREDIENTS

For the Shrimp and Noodles:
12 ounces (340 g) large raw shrimp, preferably shell-on
4 ounces (120 g) dry rice vermicelli

For the Salad:
4 ounces (120 g) finely shredded iceberg or romaine lettuce or green cabbage
1 small carrot (about 4 ounces/120 g), cut into thin matchsticks, preferably on a mandoline, or grated on the large holes of a box grater (see Notes)
½ large American or English cucumber or 1 Japanese or Persian cucumber (about 4 ounces/120 g), cut into fine matchsticks (see Notes)

1 cup (about 3 ounces/90 g) mung bean sprouts
1 ounce (30 g/about 1 cup) picked fresh mint leaves, roughly chopped
1 ounce (30 g/about 1 cup) fresh cilantro leaves and fine stems, roughly chopped
1 large grapefruit, peel and pith removed, cut into bite-sized pieces (see Notes)
½ cup (120 ml) Nước Chấm (page 343)
½ cup (80 g) roasted peanuts or Fried Peanuts (page 319), gently crushed in a mortar and pestle
Handful of homemade (page 255) or store-bought fried shallots

DIRECTIONS

(1) **For the Shrimp and Noodles:** Combine the shrimp and 2 quarts (2 l) of water in a wok or large saucepan. Set it over medium-high heat and heat until it just starts to simmer, then shut off the heat and let the shrimp cook until just barely cooked through, about 2 minutes. (You can check by cutting a shrimp in half. It should be opaque all the way through.)

(2) When the shrimp are cooked, fish them out with a metal spider or fine-mesh strainer (do not discard the cooking water) and run them under cold water to halt the cooking. Drain, remove and discard the shells, cut them in half lengthwise and rinse out any bits of dark digestive tract that run along their backs.

(3) Return the shrimp-cooking liquid to high heat and bring it to a boil. Skim off any foam that collects on top with a ladle and discard. Add the noodles, stir them with chopsticks a couple times, and cook until tender but not mushy (see the package instructions; typically 5 minutes or so). Drain the noodles, rinse them under cold running water, and drain again.

(4) **For the Salad:** Place the lettuce in the bottom of a large salad bowl. Top with cooked noodles, carrots (or đồ chua), cucumber, bean sprouts, mint leaves, cilantro leaves, shrimp, and grapefruit (along with any of its juice). Drizzle with the nước chấm, then sprinkle with peanuts and fried shallots. Serve, tossing everything together at the table.

ĐỒ CHUA (VIETNAMESE PICKLED CARROT AND DAIKON)

Yield
Makes about 1 quart

Active Time
10 minutes

Total Time
10 minutes (for best results, let rest for at least 1 day)

NOTE

For easiest results, use a mandoline or vegetable peeler to make the initial slices of carrot and daikon, then a knife to cut the slices into strips. See page 529 for instructions on how to cut carrots and daikon radish into matchsticks by hand. You can also grate the peeled carrot and daikon on the large holes of a box grater.

Đồ chua are simple quick-pickled carrots and daikon radish that accompany a wide range of Vietnamese dishes. Use them in salads, as an accompaniment to grilled meats, in sandwiches, or in fresh rice paper rolls.

INGREDIENTS

1 large carrot (about 8 ounces/225 g) peeled and cut into fine matchsticks 2 to 3 inches long

1 medium daikon radish (about 8 ounces/225 g) peeled and cut into fine matchsticks 2 to 3 inches long

1 small fresh chile, such as jalapeño, Fresno, Thai bird, or serrano, thinly sliced on a sharp bias (optional)

¼ cup (50 g) sugar

1 tablespoon (9 g) kosher salt

1 cup (240 ml) water

½ cup (120 ml) rice vinegar

DIRECTIONS

Combine the carrots, radish, chile (if using), sugar, and salt in a large bowl. Using your fingertips, massage the salt and sugar into the vegetables until dissolved. Add the water and rice vinegar. Pack the vegetables into a quart-sized mason jar. Pickles can be used immediately or, for best results, refrigerated at least overnight. Use the pickled carrots and daikon within a month.

NƯỚC CHẤM

Yield
Makes
about ½
cup

Active Time
5 minutes

Total Time
5 minutes

NOTES
Nước chấm made with lime juice will last for about a week in the refrigerator before the flavor starts to suffer. Made with vinegar, it will last indefinitely. You can make a vegetarian version of this sauce by replacing the fish sauce with equal parts light soy sauce and Maggi liquid aminos.

INGREDIENTS

1 medium garlic clove, roughly chopped
1 fresh Thai bird chile, roughly chopped (optional)
Small pinch of kosher salt
2 tablespoons (25 g) brown or palm sugar
2 tablespoons (45 ml/about 3 limes) fresh lime juice or distilled white vinegar (see Notes)
2 tablespoons (30 ml) fish sauce
¼ cup (30 ml) water or coconut water
1 ounce (30 g) very finely shredded carrot (optional)

Nước chấm is a Vietnamese sauce that varies from region to region, but all versions have a balance of sweet, acidic, and salty ingredients (usually in the form of sugar, lime juice or vinegar, and fish sauce), often flavored with garlic, and occasionally with chiles or coconut water. It's similar to Thai nam pla prik (page 257), but with a milder flavor. Use it as a dipping sauce for grilled meats, seafood, or vegetables, to dress salads, or as a dip for spring rolls.

I like making nước chấm in a mortar and pestle, which makes it very easy to break down the garlic and chiles, dissolve the sugar, and form the sauce.

DIRECTIONS

In a mortar and pestle, pound the garlic and chile (if using) with a pinch of salt until a rough paste is formed. Add the sugar, lime juice, fish sauce, and water and stir with the pestle to combine. Nước chấm can be stored in a sealed container in the refrigerator for up to a week if made with lime juice or indefinitely if made with vinegar.

HIYASHI CHŪKA

Yield
Serves 2

Active Time
20 minutes

Total Time
20 minutes

NOTE
You do not need to stick to these particular toppings. Other common toppings include shredded lettuce, slivered snap peas or snow peas, slivered cooked ham or roast pork, slivered surimi or chunks of crabmeat, slivered fresh or jarred bamboo shoots, or cooked shrimp. The important part is to use a colorful mix of toppings and to use whatever appeals to you most.

Hiyashi chūka was my grandmother Yasuko's favorite noodle dish. It literally translates from the Japanese as "chilled Chinese." The "Chinese" bit is a reference to the fact that ramen noodles are descended from Chinese lāmiàn and still considered a Chinese preparation by many Japanese people. To make it, you cook ramen noodles, chill them in cold water, then serve them with a variety of toppings, including shredded paper-thin omelet, plenty of fresh vegetables, and oftentimes slivers of ham or roast pork or seafood like shrimp, crab, or surimi (imitation crab). There are no hard and fast rules for what toppings to include, but the rule of thumb is to get a good mix of colors going. When possible, toppings should be cut into thin strips to mix with the noodles and make them easy to pick up together.

recipe continues

INGREDIENTS

For the Omelet:
2 large eggs
Pinch of sugar
Pinch of kosher salt
Vegetable oil

For the Sauce:
2 tablespoons (30 ml) water or dashi
½ teaspoon (2 g) grated fresh ginger
2 tablespoon (30 ml) shoyu or light soy
    sauce
1 tablespoon (15 ml) rice vinegar
2 tablespoons (25 g) sugar
1 tablespoon (15 ml) roasted sesame oil
1 teaspoon (5 ml) chile oil (optional)
2 teaspoons (about 5 g) toasted sesame
    seeds (optional)

For the Salad:
8 ounces (225 g) fresh ramen noodles
½ medium American or English cucumber
    or 1 Japanese or Persian cucumber
    (about 4 ounces/120 g), cut into fine
    matchsticks
1 ounce (30 g) fresh pea shoots or other
    small, tender greens (about 1 cup;
    optional)
Kernels cut from 1 ear of corn (about ¾ cup)
3 ounces (90 g) cherry or grape tomatoes,
    cut into quarters (about ¾ cup)
3 ounces (90 g) finely slivered or thinly
    sliced radish or turnip (about ½ cup)
3 to 4 scallions, white parts only, very finely
    sliced on a sharp bias or cut into hairs
    (see pages 65–66)

DIRECTIONS

(1) **For the Omelet:** Thoroughly whisk together the eggs, sugar, and salt. Rub a thin film of oil in the bottom of your wok or in a nonstick skillet. Heat over high heat until it just begins to smoke. Remove from the heat, rub another thin film of oil into it, then pour in a quarter of the egg mixture (it should bubble immediately) and swirl to form a very thin omelet. It should set almost immediately. Use a thin flexible metal spatula to release one edge of the omelet, then carefully pick it up with your fingertips or chopsticks and transfer to a cutting board. Repeat with the remaining eggs, stacking the omelets on top of each other on the cutting board, for a total of 4 omelets.

(2) Roll the omelets up like a jelly roll, then slice very thinly into strips. Set aside.

(3) **For the Sauce:** Combine the water or dashi, ginger, soy sauce, vinegar, sugar, sesame oil, chile oil, and sesame seeds (if using) in a small bowl and whisk until the sugar is dissolved.

(4) **For the Salad:** Cook the ramen according to the package directions, then drain and rinse thoroughly under cold water. Divide between 2 individual bowls (typically hiyashi chūka is served on wide, shallow bowls). Arrange the toppings on top in a radial pattern. Pour the dressing over the top or serve it in a separate bowl on the side. Serve immediately.

3.3 STIR-FRIED NOODLES

As with standard stir-fries, the most important part of stir-frying noodles is managing heat, making sure that ingredients are cooked rapidly and successively, and keeping the wok uncrowded so that ingredients sear and remain vibrant and fresh rather than steamed and drab. The major difference between stir-frying noodles and other stir-fries is the tendency of noodles to break if stirred too aggressively with a metal wok spatula or tongs. With especially delicate noodles like hor fun, many professional chefs will completely avoid using any utensils after the noodles are added, instead relying only on their ability to rapidly and effectively flip and toss the contents of the wok to combine the ingredients.

You don't have to do that. It's OK to use your spatula or tongs so long as you are gentle with them. Sure, you may break a few noodles along the way, but I promise you, they're still going to taste delicious.

How to Stir-Fry Lo Mein

Lo mein translates directly as "stirred noodles," and in Guangdong the dish typically consists of thin egg noodles—about as thin as wonton noodles or slightly thicker—that are boiled and then served topped with a sauce and toppings that can be as simple as a drizzle of oyster sauce or soy sauce with some blanched green vegetables and a fragrant oil (or lard) or more complex with braised meats, seafood, or expensive XO sauce.

In the West, lo mein are thick, yellow egg and wheat noodles that hold up well to stir-fries, retaining a nice hearty chew even after they've been coated in sauce and have sat around for a while. This is good news, because it means you can stir-fry a big batch and save the leftovers to eat later on in the week without a big dip in quality.

Here are the basic steps for stir-frying Chinese American–style lo mein.

Step 1 • Par-Boil the Noodles

The first step in any egg noodle stir-fry is to par-cook the noodles in boiling water. Some recipes suggest boiling the noodles until fully cooked, then shocking them under cold running water. This works just fine, but I prefer to take the easier route: I blanch them just until tender (about a minute), then transfer them to a bowl and toss them with a little oil to keep the noodles separated. The residual heat from the water will keep cooking them until they're ready to stir-fry a few minutes later. This also ensures that the noodles aren't too wet before being added to the wok.

Be careful: some brands sell their noodles preboiled, in which case all they need is a quick 10- to 15-second dunk in boiling water to soften them up and make them pliable before stir-frying.

Step 2 • Cook the Non-Noodle Ingredients in Batches

If you've got a powerful outdoor wok burner, you can do as they do at restaurants and add ingredients successively to the wok and build your dish that way, but on a regular home burner it means cooking in batches. For this simple stir-fry with shiitake mushrooms, cabbage, and chives, for instance, I start by cooking the shredded cabbage on its own until it chars and gets that awesomely sweet, nutty flavor that will weave its way through the whole stir-fry.

After the cabbage is done, I empty the wok, reheat it with some more oil (making sure to get it smoking hot!), and add thinly sliced shiitake mushrooms, which I had prepped and ready in a bowl conveniently placed next to my cooking station. Mushrooms contain a ton of water and empty space in their spongy flesh, so you've got to cook them long enough to let that flesh break down, concentrating their flavor. They're ready when they've stopped steaming and exuding moisture and instead are sizzling and browning.

Once the mushrooms are ready, I add a handful of chives or scallions (again, lovingly precut and cradled in their own conveniently placed bowl), stir-frying them just long enough to tame their raw bite, but leaving them nice and crisp. The shrooms and chives join the cabbage in the bowl on the side.

Step 3 • Stir-Fry the Noodles

Once all of the additional ingredients are cooked, I stir-fry the noodles (after preheating and oiling the wok again, of course). By the time you add the noodles to the wok, their surfaces should have dried out, making it easy to toss and separate them in the wok. This is the stage where you should try to be gentle with your spatula. Rather than stirring and tossing, you can gently scoop from underneath and turn the noodles over, or you can plant the head of the spatula on the near side of the base of the wok, with the concave side pointing back toward you, using the back of the spatula to move things around as you shake and toss. If you prefer to use tongs, reach for the nylon-tipped pair instead of the all-metal ones to avoid cutting the noodles up unnecessarily.

Step 4 • (Optional): Add Wok Hei

If you want to add a bit of smoky *wok hei* flavor to your stir-fried noodles, now's the time to pull out your blowtorch. You can do this directly in the wok as you stir-fry, or, if you prefer, on rimmed baking sheets outside of the wok where you can take a little more time. Just spread the cooked noodles and toppings out on a rimmed baking sheet, set the baking sheet on a heatproof surface (like your burner grates), then pass a blowtorch over them, holding the flame 2 to 3 inches above the tray and sweeping across with the torch until you smell a distinctly smoky aroma. If you're at the right distance, you should hear a little crackle as small bursts of orange flame leap off the noodles and vegetables. This is the noise and sight of oil droplets vaporizing and combusting. (For more on *wok hei*, see page 42.)

Step 5 • Add Your Aromatics, Return Everything to the Wok, and Sauce It up

When I'm ready to serve the noodles, I reheat the wok, briefly stir-fry some aromatics (say, garlic, scallions, and ginger) in oil, then return everything to the wok and add my sauce. Noodles at take-out restaurants are often swimming in gloppy sauce. I like my noodles very moderately sauced—just enough to lightly coat each strand, but not so much that it pools at the bottom of the bowl.

CHINESE AMERICAN STIR-FRIED LO MEIN WITH SHIITAKE, CHIVES, AND CHARRED CABBAGE

Yield
Serves 4

Active Time
30 minutes

Total Time
30 minutes

NOTE

Some lo mein are sold preboiled. Fresh lo mein should have a floury appearance, whereas precooked lo mein will appear shiny due to the oil added to keep the noodles from sticking. If your noodles are precooked, boil them for only 10 to 15 seconds in step 1 before draining.

INGREDIENTS

For the Noodles:
Kosher salt
1 pound (450 g) fresh lo mein noodles (see Note)
A little peanut, rice bran, or other neutral oil

For the Sauce:
1 teaspoon (5 ml) roasted sesame oil
1 tablespoon (15 ml) light soy sauce or shoyu
1 tablespoon (15 ml) dark soy sauce
1 tablespoon (15 ml) Shaoxing wine
½ teaspoon (1 g) freshly ground white pepper
1 teaspoon (4 g) granulated sugar

For the Stir-Fry:
3 tablespoons (90 ml) peanut, rice bran, or other neutral oil
8 ounces (225 g/½ large head) Napa or green cabbage, thinly sliced
6 ounces (170 g) shiitake mushroom caps, thinly sliced
4 ounces (120 g) Chinese chives or scallions, cut into 2-inch segments
1 tablespoon (8 g) minced garlic (about 3 medium cloves)
1 tablespoon (8 g) minced fresh ginger (about ¾-inch segment)
Kosher salt and freshly ground white pepper

DIRECTIONS

(1) Bring 3 quarts (3 l) salted water to a boil in your wok and cook the noodles, stirring regularly with tongs or long chopsticks, until not quite al dente and separated, about 1 minute (see Note). Drain through a fine-mesh strainer over the sink, add a drizzle of oil, toss with chopsticks to coat in the oil, then transfer the noodles to a rimmed baking sheet and spread them out in an even layer.

(2) **For the Sauce:** Combine the sesame oil, soy sauces, wine, pepper, and sugar in a small bowl and stir together until homogenous. Set aside.

(3) **For the Stir-Fry:** Heat the wok over high heat until lightly smoking. Add 1 tablespoon (15 ml) of the oil and swirl to coat. Add the cabbage and cook, stirring regularly, until tender and charred in spots about 2 minutes. Transfer to a second rimmed baking sheet and set aside.

(4) Reheat the wok until lightly smoking. Add 1 tablespoon (15 ml) of the remaining oil and swirl to coat. Add the mushrooms and cook, stirring regularly, until their moisture has evaporated and they are lightly browned and tender-crisp, about 3 minutes. Add the chives or scallions and cook, stirring, until lightly wilted, about 1 minute. Transfer to the tray with the cabbage and spread the cabbage, mushrooms, and chives out into a single layer. Place the trays of noodles and vegetables on a heatproof surface, such as on top of your burner grates.

(5) **For Smoky *Wok Hei* (optional):** Ignite your blowtorch and, holding the flame 2 to 3 inches above each tray, sweep across the vegetables and noodles until a smoky aroma reaches your nose, about 15 seconds per tray. (You should hear a distinct crackle and see small bursts of orange flame as the oil on the vegetables and noodles jumps and combusts.) Toss the noodles and the vegetables gently with a pair of tongs and torch again.

(6) Reheat the wok until lightly smoking. Add the remaining tablespoon (15 ml) oil and swirl to coat. Add the garlic and ginger and stir-fry until fragrant, about 10 seconds. Immediately add the noodles and cook, tossing and stirring, until hot. Return the vegetables to the wok and toss everything to combine. Stir the sauce and add it to the wok by pouring it around the edges. Toss everything and stir-fry until the sauce coats the noodles. Season to taste with more salt and white pepper. Transfer to a serving platter and serve immediately.

CHINESE-STYLE LO MEIN WITH OYSTER SAUCE, LETTUCE, AND BUTTER

Yield
Serves 2

Active Time
10 minutes

Total Time
10 minutes

NOTES

This recipe calls for thinner Chinese-style lo mein, typically sold as "wonton noodles," "Hong Kong chow mein," or "panfried noodles" in the United States, but honestly, any noodle or pasta you have on hand will do. If using dried or fresh noodles (fresh noodles will have a floury appearance), boil according to package instructions. If they are preboiled (they will have an oilier appearance), boil for just 15 seconds to loosen and heat them up.

INGREDIENTS

8 ounces (225 g) thin egg noodles, preferably fresh

4 to 6 ounces (120 to 170 g) iceberg or romaine lettuce, torn, or baby bok choy, divided into individual leaves

3 tablespoons (45 g) unsalted butter

¼ cup (60 ml) oyster sauce

2 scallions, cut into ¼-inch pieces

This is as simple as noodles get. All it takes is some boiled noodles and greens and a couple of pantry staples.

As opposed to the stir-fried dish typical in the United States, this version is more true to the way it's typically eaten in China: hot noodles dressed with a sauce or used to sop up the liquid from braised meats. The absolute simplest form of this dish is boiled wonton noodles tossed with oyster sauce and a fat, typically lard. My friends Chris and Steph at Chinese Cooking Demystified insist that lard is an essential flavor, and perhaps if you're seeking a true Chinese flavor, keeping rendered lard on-hand is a worthwhile use of prime refrigerator real estate. I stock it from time to time.

But late one night as I was preparing for a photo shoot for this book, I realized I didn't have any lard in my fridge. Then I realized if *I* don't have lard, most of you folks at home aren't going to have lard either (I admire those with that kind of foresight), and then what good is a so-called 10-minute recipe if you have to render lard or seek it out at the supermarket before even starting?

I don't typically have lard in my fridge, but I *do* have butter. I tried it on a whim, and it was great! Buttered oyster sauce may well become a staple flavor combination for me.

DIRECTIONS

(1) Cook the noodles according to the package instructions, adding the lettuce to the boiling water for the last 30 seconds of cooking (if using bok choy, boil it for a full minute). Drain the noodles and set aside, reserving ½ cup of the cooking liquid. Return the wok to the stove.

(2) Add the butter, oyster sauce, and a splash of the reserved noodle-cooking water to the wok and heat over high heat until bubbling and emulsified. Return the noodles and greens to the wok, remove from the heat, and break them up with a pair of chopsticks, turning and lifting them to coat in the sauce. lifting them to coat in the sauce. The sauce should be creamy and smooth, allowing the noodles to slip around. If they are clumping up, add a splash of water. If they are too loose, heat them over high heat for a few moments to reduce the sauce to the right consistency.

(3) Divide the noodles and greens between 2 bowls, top with scallions, and serve.

EASY STIR-FRIED NOODLES WITH MUSHROOMS, CARROTS, BASIL, AND SWEET SOY SAUCE

Yield
Serves 4

Active Time
30 minutes

Total Time
30 minutes

NOTES

Some lo mein are sold preboiled. Fresh lo mein should have a floury appearance, whereas precooked lo mein will appear shiny due to the oil added to keep the noodles from sticking. If your noodles are precooked, boil them for only 10 to 15 seconds in step 1 before draining. Kecap manis is a sweet Indonesian soy sauce. You can find it at Asian markets or make a similar condiment yourself following the recipe on page 291. Sambal oelek is an Indonesian-style salted chile paste. You can use any fresh or fermented hot chile paste in its place, such as sriracha.

This streamlined, simple vegetarian lo mein dish gets a big boost of flavor from sweet, aromatic Indonesian kecap manis and bright and spicy sambal oelek chile paste. It resembles *mie goreng*—Indonesian-style stir-fried noodles—but where mie goreng typically contains meat, eggs, cabbage, and tomato (or ketchup!), for this one I went with a mix of mushrooms and carrots (two vegetables my daughter can't get enough of), along with big handfuls of mung bean sprouts and basil added right at the end to preserve its bright perfume. Served with a Really Fried Egg on top, it's a dish that's equally at home on a weeknight dinner menu or a lazy weekend breakfast.

If you'd like to stick with more traditional mie goreng ingredients, start the recipe by stir-frying a few ounces of simply marinated chicken (use the Basic Stir-Fry Marinade for Any Meat on page 50) or brined shrimp (use the Brined Shrimp for Stir-Fries recipe on page 144) until almost cooked through, removing it from the wok, then proceeding with the recipe as directed, replacing the mushrooms with shredded cabbage and omitting the basil.

INGREDIENTS

For the Noodles:

Kosher salt

1 pound (450 g) fresh lo mein noodles (see Notes)

A little peanut, rice bran, or other neutral oil

For the Sauce:

1 teaspoon (5 ml) roasted sesame oil

1 teaspoon (5 ml) dark soy sauce

1 tablespoon (15 ml) light soy sauce

1½ tablespoons (22 ml) kecap manis (see Notes)

1 tablespoon (15 ml) sambal oelek or other chile sauce (see Notes)

1 teaspoon (4 g) sugar

For the Stir-Fry:

3 tablespoons (90 ml) peanut, rice bran, or other neutral oil

6 ounces (170 g) cremini or button mushrooms or shiitake mushroom caps, thinly sliced

4 ounces (170 g) carrot, peeled and cut into fine matchsticks (about ½ medium)

1 medium shallot (about 1½ ounces/45 g), thinly sliced

2 scallions, thinly sliced

2 teaspoons (5 g) minced garlic (about 2 medium cloves)

3 ounces (120 g/about 1 cup) mung bean sprouts

1 ounce (30 g/about 1 packed cup) fresh Thai or Italian basil leaves

Kosher salt and freshly ground white pepper

To Serve:

4 Extra-Crispy Fried Eggs (page 114)

Sambal oelek

DIRECTIONS

1 Bring 3 quarts (3 l) of salted water to a boil in your wok and cook the noodles, stirring regularly with tongs or long chopsticks, until not quite al dente and separated, about 1 minute (see Notes). Drain through a fine-mesh strainer over the sink, add a drizzle of oil, toss with chopsticks to coat in the oil, then transfer the noodles to a rimmed baking sheet and spread them out in an even layer.

2 **For the Sauce:** Combine the sesame oil, soy sauces, kecap manis, sambal oelek, and sugar in a small bowl and stir until the sugar is dissolved.

3 **For the Stir-Fry:** Heat the wok over high heat until lightly smoking. Add 2 tablespoons (30 ml) of the oil and swirl to coat. Add the mushrooms and cook, stirring regularly, until deeply browned, about 2 minutes. Add the carrots, shallots, scallions, and garlic and stir-fry until the carrots and shallots are tender, about 1 minute.

4 Add the remaining tablespoon (15 ml) oil, then immediately add the noodles and cook, tossing and stirring, until hot. Add the bean sprouts and basil leaves. Stir the sauce and add it to the wok by pouring it around the edges. Toss everything and stir-fry until the sauce coats the noodles, about 1 minute. Season to taste with salt and white pepper. Transfer to a serving platter and serve immediately, topped with the fried eggs and with a side of chile sauce.

YAKISOBA (JAPANESE FRIED NOODLES)

Yield
Serves 3 to 4

Active Time
15 minutes

Total Time
30 minutes

NOTES

You can typically find noodles intended for yakisoba in Japanese grocery stores, often with powdered packets of sauce included (I don't use the powdered sauce—I prefer to mix my own), and with most brands, you don't need to par-cook them at all, just run some hot water over them in the sink to loosen them up. If you can't find noodles specifically sold for yakisoba, fresh ramen or Chinese alkaline wheat noodles will work just fine. Par-boil the noodles until just shy of al dente in boiling water, drain them, toss with a little oil, and proceed as directed in the recipe.

Ao-nori, beni-shoga, and Kewpie mayonnaise can be found at any Japanese supermarket or ordered online. Ao-nori comes in little sealed pouches and should be in the dried seaweed or condiments section. Beni-shoga is sold in jars in the refrigerated section next to the *gari* (sushi ginger). Kewpie is a Japanese brand of mayonnaise that has a distinct umami kick from added MSG.

Japanese food has a bit of a split personality. On the one hand, much of the most celebrated, fanciest food—the kaiseki cuisine of Kyoto or the high-end sushi of Tokyo—is marked by its subtlety and its devotion to clean, simple flavors. But there's another side to Japanese food, a side that more resembles Homer Simpson's makeup shotgun, in which ingredients are doused in heavy sweet-and-savory sauces and a slew of condiments. If you've seen those viral videos of the Japanese chef making *omurice*—chicken-fried rice topped with an omelet with a liquid egg center and a huge ladle of ketchup-flavored demi-glace sauce—you've seen that side of Japanese food.

Yakisoba falls squarely into that side, and given its nearly hundred-year-old history in Japan, it may well be one of the progenitors of it. *Yakisoba* literally translates as "fried" (*yaki*) "noodles" (*soba*). While you may be familiar with the term *soba* in reference specifically to Japanese buckwheat noodles served in soup (a subtle dish), yakisoba are typically made with dense, Chinese-style wheat *chukasoba*, otherwise known as "ramen." It's a common street snack served at festivals, sporting events, and grade-school field days. It's typically cooked in vast quantities on a wide steel flattop called a *teppan*—the kind of flattop we'd cook burgers on in the United States. Yakisoba cooks will stir-fry cabbage, carrots, and onions, along with strips of fatty pork belly before dumping on a vast amount of par-boiled noodles, tossing everything together with a pair of short, stubby spatulas that look like mortaring trowels.

Anybody who's lived in Japan will recognize the *clang* as the trowels move back and forth, tossing the noodles, pork, and vegetables together. The dish gets finished with a sweet and savory thickened Worcestershire-style sauce, plated up, then topped with *ao-nori* (dried green seaweed) and *beni-shoga* (bright red pickled ginger). Frequently you'll also get a drizzle of Japanese-style Kewpie mayonnaise on top.*

---

* The same condiments (or a subset thereof) show up on several classic Japanese street foods, such as *okonomiyaki* (Japanese egg and cabbage pancakes) and *takoyaki* (little spherical octopus pancakes).

INGREDIENTS

For the Sauce:

2 tablespoons (30 ml) Worcestershire sauce, preferably Japanese Bulldog brand "thicker Worcestershire sauce"

2 tablespoons (30 ml) ketchup

1 tablespoon (15 ml) oyster sauce

1 tablespoon (15 ml) shoyu or light soy sauce

1 tablespoon (12 g) sugar or honey

For the Stir-Fry:

1 tablespoon (15 ml) peanut, rice bran, or other neutral oil

4 ounces (120 g) fresh pork belly or bacon, rind removed, thinly sliced, and cut into 1-inch squares

½ white or yellow onion (about 3 ounces/90 g), thinly sliced

½ medium carrot (about 3 ounces/ 90 g), cut into 2- to 3-inch matchsticks

½ small head green cabbage (about 6 ounces/170 g), thinly shredded

3 scallions, cut into 1½-inch pieces

1 pound (450 g) yakisoba noodles, rinsed under hot water to loosen them

Kosher salt and freshly ground black pepper

To Garnish:

Ao-nori, beni-shoga, and Kewpie mayonnaise (all optional; see Notes)

DIRECTIONS

(1) For the Sauce: Combine the Worcestershire sauce, ketchup, oyster sauce, soy sauce, and sugar or honey in a small bowl and stir together until the sugar is dissolved. Set aside.

(2) For the Stir-Fry: Heat the oil in a wok over medium-high heat until shimmering. Add the pork and cook, stirring and tossing, until it has rendered its fat and is starting to turn brown and crisp in spots, about 3 minutes.

(3) Increase the heat to high, then add the onion, carrot, and cabbage and stir-fry until the vegetables are tender and starting to brown slightly, about 2 minutes. Add the scallions, toss to combine, then transfer everything to a bowl and set aside, leaving some of the oil and pork fat in the wok.

(4) Reheat the wok over high heat until lightly smoking, add the noodles, and cook, tossing and stirring, until hot, about 1 minute. Return the vegetables and pork to the wok and toss everything to combine. Stir the sauce and add to the wok. Cook, tossing, until the sauce coats everything thoroughly. Season to taste with salt and black pepper. Transfer to a serving platter, sprinkle with ao-nori and beni-shoga, drizzle with Kewpie mayo (if desired), and serve.

The Many Faces of Chow Mein

Chinese noodle nomenclature in the United States can get a bit confusing. Where I grew up in New York and Boston, "lo mein" referred to thick egg noodles stir-fried with sauce. It's a slippery dish characterized by the bouncy spring of the noodle.

Chow mein, which literally translates as "stir-fried noodles," on the other hand, could refer to a few different dishes. When I was a kid, chow mein were those crunchy deep-fried noodle strips that came out of a cardboard Chun King can and were used (along with canned mandarin oranges) to top "Asian" salads or to serve under a ladle of brown soy-sauce-based gravy to drown alongside mystery meat and celery at the school cafeteria. The Chun King brand was founded by Jeno Paulucci, the convenience food magnate whose inventions include frozen pizzas and pizza rolls. It was absorbed by La Choy in 1995, which still produces the same canned fried noodles.

This version of chow mein no doubt derived from so-called Hong Kong–style panfried noodles, also known as *liang miàn huang*, or "two yellow face": a sort of noodle cake made of thin egg noodles fried until golden and crisp on both sides and served with a saucy pork and vegetable stir-fry on top.

Confusingly, "Hong Kong–style" chow mein is neither stir-fried nor originally from Hong Kong. According to Hong Kong–based Michelin writer Man Wai Leung, the dish originates from Shanghai and Suzhou on China's central coast, making its way to Hong Kong in the 1950s. It was immediately adopted and adapted by Cantonese and Teocheow communities, making its way onto the menus of Luk Yu and Lin Heung, two still-operating dim sum halls and tea houses that catered to Shanghai business tycoons at the time.

Depending on who you ask, "Hong Kong–style" chow mein could *also* refer to *chi you wang chow mein*, or "superior soy sauce fried noodles," a Cantonese preparation derived from Suzhou liang miàn huang that starts life in a similar manner—thin egg noodles boiled and then panfried in a cake—but before they're fully crisped, the cake is broken up and stir-fried with scallions, bean sprouts, and soy sauce, resulting in a dish that combines some of the tender, chewy elements of stir-fried lo-mein-style noodles, with bits of crispy noodle in each bite.

And if that's not confusing enough, when I moved out to the West Coast, I was surprised once again to discover that here "chow mein" refers to saucy stir-fried noodles similar to what we'd call "lo mein" on the East Coast, while "lo mein" would refer only to the noodles themselves. (In many respects, the West Coast nomenclature system is truer to actual Chinese definitions.) If you live in Minnesota, your chow mein may come topped with *subgum*, a saucy mix of meat and vegetables similar to what San Franciscans and New Yorkers in the 1950s would have called *chop suey*.

And if you're from Massachusetts' North Shore? Oh boy. The "chow mein sandwich," originating from the town of Fall River in the 1930s, consists of a hamburger bun overflowing with crispy fried noodles and brown gravy. That sandwich itself is a descendant of the Salem chop suey sandwich, a messy pile of bean sprouts and meat served in a burger bun that *Atlas Obscura* claims has existed since 1875.*

Is this all confusing to you? Don't worry; you don't need to unravel the tangled web of noodles that is chow mein's history to enjoy it in its various forms.

---

* Considering the hamburger bun as we know it was unveiled at the 1916 St. Louis World's Fair by future White Castle founder Walter Anderson, I would take this claim with a grain of salt . . . er, dash of soy sauce.

HOW TO MAKE CAKE-STYLE CRISPY CHOW MEIN (LIANG MIÀN HUANG)

"Oh hey! I just love these things! . . . Crunchy on the outside and a chewy center!"

I'm reminded of *The Far Side* comic with the two polar bears standing by an igloo whenever I crave crispy noodle-cake-style chow mein. The trick is in how you achieve that perfect balance.

There are several methods to cook these crispy noodle cakes. They all start with either boiling raw or dried noodles or separating store-bought par-cooked noodles to fluff them up before they go into the wok (I find that even with par-cooked noodles a quick dunk in boiling water will loosen them up and prime them for the wok).

In many restaurants, the noodles will then be deep-fried, which yields a cake that is crispy through and through. Some people may prefer this completely crispy version, but I have a strong feeling that the style was adapted more out of convenience for the cooks than for optimal eating experience. Panfrying the noodle cake in a small amount of oil takes a little more care and attention, but it results in a cake that is crispy on the outside, very gently charred in spots, but soft, tender, and chewy in the middle. Pair that with a saucy stir-fry that soaks into the crispy bits of the noodles and you've got a dish that positively sings with texture.

I find that it's very important to take your time

during the initial panfrying stage and not be shy with the oil. Many recipes call for as little as a couple teaspoons. In my testing, I've found that you need at least ¼ cup to form a really nice even layer of crispness (½ cup works even better). It may seem like a lot of oil, but you'll see as you slide the noodle cake out of the wok that the majority of the oil doesn't come along with it.

Taking your time with the noodles is also important. Try to cook them too fast and the noodles in direct contact with the wok surface will begin to burn before a crisp layer has had a chance to build up. I start my noodles in hot oil, then reduce the heat and let them take their time.

They may feel like they're sticking to the wok at first. This is OK. Do not panic. If you've ever cooked crisp-skinned pan-roasted chicken or salmon, you know that crispy skin will tell you when it's ready to release from the pan and that any attempt to force it will be met with resistance. Crispy noodles are exactly the same. When they've crisped and firmed up sufficiently, you should be able to gently loosen them from the wok so that you can start swirling—another key step for even cooking (which, incidentally, is a key step for perfect grilled cheese—keep that bread moving in the skillet!).

Once that first side is crispy and golden, I carefully slide it out onto a plate, trying to leave as much oil in the wok is possible. This allows me to invert it onto a second plate, then slide it back into the wok, a process that is much safer and more foolproof than attempting to flip it directly in the wok.

The second side cooks just like the first, with one exception: after it crisps up, I use my spatula to hold the noodles in the wok while I drain off all the excess oil, then I continue to cook the noodle cake, swirling the wok constantly, until it develops a few nice dark brown, extra-crispy parts that give it all a toasty aroma that comes through even after I top the cake with a saucy stir-fry.

When it all goes well, the dish is a textural powerhouse. Perhaps even better than igloos.

CRISPY CHOW MEIN NOODLE CAKE WITH TOPPINGS (LIANG MIÀN HUANG)

Yield
Serves 4

Active Time
30 minutes

Total Time
30 minutes

NOTE
Hong Kong–style panfried noodles may also be labeled "chow mein" or "for chow mein." They are thin egg noodles that typically come precooked (the package will say "ready to fry" or something similar). Raw noodles will have a floury appearance and should be boiled according to package directions, typically 45 to 60 seconds. Dry noodles can also be used. Follow the package directions for cooking times.

INGREDIENTS

For the Noodle Cake:
Kosher salt

8 ounces (225 g) fresh Hong Kong chow mein or panfried noodles or dried wonton noodles (see Note)

½ cup (120 ml) peanut, rice bran, or other neutral oil

To Serve:
1 recipe Shiitake and Bok Choy Topping for Crispy Chow Mein (page 357) or Shrimp Topping for Crispy Chow Mein (page 358)

DIRECTIONS

1 Bring 1 quart (1 l) of lightly salted water to a boil over high heat in your wok. Add the noodles (the wok may lose its boil; that's OK) and stir them a few times with chopsticks to break them up, then immediately drain through a colander or fine-mesh strainer. (If using raw or dried noodles, follow the package directions for cooking time—typically 45 seconds for raw and a couple minutes for dried). Spread the noodles on a rimmed baking sheet so that they can steam as they cool. Lift them and turn them with chopsticks every couple minutes to promote even cooling. Allow to cool until the noodles feel dry to the touch, about 10 minutes.

2 Transfer the noodles to a large plate and form into a circle about 10 inches in diameter. Heat the oil in your wok over medium until it registers 350°F (175°C) on an instant-read thermometer. Carefully slide the noodles into the hot oil, using a spatula to form them into a circle in the bottom of the wok and gently pat them down (don't compress them too much).

3 Cook, tilting the wok around in a circular motion to keep the oil moving, until it releases from the bottom of the wok with a few gentle nudges from a spatula, about 1 minute. Continue to cook, swirling the wok around so that the noodle cake is constantly moving until golden brown and very crispy on the first side, 8 to 12 minutes longer.

4 Slide the noodle cake back onto the plate, leaving as much oil in the wok as possible. Place a large, flat, rimless pot lid or a second plate upside down on top of the first. Holding the plate and the pot lid (or plate) together firmly, invert the noodle cake onto the pot lid (or plate), then carefully slide it back into the wok. Repeat step 3 until both sides of the cake are golden brown and crisp.

5 Holding the noodle cake in place with your wok spatula, tilt the wok to drain out any excess oil (reserve this oil for stir-fries). Return the wok to the burner, increase the heat to medium-high, and continue cooking until the noodle cake is deeply browned in spots and has a nice toasty aroma, about 2 minutes longer. Slide the cake out onto a plate and invert it onto a serving platter so that the extra-toasty side is facing up. Set it aside while you make the stir-fry topping.

Crispy Chow Mein Noodle Cake, Step by Step

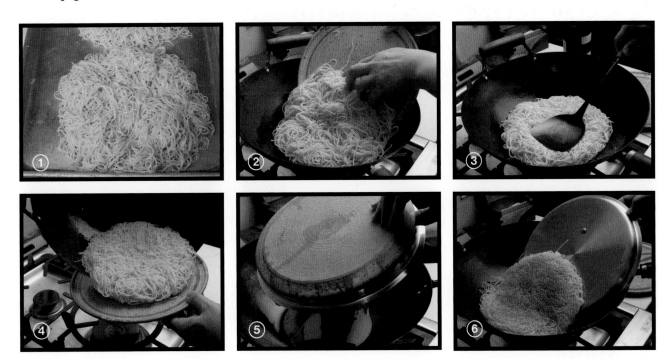

SHIITAKE AND BOK CHOY TOPPING FOR CRISPY CHOW MEIN

Yield
Serves 4

Active Time
5 minutes

Total Time
5 minutes

NOTES
You can use shiitake or a mix of any mushrooms you'd like, sliced or cut into bite-sized pieces. Use vegetarian oyster sauce and vegetable stock in place of chicken stock to make this dish vegetarian.

INGREDIENTS

For the Cornstarch Slurry:
1 tablespoon (9 g) cornstarch
2 tablespoons (30 ml) water

For the Stir-Fry:
2 tablespoons (30 ml) peanut, rice bran, or other neutral oil
8 ounces (225 g) shiitake mushrooms, stemmed and sliced (see Notes)
8 ounces (225 g) baby bok choy, leaves separated
2 medium garlic cloves (5 g), smashed and roughly chopped

3 scallions, cut into 1½-inch segments
1 tablespoon (15 ml) Shaoxing wine
2 teaspoons (10 ml) light soy sauce
2 teaspoons (10 ml) dark soy sauce
2 tablespoons (30 ml) oyster sauce
1 teaspoon (4 g) sugar
1 cup (240 ml) homemade or store-bought low-sodium chicken stock
Kosher salt and freshly ground white pepper

DIRECTIONS

(1) **For the Cornstarch Slurry:** Combine the cornstarch and water in a small bowl and stir until the cornstarch is dissolved. Set aside.

recipe continues

(2) **For the Stir-Fry:** Heat a wok over high heat until lightly smoking. Add the oil and swirl to coat. Add the mushrooms and stir-fry until they've given up most of their liquid and are starting to brown in spots, about 4 minutes. Add the bok choy, garlic, and scallions and cook, stirring, until the garlic is fragrant and the bok choy is just starting to soften, about 1 minute.

(3) Add the wine, soy sauces, oyster sauce, sugar, chicken stock, a pinch of salt, and a big pinch of white pepper. Bring to a simmer and cook for 30 seconds.

(4) Stir the cornstarch slurry and add it to the wok. Bring to a simmer and cook until the sauce is thickened into a gravy-like consistency, about 1 minute. Season with more salt and pepper to taste, then ladle the bok choy, mushrooms, and gravy on top of the noodle cake and serve.

SHRIMP TOPPING FOR CRISPY CHOW MEIN

Yield
Serves 4

Active Time
5 minutes

Total Time
5 minutes

NOTE
12.5 grams is about 1⅓ tablespoons Diamond Crystal kosher salt, 1 tablespoon Morton's kosher salt, or 2½ teaspoons table salt.

INGREDIENTS

For the Shrimp:

2 cups (500 ml) very cold water
12.5 g salt (see Note)
2 teaspoons (10 g) baking soda
12 ounces (340 g) shrimp, peeled and cut into ½-inch pieces, shells reserved separately
A cup or so of ice cubes

For the Shrimp Stock:

1 tablespoon (15 ml) peanut, rice bran, or other neutral oil
2 coin-sized slices fresh ginger
1 scallion, roughly chopped
1½ cups homemade or store-bought low-sodium chicken stock

For the Cornstarch Slurry:

2 teaspoons (6 g) cornstarch
1 tablespoon (15 ml) water

For the Stir Fry:

1 tablespoon (15 ml) peanut, rice bran, or other neutral oil
4 scallions, cut into 1½-inch pieces
½ teaspoon (2 g) sugar
1 tablespoon (15 ml) Shaoxing wine
2 teaspoons (10 ml) light soy sauce
Kosher salt and freshly ground white pepper

DIRECTIONS

(1) **For the Shrimp:** Combine the water, salt, and baking soda in a bowl and stir until the salt and baking soda are dissolved. Add the shrimp and stir to separate them and ensure the brine flows all around. Add the ice cubes and let the shrimp brine for at least 15 minutes and up to 30. Drain thoroughly and pat dry on paper towels or spin in a paper-towel-lined salad spinner.

(2) **Meanwhile, Make the Shrimp Stock:** Heat the oil in a wok over high heat until shimmering. Add the shrimp shells, ginger, and scallion and stir-fry until the shells are pink, about 1 minute. Add the stock, bring to a boil, reduce to a bare simmer, and cook until reduced to about 1 cup, about 10 minutes. Strain through a fine-mesh strainer, discard the solids, and set the stock aside until ready to stir-fry.

(3) **For the Cornstarch Slurry:** Combine the cornstarch and water in a small bowl and stir with a fork until the cornstarch is dissolved.

(4) **For the Stir-Fry:** Heat the wok over high heat until lightly smoking. Add the oil and swirl to coat. Add the shrimp and scallions and stir-fry until the shrimp are no longer translucent on the exterior, about 30 seconds. Add the reserved shrimp stock, sugar, Shaoxing wine, and soy sauce.

(5) Stir the cornstarch slurry and add it to the wok. Bring to a simmer and cook until the sauce is thickened into a gravy-like consistency, about 1 minute. Season with salt and pepper to taste, then ladle the shrimp, scallions, and gravy on top of the noodle cake and serve.

Crispy Chow Mein with "The Mix"

If you have a bag of "The Mix"—the general-purpose pork and shrimp mixture inspired by my friend Brandon Jew's recipe (page 280)—in your fridge or freezer, it's a quick and easy shortcut to a flavorful gravy for a Crispy Chow Mein Noodle Cake. To use it, stir-fry 12 ounces (340 g) of "The Mix" in a tablespoon of oil over high heat, breaking it up until the pork is fully cooked and the shrimp are no longer translucent on the outside, about 45 seconds. Deglaze the wok with a tablespoon (15 ml) of Shaoxing wine, a teaspoon (5 ml) each of light and dark soy sauce, a tablespoon of oyster sauce (15 ml), a cup of stock, and a slurry of 1 tablespoon (9 g) of cornstarch mixed with 2 tablespoons (30 ml) of water. Simmer until thickened, garnish with some sliced scallions, ladle it over the noodles, and serve.

CANTONESE SUPERIOR SOY SAUCE NOODLES (WITH BEAN SPROUTS AND SCALLIONS)

Yield
Serves 2

Active Time
15 minutes

Total Time
30 minutes

NOTE

Hong Kong–style panfried noodles may also be labeled "chow mein" or "for chow mein." They are thin egg noodles that typically come precooked (the package will say "ready to fry" or something similar). Raw noodles will have a floury appearance and should be boiled according to package directions, typically 45 to 60 seconds. Dry noodles can also be used. Follow the package directions for cooking times.

INGREDIENTS

For the Sauce:

1 tablespoon (15 ml) light soy sauce
2 teaspoons (10 ml) dark soy sauce
½ teaspoon (1 g) freshly ground white
    pepper
1 teaspoon (5 ml) Shaoxing wine
1 teaspoon (5 ml) roasted sesame oil
½ teaspoon (2 g) sugar

For the Noodles:

Kosher salt
8 ounces (225 g) Hong Kong–style panfried
    noodles (fresh chow mein; see Note)

For the Stir-Fry:

3 tablespoons (45 ml) vegetable oil
2 ounces thinly sliced yellow onion (about ½
    cup/¼ large)
4 scallions, cut into 2-inch segments and
    thinly sliced lengthwise
Small bunch Chinese chives or baby leeks,
    cut into 2-inch sections (optional)
3 ounces (about 1 cup) mung bean sprouts,
    stringy ends torn off
Kosher salt and freshly ground white
    pepper

A Hong Kong dim sum classic, these Cantonese soy sauce noodles are prized for their simplicity and combination of textures. With nothing more than noodles, onions, and bean sprouts and a simple soy-based sauce, a lot of the essence of this dish comes down to technique.

The thing that sets these noodles apart is their cooking method. As a derivative of Suzhou-style liang miàn huang (Crispy Chow Mein Noodle Cake, page 356), they begin in the same manner: boiling the noodles, then panfrying them until crisp (though not quite as crisp as for liang miàn huang). Because this noodle cake ends up stir-fried in the end, you also don't have to worry about flipping the noodles all in one go, so no need to use the two-plate inversion method here; just flip it over in pieces.

This is one of those dishes where smoky *wok hei* can really make a big improvement in flavor. To do it, I either stir-fry on my outdoor wok burner, letting the flames leap into the wok as I stir-fry the noodles and vegetables, or use the "torch *hei*" method outlined on page 44. Equally essential for *wok hei* flavor is searing the sauce by drizzling around the edge of the wok so that it falls straight onto a searing-hot surface, which alters its flavor.

DIRECTIONS

1. **For the Sauce:** Combine the soy sauces, white pepper, wine, sesame oil, and sugar in a small bowl and stir until the sugar is dissolved. Set aside.

2. Bring 1 quart (1 l) of lightly salted water to a boil over high heat in your wok. Add the noodles (the wok may lose its boil; that's OK) and stir them a few times with chopsticks to break them up, then immediately drain through a colander or fine-mesh strainer. (If using raw or dried noodles, follow the package directions for cooking time—typically 45 seconds for raw and a couple minutes for dried). Spread the noodles on a rimmed baking sheet so that they can steam as they cool. Allow to cool until the noodles feel dry to the touch, about 10 minutes.

3. **BEFORE YOU STIR-FRY, GET YOUR BOWLS READY:**

   a. Noodles
   b. Onion, scallion, chives, or leeks (if using)
   c. Mung bean sprouts
   d. Sauce
   e. Empty baking sheets for cooked ingredients
   f. Serving platter

(4) **For the Stir-Fry:** Heat a wok over medium-high heat until very lightly smoking. Add 2 tablespoons (30 ml) of the oil, swirl to coat wok, then carefully add the noodles, using your spatula to gently spread them into a single layer. They may stick a little bit at this point. That's OK. Don't try to move or stir them if they are stuck. Cook the noodles without disturbing them for 1 minute, moving the wok around a bit so that the base heats evenly over the burner.

(5) Holding your spatula upside down, gently prise off the crispy edges of the noodles from the base of the wok, working around and under the noodles until they are completely released from the wok. Carefully flip the noodles. If you practice, you should be able to flip them in a single motion using just the wok, like a pancake. Alternatively, use your spatula to flip it over in sections. It's OK if it breaks up a bit.

(6) Cook the second side like the first, then use your spatula to release the noodle cake again. Slide the noodles out into a rimmed baking sheet and spread them into an even layer.

(7) Wipe out the wok and return it to high heat until lightly smoking. Add the remaining 1 tablespoon (15 ml) of oil and swirl to coat. Add the onion, scallion, and Chinese chives or baby leeks (if using). Stir-fry until the vegetables are lightly charred and wilted, about 1 minute, then transfer them to a second rimmed baking sheet.

(8) **For Smoky *Wok Hei* (optional):** Ignite your blowtorch and, holding the flame 2 to 3 inches above each tray, sweep across the vegetables and noodles until a smoky aroma reaches your nose, about 15 seconds per tray. (You should hear a distinct crackle and see small bursts of orange flame as the oil on the vegetables and noodles jumps and combusts.) Toss the noodles and the vegetables gently with a pair of tongs and torch again.

(9) Reheat the wok over high heat until smoking. Return the vegetables and noodles to the wok. Add the mung bean sprouts. Stir the sauce and add it to the wok, swirling it around the edges so that it sears. Stir-fry rapidly, using the back of your spatula to break the noodles up and flip them through the sauce and distribute the vegetables evenly. Cook until there is no liquid sauce left at the bottom of the wok and the noodles are charred and crispy in spots.

(10) Season with salt and white pepper to taste. Transfer to a serving platter and serve.

CHOW MEIN WITH BEEF AND PEPPERS

Yield
Serves 4

Active Time
30 minutes

Total Time
30 minutes

NOTE
Hong Kong–style panfried noodles may also be labeled "chow mein" or "for chow mein." They are thin egg noodles that typically come precooked (the package will say "ready to fry" or something similar). Raw noodles will have a floury appearance and should be boiled according to package directions, typically 45 to 60 seconds. Dry noodles can also be used. Follow the package directions for cooking times.

This recipe combines tender strips of marinated beef with bell peppers, onions, and noodles for a satisfying, all-in-one meal that's equally good reheated the next day.

INGREDIENTS

For the Beef:
1 pound (450 g) beef flank steak, skirt steak, hanger steak, or flap meat, cut into ¼-inch-thick strips
½ teaspoon (2 g) baking soda
2 teaspoons (10 ml) soy sauce
2 teaspoons (10 ml) Shaoxing wine
½ teaspoon (2 g) sugar
½ teaspoon (1.5 g) cornstarch

For the Noodles:
Kosher salt
8 ounces (225 g) Hong Kong–style panfried noodles (fresh chow mein; see Note)

For the Sauce:
1 teaspoon (5 ml) roasted sesame oil
1 tablespoon (15 ml) light soy sauce or shoyu
1 tablespoon (15 ml) dark soy sauce
1 tablespoon (15 ml) oyster sauce
1 tablespoon (15 ml) Shaoxing wine

1 teaspoon (2 g) freshly ground black pepper
1 teaspoon (4 g) sugar

For the Stir-Fry:
6 tablespoons (90 ml) vegetable, peanut, or canola oil
1 green bell pepper, cored and cut into ¼-inch strips (about 1 cup)
1 red bell pepper, cored and cut into ¼-inch strips (about 1 cup)
1 medium onion, cut into ¼-inch strips from pole to pole (about 1½ cups)
2 teaspoons (5 g) minced garlic (about 2 medium cloves)
2 teaspoons (5 g) minced fresh ginger (about ½-inch segment)
3 ounces (about 1 cup) mung bean sprouts, stringy ends torn off
Kosher salt and freshly ground black pepper

DIRECTIONS

(1) Bring 1 quart (1 l) of lightly salted water to a boil over high heat in your wok. Add the noodles (the wok may lose its boil; that's OK) and stir them a few times with chopsticks to break them up, then immediately drain through a colander or fine-mesh strainer. (If using raw or dried noodles, follow the package directions for cooking time—typically 45 seconds for raw and a couple minutes for dried). Spread the noodles on a rimmed baking sheet so that they can steam as they cool. Allow to cool until the noodles feel dry to the touch, about 10 minutes.

(2) **For the Beef:** Place the beef in a medium bowl, cover with cold water, and vigorously agitate it. Drain through a fine-mesh strainer set in the sink and press on the beef with your hands to remove excess water. Return the beef to the bowl, add the baking soda, and vigorously massage the baking soda into the meat, lifting the meat, throwing it down, and squeezing it for 30 seconds to a minute. Add the soy sauce, Shaoxing

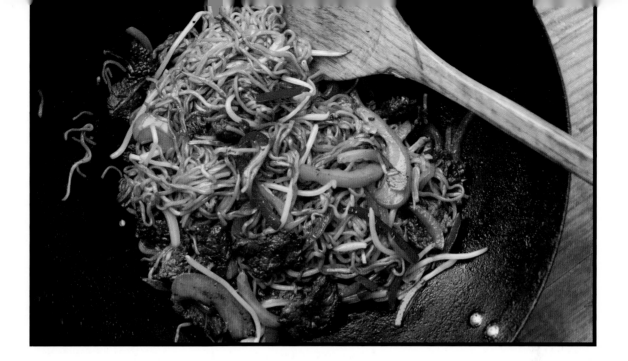

wine, sugar, and cornstarch and roughly work the marinade into the meat for at least 30 seconds. Set aside to marinate for at least 15 minutes and up to overnight.

(3) **For the Sauce:** Combine the sesame oil, soy sauces, oyster sauce, wine, pepper, and sugar in a small bowl and stir together until homogenous. Set aside.

(4) **BEFORE YOU STIR-FRY, GET YOUR BOWLS READY:**

a. Noodles

b. Marinated beef

c. Peppers and onions

d. Garlic and ginger

e. Bean sprouts

f. Sauce

g. Empty bowl for cooked ingredients

h. Serving platter

(5) **For the Stir-Fry:** Heat a wok over medium-high heat until very lightly smoking. Add 2 tablespoons (30 ml) of the oil, swirl to coat the wok, then carefully add the noodles, using your spatula to gently spread them into a single layer. They may stick a little bit at this point. That's OK. Don't try to move or stir them if they are stuck. Cook the noodles without disturbing them for 1 minute, moving the wok around a bit so that the base heats evenly over the burner.

(6) Holding your spatula upside down, gently prise off the crispy edges of the noodles from the base of the wok, working around and under the noodles until they are completely released from the wok. Carefully flip the noodles. If you practice, you should be able to flip them in a single motion using just the wok, like a pancake. Alternatively, use your spatula to flip it over in sections. It's OK if it breaks up a bit.

recipe continues

(7) Cook the second side like the first, then use your spatula to release the noodle cake again. Slide the noodles out into a rimmed baking sheet and spread them into an even layer.

(8) Wipe out the wok and return it to high heat until lightly smoking. Add 1 tablespoon (15 ml) of the remaining oil and swirl to coat. Add half of the beef and cook without moving until well seared, about 1 minute. Continue cooking while stirring and tossing until lightly cooked but still pink in spots, about 1 minute. Transfer to a bowl. Wipe out the wok and repeat with 1 tablespoon (15 ml) of the remaining oil and the remaining beef, adding the beef to the same bowl.

(9) Wipe out the wok and return it to high heat until lightly smoking. Add 1 tablespoon (15 ml) of the remaining oil and swirl to coat. Add the peppers and onions and stir-fry until lightly charred in spots and the vegetables are tender-crisp, about 1 minute. Transfer to the bowl with the beef.

(10) Reheat the wok until lightly smoking. Add the remaining tablespoon (15 ml) of oil and swirl to coat. Add the garlic and ginger and stir-fry until fragrant, about 10 seconds. Immediately add the noodles and cook, tossing and stirring, until hot. Return the beef and vegetables to the wok. Add the mung bean sprouts. Stir the sauce and add it to the wok by pouring it around the edges. Toss everything and stir-fry until the beef is fully cooked and the sauce coats the noodles. Season with salt and black pepper to taste. Transfer to a serving platter and serve immediately.

Stir-Fried Rice and Other Starch Noodles

Without the reinforcing power of gluten proteins that wheat flour brings to the table, noodles made from other types of starches—rice, mung bean, tapioca, and the like—tend to be either more delicate than wheat noodles or stickier, and your stir-frying technique has to change a bit to reflect those differences. In this section, we'll talk about some of the more common non-wheat-noodle stir-fries.

BEEF CHOW FUN

My family has no shortage of strong opinions and preferences, but if we were to collectively choose one dish that would appear on the table as our last meal together, it would undoubtedly be a perfect plate of the Guangzhou classic, beef chow fun.

According to Guangzhou's tourism board, dry-fried beef hor fun (typically called "beef chow fun" in the West) is the most popular dish in Canton (modern-day Guangzhou), eaten for breakfast, lunch, and dinner. The origins of the dish are not clear, but the story goes that it was created in 1938 by the Xus, a mother-and-son team that operated a food stall during the Japanese invasion and occupation of Canton. At the time, hor fun noodles were typically served in a starch-thickened gravy-like broth. The stall ran out of starch just as a Japanese patrolling officer and his squad stopped to order noodles.* Unable to make the saucy gravy and fearing for their lives, the mother had the idea to stir-fry the noodles in a dry style, stir-frying beef, cooking soy sauce down until it was completely absorbed by the noodles, and finishing it with scallions and bean sprouts. The family kept their lives, and dry-fried beef chow fun was born.

Over the years, my parents and two sisters have spread out across the United States, from Boston to Montana to Colorado to the West Coast, and each time one of us makes a new move, we inevitably get asked "Can you get good beef chow fun there?" Indeed, the dearth of smoky, lightly charred, dry-fried beef chow fun in my sister's adopted home of Bozeman, Montana, was one of the primary motivators for me to develop a recipe for the dish—notorious for its requirement of a powerful jet-engine-style restaurant burner—that would work for any home cook. (OK, any home cook with a decent blowtorch—which you should have by now!)

Beef chow fun is often compared to a French omelet, in that it's a simple dish whose preparation relies so much on technique that it can be used as a yardstick for a cook's skills. So what makes it so hard to perfect? Two things: *wok hei* and good tossing technique.

The Technique

Wok hei is something we've discussed at length already, but nowhere is it more important a factor in flavor than in this dish, where the smoky, singed, almost barbecued aroma of stir-fries cooked in carbon steel over intense heat, with the flame licking into the food as it cooks, is as prominent a flavoring as soy sauce or salt (or, as the case may be, MSG). If you've been waiting to pull the trigger on a powerful outdoor burner, perfect beef chow fun is the dish that should make that decision a little easier. For that reason alone, this is the only recipe in the book where I'm including specific instructions for cooking both on a high-output burner and on a home range.

Why is tossing technique so important? First and foremost, it's for the same reason tossing is important in any stir-fry: it encourages rapid cooking through the constant evaporation and condensation of steam as food is tossed through its own vapors, creating more complex aromas and flavors in the process (see "What Happens When You Toss?" on page 32 for more on the science). With chow fun, it serves a secondary role: with good enough tossing technique, you can minimize the use of a spatula or ladle, which in turn means that delicate chow fun noodles are less likely to break as they cook. This, of course, doesn't affect the way the noodles taste all that much, but it still improves the dish and is something to strive for if perfection is what you're after.

The Beef, Vegetables, and Sauce

The ingredients of beef chow fun are simple. It starts with beef. I use skirt or flank steak, which I slice thinly against the grain, then submit to the baking soda and massaging treatment to ensure that it stays extremely tender. The marinade also includes soy sauce, Shaoxing wine, and a touch of cornstarch to keep the beef nice and slippery as it cooks. I used to cook my beef by stir-frying it, but after several tests I've switched over to the hot oil "pass through" method, in which you heat up a moderate amount of oil in the wok, then fry the beef by fully submerging it in the hot oil for a few moments before draining it. It doesn't make the dish taste or feel greasy; rather, it sets the starchy coating on the surface of the beef, ensuring that all the beef is equally tender, with no overcooked or stringy spots.

A mix of alliums and bean sprouts is the classic vegetable accompaniment. I go with a mix of sliced yellow onions, scallions, and garlic, which I stir-fry together with the bean sprouts.

The sauce is also simple: It's primarily soy sauce (a mix of light and dark), which is added around the edges of the wok to develop some of those seared flavors. Some recipes for chow fun include some douchi (fermented black beans), but I personally find that they distract from the pure flavors of *wok hei* and seared soy sauce (though they can still be a good addition in situations where wok hei is not possible).

---

* Why do so many food origin stories begin when a cook is short of a specific ingredient?

The Noodles

The trickiest part of this recipe is finding the right noodles. Hor fun noodles, also called *shahe fen,* are made by steaming a thin layer of rice flour batter until it sets, then hand-cutting it into wide noodles and coating the noodles in a bit of oil to prevent them from sticking. Here's the issue: while fresh hor fun is pliable and elastic, hor fun that has been refrigerated for any length of time will be stiff. Rather than bending, it tends to crack when you attempt to stir-fry or even unfold it.

This all has to do with starch retrogradation. Cooked starches have a fluid, malleable structure. It's what makes fresh bread so stretchy and a freshly griddled corn tortilla pliable and stretchy. As they cool, starches will start to take on a crystalline structure, becoming stiffer. This process, known as starch retrogradation, is what we call *staling*, and it's what makes old bread hard to chew.* With some starches, this retrogradation is reversible: reheating a loaf of stale bread in the oven or toasting a stale English muffin will soften it up again. However, with some starches, that retrogradation is only partially reversible. This is the reason a reheated corn tortilla will never be as pliable or elastic as a fresh one and why refrigerated hor fun noodles are so difficult to work with.

Rice starch is not as bad as cornstarch when it comes to irreversible retrogradation—you can use refrigerated hor fun noodles by dropping them into boiling water and *very gently* teasing them apart to let the water flow around them until they're mostly pliable. You can even use dried wide rice noodles for chow fun. Either option will produce delicious, more-than-edible results, but if you, like me, are constantly chasing that perfect chow fun high, nothing but fresh noodles will do. Fortunately, they are among the easiest noodles to make at home. Both Grace Young and Pailin Chongchitnat have excellent rice-noodle-making guides available for free online if you'd like to try your hand at them.

Reheating Refrigerated Noodles in the Microwave

The microwave can also be a good tool for reinvigorating stale, stiff noodles that have spent too long in the refrigerator. To reheat them, place the noodles on a microwave-safe plate and put them in the microwave next to a mug of hot water (this water will steam and help keep the noodles from drying out). Microwave at 20-second intervals until the noodles feel soft and pliable all the way through (around 2 minutes total per pound of noodles). Remove the noodles from the microwave, and as soon as they're cool enough to handle, cut them as wide as you'd like, gently separate the folded noodles, and toss them in a large bowl with a drizzle of oil, occasionally fluffing them with your fingers to keep them from sticking until ready to stir-fry.

---

* Contrary to popular belief, stale bread is not necessarily dry bread, though staling and drying do often go hand in hand.

BEEF CHOW FUN ON A HOME BURNER (THE TORCH METHOD)

Yield
Serves 4

Active Time
20 minutes

Total Time
35 minutes or up
to overnight

NOTE

For best results, use freshly made hor fun noodles either from a local shop or homemade (see page 367). If using refrigerated fresh hor fun noodles or dry noodles, you will need to boil them before use: Bring 3 quarts of water to a boil in your wok. Add noodles and cook, stirring gently to break them up, until they are tender, about 1 minute (if using dry noodles, this will take a couple minutes; follow the package directions). Drain, toss with a couple teaspoons of oil to keep them separated, then spread out on a large plate or rimmed baking sheet. Allow to air-dry for at least 5 minutes.

This recipe for dry-fried beef chow fun is designed to work on a regular home burner, using a blowtorch to deliver the dish's signature smoky *wok hei*. Even without the torching step, the dish is still delicious, but I strongly recommend trying it with the torch. It makes a big difference! (See page 45 for information on what kind of torch to get.)

It has quite a few steps, but the overall process is relatively simple, and each step is designed to get the best flavor out of the simple ingredients.

INGREDIENTS

For the Beef:
8 ounces (225 g) thinly sliced beef flap meat, skirt steak, hanger steak, or flank steak
¼ teaspoon (1 g) baking soda
Kosher salt
1 teaspoon (5 ml) dark soy sauce
1 teaspoon (5 ml) light soy sauce
1 teaspoon (5 ml) Shaoxing wine
1 teaspoon (1 g) cornstarch

For the Sauce:
4 teaspoons (20 ml) light soy sauce or shoyu
2 teaspoons (10 ml) dark soy sauce
1 tablespoon (15 ml) Shaoxing wine

For the Stir-Fry
½ cup (120 ml) peanut, rice bran, or other neutral oil
½ medium yellow onion (about 3 ounces/90 g), sliced
2 teaspoons (5 g) minced garlic (about 2 medium cloves)
3 scallions, cut into 2-inch segments
3 ounces (90 g/about 1 cup) mung bean sprouts
12 ounces (340 g) hor fun (chow fun) noodles, preferably freshly made (see Note)
Kosher salt and freshly ground white pepper
MSG (optional)

DIRECTIONS

① **For the Beef:** Place the beef in a medium bowl, cover with cold water, and vigorously agitate it. Drain through a fine-mesh strainer set in the sink and press on the beef with your hands to remove excess water. Return the beef to the bowl, add the baking soda, and vigorously massage the baking soda into the meat, lifting the meat, throwing it down, and squeezing it for 30 seconds to a minute. Add the salt, soy sauces, Shaoxing wine, and cornstarch and roughly work the marinade into the meat for at least 30 seconds. Set aside to marinate for at least 15 minutes and up to overnight.

② **For the Sauce:** Combine the soy sauces and wine in a small bowl.

③ **BEFORE YOU STIR-FRY, GET YOUR BOWLS READY:**

a. **Marinated beef**
b. **A heatproof bowl with a fine-mesh strainer set in it**
c. **Noodles**
d. **Sauce**
e. **Onion, garlic, scallions, and bean sprouts**
f. **Empty rimmed baking sheets for cooked ingredients**
g. **Serving platter**

(4) **For the Stir-Fry:** Place a fine-mesh strainer in a heatproof bowl and have it ready by your wok station. Heat the oil in the wok until shimmering. It should register around 350° to 375°F (175° to 190°C) on an instant-read thermometer. With the wok over your hottest burner at the highest flame, add the beef and cook, stirring, until the pieces are separated and no longer pink, about 45 seconds. Strain the beef and oil through the fine-mesh strainer, then transfer the beef to a rimmed baking sheet and set aside. Wipe out the wok.

(5) Return the wok to high heat until lightly smoking. Add 1 tablespoon (15 ml) of the drained beef oil to the wok and swirl to coat. Add the onion, garlic, scallions, and bean sprouts and stir-fry until the vegetables are tender-crisp and charred in spots, about 1 minute. For smoky *wok hei*, ignite a blowtorch and point it into the wok while tossing, allowing the flame to directly hit the vegetables (alternatively, use the tray method explained in step 7). Transfer to the baking sheet with the beef. Spread the vegetables and beef into an even layer.

(6) Return the wok to high heat until lightly smoking. Add another tablespoon (15 ml) of the drained beef oil and swirl to coat. Add the noodles and stir-fry, being careful not to be too rough with the noodles to avoid breaking them, until the noodles are lightly charred in spots, 1 to 2 minutes. Add half of the sauce by swirling it around the edges of the wok and continue to stir-fry until the sauce is dry. Transfer the noodles to a rimmed baking sheet and carefully spread into an even layer. Wipe out the wok.

(7) **For Smoky *Wok Hei* (optional):** Ignite your blowtorch and, holding the flame 2 to 3 inches above each tray, sweep across the vegetables and noodles until a smoky aroma reaches your nose, about 15 seconds per tray. (You should hear a distinct crackle and see small bursts of orange flame as the oil on the vegetables and noodles jumps and combusts.) Toss the noodles, vegetables, and beef gently with a pair of tongs and torch again.

(8) Return the wok to high heat until smoking, then add everything back to the wok and toss to combine, being gentle with the noodles so as not to break them. Add the remaining sauce to the wok by pouring it around the edges. Cook, tossing, until the sauce is completely dry and the noodles are starting to sizzle in spots, about 1 minute. If not using the tray method explained in Step 7, ignite a blowtorch and point it into the wok while tossing, allowing the flame to directly hit the ingredients. Season to taste with salt, white pepper, MSG (if using), and more light soy sauce. Transfer to a serving platter and serve immediately.

BEEF CHOW FUN ON AN OUTDOOR WOK BURNER

NOTE

For best results, use freshly made hor fun noodles either from a local shop or homemade (see page 367). If using refrigerated fresh hor fun noodles or dry noodles, you will need to boil them before use: Bring 3 quarts of water to a boil in your wok. Add the noodles and cook, stirring gently to break them up, until they are tender, about 1 minute (if using dry noodles, this will take a couple minutes; follow the package directions). Drain, toss with a couple teaspoons of oil to keep them separated, then spread out on a large plate or rimmed baking sheet. Allow to air-dry for at least 5 minutes.

INGREDIENTS

For the Beef:

8 ounces (225 g) beef flap meat, skirt steak, hanger steak, or flank steak, thinly sliced
¼ teaspoon (1 g) baking soda
½ teaspoon (1.5 g) kosher salt
1 teaspoon (5 ml) dark soy sauce
1 teaspoon (5 ml) light soy sauce
1 teaspoon (5 ml) Shaoxing wine
1 teaspoon (1 g) cornstarch

For the Sauce:

4 teaspoons (20 ml) light soy sauce or shoyu
2 teaspoons (10 ml) dark soy sauce
1 tablespoon (15 ml) Shaoxing wine

For the Stir-Fry:

½ cup (120 ml) peanut, rice bran, or other neutral oil
12 ounces (340 g) hor fun (chow fun) noodles, preferably freshly made (see Note)
½ small yellow onion (about 3 ounces/90 g), sliced
2 teaspoons (5 g) minced garlic (about 2 medium cloves)
3 scallions, cut into 2-inch segments
3 ounces (90 g/about 1 cup) mung bean sprouts
Kosher salt and freshly ground white pepper
MSG (optional)

This recipe for beef chow fun is written to help you get the most out of a high-powered outdoor wok setup. I recommend a burner with a heat output of at least 65,000 BTU/hour, though 120–130,000 BTU/hour is even better. Work away from any flammable objects, make sure there are no hoses or things that you might trip on, and have all of your supplies ready before you start. For safety, I recommend having a heatproof landing spot where you can place your wok in the middle of cooking to prevent food from burning if you ever lose your place or need to take a quick break to regroup. Your wok burner should be off or on its lowest heat setting while you're not actively preheating or cooking. I also recommend doing a mental run-through of every step in the process before you begin cooking. It's fast and furious!

You can premix your sauce for this, but I prefer to keep my soy sauces in small plastic squeeze bottles and my Shaoxing wine in its original bottle with a pour spout fitted over the top, which makes adding all the sauces in succession simple.

DIRECTIONS

(1) **For the Beef:** Place the beef in a medium bowl, cover with cold water, and vigorously agitate it. Drain through a fine-mesh strainer set in the sink and press on the beef with your hands to remove excess water. Return the beef to the bowl, add the baking soda, and vigorously massage the baking soda into the meat, lifting the meat, throwing it down, and squeezing it for 30 seconds to a minute. Add the salt, soy sauces, Shaoxing wine, and cornstarch and roughly work the marinade into the meat for at least 30 seconds. Set aside to marinate for at least 15 minutes and up to overnight.

(2) **For the Sauce:** Combine the soy sauces and wine in a small bowl.

(3) **BEFORE YOU STIR-FRY, GET YOUR BOWLS READY:**

a. Marinated beef
b. A heatproof bowl with a fine-mesh strainer set in it
c. Noodles
d. Sauce
e. Onion, garlic, scallions, and bean sprouts
f. Large bowl for cooked ingredients
g. Serving platter

(4) **For the Stir-Fry:** Place a fine-mesh strainer in a heatproof bowl and have it ready by your wok station. Heat the oil in the wok until shimmering. It should register around 350° to 375°F (175° to 190°C) on an instant-read thermometer. With the flame on high, add the beef and cook, stirring, until the pieces are separated and no longer pink, about 45 seconds. Shut off the heat. Strain the beef and oil through the fine-mesh strainer, then transfer the beef to a bowl and set aside. Wipe out the wok.

(5) Return the wok to high heat until lightly smoking. Add 1 tablespoon (15 ml) of the drained beef oil to the wok and swirl to coat. Add the noodles and stir-fry, tilting the wok away from you so that the noodles fly directly through the jet of hot air behind the wok and the flames crackle and leap across them, until the noodles are lightly charred in spots, about 45 seconds. (Be careful not to be too rough with the noodles and avoid using the spatula or ladle as much as possible to prevent the noodles from breaking.) Add half of the sauce by swirling it around the edges of the wok and continue to stir-fry until the sauce is dry, about 30 seconds longer. Transfer the noodles to the bowl with the beef and set aside.

(6) Return the wok to high heat until smoking. Add another tablespoon (15 ml) of the drained beef oil and swirl to coat. Add the onion, garlic, scallions, and bean sprouts and stir-fry, again tilting the wok away from you so that the flames leap into it, until the vegetables are tender-crisp and charred in spots, about 30 seconds.

(7) Immediately return the noodles and beef to the wok and toss to combine. Season with a pinch of salt, white pepper, and MSG (if using). Add the remaining sauce to the wok by pouring it around the edges. Cook, tossing, until the sauce is completely dry and the noodles are starting to sizzle in spots, about 1 minute. Transfer to a serving platter and serve immediately.

PAD SEE EW WITH CHICKEN

Yield
Serves 4

Active Time
15 minutes

Total Time
30 minutes

NOTE

For best results, use freshly made hor fun noodles either from a local shop or homemade (see page 367). If using refrigerated fresh hor fun noodles or dry noodles, you will need to boil them before use: Bring 3 quarts of water to a boil in your wok. Add the noodles and cook, stirring gently to break them up, until they are tender, about 1 minute (if using dry noodles, this will take a couple minutes; follow the package directions). Drain, toss with a couple teaspoons of oil to keep them separated, then spread out on a large plate or rimmed baking sheet. Allow to air-dry for at least 5 minutes.

Pad see ew, which translates from Thai as "fried soy sauce," is one of several rice noodle stir-fries that derive from Cantonese chow fun. The process for making it is largely the same; the only real difference lies in the ingredients. In place of alliums, pad see ew includes Chinese broccoli, which I blanch briefly to set its color before stir-frying (broccolini or Western broccoli will do in a pinch). Beef can be used, but chicken, along with a fried egg, is vastly more common. Finally, in addition to soy sauce, oyster sauce (or sometimes fish sauce) is used to season the noodles. If you want to really capture the flavor of your favorite Thai takeout joint, consider using a Thai-style dark soy sauce (Healthy Boy is a popular brand).

Another difference between chow fun and pad see ew is how it's served: where chow fun is typically eaten on its own, no bowl of pad see ew is complete without a bowl of Prik Nam Som (page 256) to accompany it.

I don't consider *wok hei* as essential to the flavor of pad see ew as it is for chow fun, but if you want to get a little *wok hei* into it, you can use the same torching (or outdoor wok) procedures described in the chow fun recipes on pages 368 and 370.

INGREDIENTS

For the Chicken:
6 ounces (175 g) thinly sliced boneless, skinless dark or light meat chicken
1 teaspoon (5 ml) light soy sauce
1 teaspoon (4 g) cornstarch
¼ teaspoon (1 g) baking soda
Pinch of kosher salt

For the Sauce:
1 tablespoon (15 ml) light soy sauce
1 tablespoon (15 ml) dark soy sauce
1 tablespoon (15 ml) oyster sauce
1 tablespoon (12 g) sugar

For the Stir-Fry:
¼ cup (60 ml) vegetable oil
6 ounces Chinese broccoli (gai lan), broccoli, or broccolini, cut lengthwise so that no stems wider than ¼ inch remain

1 large egg, cracked into a small bowl
4 medium garlic cloves, minced or crushed in a mortar and pestle (about 4 teaspoons/10 to 15 g)
12 ounces (340 g) hor fun (chow fun) noodles, preferably freshly made (see Note)
Kosher salt, light soy sauce, and freshly ground white pepper

To Serve:
Bangkok-style table condiments, such as Prik Nam Som (page 256), fish sauce (such as Nam Pla Prik on page 257), sugar, and Thai chile flakes

DIRECTIONS

(1) **For the Chicken:** Place the chicken in a medium bowl, cover with cold water, and vigorously agitate it. Drain through a fine-mesh strainer set in the sink and press on the chicken with your hands to remove excess water. Combine the chicken, soy sauce, cornstarch, baking soda, and salt in a small bowl and massage with your fingertips until the cornstarch is evenly distributed. Stir vigorously with your fingertips or chopsticks for 30 seconds. Cover and set aside for at least 15 minutes while you prepare the other ingredients.

(2) **For the Sauce:** Combine the soy sauces, oyster sauce, and sugar in a small bowl and stir until the sugar is dissolved.

(3) **BEFORE YOU STIR-FRY, GET YOUR BOWLS READY:**

a. Marinated chicken   f. Noodles

b. Blanched broccoli   g. Empty bowl for cooked ingredients

c. Egg   h. Serving platter

d. Garlic

e. Sauce

(4) **For the Stir-Fry:** When ready to cook, rub the inside of a wok with a thin film of vegetable oil and heat over high heat until smoking. Add 1 tablespoon (15 ml) of the oil and swirl to coat. Add the chicken and cook, tossing occasionally until nearly cooked through, about 1 minute. Transfer to a clean bowl.

(5) Wipe out the wok and return to high heat until lightly smoking. Add 1 tablespoon (15 ml) of the remaining oil and swirl to coat. Add the broccoli and stir-fry until lightly charred in spots, about 1 minute. Transfer to the bowl with the chicken.

(6) Wipe out the wok and add the remaining 2 tablespoons (30 ml) oil. Heat until shimmering, then add the egg directly to the center of the oil, bringing the bowl right down to the surface to avoid splashing the hot oil. The egg should immediately start puffing and sputtering. Let it puff for about 15 seconds, then flip it. (It's OK if it breaks.) Add the garlic and stir-fry, breaking up the egg with your spatula until the garlic is fragrant and egg is cooked through, about 30 seconds.

(7) Add the noodles, toss the in garlicky oil, then immediately add the sauce, swirling it in around the edges. Return the chicken and broccoli to the wok and stir-fry until the sauce has cooked off and the noodles start to sizzle and char a little, about 1 minute. Season with salt and/or light soy sauce and ground white pepper to taste. Transfer to a serving platter and serve immediately with the table condiments.

PAD THAI

Given its popularity abroad and its status as the national dish of Thailand, pad Thai's history is not a particularly long one, but it is interesting. Pad Thai's development and adoption was far from a natural evolution. Rather, it was the explicit product of Thailand's troubled political climate before the start of World War II and the totalitarian government ruled by Prime Minister Plaek Phibunsongkhram. Pardon the brief history lesson—I promise we'll get back to those noodles soon.

Phibunsongkhram was a field marshal of Khana Ratsadon, the People's Party that orchestrated the lightning-fast coup d'état that ended Thailand's nearly eight hundred years of absolute monarchy during the Siamese Revolution of 1932. Siam was declared a democratic nation with a constitutional monarchy with Manopakorn Nititada appointed as its first prime minister. The democracy was not to last, as Phibunsongkhram and People's Party civilian leader Pridi Banomyong pushed the government in opposing

directions, with Banomyong pushing a leftist economic agenda and Phibunsongkhram taking totalitarian cues from Italian and German leaders.

The power struggles ended with a third-party rebellion that Phibunsongkhram was instrumental in putting down. With both popular and military support, Phibunsongkhram ascended to the role of prime minister in December of 1938 and became the de facto totalitarian dictator of what would soon be officially renamed Thailand. By 1939, surrounded on the East by French Indochina and on the West by British Burma, and with Japan's imperial invasion of China, Phibunsongkhram believed that Thailand faced an existential threat and that the key to maintaining its independence lay in creating a more "civilized" and unified Thai culture.

As Thailand entered World War II allied with Axis powers, Phibunsongkhram instituted a series of cultural mandates that controlled everything from how Thais represented themselves to foreigners to forced honoring of the flag, the military, and the national anthem, to using Thai products whenever possible.

To go along with these new mandates, Phibunsongkhram sought to create a single food that could unify the disparate cultures of northern, central, and southern Thais, that would promote good health, and that would be inexpensive to prepare. That this dish ended up being pad Thai is almost entirely chance. Phibunsongkhram's son Nitya claimed in a 2009 interview with the food studies journal *Gastronomica* that it was a dish invented by either his father's family cook or an elderly aunt that just happened to fit the bill.

According to Penny Van Esterik, nutritional anthropologist and author of the book *Materializing Thailand,* the government saw pushing a dish with multiple protein sources—peanuts, eggs, and meat—cooked over high heat in clean pans as a healthy shift away from Thai staples like rice, raw pounded chile pastes, and raw leaves. The dish was named *kuai-tiao phat thai*—Thai fried rice noodles—and the recipe was distributed across the country. The name was shortened to pad Thai, the dish took, and it's remained a Thai staple ever since.

Most foreigners are likely to identify pad Thai as a purely Thai dish. This, too, is partially by design, as later in the twentieth century and to this day the Thai government promotes pad Thai as an appealing first taste of Thailand for tourists. In Thailand, however, pad Thai is not always regarded as a Thai dish. According to Thai chef, reporter, and instructor Sirichalerm Svasti, neither noodles nor stir-frying—arguably the two key elements of pad Thai—is Thai at all; both are Chinese imports brought to the country by Chinese immigrants in the eighteenth century. The flavors, on the other hand, are distinctly Thai: sweet, sour, pungent, and hot.

The Pad Thai Pantry

The sweet-sour-pungent-hot flavor profile is built with four basic ingredients—palm sugar, tamarind pulp, fish sauce, and chiles—which is reinforced with a series of auxiliary flavors: funky dried shrimp and shrimp paste; sweet-and-tangy preserved radish; the allium aroma of garlic, shallots, and garlic chives; and the fresh crunch of bean sprouts. On top of that, you'll find four sources of protein: extra-firm tofu, crushed peanuts, scrambled egg, and shrimp.

Pad Thai may be simple to make, but there's an awful lot going on in there.

You may find recipes out there that call for white sugar in place of the palm and lime juice or even vinegar in place of the tamarind, and many recipes that omit some or all of the auxiliary ingredients. Many of these recipes will produce a tasty wokful of noodles, and if your only shopping stop for the day is the corner bodega, by all means, work with what you've got. None of these ingredients will make or break your pad Thai.

If, on the other hand, you are willing to go out of your way a bit, true pad Thai, pad Thai packed with little bursts of salty, funky flavors and crisp, crunchy, and chewy textures, pad Thai as good as any you'll find on the streets of Bangkok, can be yours. These are not the ingredients you need, but they are the ingredients you deserve.

All of these ingredients other than the garlic chives and tofu will last indefinitely in your pantry or fridge, so they will not go to waste.

- **Palm sugar** is a raw sugar sold either semimoist in jars or in small blocks. It has a unique caramely aroma that lends its flavor to dishes like pad Thai or dipping sauces like Nam Pla Prik (page 257) or Jaew (page 440).

- **Dried shrimp** have a salty, briny aroma and a pleasantly chewy texture that softens up a bit as you stir-fry them. They are great in pad Thai; can be soaked in water, chopped, and added to XO sauce (page 303—add a handful of them along with the pepperoni in my recipe); or get pounded into a green papaya salad. You can find them at Chinese, Japanese, and Southeast Asian supermarkets.

- **Shrimp paste** comes in a variety of forms, and, like the disco version of the *Star Wars* theme, is extremely funky and an acquired taste that some people will simply never acquire. My friend Leela Punyaratabhandu, author of several excellent Thai cookbooks (including *Bangkok: Recipes and Stories from the Heart of Thailand*) recommends a bright red shrimp paste in oil, which I've only ever found online. I find that Chinese shrimp pastes work just as well when I'm in the mood for some funk.

- **Preserved daikon radish** is another ingredient I would have never come across had Leela not turned me on to it. It comes in two forms: salty and sweet. The salty resembles Sichuan ya cai (preserved mustard stems) in flavor and texture, but with a stronger salty bite, while the sweet is, well, a little sweeter. The sweet stuff is what you want for pad Thai. Preserved radish is also excellent when added to fried rice or other fried noodle dishes, simmered in soups, stirred into congee (see page 249), or sprinkled into or onto Thai-style omelets (see page 168). Japanese-style pickled daikon radish can make for a semisuitable stand-in, if you are after flavor but not authenticity. Store opened packs of preserved daikon in the fridge.

- **Super firm tofu**, known as *dougan* or "dry tofu" in China, is tofu that has been pressed until it takes on a dense, almost cheese-like texture similar to halloumi or paneer. It's typically sold in Cryovacked packages and frequently dyed yellow on the exterior. I've seen it stocked at Southeast Asian markets and larger Chinese markets. Regular firm or extra-firm tofu will work fine, but this stuff adds yet another interesting texture to the pad Thai mix. Baked tofu is the next best substitute.

- **Garlic chives** are slender alliums similar to scallions but with flat, grass-like stalks rather than the hollow cylinders of scallions. I have never visited a Chinese or Southeast Asian supermarket with a produce section that did not have garlic chives on display. At Japanese supermarkets you'll see them with their Japanese name, *nira*. They have a much milder flavor than scallions, more vegetal than aromatic, so if using green onions as a substitute, I would halve the amount. Garlic chives are stir-fried into pad Thai as well as being served raw on the side (typically next to a pile of bean sprouts, and, often, slivers of raw banana blossom).

The Noodles

The noodles used for pad Thai are dried rice noodles. At the market, you can typically find a few different widths of dried noodles. Pad Thai is made with noodles about ¼ inch wide, though if you can only find thinner or thicker noodles, don't stress too much about it. Unlike chow fun or pad see ew, in which fresh noodles are rapidly stir-fried with minimal sauce, pad Thai noodles are added to the wok only partially rehydrated with a short soak in water. They will continue to absorb liquid and soften up in the wok, which is part of makes them so darn flavorful.

If there is any difficulty in pad Thai technique, it's in ensuring that the noodles are perfectly cooked—tender but not mushy—and that the sauce is completely reduced and absorbed just as this happens. That's how you end up with noodles that are tender but not mushy, with little chewy bits where the sugars in the sauce have started to caramelize a bit around their edges. This is not as difficult as it sounds; it just requires you to pay attention to what's going on inside your wok as you cook. You can tell when you are at the caramelization point because the oil will break out of the sauce and the sound of cooking will shift from the soft sputter of a simmer to the sharper crackle of frying.

There are two scenarios to be careful of:

- **If the noodles still feel tough and there's not much sauce left in the wok**, turn down the heat to slow down evaporation and give the noodles a bit more time to tenderize. In emergencies—say the sauce has completely evaporated, fat has broken out, and the ingredients are sizzling in oil rather than cooking in sauce while the noodles are still mostly raw—you can add a small splash of water to buy the noodles some extra time to soften.

In all likelihood, you're more likely to face the reverse scenario:

- **If the noodles feel like they are tenderizing faster than the sauce is reducing**, pump up the heat under the wok as high as it will go and really get things moving around in there. Both of these actions will encourage evaporation, which should help your sauce reduce in time with your noodles.

Once that frying phase has begun, you can push the noodles off to the side, then fry your shrimp and eggs. During this phase, I find it useful to position my wok a little off-center from the flame to direct the heat mainly at the section of the wok where the shrimp and eggs are cooking, slowing down the noodles until I'm ready to add my tofu, bean sprouts, and garlic chives, and give everything a final toss before serving.

PAD THAI

Yield
Serves 2
to 3

Active Time
15 minutes

Total Time
30 minutes

NOTES

Thai chile flakes are quite spicy, so adjust according to taste. You can also use Korean gochugaru or Sichuan ground er jing tiao for a milder flavor (or omit the chiles entirely). The shrimp, preserved radish, and shrimp paste are all optional ingredients. See "The Pad Thai Pantry" above for more details. For the plumpest, juiciest shrimp, follow the brining instructions on page 144. Chinese garlic chives (*nira* in Japanese markets) look like scallions but have flat leaves that look like large blades of grass. They have a milder flavor than scallions. You can use flowering chives, yellow chives, or scallions in their place if you cannot find them. If using scallions, halve the number.

INGREDIENTS

For the Noodles:
6 ounces (170 g) pad Thai noodles (¼-inch-wide dry rice noodles)

For the Sauce:
2 ounces (60 g) palm sugar or dark brown sugar
3 tablespoons (45 ml) fish sauce
3 tablespoons (45 ml) prepared tamarind pulp (see page 381)
1 teaspoon ground Thai chile (optional; see Notes)

For the Stir-Fry:
¼ cup (60 ml) vegetable oil
1 medium shallot (about 1½ ounces/45 g), thinly sliced
3 medium garlic cloves (8 g), smashed with the side of a knife and roughly chopped
2 tablespoons (5 g) dried small shrimp (optional; see Notes)
1 tablespoon (15 ml) shrimp paste (optional)
3 tablespoons (20 g) chopped preserved sweet radish (optional; see Notes)

8 ounces (225 g) large shrimp, peeled (see Notes)
2 large eggs
1 cup (about 3 ounces/90 g) mung bean sprouts
5 or 6 Chinese garlic chives (about 3 ounces/90 g), sliced on a sharp bias into 1- to 2-inch pieces (see Notes)
4 ounces (120 g) baked or super firm tofu, cut into ½- by ½- by 2-inch blocks

To Serve:
½ cup (80 g) roasted peanuts or Fried Peanuts (page 319), gently crushed in a mortar and pestle
Lime wedges
Raw Chinese garlic chives (Japanese nira)
Raw mung bean sprouts
Bangkok-style table condiments, such as Prik Nam Som (page 256), fish sauce (such as Nam Pla Prik on page 257), sugar, and Thai chile flakes

DIRECTIONS

(1) **For the Noodles:** Place the noodles in a bowl and cover with warm water. Let the noodles soak, agitating them occasionally, until they are soft enough to bend without breaking, but not mushy, about 20 minutes. Drain through a fine-mesh strainer and reserve.

(2) **For the Sauce:** Place the palm sugar in a mortar and pestle and pound until it is fully crushed. Add the fish sauce, tamarind pulp, and ground chile and grind with a circular motion with the mortar and pestle until the sugar is dissolved. If you don't have a mortar and pestle, you can crush the palm sugar on a firm countertop under a heavy pot, then stir it into the fish sauce and tamarind pulp to dissolve. (Also, get a mortar and pestle.)

③ **BEFORE YOU STIR-FRY, GET YOUR BOWLS READY:**

a. Garlic and shallots

b. Noodles

c. Sauce, dried shrimp, shrimp paste, and preserved radish (if using)

d. Raw shrimp

e. Eggs

f. Bean sprouts, Chinese garlic chives, and tofu

g. Serving platter

④ **For the Stir-Fry:** Heat 2 tablespoons (30 ml) of the oil in a wok over high heat until shimmering. Add the garlic and shallots and cook, stirring, until fragrant and softened but not browned, about 30 seconds.

⑤ Add the noodles, followed by the sauce, dried shrimp, shrimp paste, and preserved radish. Stir and toss vigorously until the noodles have absorbed about half the sauce, about 45 seconds.

⑥ Push the noodles to the side of the wok, then position the wok so that the burner is mainly heating the now-empty space. Add the shrimp to the empty space and cook them, stirring and flipping occasionally, until they are no longer translucent on either side, about 45 seconds. Toss everything in the pan together.

⑦ Push the noodles and shrimp to the side of the wok again and position the wok so that the burner is mainly heating the now-empty space. Add the remaining 2 tablespoons (30 ml) of oil, then add the eggs. Let them cook until just starting to set, about 10 seconds, then break them up with the spatula and scramble them.

⑧ Add the bean sprouts, Chinese garlic chives, and tofu, toss everything together, and stir-fry until the chives and bean sprouts are wilted and the noodles have begun to crisp and char in spots, about 1 minute longer.

⑨ Transfer to a serving platter and sprinkle with the peanuts. Serve immediately, passing lime wedges, raw garlic chives and bean sprouts, and table condiments for each diner to customize the dish as desired.

continues

Pad Thai, Step by Step

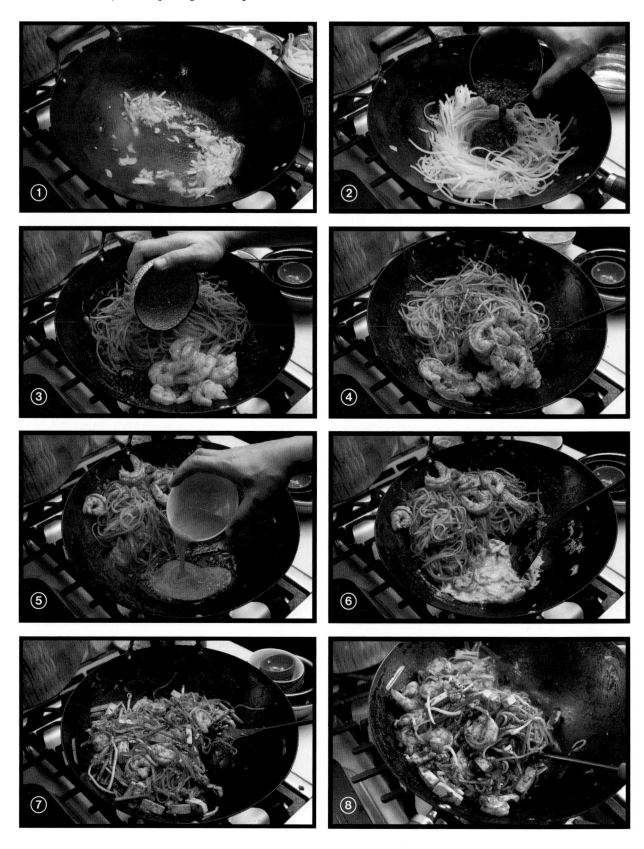

WORKING WITH TAMARIND

Tamarind is the fruit of a hardwood tree indigenous to Africa that has spread throughout Southeast Asia and South America. It produces large brown, pod-like fruits that contain a sticky, very tart pulp. When shopping for tamarind, you're likely to see it in one of three forms:

- **Tamarind concentrate** is my last choice. It comes in plastic or glass jars. You can definitely use it in a pinch, but the flavor of concentrate is usually not particularly concentrated and lacks the punch of tamarind in its more natural forms.

- **Whole tamarind fruit** are your second-best option. They are finger-shaped pods about 1 inch in diameter and 6 inches long. They typically come packed in plastic-wrapped cardboard boxes. To use whole tamarind fruit, you must first break open the hard outer pods, then soak the pulpy fruit in warm water and strain out the resulting concentrated tamarind paste.

- **Tamarind pulp** sold in block form is the best way to buy tamarind. With most ingredients, I find that the closer you can get it to its natural state, the better the flavor. With tamarind, this is not the case—the block stuff is just as good as the whole pods, and significantly easier to work with.

Tamarind pulp can be found at any Asian supermarket and most Latin markets as well. It's sold in plastic wrappers and typically stored at room temperature. Check the fresh produce aisle underneath the fresh produce display bins. Once you get it home and open the package, you can break off just as much as you need for a given recipe, rewrap the rest, and store it in the fridge for several months; its high acidity and sugar content make it an inhospitable environment for bacteria or molds to grow on. (I've never had a block of tamarind go bad on me.)

Tamarind contains lots of inedible fibers and seeds, so you need to prepare it with hot water before using it. Here's how you do it.

Step 1 • Add Hot Water

Break off as much tamarind as you need, place it in a bowl, then add a roughly equal quantity of hot water.

Step 2 • Massage

Massage the tamarind with your fingertips to loosen the pulp. Keep going, breaking up any large masses of pulp you feel. In the end it should feel like very loose, squishy mud with fibers running through it (and, depending on the brand, some hard, woody seeds).

Step 3 • Strain It

Scrape the pulp out into a fine-mesh strainer set over a clean bowl, then, using a rubber spatula, push the pulp through the strainer, going back and forth and stopping to scrape the inside of the strainer free of excess fibers every once in a while until you've extracted as much concentrated pulp as you can. Discard the fibers and seeds.

Prepared tamarind pulp can be stored in the fridge for several weeks and can be used in place of lime or lemon juice in things like salad dressings, sauces, or cocktails.

ANTS CLIMBING TREES (SICHUAN CELLOPHANE NOODLES WITH PORK AND CHILES)

Yield
Serves 2

Active Time
15 minutes

Total Time
30 minutes

NOTES

Bean thread noodles are also called *cellophane noodles* or *glass noodles*. Look for noodles made with mung bean starch. Red peppercorns can be used in place of green. Pick over your peppercorns to make sure there are no twigs or shiny black seeds. You can use store-bought or homemade hot pickled chiles (see the recipe on page 84) or use a fresh Thai bird, serrano, or jalapeño in its place. For best results, use Pixian doubanjiang imported from Sichuan. You can find it online or at a good Chinese supermarket.

INGREDIENTS

For the Noodles:

4 ounces (120 g) dry bean thread noodles (see Notes)

For the Sauce:

2 tablespoons (30 ml) light soy sauce
1 teaspoon (5 ml) dark soy sauce
1 teaspoon (4 g) sugar
½ cup (120 ml) homemade or store-bought low-sodium chicken stock or water

For the Stir-Fry:

¼ cup (60 ml) peanut, rice bran, soybean oil, or roasted rapeseed oil (caiziyou)
1 tablespoon (5 g) green Sichuan peppercorns (see Notes)
4 ounces (120 g) ground pork
4 teaspoons (10 g) minced garlic (about 4 medium cloves)
3 scallions, minced, a few tablespoons of greens reserved separately for garnish
1 pickled chile, minced (see Notes)
2 tablespoons (24 g) Sichuan broad bean chile paste (doubanjiang)
Small handful of chopped fresh cilantro

When it comes to evocative food names, it's a toss-up between the Chinese and the British. For every Toad in the Hole, Rumbledethump, or Eaton Mess in the United Kingdom, there's an Egg Flower Soup, Drunk Chicken, or Ants Climbing Trees in China. (Meanwhile we're stuck with good ol' Spam, Rocky Mountain Oysters, and S&%t on a Shingle here in the United States).

When I worked as a test cook at *Cook's Illustrated*, about once a week some of my fellow test cooks and I would take a trip to Sichuan Garden on Washington Street in Brookline Village (it's since been converted to the trendy Blossom Bar, where the original owner's son has kept the Sichuan menu, even with its new cocktail-forward, clubby vibe) where we'd order plates of beef tripe in a roasted chile vinaigrette, dry-fried green beans, and *ma yi shang shu*—Ants Climbing Trees—a dish so-named because of the way little bits of pork cling to the cellophane noodles as you lift them.

There are two variations of this dish, a drier version in which the noodles are very briefly stir-fried in oil flavored with pork, Sichuan pepper, Sichuan broad bean chile paste (doubanjiang), soy sauce, and aromatics, and a wet version that starts the same way but includes a good amount of chicken stock for the noodles to simmer in. The dry version can be quite difficult to manage (bean thread noodles tend to get very clumpy and sticky), so I usually go for the wet version. I love the way the noodles absorb the broth and turn almost jelly-like while still retaining their elastic chew.

DIRECTIONS

1. **For the Noodles:** Place the noodles in a bowl and cover with very hot water. Let soak until pliable and tender, about 15 minutes. Drain and set aside.

2. **For the Sauce:** Combine the soy sauces, sugar, and chicken stock in a small bowl and stir until the sugar is dissolved.

3. **BEFORE YOU STIR-FRY, GET YOUR BOWLS READY:**

   a. Sichuan peppercorns
   b. Pork
   c. Garlic, scallions, pickled chile, and broad bean chile paste
   d. Sauce
   e. Noodles
   f. Serving platter

4. **For the Stir-Fry:** Heat the oil in a wok over high heat until shimmering. Add the Sichuan peppercorns and cook, stirring, until fragrant, about 10 seconds. Immediately add the pork and stir-fry until the pork is cooked through and starting to brown lightly in spots, about 2 minutes.

(5) Add the garlic, scallions, pickled chile, and broad bean chile paste and stir-fry until fragrant and the fat has become a deep red, about 45 seconds. Add the sauce.

(6) When the sauce is simmering, add the noodles to the wok, laying them on top of the pork. Let them rest without moving for 30 seconds to absorb some of the sauce, then gently lift and fold the noodles and sauce on the bottom over the top. Do not stir too vigorously or the noodles may become sticky. When the sauce is mostly absorbed and reduced, fold in the reserved scallions greens and chopped cilantro. Transfer to a serving platter and serve.

4

FRYING

Why don't people deep-fry at home more often? The most common answers I hear are: it's messy, it's expensive ("What do I do with all the leftover oil?"), it's dangerous, and it's unhealthy.

Well, a wok can certainly help solve your first three problems, and we'll discuss how in detail. You're on your own for the fourth. Frying adds fat to your food, period. Contrary to the popular myth that frying at a high enough temperature reduces the amount of oil food absorbs, the opposite is in fact the case: the crisper and less soggy your fried food tastes, the more oil it has likely absorbed during cooking (and we'll get to the explanation shortly). If you're worried about the health aspects, eat a smaller portion of your General Tso's chicken or invite five friends over before you make a dozen fried spring rolls so that you're limited to two. Even better, get a gym membership or add a dog or a child to the family and burn those calories chasing them down to make sure that things not meant to be peed on are not peed on.

In this chapter we'll cover panfrying, dry frying, and deep frying in their various incarnations, including breaded, dredged, and battered foods and foods that you fry naked (that is, the food is naked, not you, unless you feel like living especially dangerously).

4.1 PANFRYING IN A WOK

Panfrying is cooking foods in a layer of oil over moderate heat. Unlike sautéing, which involves frequently tossing small pieces of food to encourage even cooking,* panfried foods are typically cooked at moderate temperatures and flipped infrequently (if at all) to promote the development of an evenly golden brown, crispy crust.

A well-seasoned flat-bottomed wok makes an excellent vessel for panfrying, and all of the panfried recipes in this section can be cooked in one. The gently sloped sides of a wok make it easy to swirl foods around without the risk of their flying out the sides or of oil splattering. It also makes it easy to slip a thin spatula underneath foods to release them.

That said, you can also use a well-seasoned carbon steel or cast iron skillet or a nonstick skillet for any of these recipes.

KOREAN-STYLE PANCAKES (BUCHIMGAE)

It's difficult to think of a simpler, faster recipe than *buchimgae*, the catchall term for panfried Korean pancakes, and there is a huge variety. They can be made from a variety of flours or ground grains—wheat, buckwheat, mung bean, or rice, for instance. They can be crunchy mung bean pancakes stuffed with bracken (an edible fern), pork, bean sprouts, and kimchi (*nokdu buchimgae*), or they can be as thin as individual cabbage leaves with a light coating of batter (*baechu buchimgae*). They can be bright red from kimchi juice and chile flakes (*kimchijeon*) or an orderly forest of dark green scallions bound together with a thin egg batter, as in Busan's famous *dongnae pajeon*.

For the simplest, all you need is flour, cornstarch, cold water, and a mix-in or two, and within ten minutes of setting foot in the kitchen you've got yourself an after-school snack, a light lunch, or a landing pad at the base of your stomach for a night of *makgeolli* (unfiltered Korean rice wine).

Aside from being simple, they're extremely adaptable. Whether you've got half a zucchini, a chunk of onion, a bunch of scallions, some wilty kale, a carrot a bit past its prime; whether it's the odd slice of bacon, chunk of ham, or bit of ground meat; whether it's frozen shrimp, fresh squid, or the end of a jar of kimchi languishing in the fridge, they will be right at home in a Korean pancake.

Recipes for wheat-flour-based Korean pancake batter can vary a bit as far as batter ingredients go, and because they're so easy and inexpensive to make, it's worth starting with my recipe and then experimenting a bit to arrive at a formula that works best for you.

Some recipes call for 100 percent wheat flour, which produces pancakes that are chewy and dense due to the gluten that develops when you mix wheat

---

* You can think of sautéing as analogous to stir-frying, but typically done over relatively lower heat with the goal of evenly cooking and softening vegetables or pieces of meat, without the hard searing or smokiness associated with stir-fries.

proteins with water. If you prefer your pancakes a little lighter and crisper, adding cornstarch or potato starch will help (I like a ratio of four parts wheat flour to one part starch by volume). Adding eggs to your batter will cause them to puff and rise a bit as they fry, resulting in a texture somewhere between an omelet and a thick crepe. Using soda water in place of regular water will create a pancake with lacier edges and a slightly puffy internal texture. Adding baking powder gives you something very close to a fluffy, Western-style pancake. (I prefer leaving the eggs and baking powder out, as I enjoy the elastic stretch of an unleavened pancake, though sometimes I'll use soda water in place of still.)

Whatever additional ingredients you add, there are two cardinal rules when making Korean pancake batter: the water must be cold (even ice cold, if you want to be exacting), and mixing should be minimal. Both of these steps ensure that you don't form too much gluten in the batter, which leads to tough, leaden pancakes. Buchimgae batter should also be significantly thinner than American-style pancake batter. It should flow off of a spoon like wet paint when you lift it up out of the mixing bowl. As for ratio of batter to mix-ins, I like to keep the batter as light as possible; the bulk of the pancake should be vegetables, seafood, or meat, with just enough batter to hold it all together.

Here's something neat: in virtually every recipe I can think of, Korean cabbage kimchi and German sauerkraut can be exchanged freely without fundamentally breaking the recipes. Try making sauerkraut pancakes or putting kimchi on your hot dog or Reuben next time. Your taste buds will be tingled and your senses enlivened. It will be a positive experience for all involved.

KIMCHI OR SAUERKRAUT BUCHIMGAE (KOREAN-STYLE PANCAKES)

Yield
Serves 4

Active Time
15 minutes

Total Time
30 minutes

NOTES

If you don't have enough kimchi juice, make up the difference in more cold water. Gochugaru are Korean chile flakes. They are not very spicy, but you can adjust the heat level of these pancakes by adding more or less or by adding a hotter chile flake or ground chile. These pancakes can be served at room temperature, but you can also keep them warm on a rack set in a rimmed baking sheet in a 200°F (90°C) oven as you cook successive batches until ready to serve. Or better yet, gather in the kitchen and eat them as they come out of the pan.

INGREDIENTS

6 ounces (170 g/about 1 cup) kimchi, thinly
    sliced, plus ¼ cup (60 ml) kimchi juice
    (see Notes)
2 ounces (60 g/about ¼ medium) onion,
    thinly sliced
2 scallions, split lengthwise and cut into
    1½-inch pieces
4 ounces (120 g/about ¾ cup) all-purpose
    flour
1 ounce (30 g/about ¼ cup) cornstarch or
    potato starch
2 teaspoons (8 g) sugar
1 teaspoon (3 g) gochugaru, more or less to
    taste (see Notes)
6 ounces (180 ml/about ¾ cup) cold water
Peanut, rice bran, or other neutral oil, as
    needed for panfrying
Pancake Dipping Sauce (page 391)

These pancakes work best with extra-old kimchi that is quite acidic. For a delicious variation, replace some or all of the kimchi with sauerkraut.

DIRECTIONS

1 Combine the kimchi, kimchi juice, onion, scallions, flour, starch, sugar, gochugaru, and water in a large mixing bowl. Stir rapidly with a spoon just until no dry flour remains (do not overmix the batter). The batter should be thin enough to flow around when you tilt the bowl.

2 Heat 2 tablespoons (30 ml) oil in the bottom of a flat-bottomed wok or an 8- to 10-inch nonstick skillet over medium-high heat until shimmering. Add just enough batter that you can spread it into a thin pancake with the back of a spoon (you should be able to make about two 10-inch pancakes, three 8-inch pancakes, or several smaller pancakes). Let the pancake cook without moving until the bottom of the pancake is set, about 2 minutes. Use a thin metal spatula to gently release the pancake from the pan if it is sticking at all.

3 Continue to cook, swirling the pancake around to encourage even browning until the first side is well browned with a few darker spots, about 5 minutes total. Use a wide spatula to carefully flip the pancake. Continue cooking until the second side is well browned, about 4 minutes longer.

4 Slide the pancake out onto a cutting board. Repeat steps 2 through 4 for the remaining pancake batter. Cut into wedges with a pizza slicer or knife and serve with the dipping sauce.

HAEMUL PAJEON (KOREAN-STYLE SEAFOOD AND SCALLION PANCAKES)

Yield
Serves 4

Active Time
15 minutes

Total Time
30 minutes

NOTE

For the seafood, use any combination of the following: shrimp, peeled, deveined, and cut into bite-sized pieces; squid, cut into thin rings or strips; fresh shucked, canned, or smoked oysters, well drained; fresh shucked clams, roughly chopped, or canned chopped clams, well drained; fresh shucked, canned, or frozen and thawed mussels, well drained. Picked fresh crabmeat, or surimi, roughly chopped; canned tuna or salmon, well drained and broken into chunks.

INGREDIENTS

8 ounces (225 g) mixed seafood (see Note)
6 scallions, split lengthwise and cut into
　　1½-inch pieces
4 ounces (120 g/about ¾ cup) all-purpose
　　flour
1 ounce (30 g/about ¼ cup) cornstarch or
　　potato starch
2 teaspoons (8 g) sugar
6 ounces (180 ml/about ¾ cup) cold water
1 large egg
Peanut, rice bran, or other neutral oil, as
　　needed for panfrying
Pancake Dipping Sauce (page 391)

These seafood and scallion pancakes can be made with any combination of shrimp, sliced squid, oysters, clams, mussels, crab, surimi, or canned tuna or salmon. You can also completely omit the seafood and double the number of scallions to make regular scallion pancakes. These pancakes can be served at room temperature, but you can also keep them warm on a rack set in a rimmed baking sheet in a 200°F (90°C) oven as you cook successive batches until ready to serve. Or better yet, gather in the kitchen and eat them as they come out of the pan.

DIRECTIONS

(1) Combine the seafood, scallions, flour, starch, sugar, water, and egg in a large mixing bowl. Stir rapidly with a spoon just until no dry flour remains (do not overmix the batter). The batter should be thin enough to flow around when you tilt the bowl.

(2) Heat 2 tablespoons (30 ml) oil in the bottom of a flat-bottomed wok or an 8- to 10-inch nonstick skillet over medium-high heat until shimmering. Add just enough batter that you can spread it into a thin pancake with the back of a spoon (you should be able to make about two 10-inch pancakes, three 8-inch pancakes, or several smaller pancakes). Let the pancake cook without moving until the bottom of the pancake is set, about 2 minutes. Use a thin metal spatula to gently release the pancake from the pan if it is sticking at all.

(3) Continue to cook, swirling the pancake around to encourage even browning until the first side is well browned with a few darker spots, about 5 minutes total. Use a wide spatula to carefully flip the pancake. Continue cooking until the second side is well browned, about 4 minutes longer.

(4) Slide the pancake out onto a cutting board. Repeat steps 2 through 4 for remaining pancake batter. Cut into wedges with a pizza slicer or knife and serve with the dipping sauce.

PANCAKE DIPPING SAUCE

Yield
Makes
½ cup

Active Time
2 minutes

Total Time
2 minutes

NOTE
You can adjust the flavor by adding thinly sliced scallions, minced garlic, roasted sesame seeds, or gochugaru (Korean chile flakes) to taste.

INGREDIENTS

3 tablespoons (45 ml) light soy sauce or shoyu
2 tablespoons (30 ml) rice or black vinegar
2 tablespoons (30 ml) water
1 teaspoon (5 ml) roasted sesame oil
1 tablespoon (12 g) sugar
1 scallion, thinly sliced
2 teaspoons minced fresh ginger (about 10 g; optional)

DIRECTIONS

Combine all the ingredients and stir until the sugar dissolves. Store in a sealed container in the refrigerator for up to 2 weeks.

How to Make Extra-Flaky Chinese-Style Scallion Pancakes (Cong You Bing)

Cong you bing ("scallion oil cakes"—i.e., flaky panfried scallion pancakes) were one of the first things I ever taught myself how to cook, way back in high school. Or, I should say, I thought I taught myself how to cook them. I mean, fried dough and scallions, right? How hard could it be?

Of course, at the time I knew nothing of gluten development, laminated pastries, or the like, and the dense, doughy blobs I was coming up with were certainly nowhere near the ideal flaky, crisp, light, multilayered affairs that the best Chinese restaurants serve. But due to an acute case of a horrible syndrome known in medical circles as *Imadethismyselfsoitmusttasteawesomosis*, I was totally oblivious to my quite obvious failure.

Here's what I did, in six easy steps:

Step 1: Combine flour and water until workable dough is formed.

Step 2: Knead a lot (I heard that kneading is good).

Step 3: Add scallions.

Step 4: Knead some more.

Step 5: Roll out with a rolling pin and fry.

Step 6: Serve with tons of salt, vinegar, and soy sauce to distract from leaden texture.

Fast-forward five or six years to me sitting in the living room watching an episode of *Yan Can Cook*, my mind rapidly being blown. This episode? Scallion pancakes, the way they're supposed to be made. The process is honestly quite simple, and ingenious. It combines two unique features: hot water dough and lamination. Here's how they work.

HOT WATER DOUGH

With most Western breads and pastries, cold or room-temperature liquid is added to flour before kneading it to develop gluten, the protein network that gives bread its springy, elastic structure. A ball of well-kneaded cold water dough will spring back if you press it and contract if you stretch it. This is why, for example, pizza dough is extremely hard to roll out until it's had at least a couple hours to rest and allow this gluten to relax.

Hot water doughs—the type used to make scallion pancakes, dumpling wrappers, Mandarin pancakes, and several other Chinese pastries—work a little differently. By adding boiling water directly to flour, you actually end up not only denaturing the proteins but smashing them into small pieces. Some degree of gluten can still form, but because cooked proteins aren't nearly as stretchy or clingy as raw ones, you won't get anywhere near the stretch or elasticity of a cold-water dough.

If airy, hole-filled bread is your goal, this is a bad thing. If, on the other hand, you're looking for tender dumpling wrappers or scallion pancakes with just a bit of tug and chew, that's precisely what you want. The beauty of a hot water dough is that it doesn't bounce back as much as a cold water dough does. This makes it extremely easy to work with and roll out. Think: play-dough. A positive boon when you've got fifty dumpling wrappers to form or when you're making scallion pancakes.

The other interesting part of scallion pancakes is the rolling method.

LAMINATED PASTRIES

Though the most famous laminated pastry in the world is probably the croissant, I'd venture to guess that scallion pancakes are the most widely consumed. What exactly is a laminated pastry? Well, unlike bread leavened biologically with yeast or quick breads leavened chemically with baking soda or baking powder, a laminated dough is leavened via fat and vapor. It consists of two basic elements: layers of lean dough separated by layers of fat.

The lean dough can be either completely unleavened (as with puff pastry, scallion pancakes, phyllo, or *pâte a brick*), leavened with yeast (as with croissants and Danish), or leavened with baking powder (as with some types of flaky, layered biscuits), each one giving you a slightly different end result. Likewise, the fat layers can be any number of fats, such as olive oil (for certain phyllo recipes), butter (for puff pastry), or, for the case of scallion pancakes, a thin sesame oil and flour paste.

The idea is that the increasingly thin layers of pastry separated with equally thin layers of fat, will separate and puff as water converts to steam and expands between the layers. It's this separating that creates the flaky, tender structure of perfect laminate pastry. With some laminate pastries, these layers are created linearly. Phyllo, for example, is built up one layer at a time, the cook manually brushing butter or oil onto each sheet before laying on the next. It's a relatively easy but time-consuming process.

Others, like puff pastry, use the power of mathematics to very quickly build up hundreds, or even thousands, of layers. Here's how it works: A thin, even slab of butter is placed on top of a layer of dough, which is then folded over the butter to completely enclose it like an envelope. Next, the entire thing gets folded into thirds and then rolled out again into the same size and shape—where you once had one layer, now you've got three. Repeat this process again, and you're up to nine layers. Most puff pastry recipes recommend a bare minimum of four folding iterations, giving you a total of 81 layers. With extremely careful handling and a cold marble surface to work on, you can fold up to eight times, which gets you a whopping 6,561 layers. Yay math!

Scallion pancakes are made by a similar method. Rather than folding over and over, the flat disks of dough are first brushed with sesame oil and flour paste, sprinkled with scallions, then rolled up, jelly-roll style. After rolling, you coil the log like a rattlesnake before flattening it out again, this time with the scallions tucked nearly inside. This technique gives you roughly three to five layers of dough. A quick fry in hot oil later and you're done. Crispy, slightly chewy, flaky, and delicious.

Want even more layers? No problem: just repeat the process to increase the number of layers by the power of two. Roll with a rolling pin into a flat circle, brush with the oil mixture, roll up like a jelly roll, coil like a snake, roll with a rolling pin a second time, brush with more oil mixture, spread with scallions, roll up like a jelly roll and coil like a snake again, then finally roll it out a third time and panfry it.

Moderate heat with a good amount of oil and constant swirling is the best way to get even browning and discrete, flaky layers.

CHINESE-STYLE SCALLION PANCAKES

Yield
Makes 4
pancakes

Active Time
15 minutes

Total Time
30 minutes

NOTES

You can make this recipe without the food processor. Just stir the flour with a wooden spoon or chopsticks in a large bowl as you add the boiling water. After it comes together, turn it out onto a floured work surface and knead for 5 minutes until satiny and smooth. Proceed as instructed. Pancakes can be made through the end of step 4, then frozen for long-term storage. Freeze flat on a rimmed baking sheet or plate, and once frozen, transfer them to a zipper-lock freezer bag, separating the pancakes with a layer of parchment or foil. Let the pancakes thaw at room temperature before panfrying.

INGREDIENTS

For the Dough:

10 ounces (285 g/about 2 cups) all-purpose flour, plus extra for dusting the work surface
1 cup (240 ml) boiling water

For the Oil Mixture:

¼ cup (60 ml) roasted sesame oil
2 tablespoons (0.6 ounce/18 g) all-purpose flour

To Cook:

2 cups thinly sliced scallion greens (about 12 scallions/100 g)
Peanut, rice bran, or other neutral oil, as needed for panfrying
Kosher salt

To Serve:

Pancake Dipping Sauce (page 391)

DIRECTIONS

(1) For the Dough: Place the flour in the bowl of a food processor (see Notes). With the processor running, slowly drizzle in about ¾ cup (180 ml) of the boiling water. Process for 15 seconds. If the dough does not come together and ride around the blade, drizzle in more water a tablespoon (15 ml) at a time until it just comes together. Transfer to a floured work surface and knead a few times to form a smooth ball. Transfer to a bowl, cover with a damp towel or plastic wrap, and allow to rest for at least 30 minutes at room temperature and up to overnight in the fridge.

(2) For the Oil Mixture: Combine sesame oil and flour in a small bowl and stir with chopsticks or a spoon.

(3) To Cook: Divide the dough into 4 equal pieces and roll each into a smooth ball. Working with one ball at a time, roll out into a disk 8 to 10 inches in diameter on a lightly floured surface. Using a pastry brush, paint a very thin layer of the sesame oil mixture over the top of the disk. Roll the disk up like a jelly roll, then twist the roll into a tight spiral, tucking the end underneath. Flatten gently with your hand, then reroll into an 8- to 10-inch disk.

(4) Paint with another layer of sesame oil mixture, sprinkle with one-quarter of the scallions, and roll up like a jelly roll again. Twist into a spiral, flatten gently, and reroll into a 7-inch disk (about 18 cm; it should just fit in the bottom of your pan).

(5) Heat 2 tablespoons (30 ml) of the oil in a flat-bottomed wok or an 8-inch carbon steel, cast iron, or nonstick skillet over medium-high heat until shimmering and carefully slip the pancake into the hot oil. Cook, shaking the pan gently, until the first side is an even golden brown, about 2 minutes. Carefully flip with a spatula or tongs (be careful not to splash the oil) and continue to cook, shaking the pan gently, until the second side is an even golden brown, about 2 minutes longer. Transfer to a paper-towel-lined plate to drain. Season with salt and cut into 6 wedges. Serve immediately with sauce for dipping. Repeat steps 3–5 with the remaining pancakes.

Scallion Pancakes, Step by Step

CHEESY SCALLION PANCAKES

Yield
Makes 4
pancakes

Active Time
15 minutes

Total Time
30 minutes

NOTES

You can make this recipe without the food processor. Just stir the flour with a wooden spoon or chopsticks in a large bowl as you add the boiling water. After it comes together, turn it out onto a floured work surface and knead for 5 minutes until satiny and smooth. Proceed as instructed. The pancakes can be made through the end of step 4, then frozen for long-term storage. Freeze flat on a rimmed baking sheet or plate, and once frozen, transfer to a zipper-lock freezer bag, separating pancakes with a layer of parchment or foil. Let the pancakes thaw at room temperature before panfrying.

INGREDIENTS

For the Dough:

10 ounces (285 g/about 2 cups) all-purpose flour, plus extra for dusting the work surface
1 cup (240 ml) boiling water

For the Oil Mixture:

¼ cup (60 ml) canola oil
2 tablespoons (0.6 ounce/18 g) all-purpose flour

To Cook:

2 cups thinly sliced scallion greens (about 12 scallions/100 g)
8 ounces (225 g) Cheddar cheese, grated
Peanut, rice bran, or other neutral oil
Kosher salt

To Serve:

Pancake Dipping Sauce (page 391)

This recipe was birthed in my kitchen fully formed one night around 2:00 a.m. while I was taking a break from a writing project. I was rummaging through my fridge and found a whole slew of leftover scallions from my scallion pancake testing, along with a block of extra-sharp cheddar cheese. Cheddar-scallion biscuits are great, so why not cheddar and scallion *bing*? I put two and two together in the form of a cheddar scallion pancake.

Once you've got the basic scallion pancake rolling method down, it's really easy to customize. Other than adding cheese, the only real difference here is swapping out roasted sesame oil for neutral canola oil—sesame oil and cheese seemed a bit much.

Rolled up, twisted, flattened into a pancake, and fried, it comes out something like fried quesadilla, but with the flaky, light layers of a scallion pancake. You won't be able to roll these quite as thin as a normal scallion pancake, so they'll take a couple extra minutes per side to cook through. Using the same technique, you can add a wide variety of fillings to your scallion pancakes, such as a ground pork and shrimp mixture ("The Mix," page 280).

DIRECTIONS

1 **For the Dough:** Place the flour in the bowl of a food processor (see Notes). With the processor running, slowly drizzle in about ¾ cup (180 ml) of the boiling water. Process for 15 seconds. If the dough does not come together and ride around the blade, drizzle in more water a tablespoon (15 ml) at a time until it just comes together. Transfer to a floured work surface and knead a few times to form a smooth ball. Transfer to a bowl, cover with a damp towel or plastic wrap, and allow to rest for 30 minutes at room temperature or up to overnight in the fridge.

2 **For the Oil Mixture:** Combine the canola oil and flour in a small bowl and stir with chopsticks or a spoon.

3 **To Cook:** Combine the scallions and cheese in a medium bowl and toss until well mixed.

4 Divide the dough into 4 equal pieces and roll each into a smooth ball. Working with one ball at a time, roll out into a disk 8 to 10 inches in diameter on a lightly floured surface. Using a pastry brush, paint a very thin layer of the sesame oil mixture over the top of the disk. Roll the disk up like a jelly roll, then twist the roll into a tight spiral, tucking the end underneath. Flatten gently with your hand, then reroll into an 8- to 10-inch disk.

(5) Paint with another layer of sesame oil mixture, sprinkle with one-quarter of the scallion and cheese mixture, and roll up like a jelly roll again. Twist into a spiral, flatten gently, and reroll into a 7-inch disk (about 18 cm, it should just fit in the bottom of your pan).

(6) Heat 2 tablespoons (30 ml) oil in a flat-bottomed wok or an 8-inch carbon steel, cast iron, or nonstick skillet over medium-high heat until shimmering and carefully slip the pancake into the hot oil. Cook, shaking the pan gently, until the first side is an even golden brown, about 2 minutes. Carefully flip with a spatula or tongs (be careful not to splash the oil), and continue to cook, shaking the pan gently, until the second side is an even golden brown, about 2 minutes longer. Transfer to a paper-towel-lined plate to drain. Season with salt and cut into 6 wedges. Serve immediately with sauce for dipping. Repeat steps 4–6 with the remaining pancakes.

Pork- and Shrimp-Stuffed Scallion Pancakes

The idea for stuffing a scallion pancake with pork and shrimp came from my friend and early cooking inspiration Ming Tsai, who made pancakes like these when we filmed an episode of his show *Simply Ming* together.

Stir-fry 8 ounces (225 g) of "The Mix" (page 280) with 1 tablespoon (15 ml) peanut, rice bran, or other neutral oil in your wok over high heat, breaking it up with a spatula, until the pork and shrimp are just barely cooked through. Drain the mixture well, toss it with the thinly sliced scallions before step 3 of the Chinese-Style Scallion Pancakes (page 394), then continue with the recipe as instructed, stuffing the pancakes with the pork/shrimp/scallion mixture instead of plain scallions. Serve with the dipping sauce

SCALLION PANCAKE BREAKFAST SANDWICHES

Yield
Serves 2

Active Time
15 minutes

Total Time
15 minutes

INGREDIENTS

4 ounces (120 g) bacon, cut into ½-inch pieces

1 raw Chinese-Style Scallion Pancake (page 394)

3 ounces (90 g) Cheddar cheese, grated

1 tablespoon (15 g) unsalted butter

2 large eggs

Kosher salt and freshly ground black pepper

Flatbreads and pancakes folded or wrapped around various fillings is a breakfast staple throughout Taiwan and parts of China. *Jianbing* are thin crêpes filled with fried egg and brushed with hoisin sauce and chile oil. Scallion pancakes can come topped with a fried egg. In Los Angeles, Taiwanese immigrants stuffed *laobing* (the generic term for any flaky, layered, unleavened pancake or flatbread) with braised beef, cucumbers, and greens, creating what's now known as the "Shandong beef roll."

At Mei Mei in Boston, siblings Irene, Andrew, and Margaret Li use scallion pancakes as the vehicle for a wide range of sandwiches, including their "Double Awesome," a scallion pancake brushed with pesto, layered with melted Cheddar cheese, then folded around a fried egg with a runny yolk.

For my scallion pancake breakfast sandwich, I like to add a bit of bacon to the mix, browning it in my wok, then using the rendered bacon fat to fry the pancakes.

Having a stack of thaw-and-cook pancakes in your freezer at all times makes this a quick and easy brunch or lunch item. You can freeze homemade raw scallion pancakes, but even store-bought frozen scallion pancakes can be truly excellent, and they cook directly from frozen (look for them in the freezer aisle of a good Asian supermarket).

DIRECTIONS

(1) Heat the bacon in a wok over medium-high heat. Cook, stirring frequently, until the bacon is rendered and crisp, about 4 minutes. Use a slotted spoon to transfer the bacon to a small bowl.

(2) Cook a scallion pancake in bacon fat, following the cooking instructions in step 5 of the Chinese-Style Scallion Pancake recipe (page 394), omitting the oil. After flipping the pancake, spread the cheese and bacon evenly over the top to melt while the second side cooks.

(3) Meanwhile, melt the butter in a cast iron, carbon steel, or nonstick skillet over medium-high heat, swirling until the foaming subsides. Add the eggs and cook to the desired doneness, flipping them halfway through the cooking if desired. Season with salt and pepper.

(4) Place one egg on each of the two quadrants on the right side of the pancake, then fold the left side of the pancake over the eggs. Slide the folded pancake with eggs out onto a cutting board, then cut in between the eggs with a sharp knife, separating the pancake into two triangular sandwiches. Serve immediately.

A Better, Faster, Easier Way to Freeze and Defrost Foods

Freezers are great for long-term storage, but they're useful only when you can defrost food quickly with minimal loss of quality. So what's the secret?

Well, time and air are the biggest enemies of frozen food. When food freezes slowly, large ice crystals form inside it. These jagged crystals can damage cell structure, which in turn causes the food to become mushy and wet after defrosting. Meanwhile, direct exposure to air leads to sublimation, which is the phase change from solid ice directly to gaseous water vapor that's responsible for freezer burn. The key to better-quality frozen food is to minimize the time it takes for your food to freeze and defrost, which means freezing flat to maximize the ratio of surface area to volume.

The shape in which you freeze your food makes a remarkable difference. To demonstrate this, I froze two separate containers, each holding a quart of water. I froze one quart in a cylindrical deli container and the other flat in a zipper-lock bag. I then placed both on the counter and let them defrost for 45 minutes. After 45 minutes, I poured out the melted water.

The ice frozen as a cylinder produced less than a cup of water. Meanwhile, the ice frozen flat produced over two cups. That's right: It defrosted more than twice as fast (and, conversely, it also froze more than twice as fast)! This can make a huge difference not just for the quality of your food, but also for convenience.

HOW TO FREEZE FOODS FLAT

For each of these methods, be sure to use a zipper-lock bag that's specifically labeled as a freezer bag, since regular zipper-lock bags are made of thinner-gauge plastic that is actually air-permeable and will not prevent freezer burn over time.

For Semisolids, Like Ground Meat and Stews

To freeze malleable solids and semisolids, like ground meat or a thick sauce, transfer your food to a zipper-lock bag. The easiest and neatest way to do this is to first label your bag with the date and the food you're going to put inside using a permanent marker. Flip the lip of the bag inside out, so that you can add food to it without the risk of getting gunk in the zipper seal. Once the bag is full, unfold the lip and seal the bag most of the way, leaving about an inch unsealed. Then squeeze out as much air as you can, working from the bottom corner opposite the opening, up toward the open seal. Once all the air is pushed out, seal up the bag, then push the contents into a flat layer. Place it on a small rimmed aluminum baking sheet and transfer it to the freezer, making sure it stays flat until it's completely frozen solid.

For Liquids, Like Soup and Stock

To store liquids, label your bag, then, starting with the bag upright, fold the edge over to give it stability (if you have a conveniently sized container, you can place the bag in the container and fold the lip over the edge of the container to keep it even more stable), and pour the liquid in. Again, seal all but an inch of the bag, then slowly lay the bag out flat, pushing the air toward the opening in the seal as you do. Seal the bag just as the last of the air escapes, transfer to a small rimmed aluminum baking sheet and freeze.

The other nice thing about freezing flat is that it helps you keep your freezer organized. Once frozen, the bags can be stacked on top of each other, or, if you prefer, stored sideways, LP record style, allowing you to flip through with ease.

For Firm Solids, Like Chicken Pieces or Steaks

Firm foods, like steaks, shrimp, and chicken pieces, may not freeze truly flat, so your best bet is to arrange them in a single layer, then remove the air from the bags. You can, of course, use a vacuum sealer, but those bags are pricey, and not everyone has a vacuum sealer at home. Instead, you can use a regular zipper-lock freezer bag, some water, and a technique called the water displacement method.

To do it, label your bag, then place your food inside and partially seal the bag, leaving just the last inch or so of the seal open. Next, lower the bag into a pot or a tub of water. As the bag is lowered, water pressure will push air out of it through the small opening you've left. Just before the bag is completely submerged, seal off that opening and pull the whole bag out of the tub. (And don't waste the water! It's perfectly safe to use for cooking or watering the garden.)

For Better Defrosting, Use Aluminum

When it comes time to defrost your food, transferring it to the fridge for a night works, but what if you're in a hurry? Running it under cold water in the sink is often recommended, but, at least where I live, water is a scarce resource, so I prefer another option: an aluminum tray.

Aluminum is one of the best conductors of heat in your kitchen. It's great at heating food quickly and evenly (that's why tri-ply pans have an aluminum core), but it's also great at channeling heat from the air into your defrosting food. I placed two identical frozen steaks on my counter, one on a wooden cutting board and the other on an aluminum tray. The one on the tray defrosted in less than half the time needed for the one on the cutting board. That's good news for quality and for safety, not to mention for your busy schedule.

The aluminum trick works equally well with foods frozen flat as it does with firmer foods, like steak, chops, fish, and shrimp—basically anything you've got that needs defrosting, including those scallion pancakes.

PANFRIED "GARLIC KNOT" PANCAKES

Yield
Serves 4

Active Time
30 minutes

Total Time
2½ hours

INGREDIENTS

12 ounces (340 g) homemade or store-
bought pizza dough

For the Filling:

2 tablespoons (30 g) unsalted butter
2 tablespoons (30 ml) extra virgin olive oil
6 medium garlic cloves (15 to 20 g),
smashed and roughly chopped
Pinch of kosher salt
½ ounce (15 g) fresh parsley, basil, or
cilantro leaves, minced (about ⅓ cup)
Vegetable or olive oil Grated Parmesan
cheese
Marinara sauce (or ranch dressing, if you
insist*) for dipping

---

* You heathen.

When I was growing up in New York, at least twice a week my lunch or dinner consisted of a slice of pizza and a couple of garlic knots. I picked my pizzeria based on those knots. The best were at Pizza Town II, a long-gone pizzeria on Broadway that always had a metal bowl full of plump knots, glistening in garlicky butter and dusted with Parmesan cheese, in the pizza display case, right underneath the autographed Paul McCartney Wings Over America tour poster. At $1.50 for a plain slice, adding three garlic knots for 50¢ was a no-brainer.

Those garlic knots are a great way for pizzerias to get extra mileage out of leftover pizza dough. One afternoon, I found myself in a similar situation, with a few extra ounces of pizza dough leftover in the fridge from the previous day's pizza party. Not wanting to fire up the oven, I wondered if I'd be able to panfry the pizza dough instead. It occurred to me that garlic knots, made by brushing pizza dough with fat and then reshaping them, are not that fundamentally different from Chinese scallion pancakes.

This led me to the idea of brushing pizza dough with garlic butter, shaping it into a flat, twisted flatbread (just like scallion pancakes), then panfrying it. The results were even better than I expected, with the fluffy, chewy pull of pizza dough, the crisp golden brown texture of panfried pancakes, and plenty of buttery, garlic- and Parmesan-scented layers.

There are a couple things to look out for. First is to make sure the pancakes have ample time to rest and rise before being fried to ensure the pancakes come out puffy and light. Second is that the pancakes have a tendency to puff up and lose contact with the wok as they fry. Careful flipping and popping the largest bubbles can mitigate this issue.

DIRECTIONS

(1) Divide the pizza dough in half and roll each into a smooth ball. Place on a countertop and cover each ball with a layer of plastic wrap followed by an overturned bowl. Let rest for 1 hour.

(2) **Meanwhile, Make the Filling:** Heat the butter and olive oil in a wok over medium heat until the butter melts and the foaming subsides. Add the garlic, season with the salt, and cook, stirring, until fragrant, about 1 minute. Add the parsley and stir to combine. Transfer to a bowl to cool.

(3) Working with one dough ball at a time, roll out the dough on a lightly oiled countertop into a circle about 8 inches in diameter. Using a spoon, spread one-quarter of the garlic/Parmesan mixture over the top of the disk. Roll disk up like a jelly roll, then twist the roll into a tight spiral,

recipe continues

tucking the end underneath. Flatten gently with your hand, then reroll into an 8-inch disk. Repeat with the second dough ball. Cover the disks with plastic wrap and let rise at room temperature until roughly doubled in volume, about 1 hour longer.

(4) When ready to cook, heat ¼ cup (60 ml) oil in a flat-bottomed wok or a 10-inch carbon steel, cast iron, or nonstick skillet over medium-high heat until shimmering and carefully slip pancake into the hot oil. Cook, shaking the pan gently until the first side is an even golden brown, about 3 minutes, using tongs or a small spatula to release air trapped underneath and pressing down any bubbles that may form (you may need to make a tear in the pancake to let air escape from underneath if it is puffing excessively). Carefully flip with a spatula or tongs (be careful not to splash the oil) and continue to cook, shaking the pan gently, until the second side is an even golden brown, about 3 minutes longer. Transfer to a paper-towel-lined plate to drain. Repeat with the second pancake.

(5) Brush the cooked pancakes with the remaining garlic mixture and dust with Parmesan. Cut into wedges and serve immediately with marinara sauce for dipping.

EASY TORTILLA "JIAN BING"

Yield
Serves 1

Active Time
10 minutes

Total Time
10 minutes

NOTE
Feel free to add any kind of filling to these folded sandwiches, including strips of fried chicken, bacon, ham, extra scrambled eggs, greens, or stir-fried corn.

INGREDIENTS

1 tablespoon (15 ml) peanut, rice bran, or other neutral oil

One 8- to 10-inch flour tortilla

1 large egg

1 scallion, thinly sliced

Small handful of fresh cilantro leaves and fine stems, roughly chopped

Small sprinkle white or black sesame seeds

Pinch of kosher salt

2 teaspoons (10 ml) hoisin sauce

2 teaspoons (10 ml) homemade (page 310) or store-bought chile oil

July 19, 2014, Beijing, China:

This morning we had jian bing, *the Chinese-style egg-filled crepes found in every major metropolitan city in the country, for breakfast. It's a dish so damn delicious that I can't fathom why it hasn't become a staple food in Chinatowns all across the U.S.* It's essentially a batter-based crepe cooked with an egg smeared into one side, along with cilantro and scallions, that then gets brushed with a few sauces (hoisin or a similar bean sauce and a ground chile oil), then folded up, often with a* baocui *inside. The baocui is a puffed, crisply fried cracker that's a specialty of Beijing.*

Essentially what you've got is a bit of crisp carb wrapped in soft carb action. We ordered ours with a piece of battered fried chicken wrapped up in there with the cracker. As the whole thing steams, the inner cracker softens a bit, but you still get an awesome mix of texture and flavors.

In the intervening years since I wrote that travel diary entry, I've seen jian bing vendors start popping up in the United States on both coasts, so at least a few people had the same idea.

At home, I've taken to making a quick, cheaty version of the dish using store-bought flour tortillas.

To make it, I start by panfrying a flour tortilla in the bottom of my wok. Meanwhile, I whisk together an egg with some cilantro and scallions, which I then pour over the tortilla and spread around with the edge of a spatula until the tortilla is coated in a layer of the egg mixture. As soon as the first side is crisp, I flip the whole thing over, egg side down, to fry.

Finally, I flip it again and brush the egg with some hoisin sauce and chile oil before folding it up into a neat triangle. More adventurous cooks can try folding the tortilla with the egg layer on the outside for a more authentic take. It's not quite as glorious as the crepe-based original, but it's got texture, flavor, and is a fantastic (and fantastically quick) breakfast or snack in its own right.

recipe continues

---

*   Or perhaps it has and I just don't know where to look.

DIRECTIONS

(1) Heat the oil in a flat-bottomed wok or a carbon steel, cast iron, or nonstick skillet over medium heat until shimmering. Add the tortilla.

(2) As the tortilla cooks, whisk together the egg, scallion, cilantro, sesame seeds, and salt in a small bowl. Pour the mixture on top of the tortilla and spread it around into a thin, even layer using a rubber spatula or the end of a metal spatula. Continue cooking until the tortilla is golden brown and crisp on the first side, about 3 minutes total. Flip the whole thing over so that the egg is facing down. Reduce the heat to medium-low, and cook until the egg is set, about 30 seconds. Flip the tortilla again so the egg side is up.

(3) Brush the egg with hoisin sauce and chile oil. Fold the whole thing in half to form a semicircle, then in half again, forming a quarter-circle. Slide it out of the pan, wrap with a napkin, and eat it with your hands.

Panfried Dumplings

My earliest cooking memories involve sitting cross-legged on the worn-out, seventies-style bright orange shag carpet at the low, wide Japanese oak table in our living room. Every couple months, my mom would plant me and my sisters there in front of the television with a bowl of gyoza filling and a stack of store-bought dumpling wrappers. Rather than the traditional pork filling, my mom made hers with ground beef—the stretch of Riverside Drive by our apartment, between the Cotton Club and 132nd Street, used to be home to a number of large-scale meat cutters and butcher shops, and hamburger was cheap. My sisters and I would sit there, stuffing and folding dumplings, placing them in neat rows on baking sheets.

My mom would panfry a batch of them for dinner that night, deep-fry some to stick in our lunch boxes the next day, and freeze the rest. We'd eat them every other week or so until the supply was depleted and we'd make a new batch.

That Japanese oak table, which my grandparents shipped over from Japan in the seventies, is now in my living room in Seattle. We don't have a TV in our living room, but I still use it to stuff dumplings, and ever since reaching "big kid" age, my daughter, Alicia, helps make them. (She's been an expert at eating them for years.)

The world of fillings-stuffed-into-dough-then-steamed-boiled-or-fried is vast, stretching from Japanese *gyoza* to Chinese *guo tie* and *har gao*, to Tibetan *momos*, Turkish *manti*, or even Polish *pierogi*. There's something extraordinarily satisfying about biting into a perfect dumpling—the tug of dough, the burst of steam, that first hit of flavorful filling—that seems to surpass cultural boundaries. Have you ever met anyone who doesn't like dumplings? Didn't think so.

The hardest part of making dumplings at home is forming and rolling out the dough, and it's not 100 percent necessary—after all, the gyoza we made growing up were made with store-bought wrappers, as is typical of the Japanese gyoza, whether homemade or from a restaurant. Thicker Chinese-style store-bought wrappers also work just fine for Chinese guo tie or *jiao zi*.

That said, even homemade wrappers are not particularly hard to do. Like scallion pancakes, dumpling wrappers are made with a hot water dough, which behaves much more like a thick paste than a stretchy bread dough. It's malleable stuff that doesn't snap back, making it easy to roll out into even, thin circles with the help of a small rolling pin or wooden dowel (even a beer or wine bottle will do in a pinch). After steaming or boiling, it becomes slightly translucent, with a pleasant springiness that contrasts with a crunchy base when fried.

HOW TO STUFF AND SHAPE DUMPLINGS

Before starting to form dumplings, you need to set up a work space to make the process more efficient (believe me, after years of doing this the inefficient way, I can tell you how much of a difference good mise en place makes).

Here's what you'll want for each person:

- A cutting board, preferably wood (the wrappers will not stick to wood as easily)

- A stack of homemade or store-bought round dumpling wrappers, kept under plastic wrap or a dense, clean kitchen towel to prevent them from drying out

- A bowl of filling with a spoon or small offset metal spatula for spreading it

- A small bowl of water for moistening the edges of the dumpling wrapper

- A clean dish towel for wiping your fingers and cutting board and keeping them dry in between dumplings

- A rimmed baking sheet lined with parchment paper to place your finished dumplings.

If you're using frozen store-bought dumpling wrappers, make sure that they are fully thawed before you start.

How to Form Traditional Pleated Dumplings

This is the most traditional way to form Japanese gyoza or Chinese guo tie or jiao zi. It's also a method that takes a little practice. Don't worry if your dumplings don't look great at the beginning—so long as the wrappers are closed around the filling they will taste just fine.

If you find it hard to hold the dumpling up in the air while you pleat the wrappers, you can place the skin on your cutting board. The shape will come out slightly different, but it should still be fine. I've been making these dumplings since grade school, and it still took years before I got to the point where I could make them entirely in my hands and far longer until I was good enough to hit the thirty-seconds-per-dumpling barrier. I've seen professional dumpling makers bang them out in under ten seconds apiece!

Step 1 • Spoon in the Filling

I'm a chronic overstuffer. Whether it's a burrito, a taco, or a simple sandwich, if I have the opportunity to put way more filling into something than it can reasonably handle, it's a good bet that I won't miss that chance. Dumplings are no exception, and I have to consciously remind myself not to put as much filling in there as I'd like. If this is your first go-around, you may want to stick with as little as a teaspoon or two. Once you get good at shaping, you'll be able to bump that amount up to about a tablespoon.

There's one real key to dumpling filling, though— one that took me years to discover: do not place your filling in the center of the dumpling in a cute little ball. This is a surefire way to end up squeezing filling out of your dumpling around the edges, ruining the seal.

Instead, it's much better to spread the filling in a disk-shaped layer. This way, the filling will bend and conform with your wrapper as you start folding.

Step 2 • Moisten the Edge

Dip the very tip of your finger in water and very lightly moisten the edge of the wrapper, then dry your finger carefully on the clean towel. It's important not to let the edge of the wrapper get too wet.

Step 3 • Pinch the Seam

Gently support the dumpling with the middle and ring fingers of your right hand, using your left hand to keep the dumpling folded like a taco. Use the thumb and forefinger of your right hand to pinch the near seam shut.

Step 4 • Pleat along One Side

Continuing to gently support the dumpling, start using the thumb and forefinger of your left hand to feed the edge of the filling into your right thumb and forefinger, forming small pleats on the near edge. The ring finger and pinky of your left hand should be supporting the far end of the dumpling, making sure that the filling doesn't get squeezed out.

Step 5 • Keep Crimping!

Continue crimping the seam until you reach the far corner, making sure to squeeze out any excess air as you go.

continues

Step 6 • Shape the Dumpling

Once the dumpling is crimped, you'll find that it forms a natural crescent shape with the crimped edge on the outer portion of the curve. Place the dumpling flat on the cutting board and use your fingers to adjust the shape of the crescent so that the bottom lies flat and the sides are plumped outward. Transfer the finished dumpling to the baking sheet, wipe your fingers clean, and start on the next one.

And hop to it—these dumplings aren't going to stuff themselves!

How to Form Simplified Pleated Gyoza

Are you finding the traditional pleat a little too difficult? No worries: even folding the gyoza in half to form half-moons will get the job done, so long as you squeeze out excess air. But there's another method that is far simpler than the one-sided pleat. The trick is to pleat each half of the dumpling working from the center out, with the pleats facing the center. The left side should be a mirror image of the right. This method also lets you rest the dumpling on your cutting board the whole time.

Step 1 • Seal the Center

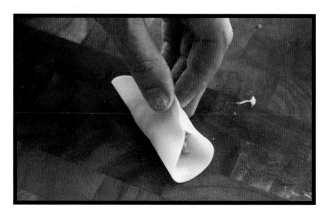

Start by placing the filling on the skin and moistening the edge just as with the standard method. Lift the front and back edges like a taco and seal them in the center.

Step 2 • Form Pleats

Keeping the center pinched, start forming pleats along the front edge, folding the pleats so that they point toward the center, sealing the skin as you go, and working from the center to the right corner.

Pinch in the center.

Continue adding pleats until you get to the corner, then seal the dumpling shut, making sure you squeeze out any air as you go.

Repeat the pleating process on the left edge, with the pleats again pointing toward the center, until the dumpling is completely sealed.

Step 3 • Shape the Dumpling

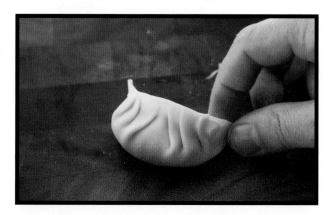

Plump up the dumpling, flattening the bottom and forming a nice crescent. Transfer the dumpling to the parchment sheet and repeat.

HOW TO FREEZE DUMPLINGS

Once you've completed all your dumplings, they are ready to cook immediately or to freeze for later use. To freeze, place the entire tray of dumplings into the freezer uncovered and let them rest until fully frozen, about half an hour, then transfer the frozen dumplings to a zipper-lock freezer bag, squeeze out as much air as possible, seal the bag, and store the dumplings for up to 2 months. The dumplings can be cooked straight from frozen.

HOW TO COOK DUMPLINGS

There are multiple ways to cook dumplings—boiling, steaming, and deep frying—as well as hybrid methods, which involve steaming or boiling followed by panfrying or using the "potsticker" method.

Boiling is the simplest method and results in a relatively thick, soft-skinned specimen. Just toss them into a wokful of boiling water, wait until they float, then let them cook for an extra minute or two to ensure the filling is cooked through. Remove them from the wok with a spider, transfer them to a plate, and serve with dipping sauce.

Steaming is also quite simple, provided you have a bamboo steamer for your wok (if you don't, you should). This method produces dumplings with a slightly thinner, stretchier skin. Superior, if you ask me. Remember to line your steamer basket with cabbage leaves, parchment, or a reusable silicone liner to prevent sticking. Another advantage of steaming is that with multiple stacking baskets, you can steam a huge quantity of dumplings at once. Bring a few inches of water to a strong boil in a wok, then place the steamer baskets directly in the wok and allow the dumplings to steam until cooked through, 10 to 12 minutes. Transfer the steamer basket directly to a large plate and serve.

Deep frying dumplings by lowering them into a hot wokful of oil (around 325°F/165°C is a good temperature to aim for) and letting them fry until cooked through (4 to 5 minutes) will cause their wrappers to blister and crisp up. Retrieve them with a spider and drain on a rack or on paper towels. They can be served hot, but fried dumplings are also great served cold the next day, when the crispy wrappers absorb sauce very well and retain some of their crispness (fried dumplings are a favorite for bento-style packed lunches in Japan).

Panfrying is my favorite way to cook dumplings, and there are two ways to do it. The first method is to start by steaming or boiling them, allow them to cool and air-dry slightly, then finish them by frying in a couple tablespoons of oil heated in a wok over moderate heat until their bottoms are golden brown and crispy. This method is simple to pull off and especially good if you are cooking a large quantity of dumplings: start by steaming them all in a series of stacking bamboo steamers. Once they're all cooked through, empty the wok, heat up some oil, and panfry in batches, letting guests eat the dumplings while they're still hot.

The potsticker approach is a little more streamlined, but it works only for smaller batches of dumplings and has a little more room for error. Even in the most well-seasoned, slickest of woks, there's still a good chance of the dumplings sticking (they are, after all, called "potstickers"), so I recommend setting the wok aside (!) and using a nonstick skillet for this method.

THE POTSTICKER METHOD, STEP BY STEP

This technique gives you dumplings with a crisp bottom and chewy steamed top. To achieve this, you start by frying the raw dumplings until crisp, then steaming them under a cover to cook the filling and the top of the wrapper through, and finally refrying them until the bottoms crisp up again. These days it's also in vogue to use a starch slurry in place of plain water during the steaming step, which creates a lacy sheet of crispy fried starch that can bind all of the dumplings together. In Japan, this technique is called *hanetsuki gyoza*, or "dumplings with wings."

Step 1 • Fry

Fry the raw or frozen gyoza over moderate heat in a couple tablespoons of oil with their flat side down in a cast iron or nonstick skillet, swirling the pan as they cook so that they crisp up evenly.

Step 2 • Continue until Golden

Keep frying (and don't stop swirling!) until golden brown and blistered evenly across the bottom surface.

Step 3 • Add Water

Add about ½ cup of water to the skillet (if using an 8- or 10-inch skillet, or ¾ cup if using a 12-inch skillet) all at once (adding it rapidly will minimize the amount of spattering and keep things neater.

Step 4 • Cover and Cook

Increase the heat to medium-high, then cover the pan immediately.

Step 5 • Cook Through

As the water evaporates, it'll gently steam the tops of the dumplings, cooking the filling through and steaming the wrapper to a perfect tender-stretchy texture over the course of a few minutes.

Step 6 • Refry

Remove the lid and keep cooking until the water has completely evaporated. If cooking the dumplings on their own, swirl the pan gently to promote even cooking and ensure the dumplings aren't sticking to the bottom. If adding a starchy layer, you'll notice it start to crisp up and start to pull away from the edges of the pan. Encourage it to lift using a thin metal spatula and move the pan around the flame to promote even browning of that layer.

continues

Step 7 • Extra Crisp!

Keep on cooking until the dumplings are extra-crisp on the bottom (and I mean crisp!).

Step 8 • Invert onto a Plate and Serve

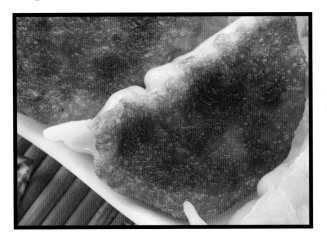

Off the heat, invert a plate over the top of the pan, then flip the whole thing over so that the dumplings invert onto the plate with their crisp sides facing up. Serve immediately with dipping sauce.

HOW TO MAKE "DUMPWINGS"

These days it's in vogue to use a starch slurry in place of plain water during the steaming step, which creates a lacy sheet of crispy fried starch that can bind all of the dumplings together and add a nice extra crunchy element to the dish. In Japan, this technique is called *hanetsuki gyoza*, or "dumplings with wings." I just call them "Dumpwings."

The process is simple. To do it, follow the potsticker method. In step 3, rather than adding plain water to the pan, add a starchy slurry made by stirring together 1 tablespoon (9 g) cornstarch or tapioca starch (the latter will produce a more crackly, glass-like lace), 1 teaspoon all-purpose flour, and ½ cup (120 ml) water until no lumps remain (double these amounts if using a 12-inch-skillet). Proceed exactly as directed. The slurry will get very thick and bubbly and look all sorts of wrong as the dumplings steam. Don't worry; just let it keep cooking down. As the starchy liquid evaporates, eventually a layer of crispy starch will get left behind and start to brown. At first you'll notice the starchy layer start to lift up off the pan around the edges. Continue cooking until it is extra-crisp and brown, then use a very thin metal spatula to gently release the whole layer of dumplings off the bottom of the skillet. Place an inverted plate on top and flip everything together so that the "dumpwings" end up lacy side up on the plate.

While this technique can be done in cast iron or in a carbon steel wok, this is one case where I strongly recommend a good nonstick skillet as it'll greatly minimize the risk of having the starchy layer stick to the pan.

HOMEMADE DUMPLING WRAPPERS

Yield
Makes about 40 dumpling wrappers

Active Time
30 minutes

Total Time
1 hour

NOTES

You can make this recipe without the food processor. Just stir the flour with a wooden spoon or chopsticks in a large bowl as you add the boiling water. After it comes together, turn it out onto a floured work surface and knead for 5 minutes until satiny and smooth. Proceed as instructed. Use about 1 pound (450 g) dumpling filling of your choice (recipes follow).

INGREDIENTS

2 cups (10 ounces/280 g) all-purpose flour, plus more for dusting
1 cup (240 ml) boiling water

DIRECTIONS

1. Place the flour in the bowl of a food processor. With the machine running, slowly drizzle in the water just until a cohesive dough is formed (you probably won't need all the water). Allow the dough to ride around the processor for 30 seconds. Form into a ball using floured hands and transfer to a bowl. Cover with a damp towel and let rest for at least 30 minutes.

2. When ready to stuff, divide the rested dough into 4 equal pieces, divide each piece in half, then divide each of those 8 pieces of dough into 5 small balls, making 40 balls total. On a well-floured work surface, roll each ball into a round 3½ to 4 inches in diameter. Dust the wrappers with flour, stack them, and keep under plastic until you're ready to use them. For better results, I recommend working with a partner, with one person in charge of rolling wrappers and the other stuffing and shaping them as soon as they're rolled.

PORK AND SHRIMP DUMPLINGS

Yield
Makes
about 40
dumplings

Active Time
30 minutes

Total Time
1 hour

NOTES

You can use any filling in place of the pork and shrimp filling here (such as the fillings on pages 415, 417, and 418). If you have a batch of "The Mix" (page 280) handy, you can also use that here as dumpling filling. Three chopped scallions can be used in place of the garlic chives.

INGREDIENTS

8 ounces (225 g) ground pork
6 ounces (170 g) raw peeled shrimp, roughly
    chopped into ¼-inch pieces
¼ teaspoon freshly ground white pepper
2 teaspoons (10 ml) soy sauce
2 teaspoons (5 g) minced garlic (about 2
    medium cloves)
2 teaspoons (5 g) minced fresh ginger
    (about ½-inch segment)
8 Chinese garlic chives, finely chopped
    (see Notes)
2 teaspoons (9 g) sugar
1 teaspoon (4 g) cornstarch
¼ teaspoon baking soda
40 dumpling wrappers, homemade (page
    413) or store-bought

DIRECTIONS

(1) Combine all the filling ingredients (see Notes) in a bowl and mix vigorously with your fingertips until the mixture feels slightly tacky, about 1 minute.

(2) To form dumplings, smear 2 to 3 teaspoons (10 to 15 g) of filling in the center of a wrapper. Moisten the edges of the wrapper with a wet fingertip or a pastry brush. Fold in half and pinch the bottom right corner closed. Pleat the front edge of the wrapper repeatedly, pinching the edge closed after each pleat until the entire dumpling is sealed. Place the dumpling on your cutting board and plump it up into shape. (See page 406 for detailed instructions for shaping.)

(3) Transfer the sealed dumplings to a parchment-lined rimmed baking sheet. Freeze the dumplings for future use (see page 409 for freezing instructions) or cook by boiling, steaming, deep frying, or panfrying (see page 409 for detailed cooking instructions).

How to Taste Raw Meat Mixtures for Seasoning

It's not easy to predict whether your dumpling filling is properly seasoned, especially if you've added a salt-purged vegetable (like cabbage) to the mix. To test for seasoning, I turn to my friend Chef Mike (aka the microwave). All you have to do is take a dime-sized bit of filling and place it on a microwave-safe plate and microwave it just until it's cooked through (this takes only 10 seconds or so). That way I can taste it and add more salt, sugar, white pepper, or other seasonings until it tastes right to me.

If you don't have a microwave, you can panfry a small amount of filling to check for seasoning instead.

JAPANESE-STYLE PORK AND CABBAGE GYOZA FILLING FOR DUMPLINGS

Yield
Makes
enough
for 40
dumplings

Active Time
15 minutes

Total Time
30 minutes

NOTES

To form and cook dumplings, see pages 405–14.

This recipe calls specifically for Diamond Crystal kosher salt. If using Morton's kosher salt, use two-thirds as much. If using table salt, use only half as much. See "How to Purge Cabbage or Other Greens, Step by Step" (page 416) for more detailed instructions for purging cabbage.

INGREDIENTS

12 ounces (340 g) finely minced Napa cabbage (about ½ medium head)

2 teaspoons (6 g) kosher salt (see Notes)

12 ounces (340 g) ground pork shoulder

¾ teaspoon (about 2 g) freshly ground white pepper

2 medium garlic cloves, minced (about 2 teaspoons/8 g)

1 teaspoon (3 g) minced fresh ginger (about ¼-inch segment)

2 ounces (60 g/about 2 whole) scallions, minced

2 teaspoons (8 g) sugar

Gyoza are Japanese-style dumplings made with pork or chicken and cabbage and typically served in ramen shops. I've seen many different methods of mixing gyoza filling, ranging from folding it gently together to processing it into a paste in a food processor to kneading it with a stand mixer. After testing them side by side, I find that in general more kneading leads to better texture. Kneading helps unravel pork proteins, which then cross-link with each other, giving the filling better structure and a little bit of springiness. This protein network also helps trap juices, ensuring that the filling stays moist—underkneading leads to a dumpling filling that resembles a dry meatball sitting in a puddle of leaked liquid. Not so great.

Still, I don't find it necessary to whip out the heavy equipment just for this process. Instead, I knead the filling vigorously by hand, picking it up by the handful, squeezing it through my fingers, lifting from the bottom and folding over the top, and generally being as rough with it as I care to be. Like a good sausage, once the mixture starts to turn a little tacky and sticky, you're there.

This filling is what you can expect to find in Japanese ramen shops and *izakaya* (drinking halls). Like ramen, dumplings came to Japan by way of China, but they've since been adapted to local tastes. Japanese gyoza are frequently made with store-bought wrappers, so don't feel compelled to match this filling with homemade wrappers.

DIRECTIONS

(1) **For the Cabbage (see Notes):** Combine the cabbage and 1½ teaspoons (4 g) of the salt in a large bowl and toss to combine. Transfer to a fine-mesh strainer and set it over the bowl. Let stand at room temperature for 15 minutes.

(2) Transfer the cabbage to the center of a clean dish towel and gather up the edges. Twist the towel to squeeze the cabbage, wringing out as much excess moisture as possible. Discard the liquid.

(3) Combine the pork, drained cabbage, remaining ½ teaspoon (2 g) salt, the white pepper, garlic, ginger, scallions, and sugar in a large bowl and knead and turn with clean hands until the mixture is homogenous and starting to feel tacky/sticky. Transfer a teaspoon-sized amount to a microwave-safe plate and microwave on high power until cooked through, about 10 seconds. Taste and adjust the seasoning with more salt, white pepper, and/or sugar if desired.

How to Purge Cabbage or Other Greens, Step by Step

Purging cabbage or other vegetables of excess liquid is a key first step when adding them to dumpling fillings. Here's how you do it.

Step 1 • Cut Out the Core

Start by splitting a head of cabbage in half and cutting out the firm core. I played with various ratios of cabbage to pork and found that most recipes don't use quite enough cabbage. I use a full pound of cabbage for every pound of pork. This makes enough filling for 40 to 50 plump dumplings.

Step 2 • Shred the Cabbage

Use a sharp chef's knife to very thinly slice the cabbage. If you've got one, you can also shred the cabbage in a food processor fitted with the large grating disk.

Step 3 • Mince the Cabbage

After shredding the cabbage, finely mince it by rocking a sharp chef's knife over it back and forth or by pulsing it in a food processor fitted with a standard blade.

Step 4 • Salt and Wait

Here comes the moisture-removal step. Salting the cabbage and letting it rest for about 15 minutes harnesses the power of osmosis to draw liquid out from inside its cell walls.

I use 1 teaspoon (4 g) of kosher salt for every 8 ounces (225 g) of cabbage, letting it drain in a strainer set over a bowl. Once the cabbage has had time to rest, I transfer it to the center of a clean kitchen towel.

Step 5 • Wring out Excess Moisture

Draw up the edges of the towel and squeeze the heck out of the cabbage. Seriously. Squeeze the heck out of it. If there is still liquid coming out, you haven't squeezed hard enough. By the time you're done, the cabbage should have lost almost three-quarters of its volume and at least half its weight.

MY MOM'S BEEF AND VEGETABLE FILLING FOR DUMPLINGS

Yield
Makes
enough
for 40
dumplings

Active Time
10 minutes

Total Time
10 minutes

NOTE
To form and cook dumplings, see pages 409–14.

INGREDIENTS

4 ounces (120 g) frozen spinach
12 ounces (340 g) ground beef
2 ounces (60 g/about ½ small) carrot,
    peeled and grated on the large holes of
    a box grater
2 teaspoons (10 ml) soy sauce
2 teaspoons (5 g) minced fresh ginger
    (about ½-inch segment)
2 scallions (about 60 g), minced
1 tablespoon (12.5 g) sugar
1 teaspoon (4 g) cornstarch
½ teaspoon (2 g) freshly ground white
    pepper

When I was growing up, ground beef was a far more common meat in my mom's kitchen than ground pork. This was both a product of our proximity to several meat-packing plants near our apartment building in Morningside Heights and a practical way for her to be able to use the same bulk pack of ground beef for dumplings, mapo tofu, Italian American meat sauces, meat loaf, Hamburg steak, and the like. Rather than the cabbage typical of Japanese gyoza, her dumplings featured frozen spinach and carrots. Frozen spinach was practical, and carrots were her way of getting more vegetables into us.

DIRECTIONS

(1) Place the frozen spinach in a bowl and cover with hot water. Let sit for 5 minutes, until thawed. Drain through a fine-mesh strainer, then squeeze out as much excess moisture as you can by using your hands or by wrapping the spinach in a clean kitchen towel, gathering the ends, and twisting (see "How to Purge Cabbage or Other Greens, Step by Step" (page 416) for detailed photos of the squeezing process). Discard excess liquid.

(2) Combine all the ingredients in a bowl and mix vigorously with your fingertips until the mixture feels slightly tacky, about 1 minute.

VEGETARIAN EGGPLANT, MUSHROOM, AND CARROT FILLING FOR DUMPLINGS

Yield
Makes enough for 60 to 80 dumplings

Active Time
20 minutes

Total Time
20 minutes, plus time to cool

NOTES

To form and cook dumplings, see pages 409–14.

If you don't use up all the filling, extra can be placed in a zipper-lock freezer bag with the air squeezed out, pressed flat, and frozen for future use.

INGREDIENTS

1 pound (450 g/about 2 medium) Japanese or Chinese eggplant, stems removed, cut into 2-inch chunks

2 tablespoons (30 ml) peanut, rice bran, or other neutral oil

4 ounces (120 g/about 1 small) carrot, peeled and grated on the large holes of a box grater or very finely diced by hand

4 ounces (120 g/about 12 medium) shiitake mushrooms, stems removed, caps minced

2 teaspoons (5 g) minced garlic (about 2 medium cloves)

2 teaspoons (5 g) minced fresh ginger (about ½-inch segment)

2 scallions, minced

1 tablespoon (15 ml) Shaoxing wine

1 tablespoon (15 ml) light soy sauce or shoyu

1 teaspoon (5 ml) dark soy sauce

1 tablespoon (15 ml) red, brown, or yellow miso paste

2 teaspoons (about 4 g) dried fermented black beans (douchi), roughly chopped

Salt and freshly ground white pepper

One of the issues I have with common vegetarian dumpling fillings is their texture. Meat is made of muscle cells, and muscle cells are particularly good at forming strong, elastic networks. This is a physiological thing. Our muscles need to be able to contract and change shape without breaking, bursting, or tearing. Plant cells, on the other hand, are rigid in structure, designed to hold their shape rather than bend or pull. This is why meat-based dumpling fillings tend to have a denser, more coherent texture even without the wrapper, while vegetable-based fillings often feel like a collection of bits and pieces held together by the dumpling skin alone. This also makes many vegetable-based fillings difficult to work with, as they have a tendency to fall out of wrappers as you try to wrap them.

Enter eggplant. If you've read my book *The Food Lab*, you'll know that I use eggplant to improve the texture and moisture-retaining capabilities of ground turkey in my turkey burgers. The same characteristics—eggplant's ability to retain moisture and fat, as well as its dense texture and ability to soak up flavors—make it a wonderful choice for a dumpling filling.

I start by steaming cut eggplant to tenderize it, then stir-fry it with carrot and shiitake mushroom, along with garlic, ginger, a dash of miso paste, and some fermented black beans. The filling is dense, umami-packed, and very satisfying, and it behaves very similarly to meat-based fillings, making it quite easy to work with.

DIRECTIONS

(1) Bring a couple inches of water to a boil in your wok. Arrange the eggplant pieces in a single layer in a bamboo steamer insert (stack 2 steamers if necessary), cover, and steam until the eggplant is completely tender, about 10 minutes. Set aside.

(2) Empty the wok and heat over high heat until lightly smoking. Add the oil and swirl to coat. Add the carrot, mushrooms, garlic, ginger and scallions and stir-fry until the mushrooms and carrots are lightly softened, about 2 minutes. Add the wine, soy sauces, miso paste, and fermented black beans and stir-fry until the miso paste is fully incorporated, about 1 minute.

(3) Add the eggplant, reduce the heat to medium-low, and cook, stirring and mashing with a whisk, potato masher, or pastry cutter, until the eggplant is completely broken down and the mixture is thickened, about 2 minutes. Season with salt and white pepper to taste. Transfer the mixture to a rimmed baking sheet or a large plate and spread into an even layer. Refrigerate until completely cooled before using.

4.2 DEEP FRYING IN A WOK

Panfrying works well in a wok but can also be done just fine in a skillet. Where woks *truly* excel is in the realm of deep frying. For stovetop use, there's no vessel that beats it. What makes a wok so good for deep frying? Glad you asked. We'll talk about that, as well as every other question you may have about deep frying before we get to the recipes.

All of Your Deep-Frying Questions Answered

Q *Why is a wok the ideal vessel for deep frying?*

A It's all in the shape. The flared sides of a wok offer several advantages over the vertical sides of a Dutch oven or saucepan.

It's safer. Adding food to hot oil creates bubbles of water vapor that can begin to pile up on top of each other. In a tall, narrow pot, there's only one way for them to go: up and over. A wok, with its flared sides, on the other hand, provides plenty of extra space for those bubbles to spread out. Their surface area increases, weakening their structure and causing them to pop.

It's less messy. Deep frying food inevitably causes oil spatter. In a straight-sided pot, those oil droplets end up on your range (or floor). The flared sides of a wok catch a much larger proportion of these droplets, keeping your cooktop neat and clean.

It offers more space for maneuvering. The sloping sides of a wok make it easy to grab food with a spider or a pair of long chopsticks. It also prevents pieces of food from piling up on top of each other. Both of these factors lead to more efficient, even frying.

THE TOOLS

Q *Do I need any special tools to deep-fry?*

A At a bare minimum you'll need these three tools (and a willingness to leave your fears at the kitchen door).

→ **A wok.** This is the ideal frying vessel for a home kitchen.
→ **A thermometer.** Maintaining the right temperature is essential for effective deep frying. I recommend either a leave-in deep-fry thermometer with a pot clip or a good instant-read thermometer like the Thermapen from Thermoworks or the more budget-friendly Thermopop.
→ **A wire-mesh spider**, for maneuvering foods as they fry, lifting foods out of the fryer as they finish, and fishing out bits of debris from the oil to keep it relatively clean during frying.

Additionally, you'll probably also want:

→ **A wire resting rack.** This can be a semicircular rack that rests on the lip of your wok and allows oil to drip from fried foods back into the wok below, or it can be a wire rack that fits into a rimmed baking sheet that you keep next to your wok.
→ **A fine-mesh strainer** to filter used oil through before storing and reusing.
→ **A sealable container** to store your deep-frying oil between uses (and to discard used oil). An old empty oil container with a screw-top lid works well for this.
→ **A funnel** to facilitate transferring used oil to the container.
→ **A fire extinguisher** for worst case scenarios. Make sure it's one designated for oil fires (a water-based extinguisher will only make oil fires worse).

HOW FRYING WORKS

Q *What exactly happens when you deep-fry foods, and why are deep-fried foods so delicious?*

A Deep frying breaks down to a few key processes:

→ **Dehydration:** Virtually all foods that we fry contain some amount of moisture. While water boils at 212°F (100°C), fat for deep frying is typically heated much hotter, between 300°F (150°C) and 400°F (205°C). As soon as food is lowered into the fat, energy from the hot oil is used to convert moisture from the food into steam. This is what causes the rapid bubbling that you see during frying[*] and an important first step in deep frying. The most obvious benefit of dehydration is that it allows batters and breadings to become crisp. However, it's also important to note that until a significant amount of surface moisture has evaporated, it's very difficult for the temperature of your food to surpass the boiling point of water. This makes dehydration a vital first step for . . .
→ **Browning and Caramelization**: The former, which food scientists call "Maillard browning" (pronounced "may-yard"), is the process by which proteins and carbohydrates break down into their constituent parts, then recombine to form a cascading series of new compounds that give browned foods their complex, toasty, roasty aroma. The latter is a similar process that occurs to sugars when heated. Both of these processes occur only after enough moisture has evaporated to allow the food being fried to reach temperatures that exceed the boiling point of water.
→ **Expansion**: Wet, dense batters become puffy, light, and crisp because of the expansion of gases trapped within them (in the case of

---

[*] You may have heard the expression "boiling oil." In fact, during frying, it's not the oil that is boiling, it's the water in the food. Under normal circumstances, oil cannot boil—its boiling temperature is well above its smoke point (the temperature at which it emits smoke) and flash point (the temperature at which it will spontaneously erupt into flames).

batters that rely on baking powder or yeast to produce carbon dioxide gas, batters made with soda water, or batters in which egg whites are whipped up to incorporate air, for instance), as well as the rapid transformation of water to water vapor. In some batters, alcohol, which has a relatively low boiling point and thus converts to vapor more violently and rapidly, can be used to increase this effect. (Several of the recipes in this section include batters made with vodka for this reason.)

→ **Protein coagulation:** When heated, the structure of raw proteins will tighten. This, in conjunction with dehydration, is what makes loose batters and breadings form rigid, crisp structures.

→ **Oil absorption:** When water leaves foods in the form of steam, this leaves empty gaps where oil is subsequently absorbed. Generally, the higher the temperature of your oil, the more water is forced out and the more oil your food will absorb. Bear in mind that excess oil absorption is *not* what makes foods taste greasy. More on that in a moment.

Q *OK . . . that's a lot happening at once. How do I make sure that it all gets done at the same time?*

A So long as you're following a well-tested recipe (or have enough experience and knowledge under your belt to improvise) and you're carefully monitoring oil temperature, it doesn't require much work at all. The beauty of deep frying is that all of those things happen at once with very little work on the part of the cook. A good—and more importantly, safe—fry cook's job boils down to a few things:

→ **Keep the wok handle facing the back of the stovetop**, and if possible, place the wok on a back burner to minimize the chance that it will get bumped or pushed off the stovetop. Make sure that you have space to work—now is not the time for friends or toddlers to crowd the kitchen.

→ **Properly maintain oil temperature**. Letting the oil get too hot or too cold will lead to food that's greasy and undercrisped or burnt and acrid tasting (and raw in the middle). Keep an eye on your oil temperature using an instant-read thermometer or a leave-in deep-frying thermometer at all times during the process.

→ **Keep it separated.** You've got a handful of vegetables in a bowl of tempura batter. If you drop them into the oil all at once, they'll form a single large battered vegetable raft. What's worse is that the vegetables and batter trapped in the middle of the raft won't cook properly, leading to pockets of raw batter. Instead, always remember to lower foods into the oil one piece at a time to ensure that they stay separated and cook evenly. Lowering larger pieces of food in slowly will also allow coatings to expand, which will buoy up the food and ensure that they don't sink and stick to the bottom of the wok.

→ **Don't fear the fat**. Hot fat can sense fear, and this is a lesson you'll learn the first time you hold your hand high above the oil, causing it to splash onto your arm or feet as you drop food into it. Instead, bring your hand right down above the surface of the oil and lower the food into it to minimize splashing.

→ **Keep things moving**. Have you ever noticed that a cold day feels much colder when there's a breeze? This is because on still days the air around your body will warm up. A breeze will continuously expose you to fresh cold air. A similar thing happens during deep frying: as a piece of food cooks in a wok, the oil directly surrounding it will lose energy and be at a relatively low temperature, rendering frying inefficient. Continuously agitating the oil and keeping food moving with a spider, tongs, or chopsticks will ensure that it is constantly hit with fresh, hot oil so that it fries efficiently and evenly.

→ **Let delicate crusts set**. The only time you should ignore the previous rule is right when your food is first added. Agitating too early can lead to crusts that break off the food. Make sure to let batter and breading begin to set before you start moving food around. This typically takes 10 to 15 seconds.

→ **Keep your oil clean**. As you deep-fry food, you'll find that bits of batter, panko crumbs, or errant vegetable scraps will begin to collect. Those bits of stuff will cause your oil to break down faster or can burn and end up stuck to the exterior of the next batch of food you fry. When I'm frying, I keep a small heatproof container next to my wok. This container has two purposes: First, as I fry I can continuously fish out and discard unwanted detritus in the fry oil. Second, it's a good place to rest my frying implements when they aren't in my hands.

→ **Don't drink and fry**.

ALL ABOUT OIL

Q *What's the best oil for deep frying?*

A With deep frying, you typically want a fat that has a relatively neutral flavor (no extra virgin olive oil or roasted sesame oil!)* and a relatively high smoke point, though as long as you're monitoring temperature carefully, virtually any oil will have a high enough smoke point for deep frying. Fats with a higher percentage of saturated fat (vs. mono- or polyunsaturated fat) will typically yield crisper end results, and the fat will be more stable, which means you can reuse it more times before it starts to break down. However, if a fat is *too* saturated, it can solidify and turn waxy or pasty in your mouth. This is not a good thing.†

I find that for deep frying, peanut oil, rice bran oil, and vegetable shortening produce the best results. Soybean oil, corn oil, and vegetable oil (which is typically composed mostly of soybean oil these days) are also good choices and are generally less expensive.

Q *Is it possible to overheat my oil? What's the danger if I do?*

A As fats heat up, they eventually start breaking down, forming dangerous compounds called *free radicals* and *acrolein*, a chemical that can give foods an acrid, burnt flavor. The longer a fat is held at a high temperature, the more concentrated these compounds become. The temperature at which this concentration occurs is correlated to an oil's smoke point—the temperature at which those volatile compounds start vaporizing in sufficient quantities to produce a visible bluish smoke, although there are exceptions. Extra-virgin olive oil, for instance, has a relatively low smoke point at 375°F (190°C), but, due to its high antioxidant content, is generally more stable than other fats at high temperatures.

That said, if you notice that your oil is smoking, you've heated it beyond typical deep-frying temperatures and you should immediately remove it from the heat. Adding some fresh, cooler oil is the best way to rapidly cool it. Do not put it in the sink or add water or ice!

Beyond the smoke point is a temperature called the *flash point*—this is the temperature at which actual flames may start flickering and leaping across the surface of the oil spontaneously. Don't let your oil get this hot.

Here's a chart of common cooking fats, their smoke points, flash points, and saturated fat content.

---

* There are exceptions, and sometimes you really want those flavors in your food. Roman-style fried artichokes are typically fried in extra virgin olive oil, for instance, and I've been to tempura shops in Tokyo that fry in nothing but sesame oil.

† Unless you're planning on eating the Merciless Pepper of Quetzalacatenango.

FAT	SMOKE POINT	FLASH POINT	SATURATED FAT CONTENT
Safflower Oil	510°F/265°C	600°F/315°C	9%
Palm Oil	490°F/260°C	615°F/320°C	50%
Light/Refined Olive Oil	465°F/240°C	600°F/315°C	13%
Rice Bran Oil	450°F/230°C	615°F/320°C	25%
Soybean Oil	450°F/230°C	625°F/330°C	15%
Peanut Oil	450°F/230°C	635°F/335°C	17–20%
Clarified Butter	450°F/230°C	565°F/295°C	62%
Corn Oil	450°F/230°C	620°F/325°C	13%
Canola Oil	450°F/230°C	620°F/325°C	7%
Sunflower Oil	440°F/225°C	610°F/315°C	11%
Vegetable Oil	400°–450°F / 205°–230°C	590–610°F / 310°–320°C	15%
Vegetable Shortening	390°F/195°C	590°F/310°C	31%
Grapeseed Oil	390°F/195°C	610°F/315°C	10%
Lard	390°F/195°C	620°F/325°C	40%
Coconut Oil	385°F/195°C	565°F/295°C	86%
Extra Virgin Olive Oil	375°F/190°C	600°F/315°C	13%

Q *I've heard that properly deep-fried food doesn't absorb much oil at all. Is this true?*

A I believed this for a long time. The argument I heard went something like this: If you fry food at a high enough temperature, the outward force of water evaporating will prevent oil from being absorbed into foods. This is an appealing explanation, but it's unfortunately incorrect. A 1997 study in the *Journal of Food Engineering* on how various factors affect oil absorption in tortilla chips found that while it is true that relatively little oil absorption takes place during the frying process itself (around 20 percent of total oil absorbed), the moment that you remove it from the hot fat, it cools rapidly, causing pressure within open pore spaces in the chip to drop. The surface tension of the oil simultaneously experiences a rapid increase. These two factors cause oil on the surface of the chip to flow very rapidly into the interior—about 64 percent of a chip's total oil absorption takes place during cooling, and the vast majority of that absorption takes place within the first 10 seconds after the chip is removed from its oil bath.

The amount of oil that is absorbed is related to the amount of space that is freed up by the evaporation of liquids from within the food. Typically, the longer you fry a food and the hotter it is fried, the more water is forced out, thus the more fat it absorbs as it cools. Fat absorption is also related to oil freshness: the fresher the oil, the more fat gets absorbed into the food (and consequently the less fat is left on its surface).

Q *But wait a minute. I've had food that was fried at too low a temperature, and it tastes greasier than food fried at the right temperature. What gives?*

A There are two reasons for this. The first is that when food is fried at too low a temperature, more water is left inside it. More water inside means less room for surface oil to get absorbed as it cools, which in turn leads to more oil left on the surface of the food, making the food look and feel greasier than its properly fried counterpart. The second reason is that improperly fried foods will still have a lot of moisture left in their batter or breading, preventing them from crisping properly. This sogginess combined with the surface grease is what we perceive as greasiness on our fingers and tongues.

Note that the total amount of oil added to fried foods doesn't significantly change whether the food is fried properly or not, nor whether the oil is old or fresh. What changes is the *distribution* of that oil, as well as the moisture content of the coating, and our subjective sensation of greasiness.

Q *I see. I'm a little concerned about my calorie intake though. Is there any way to actually reduce the amount of oil added to fried foods?*

A On an industrial scale, products like low-fat potato chips are made on specialized equipment that centrifuges food as soon as it comes out of the frying medium, which, like a salad spinner, causes liquids on its surface to be drained away before they can be absorbed. At home, you can mimic this technique by lining a salad spinner with several layers of paper towels (the sides and the bottom—this is to prevent hot

oil from melting the salad spinner). Retrieve food from the fryer using a spider, give it a few good up-and-down shakes to get excess oil off, then immediately transfer it to the salad spinner and give it a spin (the goal is to get it spinning within 5 to 10 seconds of removal from the oil).

If that seems too involved, simply draining on paper towels can decrease oil absorption by around 25 percent in most cases, although resting on paper towels can cause the part of the food that is in contact with the towel to soften and become soggy if it's left for too long (by contrast, resting food on an open rack will not cause sogginess).

In my opinion, the easiest (and best) way to reduce calorie intake from fried foods is to just reduce your portion size and realize that the foods in this chapter are not everyday fare.

Q *I'm interested in deep frying at home, but it seems like such a waste of oil. Can I reuse the oil for other purposes?*

A You can filter oil and reuse it for deep frying (generally multiple times), stir-frying, or sautéing, although oil's useful life span will depend on what you've been frying in it. In general, the more particulate matter there is on the fried food, the shorter the life span of the oil and the more thoroughly you'll need to filter it before reusing.

In order of easiest on your oil to toughest, here's what we've got:

→ **Foods coated in a wet batter** (such as tempura, page 471, or Korean Fried Chicken, page 460): These foods are very gentle on your oil, especially if you try to minimize dripping when transferring the battered food to the oil.
→ **Foods fried naked** (such as Fried Shishito Peppers, page 431, or Crispy Fried Pork Belly, page 434): These foods require no filtering or straining after you're done frying. They tend to be a little bit harder on your oil than wet-battered foods, especially meats, such as Málà Salt and Pepper Chicken Wings (page 452) or

Dry-Fried Beef (page 436), which will expel protein-rich juices that can increase the rate at which oil begins to break down.

→ **Foods that are breaded with panko or bread crumbs** (such as Katsu, page 465, or Korokke, page 467): Panko bread crumbs increase the surface area of food, which can make for some supremely crunchy results, but that increased surface area also means increased contact points with the oil, which in turn leads to more rapid breakdown. Additionally, no matter how carefully you apply your breading, bread crumbs are going to fall off and sink, making contact with the hot bottom surface of the wok, causing them to darken and burn, which in turn hastens the rate at which oil breaks down.

→ **Foods that are coated in a floury dredge** (such as General Tso's, page 485, or Orange Peel Beef, page 494): Floury dredging mixtures will shed off a ton of fine particles into your oil. This means lots of surface contact with food, which in turn means faster oil breakdown. Moreover, fine particles like flour can't be fished out with a fine-mesh strainer, which means they end up spending a longer time in the oil in a given frying session.

Q *What do I do after frying if I want to keep my oil for reuse?*

A First, use a spider to clear out any large bits of stuff from the oil. Next, let it cool. As any fry cook who has forgotten to shut off the fryer until just before nightly cleaning can tell you, straining and storing hot oil is not a fun project. Push your wok to the back of your stove, put a lid on it to prevent dust or other stuff from falling into it, and leave it alone. The ideal temperature is just cool enough that you can handle it without danger of burning yourself (cooler oil is more viscous, which makes it harder to strain effectively).

Once the oil has cooled, you can strain it. If you've been cooking battered foods or foods breaded in large panko crumbs, a simple pass

through a fine-mesh strainer is sufficient. For foods that have been dredged in a floury coating, you should line that fine-mesh strainer with paper towels, a coffee strainer, or several layers of cheesecloth to give it a finer filter. Transfer the filtered oil to a container that just fits it and has a tight-fitting lid (mason jars of various sizes work well for this). Store the oil in a dark pantry or in the refrigerator until you need it next.

Q *How do I know my oil is past its prime?*

A If your oil produces bubbles that collect and float on its surface rather than immediately popping, that's a good sign that your oil is no longer going to fry effectively. It may also start developing fishy off-aromas. Finally, foods cooked in oil that's too old won't crisp or brown properly.

Q *How should I discard used oil?*

A Small amounts of used oil can be poured down the drain with some soap and hot water. For anything more than ¼ cup or so, it should be transferred to a container using a funnel and discarded. Some folks are lucky enough to have municipal oil recycling. Others will have to discard the oil in the container in the regular garbage bin (check with your city to figure out where your oil should be going).

Q *So why can't I keep using the same oil indefinitely? What exactly is happening in there?*

A Two things: oxidation and hydrolysis. Oxidation is the process of large fat molecules, composed of three fatty acid chains attached to a glycerol backbone, breaking down into smaller and smaller constituent parts: first into free fatty acids, peroxides, and dienes, then into carbonyls, aldehydes, and trienes, and finally into tertiary products like foul-smelling ketones and short-chain hydrocarbons.

Oxidation is something that occurs even when you aren't frying with your oil. If you've ever opened up a bottle of canola oil that your roommate has stored above the stove or on the windowsill (you would never do that, right?) and noticed a sticky, tacky feel around the mouth of the jar and a sort of fishy aroma, you're familiar with oxidized oil. Hydrolysis occurs when you combine oil, water, and heat (in other words, every time you fry something), and it can significantly speed up the process of oxidation.

Eventually, when oil has broken down enough, the properties that made it such a good cooking medium—its ability to effectively transfer heat and remove moisture, for instance—start to lessen. This is why old oil yields soggy fried food.

Q *Got it. So oxidation is the enemy. How do I stop it? What tools do I have at my disposal?*

A Oil is in a constant state of increasing oxidation, and there's nothing you can do to stop it. That said, you can slow it down significantly by controlling its storage environment and use. There are a few factors that will increase the oxidation rate of oil.

→ **Light increases oxidation.** I keep oils that I use every day and leave on the counter in tinted glass or lightproof metal containers. Oils that I use infrequently I store away in a dark pantry between uses.

→ **Heat increases oxidation**. If you keep oil on your countertop for everyday use, keep it well to the side of your stove (not, for instance, on the hot backsplash or in a cupboard above your cooktop).

→ **Moisture increases oxidation.** Make sure that when you strain and store your oil for reuse there is no layer of watery liquids at the bottom.

If there is, carefully pour the clear oil off the top, then discard the watery layer. Transfer the oil to a clean, dry container. Additionally, make sure to keep stored oil well sealed so that humidity can't find its way in.

→ **Air contact increases oxidation**. Store oil in a container that fits it. A small amount of oil in a large container that has a big headspace of air will oxidize faster than the same oil in a container with just a bit of headspace.

DEEP FRYING AT RESTAURANTS VS. AT HOME

Q *Why do foods deep-fried at restaurants frequently come out better than my attempts at home?*

A There are a few answers to this question. First and foremost, it's the equipment. A restaurant deep fryer holds a very large volume of oil, typically around 40 pounds (about 12 gallons). It's the Imperial Star Destroyer to the Corellian Corvette you have at home. A larger volume of oil means that there is a relatively low drop in temperature when you add room-temperature or cold foods to it, which in turn means more efficient frying. A large volume of oil also gives a good fry cook the ability to really keep the food moving around, constantly exposing it to fresh hot oil, which increases both the rate and the evenness of cooking.

To effectively overcome this handicap, it's important to fry in small enough batches that your oil doesn't significantly drop in temperature, and, more importantly, it's important to carefully monitor oil temperature throughout the process. Most recipes will call for preheating the oil to a temperature *higher* than your actual frying temperature, to compensate for the sudden drop in temperature the oil will experience when you add food to it.

Q *Wait—if my oil at home is good for only a half dozen or so batches of fried foods, how the heck does a restaurant manage? Do they switch out their oil every half dozen orders?*

A Again, restaurants have an advantage here. As far as ingredients go, a restaurant has access to specialty oils that are formulated to have extra-long useful life spans. A commercial deep fryer also has the advantage that its heating element or tubes are elevated from the floor of the oil compartment. At home, when a bit of panko falls off your food, it lands on the bottom of the wok, where the oil is the hottest, causing it to burn relatively rapidly. In a restaurant deep fryer that panko falls *below* the heating elements, which keeps it from burning.

TROUBLESHOOTING FRIED RECIPES

Q *I'm trying to adapt a recipe I have and keep finding that my food comes out overbrowned/underbrowned/raw in the middle/too tough/ etc. What can I do to fix it?*

A It depends on the type of coating you're using and the size of the pieces of food you're cooking. Any decent recipe should give you appropriate cooking temperatures, but what if you're trying to create a new recipe or modify one that you've already found success with?

Here are a few simple rules that will help you troubleshoot or make adjustments to recipes as you modify them.

→ **If your coating is browning before the food is fully cooked:** Lower the fry temperature and increase cook time. This allows for the food inside to cook before the coating starts to burn. You can also consider modifying the recipe for your coating. Sugar and some spices, such as dried herbs or paprika, will increase the rate at which coatings brown. Reducing or eliminating them from the recipe should help. Wheat flour,

which is high in protein, also browns faster than cornstarch, potato starch, or rice flour. Replacing part of your wheat flour with one of those should decrease the browning rate.

→ **If your coating looks perfect but the food inside is overcooked:** Raise the fryer temperature and decrease cook time. Less time in the fryer means less time to overcook, while a higher temperature means more browning in less time.

→ **If you are converting a recipe for small pieces of food to work for larger pieces of food:** Lower the temperature and increase cook time. Larger chunks of food take a longer time to cook through to the center, which means that you need to lower the oil temperature a bit to avoid burning the coating on the exterior. For instance, while thin chicken fingers work just fine with a 4- to 5-minute fry at 350°F, a bone-in chicken thigh might take closer to 10 to 12 minutes at 300°F.

→ **Conversely, the smaller the food, the higher the fry temperature and the lower the fry time.**

→ **If the coating on your breaded or battered foods feels tough:** Most likely the overdevelopment of gluten, derived from wheat flour, is to blame. Replace part of the wheat flour with cornstarch, potato starch, or rice flour and make sure to fry your food immediately after you've covered it in your coating of choice (the longer wheat flour sits around wet before frying, the more gluten it will develop).

Frying Naked

Foods fried naked are foods fried directly in oil, no intervening layer of breading or batter necessary. Frying naked takes full advantage of the flavor and texture development potential of frying. Vegetables like Brussels sprouts, broccoli, and shishito peppers acquire a sweet nuttiness. Eggs come out puffy and crisp. Dry-fried meats become more porous, allowing sauces and flavors to really soak into them. The major downside of naked-fried foods is that without a layer of crisp breading or batter to protect them, they can come out quite greasy tasting. To combat this flavor, most naked-fried foods do best when paired with sharp, acidic, flavorful sauces that cut through the extra fat.

FRIED BRUSSELS SPROUTS WITH FISH SAUCE, SHALLOTS, AND CHILES

When you fry them, Brussels sprouts become everything you love about Brussels sprouts with none of their downside. The nutty aroma. The mildly sweet flavor. The just-tender-but-still-crisp interior. All that coupled with crisply frizzled edges and tiny pockets perfect for coating in sauce. It's a flavor bomb, and your mouth is squarely in the blast zone.

The goal is to get the exteriors to brown and frizzle just as the interiors barely finish cooking. It's a pretty foolproof technique—the only way to go wrong is if you try to add too many sprouts at once or you don't use enough oil; the temperature will drop and your sprouts will end up overcooking by the time they crisp properly, leaving you with soft, greasy centers. But barring that, all you gotta do is heat your oil, dump your sprouts in, and wait.

A few minutes later, they emerge. Crisp, golden brown, and glistening. Want to get extra fancy? Throw a few sliced shallots in there with 'em. They frizzle up in just about the same time, becoming as sweet and aromatic as the best onion ring. You can eat everything as is with just some salt and pepper, but they're even better in a Thai-style dressing with fish sauce, lime juice, and hot chiles.

recipe continues

Yield
Serves 4

Active Time
20 minutes

Total Time
20 minutes

NOTE
Some folks may find this amount of Thai bird chiles to be quite hot. Use your discretion. You can also replace the Thai birds with a milder chile like jalapeño or Fresno.

INGREDIENTS

2 to 3 fresh Thai bird chiles, roughly chopped (see Note)

3 medium garlic cloves (8 g)

1 tablespoon (15 ml) palm or light brown sugar

1 tablespoon (15 ml) fish sauce

1 tablespoon (15 ml) fresh lime juice

Handful of roughly chopped fresh cilantro leaves and fine stems

3 quarts (1.5 l) peanut, rice bran, or other neutral oil

1 pound (450 g) Brussels sprouts, stems trimmed, outer leaves removed, split in half

3 medium shallots (about 4½ ounces/130 g), thinly sliced

DIRECTIONS

(1) Pound the chiles and garlic in the bowl of a mortar and pestle until a rough paste is formed. Add the sugar and pound until dissolved (the mixture will be quite sticky). Use the pestle to incorporate the fish sauce and lime juice by stirring it in with a circular motion. Stir in the cilantro leaves.

(2) Line a rimmed baking sheet with a triple layer of paper towels. In a wok, heat the oil to 400°F. Add the Brussels sprouts and shallots. Oil temperature will drop to around 325°F. Adjust the heat to maintain this temperature. Cook, stirring and agitating with a spider until the Brussels sprouts are deep golden brown, about 4 minutes. Transfer to the paper-towel-lined baking sheet and shake to blot off excess oil.

(3) Transfer the sprouts and shallots to a large bowl and add the dressing. Toss to combine and serve.

FRIED BROCCOLI WITH HONEY AND BALSAMIC VINEGAR

Yield
Serves 4

Active Time
20 minutes

Total Time
20 minutes

INGREDIENTS

3 tablespoons (45 ml) honey

1 tablespoon (15 ml) balsamic vinegar

2 tablespoons (15 g) drained capers, roughly chopped

Handful of minced fresh parsley leaves

3 quarts (1.5 l) peanut, rice bran, or other neutral oil

1¼ pounds (565 g) broccoli, florets separated and cut into bite-sized pieces, stems peeled and cut on a bias into ½-inch-wide planks

2 ounces (60 g/about ⅓ cup) pine nuts

3 medium shallots (about 4½ ounces/130 g), thinly sliced

Kosher salt and freshly ground black pepper

As with Brussels sprouts, broccoli gets an intensely nutty, sweet aroma when deep-fried. Honey, balsamic vinegar, pine nuts, and capers complement this nuttiness. This recipe also works well with cauliflower.

DIRECTIONS

1. Combine the honey, vinegar, capers, and parsley in a large bowl and set aside.

2. Line a rimmed baking sheet with a triple layer of paper towels. In a wok, heat the oil to 400°F. Add the broccoli, pine nuts, and shallots. Oil temperature will drop to around 325°F. Adjust the heat to maintain this temperature. Cook, stirring and agitating with a spider until the edges of the broccoli are deep golden brown, about 4 minutes. Transfer to the paper-towel-lined baking sheet and shake to blot off excess oil.

3. Transfer the broccoli mixture to the bowl with the dressing. Toss to combine, season with salt and pepper to taste, and serve.

FRIED SHISHITO PEPPERS

Yield
Serves 3 to 4 as a snack or side dish

Active Time
5 minutes

Total Time
5 minutes

INGREDIENTS

12 ounces (340 g) shishito or padrón peppers

1 quart (1 l) peanut, rice bran, or other neutral oil

Kosher salt

Shishito peppers are small Japanese peppers with thin skins and a grassy flavor, similar to Spanish padrón peppers but larger. They are typically mild, but once in a while you'll bite into a hot one. This is the simplest recipe in the book, requiring nothing but peppers, oil, and a bit of salt.

DIRECTIONS

Line a bowl with a triple layer of paper towels. In a wok, heat the oil to 350°F. Add the peppers all at once (they will sputter and spit a bit). Cook, agitating with a spider, until blistered all over, about 20 seconds. Transfer to the bowl, season with salt, and toss to blot off excess oil. Serve immediately.

CRISPY FRIED PORK BELLY

One of the most glorious sights to behold at a Thai market is the *mu krop* vendor, with slabs of golden-brown pork belly. Order some belly and they'll cut off a chunk with a cleaver, cracking through the thick, blistered surface and revealing pale white, tender, juicy meat and fat underneath. It's a classic ingredient in dishes like *pad khana mu krop* (Stir-fried Chinese broccoli with pork belly, page 206). In the Philippines it's known as *lechon kawali* (*lechón* is the Spanish word for "suckling pig," while *kawali* is the Filipino word for "wok")

and comes served with a hot and vinegary dipping sauce, sometimes flavored with pork liver. In Adri's native Colombia, it's *chicharrón*, and in China a similar roasted version is *sio bak*. There's a reason crispy pork belly is popular across multiple cultures around the world.

Why does pork skin puff and blister when you fry it? It's all thanks to moisture within the rind that suddenly turns to steam, causing rapid expansion that puffs up the skin into bubbles that then dehydrate and set in the hot fat. But it's not as simple as dropping a piece of pork belly into hot oil. Try that and you end up with pork rind that is impossibly tough and chewy.

You know how difficult it is to blow up a rubber balloon fresh from the package, but if you stretch it out with your hands a few times to loosen it up, it becomes much easier? We have to take the same approach with bubbles of pork skin, but rather than loosening it up by stretching it with our hands, we'll loosen it up by par-cooking it, breaking down some of the tough connective tissue.

The first step is to simmer the pork belly in water spiked with vinegar and salt for an hour. This causes the meat to start constricting, which in turn pushes out impurities and gunk that would cause the fried belly to discolor and turn blotchy. The connective tissue will begin to soften at this stage, and some of the fat will begin to render as well. Finally, it tightens up its structure enough to allow you to score the rind, which allows the skin to expand more during its final puffing stage. For more flavor, you can add aromatics to the water at this stage, such as bay leaves, peppercorns, and garlic.

There are a few ways to score pork rind. If you've got a sharp knife and a bit of patience, you can cut a series of shallow parallel or cross-hatched lines into it, making sure to score only the topmost layer—if you score into the flesh, juices get pushed out during cooking that prevent the rind from crisping properly.

The other alternative is to use a sharp metal skewer or fork to repeatedly poke it (go for around fifteen to twenty holes per square inch of rind), or to use a jaccard—a tool made for tenderizing meat that consists of dozens of sharp skewers attached to a single handle (you can find them online for around $25). If you use any of these methods, the same caveat applies: be careful not to poke into the actual meat underneath the rind; a very light prick is all it needs.

Just like French fries, crispy pork belly benefits from double cooking (triple cooking if you count the initial boil): once at a relatively low temperature to break down the connective tissue further and begin to dehydrate the crust, then a rest at room temperature, followed by a second fry at a higher temperature. The problem is that during this first fry, your pork belly will still have pockets of moisture in the rind that can pop very explosively as pressure builds up from the conversion of water to steam. This can cause frightening and dangerous oil spatters.

To prevent this problem, I like to swap out that initial fry with a stay in the oven, roasting the pork belly at around 375°F (190°C) for 20 to 30 minutes to drive off excess moisture and prime the rind for the final puffing and crisping stage.

Once the pork belly has had a chance to cool, I carefully lower it into a wok with a few inches of hot oil, positioning the pork belly so that the rind is facing up and emerging from the oil a bit. This allows you to ladle hot fat over the top of the pork belly. As you do so, you'll see an immediate and dramatic puffing of the skin as it forms thousands of microblisters, each one adding surface area and crunch. Leaving the pork belly rind up and emerging from the boil during this stage minimizes pressure on the rind, which is what allows the skin to puff so dramatically.

Once the rind has fully puffed, you can carefully turn it over so the rind is submerged in the oil, allowing it to finish crisping and browning.

Take the pork belly out and let it rest on a rack for a few moments to cool, then scrape a knife across its surface and marvel at the crispy, bubbly skin you've just created. Surely such an accomplishment deserves some kind of reward. Luckily, this is the kind of accomplishment that has the reward built right in.

CRISPY FRIED PORK BELLY

DIRECTIONS

(1) Place the pork belly in a wok, rind side up. Cover with water, then add the vinegar, peppercorns, bay leaves, garlic, and 2 tablespoons (20 g) of the salt. Bring to a boil, reduce to a bare simmer, cover, and cook for 1 hour. Transfer the pork belly to a cutting board and allow it to rest until cool enough to handle. Discard the water and aromatics.

(2) Place an oven rack in the center position and preheat the oven to 375°F (190°C). Using a fork, a handful of metal or bamboo skewers, or a metal jaccard, poke holes all over the surface of the rind, being careful to pierce only the very surface of the rind (do not pierce the meat underneath). You can also use a very sharp knife to thinly score the rind at ¼-inch intervals.

(3) Combine the remaining tablespoon (10 g) salt and the baking soda, then rub it all over the pork belly, using your palms to really rub it in. Place the pork belly on a rack set in a rimmed baking sheet and let it rest for 15 minutes. Transfer to the oven and roast until the surface of the pork is very dry, about 25 minutes. Remove the pork from the oven and allow to cool for 15 minutes.

(4) Heat the oil in the wok over medium heat until it registers 325°F (160°C) on an instant-read thermometer. Using tongs and a wide wok spatula, carefully lower the pork belly into the oil, skin side up (the skin should be emerging from the oil). Use the spatula to splash hot oil over the top of the pork belly. You should immediately start to see the skin puffing and blistering. Continue basting the hot oil over the skin until no new bubbles form and the skin starts to crisp a bit, about 3 minutes.

(5) Carefully flip the pork belly skin side down, being careful not to splash the hot oil. Increase the heat to high and cook, moving the pork belly around and splashing it with hot oil until deeply golden brown and crispy on all sides, 3 to 4 more minutes.

(6) Transfer the pork belly back to the wire rack set in a rimmed baking sheet, skin side up, and allow it to cool slightly. Use a sharp knife or cleaver to cut the pork belly into thick slices, then cut the slices into bite-sized chunks. Serve immediately with Sukang Sawsawan or Nam Pla Prik.

Yield
Serves 6

Active Time
30 minutes

Total Time
2 hours

NOTE

Look for rind-on pork belly with a relatively even ratio of fat to lean. Sometimes pork belly has hair or discoloration on its rind. If your pork belly looks anything but pristine, I would suggest passing a blowtorch briefly across its surface, then scraping it firmly with a knife to clean it.

INGREDIENTS

One 2-pound (900 g) slab rind-on pork belly
2 tablespoons (30 ml) distilled white vinegar
1 tablespoon (8 g) whole black peppercorns
3 dried bay leaves
1 head garlic, split in half horizontally
3 tablespoons (35 g) kosher salt
½ teaspoon (2 g) baking soda
2 quarts (2 l) peanut, rice bran, or other neutral oil

To Serve:

Sukang Sawsawan (Philippine Chile-Vinegar Dipping Sauce, page 435) or Nam Pla Prik (page 257) for serving

SUKANG SAWSAWAN (PHILIPPINE CHILE-VINEGAR DIPPING SAUCE)

Yield
Makes
1 cup

Active Time
5 minutes

Total Time
5 minutes

NOTES
You can use other types of chiles to suit your heat tolerance and flavor preference, such as jalapeño (mildest), Fresno (hotter), or Scotch bonnet (blazing). Cane vinegar is a Philippine-style vinegar made from sugarcane. If you can't find it, you can use white vinegar or rice vinegar in its place.

INGREDIENTS

1 teaspoon (3 g) black peppercorns

4 medium garlic cloves (10 to 15 g), roughly chopped

2 to 3 fresh Thai bird chiles, roughly chopped (see Notes)

2 ounces (60 g/about ¼ small) red onion, roughly chopped

1 teaspoon (3 g) kosher salt, plus more as needed

2 tablespoons (25 g) granulated or light or dark brown sugar, plus more as needed

1 tablespoon (15 ml) light soy sauce or shoyu or fish sauce

¾ cup (180 ml) cane or coconut vinegar (see Notes)

Sawsawan is the Filipino word for a variety of sauces that accompany barbecued and fried meats. This particular version is vinegary and spicy, tempered with a bit of sugar and flavored with garlic and onions. It can be made in advance and stored in a jar in your fridge for several months. The flavor will improve with time. As with most sauces and dips that use fresh aromatics, you get much better flavor out of them by pounding them in a mortar and pestle.

DIRECTIONS

(1) Grind the peppercorns in a large mortar and pestle until roughly ground. Add the garlic, chiles, onion, and salt and pound with the pestle until a rough paste is formed. Add the sugar and grind with a circular motion until the sugar is dissolved and the paste turns sticky, about 30 seconds.

(2) Add the soy sauce or fish sauce. Slowly add the vinegar while grinding with a circular motion. Taste and season with more salt or sugar to taste. Transfer to a sealable jar and store in the refrigerator for up to several months. The sauce will improve the most dramatically after a day in the fridge but will continue to get better with time.

Dry Frying

Dry frying is a technique used in Sichuan cuisine. The general idea is to cook your main ingredient—whether it's a protein (typically beef, lamb, or pork) or a vegetable (like long beans, green beans, or Chinese broccoli)—in a relatively large amount of moderately hot oil without any kind of batter or protective coating. As it cooks, the intense heat drives off interior moisture, thereby concentrating its flavor. Simultaneously, the exterior becomes desiccated (hence "dry" frying) and browned.

After their initial par-frying stage, dry-fried foods are very briefly stir-fried with a small amount of strongly aromatic ingredients, which get absorbed into the recently desiccated surfaces. Generally, there's no real "sauce" to speak of, so if you're the kind of person who likes to pour juices on top of rice, these aren't the droids you're looking for. Move along.

The result is intensely flavored food with a uniquely chewy, crisp texture.

SICHUAN DRY-FRIED BEEF

While some recipes for dry-fried beef call for using a very small amount of oil (2 tablespoons or so) for the initial fry for the sake of convenience, I find that you really don't get the same dehydrating effect; the food ends up steaming or searing instead. It's a little more work, and requires you to strain and save the excess oil (I keep oil I've used for dry frying in the fridge, since it tends to turn rancid faster than other types of used oil), but the final results are worth it.

While restaurants operate by dunking proteins directly into hot oil, I find that starting with cold oil and meat and heating them together is a much safer, burn-and-splatter-proof method that leads to comparable results (it won't work for vegetables). The oil starts out looking cloudy and emulsified, but as the moisture slowly evaporates, it'll begin to resemble a regular deep fry. This is when you need to start tasting and checking for doneness.

The beef is done when it's chewy on the exterior, still slightly moist in the center, with a few crisp bits here and there. It's then ready to stir-fry with its spicy, vinegary sauce.

Yield
Serves 3
to 4

Active Time
30 minutes

Total Time
45 minutes

NOTES

The shredded dried chiles make this dish pretty hot. You can omit them or cut back on them to make a milder version. The strained oil can be cooled, then stored in a sealed container in the fridge for another use. Chinese celery and carrots are typical vegetables in this dish, but slivered bell peppers would work instead of or in addition to them.

INGREDIENTS

1 pound (450 g) flank steak, cut into fine matchsticks (see page 116)

1 cup (240 ml) peanut, rice bran, or other neutral oil

2 teaspoons (5 g) minced garlic (about 2 medium cloves)

2 teaspoons (5 g) minced fresh ginger (about ½-inch segment)

2 tablespoons fermented chile bean paste (doubanjiang)

6 dried hot chiles, such as er jing tiao or árbol, seeded and cut into fine shreds with kitchen shears (see Notes)

½ teaspoon (2 g) ground Sichuan peppercorns

2 Chinese or regular celery stalks, cut on a sharp bias into ¼-inch slices

1 medium carrot (about 6 ounces/170 g), cut into fine matchsticks (see page 86)

1 tablespoon (15 ml) soy sauce

1 tablespoon (15 ml) Chinkiang or black vinegar

1 tablespoon (15 ml) Shaoxing wine

2 teaspoons (8 g) sugar

Kosher salt

DIRECTIONS

(1) Line a large plate with a double layer of paper towels. Combine the steak and oil in wok and cook over medium-high heat, stirring occasionally. The beef will initially give off lots of moisture and eventually begin sizzling and frying. The beef is done when deep brown, crisp at the edges, but still pliant, about 10 minutes. Remove from the oil with a slotted spoon, drain on the paper-towel-lined plate, and transfer to a medium bowl.

(2) Carefully pour the hot oil out of the wok through a fine-mesh strainer set in a heatproof container (such as a large saucepan).

(3) Wipe out the wok and heat over high heat until smoking. Reduce the heat to medium-high, add 2 tablespoons (30 ml) of the strained oil, and swirl to coat. Immediately add the garlic, ginger, and chile bean paste and stir-fry until the oil turns red, about 30 seconds.

(4) Increase the heat to high. Add the hot chiles, Sichuan peppercorns, drained beef, celery, and carrots and stir-fry until the celery and carrots are tender-crisp, about 1 minute.

(5) Add the soy sauce, vinegar, and wine by swirling it around the edges of the wok. Add the sugar. Toss everything together and stir-fry until there is no liquid remaining in the wok and the beef is coated in a layer of sizzling spices, about 1 minute longer. Season with salt (it may not need any) to taste. Transfer to a serving platter and serve.

How to Shred Dry Chiles

You can buy preshredded small hot chiles for dishes like Sichuan Dry-Fried Beef at a Chinese supermarket, but it's easy enough to do with a pair of sharp kitchen shears. Hold each chile by the stem end, then snip them at a very sharp bias as thin as your scissors allow. Don't worry about the seeds for now.

As you finish with each chile, discard the stem ends. Once all your chiles are snipped, shake the pile of shredded chiles with your fingertips and most of the seeds should fall right out. Transfer the shredded chiles to a sealable container and discard the seeds left on the cutting board. (A few seeds might hitch a ride with the shredded chiles. This is fine.)

NUA KEM (THAI-STYLE BEEF JERKY)

Yield
Serves 3 to
4 as a snack
or appetizer

Active Time
20 minutes

Total Time
5 to 6 hours total
if using sun-
drying method, 2
to 3 hours total if
using the oven

NOTES
The initial marinating and drying steps can be done up to several days in advance, leaving just the final dry-fry step before serving. This dish is typically served with *jaew*, sticky rice, som tam (green papaya salad; page 619), but it is equally tasty with many other dipping sauces, such as Nam Pla Prik (page 257), *sukang sawsawan* (page 435), or your favorite bottled sriracha (I recommend Shark brand).

When Nua Kem appears on menus in Thai restaurants in the West, it's almost always described as "Thai Beef Jerky," but this is not an accurate description, as it is far juicier than any preserved beef snack I've ever had. It's made by marinating beef strips in a mixture of soy sauce, fish sauce, and sugar, letting the beef strips dry in the sun until the marinade forms a dry pellicle (an oven at its lowest setting works fine if you are squeamish about leaving raw meat outside in the sun), then deep frying it until the surface is deeply caramelized with a texture that's halfway between crispy and chewy and a juicy, flavorful core. The dehydrated surface of the beef makes it a perfect sponge for soaking up a flavorful *jaew* dipping sauce (page 440).

DIRECTIONS

(1) In a medium bowl, combine the soy sauce, fish sauce, sugar, and white pepper until the sugar is dissolved. Add the beef strips and toss to coat thoroughly.

2 teaspoons (10 ml) light soy sauce or shoyu

2 tablespoons (30 ml) fish sauce

1 tablespoon (12 g) palm, light or dark brown, or granulated sugar

½ teaspoon (2 g) freshly ground white pepper

1 pound (450 g) flank or skirt steak, cut against the grain into ½-inch slivers

2 cups (480 ml) peanut, rice bran, or other neutral oil

1 recipe *Jaew* (page 440) for dipping

(2) Spread the beef out onto a wire rack set in a rimmed baking sheet. If the weather is hot and sunny, place the beef outside in the sun, flipping every 45 to 60 minutes, until the surface feels dry to the touch. Alternatively, place the beef in an oven preheated as low as it will go (aim for a minimum of 125°F and a maximum of 175°F, the lower the better) and let it dry out, turning every 30 to 45 minutes, until the surface feels dry to the touch. Proceed immediately to step 3 or transfer the beef to a sealed container and store in the refrigerator for up to 5 days before proceeding.

(3) When ready to serve, heat the oil in a wok over high heat until it registers 325°F on an instant-read thermometer. Add the beef and cook, stirring it constantly and adjusting the heat to maintain a temperature between 275° and 325°F, until it is well browned and crisp at the edges but still pliant, about 5 minutes. Transfer to a paper-towel-lined plate to drain. Serve immediately with *jaew*.

JAEW

Yield
Makes 1 cup

Active Time
10 minutes

Total Time
10 minutes

NOTE

Prik pon is roasted and ground dried chiles from Thailand. *Khao khua* is toasted glutinous rice powder. You can find both ingredients at any Southeast Asian specialty market, most large Asian supermarkets with a Southeast Asian section, or from an online retailer.

INGREDIENTS

4 medium garlic cloves (about 10 g)
1 tablespoon (about 8 g) palm sugar
1 tablespoon (about 8 g) *prik pon* (see Note)
1 tablespoon (about 8 g) *khao khua* (see Note)
½ cup (120 ml) fish sauce, plus more to taste
3 tablespoons (45 ml) lime juice from about 3 limes, plus more to taste
1 medium shallot (about 1½ ounces/45 g), thinly sliced, plus more to taste
Handful of fresh cilantro leaves, finely chopped (about 20 g)

Nam pla prik (page 257), made with fresh chiles and fish sauce, may be the most well-known Thai dipping sauce, but *jaew*, its tangier, more aromatic cousin made with fresh aromatics and dried chiles, is my favorite. It goes wonderfully well with any kind of grilled meat and is the classic accompaniment to *kai yang* (Thai-style grilled chicken; you can find my recipe for it on SeriousEats.com) or *mu ping* (grilled pork skewers). It's also great as a dip for *nua kem* (page 438).

While it's possible to make the sauce with any dried chile, I urge you to seek out or special-order Thai-style roasted and ground dried chiles (*prik pon*), which have an intense heat and a flavor that's equal parts fruity and smoky. The other specialty ingredient you'll need is *khao khua*, which is glutinous rice (also sold as "sweet rice" or "sticky rice"; see pages 221–22 of the rice guide) that has been toasted and ground into a powder. You can find it at any Southeast Asian market or online retailer, or you can make it yourself by stirring ½ cup of dry glutinous rice in a wok over medium heat until it is toasty brown all over, then grinding it in a mortar and pestle or a spice grinder.

Note that even without the special ingredients you can make a delicious dipping sauce using any type of ground dried chiles in place of the *prik pon* and omitting the *khao khua* (just don't tell any Thai food purists you know).

DIRECTIONS

Combine the garlic and palm sugar in a mortar and pound to a paste with a pestle. Add the *prik pon*, *khao khua*, fish sauce, and lime juice and stir with the pestle until the paste is fully dissolved into the liquid. Stir in the shallots and cilantro leaves. Adjust to taste with more fish sauce, lime juice, or ground chile.

Starch-Coated Fried Foods

Starch-coated fried foods don't have the hard *crunch* of foods that are more heavily battered or breaded in mixtures made with wheat flour, but they do have a thin, mildly crispy shell that forms a good surface for sauce or dips to adhere. Starch coatings are also good for preserving the natural flavor of the fried main ingredient.

CHONGQING-STYLE DRY-FRIED CHICKEN

"La zi ji," I said, timidly.

A confused stare.

"La ZI ji?"

More confusion.

"LA ZI JI."

A sudden burst of recognition. "Ah, *la zi ji!*" exclaimed the host at the hostel Adri and I were staying at in Chongqing.

That's exactly what I said! I couldn't help thinking to myself. Apparently my inflection confused our host, who was trying her earnest best to help us out. She grabbed a map and drew a circle around a building, indicating which restaurant I should go to. I'd have to repeat the same exchange twice more—once with the host of the restaurant and once with the server—before I finally got what I was after: dry-fried chicken tossed in a giant pile of dried chiles and Sichuan peppercorns.

The dish I was served was immediately familiar to me: golden bits of fried chicken nestled into an overwhelmingly large pile of dried chiles whose aroma mingled with the piney,

recipe continues

<table>
<tr><td>Yield
Serves 4</td><td>Active Time
15 minutes

Total Time
40 minutes</td></tr>
</table>

NOTES

For more information on dried Sichuan chiles, see pages 313–15. Note that when eating this dish, the chiles are not meant to be eaten; they are there for aroma and visual appeal. The strained oil can be cooled, then stored in a sealed container in the fridge for the next time you deep-fry.

INGREDIENTS

For the Dry-Fried Chicken:

1 pound (450 g) boneless, skinless chicken thigh, cut into ½-inch chunks

2 teaspoons (10 ml) light soy sauce or shoyu

2 teaspoons (10 ml) Shaoxing wine

2 teaspoons (8 g) kosher salt

1 large egg

1 tablespoon cornstarch or potato starch

2 quarts (2 l) peanut, rice bran, or other neutral oil

For the Stir-Fry:

2 tablespoons (15 g) minced garlic (about 6 medium cloves)

2 tablespoons (15 g) minced fresh ginger (about ¾-inch segment)

2 scallions, thinly sliced

1½ ounces (45 g/about 1 cup) dried er jing tiao chiles, cut into 1-inch pieces (see Notes)

1½ ounces (45 g/about 1 cup) dried chao tian jiao chiles, cut into 1-inch pieces (see Notes)

1 tablespoon (8 g) Sichuan or Korean chile flakes

2 tablespoons (about ½ ounce/20 g) green or red Sichuan peppercorns

1 teaspoon (4 g) sugar

¼ cup (40 g) roasted peanuts or Fried Peanuts (page 319)

2 tablespoons (15 g) toasted sesame seeds

citrusy scent of Sichuan peppercorns. The tastes were also familiar: crispy, slightly chewy bites of chicken whose flavor was intensified through dry frying, a mouth-numbing quantity of Sichuan peppercorn, and a chile heat that, while not overwhelming, certainly built up as I powered through the plate.

The main difference in the version I had in Chongqing versus the majority of the versions I've had in the United States was the presence of bones. In the Sichuan original, the chicken is chopped up bones and all, and as a diner you're expected to suck the bits of meat and marrow off them in your mouth, spitting out the little shards onto a plate as you eat. I've had it this way a handful of times in the United States, but I've got to admit, it's a whole lot more work in a dish that already has you picking through piles of peppers in search of juicy nuggets. In the U.S., the chicken is often fried with a very light batter or dredging, which I usually do as well.

Once you get over the barrier of deep frying (and you should be over that barrier by now), it's a surprisingly easy dish to make at home. Some recipes recommend frying the chicken once before stir-frying it, but I find that, as is nearly always the case with fried foods, a double-fry with a rest in between produces better results.

Why is this? The trouble with an extended single fry is that by the time the exterior is perfectly crispy, the chicken on the interior is liable to overcook significantly, leading to dry, chewy bites. By frying once, allowing the chicken to rest, then frying again, you can drive more moisture off the exterior, while still ensuring that the chicken in the center doesn't ever get so hot that it dries out. The result is chicken with a crisper exterior and juicier center.

The only difficulty you may find is in procuring the right ingredients. The dish relies on a mix of chiles—er jing tiao and chao tian jiao at the very least, with the addition of *deng long jiao* (Sichuan lantern chiles) if you want the most complex combination of aroma and heat. Green Sichuan peppercorns, with their more intense numbing factor, are also preferable to red in this dish. You can find most of these ingredients online or at a very well-stocked Chinese supermarket, but even if you're just using árbol chiles and red Sichuan peppercorn, you're in for a numbing-good time.

DIRECTIONS

(1) **For the Chicken:** Combine the chicken, soy sauce, Shaoxing wine, salt, egg, and starch in a medium bowl. Massage with your hands until the chicken is sticky and thoroughly coated in the starch mixture. Set aside to marinate for at least 15 minutes and up to 1 hour.

(2) In a wok, heat the oil to 350°F (175°C). Add the chicken and cook, agitating it to separate the pieces and adjusting the heat to maintain an oil temperature of 300° to 325°F (150° to 160°C), until the chicken is pale golden brown and starting to crisp up around the edges, about 1 minute. Remove the chicken with a spider and transfer to a rimmed baking sheet. Allow the chicken to cool for 5 minutes.

(3) **For the Stir-Fry:** Heat the oil in the wok to 400°F (190°C). With the wok set over high heat, add the chicken and cook, agitating and stirring it until the pieces are crispy and deep golden brown, about 45 seconds. Remove the chicken with a spider and return it to the rimmed baking sheet. Carefully pour the hot oil out of the wok through a fine-mesh strainer set in a heatproof container (such as a large saucepan).

(4) Wipe out the wok and return it to high heat until smoking. Reduce the heat to medium, then add 3 tablespoons (45 ml) of the strained oil and swirl to coat. Add the garlic, ginger, scallions, dried chiles, chile flakes, and Sichuan peppercorns. Stir-fry until fragrant, about 30 seconds. Return the chicken to the wok along with the sugar, peanuts, and sesame seeds and stir-fry for an additional 30 seconds. Transfer to a serving platter and serve immediately.

KARAAGE (JAPANESE-STYLE MARINATED FRIED CHICKEN)

The etymology of the word *karaage (kah-ra-ah-geh)* is not completely clear. The *age* part of it is the Japanese word for "frying." That much is agreed upon. But the *kara* part could mean two different things depending on exactly how it's spelled. It's more commonly spelled with the character 唐, a reference to the Tang Dynasty in China, the origin of the style of frying. However, there is little to suggest that the dish karaage is actually Chinese in origin, so some newspapers and food writers use the character "空" instead, which translates as "empty."

This latter makes sense. Typical methods of frying in Japan include a batter (as with tempura) or a bread crumb coating (as with katsu), but with karaage, bits of food are simply dusted in flour or starch before being fried. I asked my mom what karaage means to her. Her response was "not katsu and not tempura."

You may have heard the term *tatsutaage*. Technically, tatsutaage involves marinating meat before dusting and frying it, while karaage involves no marinade, but these days the two terms are generally used interchangeably, and nobody would bat an eye if ordering karaage produced something with some soy and ginger flavor built right in with a marinade. Similarly, while *karaage* technically refers to any food cooked in that style (pork, octopus, and burdock are common choices), if there is no qualifier attached to it, chicken thigh is the default choice.

A basic karaage marinade contains ginger, sake, and soy sauce, though if you'd like, you can add any number of other flavors. Garlic and sesame oil are common choices, as is mirin, oyster sauce, or even Kewpie mayonnaise. My mom would marinate hers with soy sauce, sake, and ginger, then dust it in potato starch cut with Japanese curry powder before deep frying it.

The soy sauce is the real key to good karaage. It contains two factors that improve chicken: salt and protease enzymes. As muscle proteins heat up, they constrict, which squeezes juices out of meat, toughening it and making it dry out. The salt in marinades, brines, and dry rubs dissolves muscle proteins. This reduces their proclivity to constrict, which in turn leaves meat that's been treated with salt juicier and more tender. Proteases are enzymes in soy sauce that behave in a similar manner, breaking down proteins and enhancing the effect of salt (powerful proteases are how papaya juice, pineapple juice, and commercial meat tenderizers tenderize meats).

As for the starch coating, karaage is *never* as crisp as, say, southern fried chicken. The thin layer of starch on it is less about creating a crunchy shell and more about protecting the outer layers of meat from desiccating or turning stringy. Still, double-frying the chicken—once at a low temp and then again at a higher temperature—will make it extra crisp (are you beginning to notice a theme here?)

CHICKEN KARAAGE (JAPANESE-STYLE FRIED CHICKEN WITH SOY, SAKE, AND GINGER MARINADE)

Yield
Serves 4

Active Time
15 minutes

Total Time
30 minutes

NOTES

You can use skin-on or skinless chicken thighs for this, according to preference. Potato starch will produce a slightly crisper texture than cornstarch, but either works. The used oil can be strained and saved for another use.

INGREDIENTS

1 pound (450 g) boneless chicken thighs (about 4 thighs), trimmed of excess fat and cut into rough 1-inch chunks (see Notes)

1 tablespoon (8 g) minced fresh ginger (about ½-inch segment)

1 tablespoon (15 ml) light soy sauce or shoyu

1 tablespoon (15 ml) sake

½ teaspoon (2 g) kosher salt

⅓ cup (45 g) potato starch or cornstarch (see Notes)

⅓ cup (45 g) all-purpose flour

1 quart (1 l) peanut, rice bran, or other neutral oil

1 lemon, cut into wedges

This simple karaage recipe is an ideal accompaniment for sake or a cold, crisp beer. It's also good served cold in a lunch box. Lemon wedges are the simplest accompaniment, but you can also serve them with Japanese-style Kewpie mayonnaise or with a dusting of shichimi togarashi, a Japanese seven-spice blend.

For flavor variations, try adding any of the following to the marinade:

→ **2 cloves garlic, minced**
→ **1 tablespoon (15 ml) oyster sauce**
→ **1 tablespoon (8 to 10 g) Japanese curry powder (such as S&B Oriental Curry Powder)**
→ **¼ cup (30 to 40 g) raw or toasted white or black sesame seeds added to the starch/flour mixture**

DIRECTIONS

(1) Combine the chicken, ginger, soy sauce, sake, and salt in a medium bowl and toss until the chicken is thoroughly coated in the marinade. Cover and refrigerate for at least 30 minutes and up to 24 hours.

(2) Combine the starch and flour in a large bowl. Remove the chicken pieces from the marinade and toss in the flour mixture until well coated. Place in a fine-mesh strainer held over the sink and shake to remove excess starch and flour.

(3) In a wok, heat the oil to 350°F (175°C). Add the chicken and cook, agitating it to separate the pieces and adjusting the heat to maintain an oil temperature of 300° to 325°F (150° to 160°C), until the chicken is pale golden brown, barely cooked through, and starting to crisp up around the edges, around 1½ minutes. Remove the chicken with a spider and transfer to a rimmed baking sheet. Allow the chicken to cool for 5 minutes.

(4) Heat the oil in the wok to 400°F (190°C). With the wok set over high heat, add the chicken and cook, agitating and stirring it until the pieces are crispy and deep golden brown, 45 seconds to 1 minute. Remove the chicken with a spider, drain, then transfer to a serving platter. Serve chicken with lemon wedges.

AGEDASHI TOFU (FRIED TOFU WITH SOY-DASHI)

Yield
Serves 4

Active Time
30 minutes

Total Time
30 minutes

NOTES

Homemade or store-bought tsuyu can be used in place of the dashi, soy, and mirin mixture in step one. Dilute tsuyu at a ratio of 1½ cups (360 ml) water to ½ cup (120 ml) tsuyu. For best flavor, use homemade dashi (pages 519–21). Alternatively, you can use powdered Hondashi, available at Asian markets or occasionally in the international aisle of a well-stocked supermarket. The used oil can be strained and saved for another use.

INGREDIENTS

For the Soy-Dashi (see Notes):

1½ cups (360 ml) dashi (see Notes)

3 tablespoons (45 ml) mirin

2 tablespoons (30 ml) light soy sauce or shoyu

For the Tofu:

⅓ cup (45 g) potato starch or cornstarch (see Notes)

⅓ cup (45 g) all-purpose flour

One 12.3-ounce/340 g) package firm or extra-firm silken tofu, cut into ¾-inch cubes

1 quart (1 l) peanut, rice bran, or other neutral oil

2 scallions, finely sliced, slices stored in ice water until ready to use (optional)

Large pinch of katsuobushi (optional)

2 ounces (60 g) grated daikon radish (optional)

In the West, we tend to be obsessed with crispy, crunchy foods. If you work hard to get something crispy, it had better *stay* crispy until it gets in your mouth. In Japan, on the other hand, fried foods are frequently intentionally allowed to soften. Crispy fried tofu is marinated in soy sauce and mirin until soft, then stuffed with rice for *inarizushi*. Crisp tempura shrimp served saturated in broth with noodles is a classic udon or soba shop menu item.

The idea is that a puffy fried coating, with its open pores and light texture, is like a sponge: it's a very effective medium for absorbing and holding on to broth and sauce. With agedashi tofu, for instance, silken tofu is dusted in starch, deep-fried until crisp, then served in a shallow pool of dashi seasoned with soy sauce and mirin (you can use homemade or store-bought concentrated tsuyu to make this broth; see the recipe on page 231). The coating softens and absorbs the broth, which effectively seasons every bite of tofu.

This is one of my favorite dishes and a favorite of my daughter as well (who has been eating it since she was around 6 months old).

DIRECTIONS

(1) **For the Soy-Dashi:** Combine the dashi, mirin, and soy sauce in a small saucepan and heat over medium-high heat until barely simmering. Reduce the heat, cover, and keep warm until ready to use.

(2) **For the Tofu:** Combine the starch and flour in a large bowl and toss the tofu in the flour mixture until well coated. Place in a fine-mesh strainer held over the sink and shake gently to remove excess starch and flour.

(3) In a wok, heat the oil to 375°F (190°C). Add the tofu and cook, agitating it to separate the pieces and adjusting the heat to maintain an oil temperature of 325° to 350°F (160° to 175°C), until the tofu is golden brown and crisp, about 2 minutes. Remove the tofu with a spider, drain, and transfer to serving bowls. Pour the hot dashi mixture over the tofu, garnish with scallions, katsuobushi, and grated daikon (if using), and serve.

CANTONESE PEPPER AND SALTY SHRIMP

I can't say that Phoenix Garden, with its slightly-too-gloppy sauces, dingy tables, and mildly rude waitstaff served the best or even the most authentic Cantonese cuisine in New York, but my oh my, how it's fed me and my family over the years. When we first moved to New York in 1983, it was located in the Elizabeth Street mall. We'd wait in line for an hour or more under the glow of greenish blue fluorescent lights shining through a dim, greasy haze just to get a taste of its crisp and juicy salt and pepper shrimp, served in their crunchy shells, piled high with fresh garlic and chiles. There is still no shrimp in the world that can touch Phoenix Garden's in its heyday.

That haze, incidentally, was no doubt due to years of poorly maintained ventilation hoods, which eventually led to the fire that forced them to close. For years we resorted to driving across the George Washington to hit their New Jersey counterpart, Phoenix Garden II. I'm still unclear on whether the man who ran the Jersey branch was really the identical twin of the New York branch operator or if it was all just a prank, but either way, their dry-fried chow fun and clams in black bean sauce had just as much *wok hei* as ever.

Their third and final incarnation on 40th Street and 2nd Avenue, run by the sons of the original owner, closed in the late 2010s, well after my sisters and I had already moved out of the area, which means that since then we've had to make those shrimp for ourselves. This recipe, intended to mimic the ones from Phoenix Garden, is one I developed specifically for my sister Pico, to help her re-create those crispy and salty shrimp even in the middle of a landlocked Montana winter.

It's actually surprisingly simple: butterfly some shell-on shrimp (the largest you can get), give them a baking soda brine to plump them up, toss with cornstarch, then deep-fry them just until they're crispy. Finally, stir-fry them with aromatics and a salt and pepper blend.

That salt and pepper blend can be as simple as ground white pepper and salt, but if you want the best flavor, it pays to not only toast the white peppercorns before grinding them but to actually toast the salt as well. Toasting salt in a carbon steel wok will give it a yellowish brown tinge and the distinct smoky aroma of *wok hei* as smoky vapors from the pan leave deposits on the surface of the salt (see "Toast Your Salt to Add Wok Hei to Any Dish," page 451).

recipe continues

Yield	Active Time
Serves 4	20 minutes
	Total Time
	35 to 40 minutes

NOTES

12.5 grams is about 1⅓ tablespoons Diamond Crystal kosher salt, 1 tablespoon Morton's kosher salt, or 2½ teaspoons table salt. The shrimp in this dish are meant to be eaten shell and all, though you can peel the shells as you eat if you don't like their texture. I like to butterfly the shrimp for this recipe, slitting open the shell along the back so that the shrimp increases in surface area as it fries (see step-by-step directions on page 449). If you buy EZ-peel shrimp, they come already butterflied, making them ideal for this dish. The strained oil can be cooled, then stored in a sealed container in the fridge for another use.

INGREDIENTS

For the Shrimp:

½ liter (500 g/about 2 cups) very cold water

12.5 g salt (see Notes)

10 g (about 1½ teaspoons) baking soda

1 pound (450 g) large shell-on shrimp, deveined and butterflied (see Notes)

A cup or so of ice cubes

¼ cup (30 g) cornstarch

1 quart (1 l) peanut, rice bran, or other neutral oil

For the Stir-Fry:

10 medium garlic cloves (30 to 40 g), thinly sliced

4 scallions, thinly sliced

1 hot green chile, such as Chinese cowhorn, Anaheim, jalapeño, or serrano, thinly sliced

1 hot red chile, such as Fresno or red serrano, thinly sliced

2 teaspoons (15 g) Dry-Roasted Salt and Pepper Blend (see page 450)

DIRECTIONS

(1) **For the Shrimp:** Combine the water, salt, and baking soda in a bowl and stir until the salt and baking soda are dissolved. Add the shrimp and stir to separate them and ensure the brine flows all around. Add the ice cubes and let the shrimp brine for at least 15 minutes and up to 30. Drain well.

(2) Bring 2 quarts (2 l) water to a boil in your wok. Drain the shrimp and add to the boiling water. Cook, stirring, until the shrimp are beginning to get firm and are bright pink, about 45 seconds. Drain well and transfer to a rimmed baking sheet or large plate to air-dry for a few minutes. Transfer to a bowl and toss with the cornstarch until all the shrimp are thoroughly coated.

(3) Wipe out the wok, add the oil, and heat to 400°F (200°C). With the wok over high heat, add half the shrimp and cook, agitating and stirring the shrimp constantly until crispy and barely cooked through, about 1 minute. Remove the shrimp with a spider and transfer them to a tray or large plate. Reheat the oil to 400°F (200°C) and repeat with the remaining shrimp. Carefully pour the hot oil out of the wok through a fine-mesh strainer set in a heatproof container (such as a large saucepan).

(4) **For the Stir-Fry:** Wipe out the wok and return it to high heat until smoking. Add 2 tablespoons (30 ml) of the strained oil and swirl to coat. Add the garlic, scallions, and green and red chiles and stir-fry until fragrant, about 30 seconds. Add the shrimp and the salt and pepper blend and toss to coat. Transfer to a serving platter and serve immediately.

How to Prepare Shrimp for Pepper and Salty Shrimp

Cantonese pepper and salty shrimp is best made with whole shell-on shrimp. If you can find live shrimp with their heads intact, this is your best option. If you cannot find live shrimp, go for headless frozen shrimp.

EZ-peel shrimp are the easiest option for this dish, as they require no prep work at all. For other options, here's what you need to do.

Step 1 • Snip the Beak and Antennae

If using live shrimp, place them in a single layer on a tray in the freezer for several hours to humanely kill them. Thaw before proceeding.

Head-on shrimp have a sharp pointed beaklike protrusion at the front of their heads that can prick diners if they aren't careful. Snipping it off with a pair of kitchen shears helps preclude this. I also snip the antennae off at the base. They aren't edible and make for messy presentation.

Step 2 • Snip off the Legs

Hold the shrimp in one hand, straightening out its back so that all of its legs are exposed. Use kitchen shears to trim them off.

Step 3 • Butterfly and Devein

Slip your kitchen shears underneath the first segment of the shrimp's abdomen (for shell-on shrimp, that's the first segment behind the carapace of the head) and snip along the shrimp's back down to the last segment before the tail. (You should cut through a total of five segments.) Rinse the shrimp, opening up its back with your fingers and pulling out any bits of dark digestive tract you see in the process.

DRY-ROASTED SALT AND PEPPER BLEND

Yield
Makes
½ cup
(about
75 g)

Active Time
30 minutes

Total Time
30 minutes

NOTES
You can omit the Sichuan peppercorns if you'd like. You can also grind the toasted salt and pepper in an electric spice grinder. Allow it to cool completely after toasting before grinding.

INGREDIENTS

6 tablespoons (about 60 g) white
    peppercorns
4 teaspoons (about 16 g) green or red
    Sichuan peppercorns (optional)
¼ cup (35 g) kosher salt

Dry-roasting salt and pepper in a wok before grinding it gives it a toasty, lightly smoky aroma. This comes in part from the flavors developed by toasting spices, but it also comes from vaporized polymers and oil from the wok leaving deposits on the surface of the salt. Roasted salt and pepper can enhance smoky *wok hei* flavor in food even when the food has never seen the inside of a wok. Try a pinch on roasted or seared vegetables or meat, to season your salad, or anywhere you want a hint of smokiness.

DIRECTIONS

(1) Heat all the ingredients in a dry wok over medium heat, tossing and stirring frequently, until very toasty and fragrant, 7 to 10 minutes. Note that this may create some smoke, so use a vent hood if you have one, or at the very least get a good cross-breeze going through your kitchen space.

(2) Transfer to a large plate or tray and let cool completely. Transfer to a heavy mortar and pestle or a spice grinder and grind into a powder. Let cool completely, then store in a sealed container in the pantry indefinitely.

Toast Your Salt to Add Wok Hei to Any Dish

Toasting salt in a wok is a traditional technique for dishes like Cantonese salt and pepper shrimp. Tasted side by side, toasted salt acquires a lightly smoky aroma reminiscent of good *wok hei* (see page 42). It also visibly changes color, acquiring a yellowish brown hue. However, NaCl (sodium chloride, i.e., table salt) is a very stable molecule that should not react through heating at normal wok ranges (it doesn't melt until a whopping 1,473°F/801°C), and the kosher salt I use (Diamond Crystal) is 99.83 percent pure sodium chloride (some salts have iodine or anti-caking agents added, which could alter their color when heated).

So what was causing the color and flavor change? I posed this question over social media, where several metallurgists and chemists chimed in with suggestions for experiments.

First, I tried heating salt in a stainless steel skillet side by side with a carbon steel wok. After 5 minutes at around 600°F (315°C), the salt in the stainless steel skillet remained unchanged compared to a raw control, while the salt in carbon steel had turned brownish yellow. This confirmed that it's not a chemical change solely in the salt; it has to have something to do with either the carbon steel itself or the seasoning on the surface of the steel. I noted that the carbon steel pan smoked during this operation, while the stainless steel did not, due to the seasoning on the surface of the carbon steel.

Some folks suggested that if iron was leaching off into the salt, then a powerful magnet should affect the salt, so I tried passing a strong rare earth magnet over the brown salt. There was no movement at all. Next, I tried dissolving the salt in a glass of water. *Aha!* The salt dissolved completely but left a brown deposit on the surface that collected in little clumps. Rubbing the deposit in my fingers revealed that it was composed of tiny particles. This

seemed to confirm my suspicion that the color and flavor comes from deposits from the seasoning that are vaporizing during the toasting process.

If this were the case, then the salt should acquire color and flavor in the presence of smoke from the seasoning, even if it's not in direct contact with the wok itself. So to test this, I made a small aluminum foil boat and filled it with a layer of salt. I also filled a stainless steel spoon with salt. I placed these two vessels in the bottom of my wok, placed a lid over the top, then heated the wok.

Both salts acquired the brownish yellow tinge of toasted salt. Moreover, the steel spoon, foil boat, and lid of the wok also acquired a similar yellowish brown haze.

All of this together indicates that the color and flavor of toasted salt comes from deposits from the oil/polymers vaporizing from the wok itself—the same stuff that contributes to the smoky flavor of *wok hei*. Given that the toasted salt has some of that *wok hei* flavor, this makes perfect sense. It's also worth noting that using this toasted salt to season your food in place of regular will impart some smokiness to it, even if it hasn't been cooked in a wok.

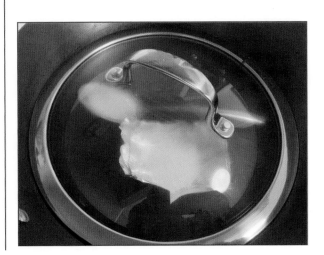

MÁLÀ SALT AND PEPPER CHICKEN WINGS

Yield
Serves 4
to 6

Active Time
30 minutes

Total Time
30 minutes

NOTES

This recipe makes more toasted málà salt than you need. Save it for another use (it's an excellent rub for roasted or smoked meats, for grilled or broiled vegetables or tofu, or sprinkled on any fried foods). The used oil can be strained and saved for another use.

INGREDIENTS

For the Wings:

1½ pounds (700 g) chicken wings, separated into drums and flats
1 tablespoon (12 g) kosher salt
½ cup (60 g) potato starch

For the Toasted Málà Salt:

1 tablespoon (6 g) whole cumin seeds
1 tablespoon (3 g) red or green Sichuan peppercorns
2 teaspoons (4 g) fennel seeds
1 teaspoon (2 g) white peppercorns
1 star anise pod, broken into pieces, dark seeds discarded
4 small hot dried chiles, such as chao tian jiao, árbol, or Japones
2 tablespoons (24 g) kosher salt
2 tablespoons (25 g) light or dark brown sugar

To Cook:

3 quarts (3 l) peanut, rice bran, or other neutral oil
4 scallions, thinly sliced
Handful of fresh cilantro leaves and fine stems, roughly chopped

These deep-fried crunchy chicken wings get tossed in a hot-and-numbing toasted spice and salt mixture with a hint of sweetness that draws inspiration from some of the street snacks in Sichuan and Shaanxi. For the spice coating, I toast cumin, fennel, star anise, white pepper, Sichuan peppercorns, and whole dried chiles with salt in a dry wok until intensely aromatic, then grind them and combine them with brown sugar.

Incidentally, this mixture makes a wonderful barbecue rub for slow-smoked ribs or pork shoulder.

DIRECTIONS

(1) **For the Wings:** In a large bowl, toss the wings with the salt until well coated. Add the starch and toss until the wings are coated. Place in a fine-mesh strainer held over the sink and shake to remove excess starch. Arrange wings in a single layer on a baking sheet and set aside.

(2) **For the Toasted Málà Salt:** Combine the cumin, Sichuan peppercorns, fennel, white peppercorns, star anise, chiles, and salt in a wok. Heat over medium heat, tossing and stirring frequently, until very toasty and fragrant, 7 to 10 minutes. Note that this may create some smoke, so use a vent hood if you have one, or at the very least get a good cross-breeze going through your kitchen space.

(3) Transfer to a large plate or tray and let cool completely. Transfer to a heavy mortar and pestle or a spice grinder and grind into a powder. Let cool completely, then add the brown sugar and toss to combine.

(4) **To Cook:** Heat the oil to 400°F (205°C) in the wok. Add the chicken wings, agitating with a spider or chopsticks to separate the wings. Adjust the heat to maintain a temperature of 325° to 350°F (160° to 175°C) as the wings cook, agitating and moving them regularly until they are golden brown and very crisp, about 8 minutes. Drain the chicken, then transfer to a large bowl.

(5) Add the scallions and cilantro and season generously with the spice mixture as you toss everything together. Serve immediately.

CANTONESE STIR-FRIED LOBSTER WITH GINGER AND SCALLIONS

I have fond memories of little me in my precollege years heading out to Boston's Chinatown with my dad and two sisters to East Ocean City, home of the finest dry-style beef chow fun in the world (at least according to my little sister). The best trips were the ones where we'd stand in front of the giant tanks they keep at the front of the restaurant and pick out our dinner for the night. Sometimes it was spider crabs (the waiters would fish one out and hold its massive legs out at arm's length), sometimes hairy crabs, but in the summer season it was lobsters.

The crustacean would get scuttled off into the kitchen to meet its maker while we sat at our table picking at razor clams with black bean sauce, shrimp-paste-stuffed hot green chiles, and live Maine sweet shrimp stir-fried plain in the shell with a dish of mild soy sauce for dipping the bodies into as you sucked the juices out of the heads.

When the lobster finally reemerged, it would come out chopped into large chunks, their surfaces crisp, lacy, and coated in a thin veneer of sauce. Tossed with slivers of ginger and sliced scallions, their primary aroma was sweet and spicy, the briny flavor of the lobsters coming through only once you started eating them.

There are no two ways about it. Eating Cantonese-style lobster with ginger and scallions is a gentlemen-start-your-wet-naps type of messy affair. The only way to get the meat out of the bones—particularly the slender knuckles and claws—is to poke, pry, and suck until you've removed every last scrap. I like that kind of meal—it makes you really work for your food and makes the whole event last a bit longer.

recipe continues

Yield
Serves 4

Active Time
40 minutes

Total Time
40 minutes

NOTES

Follow the step-by-step photos for details on how to break down the lobster. The strained oil can be cooled, then stored in a sealed container in the fridge for another use.

INGREDIENTS

For the Sauce:

1 tablespoon soy sauce

2 teaspoons (about 6 g) cornstarch

¼ cup (80 ml) Shaoxing wine or dry sherry

½ cup (120 ml) homemade or store-bought low-sodium chicken stock

For the Lobster:

2 lobsters, preferably soft-shell, about 1¼ pounds (575 g) each

¼ cup (30 g) cornstarch

1 quart (1 l) peanut, rice bran, or other neutral oil

For the Stir-Fry:

10 medium garlic cloves (30 to 40 g), thinly sliced

4 scallions, thinly sliced

1 long green chile (such as Chinese cowhorn or Anaheim), jalapeño, or serrano pepper, thinly sliced

1 hot red chile, such as Fresno or red serrano, thinly sliced

2 teaspoons (15 g) Dry-Roasted Salt and Pepper Blend (page 450)

12 yellow chives, cut into 2-inch pieces (optional)

These days I've worked my way through enough recipes that I'm happy with where I'm at with my current version. I like a little bit of heat in my dish, so I add a single long Chinese hot green chile, as well as a handful of yellow chives, which have a milder, sweeter flavor than their green counterparts, like a very tender, young leek.

The cooking process is threefold, but each step is fast, so it doesn't take more than half an hour from start to finish. The lobster first gets steamed (you can do it in a steamer or directly in the wok, as I do) just until it starts to cook through and firms up a bit. You then break it down and cut it into chunks, shell and all. A heavy cleaver helps here, but a good chef's knife will work. The chunks are then coated in cornstarch and deep-fried for another moment until crisp on the exterior.

Finally, the lobster chunks get stir-fried with the aromatics along with a very small amount of sauce made from rice wine, soy sauce, and chicken stock lightly thickened with cornstarch. The crisp, lacy exteriors of the fried lobster pieces are the perfect surface for the aromatic sauce to cling to. It's one of the tastiest (not to mention most impressive and unique) ways to eat lobster I know.

DIRECTIONS

(1) **For the Sauce:** Combine the soy sauce and cornstarch in a small bowl and mix until the cornstarch is dissolved. Stir in the wine and chicken stock. Set aside.

(2) **For the Lobster:** Add 1 inch of water to a pot or wok and bring to a boil. Add the lobsters, cover, and steam for 3 minutes (you can use a wire rack steamer or just put the lobsters directly in the wok). Remove and transfer to a cutting board. Allow to cool slightly. Discard the water and wipe out the wok.

(3) Twist off the tail and claws from the lobsters. Remove the guts from the lobster heads and rinse clean for garnish. Using a heavy chef's knife or cleaver, split the tails in half lengthwise, then into thirds crosswise, forming 6 pieces. Transfer to a large bowl. Cut both knuckles from each claw and add to the bowl with the tails. Remove the small side of each claw by breaking it off by hand and add to bowl. Cut each claw in half, exposing the meat, and add to the bowl. Add the starch and toss to coat.

(4) Heat the oil to 375°F (190°C) in a large wok, adjusting the heat as necessary to maintain the temperature. Carefully add the lobster pieces to the hot oil one piece at a time until half of them have been added. Fry, agitating occasionally with a spider, until the cornstarch coating is crisp and pale golden brown, about 1½ minutes. Transfer the lobster pieces to a colander set in a bowl to drain. Repeat with the remaining lobster. Carefully pour the hot oil out of the wok through a fine-mesh strainer set in a heatproof container (such as a large saucepan).

(5) **For the Stir-Fry:** Wipe out the wok and return it to high heat until smoking. Add 2 tablespoons (30 ml) of the strained oil and swirl to coat. Add the garlic, scallions, and green and red chiles and stir-fry until fragrant, about 30 seconds. Add the lobster and the salt and pepper blend and toss to coat. Stir the sauce mixture and add to the wok, pouring it around the edges. Cook, stirring and tossing constantly until the mixture has bubbled and thickened, coating the lobster and vegetables. Immediately transfer to a serving platter, garnish with the lobster heads and the yellow chives (if using), and serve.

Cantonese-Style Stir-Fried Lobster, Step by Step

Step 1 • Steam the Lobsters

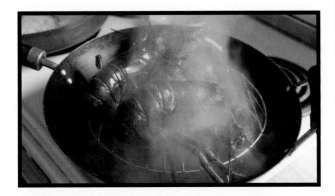

To kill a lobster, place the tip of a heavy knife in the center of the head. Plunge it into the head rapidly, splitting it between the eyes to instantly kill it.

The lobsters start with a quick steam, which you can do directly in the wok. Get the water boiling, add the lobsters, cover, and cook for just a few minutes to set the flesh.

Step 2 • Break Them Down

Break the lobsters into tail and claw/knuckle pieces, removing the guts and rinsing out the heads for garnish.

Step 3 • Chop the Tails

Cut the tails in half lengthwise, then split each half into three pieces.

continues

Step 4 • Split the Claws

Cut the knuckles off the claws in between the joints. Remove the small pincher by breaking it off a bit and cutting through the meat and cartilage with the tip of a sharp knife. Split the large pincher in half with a heavy knife. If the shell is very tough, you may need to crack it with a cleaver or by placing it under a towel and rapping it hard with the back of a knife.

Step 5 • Toss with Starch

Toss the lobster pieces in cornstarch to coat.

Step 6 • Fry in Batches

Heat oil in the wok to 350° to 375°F and cook the lobster in batches, agitating it as it cooks. You want to cook just until it gets crisp, about a minute, then drain it immediately.

Step 7 • Stir-Fry the Aromatics

Heat the wok until smoking hot, then add the aromatics and start stir-frying, tossing them constantly.

Step 8 • Stir-Fry the Lobster

Add the lobster meat along with the sauce. Stir-fry just until the sauce has thickened and coats the lobster and vegetables in a glossy sheen. Don't overcook that lobster!

Battered and Dredged

Batters are liquids thickened with flour or starch that are used to give either a puffy coating to fried foods—as with tempura—or an eggshell-like crispy coating—as with Korean fried chicken. Both serve a triple purpose:

- They add texture and crunch to the exterior of the food.

- They insulate the food within from the violent heat of the oil, making for moister, juicier results.

- They provide a surface for sauces and dips to cling.

Dredged foods are similar to battered foods, but rather than adding all of the starch directly to the liquid coating, some or all of it is added as a separate step by tossing liquid-coated foods in a starchy mixture just before frying.

KOREAN FRIED CHICKEN

Years ago, when Adri ran in her first 5k race, the only thing she asked for to celebrate with? Not Champagne, not a night on the town, not even a her-choice no-questions-asked movie night. All she wanted was fried chicken.

The thing is, we don't eat it that often round these parts. A few times a year, max. So when we do get around to it, it had darned well better be the best fried chicken out there. And when it comes to frying chicken, nobody—and I mean nobody—does it better than Korea. My apologies to all you Southerners.

Korean fried chicken (or KFC as those in the know call it) differs vastly from American-style fried chicken. Rather than the craggy, crusty, significant coating you'd get on a Popeye's drumstick, you get an eggshell-thin, ultra-crisp crust around a drippingly juicy interior.

The end goal is clear, but getting there required a bit of bushwhacking.

The Batter

For my testing, I used chicken wings, which cook quickly and are easy to find in uniform sizes.

Korean fried chicken typically uses a thin, thin batter that barely coats the wing to get that eggshell-thin crack. My first task was to figure out a way to get that batter to stick. Chicken skin will naturally repel water-based liquids (it had better; otherwise chickens would soak up water like a sponge any time it rained). Try dipping chicken straight out of the package into a batter, and you'll find that it just runs straight off. Just like a painter rolling on a layer of primer to make sure the paint sticks to the walls, my chicken needed some kind of pretreatment.

I tried a variety of tactics, including air-drying overnight (successful but time consuming), salting to carefully draw out moisture and then drying (works!), coating with a salt and baking powder mixture (also works—the baking powder raises the pH of the surface and increases its surface area by creating tiny bubbles of protein-rich liquid, allowing it to crisp better), and tossing in plain cornstarch to absorb some surface moisture and create a rougher texture for the batter to adhere to.

The best was actually a combination of all four methods: I tossed the chicken wings in a mixture of cornstarch, kosher salt, and baking powder before spreading them out on a rack and letting them air-dry for about an hour (overnight is better, but even as little as 15 minutes will work). Once the coating was in place, I had no trouble getting my batter to stick. But which batter is best?

No. 2: The Starch

The goal of frying is twofold: First, hot oil causes moisture and air inside the batter to evaporate, leaving you with a dried-out crust in place of a wet slurry. Next, protein networks within the batter will harden, making your batter stiff and crisp. While all this is going on, you're also browning both proteins and carbohydrates, creating new flavorful compounds. So three things.

Among frying's goals are such diverse elements as drying, hardening, and browning with ruthless efficiency.

Where does the recipe for batter fit into this? Well, working with batter is a balancing act between crispness and structure. See, when you mix flour with water, a sticky gluten network begins to form. Some gluten development is necessary—it provides structure and support. But too much gluten development can lead to tough or leathery crusts.

Take a look at these two wings, one made with a pure water and flour batter, the other made with a cornstarch and water batter. Cornstarch is a pure starch,

meaning that its protein content is essentially zero and it produces no gluten when combined with water.

Using 100 percent flour gives you a thing that is leathery and greasy—too much gluten forms, making the coating too robust. On the other hand, 100 percent cornstarch produces a coating that is powdery with relatively little browning (the proteins in flour aid with browning). To get a crust that's both robust and crisp, you need to use a combination of tactics.* Still, I wanted my wings to be a little bit crunchier, so I pressed on.

The conundrum I was facing was this one: On the one hand, I wanted my batter extra-thin in order to form an eggshell-thin crust around the chicken wing that wasn't too tough. On the other hand, adding extra water to a flour and starch slurry actually *increases* the toughness of the fried coating.

Sounds weird, doesn't it? Shouldn't a wetter batter lead to a more tender crust? The culprit is, once again, excess gluten. The proteins that link to form gluten actually have an easier time doing it in a thinner batter, where they have the ability to slosh around and bump into each other more than they do in a thicker batter. This is why a relatively dry bread dough requires lots of manual kneading to create a gluten network, while with a thin pancake batter you can overdevelop gluten with just a few too many whisks.

So what was the solution?

Booze Clues

Fans of British chef Heston Blumenthal will recognize vodka as one of the ingredients in his Perfect Fish & Chips recipe. When he presented the idea, initially the thought was that the volatility of the vodka (that is, its propensity to evaporate quickly) would cause it to jump out of the batter faster as it fried, allowing the batter to dehydrate quicker and thus brown faster and crisp up better in the same amount of time. At that task, it serves admirably.

But for my purposes, there's an even more important factor it brings to the table: limiting gluten development.

---

* Similarly, if you want someone to talk, the comfy chair is not good enough. You must also poke them with the soft cushions.

Back when I was working at *Cook's Illustrated*, I came up with a recipe which we dubbed Foolproof Pie Dough. It relied on the same principle to achieve the same goals: better hydration in dough/batter while simultaneously limiting gluten development. The idea is that since 80-proof vodka is 40 percent alcohol and gluten does not form in alcohol, you can add more vodka to a batter than you would be able to with water, while maintaining the same (or even a diminished) level of gluten formation.

This is precisely what I'm looking for with my fried chicken.

I fried off two batches of chicken wings, one coated with a batter of flour, starch, a touch of baking powder, and water, and the other with some of the water replaced by vodka. Exact same proportions, totally different results: the vodka batter comes out noticeably crisper and lighter, with more of those texture-enhancing, sauce-grabbing microblisters.

Even better: with a vodka-based batter, the useful shelf-life of a premixed batter is drastically extended. You can mix this batter, go catch an episode of Wang Gang on YouTube, walk the dogs, play a round of Dinosaur Escape with the toddler, start on your income tax return, and it'll *still* produce thin, perfectly crisp chicken.

As with all fried chicken, allowing it to cool and then frying it briefly a second time will help produce extra-crispy results and a crust that stays shatteringly crisp even after it's been sitting in a sticky sauce.

This chicken is excellent with either a soy and ginger glaze or a sweet Korean chile glaze (recipes follow), but feel free to use your favorite wing sauce with them.

EXTRA-CRISPY KOREAN FRIED CHICKEN

Yield
Serves 4

Active Time
1 hour

Total Time
1½ hours (to overnight)

NOTE

For this recipe I prefer whole wings with the wing tips still attached, if you can find them. The vodka in this recipe will evaporate almost completely during cooking, leaving behind no alcohol in the coating. If you cannot have alcohol in your home, you can replace the vodka with an additional ½ cup (120 ml) of water mixed with 3 tablespoons (45 ml) of distilled vinegar, though the results will not be quite as crisp.

INGREDIENTS

For the Chicken:

1 tablespoon (12 g) kosher salt
⅓ cup (1.5 ounces/45 g) cornstarch
½ teaspoon (2 g) baking powder
3 pounds (about 1.5 kg) chicken wings and drumsticks (see Note)

To Fry:

¾ cup (3 ounces/90 g) cornstarch
¾ cup (3.75 ounces/110 g) all-purpose flour
½ teaspoon (2 g) baking powder
1 tablespoon (12 g) kosher salt, plus more as needed
¾ cup (180 ml) cold water
¾ cup (180 ml) vodka
3 quarts (3 l) peanut, rice bran, or other neutral oil
1 recipe Sweet Soy-Ginger Glaze (page 461) or Sweet and Spicy Korean Chile Sauce (page 461) (optional)

DIRECTIONS

(1) **For the Chicken:** Combine the salt, cornstarch, and baking powder in a large bowl and mix until homogenous. Add the chicken and toss until every surface is coated in the mixture. Transfer to a wire rack set in a rimmed baking sheet, shaking vigorously as you go to get rid of any excess coating. Transfer to the refrigerator and let rest, uncovered, for at least 30 minutes and up to overnight.

(2) **To fry:** Combine the cornstarch, flour, baking powder, and kosher salt in a large bowl and mix until homogenous. Add the water and vodka and whisk until a smooth batter is formed, adding up to 2 tablespoons more water if the batter is too thick. It should have the consistency of thin paint and fall off the whisk in thin ribbons that instantly disappear as they hit the surface of the batter in the bowl.

(3) Heat the oil in a wok to 350°F (175°C).

(4) Add one-third of the chicken to the batter. Working one piece at a time, lift the chicken and allow the excess batter to drip off, using your finger to get rid of any large pockets or slicks of batter. Carefully lower the chicken into the hot oil. Repeat with the remaining pieces in the first batch. Adjust the heat to maintain a temperature of 300° to 325°F (150° to 160°C) throughout the cooking. Fry, using a metal spider or slotted spatula to rotate and agitate the chicken as it cooks until evenly golden brown and crisp all over, about 8 minutes. Transfer to a wire rack set in a rimmed baking and season immediately with salt.

(5) When all chicken is cooked, allow to cool for 10 minutes, then reheat the oil to 375°F (190°C). Refry chicken in two batches, maintaining the oil temperature at 325° to 350°F (160° to 175°C) and frying each batch until shatteringly crisp, about 3 minutes, then returning it to the rack to cool.

(6) Serve the chicken plain or toss with Sweet Soy-Ginger Glaze or Sweet and Spicy Korean Chile Sauce or your favorite wing sauce or seasoning.

SWEET SOY-GINGER GLAZE

Yield	Active Time
Makes about ¾ cup	10 minutes
	Total Time
	10 minutes

NOTE

Korean chile flakes have a mild heat. You can substitute any mild chile powder or flakes, such as er jing tiao or ancho.

INGREDIENTS

½ cup (120 ml) soy sauce
2 tablespoons (30 ml) rice vinegar
¼ cup (60 ml) mirin
¾ cup (150 g) light or dark brown sugar
2 teaspoons (5 g) minced garlic (about 2 medium cloves)
2 teaspoons (5 g) minced fresh ginger (about ½-inch segment)
½ teaspoon gochugaru (Korean chile flakes; see Note)
2 teaspoons (10 ml) roasted sesame oil
1 tablespoon (9 g) cornstarch
1 tablespoon (15 ml) water
2 tablespoons (15 g) toasted sesame seeds
2 scallions, thinly sliced

DIRECTIONS

Heat the soy sauce, vinegar, mirin, brown sugar, garlic, ginger, gochugaru, and sesame oil in a small saucepan over medium heat, whisking until the sugar is dissolved. Combine the cornstarch and water in a small bowl and whisk it into the sauce. Bring to a boil and cook until the sauce is slightly reduced and thickened, about 3 minutes. Transfer to a bowl and allow to cool for 5 minutes. Stir in the sesame seeds and scallions. Serve with Korean Fried Chicken.

SWEET AND SPICY KOREAN CHILE SAUCE

Yield	Active Time
Makes about ¾ cup	10 minutes
	Total Time
	10 minutes

INGREDIENTS

¼ cup (60 g) gochujang
2 tablespoons (30 ml) light soy sauce or shoyu
1 tablespoon (15 ml) rice vinegar
3 tablespoons (35 g) dark brown sugar
2 teaspoons (5 g) minced garlic (about 2 medium cloves)
2 teaspoons (5 g) minced fresh ginger (about ½-inch segment)
1 tablespoon (15 ml) roasted sesame oil

DIRECTIONS

Combine the gochujang, soy sauce, vinegar, sugar, garlic, ginger, and sesame oil in a large bowl and whisk to combine. Gochujang can be inconsistent in its thickness. Add up to 2 tablespoons (30 ml) water until the sauce is just barely thin enough to drip off a spoon when inverted. Serve with Korean Fried Chicken.

JAPANESE KATSU AND THE MAGIC OF PANKO COATING

If you weren't familiar with Japanese cuisine, you might not think there was anything particularly Japanese about katsu, a simple dish of breaded and fried cutlets. But if you've ever been in a Japanese shopping mall food court, you've seen that, just like pizza in the United States, katsu has established itself so firmly in the food culture that it could be considered a national comfort-food staple. It's an easy dish to love. Juicy chicken or pork cutlets in an incredibly crisp layer of golden brown bread crumbs, with a sweet and savory sauce and a side of crisp shredded cabbage and steamed white rice. It's a simple and delicious weeknight meal, whether you buy it at the food court or fry it in your own kitchen.

Given how popular panko-style bread crumbs are these days, even in non-Japanese recipes, there's not really a fundamental difference between katsu and any other style of breaded and fried cutlets. Only two things distinguish it. First, katsu *must* be made with panko crumbs (as opposed to European-style breaded cutlets). And second, it must be served with katsu sauce. Katsu simply wouldn't be katsu without a big ol' drizzle of the thick, savory-sweet, Worcestershire-esque stuff.

I have a recipe for my own homemade version of the sauce that'll kick you in the mouth with flavor, but in all honesty, to me katsu sauce is sort of like ketchup: the homemade version will never beat Heinz. Except, in the case of katsu sauce, the brand is Bull-Dog. The white-capped bottle has been a fixture in my fridge from the time of my very earliest memories, and its flavor is intimately linked to katsu in my mind.

The word *katsu* is *gairaigo*, the Japanese term for words borrowed from other languages. The simplest phonetic translation of "cutlet" to Japanese vocalizations is *katsuretsu*, which in turn is shortened to *katsu*. Add *ton*—the Sino-Japanese word for "pork"—to the front of that and you've got *tonkatsu*, or breaded fried pork cutlets (not to be confused with *tonkotsu*, which is pork-based ramen broth). Got it? Good. Let's move on to more fun stuff.

Meat Choices

Katsu is most often made using pork, with chicken coming in a close second, though beef or even ham or hamburger is not uncommon in parts of Japan. I typically stick with pork or chicken, or firm tofu or tempeh if I'm in the mood for a nonmeaty version.

When using pork, you want cutlets that are nice and fatty so that they stay juicy while cooking. My favorite is pork sirloin cutlets. You could also use pork loin cutlets, from either close to the shoulder (blade chops) or as close to the sirloin as possible. (Chops cut from the back end of the blade are essentially the same as those cut from the front end of the sirloin, where the two sections meet.) Avoid center-cut rib chops, which are better when thick and pan-seared or grilled. So long as it's got good striations of fat and a mix of light and dark meat, it'll work out fine.

Ask for cutlets that are between four and five ounces apiece and pound them gently to a quarter-inch thickness. The easiest way I've found to do this is to split open the sides of a heavy-duty zipper-lock bag, place the cutlet inside, and gently pound it with a meat mallet or the bottom of a heavy skillet. Mindless bludgeoning can lead to torn meat and holes: You want to use firm but gentle pressure, working at the uneven spots.

With chicken, either breasts or thighs will do just fine, though they need to be treated a little differently.

Boneless, skinless chicken thighs can be treated very much like pork cutlets: just pound them inside a zipper-lock bag. Whole chicken breast halves are too big (especially considering the massive chickens you find at the supermarket these days), so the first step is to split them into cutlets. It's easy to do—if you've never done it before, just follow the step-by-step guide on page 54.

The other problem with chicken breast is that it's lean and prone to drying out, but a quick brine solves that problem. Take a look at these two breast slices:

The slice on the left was brined and remains smooth and juicy, while the unbrined cutlet on the right dries out more.

Was the nonbrined chicken bad? No, not by any means. But if you're in a rush, I'd strongly suggest using chicken thighs or fattier pork cutlets, both of which are less prone to drying out than chicken breast. If using breasts, I'd salt them and let them rest for a minimum of three to four hours.

Breading

Katsu is made using the classic breading technique of dredging in flour, dipping in egg, and coating with bread crumbs. The easiest way to do this is to place flour, beaten eggs, and panko in three shallow bowls, pie plates, or rimmed plates. Working with one cutlet at a time, transfer it to the flour with one hand (designate this the "dry" hand) and turn to coat, then pick it up with the same hand and transfer to the egg plate. Using your other hand (the "wet" hand), turn it to coat in the egg, lift, let the excess drain off, and transfer to the bread crumbs. Using your dry hand, lift bread crumbs and scoop them on top of the cutlet, then press down so they adhere. Once it's thoroughly coated, you

can safely lift the cutlet with your dry hand, flip, and continue pressing crumbs into it until a thick layer is built up all over.

Transfer the breaded cutlet to a plate and repeat with the remaining ones.

One thing I'd always wondered about: Why do we bother dipping cutlets in flour before we dip them in egg? Surely the egg is gonna stick to a bare chicken cutlet well enough to get a good coating of bread crumbs, isn't it?

I tested it out, cooking two cutlets side by side, one with the standard flour/egg/bread crumb treatment and the other with just egg and bread crumbs. Here's what they looked like:

You can plainly see that the flour does indeed help create a more even coating, which in turn leads to more even browning. If you've ever tried to paint a wall without first laying on a coat of primer, you're familiar with the patchy effect seen in the cutlet on the right. Flour is like the primer of the breaded-and-fried-cutlet world. Flouring also helps produce juicier meat: because the chicken with no flour had bald patches where the coating was completely stripped away, some of the delicate chicken meat came in direct contact with the hot oil, causing it to turn stringy and dry in spots. Skipping the flour is a tempting shortcut, but it's one that should be avoided.

Frying

Frying katsu is very straightforward and can be done either in a skillet in a shallow amount of fat or in a wok with a deeper fat layer. I prefer doing it in a wok, as you get more even browning all over with minimal fussing. Many recipes recommend flipping only once during cooking, but I found that flipping multiple times actually resulted in more evenly browned cutlets. The key is to let them cook on the first side until the breading is set enough that you can flip without scraping it off. About a minute and a half is good. Then cook on the second side for another minute and a half and spend the remaining time flipping the cutlets frequently until they're perfectly golden brown.

Katsu is typically served with chopsticks, which means you'll need to cut it up in the kitchen before it hits the table. Use a sharp knife to cut the cutlets into thin strips.

Serve the katsu with finely shredded cabbage (an inexpensive mandoline makes short work of that), some lemon wedges, and a good drizzle of katsu sauce. If you want to go full-on Japanese, some steamed white rice with Japanese pickles also makes a great side dish.

It's a cutlet! It's Japanese schnitzel! It's Asian Milanese! It's katsu! Call it whatever you want. I call it delicious.

JAPANESE KATSU

Yield
Serves 3
to 4

Active Time
30 minutes

Total Time
30 minutes (plus
4 to 8 hours, if
resting chicken
breast meat
before cooking)

INGREDIENTS

2 boneless, skinless chicken breast
halves, about 8 ounces (225 g) each;
or 4 boneless, skinless chicken thighs,
4 to 5 ounces (110 to 140 g) each; or
4 boneless pork sirloin cutlets, 4 to 5
ounces (110 to 140 g) each
Kosher salt and freshly ground black
pepper
1 cup (about 5 ounces/140 g) all-purpose
flour
3 large eggs, thoroughly beaten
1½ cups (about 5 ounces/140 g) Japanese-
style panko bread crumbs
1 quart (1 l) peanut, rice bran, or other neutral
oil

To Serve:

Finely shredded green cabbage
Lemon wedges
Steamed rice
Japanese-style pickles (*sunomono*;
optional)
Tonkatsu sauce, homemade (page 467) or
store-bought

DIRECTIONS

(1) **If Using Chicken Breasts:** Cut each breast half into 2 cutlets (see page 54 for step-by-step instructions). Place them, one at a time, in a heavy-duty zipper-lock bag and pound gently to ¼-inch thickness, using a meat mallet or the bottom of a heavy 8-inch skillet. Season generously with salt and pepper. For best results, let them rest in the refrigerator for at least 4 hours and up to overnight after seasoning. Proceed to step 3.

(2) **If Using Chicken Thighs or Pork Cutlets:** Place thighs or cutlets, one at a time, in a heavy-duty zipper-lock bag and pound gently to ¼-inch thickness, using a meat mallet or the bottom of a heavy 8-inch skillet. Season generously with salt and pepper. Proceed immediately to step 3.

(3) Fill 3 wide, shallow bowls or high-rimmed plates with flour, beaten eggs, and panko, respectively. Working with one thigh or cutlet at a time, dredge in flour with your first hand, shaking off excess. Transfer it to the egg dish, then turn the thigh or cutlet with your second hand to coat both sides. Lift and allow excess egg to drain off, then transfer it to the bread crumb mixture. With your first hand, scoop bread crumbs on top of the thigh or cutlet, then gently press, turning to ensure a good layer of crumbs on both sides. Transfer the thigh or cutlet to a clean plate and repeat with the remaining meat. If this is done properly, your first hand should touch only dry ingredients, while your second hand should touch only wet, making the process less messy.

(4) Heat the oil in a wok over high heat until it registers 350°F (175°C) on an instant-read thermometer. Using tongs or your fingers, gently lower the cutlets into hot fat, laying them down away from you to prevent hot fat from splashing toward you. Fry, adjusting the heat as necessary for a steady, vigorous bubble (around 300° to 325°F; 150° to 160°C), gently swirling the wok and rotating the cutlets for even browning, until the bottom side is set, about 1½ minutes. Flip the cutlets and fry until the other side is set, about 1½ minutes longer. Continue cooking, swirling frequently and flipping occasionally, until well browned on both sides, about 3 minutes longer. Transfer to paper towels to drain and season with salt right away.

(5) Slice the katsu into thin strips and serve immediately with shredded cabbage, lemon wedges, rice, Japanese pickles (if desired), and tonkatsu sauce.

How to Cut Chicken Breasts into Cutlets

Learning how to cut a chicken breast into thin cutlets is an essential skill for weeknight cooking. Thinner chicken cutlets cook more rapidly than full-sized breasts and are ideal for searing or breading and frying in dishes like chicken katsu.

The most difficult step is the cutting: it requires a sharp knife and a bit of practice. If you're still a little green in the kitchen, you'll probably make a few holes in your chicken breasts before you get the hang of it—no worries; they'll still taste just as good.

Once you've got the breast split, the pounding is fun and easy. The key is not to pound too hard, which gives you less control over the final thickness and can lead to holes in your meat. So easy does it, OK?

Step 1 • Split the Breast

Place a boneless, skinless chicken breast, with the tender removed, on a cutting board, and hold it flat with the palm of your nonknife hand. Using a sharp chef's, boning, or fillet knife, slice the chicken breast horizontally into two even pieces. It helps if you do this close to the edge of the cutting board.

Step 2 • Open the Bag

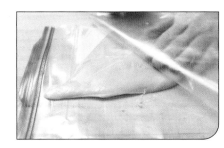

Using your knife, split a gallon-sized zipper-lock bag along both edges so that it can be opened up into a flat sheet. Alternatively, you can use layers of plastic wrap, though plastic wrap has a tendency to tear during pounding. Place the chicken between the layers of plastic and spread the plastic out tight to avoid wrinkles, which can leave imprints on the meat's surface.

Step 3 • Pound the Chicken

Use a meat mallet or the bottom of a sturdy eight-inch skillet to gently pound the chicken. When pounding, go slow and steady to avoid making holes. Rather than moving the pan directly up and down, use slight lateral motions to gently coax the chicken into shape. The goal is an even thickness and form.

Step 4 • Done!

When finished, the chicken should be an even quarter inch in thickness all around.

HOMEMADE TONKATSU SAUCE

Yield
Makes about 1 cup

Active Time
5 minutes

Total Time
5 minutes

INGREDIENTS

½ cup (120 ml) ketchup
¼ cup (60 ml) Worcestershire sauce
1 tablespoon (15 ml) light soy sauce or shoyu
1 tablespoon (12 g) sugar

Tonkatsu sauce is a thick, brown sauce somewhere between Worcestershire sauce and gravy. It's great on all kinds of panko-crusted fried foods.

DIRECTIONS

Combine all the ingredients and stir together until the sugar is dissolved. Tonkatsu sauce can be stored in the fridge indefinitely.

KOROKKE (JAPANESE POTATO CROQUETTES)

Like tempura and katsu, *korokke* is yet another popular Japanese food that was introduced from another culture and has kept its name. Korokke (pronounced "ko-roh-keh") comes from the French *croquette*, and like French croquettes or Spanish *croquetas*, it consists of a soft filling—most often mashed potatoes—coated in bread crumbs and deep-fried. Korokke are larger than your average croquette: fat oblong disks about the size of an old Nokia brick phone.

Frequently, folks will fold ground meat or vegetables into the potato mixture. My mom used them as a way to incorporate whatever vegetables she had kicking around the freezer or vegetable drawer. She'd generally start by sautéing a bit of onion and ground beef (from the same bulk packs that she'd use for gyoza filling, mapo tofu, and spaghetti with meat sauce), which she would drain and fold into some coarsely mashed potatoes. If there was frozen corn, peas, or spinach in the freezer, there's a good chance some of them would end up in the croquettes, as would diced carrots, canned tuna, frozen broccoli, leftover rotisserie chicken, or ham. Occasionally we'd be surprised by a gooey pocket of grated cheese. My older sister, Aya, insists that my mom stuck chicken livers in them once. I don't remember that, but I'd believe it if those livers were on sale.

They can be served hot, but are just as frequently served cold. They can be eaten with a fork and knife on a plate, packed into a box and eaten from a napkin during a long car ride, or bought from the 7-Eleven display case tucked in between two slices of soft white bread. (Yes, that's potato, bread crumbs, and bread for some sweet carb on carb on carb action with each bite.)

recipe continues

Just about the only universals for korokke are that they are coated in a golden crust of panko-style bread crumbs and drizzled with sweet and salty tonkatsu sauce.

In fact, I almost feel silly giving a recipe for korokke, because as far as I'm concerned, they are the least prescriptive thing out there. There are only three real rules when it comes to adding stuff to korroke:

- **Make sure the add-ins are cooked**. The croquettes will heat up as they fry, but uncooked vegetables and meat will not reliably cook through. This means sautéing any raw meat and blanching or sautéing vegetables. (Frozen vegetables are typically preblanched and thus don't need to be cooked separately before being added.)

- **Don't add anything too wet**. Wet ingredients will cause the korokke to build up steam inside. If it's bad enough, the steam build-up will pop a hole in the crust and fat will leak inside, turning them greasy soft. Drain sautéed or blanched vegetables well, and either cook ground meat until all the liquid has evaporated or drain before incorporating.

- **Make sure there's enough potato to bind everything together.** Whatever you decide to add to korokke, they need to be able to hold their shape easily before you bread and fry them, which means they should comprise at least 50 percent potato.

We always had a box of Idahoan or Hungry Jack in the pantry, though I rarely remember eating instant mashed potatoes growing up. It was just this past year, at forty-one years old, that I discovered what those dehydrated mashed potato flakes were doing there: My mom used them to thicken up korokke filling if she accidentally made it too wet or did not have enough real potatoes to bind everything together. The trick works really well!*

---

* And for what it's worth, I maintain that instant mashed potatoes are among the best convenience foods out there – provided you rehydrate them with equal parts milk and butter and load them up with plenty of salt and pepper.

Yield	Active Time
Makes 12 to 16	30 minutes
	Total Time
	1 hour

NOTES

Breaded korokke can be frozen before frying. You can then fry them directly from the freezer (add 2 minutes to total frying time if frying from frozen). Feel free to omit any of the filling ingredients or to add whatever other ingredients you'd like. Common additions would be frozen vegetables such as peas, green beans, corn, or spinach (thawed and drained of excess liquid), grated cheese, canned tuna, pulled chicken meat, or sautéed minced mushrooms. If adding ingredients, just make sure they are cooked (frozen vegetables do not need to be cooked), dry, and that at least 50 percent of the mixture is composed of potato. If your mixture has trouble holding together, add instant mashed potatoes a tablespoon at a time to help bind.

INGREDIENTS

2 pounds (900 g) russet potatoes, peeled and cut into 2-inch chunks
Kosher salt
1 tablespoon (15 ml) peanut, rice bran, or other neutral oil
8 ounces (225 g) lean ground meat
1 small onion (about 4 ounces/120 g), minced
2 medium garlic cloves, minced (about 2 teaspoons/5 g)
1 small carrot (about 4 ounces/120 g), peeled and minced
2 tablespoons (30 g) unsalted butter, cut into a few thin pats
Freshly ground black pepper

For the Coating:

1 cup (about 5 ounces/140 g) all-purpose flour
3 large eggs, thoroughly beaten
1½ cups (about 5 ounces/140 g) Japanese-style panko bread crumbs

To Cook:

1 quart (1 l) peanut, rice bran, or other neutral oil

To Serve:

Tonkatsu sauce, homemade (page 467) or store-bought

DIRECTIONS

(1) In a large saucepan, cover the potatoes with cold water seasoned with a big pinch of salt. Bring to a boil over high heat, reduce to a simmer, and cook just until the potatoes can be pierced easily with a knife or a skewer (10 to 15 minutes after coming to a boil). Drain well, return them to the saucepan, and allow to steam-dry until cool enough to handle.

(2) Meanwhile, heat the oil in a wok over heat until shimmering. Add the meat and cook, breaking it up with a wok spatula or a potato masher, until it is no longer pink, about 2 minutes. Add the onion, garlic, and carrots and cook, stirring and tossing frequently, until the vegetables are softened and any exuded liquids have evaporated, about 5 minutes. Add the butter and remove from the heat.

(3) Using a potato masher, roughly mash the potatoes until no chunks larger than ½ inch remain. Sprinkle generously with salt and pepper. Add the meat and vegetable mixture and fold everything together with a spatula to incorporate. Taste the mixture and season with salt or pepper to taste.

(4) When cool enough to handle, pick up about 4 ounces (120 g) of the mixture and form it into a ¾- to 1-inch-thick oblong patty about the size and dimensions of a computer mouse. Transfer to a baking sheet or large plate. Continue forming patties until all the mixture is used up. Refrigerate patties until quite cool, 15 to 30 minutes, before continuing.

(5) **For the Coating:** Fill 3 wide, shallow bowls or high-rimmed plates with flour, beaten eggs, and panko, respectively. Working with one patty at a time, dredge in flour with your first hand, shaking off the excess. Transfer

recipe continues

to the egg dish, then turn the patty with your second hand to coat both sides. Lift and allow excess egg to drain off, then transfer the patty to the bread crumb mixture. With your first hand, scoop bread crumbs on top of the patty, then gently press, turning to ensure a good layer of crumbs on both sides. Return the patty to the tray or plate and repeat with the remaining patties. If this is done properly, your first hand should touch only dry ingredients, while your second hand should touch only wet, making the process less messy. Breaded patties can be stored in the refrigerator for several days or frozen and stored in the freezer for several months.

(6) **When Ready to Cook:** Heat the oil in a wok over high heat until it registers 350°F (175°C) on an instant-read thermometer. Using tongs or your fingers, gently lower patties into hot fat, adding only as many as you can fit in a single layer (4 to 6 patties). Fry, adjusting the heat as necessary for a steady, vigorous bubble (around 300° to 325°F; 150° to 160°C), gently swirling the wok and turning the patties occasionally for even browning, until crisp and golden brown all over and hot in the center, about 4 minutes total (or 6 minutes if cooking from frozen).

(7) Transfer cooked patties to a paper-towel-lined plate and season with salt. Serve korokke hot, at room temperature, or chilled, with tonkatsu sauce.

Kabocha Squash or Sweet Potato Korokke

Korokke can be made with squash or sweet potato in place of the mashed potatoes. For sweet potatoes, the same technique can be used, simply substituting sweet potato for the potato. For kabocha squash, split 2 pounds of squash (no need to remove the skin), scrape out the seeds, cut into large chunks, and cook them in a bamboo steamer or metal steamer insert until just tender (about 20 minutes), discard the stem, and use in place of boiled potatoes in the recipe.

TEMPURA

Tempura is one of Japan's oldest and most popular culinary traditions. Tempura-style batters were introduced to Japan by Portuguese missionaries in the sixteenth century. The word itself is a loan word from Portuguese.* *Tempora* referred to the period of time during which missionaries refrained from eating meat, instead eating fried seafood. In modern Japan, tempura ranges from inexpensive, everyday fare you can find at food courts and shopping malls to fancy, multi-course all-tempura meals prepared by a single tempura master. I remember having one such meal

at Tsunahachi, a Tokyo tempura shop that has been serving tempura fried in sesame oil since 1923. The meal was superb, but it was made extra memorable when the live *kuruma-ebi* (Japanese tiger prawn) the chef presented before he was to dispatch and deep-fry it leapt off the plate and into my mother's purse in a last-ditch escape attempt. (He was delicious.)

I am no tempura master, but as a cook at a sashimi restaurant, I've fried enough tempura in my time to pick up a few tips. All of the basic rules of deep frying I went over earlier in this chapter apply to tempura as well, but there are three especially important factors that can mean the difference between a light, airy, crisp coating and a soggy or thick coating:

- **Do not overmix the batter**. Once you add the liquid, your goal is to incorporate the liquid and batter as rapidly as possible, then stop stirring, as any extra stirring will encourage gluten development, robbing the batter of its light crispness. The best

way I've found to mix tempura batter is to put the dry mixture in a wide bowl, add your liquid all at once, then stir rapidly with a pair of chopsticks in one hand, while vigorously shaking the bowl with the other. When finished, the batter should not have any watery liquid remaining, but it should still have plenty of bubbles and lumps.

- **Use ice-cold soda water or a vodka/soda water mixture**. Keeping the liquid cold inhibits gluten formation. Soda water adds bubbles to the mix, which will lighten the batter as it fries. Vodka will limit gluten development while also increasing the volatility of the batter, leading to faster frying and a lacier texture.

- **Keep the food moving in the oil**. Once the food goes into the fryer, do not let it sit still. Keep it moving by using a spider to continuously spin it, flip it, and splash it with fresh oil to encourage fast, even cooking.

---

* Japanese has several such Portuguese loan words, such as *paraiso* (paradise) and *shabon* (soap).

ALL-PURPOSE TEMPURA BATTER AND DREDGING MIXTURE

Yield
Makes 4
cups

Active Time
2 minutes

Total Time
2 minutes

This all-purpose tempura and dredging mixture is the recipe we use for several of the fried dishes we've served over the years at my restaurant Wursthall (at least it was the recipe we used up until we found a similar commercial tempura mix we liked). Gently mixed with soda water, it forms an excellent tempura-style batter for our tempura-fried sauerkraut (find the recipe on page 477). We season it with spices, mix it with buttermilk and eggs, marinate chicken in it overnight, then dredge that chicken in more of the dry mixture before double-frying it to make our most popular menu item, the Korean hot fried chicken sandwich. Whether as the base for a batter or a dredging mixture, it fries up light and crisp.

INGREDIENTS

2 cups (8 ounces/225 g) rice flour
2 cups (10 ounce/300 g) all-purpose flour
1 tablespoon (15 g) baking powder
1 tablespoon (15 g) fine salt

DIRECTIONS

Whisk together all the ingredients in a bowl. Store in a cool, dark pantry when not in use.

How to Prepare Common Tempura Ingredients

INGREDIENT	PREPARATION
VEGETABLES	
Avocados	Remove the skin and pit and cut into thick wedges.
Bell peppers	Cut into ½-inch-wide rings or strips.
Broccoli and cauliflower	Cut into 1-inch florets.
Butternut squash	Peel, seed, and cut into ¼-inch slices.
Cabbage or sauerkraut	Finely shred.
Carrots	Peel and cut into ¼-inch slices or planks.
Eggplants	Cut into ½-inch rounds.
Green beans	Trim the ends.
Kabocha squash	Remove seeds and cut into ¼-inch slices.
Kale	Remove the central tough stem from each leaf.
Mushrooms	Clean and thinly slice or leave thin mushrooms like shiitake or oyster whole.
Okra	Trim the stem ends.
Onions	Cut into ½-inch rings or finely shred.
Sweet potatoes	Peel and cut into ¼-inch slices.
Zucchini and summer squash	Cut into ½-inch rounds or sticks.
SEAFOOD	
Fish	Cut into thin fillets or strips.
Shrimp	Peel, leaving the final tail section intact if desired, and remove the legs. Flatten each shrimp and insert a wooden skewer or toothpick lengthwise to keep it straight while it fries; remove the skewers after cooking.
Squid	Cut the tubes into thin rings. Leave the tentacles whole or cut into individual tentacles.

TEMPURA VEGETABLES OR SEAFOOD

Yield
Serves 3
to 4

Active Time
15 minutes

Total Time
15 minutes

INGREDIENTS

2 quarts (2 l) peanut, rice bran, or other
    neutral oil
1 cup All-Purpose Tempura Batter and
    Dredging Mixture (page 472)
¼ cup (60 ml) 80-proof vodka
⅔ cup (160 ml) ice-cold soda water
12 ounces (340 g) vegetables or seafood,
    prepared for tempura (see page 474)

To Serve (optional):
Lemon wedges or dipping sauce of your
    choice (recipes follow) on pages
    475–76

Following the chart on page 473, prepare up to 12 ounces (340 g) of ingredients to fry per batch of batter. Mix fresh batter for subsequent batches. For extra crunch, drizzle excess batter off of your fingertips on top of vegetables and seafood immediately after adding them to the hot oil.

DIRECTIONS

(1) Heat the oil to 375°F (190°C) in a wok over high heat, then adjust the heat as necessary to maintain the temperature. Line a large plate or baking sheet with a double layer of paper towels.

(2) Add the batter mix to a large bowl. Add the vodka and soda water and, holding the bowl with one hand and chopsticks in the other, shake the bowl back and forth while vigorously stirring with chopsticks until the liquid and dry ingredients are just barely combined. There should still be many bubbles and pockets of dry flour.

(3) Add the vegetables (or seafood) to the batter and fold gently with your hand to coat. Pick up a few pieces at a time, allowing excess batter to drip off, and transfer to the hot oil, getting your hand as close as possible to the surface before sliding them into the oil one piece at a time. Increase the heat to high to maintain the temperature as close to 350°F (175°C) as possible and add the remaining vegetables (and/or shrimp) a few pieces at a time. Immediately start agitating them with chopsticks or a spider, separating the vegetables, flipping them, and constantly exposing them to fresh oil. Continue frying until the batter is completely crisp and pale blond, about 1 minute.

(4) Transfer the tempura to a paper-towel-lined plate or baking sheet and immediately sprinkle with salt. Serve with lemon or dipping sauce.

SOY-DASHI DIPPING SAUCE FOR TEMPURA

Yield
Makes 1
cup

Active Time
5 minutes

Total Time
5 minutes

NOTE

Hondashi is powdered dashi that can be found at any Japanese market and most well-stocked supermarkets. You can also combine ¼ cup Homemade Concentrated Mentsuyu (page 231) with ¾ cup water for this sauce.

This balanced mix of savory dashi, salty soy sauce, and sweet mirin is the classic accompaniment for tempura.

INGREDIENTS

¾ cup (180 ml) homemade dashi (pages 519–21), or the equivalent in Hondashi (see Note)
3 tablespoons (45 ml) mirin
1 tablespoon (15 ml) light soy sauce or shoyu

To Serve:
2 ounces (60 g) daikon radish, grated into a pulp on the smallest holes of a box grater

DIRECTIONS

Combine all the ingredients. Soy dashi can be stored in the refrigerator for up to 4 days.

VINEGAR-CARAMEL DIPPING SAUCE FOR TEMPURA

Yield
Serves 4

Active Time
15 minutes

Total Time
15 minutes

This vinegar-caramel dipping sauce is based on Italian agrodolce (sweet and sour) sauce, a common pairing with *fritto misto*, fried seafood. It's simple and especially delicious with tempura-fried pumpkin or sweet potato slices.

INGREDIENTS

½ cup (3½ ounces/100 g) sugar
¼ cup (60 ml) water
Pinch of salt

½ cup (120 ml) white wine or champagne vinegar
1 fresh hot red chile, such as Fresno, red serrano, or Thai bird, thinly sliced

DIRECTIONS

Heat the sugar, water, and salt in a medium saucepan over medium heat. Stir with a fork until it comes to a boil. Continue cooking, swirling the pan gently, until it darkens to a golden honey color, about 6 minutes. Immediately add the vinegar all at once (it will bubble fiercely) as well as the chile, stir until the caramel is dissolved, then remove from the heat and let cool. The sauce can be stored in the refrigerator for several months.

GOCHUGARU YOGURT RANCH DRESSING

Yield
Makes about 1 cup

Active Time
5 minutes

Total Time
5 minutes

This ranch-style dressing seasoned with Korean chile flakes is delicious as a dip for tempura (we used to serve it with our tempura sauerkraut at Wursthall) and other fried foods. It's also just great on a simple salad or as a dip for raw vegetables. I find that the combination of granulated garlic and fresh garlic is essential for that "ranchy" flavor.

INGREDIENTS

½ cup (120 ml) full-fat Greek-style yogurt
¼ cup (60 ml) mayonnaise
2 teaspoons (6 g) granulated garlic
1 teaspoon (3 g) granulated onion
2 teaspoons (5 g) minced fresh garlic (about 2 medium cloves)
½ ounce (15 g) fresh dill, minced

1 teaspoon (3 g) freshly ground black pepper
¼ ounce (8 g) fresh chives, minced
1 tablespoon (15 g) fresh lemon or lime juice (from 1 lemon or lime)
2 teaspoons (6 g) gochugaru
Kosher salt

DIRECTIONS

Combine all the ingredients in a medium bowl and whisk until homogenous. Season to taste with salt. The dressing can be stored in the fridge for up to 2 weeks.

HONEY-MISO MAYONNAISE FOR TEMPURA

Yield
Makes 1 cup

Active Time
5 minutes

Total Time
5 minutes

This sweet and savory mayonnaise is based on a recipe I learned as a cook at Ken Oringer's UNI in Boston, and makes an excellent dip for tempura (or French fries, for that matter) or raw vegetables, especially cucumber.

INGREDIENTS

¾ cup (180 ml) mayonnaise
2 tablespoons (35 g) yellow miso paste

2 tablespoons (30 ml) honey
1 tablespoon (15 ml) rice vinegar

DIRECTIONS

Combine all the ingredients in a medium bowl and whisk until homogenous. Honey-miso mayonnaise can be stored in the refrigerator for several weeks.

TEMPURA SAUERKRAUT AND ONIONS

Yield
Serves 3
to 4

Active Time
15 minutes

Total Time
15 minutes

NOTE
Replace half of the sauerkraut with finely shredded cabbage kimchi for a spicier variation

INGREDIENTS

2 quarts (2 l) peanut, rice bran, or other neutral oil

12 ounces (340 g) sauerkraut

2 ounces (60 g) red or yellow onion, thinly sliced

1 ounce (30 g) homemade or store-bought pickled chiles (page 84), thinly sliced

1 cup All-Purpose Tempura Batter and Dredging Mixture (page 472)

¼ cup (60 ml) 80-proof vodka

⅔ cup (160 ml) ice-cold soda water

To Serve:

Gochugaru Yogurt Ranch Dressing (page 476)

This recipe is something that came in a flash of inspiration in October of 2019. I was working on a new formula for the fried chicken sandwich at Wursthall with my sous-chef Erik Drobey and experimenting with various homemade and commercial tempura mixes. One of the cooks, Carlos Gonzalez, was stocking the line with sauerkraut for the night. On a whim, I grabbed a handful and dropped it into a bowl of tempura batter along with some slivered red onions (that I pulled out of our burger station) and some of the pickled Fresno chiles we serve with our queso pretzel dip. I mixed them all up, then drizzled them into the fryer.

I was floored by how delicious the concoction was. The sauerkraut acquired the nutty aroma of roasted cabbage, while onion added some sweetness, tempered by a bit of heat from the Fresnos. Tempura is light to begin with, but the acidity from the sauerkraut and chiles made it even brighter. It was delicious enough that we put it on the menu a week later, serving it with a Gochugaru Yogurt Ranch Dressing (page 476). The changes we had to make for operations when the coronavirus hit forced us to pull it off the menu a few months later, but I am confident that my relationship with tempura sauerkraut is far from over.

DIRECTIONS

1. Heat the oil to 375°F (190°C) in a wok over high heat, then adjust the heat as necessary to maintain the temperature. Line a large plate or baking sheet with a double layer of paper towels.

2. Place sauerkraut in a fine-mesh strainer set over the sink and squeeze as much moisture out of it as you can. Add the onions and chiles and toss everything until well mixed.

3. Add the batter mix to a large bowl. Add the vodka and soda water and, holding the bowl with one hand and chopsticks in the other, shake the bowl back and forth while vigorously stirring with chopsticks until the liquid and dry ingredients are just barely combined. There should still be many bubbles and pockets of dry flour.

4. Add the sauerkraut/onion/chile mixture and toss to coat. Pick up a small handful in loose fingertips, let the excess batter drip back into the bowl, then slowly sprinkle the mixture into the oil. Continue adding until all the mixture is in the oil. Increase the heat to high to maintain the temperature as close to 350°F (175°C) as possible. Immediately start agitating with chopsticks or a spider, breaking up the largest clumps but allowing the mixture to stay tangled. Continue frying until the batter is completely crisp and pale blond, about 1 minute total.

5. Transfer the tempura to a paper-towel-lined plate or baking sheet and immediately sprinkle with salt. Serve with Gochugaru Yogurt Ranch Dressing.

4.3 CRISPY-AND-SAUCY RECIPES, THE CHINESE AMERICAN WAY

I think it's high time that General Tso gets his chicken recognized as one of the national dishes of the United States. After all, ask yourself the question that Jennifer 8. Lee, journalist and author of *The Fortune Cookie Chronicles*, asked in a 2008 TED Talk: how many times a year do you eat Chinese food versus the supposedly all-American apple pie?

For me, the ratio is easily 30 to 1, Chinese food to apple pie. Indeed, in most years, that ratio would become a mathematically undefined, divide-by-zero situation.

According to a very brief internet search, there were 46,700 Chinese restaurants in the United States in 2015—more than all of the McDonald's, Burger Kings, Wendy's, Taco Bells, and Kentucky Fried Chickens combined. And whether it's called General Tso's (as it is where I grew up in in New York), General Gau's (the way I knew it through my college years in New England), Cho's, Chau's, Joe's, Ching's, Chang's (as it's called at Chinese American shopping mall staple P. F. Chang's), or, as they call it in the navy, Admiral Tso's, walk into any one of those restaurants and chances are you'll find it on the menu.

Its origins are still up for debate. Its namesake general, Zuo Zongtang, almost certainly never tasted the dish before his death in 1885, and, as Lee discovers, his descendants—many of whom still reside in the general's hometown of Xiangyin—don't recognize the dish as a family heirloom or even as particularly Chinese for that matter.

As my friend Francis Lam reported in a 2010 article for Salon.com, Ed Schoenfeld, proprietor of New York's Red Farm and perhaps the world's foremost expert on Chinese American cuisine, traces its origins to Chef Peng Jia, a Hunanese chef who fled to Taiwan after the 1949 revolution. Made with unbattered large chunks of dark-meat chicken tossed in a tart sauce, it was more savory than sweet. It wasn't until a New York–based chef, Tsung Ting Wang (better known as T. T. Wang), learned the recipe from Peng in Taiwan, brought it back, added a crispy deep-fried coating and sugar to the sauce, and changed the name to General Ching's, that it stuck (the sugary sauce and the name), eventually making its way onto Chinese menus across the country and the globe (the name got changed a bit in the process). It's so popular that an entire feature-length film on its origins—*The Search for General Tso*—debuted in 2014 at the Tribeca Film Festival.

It makes sense: As Americans we like our food sweet, we like it fried, and man, do we love chicken.

General Ching's chicken wasn't the only dish that chef T. T. Wang adapted and popularized at New York's Shun Lee Palace between its opening in 1971 and his passing in 1983. He can be credited with popularizing—if not outright creating—orange beef and crispy whole deep-fried sea bass. The former consists of slices of beef breaded and deep-fried until crisp, then tossed with a sweet and tangy sauce flavored with dried orange peel, and has since become a staple at Chinese American restaurants on the East Coast. Why chicken, beef, and fish? Chef Wang and his business partner Michael Tong were always acutely aware of their popularity among New York's Jews. Indeed, there's a custom among many families in the New York Jewish community of ordering Chinese food on Christmas Day, which can likely be traced back to Shun Lee and its other midtown competitors.

Since then, the repertoire of crisply fried foods tossed in a sticky sweet-sour-savory sauce has expanded as it made its way across the country. Andy Kao, the executive chef of the California-based chain Panda Express, created their signature orange chicken in 1987. It's now served at their over two thousand locations, alongside their "Beijing Beef," a stir-fry of bell pepper, onion, and crispy fried beef strips in a General Tso–style dark, sweet, and vinegary sauce, and their "Honey Walnut Shrimp," which, again, is crunchy, sweet, tangy, and deep-fried.

The details of these dishes vary—the protein, the vegetables, the sauce—but the basics are the same: food coated in a crisp, craggy, deep-fried coating that Colonel Sanders himself would be proud of (what is it with military titles and fried chicken anyway?), tossed in a powerfully flavored, glossy, thickened sauce that completely coats the chunks but does not render them soggy or soft (at least, it shouldn't). Throw it all on a plate with some steamed white rice and you've got some of America's most popular dishes.

Even at the chains, these dishes are undeniably delicious. But my goal at home was to take the same idea and really max out all of its stats. Shatteringly crisp. Shockingly aromatic. Explosively flavorful. And other adverbial phrases as well. I'm smart enough to know that one should never get involved in a land war in Asia, but luckily, this was a battle I could fight in my own kitchen at home. I rolled up my sleeves and headed into the fray.

The Coating

To start my testing, I scanned through various books and online resources, pulling out recipes that claimed to solve some of the problems I was looking at—namely, a crazy crunchy fried coating that doesn't soften up when the chicken gets tossed with sauce. Though similar, there were variations across the board in terms of how thick the marinade should be (some contained only soy sauce and wine, others contained eggs, and still others were a thick batter), whether or not to toss with dry starch or flour after marinating, and whether to use light or dark meat.

I put together a few working recipes that seemed to run the gamut of what's out there to test which approach gave the best initial results, including:

- Thin marinade of soy sauce and wine; tossed in cornstarch before frying

- Egg-white-based marinade; tossed in cornstarch before frying

- Whole-egg-based marinade; tossed in cornstarch before frying

- Egg-based batter made with cornstarch; no dry coating before frying

- Egg-based batter made with cornstarch; dry coating before frying

- Egg-based batter made with flour and cornstarch; no dry coating before frying

- Egg-based batter made with flour and cornstarch; dry coating before frying

Here are a few of the results:

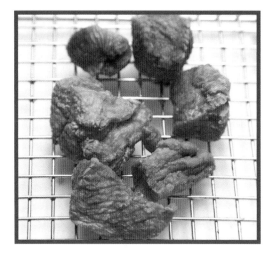

A simple cornstarch coating.

An egg-based batter with just enough cornstarch to thicken it; no dry coating afterward.

A thick and eggy marinade; dry cornstarch coating afterward.

No eggs at all, just a liquid marinade; cornstarch coating afterward.

They all look alright, but none of them stayed crisp for long, even before they were added to the sauce. From the testing, one thing was certain: a thicker, egg-based marinade is superior to a thin marinade, which produced chicken that was powdery and a crust that turned soft within seconds of coming out of the fryer. Adding a bit of starch to the marinade before tossing it in a dry coat was even better.

The other takeaway? Dark meat is the way to go. Breast meat comes out dry and chalky, a problem that can be mitigated with some extended marinating (the soy sauce in the marinade acts as a brine, helping it to retain moisture), but the process adds time to an already lengthy recipe, and even brined white meat is nowhere near as juicy as dark meat, and who are we kidding? General Tso's is never going to be health food. Break out the thighs for this one.

Since none of the existing techniques I found gave me quite the coating I was looking for, I decided to start expanding my search, pulling out all of the chicken-frying tricks in the book.

What about double dipping? I started my chicken pieces in a thick marinade made of egg white, soy sauce, wine, baking powder, and cornstarch (I found that adding baking powder to the batter helped keep it lighter as it fried), then dipped it into a mixture of cornstarch, flour, and baking powder (a mixture of cornstarch and flour browns a little better than straight up starch). After that I moved it back to the wet mixture, and again into the dry, creating an extra-thick coating.

Extra-thick coatings produce extra-crunchy chicken for sure. Too crunchy, unfortunately. Getting close to a quarter inch thick in parts, the coating made the General Tso's taste more like tough crackers than anything. Extra leavening didn't help. I went for a different approach, this time looking to my Extra-Crispy Korean Fried Chicken (page 460) for some clues.

The solution there? Use a thin slurry of cornstarch that's been cut with vodka, which both speeds up evaporation (and therefore crisping) and limits gluten development in batters, reducing their toughness, so I tried coating chicken thigh pieces with the exact same batter that I used for my fried chicken recipe before tossing it in sauce and tasting it.

It was an improvement on the stay-crisp-when-wet front for sure, but it wasn't exactly what I was looking for in General Tso's. It needed more craggy nooks and crannies to capture that sauce.

With the idea of nooks and crannies in my head, my thoughts immediately jumped to the American-style fried chicken recipe I developed for my first book, *The Food Lab*. It's my favorite fried chicken trick: drizzling some wet batter into the dry dredging mixture to build up little nuggets of crust that adhere to the chicken and add surface area as it fries.

By combining that method with the vodka trick I learned from my Extra-Crispy Korean Fried Chicken, I ended up with even better end results. The best of both worlds:

I mean, just look at that exterior texture! And the best part? Those sauce-catching crags stay crisp for a long time—so crisp that even microwaved the next day, the chicken is almost as good as it was freshly fried. (And, if you are inclined to add a double-fry to the process, it stays crispy for *days*.)

Extra-Crispy Fried Chicken or Beef for Chinese American Dishes, Step by Step

I had the general in my crosshairs; all that was left to do was pull the trigger. With just a bit of tweaking and streamlining, here's where we end up, step by step. The same process works for any dish where fried nuggets end up tossed in a thickened sauce, such as General Tso's or orange peel beef. Only the flavors in the marinade change slightly.

Step 1 • Mix the Marinade

I start with a marinade of an egg white mixed with a couple tablespoons of dark soy sauce, a couple tablespoons of Shaoxing wine, and a couple tablespoons of vodka.

Step 2 • Marinate the Meat

After setting aside half the marinade (I'm going to use it to moisten up my dry coating later on), I add 3 tablespoons of cornstarch, ¼ teaspoon of baking soda (no need for baking powder here, as the wine adds the acidic element that reacts with the soda), and a pound

of chicken (or beef, shrimp, tofu, etc.), tossing it all with my fingers until the chicken is thoroughly coated.

At this stage you can refrigerate the meat for up to a few hours, or you can plow straight through the rest of the recipe with a shortened marinating period. It makes very little difference.

Step 3 • Combine the Reserved Marinade and the Dredging Mixture

Next up, I add that reserved marinade to my dry ingredients: ½ cup each of flour and cornstarch, along with ½ teaspoon of baking powder and ½ teaspoon of salt.

Step 4 • Mix and Form Crumbles

I mix it all together with my fingertips or a whisk. At this stage the mixture should look coarse and crumbly, with a few big nuggets of the flour-marinade mixture.

Step 5 • Add the Meat and Coat

With the dry mix made, I add the chicken. You can just dump all the chicken in and then work on carefully separating and coating each piece in the mixture, pressing firmly so that it adheres (you will get messy hands using this method), or you can use my preferred method, which takes a bit more practice: Holding the dry mix in one hand and tossing constantly, drop individual pieces of chicken in one by one with your other hand. As you toss, the chicken pieces should all get individually coated.

Step 6 • Deep-Fry

All of the normal caveats about deep frying hold true here: use a thermometer to regulate temperature (350°F/175°C was the right temperature for this application), add pieces one at a time and gently lower them into the hot oil (don't drop them!), and keep things moving so that they fry rapidly and evenly, which in turn will help them get crisper faster.

Once they are crispy and cooked through (about 4 minutes or so), you can drain them and toss them with your sauce, or if you want even better results, drain them, let them cool completely (they can be stored up to a few days uncovered in the fridge), then fry them a second time at 375°F (190°C) just until they recrisp, about 2 minutes.

They get crisp. I mean CRISP. You could take those double-fried nuggets to the beautiful Mount Airy Lodge in the Poconos, dance into the night with them, relax in a heart-shaped jacuzzi, share a bottle of Champagne, cuddle up next to the fire, and fall asleep with them in your arms, and they'll *still* be crispy the next morning. (Not that I've actually tested this.)

Step 7 • Toss with the Sauce

Since your wok will be occupied with the deep fry, you can stir-fry secondary ingredients and premix your sauce before the frying process, then finish everything by tossing it all together in a saucepan or skillet on a second burner as soon as your crispy nuggets are finished frying.

It takes a bit of work to get the sauce to coat every surface, but you will be rewarded when all's said and done. Greatly rewarded.

GENERAL TSO'S SAUCE

Though Chinese restaurants often brand General Tso's with a token chile or two next to its number on the menu, its flavors are really more sweet and savory with a bracing hit of acidity than actually spicy. Shaoxing wine, soy sauce, rice vinegar, chicken stock, and sugar are the base ingredients, and they all get thickened up into a shiny glaze with a bit of cornstarch.

I looked at several existing recipes and tasted versions of the sauce from restaurants all around New York and San Francisco. Most restaurant versions are syrupy sweet, while home recipes range from being cloying to containing almost no sugar at all. I found that plenty of sugar is actually a good thing in these sauces, but that the sugar has to be paired with enough acidity to balance it out. I settled on a mixture of 2 tablespoons (30 ml) of wine and 2 tablespoons (30 ml) vinegar along with a full ¼ cup (50 g) of granulated sugar. Soy sauce, sesame oil, and chicken stock, along with the classic trio of ginger, garlic, and scallions and a few whole dried chiles rounded out the flavors.

At restaurants, the fried stuff would get cooked either in a deep fryer or in a dedicated frying wok while the cook makes the sauce and builds the rest of the stir-fry in a separate wok. The fried ingredients would then get dumped into the wok and tossed before serving. At home, however, with my wok dedicated to deep frying, I have to rely on a separate skillet or saucepan to make my sauce.

I was worried that without the high heat of a wok my sauces would not come out as flavorful, so I made two batches side by side. One I made the traditional way:

oil heated until smoking hot, with the aromatics added in and stir-fried for just 30 seconds or so before adding in the liquid ingredients and letting the sauce simmer and thicken. The second I made by starting the same aromatics in a cold skillet with oil, heating them while stirring until aromatic, then adding the liquids.

I fully expected the high-heat version to have superior flavor, but when I compared them in a blind taste test, nearly everyone actually preferred the version made in the skillet: the garlic, ginger, and scallion flavor was more subtle and blended more smoothly with the other ingredients. The great part about General Tso's (and, in fact, any of the crispy-and-saucy recipes in this section) is that you can make the sauce well in advance—heck, you can even make it the day before if you'd like—and just warm it up to toss with the chicken when it's good and ready for it.

GENERAL TSO'S CHICKEN

Yield
Serves 4
to 6

Active Time
45 minutes

Total Time
1 hour or up to
several days

This is my version of the Chinese American classic. A vodka-based batter and a double-fry makes the chicken extra crispy. Crispy enough that you can coat it in the sweet, sour, and mildly spicy sauce and let it sit for hours or days without losing its crispiness. Even reheated in the microwave, you'll feel its crunch.

INGREDIENTS

For the Marinade and Chicken:
1 large egg white
1 tablespoon (15 ml) light soy sauce or
  shoyu
2 tablespoons (30 ml) Shaoxing wine
2 tablespoons (30 ml) 80-proof vodka
¼ teaspoon (1 g) baking soda
3 tablespoons (9 g) cornstarch
1 pound (450 g) boneless, skinless
  chicken thighs, cut into ½- to ¾-inch
  chunks

For the Dry Coating:
½ cup (2½ ounces/70 g) all-purpose
  flour
½ cup (2 ounces/60 g) cornstarch
½ teaspoon (3 g) baking powder
½ teaspoon (3 g) kosher salt

For the Sauce:
2 tablespoons (30 ml) light soy sauce or
  shoyu
1 tablespoon (15 ml) dark soy sauce
1 tablespoon (3 g) cornstarch
2 tablespoons (30 ml) Shaoxing wine
2 tablespoons (30 ml) distilled white
  vinegar
3 tablespoons (45 ml) homemade or
  store-bought low-sodium chicken
  stock or water
¼ cup (50 g) sugar
1 teaspoon (5 ml) roasted sesame oil
2 teaspoons (10 ml) peanut, vegetable, or
  canola oil
2 teaspoons (5 g) minced garlic (about 2
  medium cloves)
2 teaspoons (5 g) minced fresh ginger
  (about ½-inch segment)
1 scallion, minced, plus 6 to 8 scallions,
  white and pale green parts only, cut
  into 1-inch lengths
8 small dried hot chiles, such as chao tian
  jiao, árbol, or Japones, or ½ teaspoon
  hot red pepper flakes

To Finish:
2 quarts (2 l) peanut, rice bran, or other
  neutral oil
Steamed rice, for serving

DIRECTIONS

(1) **For the Marinade and Chicken:** Beat the egg white in a large bowl until broken down and lightly foamy. Add the soy sauce, wine, and vodka and whisk to combine. Set aside half of the marinade in a small bowl. Add the baking soda and cornstarch to the large bowl and whisk to combine. Add the chicken to the large bowl and turn it with your fingers to coat thoroughly. Set aside while you prepare the remaining ingredients or marinate in the refrigerator up to overnight before continuing.

recipe continues

(2) **For the Dry Coating:** Combine the flour, cornstarch, baking powder, and salt in a large bowl. Whisk until homogenous. Add the reserved marinade and whisk until the mixture has coarse, mealy clumps. Set aside.

(3) **For the Sauce:** Combine the soy sauces and cornstarch in a medium bowl and stir with a fork until no lumps remain. Add the wine, vinegar, chicken stock, sugar, and sesame oil and stir to combine. Set aside.

(4) Combine the oil, garlic, ginger, minced scallions, and red chiles in a large skillet and cook over medium heat, stirring, until the vegetables are aromatic and soft but not browned, about 3 minutes. Stir the sauce mixture and add to the skillet, making sure to scrape out any sugar or starch that has sunk to the bottom. Cook, stirring, until the sauce boils and thickens, about 1 minute. Add the scallion segments. Remove from the heat.

(5) **To Finish:** Heat the oil in a wok over high heat until it registers 350°F (175°C) on an instant-read thermometer, then adjust the heat to maintain the temperature. Working one piece at a time, transfer the chicken from the marinade to the dry coating mixture, tossing after each addition to coat the chicken. When all the chicken has been added to the dry coating, toss with your hands, pressing the dry mixture onto the chicken so it adheres and making sure that every piece is coated thoroughly.

(6) Lift the chicken one piece at a time, shake off the excess coating, and carefully lower it into the hot oil (do not drop it). Once all the chicken has been added, cook, agitating with long chopsticks or a spider and adjusting the heat to maintain a temperature of 325° to 350°F (160° to 175°C), until the chicken is cooked through and very crispy, about 4 minutes. Remove the chicken with a spider and transfer to a paper-towel-lined bowl to drain.

(7) **Optional Double-Fry, for Extra-Crispy Results:** Let the chicken cool completely on the countertop, or let it rest uncovered in the fridge for up to two nights. Meanwhile, strain the oil and discard any solids. Reheat the oil to 375°F (190°C), return the chicken to the oil, and refry, agitating constantly, until crispy, about 2 minutes. Remove the chicken with a spider and transfer to a paper-towel-lined bowl to drain.

(8) Add the chicken to the skillet with the sauce. Toss the chicken, folding it with a rubber spatula until all pieces are thoroughly coated. Serve immediately with rice.

Popeye's + Your Wok = Excellent General Tso's

I want to preface this by saying this idea was not mine, and in no way can I claim credit for it. It came from a conversation I had with a *Serious Eats* reader in 2011, who told me that he had started making my kung pao chicken recipe, only to realize that he had no chicken at home. What he did have, on the other hand, was leftover Popeye's chicken nuggets. So he improvised.

The idea seemed absolutely brilliant, especially for Chinese American dishes traditionally made with fried nuggets of chicken, so I tried it. I picked up a couple boxes of Popeye's chicken nuggets and fried shrimp, then added them directly to batches of General Tso's, orange chicken, and sesame chicken sauces. They were terrific. Not quite as crisp as the homemade stuff, of course, but if you're craving some of these dishes and simply don't feel like deep frying at home, this hack may well be just the right fit for your dinner plans. Pro tip: if you *refry* fridge-cold leftover fried chicken (whether homemade or fast food), it comes out extra-crisp.

THE GENERAL'S EXTENDED FAMILY

My high school physics teacher, Mr. Harless, always told me, "Kenji, your goal in life should be to work hard to become as lazy as you can be." During my first semester at college, when all classes were taken on a pass/fail basis, I took him at his word by being the student in my thermodynamics class who got the lowest possible passing grade. I'm pretty sure that's not what Mr. Harless meant, but my TA bought me a six-pack of beer for the accomplishment, so . . . thanks, Mr. Harless?

What he did mean was this: If you take the time to solve one problem, you should do your darnedest to make sure that the lessons you learn while solving it are applied to other, similar problems so that you can kill multiple birds with one stone.*

Prime example: take all the lessons I learned during months of testing recipes for General Tso's chicken and apply them to its very similar partners-in-crime on the Chinese American lunch special menu— orange chicken, sesame chicken, Springfield-style cashew chicken, and orange peel beef.

Hey, Mr. Harless, look what I did: I can now get takeout-style Chinese American chicken dishes, and I don't even have to pick up the phone! How's that for lazy?

---

* In this case, confusingly, the stone in the metaphor is actually a bird, while the birds are, in fact, saucy and crispy Chinese American dishes.

CALIFORNIA-STYLE ORANGE CHICKEN

Yield
Serves 4
to 6

Active Time
45 minutes

Total Time
1 hour or up to
several days

Orange chicken was invented in Hawaii in 1987 by Andy Kao, the executive chef of Panda Express. In a 2017 NPR interview on the thirtieth anniversary of the dish, Panda Express co-founder Andrew Cherng explained that their orange chicken was a variation of General Tso's. It sold well. Very well. Its popularity is a large part of Panda Express's success; it's the country's most successful Asian restaurant chain, with over 2,200 locations as of 2019.

If we are to believe their published nutritional information and ingredients lists, their sauce is made mostly from water, sugar, distilled white vinegar, and soy sauce, thickened with starch and getting its oranginess from orange extract rather than fresh oranges. At home you can make yourself a brighter, fresher-tasting sauce by ditching the extract and using fresh oranges instead, incorporating the juice as well as strips of zest into the sauce. In most cases I'd recommend being very careful not to grab any of the bitter pith when zesting citrus, but here a touch of bitterness is actually a welcome addition to the otherwise extremely sweet sauce.

For the aromatics, I stick with just garlic and ginger here, leaving out the scallions until the very end as a garnish (although you should do it however you're inclined) and adding a tiny pinch of pepper flakes for a hint of heat (you could also use whole dried chiles, if you'd like).

INGREDIENTS

For the Marinade and Chicken:
1 large egg white
1 tablespoon (15 ml) light soy sauce
    or shoyu
2 tablespoons (30 ml) Shaoxing wine
2 tablespoons (30 ml) 80-proof
    vodka
¼ teaspoon (1 g) baking soda
3 tablespoons (9 g) cornstarch
1 pound (450 g) boneless, skinless
    chicken thighs, cut into ½- to
    ¾-inch chunks

For the Dry Coating:
½ cup (2½ ounces/70 g) all-purpose
    flour
½ cup (2 ounces/60 g) cornstarch
½ teaspoon (3 g) baking powder
½ teaspoon (3 g) kosher salt

For the Sauce:
2 tablespoons (30 ml) light soy sauce
    or shoyu
1 tablespoon cornstarch
3 tablespoons (45 ml) distilled white
    vinegar
½ cup (120 ml) fresh orange juice,
    plus three 2-inch long strips zest,
    from about 3 oranges (see Note)

¼ cup (50 g) sugar
1 teaspoon (5 ml) roasted sesame oil
Small pinch of hot red pepper flakes
2 teaspoons (10 ml) peanut,
    vegetable, or canola oil
2 teaspoons (5 g) minced garlic
    (about 2 medium cloves)
2 teaspoons (5 g) minced fresh ginger
    (about ½-inch segment)

To Finish:
2 quarts (2 l) peanut, rice bran, or
    other neutral oil
Steamed white rice, for serving
Sliced scallions, for serving

DIRECTIONS

(1) **For the Marinade and Chicken:** Beat the egg white in a large bowl until broken down and lightly foamy. Add the soy sauce, wine, and vodka and whisk to combine. Set aside half of the marinade in a small bowl. Add

the baking soda and cornstarch to the large bowl and whisk to combine. Add the chicken to the large bowl and turn it with your fingers to coat thoroughly. Set aside while you prepare the remaining ingredients or marinate in the refrigerator up to overnight before continuing.

(2) **For the Dry Coating:** Combine the flour, cornstarch, baking powder, and salt in a large bowl. Whisk until homogenous. Add the reserved marinade and whisk until the mixture has coarse, mealy clumps. Set aside.

(3) **For the Sauce:** Combine the soy sauce and cornstarch in a medium bowl and stir with a fork until no lumps remain. Add the vinegar, orange juice, orange zest, sugar, sesame oil, and pepper flakes and stir to combine. Set aside.

(4) Combine the oil, garlic, and ginger in a large skillet and cook over medium heat, stirring, until aromatic and soft but not browned, about 2 minutes. Stir the sauce mixture and add to the skillet, making sure to scrape out any sugar or starch that has sunk to the bottom. Cook, stirring, until the sauce boils, reduces, and thickens to the point where it can easily coat the back of a spoon, about 5 minutes. Remove from the heat.

(5) **To Finish:** Heat the oil in a wok over high heat until it registers 350°F (175°C) on an instant-read thermometer, then adjust the heat to maintain the temperature. Working one piece at a time, transfer the chicken from the marinade to the dry coating mixture, tossing after each addition to coat the chicken. When all the chicken has been added to the dry coating, toss it with your hands, pressing the dry mixture onto the chicken so it adheres and making sure that every piece is coated thoroughly.

(6) Lift the chicken one piece at a time, shake off excess coating, and carefully lower it into the hot oil (do not drop it). Once all the chicken has been added, cook, agitating with long chopsticks or a spider and adjusting the heat to maintain a temperature of 325° to 350°F (160° to 175°C), until the chicken is cooked through and very crispy, about 4 minutes. Remove the chicken with a spider and transfer to a paper-towel-lined bowl to drain.

(7) **Optional Double-Fry, for Extra-Crispy Results:** Let the chicken cool completely on the countertop, or let it rest uncovered in the fridge for up to two nights. Meanwhile, strain the oil and discard any solids. Reheat the oil to 375°F (190°C), add the rested chicken, and refry until crispy, about 2 minutes. Remove the chicken with a spider and transfer to a paper-towel-lined bowl to drain.

(8) Add the chicken to the skillet with the sauce. Toss the chicken, folding it with a rubber spatula until all pieces are thoroughly coated. Serve immediately with rice and sliced scallions.

SESAME CHICKEN

Yield
Serves 4
to 6

Active Time
45 minutes

Total Time
1 hour or up to
several days

INGREDIENTS

For the Marinade and Chicken:

1 large egg white
1 tablespoon (15 ml) light soy sauce or shoyu
2 tablespoons (30 ml) Shaoxing wine
2 tablespoons (30 ml) 80-proof vodka
¼ teaspoon (1 g) baking soda
3 tablespoons (9 g) cornstarch
1 pound (450 g) boneless, skinless chicken
    thighs, cut into ½- to ¾-inch chunks

For the Dry Coating:

½ cup (2½ ounces/70 g) all-purpose flour
½ cup (2 ounces/60 g) cornstarch
½ teaspoon (3 g) baking powder
½ teaspoon (3 g) kosher salt

For the Sauce:

2 tablespoons (30 ml) light soy sauce or
    shoyu
2 tablespoons (30 ml) dark soy sauce
1 tablespoon (3 g) cornstarch
2 tablespoons (30 ml) Shaoxing wine
2 tablespoons (30 ml) distilled white
    vinegar
3 tablespoons (45 ml) homemade or store-
    bought low-sodium chicken stock or
    water
5 tablespoons (65 g) sugar
1 tablespoon (15 ml) roasted sesame oil
2 teaspoons (10 ml) peanut, rice bran, or
    other neutral oil
2 teaspoons (5 g) minced garlic (about 2
    medium cloves)
2 teaspoons (5 g) minced fresh ginger
    (about ½-inch segment)
2 to 3 tablespoons (15 to 25 g) toasted
    sesame seeds

To Finish:

2 quarts (2 l) peanut, rice bran, or other
    neutral oil
Steamed rice for serving

Once you start with that General Tso's base, sesame chicken is even easier than orange chicken. The main difference is that sesame chicken tends to be a little sweeter (if you can imagine that) than General Tso's, with no heat, along with a little more sesame oil and a big shower of sesame seeds added at the end.

DIRECTIONS

1. **For the Marinade and Chicken:** Beat the egg white in a large bowl until broken down and lightly foamy. Add the soy sauce, wine, and vodka and whisk to combine. Set aside half of the marinade in a small bowl. Add the baking soda and cornstarch to the large bowl and whisk to combine. Add the chicken to the large bowl and turn it with your fingers to coat it thoroughly. Set aside while you prepare the remaining ingredients or marinate in the refrigerator up to overnight before continuing.

2. **For the Dry Coating:** Combine the flour, cornstarch, baking powder, and salt in a large bowl. Whisk until homogenous. Add the reserved marinade and whisk until the mixture has coarse, mealy clumps. Set aside.

3. **For the Sauce:** Combine the soy sauces and cornstarch in a medium bowl and stir with a fork until no lumps remain. Add the wine, vinegar, chicken stock, sugar, and sesame oil and stir to combine. Set aside.

4. Combine the oil, garlic, and ginger in a large skillet and cook over medium heat, stirring, until aromatic and soft but not browned, about 2 minutes. Stir the sauce mixture and add to the skillet, making sure to scrape out any sugar or starch that has sunk to the bottom. Cook, stirring, until the sauce boils, reduces, and thickens to the point where it can easily coat the back of a spoon, about 1 minute. Stir in the sesame seeds and remove from the heat.

5. **To Finish:** Heat the oil in a wok over high heat until it registers 350°F (175°C) on an instant-read thermometer, then adjust the heat to maintain the temperature. Working one piece at a time, transfer the chicken from the marinade to the dry coating mixture, tossing after each addition to coat the chicken. When all the chicken has been added to the dry coating, toss it with your hands, pressing the dry mixture onto the chicken so it adheres and making sure that every piece is coated thoroughly.

6 Lift the chicken one piece at a time, shake off the excess coating, and carefully lower it into the hot oil (do not drop it). Once all the chicken has been added, cook, agitating with long chopsticks or a spider and adjusting the heat to maintain a temperature of 325° to 350°F (160° to 175°C), until the chicken is cooked through and very crispy, about 4 minutes. Remove the chicken with a spider and transfer to a paper-towel-lined bowl to drain.

7 **Optional Double-Fry, for Extra-Crispy Results:** Let the chicken cool completely on the countertop or let it rest uncovered in the fridge for up to 2 nights. Meanwhile, strain the oil and discard any solids. Reheat the oil to 375°F (190°C), add the rested chicken, and refry until crispy, about 2 minutes. Remove the chicken with a spider and transfer to a paper-towel-lined bowl to drain.

8 Add the chicken to the skillet with the sauce. Toss the chicken, folding it into the sauce with a rubber spatula until all pieces are thoroughly coated. Serve immediately with rice.

SPRINGFIELD-STYLE CASHEW CHICKEN

Yield
Serves 4
to 6

Active Time
45 minutes

Total Time
1 hour or up to
several days

The very first battered, fried, and sauced Chinese American dish might be from Springfield, Missouri, where Wing Yin Leong, a Chinese immigrant and American World War II hero, created Springfield-Style Cashew Chicken in late 1963, shortly after opening his restaurant Leong's Tea House, a full eight years before General Ching's appeared in New York. According to Leong, the dish was an attempt to cater to the local taste for fried chicken. Rather than serving it with mashed potatoes, he served it with rice. Instead of a roux-thickened chicken gravy, he thickened his with starch and flavored it with oyster sauce, topping the whole thing off with a handful of scallions and cashews. Leong passed away in July 2020, but his cashew chicken has become a staple in Springfield, served at Chinese restaurants and school cafeterias alike.

David Leong (the American name that Wing Yin adopted) has been very generous with his recipe, and you can easily find it online. The chicken itself is essentially southern-style American fried chicken, with a milk- and egg-based dredging mixture that calls for regular all-purpose flour flavored with garlic powder, cayenne, and white pepper.

The recipe in this book is partially inspired by his recipe, but it implements a few of the techniques and tips I've picked up through my other experiments and research in Chinese American fried chicken, as well as some personal preferences in my southern-style fried chicken (such as copious amounts of black pepper in place of the white). I strongly urge you to look up Leong's original recipe and compare it to this one, then make your own calls as to what flavors and techniques you want to incorporate to make it your own.

INGREDIENTS

For the Marinade and Chicken:
1 large egg
1 tablespoon (15 ml) light soy sauce or shoyu
2 tablespoons (30 ml) 80-proof vodka
¼ cup (60 ml) buttermilk or whole milk
¼ teaspoon (1 g) baking soda
⅓ cup (2 ounces/60 g) all-purpose flour
½ teaspoon (1 g) freshly ground black pepper
½ teaspoon (1 g) garlic powder
¼ teaspoon (0.5 g) cayenne
1 teaspoon (5 ml) roasted sesame oil
1 teaspoon (3 g) chicken bouillon powder or salt

1 pound (450 g) boneless, skinless chicken thighs, cut into ½- to ¾-inch chunks

For the Sauce:
1½ cups (360 ml) homemade or store-bought low-sodium chicken stock or water
¼ cup (60 ml) oyster sauce
2 tablespoons (30 ml) light soy sauce
1 teaspoon (4 g) sugar
½ teaspoon (1 g) freshly ground black or white pepper
½ teaspoon (5 ml) roasted sesame oil
1 teaspoon (2.5 g) minced fresh ginger (about ¼-inch segment)
1½ tablespoons (4.5 g) cornstarch
2 tablespoons (30 ml) water

For the Dry Coating:
½ cup (2.5 ounces/70 g) all-purpose flour
½ cup (2 ounces/60 g) cornstarch
½ teaspoon (3 g) baking powder
1½ teaspoons (3 g) freshly ground black pepper
1 teaspoon (2 g) garlic powder
¼ teaspoon (0.5 g) cayenne
½ teaspoon (3 g) kosher salt

To Finish:
2 quarts (2 l) peanut, rice bran, or other neutral oil
½ cup (75 g) raw cashews
2 scallions, sliced
Steamed rice, for serving

DIRECTIONS

(1) **For the Marinade and Chicken:** Whisk together the egg, soy sauce, vodka, buttermilk, baking soda, flour, black pepper, garlic powder, and cayenne in a large bowl. Add the chicken and turn it with your fingers to coat thoroughly. Set aside while you prepare the remaining ingredients or marinate in the refrigerator up to overnight before continuing.

(2) **For the Sauce:** Combine the chicken stock, oyster sauce, soy sauce, sugar, pepper, sesame oil, and ginger in a small saucepan. Combine the cornstarch and water in a small bowl and stir with a fork until the cornstarch is dissolved. Add to the saucepan and stir to combine. Cook the sauce over medium heat, stirring, until it boils, reduces, and thickens to the point where it can easily coat the back of a spoon, 5 to 10 minutes total. Set the sauce aside and keep warm.

(3) **For the Dry Coating:** Combine the flour, cornstarch, baking powder, black pepper, garlic powder, cayenne, and salt in a large bowl. Whisk until homogenous.

(4) **To Finish:** Heat the oil in a wok over high heat until it registers 350°F (175°C) on an instant-read thermometer, then adjust the heat to maintain the temperature. Drizzle a few tablespoons of the chicken marinade into the dry coating mixture and work it in with your fingertips to form little clumps of flour. Working one piece at a time, transfer the chicken from the marinade to the dry coating mixture, tossing after each addition to coat the chicken. When all the chicken has been added to the dry coating, toss it with your hands, pressing the dry mixture onto the chicken so it adheres and making sure that every piece is coated thoroughly.

(5) Lift the chicken one piece at a time, shake off excess coating, and carefully lower the chicken into hot oil (do not drop it). Once all the chicken is added, cook, agitating with long chopsticks or a spider and adjusting the heat to maintain a temperature of 300° to 325°F (150° to 160°C), until the chicken is cooked through and very crispy, about 4 minutes. Remove the chicken with a spider and transfer it to a paper-towel-lined bowl to drain.

(6) **Optional Double-Fry, for Extra-Crispy Results:** Let the chicken cool completely on the countertop, or let it rest uncovered in the fridge for up to two nights. Meanwhile, strain the oil and discard any solids. Reheat the oil to 375°F (190°C), add the rested chicken, and refry until crispy, about 2 minutes. Remove the chicken with a spider and transfer it to a paper-towel-lined bowl to drain.

(7) Add the cashews to the oil and fry until pale golden brown, about 45 seconds (the cashews will continue to darken after you remove them from the oil; do not overcook). Transfer to the bowl with the chicken.

(8) Transfer the chicken and cashews to a serving platter. Ladle the gravy on top, sprinkle with the scallions, and serve immediately with rice.

ORANGE PEEL BEEF, BY WAY OF SICHUAN AND OLD NEW YORK

Growing up in New York, I remember orange peel beef being on virtually every Shun Lee–inspired Hunan- or Sichuan-style Chinese American restaurant around. It consisted of thin slices of crisply fried beef with a dark and intensely flavorful sauce made with dried chiles and *chen pi,* aromatic and slightly bitter dried Chinese mandarin peels (see "How to Buy and Store *Chen Pi"*). I loved it dearly. These days, as many of those old-school New York joints faded away and were replaced by a range of other regional restaurants (including more authentically Sichuanese spots), that style of orange beef is harder to come by. It's especially sparse on the West Coast, where ordering orange beef will frequently get you a dish that's more similar to Panda Express–style orange chicken with beef in place of the chicken—sweeter, less spicy, and lacking the bitter complexity of the original.

Shun Lee's orange peel beef has its roots in *chen pi niu rou* ("dried tangerine peel beef"), a Sichuan dish made with thin slices of lean beef that's dry-fried, then cooked in a sauce flavored with chen pi, chiles, warm spices like star anise and cinnamon, aromatics like ginger and garlic, and sugar. The sauce is cooked down until completely dry, leaving an intensely flavored syrup coating the beef.

My recipe pays homage to both versions by pairing the sauce of the Sichuan original with the crispy fried beef of Shun Lee's New York version. While I typically recommend flank or skirt for stir-fries, for this kind of dish the tighter grain of tenderloin, bottom round, or top sirloin works better. If you'd like to try something more similar to the Sichuan original, you can replace the beef marinade and frying steps in this recipe with the dry-frying process outlined on page 436.

INGREDIENTS

For the Marinade and Beef:
1 large egg white
1 tablespoon (15 ml) light soy sauce or shoyu
2 tablespoons (30 ml) Shaoxing wine
2 tablespoons (30 ml) 80-proof vodka
¼ teaspoon (1 g) baking soda
3 tablespoons (9 g) cornstarch
1 pound (450 g) beef tenderloin, bottom round, top sirloin, flatiron, flap meat (sirloin tip), skirt steak, or tri-tip, cut into ribbons approximately 1 by 2 by ¼ inch

For the Dry Coating:
½ cup (2.5 ounces/70 g) all-purpose flour
½ cup (2 ounces/60 g) cornstarch

½ teaspoon (3 g) baking powder
½ teaspoon (3 g) kosher salt

For the Sauce:
1 tablespoon (15 ml) light soy sauce or shoyu
1 teaspoon (5 ml) dark soy sauce
2 teaspoons (6 g) cornstarch
2 teaspoons (10 ml) peanut, rice bran, or other neutral oil
2 teaspoons (2 g) whole red Sichuan peppercorns
2 teaspoons (5 g) minced garlic (about 2 medium cloves)
2 teaspoons (5 g) minced fresh ginger (about ½-inch segment)
4 small hot dried chiles, such as chao tian jiao, árbol, or Japones
1 star anise pod

1 cinnamon stick
3 tablespoons (35 g) sugar
3 tablespoons (45 ml) distilled white vinegar
2 teaspoons (10 ml) roasted sesame oil
4 strips (about 10 g) chen pi (see Note)
1 cup (240 ml) homemade or store-bought low-sodium chicken stock or water
2 scallions, cut into 1-inch segments
Kosher salt

To Finish:
2 quarts (2 l) peanut, rice bran, or other neutral oil

Yield	Active Time
Serves 4 to 6	45 minutes
	Total Time
	1 hour and 15 minutes or up to several days

NOTE

Chen pi is dried mandarin peel. You can order it from online retailers or from better-stocked Chinese supermarkets or Chinese herbal medicine shops. If you cannot find it, you can use four strips of mandarin, tangerine, or satsuma peel removed from a fresh fruit. If using fresh peel, omit the soaking process in step 3. In step 5, add the fresh peels along with 1 cup of water in place of the chen pi and their soaking water.

DIRECTIONS

(1) **For the Marinade and Beef:** Beat the egg white in a large bowl until broken down and lightly foamy. Add the soy sauce, wine, and vodka and whisk to combine. Set aside half of the marinade in a small bowl. Add the baking soda and cornstarch to the large bowl and whisk to combine. Add the beef to the large bowl and turn it with your fingers to coat thoroughly. Set aside while you prepare the remaining ingredients or marinate in the refrigerator up to overnight before continuing.

(2) **For the Dry Coating:** Combine the flour, cornstarch, baking powder, and salt in a large bowl. Whisk until homogenous. Add the reserved marinade and whisk until the mixture has coarse, mealy clumps. Set aside.

(3) **For the Sauce:** Combine the soy sauces and cornstarch in a small bowl and mix with a fork until no lumps remain. Set aside.

(4) Heat the oil and Sichuan peppercorns in a large saucepan or skillet over medium heat until fragrant, about 1 minute. Remove the Sichuan peppercorns with a slotted spoon and discard. Add the garlic and ginger and return to medium heat. Cook, stirring, until aromatic and soft, but not browned, about 2 minutes. Add the chiles, star anise, and cinnamon and cook, stirring frequently, until a toasty aroma hits your nose, about 30 seconds.

(5) Add the sugar, vinegar, sesame oil, chen pi, and chicken stock. Bring to a bare simmer and cook for 10 minutes. Stir the soy sauce/starch mixture and add it to the sauce. Continue to cook, stirring, until the sauce boils and thickens to the point where it can easily coat the back of a spoon, about 1 minute. Add the scallions. Season the sauce with salt to taste and remove from the heat.

(6) **To Finish:** Heat the oil in a wok over high heat until it registers 350°F (175°C) on an instant-read thermometer, then adjust the heat to maintain the temperature. Working one piece at a time, transfer the beef from the marinade to the dry coating mixture, tossing after each additions to coat the beef. When all the beef has been added to the dry coating, toss it with your hands, pressing the dry mixture onto the beef so it adheres and making sure that every piece is coated thoroughly.

(7) Lift the beef one piece at a time, shake off excess coating, and carefully lower it into the hot oil (do not drop it). Once all the beef has been added, cook, agitating with long chopsticks or a metal spider and adjusting the heat to maintain a temperature of 325° to 350°F (160 to 175°C), until the beef is cooked through and very crispy, about 4 minutes. Remove the beef with a spider and transfer to a paper-towel-lined bowl to drain.

recipe continues

8 **Optional Double-Fry, for Extra-Crispy Results:** Let the beef cool completely on the countertop, or let it rest uncovered in the fridge for up to two nights. Meanwhile, strain the oil and discard any solids. Reheat the oil to 375°F (190°C), add the rested beef, and refry until crispy, about 2 minutes. Remove the beef with a spider and transfer to a paper-towel-lined bowl to drain.

9 Add the beef to the skillet with the sauce. Toss the beef, folding it with a rubber spatula until all pieces are thoroughly coated. Serve immediately with rice.

How to Buy and Store Chen Pi (Dried Mandarin Peel)

Hunan- or Sichuan-style orange peel beef is traditionally made with chen pi, the dried peel of a specific type of mandarin from Xinhui in Guangdong province. The fruits are small and spherical with orange flesh hidden under a thin rind that's picked while it's still green. To produce chen pi, the rinds are removed whole (with

their underlying pith), strung up, then hung in the open air for two to three weeks, during which time they dry, intensify in flavor, and acquire a dark brown hue. They've been used in traditional Chinese medicine since at least the first century, and they make a wonderfully aromatic, slightly bitter infusion. (You tea nerds out there may have also seen whole Xinhui mandarin rinds filled and aged with pu'er tea, meant to be steeped all together.)

In all honesty, the flavor doesn't resemble fresh oranges at all, and recipes for orange beef that call for fresh orange juice or orange peel are a far cry from both the Chinese original and the Chinese American version, which, at its best, is still made with actual chen pi.

Thankfully, chen pi is relatively easy to find in the United States, both from online retailers or in the dried ingredient or herbal section of a Chinese supermarket, or you can make them yourself if you have access to underripe mandarins, tangerines, satsumas, or any other thin-skinned orange citrus fruit. Traditionally, the rind of the fruit is carefully scored into thirds, then peeled off the fruit in a single piece resembling a three-petaled flower. If you want to try making it yourself, you can take the peel off however you like, so long as the pieces remain relatively large and chunky and are free of any of the underlying fruit. You can string them up if you'd like, but it's just as effective (and easier) to spread them on a wire rack set in a rimmed baking sheet and leave them out on the porch in the sunlight for a couple of weeks.

Like dried chiles, chen pi should be dry but still leathery and pliable. They can be stored in an airtight container in a cool, dark pantry for several months or in a zipper-lock freezer bag in the freezer indefinitely.

How to Make Tofu Worth Eating

I happen to be of the mind that even plain soft tofu with a little drizzle of soy sauce is excellent, but if you, or someone you love, needs some convincing that tofu can be texture-packed and delicious, then a bit of extra crispness and browning through panfrying or deep frying is a good direction to go.

There are three basic techniques when it comes to frying tofu, and for each technique a particular type of tofu is best.

- **Panfried tofu** is tofu that is cooked in a thin layer of oil until crispy and well browned. For panfried tofu, you'll need firm or extra-firm cotton-style tofu.

- **Deep-fried or puffy tofu** is tofu that is deep-fried with no coating. As it fries, the exterior forms an airtight barrier that traps in moisture, causing it to puff up as it cooks. Deep-fried tofu can be served on its own with a dipping sauce or incorporated into stir-fried dishes. For deep-fried tofu, I prefer firm or extra-firm silken-style tofu or a soft cotton-style tofu to emphasize the textural contrast between crisp exterior and tender interior.

- **Coated and fried tofu** is tofu that's coated in a starchy dredge or batter. This can be served as is with a dipping sauce or stir-fried with a sauce. For this technique, firm or extra-firm cotton-style tofu is best (with the exception of Agedashi Tofu, page 446, which is made with silken tofu).

TOFU VARIETIES

There is a huge range of tofu and related products throughout Asia, but for our purposes we'll talk about the two major forms: silken and cottony. All tofu is made by adding a coagulant to soy milk, which causes its proteins to bind together, producing a jelled matrix of tangled proteins in a process similar to how milk is coagulated to form cheese. Silken tofu and cottony tofu are made using two different coagulating agents, slightly different processes, and have different culinary uses. Within these two categories you'll find varying degrees of firmness from custardy soft to very firm and meaty, depending on their final water content. Some brands of tofu in the West conflate "soft" with "silken," but the two are orthogonal measures (that is, it is possible to have soft cottony tofu just as it's possible to have firm silken tofu).

Silken tofu, known as *kinugoshi-dofu* in Japan, *yeon-dubu* in Korea, and *huah doufu* or *shigao doufu* in China, is made by adding a gypsum (calcium sulfate) solution to soy milk. The gypsum causes soy proteins to coagulate into a stable matrix that is left untouched. Typically, silken tofu is coagulated directly in its packaging (which is why it conforms to the shape of its plastic container or cardboard Tetra Pak), and because it is uncut and undrained, it has a very high moisture content and a smooth texture that shears rather than crumbles.

As silken tofu is undrained, its moisture content is

similar whether firm or soft. (Its firmness is related to the amount of coagulant added.) Because of this, even the firmest silken tofu will be relatively tender compared to cottony-style tofus labeled "soft."

Silken tofu is frequently enjoyed cold and simply dressed (as in Japanese hiyayakko, page 621), or cooked in soups and stews. I like to use firm or extra-firm silken tofu for dishes like Mapo Tofu (page 598); while not the traditional choice, it's the closest you can find to the style of soft tofu typically used.

Cottony or *pressed tofu*, known as *momendofu* in Japan, *mo-dubu* in Korea, and *laodoufu* in China, is made by adding magnesium chloride or calcium chloride (*nigari* in Japan or *lushui* in China) to soy milk. This creates a spongy, fine-textured curd that, like milk proteins during cheese making, will precipitate, leaving water behind. The unstrained curd is known as *sundubu* in Korea or sold as "extra-soft" in the West. To make firmer styles of cottony tofu, the curds are strained, packed in cloth-lined molds, and pressed to remove excess moisture. Depending on how much moisture is expressed, you get different firmnesses.

Cottony tofu will have the impression of the cloth mold on its surface. It has a more crumbly texture than silken tofu. Cottony tofu can stand up to more vigorous cooking techniques, like panfrying, deep frying, or stir-frying.

HOW TO PANFRY TOFU

Crispness comes from the dehydration of the exterior layer of proteins in your tofu slices, while browning occurs when those proteins and carbohydrates are exposed to temperatures above around 300°F or so, precipitating the Maillard reaction. The key to great panfried tofu is drying it. The drier you get your tofu to begin with, the more efficiently those crisping and browning reactions will take place and the better the contrast between crisp exterior and moist, tender interior will be.

Note that when I say to dry your tofu, that's a

fundamentally different thing than pressing moisture out of your tofu. Pressing moisture out of your tofu by placing it between layers of towels and weighting it down will squeeze moisture out of its interior in a process that's similar to how tofu was treated before it went in the package to begin with. Doing this will turn medium tofu into firm tofu, firm tofu into extra-firm, and so on. There's not a very compelling reason to do this, unless you happen to have only tofu that's softer than what the recipe calls for.

No, when I say to dry your tofu, I'm talking about the surface of the tofu. Tofu comes packed in water, so when it comes out of that package, it's wet. Your goal is to get the surface nice and dry while still leaving the interior moist. You can do this by very gently pressing your tofu with paper towels or by microwaving it briefly, but I find that the most reliable method is to do what Andrea Nguyen, author of *Asian Tofu*, suggests: pour hot salted water over it.

It may seem counterintuitive to add water to something you're trying to dry out, but boiling water will actually cause the tofu to squeeze out more moisture, bringing it to the surface and making it easier to blot off, while the salt gently seasons the slices. Hot water also evaporates much faster than the cold water on refrigerated tofu.

No matter which method you choose—pressing the tofu between towels or pouring salted boiling water on top and then blotting—your tofu should be dry to the touch before you panfry it. Have you ever stuck out your tongue and left it out for few minutes to see how dry it can get? That's what your tofu should feel like.

Once the tofu is nice and dry, it can go straight into a well-oiled wok or skillet over moderate heat until deep brown and crispy on both sides, using a thin metal spatula to flip the slices as they crisp. Taking your time is key: the more gently you brown the slices, the more evenly and deeper brown you can get them without burning them.

SIMPLE PANFRIED TOFU WITH SOY-GARLIC DIPPING SAUCE

Yield
Serves 4

Active Time
10 minutes

Total Time
15 minutes

NOTE
I like cutting the tofu into two-bite slabs, but you can cut them into whatever size you wish, so long as they are ½ inch thick.

INGREDIENTS

For the Sauce:
3 tablespoons (45 ml) light soy sauce or shoyu
1 tablespoon (15 ml) water
2 teaspoons (8 g) sugar
1 tablespoon (8 g) minced garlic (about 3 medium cloves)
2 teaspoons (10 ml) roasted sesame oil
1 scallion, thinly sliced
Big pinch of roasted sesame seeds
Chile sauce (such as sambal oelek or sriracha)

For the Tofu:
One 12-ounce (340 g) block firm tofu, cut into rectangular ½-inch slabs roughly 2 by 1½ inches each (see Note)
2 tablespoons (30 ml) peanut, rice bran, or other neutral oil
2 scallions, sliced

Panfried tofu has an open, spongy texture on its surface, which makes it great for picking up a simple soy-based dipping sauce.

DIRECTIONS

(1) **For the Sauce:** Combine all the sauce ingredients in a small bowl and stir with a fork until the sugar dissolves.

(2) **For the Tofu:** Place the tofu slices in a colander or fine-mesh strainer set in your sink, laying them out in as close to a single layer as possible. Bring a pot or kettle full of water to a boil. Pour the boiling water over the tofu slices, then let the tofu slices cool and air-dry for a few minutes. They should feel slightly tacky and dry to the touch, like a cat's tongue.

(3) Heat a wok over high heat until lightly smoking. Reduce the heat to medium, add the oil, and swirl to coat. Add the tofu one piece at a time in a single layer (the tofu should come up the sides of the wok a little) and cook, occasionally swirling the pan gently, until crisp on the first side, about 5 minutes. (If the tofu sticks at all, let it cook undisturbed for a couple of minutes before gently prising it off the wok with a thin metal spatula). Slide the tofu out of the wok onto a large plate and return the wok to medium heat.

(4) Flip the tofu pieces (they may be stuck together on the edges and have to be gently prised apart), then return them to the wok and cook the second side, swirling the pan gently, until crisp on the second side, about 5 minutes longer. Transfer to a serving platter, sprinkle with scallions, and serve immediately.

PANFRIED TOFU WITH GARLIC AND BLACK BEAN SAUCE

Yield
Serves 4

Active Time
30 minutes

Total Time
35 minutes

INGREDIENTS

For the Tofu:
One 12-ounce (340 g) block firm tofu, cut
    into 1-inch squares ½ inch thick

For the Sauce:
1 tablespoon (15 ml) Shaoxing wine
1 tablespoon (15 ml) light soy sauce
1 teaspoon (5 ml) dark soy sauce
3 tablespoons homemade or store-bought
    low-sodium chicken stock or water
1 teaspoon (4 g) sugar

For the Cornstarch Slurry:
2 teaspoons (6 g) cornstarch
1 tablespoon (15 ml) water

For the Stir-Fry:
3 tablespoons (45 ml) peanut, rice bran, or
    other neutral oil
1 tablespoon (7.5 g) minced garlic (about 3
    medium cloves)
2 teaspoons (5 g) minced fresh ginger
    (about ½-inch segment)
1 scallion, white and pale green parts only,
    chopped into ¼-inch pieces
2 tablespoons (about 12 g) dried fermented
    black beans (douchi), roughly chopped

This simple tofu dish combines the panfrying with a quick toss in a black bean sauce. I love the contrast in textures between the crisply browned crust of the tofu, the spongy interior, and the silky sauce that coats it all.

DIRECTIONS

(1) For the Tofu: Place the tofu slices in a colander or fine-mesh strainer set in your sink, laying them out in as close to a single layer as possible. Bring a pot or kettle full of water to a boil. Pour the boiling water over the tofu slices, then let the tofu slices cool and air-dry for a few minutes. They should feel slightly tacky and dry to the touch, like a cat's tongue.

(2) For the Sauce: Combine the Shaoxing wine, soy sauces, chicken stock or water, and sugar in a small bowl and stir together until homogenous. Set aside. Combine the cornstarch and water in a separate small bowl and stir with a fork until the cornstarch is dissolved.

(3) For the Stir-Fry: Heat a wok over high heat until lightly smoking. Reduce the heat to medium, add 2 tablespoons (30 ml) of the oil, and swirl to coat. Add the tofu one piece at a time in a single layer (the tofu should come up the sides of the wok a little) and cook, occasionally swirling the pan gently, until crisp on the first side, about 5 minutes. (If the tofu sticks at all, let it cook undisturbed for a couple of minutes before gently prising it off the wok with a thin metal spatula and swirling the wok to ensure nothing is sticking). Slide the tofu out of the wok onto a large plate and return the wok to medium heat.

(4) Flip the tofu pieces (they may be stuck together on the edges and have to be gently prised apart), then return them to the wok and cook the second side, swirling the pan gently, until crisp on the second side, about 5 minutes longer. Slide the tofu back out onto a plate and set aside.

(5) Return the wok to high heat until lightly smoking. Add the remaining 1 tablespoon (15 ml) oil and swirl to coat. Immediately add the garlic, ginger, scallions, and black beans and stir-fry until fragrant, about 10 seconds. Stir the sauce and add to the wok by pouring it around the edges. Stir the cornstarch slurry and add it to the wok. Cook, stirring, until the sauce thickens, about 15 seconds. Return the tofu to the wok and toss to coat in sauce. Transfer to a serving platter and serve immediately.

KOREAN-STYLE SPICY BRAISED TOFU (DUBU JORIM)

Yield
Serves 4

Active Time
20 minutes

Total Time
25 minutes

INGREDIENTS

For the Sauce:

3 tablespoons (45 ml) light soy sauce or shoyu
¼ cup (60 ml) water
2 teaspoons (8 g) sugar
2 teaspoons (5 g) minced garlic (about 2 medium cloves)
2 teaspoons (10 ml) roasted sesame oil
1 scallion, thinly sliced
1 tablespoon (8 g) gochugaru (Korean chile flakes), more or less as desired
Big pinch of toasted sesame seeds

For the Tofu:

One 12-ounce (340 g) block firm tofu, cut into ½-inch slabs
2 tablespoons (30 ml) peanut, rice bran, or other neutral oil

While we typically think of braising as a long, slow process used to tenderize tough cuts of meat, there are quite a few quick-braised dishes. Braising is a hybrid cooking technique that begins with frying to create browned flavors and add texture to the surface of the food being cooked, followed by simmering it in a liquid. *Dubu jorim* starts with panfrying tofu and is finished by simmering it in a spicy soy sauce. It fits the criteria perfectly, which makes it a braised dish that takes only 25 minutes to cook from start to finish!

DIRECTIONS

(1) **For the Sauce:** Combine all the sauce ingredients in a small bowl and stir with a fork until the sugar dissolves.

(2) **For the Tofu:** Place the tofu slices in a colander or fine-mesh strainer set in your sink, laying them out in as close to a single layer as possible. Bring a pot or kettle full of water to a boil. Pour the boiling water over the tofu slices, then let the tofu slices cool and air-dry for a few minutes. They should feel slightly tacky and dry to the touch, like a cat's tongue.

(3) **For the Stir-Fry:** Heat a wok over high heat until lightly smoking. Reduce the heat to medium, add the oil, and swirl to coat. Add the tofu one piece at a time in a single layer (the tofu should come up the sides of the wok a little) and cook, occasionally swirling the pan gently, until crisp on the first side, about 5 minutes. (If the tofu sticks at all, let it cook undisturbed for a couple of minutes before gently prising it off the wok with a thin metal spatula and swirling the wok to ensure nothing is sticking). Slide the tofu out of the wok onto a large plate and return the wok to medium heat.

(4) Flip the tofu pieces (they may be stuck together on the edges and have to be gently prised apart), then return them to the wok and cook the second side, swirling the pan gently, until crisp on the second side, about 5 minutes longer. Slide the tofu back out onto a plate and set aside.

(5) Reduce the heat to medium-low, add the sauce to the wok, and cook, turning the tofu occasionally, until the sauce is reduced to a syrupy glaze that coats each piece, about 2 minutes. Serve immediately.

HOW TO DEEP-FRY TOFU

Deep frying tofu is extraordinarily simple. You just . . . deep-fry it. That's it. No special pretreatment needed, no coating necessary. You can, if you want, dry the surface as for panfried tofu, which will make lowering the tofu into the hot oil a little bit less spatter-prone, but it won't significantly change the cooking time at all.

As with all deep frying, maintaining the oil temperature and keeping things moving is key to effective, even frying. For fried tofu, I like to use soft to medium cottony tofu, which really accentuates the contrast between the tender, moist interior and the crisp exterior.

As tofu deep-fries, you'll notice that it puffs up like a balloon. This looks very cool, but unfortunately, as in a collapsing soufflé, that puffing doesn't last. As soon as it comes out of the oil, the water vapor and expanded air inside that was keeping it puffed will cool and contract, causing it to deflate.

Deep-fried tofu can be used in a very similar manner to panfried tofu: either on its own with a dipping sauce, finished with a brief stir-fry, or braised for a bit longer. In fact, you can substitute deep-fried tofu in any of the panfried tofu dishes in the previous section.

SHRIMP-STUFFED FRIED TOFU

Yield
Serves 4
to 6

Active Time
30 minutes

Total Time
30 minutes

NOTE
The first few times you try this dish you may find that the shrimp balls pop out of the tofu as they fry. This is no big deal. If that happens, just replace them while plating. I promise it will still be delicious.

Whenever my family went out for Cantonese food, my mother would invariably order the stuffed tofu. It's not a common menu item these days, as many of the old New York–style Chinese American spots are being replaced (for better or worse) by a wider range of regional Chinese restaurants, but some of the old-school New York restaurants still have it. For now.

Thankfully, it's a very simple dish to make at home. You start by making a little divot in the top of a cube of soft tofu. Into that divot goes a chopped shrimp mixture coated in cornstarch. You then deep-fry the whole thing and serve it shrimp side up with a soy-based dipping sauce.

DIRECTIONS

(1) **For the Shrimp Filling:** Finely chop the shrimp with a cleaver or chef's knife. Combine the chopped shrimp, sesame oil, wine, soy sauce, cornstarch, white pepper, and salt in a small bowl. Stir with a fork until the mixture is sticky and holds its shape easily. Alternatively, place all the ingredients in a mini-chopper and process until a sticky paste is formed.

(2) **For the Sauce:** Combine the soy sauce, water, sugar, and scallion whites in a small bowl and stir until the sugar is dissolved. (Reserve the scallion greens for garnish in step 8.) Set aside.

INGREDIENTS

For the Shrimp Filling:

4 ounces (120 g) shrimp, peeled
½ teaspoon (2.5 ml) roasted sesame oil
¼ teaspoon (1.25 ml) Shaoxing wine
¼ teaspoon (1.25 ml) light soy sauce or shoyu
½ teaspoon (1.5 g) cornstarch, plus more
    for dusting
Tiny pinch of freshly ground white pepper
Big pinch of kosher salt

For the Sauce:

2 tablespoons (30 ml) light soy sauce
1 tablespoon (15 ml) water
1½ teaspoons (6 g) sugar
1 scallion, thinly sliced, greens and whites
    reserved separately

For the Tofu:

One 12-ounce (340 g) block soft tofu

To Finish:

2 quarts (2 l) peanut, rice bran, or other
    neutral oil

(3) **For the Tofu:** Cut the block in half horizontally, leaving the top and bottom halves stacked. Cut lengthwise down the center, then crosswise twice, giving you a total of 12 rectangular blocks of tofu. Arrange them on a large plate. Using a ¼-teaspoon measure, scoop out a small divot in the center of the top of each tofu block.

(4) Fill a shallow dish with a layer of cornstarch. Using a ¼-teaspoon measure, pick up small heaps of the shrimp mixture, drop them into the cornstarch, and roll to coat. You don't need to be too precise, but your goal is to divide the mixture into 12 roughly equal-sized balls.

(5) Use chopsticks or your fingers to pick up a shrimp ball and place it in the divot on a block of tofu, pressing gently to stick it into place. Repeat with the remaining shrimp balls and tofu blocks.

(6) Pick up one block of tofu at a time, invert it so that the shrimp side is facing down, and gently press it into the plate of cornstarch, lightly flattening the shrimp ball and adding a thin layer of cornstarch to the top of the tofu block. Return the tofu block to the large plate, shrimp side up, dusting off any excess cornstarch.

recipe continues

7 **To Finish:** Heat the oil in a wok over high heat until it registers 375°F (190°C) on an instant-read thermometer. Carefully add the tofu to the oil one piece at a time. Adjust the heat to maintain a temperature between 350° and 375°F (175° and 190°C) and fry, moving the tofu around gently to avoid knocking the shrimp filling out, until golden brown and very crisp, about 4 minutes. Transfer to a paper-towel-lined plate to drain.

8 Arrange on a serving platter shrimp side up, sprinkle with the reserved scallion greens, and serve immediately with the dipping sauce.

Should I Marinate Tofu?

It seems like a no-brainer to marinate tofu, but I'd actually advise against it. While nonsilken tofu does have a somewhat spongy texture that will absorb marinades, you end up with tofu that browns too fast and tastes like raw marinade on the inside. I prefer keeping the tofu tasting like tofu, using a sauce applied after cooking to lend it flavor if it needs it.

Similarly, a dusting of spices can be tasty if the spices are fresh, properly toasted, and balanced, but again, you want to apply them after cooking the tofu. Tofu simply takes too long to crisp up properly to be able to season it before cooking without running the risk of burning those spices up.

CRISPY-AND-SAUCY DEEP-FRIED TOFU

There are some days when you lounge around in your pajamas on the couch, others where nary a piece of fabric girds your loins from dawn to dusk, and still others where a heavy winter coat and a pair of long johns are appropriate. Similarly, sometimes your fried tofu needs no coating, and other times you'll be glad to have it.

If tofu is destined for a Chinese American saucy stir-fry, you'll want to give them a crispy coating that can both absorb a bit of sauce and provide a layer of protection so that the tofu can stay crisp even after saucing. I tried coating tofu with various blends of flour, potato starch, rice flour, and cornstarch, both panfrying and deep frying, and found that the crispest, cleanest-tasting results came from a deep fry in a simple coating of cornstarch. Unfortunately that crispness is short-lived. This is fine for dishes like Agedashi Tofu (page 446), in which the softened coating is part of the appeal, but not great for a saucy stir-fry.

A flour-based coating like I'd use for beef or chicken had a hard time sticking to tofu, but what about a wet batter instead? I'd spent a long time working out the batter recipe for my Korean Fried Chicken (page 460). Would the same coating work on my tofu?

Indeed it did: a quick dredge in dry cornstarch followed by a dip into a cornstarch, water, and vodka mixture before a plunge into a wok with a couple quarts of 350°F oil resulted in ultra-crisp bites of tofu that stay crisp even after you finish them off in a stir-fry, and once the tofu is fried and crisp, you can incorporate it in place of meat into virtually any stir-fry. It's especially tasty with crispy-and-saucy Chinese American dishes, like General Tso's tofu, sesame tofu, or this Crispy Tofu with Broccoli and Garlic Sauce. To keep things vegan, make sure to use vegan stock or water in place of chicken stock wherever it's called for.

CRISPY FRIED TOFU WITH BROCCOLI AND GARLIC SAUCE

Yield
Serves 4

Active Time
40 minutes

Total Time
40 minutes

INGREDIENTS

For the Sauce:
¼ cup (60 ml) Shaoxing wine or dry sherry
¼ cup (60 ml) homemade or store-bought low-sodium vegetable stock or water
2 tablespoons (30 ml) light soy sauce or shoyu
2 tablespoons (30 ml) distilled white vinegar
1 tablespoon (15 ml) fermented black bean sauce
2 tablespoons (25 g) sugar
1 teaspoon (5 ml) roasted sesame oil

For the Cornstarch Slurry:
2 teaspoons (6 g) cornstarch
1 tablespoon (15 ml) water

For the Tofu:
½ cup (2.5 ounces/70 g) all-purpose flour
½ cup (2 ounces/60 g) cornstarch
½ teaspoon (3 g) baking powder
½ teaspoon (3 g) kosher salt
½ cup (120 ml) cold water
½ cup (120 ml) vodka
2 quarts (2 l) peanut, rice bran, or other neutral oil
12 ounces (340 g) extra-firm tofu, cut into ½- by 2- by 1-inch slabs, blotted dry with paper towels

For the Broccoli:
1 pound (450 g) broccoli or broccolini, cut into bite-sized pieces

For the Stir-Fry:
2 teaspoons (5 g) minced garlic (about 2 medium cloves)
2 teaspoons (5 g) minced fresh ginger (about ½-inch segment)
Steamed rice, for serving

DIRECTIONS

(1) **For the Sauce:** Combine the wine, stock, soy sauce, vinegar, black bean sauce, sugar, and sesame oil in a small bowl and whisk to combine. Set aside. Combine the cornstarch and water in a separate small bowl and stir with a fork until the cornstarch is dissolved.

(2) **For the Tofu:** Whisk together the flour, cornstarch, baking powder, and salt. Add the water and vodka and whisk until a smooth batter is formed, adding up to 2 tablespoons (30 ml) water if the batter is too thick. It should have the consistency of thin paint and fall off the whisk in thin ribbons that instantly disappear as they hit the surface of the batter in the bowl. Add the tofu slices and carefully fold to coat.

(3) Heat the oil in a wok over high heat until it registers 350°F (175°C) on an instant-read thermometer, then adjust the heat to maintain the temperature. Working one piece at a time, lift the tofu and allow excess batter to drip off. Carefully lower it into the hot oil. Repeat with the remaining tofu until the wok is full. Fry, using a metal spider or slotted spatula to rotate and agitate the pieces as they cook, until evenly pale golden and crisp all over, about 6 minutes. Remove the tofu with a spider and transfer to a paper-towel-lined bowl to drain.

(4) **Optional Double-Fry, for Extra-Crispy Results:** Let the tofu cool completely on the countertop, or let it rest uncovered in the fridge for up to two nights. Meanwhile, strain the oil and discard any solids. Reheat the oil to 375°F (190°C), add the rested tofu, and refry until crispy, about 2 minutes. Remove the tofu with a spider and transfer to a paper-towel-lined bowl to drain.

(5) **For the Broccoli:** Strain the oil through a fine-mesh strainer into a heat-proof container. Wipe out the wok with a paper towel and add 1 quart (1 liter) of lightly salted water. Bring to a boil over high heat. Add the broccoli, stir well, cover, and boil, shaking the pan occasionally, until bright green but still quite firm, about 1 minute. Drain the broccoli and spread into a single layer on a sheet tray or large plate.

(6) **For the Stir-Fry:** Return the wok to high heat until lightly smoking. Add 1 tablespoon (15 ml) of the strained oil and swirl to coat (save the remaining oil for another use). Add half of the broccoli and stir-fry until tender-crisp, about 1 minute. Return it to its tray. Wipe out the wok and return it to high heat until lightly smoking. Add another tablespoon (15 ml) of the strained oil and swirl to coat. Add the remaining half of the broccoli and stir-fry until tender-crisp, about 1 minute. Return all the tofu and broccoli to the wok along with the garlic and ginger. Stir-fry until fragrant, about 30 seconds.

(7) Stir the sauce and add it to the wok. Stir the cornstarch slurry and add a splash. Cook, tossing, until the sauce thickens, about 30 seconds. Adjust the sauce consistency with more cornstarch slurry if it is too thin or a splash of water if it is too thick. Transfer to a serving platter and serve immediately with steamed rice.

5

SIMMERING AND BRAISING

—

As someone who grew up fishing, for many years I thought it was all about catching fish. Whether it was snaring a fat rainbow trout on a Royal Wulff or hooking into that striper off Stellwagen Bank on a live pogie at the mouth of the Massachusetts Bay, fishing was about the *action*. It's only now, when I think back on fishing trips with my father and sisters, that I realize the vast majority of my pleasant memories are from the more subtle parts of fishing. Standing in waders off the icy banks of the Gallatin River by my sister's home in Montana. Riding out on Boston Harbor in my dad's boat, eating bologna sandwiches* and Cape Cod chips. The action is great, but there's a whole lot more to fishing than that.

Likewise, it's easy to associate woks with extreme cooking—the intense heat of a Cantonese stir-fry, the nose-tingling aroma of chiles and Sichuan peppercorns toasting, the food leaping and dancing through live flames. In this chapter I want to focus on the quieter side of wok cooking: simmering and braising. Techniques that can push tough cuts of meat or starchy root vegetables into tender, savory submission. Brothy recipes that range from the subtlest bowl of miso soup to the most intense Thai curry or kimchi stew.

This is the calmer side of wok cooking. Let's start with the basics: making and using stock.

Stock Basics

Stock and broth are both made by simmering together vegetables and, usually, animal bones and connective tissue. They can be watery and thin in texture (as in the case of a vegetable stock) or thick and gelatinous (animal connective tissue will break down into gelatin, which adds body to stocks). They can be made with raw bones and vegetables, or they can be made with roasted ingredients. They may contain aromatics, such as peppercorns or bay leaves or ginger, or they can be as simple as a chicken carcass simmered in water.

There's plenty of linguistic debate on the difference between stock and broth (and that's before we even get into the opaque, milky-white quagmire of

so-called "bone broths"). Some (including me in the past) would say that the inclusion of connective tissue and bones is what differentiates stock from broth. Others would say that stocks are basic building blocks for cooking, while broths have already been seasoned with salt and are ready to drink. In all honesty, it doesn't matter much, and the terms can generally be used interchangeably.

What *does* matter is the way in which you make or buy them and how you utilize them in your cooking. Let's take stock of the basics.

---

* Alright, I confess, there's a reason those events were particularly memorable. That icy day on the Gallatin was the first time my wife, Adri, had ever tried fly fishing. After 45 minutes standing thigh-high in ice water in rented waders, she called it quits. I helped her out of her waders only to discover that they had a hole in them and that icy water had been sloshing around her legs the entire time; I asked her why she hadn't said anything, and she said, "I thought it was normal. I didn't want to seem like a wimp!" As for the bologna incident, we weren't just eating it; we were eating eye and nose holes into the slices, laying them over our faces, and calling each other bolognaface, as you do.

Q *What's the difference between Western and Asian stocks and broths?*

A Fundamentally, not much. Both Western and Asian stocks are made by simmering ingredients in water to draw out their flavor for use in other dishes. In both Western and Asian cuisines, making stock can be a means to extract more flavor and nutrients from ingredients that would otherwise be discarded (a chicken carcass or ham bone with the meat removed, the tough stems of herbs, vegetable trimmings, dry aromatics, etc.), a way to introduce more flavor to a dish (by using stock in place of water, for instance), or both.

In fact, to try to divide stocks into these East vs. West categories, I'm forced to make some extremely broad generalizations, so please note that if you really want to get a full understanding of the breadth of techniques used to make stock and the wide range of scenarios in which it's used, you'll need to dive deeper into an individual cuisine than this book allows for.

Many of the differences come down to ingredient choice. In Western cuisines, stock is typically made with animal bones and connective tissue, along with mirepoix, the classic combination of carrot, celery, and onion. Frequently other types of alliums, such as leeks or garlic, will also be included, as will herbs and aromatics like bay leaves, peppercorns, parsley, or thyme. While pork stock, venison stock, lamb stock, and others exist, by far the most common animal parts used for stock in the West are chicken carcasses, veal bones (which offer a ton of connective tissue and yield very rich, gelatinous stock), and fish bones for quick *fumets*.

In contrast, meat-based Asian stocks will frequently feature ingredients like fresh ginger, scallions, and garlic as their main vegetal elements, or they may use charred onions and ginger (as with some ramen or pho broths). Chicken is still a popular stock choice, but depending on the country and region pork (especially gelatin-rich pork trotters and heads), ham, mutton, and beef

are used as well. Dried seafood is used extensively in broths throughout Asia. It can be subtle, as with Japanese dashi, made only with dried sea kelp and dried bonito, or it can be an intense flavor enhancer, as with the dried flounder, scallop, or shrimp added to Chinese "superior stock" when making an aromatic wonton soup base.

Aromatic choices can vary wildly throughout Asia as well. Classic Thai tom yam soup is flavored with a slew of fresh aromatics: lemongrass, galangal, makrut lime leaf, shallot, garlic, chiles, etc. The deep red broth for Taiwanese beef noodle soup features warm spices like fennel, star anise, and cinnamon. South Vietnamese pho might be seasoned with rock sugar and herbs like culantro and lemon basil, while North Vietnamese pho focuses on the cleaner, simpler flavors.

The point is, there's variation in stock, and an awful lot of it.

Q *When should I make homemade broth, and when is it OK to use store-bought?*

A I use store-bought stocks and concentrated bouillon pastes, powders, and cubes pretty extensively at home. I also make and use an awful lot of homemade stocks. The only situation where I find homemade stock—or, at the very least, well-doctored store-bought stock—to be essential is when making brothy, aromatic soups. Dishes like wonton soup (page 554) or Chicken and Ginger Soup (page 544) rely on well-seasoned stocks flavored with a specific set of aromatics, and without those specific aromatics, they just won't taste right.

For soups that rely on many other seasonings—Hot and Sour Soup (page 546), or Tom Yam Kung (page 597), for instance—starting with a homemade stock will help, but it won't make or break the dish. Likewise, when stock is an ingredient in the sauce for a stir-fry, or in the simmering liquid for Japanese-stye donburi—such as Gyudon (page 235) or

Oyakodon (page 233)—using homemade stuff will improve the flavor and texture of the final dish, but using store-bought stock or even water with a dash of bouillon in place of chicken stock, or granulated Hondashi in place of fresh dashi, will get the job done.

 Q *How long does a stock need to simmer?*

A It all depends on what ingredients you're adding to it. For the most part, aromas are extracted relatively quickly. That means that after the first 20 to 30 minutes those thin slices of ginger, the onion chunks, the garlic, the dry spices, the herbs have all given up about as much as they're going to give. With meat and bones flavor takes a little bit longer to extract. The exact timing can vary depending on the specific animal you're using and the size of the pieces, ranging from around 45 minutes for chopped chicken carcasses and wings to several hours for whole chicken carcasses and meaty chunks of beef shin or pork trotters.

Connective tissue, mainly collagen, is the fibrous or rubbery white sinews and yellowish tissues that keep meat attached to bones and bones connected with each other. Collagen is also what gives skin its elastic stretchiness. When making stock, we aren't trying to extract collagen per se. Rather, we're trying to convert that collagen into gelatin. In its natural state, collagen is a tightly wound protein made of three tightly interwound strands (its structure is known as a *triple helix*). As collagen is cooked in the presence of water, it unravels and hydrolyzes, forming gelatin, a series of proteins and peptides that range in weight and length but have the ability to form a loosely interconnected matrix that gives stock body when hot, and causes it to solidify into a jelly-like mass when cooled. Depending on the concentration of gelatin, this jelly will range from a slightly viscous liquid to a substance as firm and bouncy as a rubber ball.

Collagen transformation depends not just on the presence of heat and water, but on *time* as well. So while the flavor of a chicken stock may not change that much after the first hour or so of simmering, it'll continue to gain body over the course of a few hours as gelatin is extracted. Collagen comes in many different forms, and as a general rule, the more support work collagen has to do, the more time it takes to fully extract and convert into gelatin for a stock.

Collagen in pork bones, for instances, takes longer to extract than in lighter chicken carcasses. In veal bones, it takes longer still—many veal stock recipes call for 12- or even 24-hour simmering times. Fish, which spend their life supported in the semi-weightless environment of the ocean, on the other hand, have very fast-extracting collagen. Boil a fish carcass and you won't see much change after a mere 45 minutes.

This chart gives you a good idea of how long you can expect to simmer ingredients for flavor and collagen extraction. When designing your own broth, it's easy enough to dump everything into the pot and strain it out when you feel like it's finished (how I make 75 percent of my broths at home), but if you want to maximize flavor and body, start with the most long-cooking ingredients (such as bones with lots of connective tissue) and progressively add shorter-cooking ingredients (such as vegetables and aromatics), timing it so that everything finishes around the same time. (Overboiling aromatics can actually cause a broth to slowly lose aroma—if you can smell an aromatic compound in the air, it's no longer in the pot.)

Note that younger animals in general have more connective tissue and fewer fully developed muscles, which means, for instance, that with enough time, veal bones will give up much more gelatin than beef bones.

Common Stock Ingredients and Their Cooking Times

INGREDIENT	TIME FOR FLAVOR	TIME FOR BODY	NOTES
Shellfish shells	30 minutes	N/A	Roast or sauté shellfish carcasses for more flavor
Fish carcasses	45 minutes	45 minutes to 1½ hours	Roughly chop with a cleaver.
Dried seafood (such as shrimp, scallops, or flounder)	45 minutes to 1 hour	N/A	
Chicken carcasses	1 hour	4 hours	Roughly chop with a cleaver. Wings and feet lend more body (but are not as flavorful).
Pork bones	1½ hours	4 to 6 hours	Roast or sauté if browned flavors are desired.
Lamb bones	1½ hours	4 to 6 hours	Roast or sauté if browned flavors are desired.
Pork trotters	N/A	6 to 8 hours	Boil briefly, then drain, scrub, and add fresh water for cleaner-tasting, clearer stock.
Beef bones	2 to 3 hours	4 to 6 hours	Boil briefly, then drain, scrub, and add fresh water for cleaner-tasting, clearer stock.
Veal bones	2 to 3 hours	12 to 24 hours	Roast or sauté if browned flavors are desired.
Chopped vegetables (such as carrots, onions, or celery)	45 minutes	N/A	Roast or sauté if browned flavors are desired.
Herbs (such as parsley, thyme, or cilantro)	30 minutes	N/A	
Dry spices (such as star anise, cinnamon, cloves, black peppercorns, or Sichuan peppercorns)	30 minutes	N/A	Toast in a dry wok or skillet before using.
Thin, sliced, or pounded aromatics (such as shallots, garlic, ginger, scallions, makrut lime, or lemongrass)	20 to 30 minutes	N/A	Smashing aromatics in a mortar and pestle or with the spine or flat side of a knife will speed up extraction.

Q *What exactly is body, and why is it so desirable?*

A Body is what gelatin adds to your stock. It's a synonym for *viscosity*. The more gelatin-rich your broth, the more viscous it will be, and the more viscous a broth, the richer it feels in your mouth and the longer its flavor will linger. In Western cuisine, this richness is often concentrated by reducing stocks into *jus* or *demi-glace*—a stock so concentrated that it can glaze meat and vegetables in a rich, sticky coating. In Asian cuisines, you're most likely to find these kinds of sticky, extra-rich broths in long-simmered broths like ramen, pho, or Taiwanese beef noodle soup (page 608), or in Shanghai-style xiao long bao or sheng jian bao (steamed and panfried soup buns, respectively), with their lip-smacking liquid centers of sticky pork broth.

 Does my stock have to have body for it to be tasty?

No, not at all! In fact, many light broths, such as dashi, will have no more body than plain water. Other times body is added to the stock in the form of a thickener—the cornstarch slurry added to Egg Drop Soup (page 545) or Hot and Sour Soup (page 546), for instance. In those cases, the gelatin content of your starting broth will have relatively little effect on the final texture of the soup, so feel free to use a shorter-simmered stock or to doctor up store-bought stock.

 Oh, speaking of store-bought stock, is it any good?

Store-bought, low-sodium chicken stock or broth is the only type of store-bought stock I'd recommend. Low sodium is essential for controlling the salt content of your finished dish, especially because oftentimes stir-fries are plenty salty to begin with and adding a salty store-bought stock may push it over the edge. In general, store-bought chicken stock has more actual chicken in it compared to the beef content of store-bought beef stock (which is mostly hydrolyzed soy protein and other flavor enhancers as opposed to actual beef). I have not found a store-bought vegetable stock that I would recommend (though if you have a brand you enjoy, by all means use it).

Feel free to use store-bought stock as a component in stir-fry sauces or in any soup recipe that doesn't specifically call for unique aromatics or animal parts.

What about powdered or concentrated bouillon?

Powdered bouillon will do in a pinch for most stir-fry sauces, though powdered bouillon tends to be extremely salty, so be very careful about not overseasoning your finished dish if using any powdered bouillon. (It's a good idea to omit any added salt from the sauce and add it to taste at the end.) Even better is Better Than Bouillon, a brand of concentrated stock bases that have markedly better flavor than the powdered stuff. I keep a jar of their lower-sodium chicken base and their beef base in my fridge all the time. As with store-bought vegetable broth, store-bought vegetable powder or concentrated bouillon tends to be subpar.

Concentrated dashi, sold under the brand name Hondashi, is an excellent approximation of homemade dashi, and I find a number of uses for it (see page 515 for more on dashi). It's worth keeping a jar of it around.

How can I doctor up store-bought stock to work in other dishes?

The most effective, tasty, and fastest way to substitute store-bought stock for homemade is to doctor it up by omitting the main meat-based ingredient in a stock recipe but keeping the aromatics. For instance, my Everyday Chicken and Ginger Stock recipe (page 542) calls for chicken pieces, sliced ginger, and scallions simmered together for an hour. You can start with a carton of low-sodium chicken broth, add some ginger and scallions to it, and let it simmer for 20 to 30 minutes to extract flavor form the ginger and scallions and cut that recipe time in half.

Basic Stocks

It feels silly to offer recipes for stock that call for very precise amounts of chicken carcasses or a weighed-out piece of kombu. It feels like giving someone the formula for the perfect bubble bath, or returning the potpourri because the ratio of rose petals to pinecones isn't exactly right.

The truth is, unless you are working at a restaurant where consistency from batch to batch is key, exact measurements are really not important. Stock really should be thought of as a way to use up scraps—the leftover chicken carcass or the scallions languishing in the vegetable drawer. When I make stock at home, I eyeball everything and make use of what I've got. I'll freeze chicken carcasses, spare leg bones, wing tips, and necks until I've got a gallon bag full of them, then I'll throw them into a pot and start making stock. If I've got some scallions and ginger on hand, I might go with a simple Chinese-style stock, throwing in a ham bone or some slices of bacon for cured pork flavor if I'm feeling in the mood. If I've got shrimp shells leftover from a batch of shrimp and pork dumplings, maybe my hot and sour soup will get a little hit of shrimp flavor this time. If I happened to have been out picking mandarins from the garden, I might grab a few mandarin leaves and add them to my tom yam.

The point is, you can follow recipes for stock, but please, do not let a recipe restrict you from improvising or making do with what you've got on hand.

More complex stocks are best made in bulk, as the cooking time and effort is nearly the same whether you're making a quart or a gallon. Excess stock can be frozen flat in zipper-lock bags (see page 399). Once they are frozen, you can break off however much you need for a given recipe and return the rest to the freezer.

DASHI: THE WORLD'S SIMPLEST STOCK IS LIQUID UMAMI

More than soy sauce, more than sake, more than miso, it's dashi, a simple seaweed-based stock, that is the essential flavor of Japanese cuisine. It's used in soups, sauces, and dips. It's used for simmering vegetables and braising meat. If you've eaten any Japanese food, whether it's a simple cup of miso soup, a hearty bowl of ramen, or a multicourse *omakase* menu at a sushi restaurant, you've tasted dashi.

And here's the good news: It's incredibly easy to make. You will, of course, run into folks who insist that perfecting dashi is an art, or that only the most devoted cooks who have apprenticed for decades under a master can understand what true dashi is. It's OK if they want to believe that. Were my grandmother still alive, she'd giggle at the thought of something so simple being taken so seriously.

We call dashi "stock," but unlike most stocks, dashi is quick. It's very much like brewing a cup of tea, and just like tea, it's finished in a matter of minutes.

The most common dashi is made from two ingredients: kombu (giant sea kelp) and katsuobushi (smoked, dried bonito). Sometimes other ingredients, such as *niboshi* (small dried sardines) or dried shiitake mushrooms can be added to the mix as well, and a simple stock made with just kombu and shiitake mushrooms makes an excellent vegan dashi that can be used just like regular dashi.

You may notice a common theme among all the dashi ingredients: umami. Kombu is rich in the umami-triggering compound glutamic acid. And, in fact, kombu was the primary source of commercial monosodium glutamate (MSG) production until modern methods of synthesis were developed (see "The Truth about MSG," page 50 for more about it). Dried bonito and sardines contain inosinates, while mushrooms contain guanylates, two more organic compounds that enhance the umami effect of glutamic acid, making them several times more effective.

Like saltiness, umaminess is a flavor enhancer. Dishes cooked with or in dashi have a uniquely savory, satisfying quality.

Shopping for Basic Dashi Ingredients

Process-wise, dashi is one of the least intimidating recipes out there. The ingredients might throw you off, however. When I was growing up, finding kombu and katsuobushi meant a trip to the Japanese supermarket. These days I've seen both ingredients at well-stocked Western supermarkets, and certainly they're widely available online.

Kombu comes in a few varieties. I generally look for **hidaka kombu**, which is dark green to black in color, about 3 inches wide, with very lightly curled edges. It's usually the cheapest one at the store. It's also the most versatile, becoming tender and pliable when cooked, which means that after making dashi you can continue to cook it down to make *kombu tsukudani* (page 520), a rice topping that packs an intense umami punch.

Other common kombu varieties are:

- **Rishiri kombu**, which is dark brown in color with heavily ruffled edges and makes a strongly flavored, saline broth

- **Rausu kombu**, which has thin, wide fronds and plenty of powdery mineral deposits. It's great for making dashi, though it's usually a little pricier than Hidaka kombu and not as versatile for cooking.

- **Ma kombu,** sometimes referred to as the "king of kombu," it is the most subtle of the lot, producing very clear, lightly sweet and saline dashi. It commands a high price.

Katsuobushi is fermented, smoked, and dried bonito. In block form it resembles a solid block of wood and is one of the most well-preserved foods in the world. I remember discovering a block of katsuobushi in a forgotten drawer at Uni in Boston. I asked Ken Oringer, the chef, how long it had been there, and he told me it had been in that drawer since opening day, a good four years previous. It felt just like a fresh block (though by that point, its flavor and aroma had deteriorated).

If you want to get super fancy, you can find these solid blocks at specialty shops or online retailers and shave it yourself on a specialized wooden box. You'll find katsuobushi ranging from the simplest *arabushi* style, which is aged for about a month and has a dark brown, wood-like appearance, to the pricier *honkarebushi* style, which is dried, then sprayed with a mist of *Aspergillus glaucus*, a mold that gives it a deeper umami flavor and a brown, powdery rind.

In my grandmother's time it was common for katsuobushi to be shaved fresh for cooking. These days not many people in your average Japanese household do this. Instead, they buy katsuobushi preshaved from the supermarket. Here you'll find a wider variety of options than for kombu, and once again, the cheaper stuff is what you want when making dashi. Stock-grade katsuobushi will come in large shavings about the size of rabbit bedding. I buy mine in large plastic bags of between 3 and 4 ounces.

The much finer katsuobushi, about the size and shape of slender pencil shavings, and generally with a paler pink color, is used to garnish dishes. A small pinch of fine-shaved katsuobushi is a classic topping for a cold spinach salad dressed in dashi (*ohitashi*) or on top of a block of silken tofu that's been drizzled with shoyu, one of my favorite snacks growing up (and now one of Alicia's favorite snacks as well). I keep both stock- and topping-grade katsuobushi in my pantry.

Once a package is opened, it can be stored in a sealed container in a dark pantry for a few months, or in the freezer for up to a year.

Niboshi are small dried sardines. They can add an extra-strong boost of guanylates to dashi, enhancing its umami flavor. Typically the head and guts of niboshi are removed before making the stock, as they can have an unpleasantly fishy aroma. I rarely add niboshi to dashi, and when I do, I generally don't bother with gutting them either. That fishy aroma is a conscious decision. If you're interested in experimenting with niboshi, open up a packet and sniff the bag. If they smell delicious to you, you'll probably enjoy them in your dashi as well.

Instant Dashi

The fastest, easiest way to get passable dashi in your kitchen is to simply use Hondashi, a dry granulated form of dashi made by the Aji-No-Moto company. Is it the most subtle, delectable dashi in the world? Not by a long shot. Will it do in dishes where you mix it with soy sauce and mirin or use it to simmer more robustly flavored ingredients? Absolutely. Tasted side by side, miso soup made with Hondashi will taste flat and one-dimensional compared to real dashi, but even one-dimensional miso soup is delicious and satisfying.*

To be honest, I use powdered Hondashi more frequently than I make dashi from scratch.

The other useful form of instant dashi is in premixed infusions. These are essentially tea bags that, instead of tea, contain premixed dashi ingredients. Most frequently it's a combination of kombu, katsuobushi, shiitake mushroom, and niboshi or *urume* (another type of dried sardine-like fish). You steep them in hot water exactly like tea, and a few minutes later you've got excellent dashi, ready to go. You'll find these stocked next to the Hondashi at the Japanese supermarket or from online retailers.

Ichiban and Niban Dashi

The two major types of dashi are *ichiban*-dashi—or first dashi—and *niban*-dashi—second dashi. Ichiban dashi is the first extraction of kombu and katsuobshi, and it's used primarily in restaurants. The idea is to use a great deal of kombu and bonito, steeped at a relatively low temperature. By doing so, you develop a light broth without extracting many of the heavier, stronger flavors. At the same time, by not allowing the liquid to simmer, you get stock that is crystal clear and suitable for clear, lightly garnished soups (*suimono*) that form an essential part of a traditional multicourse Japanese meal. It's also not something most folks bother with at home (I certainly don't).

Niban dashi is made by taking the spent bonito flakes and kombu from the first dashi, covering it with more water, then simmering it for a longer period of time—ten minutes or so is normal—to extract what's left of the flavor. What results is a much more intense, slightly cloudy, smoky, briny broth. In restaurants this broth is suitable for making sauce, braising meats, simmering vegetables, and other uses where it's a base flavor for other ingredients.

From a half ounce of kombu and a half ounce of dried bonito flakes, you end up with about a quart each of ichiban and niban dashi.

Alternatively, you can do what I do: skip the ichiban dashi and just make lightly simmered dashi from the get-go. You end up with about a quart and a half of dashi that is heavier than ichiban dashi, but more complex in flavor than niban dashi. It's ideal for home use.

---

* It's especially good for hangovers!

How to Make Dashi

There is much debate over how to properly make dashi. At the sashimi bar I used to work at, we made our ichiban dashi by placing kombu in cold water in the morning, letting it steep until the early afternoon, then bringing the water to a bare simmer, removing it from the heat, adding our katsuobushi, letting that steep for five minutes, then straining everything out. (We'd then further simmer the kombu and katsuobushi for niban dashi, or, frequently, until the kombu was tender enough to thinly slice and use as a garnish for a number of dishes.)

The idea is that when simmered, kombu will impart a few mildly bitter flavors that can upset delicate palates. I've never had a problem with it. Katsuobushi definitely tastes different depending on whether it's been steeped, simmered, or boiled. Steeped, you get a very light, smoky, umami flavor. Simmered, it starts to pick up some lightly fishy flavors with a hint of sourness. Boil it for any period of time, and you end up with a noticeably sour, fishy broth. I don't recommend boiling katsuobushi.

For my homemade dashi, I take a simple approach: I combine the kombu and water, bring it to a bare simmer, let it simmer for five minutes, add the katsuobushi off heat, steep for five more minutes, then strain it off for use. If I'm feeling extra ambitious, I'll let the kombu steep in the cold water for longer before heating it up (even overnight on the countertop at room temperature will work).

BASIC DASHI

Yield
Makes 1½
quarts

Active Time
5 minutes

Total Time
10 minutes or up
to overnight

NOTES

Kombu is giant sea kelp, and katsuobushi is dried smoked bonito shavings. They can be found at Japanese or well-stocked Western supermarkets. You can omit the initial cold-steeping step for faster dashi. Strained katsuobushi makes an excellent and healthy snack for pets (or humans, if you are so inclined), or you can cook it down into homemade *furikake* (rice seasoning; see the recipe on page 521). If you used hidaka kombu (see page 516), you can cut it into slivers and cook it down into Tsukudani (page 520).

INGREDIENTS

1½ quarts (1.5 l) water
½ ounce (15 g) kombu (approximately
    4-by-6-inch piece; see Notes)
¾ ounce (20 to 25 g/about 1½ cups)
    katsuobushi (shaved bonito flakes; see
    Notes)

DIRECTIONS

(1) Combine the water and kombu in a saucepan or wok. Cover and let steep at room temperature for several hours or up to overnight (optional, see Notes).

(2) Bring to a bare simmer over medium-high heat, keeping an eye on it and adjusting the heat so that it never gets above a bare simmer. Let it simmer very gently for 5 minutes. Remove from the heat, add the katsuobushi, let steep for 5 minutes, then strain through a fine-mesh strainer, discarding or reserving the solids for another use (see Notes). Dashi can be stored in a sealed container in the fridge for up to 5 days or in the freezer for several months.

Vegan Kombu Dashi

The simplest form of vegan dashi can be made with just kombu and water. Follow the directions for dashi, omitting the katsuobushi flakes but following the steeping and heating steps exactly as directed.

Vegan Shiitake Dashi

Follow the directions for dashi, using ½ ounce (15 g) of dried shiitake mushrooms in place of the katsuobushi. Follow the steeping and heating steps exactly as directed. Steeped shiitake mushrooms can be added to soup, stews, and stir-fries.

TSUKUDANI FROM SPENT KOMBU

Yield
Makes about ½ cup

Active Time
15 minutes

Total Time
25 minutes or longer, depending on the kombu

NOTES

You can use just kombu or a mix of kombu and niboshi (if you made dashi with niboshi). Don't worry if a bit of stray katsuobushi makes its way into the pot.

INGREDIENTS

Kombu left over from 1 batch of dashi
Niboshi left over from 1 batch of dashi (optional)
2 tablespoons (30 ml) light soy sauce or shoyu
2 tablespoons (30 ml) sake
2 tablespoons (30 ml) mirin
1 teaspoon (4 g) sugar
Water
1 teaspoon (3 g) toasted white or black sesame seeds

Tsukudani is a dish named after the small island city of Tsukadajima, which is now the Chūō ward in present-day Tokyo. It's a side dish that's served as an accompaniment to rice, made by simmering seaweed or fish in soy sauce and mirin. The high salt content of the soy sauce and sugar content of the mirin is further concentrated as the liquid reduces into a sticky glaze, which effectively preserves the seafood. It's been a popular side dish in Japan since the seventeenth-century Edo period.

It hits all three of the major Japanese flavors: salty, sweet, and umami. Because it's so intense, a little goes a long way. My grandmother kept various flavors of tsukudani in her fridge at all times, pulling out a pinch with a pair of chopsticks to put on top of her hot rice. A few teaspoons of the stuff is enough to season a full serving of rice.

DIRECTIONS

1. Cut the spent kombu into 1½-inch strips, then cut those strips crosswise as thin as you can to form short, floppy matchsticks.

2. Combine the kombu, niboshi (if using), soy sauce, sake, mirin, sugar, and enough water to cover in a wok or skillet and stir until the sugar is dissolved. Cook over low heat, stirring occasionally with chopsticks, until the liquid has completely reduced and the mixture is thick and syrupy, 15 to 20 minutes. Taste a piece of kombu. It should be very tender. If it is still firm or tastes chalky or raw in the center, add another ½ cup (120 ml) of water, stir, and let it reduce again. Repeat until the kombu is tender.

3. Stir in the sesame seeds. Transfer the mixture to a sealable container, let it cool completely, then store in the fridge. Use straight from the fridge to top bowls of rice. Store in the fridge for several months or up to a year.

HOMEMADE FURIKAKE FROM SPENT KATSUOBUSHI

Yield
Makes
about
¾ cup

Active Time
15 minutes

Total Time
25 minutes

NOTE

Ao-nori is crumbled green seaweed used as a topping for many Japanese street food and rice dishes. Cooling the furikake on an aluminum pan will help it cool quickly and evenly (see page 4 on why aluminum is so good at heating and cooling foods).

INGREDIENTS

Katsuobushi left over from 1 batch of dashi (or ½ ounce/15 g dried katsuobushi moistened with a few tablespoons of water)

2 teaspoons (10 ml) shoyu or light soy sauce

2 teaspoons (8 g) sugar

1 tablespoon (15 ml) mirin

2 tablespoons (16 g) toasted white or black sesame seeds

Up to 2 tablespoons additional dry ingredients, such as dried small shrimp, dried small anchovies, ao-nori (see Notes), freeze-dried shiso, togarashi, or finely crumbled nori

Homemade and store-bought furikake have the same culinary uses (sprinkling over steamed rice or, if you're my wife, Adri, eating out of hand as a snack), but they are quite different in texture and flavor. One is not better than the other; they're just . . . different. As with Kraft mac and cheese and the homemade stuff, sometimes you crave one, sometimes you crave the other, and there's no need to judge anyone on their preference.

The main difference is that commercial mixes typically include a host of freeze-dried ingredients, like egg yolks, wasabi, or shiso. They also use industrial machinery to carefully dry out katsuobushi that has been cooked with soy sauce and sugar into crunchy granules, whereas homemade furikake tends to have a more mixed texture with some crispy bits and some softer clumps.

Both store-bought furikake and this recipe, based closely on the furikake recipe from the Yokohama-born recipe developer Namiko Chen of the site Just One Cookbook, are better than the vast majority of "furikake mix" recipes you'll find online these days, which typically consist of nothing more than throwing together a dry mixture of nori, sesame seeds, shaved bonito flakes, and perhaps some togarashi or other chile together. For me, the process of cooking down the ingredients with soy sauce and sugar is an essential part of the flavor profile of furikake. Once you've got that bit under your belt, feel free to experiment with adding other ingredients, like poppy seeds, extra-small dried anchovies, or dried shrimp.

When making the furikake, note that, just like all sugary concoctions, its texture while hot does not reflect its texture when fully cooled. The furikake may seem moist and soft in the pan, but as it starts to cool, it'll firm up and start getting crispy.

DIRECTIONS

(1) **If Using Katsuobushi Left Over from Dashi:** Place the katsuobushi in a wok or a wide skillet or saucepan and cook over low heat until the individual pieces dry out and start to separate from each other as you stir, 10 to 15 minutes. Watch carefully, especially toward the end, to make sure that large clumps of moist katsuobushi get broken up and that small pieces don't burn. I find that chopsticks are the best tools for separating clumps of moist katsuobushi and spreading them around.

recipe continues

② Add the soy sauce, sugar, and mirin and continue to cook, stirring with chopsticks, until the liquid has completely evaporated and the katsuobushi starts to stick together in moist clumps that settle gently when you pile them up, about 10 minutes. You may notice the sugar starting to caramelize lightly on the bottom or sides of the pan, or you may smell a faint aroma of caramel. This is an indication the katsuobushi is done.

③ Transfer the katsuobushi to a rimmed metal pan, preferably aluminum (see Notes), using your fingertips to break it up into small bits as it cools. Once it's completely cooled, transfer to a bowl, add the sesame seeds and whatever other ingredients you are adding, then get in there with your fingertips, squeezing and crumbling the dried katsuobushi until it is as fine as you'd like it. Store at room temperature in a sealed container for up to 2 months.

Done with Dashi? Don't Throw Anything Out!

When making a Western-style meat stock, there's not all that much you can do with the solid bits you've strained out when you're done. I add carrots and celery to my dog's dinner (make sure not to do this with onions, garlic, or any other allium—they are poisonous to dogs), but the spent carcasses and aromatics end up in the compost bin.

Dashi is a different story. With dashi, both the kombu and the katsuobushi can be repurposed into delicious toppings for rice: tsukudani from the kombu and niboshi and furikake from the katsuobushi.

Thankfully, because dashi is so simple, it's also easy to sort and separate the kombu and katsuobushi after draining the dashi. Niboshi have a tendency to get tangled up in the katsuobushi, but fortunately, tsukudani doesn't get hurt when a bit of stray katsuobushi ends up in it, and likewise a few stray niboshi won't harm your furikake, so no need to be meticulous about separating everything.

The best thing about these preparations is that they both have an extremely long shelf life and can be added directly to cooked rice straight from the pantry (in the case of furikake) or the fridge (in the case of tsukudani).

MISO SOUP

There were many reasons for the middle school version of me to pretend to be sick so I could stay home from school. I once faked a cold for an entire week so I could finish beating the Legend of Zelda, then faked it again the week after so I could finish reading *The Neverending Story* (a classic, every bit as magical as the film, and now a favorite of my daughter as well). But the best part of staying home sick: as much miso soup as my mom could make. Next to rice, miso soup was the food I consumed most growing up, and it's still one of my favorite comfort foods.

Basic miso soup is nothing more than dashi and miso, and the secret to great miso soup is to start with great dashi. We already know how to do that. The rest is simple.

As for the miso itself, you can use whatever shade of fermented soybean paste you'd like. White miso, red miso, and dark miso are all used in various regions of Japan.

You want to ensure that the miso is entirely lump-free as it gets incorporated into the broth. There are a couple ways to do this. Some folks treat it sort of like a béchamel, starting with miso in the pot and slowly adding hot broth in a steady stream, stirring vigorously with chopsticks or a whisk as the water gets incorporated.

I find it easier to use a whisk and a fine-mesh strainer. I start by pushing the top of a whisk directly into the container of miso, twisting as I pull it out to grab as much miso as I need (about a tablespoon per cup of dashi).

Next, I submerge a fine-mesh strainer into the pot of hot dashi. I add the miso to the inside of the strainer, swirling the whisk and pressing it until all the miso has passed through the strainer and only the large, grainy chunks remain, making them easy to discard.

As for other ingredients, it's up to you. I love the texture and flavor of wakame, a dried seaweed. You can reconstitute it separately in hot water, but personally, I don't have the patience—I just add it to my hot soup and let it soften on its own. Firm silken tofu cubes are a must for me—I love their slippery texture as they heat up in the broth—as are scallions. If I'm feeling like a miso soup lush, I'll go ahead and add some *hon shimeji* or slippery nameko mushrooms to the mix. Small clams or cockles are also a classic, delicious addition to miso soup.

Even with homemade dashi, miso soup takes all of 15 minutes to make 100 percent from scratch, which is something I appreciate on mornings when I've had a bit too much sake the night before: It's extremely easy on sensitive stomachs and about as good a hangover cure as I know.

Yield
Serves 4

Active Time
5 minutes

Total Time
5 minutes

NOTE

You can add a wide range of vegetables to miso soup. Try fresh tender greens like spinach or pea shoots or thinly sliced seasonal vegetables like radish, carrot, onion, or turnip. Heartier greens like cabbage, bok choy, or chard are also great thinly sliced. You can add squares of fried tofu, thin slices of bacon, or bits of shredded chicken or thinly slivered pork. Leftover rice and scrambled egg drizzled into the hot soup are also delicious, as are tiny cockles or clams, added at the end and simmered just until they open. Any kind of mushroom, cut into thin shavings or spoon-sized pieces, is a welcome addition to miso soup as well. All of these ingredients should be added at the start of step 2 so they can be simmered very gently before serving.

recipe continues

INGREDIENTS

1½ quarts (750 ml) dashi

6 tablespoons (90 g) white, red, or brown miso paste

6 ounces (170 g) firm silken tofu, cut into ½-inch cubes

¼ ounce (7.5 g/about 2 tablespoons) dried wakame seaweed (optional)

2 whole scallions, thinly sliced (optional)

DIRECTIONS

(1) Bring the broth to a subsimmer in a medium saucepan or wok (bubbles should just start escaping the bottom of the pot, but there should be no vigorous simmering or boiling), then reduce the heat to low to keep it hot but not boiling. Use a whisk to scoop the miso paste out of its container (or add the paste directly to the strainer using a spoon). Use a whisk or spoon to press the paste through the strainer into the broth, swirling and shaking the strainer to encourage it. Discard any large grains that don't pass through.

(2) Add the tofu and wakame and simmer gently until the wakame has rehydrated, about 5 minutes. Garnish with scallions (if using) and serve immediately.

Shopping for and Storing Miso Paste

At a regular supermarket you're likely to see two types of miso: light miso and dark miso. At the Japanese market, you'll find a vast rainbow of browns, from light brown to dark brown to kinda orangey reddish brown.*

All miso is made through the same basic process. A grain or a pulse—typically soybeans, though barley, rice, millet, rye, and, more recently, chickpeas and quinoa—is ground and fermented with salt and the fungus *Aspergillus oryzae* (*koji* in Japanese). The resulting protein-rich paste has a salty-savory flavor that can range from heavy and funky to light and mildly sweet. Typically, the darker the color of the miso, the higher the proportion of soybeans used and the stronger the flavor. At home I keep three varieties of miso in my fridge:

→ **Akamiso** (red miso) is a dark red miso that has a rich flavor and is excellent in miso soup, in hearty stir-fries and marinades (such as for Broiled Miso Eggplant, page 243), in noodle soups, or in dips for grilled or fresh vegetables.

→ Regular **shiromiso** (white miso) is a pale yellow miso with a lighter flavor that works well in salad dressings (Sesame-Ginger Vinaigrette, page 620), marinades, light miso soup, and in lighter stir-fries (such as Stir-Fried Kabocha Squash with Sake and Miso, page 199).

→ **Saikyo miso** is a variety of white miso from Kyoto that is especially smooth in texture and sweet, due to the high rice content in its mash. It is used to prepare *saikyo-yaki*—miso-marinated broiled fish, such as the Miso-Glazed Broiled Black Cod or Salmon (page 242).

Miso has long been used as a preservative (before refrigeration, fish was packed in soybean or rice miso to preserve it—this combination of fish with rice is the origin of modern sushi), and it has an excellent shelf life. Kept in a sealed container in the fridge, it'll last for months or even years. Miso often comes sold in resealable containers, though sometimes it's sold in plastic bags. If I buy it in plastic bags, I snip off the corner, squeeze out what I need, then pack the whole bag into a separate sealable container for storage in the fridge.

---

* The color that Bob Ross would call "burnt ochre"

Hondashi = Umami Supremacy

Dashinomoto (literally "foundation of dashi") or instant dashi, is granulated dry dashi and an indispensable ingredient in my own pantry. On paper, it is to dashi what powdered chicken bouillon is to chicken stock or beef bouillon is to beef stock. Unlike powdered bouillons, however, it's a legitimately useful stand-in for the real stuff in many applications. The most popular brand is Hondashi, made by the Aji-No-Moto corporation, the same company that built its empire through the discovery and extraction of monosodium glutamate. The name is a contraction of the words *hontou* ("for real") and *dashi*, and true to its name, it's really made from dashi, albeit propped up with a host of other flavor enhancers.

It's made by evaporating and freeze-drying actual dashi, then combining it with monosodium glutamate (MSG), disodium inosinate, disodium succinate (which provide a multiplying effect for MSG), salt, and sugar. Where powdered chicken bouillons taste mainly of salt, granulated dashi is an absolute umami *bomb*, and because it's relatively low in sodium, it's useful for adding umami backbone to a host of dishes, even in places where you wouldn't typically incorporate actual dashi.

In *The Food Lab*, I wrote extensively about how to use umami bombs like anchovies, fish sauce, and Marmite in Western soups and stews to bolster their meaty flavors. Add instant dashi to that list. A teaspoon added to a pot of Tex-Mex chili con carne, French boeuf bourguignon, or even Italian ragù Bolognese will instantly boost its flavor, and because Hondashi is so subtle in flavor, it doesn't leave your stews with any kind of fishiness.*

Because it comes as dry granules, it can be incorporated to add umami flavor to dishes where added liquids would not be appropriate, such as sprinkled onto popcorn, blended into mayonnaise, or used in dry rubs for grilling or roasting.

Here are a few of my favorite uses:

Hondashi Eggs

Beat ½ teaspoon (about 1 g) Hondashi and a pinch of salt into every two eggs when making scrambled eggs for an umami boost. Or sprinkle Hondashi directly onto hard- or soft-boiled eggs while eating them.

Hondashi Mayonnaise

Whisk ½ teaspoon (about 1 g) Hondashi, ½ teaspoon (2 g) sugar, and 1 teaspoon (5 ml) rice vinegar into a cup of mayonnaise to make a quick Japanese-style mayo (think: Kewpie) that is especially good on steamed and chilled vegetables.

Hondashi Popcorn

Grind together 1 teaspoon (about 2 g) Hondashi, 1 teaspoon (3 g) kosher salt, and 1 teaspoon (4 g) sugar in a mortar and pestle or spice grinder. Add furikake (page 521), *ao-nori* (dried green seaweed), toasted sesame seeds, and/or shichimi or ichimi togarashi (Japanese seven-spice or chile blend) to taste, then toss it with a bowl of buttered popcorn.

Hondashi Risotto, Oats, and Grits

Season risotto, oats, grits, polenta, or other saucy grains with Hondashi in place of salt for an umami boost and a subtle oceany aroma. This is especially great for seafood-based dishes like shrimp and grits or a seafood risotto.

Note that while Hondashi is the most popular brand out there, it has quite a few competitors. Kayanoya is a premium brand that I would recommend for dishes in which the dashi is front and center, such as miso soup or simmered vegetable dishes.

---

* Note: there are versions of Hondashi and other instant dashi that include stronger fishy-smelling ingredients, like sardines or mackerel. I would not use those for Western dishes!

Dashi-Simmered and Dashi-Dressed Dishes

Now that we know how to make great dashi (see page 525), let's put it to use in the simplest Japanese dishes: *nimono*. Nimono are cooked by simmering fresh ingredients in *shiru*, a seasoned broth. Shiru can be seasoned with a number of ingredients, but dashi with soy sauce, sake, mirin, and sugar is the most common. Miso and other ingredients like vinegar or citrus juice might also make an appearance in some nimono. They can range from simple vegetable preparations to more complex meat and vegetable stews, but their preparation is never more complicated than "put this stuff together, add some broth, and cook it until it's done."

Nimono are traditionally prepared in wide terracotta casserole dishes covered with an *otoshibuta*, a lid that is purposely made smaller than the cooking vessel so that it drops directly onto the food, keeping it submerged as it simmers. This allows ingredients to cook gently in a single, even layer. A wok or a wide sauté pan does the same job very well, provided you make your own otoshibuta for it. This is easy to do with a sheet of parchment paper.

HOW TO MAKE A PARCHMENT PAPER OTOSHIBUTA

Cutting a sheet of parchment paper into a circle that fits whatever vessel you are using is simple. It's useful for lining a bamboo steamer basket when steaming dumplings. It's great for Japanese-style simmered dishes as it keeps ingredients moist while allowing evaporation. It's also useful for Western-style stews and braises when you want to have some of the benefits of lidless cooking (more evaporation and browning in the oven) and lid-on cooking (gentler cooking of ingredients, protection against the top of the stew drying out).

Here's how you do it.

Step 1 • Fold a Sheet of Parchment into Quarters

Starting with a flat sheet of parchment paper larger than the size of your cooking vessel, fold it in half once, then again in the perpendicular direction. It helps to use flat sheets of parchment rather than parchment from a roll (though either will work).

Step 2 • Fold into a Triangle

Fold the parchment into a right triangle with its point at the intersection of the first two folds (the center of the unfolded parchment sheet).

Step 3 • Make the Triangle More Slender

Continue to fold the parchment one or two more times to form a more slender triangle, always keeping the vertex of the fold at the same central point.

Step 4 • Trim the Edges

Hold the triangle with the acute tip at the center of your cooking vessel. With a pair of kitchen shears, trim the back edge of the triangle so that its height ends up slightly smaller than the radius of the cooking vessel. If using a flat-bottomed wok to cook, make the height slightly *larger* than the flat-bottomed area of your wok.

Step 5 • Trim the Tip

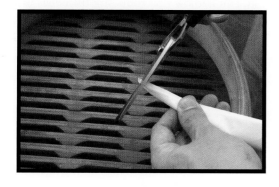

Cut off the top ½ inch or so of the triangle. This will create a hole for steam to vent through, which keeps your parchment lid from puffing up off the surface of the liquid.

Step 6 • Cut Notches

If using to line a steamer basket, cut little notches up and down both edges, spacing them about an inch apart.

Step 7 • Unfold

Unfold your parchment lid and marvel at how perfectly it fits your pot.

SIMMERED DAIKON RADISH (DAIKON NO NIMONO)

Yield
Serves 4

Active Time
5 minutes

Total Time
25 to 30 minutes

NOTES

Hondashi is powdered dashi that can be found at any Japanese market and most well-stocked supermarkets. The daikon for this recipe looks best when it is slightly beveled around its sharp corners. See page 529 for step-by-step instructions on how to prepare daikon for braising. The daikon can be served as is, or you can add some other ingredients. Pick one or two of the suggested serving accompaniments to keep things simple.

INGREDIENTS

2 cups (480 ml) homemade dashi (pages 519–21), or the equivalent in Hondashi (see Notes)

1 tablespoon (15 ml) light soy sauce

2 tablespoons (30 ml) sake

1 tablespoon (15 ml) mirin

1 teaspoon (4 g) sugar

1 daikon radish (about 1 pound/450 g), peeled, cut into 1½-inch slices, and beveled (see Notes)

To Serve (all optional; see Notes):

Small handful of leafy greens such as spinach, baby bok choy, or tatsoi, simmered with the daikon in the broth for the last few minutes

½ cup (70 g) frozen edamame added to the broth for the last minute of cooking to defrost

Finely julienned fresh ginger, thinly sliced scallions, or toasted sesame seeds scattered on top

A small dab of wasabi added to each piece

A small dollop of Sweet and Spicy Miso Dip (page 617) added to each piece

Daikon radish simmered in dashi with a touch of soy sauce, sake, mirin, and sugar is a classic Japanese preparation that is great hot, at room temperature, or straight out of the fridge. Daikon gets this really uniquely juicy-crunchy texture when simmered. It's hard to describe, almost like biting into a crisp, dashi-filled water balloon. For a vegetable-based side dish, it packs a ton of flavor.

Some folks like to reduce the broth until it's almost a glaze, giving the daikon a very intense savory-sweet flavor. I usually leave my broth a little lighter, which lets you serve the daikon in a bowl with plenty of broth (some leafy greens or edamame added to the simmering liquid right at the end is nice). The daikon is peeled and cut crosswise into disks, then the edges are lightly beveled (you can do this with a vegetable peeler or a knife). The technique, known as *mentori* in Japan, is about more than just appearance: beveling the edges protects the radishes from splitting or falling apart as they simmer gently in the broth. If you've ever built a table or dresser for a child, you'll know that rounding the edges protects the child *and* the furniture. A similar technique is used for potatoes in *nikujaga* (beef and potato stew, page 532). Daikon cooks through in about 20 minutes at a simmer, but it can go for up to 45 without falling apart (assuming you've given it the mentori treatment). It's hard to overcook the daikon, so there's no big risk involved with experimenting in reducing the liquid as much or as little as you like.

If you plan on serving the daikon cold or have leftovers, I'd suggest transferring it to a zipper-lock bag and removing as much air as possible by sealing all but the last inch of the bag, squeezing out the air, and sealing it just before the liquid starts to come out. Place the bag on a flat plate or small rimmed tray (to catch any juices that might leak out) and store in the fridge for up to a few days. The broth will continue to add flavor to the daikon as it rests.

DIRECTIONS

(1) Combine the dashi, soy sauce, sake, mirin, and sugar in a flat-bottomed wok or wide skillet or sauté pan. Add the daikon pieces and arrange in a single layer (it's OK if the daikon is not completely submerged).

(2) Bring to a bare simmer, cover (for best results use an otoshibuta or parchment lid; see page 526), and cook, adjusting the heat to maintain a very gentle bubble and flipping the daikon pieces over carefully once every 10 to 15 minutes, until the daikon is completely tender and the liquid is reduced as much as you'd like it (depending on whether you simmer

for 20 or up to 45 minutes, the broth will have more subtle or powerful flavor—taste and use your own judgment as to when to stop).

(3) **To Serve:** Add any optional serving ingredients, transfer to a plate, and serve. Simmered daikon can also be stored in its broth in a sealed zipper-lock bag with the air squeezed out of it in the fridge for up to a few days. It's excellent served cold.

Shopping for, Storing, and Preparing Daikon Radish

Daikon radish, known as *mooli* in parts of the United Kingdom (after its Hindi and Urdu name) is a large white root vegetable with a crisp, watery texture and a mild flavor that's slightly peppery when raw and becomes very savory with a mild sulphury aroma* when pickled or cooked. It's a hugely important vegetable in Japanese cuisine, where it is grated fresh and stirred into dipping sauces for noodles or tempura, simmered in broth, added to soups and stews, or pickled and used as a topping for rice.

When shopping for it, look for daikon with smooth, firm skin, bright, fresh-looking greens (if they are still attached), and a straight, cylindrical body (which makes it easier to cook with). Daikon can be stored in a bag in your crisper drawer for a week or longer. Daikon that has started to turn a little limp can't be used for grating, but it still works just fine for pickling or simmering.

One of the problems with simmering daikon is that it tends to break around sharp corners, which can cause bits of the vegetable to fall into and cloud the broth, making for a less-than-ideal presentation. To solve this issue, Japanese cooks use a technique called *mentori*, in which the edges of a vegetable are chamfered or beveled to ease sharp angles. The technique is similar to the French technique of chamfering potatoes for *pommes de terre fondantes* and indeed works well for stewed potatoes, such as in *nikujaga* (page 532)

Step 1 • Peel the Daikon

Use a vegetable peeler to remove the skin from the daikon.

Step 2 • Cut the Daikon

Cut the daikon into 1½-inch disks.

Step 3 • Bevel the Edges

Use a sharp knife or a vegetable peeler to make an ⅛-inch bevel around the edges of the sliced daikon. The finished daikon should have a chamfered, lozenge-like shape.

---

*　Let's just say it: Daikon radish smells kinda like farts. But in a good way, like cute baby farts.

KNIFE SKILLS

SIMMERED KABOCHA SQUASH (KABOCHA NO NIMONO)

Yield
Serves 4

Active Time
5 minutes

Total Time
25 to 35 minutes

Japanese kabocha squash simmered in seasoned dashi has a dense, fleshy texture and a really nice balance of sweet flavors from the squash, mirin, and sugar, balanced by savory dashi and soy sauce. Because kabocha has natural sweetness, I omit the sugar I use to simmer daikon. The heat of ginger goes particularly well with simmered kabocha, as does a sprinkle of shichimi togarashi (Japanese seven-spice blend).

INGREDIENTS

2 cups (500 ml) homemade or instant dashi
1 tablespoon (15 ml) light soy sauce
2 tablespoons (30 ml) sake
1 tablespoon (15 ml) mirin
½ kabocha squash (about 1 pound/450 g), seeded and cut into 1½-inch chunks (see page 200 for step-by-step instructions)
1 coin-sized slice fresh ginger

DIRECTIONS

1 Combine the dashi, soy sauce, sake, and mirin in a flat-bottomed wok or wide skillet or sauté pan. Add the kabocha pieces and arrange in a single layer (it's OK if the squash is not completely submerged).

2 Bring to a bare simmer, cover (for best results use an otoshibuta or parchment lid; see page 526), and cook, adjusting the heat to maintain a very gentle bubble until the kabocha is tender but not falling apart, 20 to 30 minutes. Serve immediately or, for best flavor, allow the squash to cool in the broth and reheat briefly before serving.

SIMMERED GREENS WITH SOY DASHI AND KATSUOBUSHI (OHITASHI)

Yield
Serves 2
to 4

Active Time
10 minutes

Total Time
10 minutes

NOTES
You can use any tender greens that are suitable for blanching for this recipe. Greens can be blanched in advance, dressed, and stored in the fridge for up to a couple days before serving if desired. Hondashi is powdered dashi that can be found at any Japanese market and most well-stocked supermarkets.

INGREDIENTS

For the Greens:
Kosher salt
5 ounces (145 g) tender greens, such
    as spinach, baby kale, beet greens,
    watercress, or mizuna

For the Sauce:
1 tablespoon (15 ml) mirin
2 teaspoons (10 ml) sake
2 teaspoons (10 ml) shoyu or light soy sauce
⅓ cup (80 ml) homemade dashi (pages
    519–21) or the equivalent in Hondashi
    (see Notes)

To Serve:
Toasted sesame seeds and shaved
    katsuobushi

Simmered greens that are chilled and served with a soy dashi marinade are a staple side dish in Japan. They can be made with spinach, *shungiku* (chrysanthemum greens), dandelion greens, beet greens, turnip greens, watercress, etc. As long as the greens are edible, they will work in this dish. The key to this dish is drying the greens very thoroughly after blanching so that the water they retain doesn't water down the sauce. You can use your hands, but for best results wrapping the greens in a kitchen towel and twisting the ends to wring out excess moisture is the most effective method I know.

DIRECTIONS

(1) **For the Greens:** Bring a wok full of lightly salted water to a boil over high heat. Add the greens. Cook, stirring occasionally, until wilted but still bright green, about 1 minute. Immediately drain and rinse under cold running water until completely cold.

(2) Place the drained greens in the middle of a clean kitchen towel or a triple layer of cheesecloth. Gather up the ends of the towel to form a sack. Hold the sack over the sink, then twist the ends together to tighten the sack. Continue twisting and squeezing the sack to press out as much excess moisture as possible from the greens.

(3) **For the Sauce:** Combine the mirin, sake, soy sauce, and dashi in a medium bowl.

(4) Transfer the greens to the bowl and toss to coat in the sauce. The greens can be stored in the sauce in the refrigerator for up to 2 days.

(5) **To Serve:** When ready to serve, transfer the greens to a serving platter and pour the excess marinade around them. Sprinkle with the sesame seeds and katsuobushi and serve.

JAPANESE BEEF AND POTATO STEW (NIKUJAGA)

Yield
Serves 4

Active Time
20 minutes

Total Time
40 minutes

NOTE

Thinly sliced rib eye, short rib, or chuck roll intended for shabu, sukiyaki, or bulgogi all work for this dish. You can also use thinly sliced pork loin or belly, ground pork, or no meat at all.

INGREDIENTS

One 8-ounce (225 g) package shirataki noodles, drained
1 tablespoon (15 ml) peanut, rice bran, or other neutral oil
1 small onion, cut into ¼-inch slivers
8 ounces (225 g) thinly sliced or ground beef (see Note)
1 medium carrot, peeled and cut into 1½-inch chunks
1 large russet potato, peeled and cut into 1½-inch chunks
2 cups (500 ml) homemade or instant dashi
3 tablespoons (45 ml) light soy sauce
¼ cup (60 ml) sake
2 tablespoons (30 ml) mirin
1 tablespoon (12 g) sugar
½ cup frozen peas (optional)

Created by the Imperial Japanese Navy in the nineteenth century, *niku-jaga* (literally "meat and potatoes") was a conscious effort by Japanese naval chefs to create a version of the beef stew served to the British navy. The resulting dish combined some traditionally British ingredients—beef, onions, potatoes, and carrots—with the Japanese flavors of dashi, mirin, sake, and soy sauce, as well as the addition of shirataki noodles, which become infused with the flavor of the broth as they simmer. (See page 300 for more on shirataki noodles.)

Unlike Western beef stews, which use larger chunks of meat cooked until meltingly tender, nikujaga uses thinly sliced or ground beef and is cooked only until the vegetables are tender and the broth is reduced and intensified.

DIRECTIONS

(1) Transfer the shirataki noodles to a colander or strainer. Rinse under cold running water for 30 seconds, then set over a bowl to drain.

(2) Heat the oil in a wok or a saucepan over medium-high heat until shimmering. Add the onion and cook, stirring, until lightly softened, about 1 minute. Add the meat and cook, stirring, until only a few lightly pink bits remain.

(3) Add the carrots, potatoes, and drained shirataki noodles and toss to combine. Add the dashi, soy sauce, sake, mirin, and sugar and stir to combine. Bring to a bare simmer, skim any foamy scum with a skimmer or ladle and discard, cover (for best results use an otoshibuta or parchment lid; see page 526), and cook, adjusting the heat to maintain a very gentle bubble, until the vegetables are very tender, 20 to 30 minutes. Stir in the peas, if using. Serve immediately, or for best flavor, allow to cool and reheat briefly.

Nikujaga, Step by Step

MY BOILED EGG OBSESSION

Boiled eggs that slip cleanly and reliably out of their shells have been something of an obsession of mine for well over two decades. It began when it was my job to boil and peel dozens of soft-cooked eggs to top the blanched asparagus we served at No. 9 Park in Boston, one of my first restaurant jobs. Testing what factors affect egg peelability was the subject of my very first "Food Lab" article on *Serious Eats* in 2009, as well as my first cooking column for the *New York Times* in 2019. Over the course of my life I have boiled, pressure-cooked, baked, steamed, and simmered tens of thousands of eggs and have had over a hundred different volunteers peel those eggs double-blind (that is, neither I nor the testers knew how the eggs being peeled were cooked until after the experiment was over, in order to eliminate any possible bias) to determine what truly matters and what doesn't. You may say that my obsession borders on the eggstreme. I'd simply say that I've got egg peeling down to an eggsact science.

In all that testing, I've managed to boil it down to one all-important factor: the temperature at which you start cooking the eggs. Everything else is details.

The six eggs on the left were started in cold water, while the six on the right were lowered into boiling water.

Starting eggs in cold water coagulates egg-white proteins, which causes them to bond tightly to the inner membrane of the shell. Starting them in already-boiling water or a preheated steamer gets those proteins to set up quickly, before they have a chance to bond to the shells. The difference is night and day: when peeled, cold-water eggs are nine times more likely to experience major flaws (completely torn egg whites) and twice as likely to produce minor flaws (small divots and imperfections in the whites).

Aside from that factor, little else makes a difference. Old eggs peel just as well as fresh eggs (I compared eggs that were laid the same morning with eggs that were between two weeks and one month old). Vinegar, baking soda, or salt added to the water made no discernible difference. Room-temperature eggs will cook about a minute faster than cold eggs but are no easier or more difficult to peel. Pressure-cooked eggs are easy to peel, but they are also noticeably tougher than steamed or boiled eggs. Baked eggs stick impossibly to the shell, take forever, and have a strong, sulfurous aroma (I'm convinced baked eggs are some kind of bad yolk).

Happily, I've found that it makes no difference to peelability whether your eggs are fully submerged in boiling water or simply resting in a covered pot with an inch or so of rapidly boiling water. In fact, eggs that are cooked in the latter manner come out a bit more tender than those that are boiled the entire way through (because boiling water is a more effective and violent means of heat transfer than steam).

The wok is also an ideal egg-steaming vessel. A saucepan, with its tall sides, makes it difficult to gingerly lower eggs to the bottom without accidentally cracking them. The gently sloped sides of a wok make it easy.

There's only one other factor that made a noticeable difference in the appearance of the finished eggs: pricking the fat end with a pin.

The fat end of an egg has a small pocket of air that grows larger as an egg gets older (egg shells are porous, and as water from inside the egg evaporates, air comes in to take its place). When it's large enough, it can cause a dimple to appear in the cooked egg and may also lead to a blowout as that air expands during cooking. Pricking the fat end with a pushpin before steaming them will allow gases trapped in the fat end to escape as they expand, leading to lower chances of a cracked egg and eliminating that dimpled end.

PERFECTLY PEELABLE STEAM-BOILED EGGS

Yield
Makes 1
to 12

Active Time
2 minutes

Total Time
15 minutes

NOTE
If you keep your eggs on the counter (as you should if you are in Europe, you buy your eggs directly from the farmer, or you keep a backyard flock), reduce cooking times by 1 minute.

INGREDIENTS

1 to 12 large eggs, straight from the fridge
(see Note)

This technique will produce eggs that slip cleanly out of their shells at least 87 percent of the time (I am not aware of any technique known to science that produces reliably peelable eggs at a higher rate than that!).

DIRECTIONS

1. Bring 2 quarts (2 l) of water to a hard boil inside a wok over high heat. Meanwhile, prick the fat end of each egg with a pushpin to create a small hole for air to escape.

2. When the water is boiling, gently lower the eggs into the wok by rolling them down the side and releasing them just before your hand touches the water. Once all the eggs are added, cover the wok and set a time: 6 minutes for soft cooked (a warm liquid yolk and firm whites); 8½ minutes for medium (a translucent, fudgy yolk); or 11 minutes for hard (a yolk that is just barely firm all the way through).

3. When the eggs are done, remove the wok from the heat and drain off the water. Peel the eggs immediately under cold running water or transfer them to a plate, let them cool completely, and store in the refrigerator for up to 2 days before peeling and using.

AJITSUKE TAMAGO

Yield
Makes 6
eggs

Active Time
5 minutes, plus
time to boil the
eggs if starting
from raw

Total Time
4 to 12 hours

INGREDIENTS

1 cup (240 ml) water
1 cup (240 ml) sake
½ cup (120 ml) soy sauce
½ cup (120 ml) mirin
½ cup (100 g) sugar
6 soft- or medium-boiled eggs, peeled
   (page 535)

Ajitsuke tamago (Japanese for "flavored eggs") are boiled eggs that are marinated in a mixture of sake, soy sauce, mirin, and sugar until the exteriors are lightly dyed brown and the eggs pick up a sweet and savory flavor. They're a common addition to bowls of ramen, but they're also delicious on their own and a recipe worth keeping under your belt.

Now, you could just pour your marinade into a bowl and add your eggs. That'll work. Sort of. The problem is that hard-boiled eggs are more buoyant than the sweet-salty marinade and thus float to the top and poke their heads out, resulting in uneven marination. One common solution for this is to put the eggs and the marinade into a plastic zipper-lock bag and carefully remove all the air from it, forcing the liquid to spread around the eggs. It works, but it's a little messy to do. A much easier technique is to simply cover the tops of the marinating eggs with a paper towel.

The towel wicks liquid up and around the eggs, making sure that all sides get even exposure to marinade. It's a technique I use all the time for all kinds of preparations—keeping vegetables submerged in their pickling liquid, for example, or keeping peeled artichokes submerged in lemon water to prevent discoloration.

DIRECTIONS

(1) Combine the water, sake, soy, mirin, and sugar in a medium bowl and whisk until the sugar is dissolved.

(2) Place the eggs in a bowl that just barely fits them all. Pour the marinade on top until the eggs are covered or just floating. Place a double layer of paper towels on top and press down until completely saturated in liquid to help keep the eggs submerged and marinating evenly. Refrigerate for at least 4 hours and up to 12. Discard the marinade after 12 hours. Store the eggs in a sealed container in the fridge for up to 3 days. Serve cold or reheat by boiling for a couple of minutes in water or in noodle soup broth.

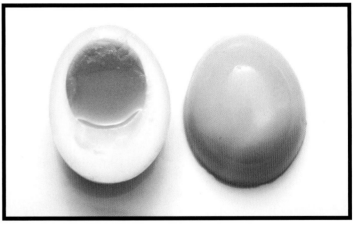

The Limits of Marination

When I was in college and living in a house shared by fifty people, I remember getting an email once from a resident offering free chicken breasts to whoever wanted them. His claim: "they've been marinating for three whole days, so they're going to be super tender and tasty as f*&k."

I don't know any college student who'd turn down free food, so I took them, grilled them, and served them to some friends for dinner. The consensus? They were awful. Mushy and mealy with a chalky texture that was completely offputting. The lesson I learned that day? With marinades, longer does not necessarily equal better. Marinades can be great for seasoning the outer layers of a food, but letting your food sit in a marinade for too long can wreak chemical havoc on its texture.

With acidic marinades—like the Italian-style dressing those chicken breasts had been marinated in—denaturation of proteins can cause foods to turn mushy and rapidly give up their moisture when heated.

With ajitsuke tamago, there's another culprit: salt.

We all know that salt can have a powerful effect on food, right? In the case of bacon or ham, for instance, salt not only draws moisture out from the interior of the food; it also dissolves some of the proteins in the muscle, causing it to tighten and change in texture (ever notice how different bacon feels from fresh pork belly?).

So it is with ajitsuke tamago. A few hours in a marinade and you'll get an egg with a delightfully sweet and salty flavor on its outer layer. The flavor is powerful enough to season the whole bite, despite the fact that it's only penetrated a millimeter or two. Let the egg sit in that salty marinade for too long, however, and you'll see the marinade slowly work its way into the center of the egg. Eventually it'll even reach the yolk, causing it to firm up and set into an almost fudge-like texture. Not what we're after.

Pictured is an egg that I marinated for three whole days before slicing in half.

As you can see, nearly all of the yolk has been hardened (a small amount of liquid remains in the very center—give it another day or two, and it would have been hard all the way through). Eating this egg is also quite unpleasant. The white is hard, dry, and extremely rubbery, and the parts of the yolk that have been cured are hard set, sticky, and chewy in a manner most unpleasant. This process is taken to the extreme to make the infamous Chinese thousand-year-old eggs, in which raw duck eggs are buried in a salty mixture of tea ashes until cured all the way through to the center. The resultant eggs are as hard as a hard-boiled eggs but have never seen heat.

KATSUOBUSHI DEVILED EGGS

Yield
Makes 8
deviled egg
halves

Active Time
20 minutes, plus
time to boil the
eggs if starting
from raw

Total Time
20 minutes, plus
time to boil the
eggs if starting
from raw

NOTE
Karashi is powdered Japanese mustard. If you
don't have it, you can use dried Chinese or
English hot mustard in its place or 2 teaspoons
(10 ml) of hot prepared English or Dijon mustard.

INGREDIENTS

6 hard-boiled eggs, peeled (page 535)
2 teaspoons (10 ml) rice vinegar or distilled
    white vinegar
1 teaspoon (2 g) powdered *karashi* (see
    Note)
3 tablespoons (45 g) mayonnaise
1 teaspoon (3 g) Hondashi
Kosher salt

To Finish:

Thinly sliced scallions
Shichimi togarashi
Shaved katsuobushi
Coarse sea salt, such as Maldon or fleur
    de sel

I am a deviled egg *fiend*. They've been on the menu at Wursthall since
before we even opened and have remained one of the most popular appetizers. The ones we serve there are an extra-mustardy affair with spicy
German mustard in the filling and pickled mustard seeds spooned on
top—you can find my recipe for free online if you search for "Wursthall
Deviled Eggs," or just stop by the restaurant and try them yourself. But
this version, made with Japanese mustard and Hondashi, and topped with
katsuobushi flakes, is another favorite of mine.

DIRECTIONS

(1) Cut the eggs in half lengthwise. Place all the yolks in the bowl of a food
processor. Select 8 of the best-looking egg white halves, rinse in cold water
to clean out any excess yolk, and set aside; reserve the remaining 4 whites
for another use. Add the vinegar, karashi, mayonnaise, and Hondashi to
the food processor or mini chopper and process until smooth, scraping
down sides of the bowl as necessary. Season with salt to taste.

(2) Transfer the yolk mixture to a zipper-lock bag or a piping bag fitted
with a piping tip. Filling and egg white halves can be stored in the refrigerator up to overnight before the eggs are filled and served.

(3) **To Finish:** If using a zipper-lock bag to pipe, cut off a corner of the
bag. Pipe a small dollop of filling onto a serving platter and place an egg
white on top of it to secure it in place. Pipe the filling mixture into the
egg white, overstuffing it. Repeat with the remaining egg white halves
and filling. Top with scallions, togarashi, katsuobushi, and coarse salt and
serve immediately.

KOREAN SOFT TOFU AND KIMCHI SOUP (KIMCHI SOONDUBU JJIGAE)

Yield
Serves 4
to 6

Active Time
15 minutes

Total Time
30 minutes

NOTES

The broth for this soup is typically made with sea kelp (kombu) and dried anchovies. You can make a dashi with those two ingredients (page 519) or just use whatever dashi you'd like. I like adding kimchi to the soup, though it's not a necessary ingredient. Kimchi contains probiotics and will continue to ferment in your fridge after you buy it, eventually gaining a bubbly effervescence. That bubbly, extra-sour kimchi is perfect for this dish. Other good additions are several ounces of daikon radish cut into small cubes, whole enoki or beech mushrooms, cockles, clams, or shrimp. Any additions should be added with the dashi in step 3 and simmered just until cooked through (about 15 minutes for radish or 2 to 3 minutes for mushrooms and shellfish). If you use a mushroom-based vegan dashi (page 519) and a vegan kimchi (check the label; most kimchi is made with anchovies—vegan kimchi will typically be labeled as such on the front of the container), the dish is entirely vegan.

INGREDIENTS

1 cup (225 g) very fermented kimchi with juice (optional; see Notes)

1 tablespoon (15 ml) vegetable oil

6 scallions, cut into 1-inch segments

1 tablespoon (8 g) minced garlic (about 4 medium cloves)

2 tablespoons (30 g) gochujang

1 tablespoon (15 ml) light soy sauce, plus more to taste

3 tablespoons (20 g) gochugaru (Korean chile flakes), more or less to taste

1 quart (1 l) dashi (see Notes)

1½ pounds (680 g) soft tofu, preferably Korean soondubu

1 large egg per serving (optional)

A mainstay of the Korean table, *jjigae* literally translates as "stew," and there are hundreds of common varieties. When I have a cold, there are few things I crave more than a steaming hot bowl of *soondubu jjigae*—soft tofu stew. I grew up right across the George Washington Bridge from Palisades Park, the municipality that, with a full 52 percent of its residents being of Korean descent, represents the most concentrated Korean population in the country. I made it a habit to make the trek across the bridge to nearby Fort Lee for soondubu jjigae from Soft Tofu Restaurant (that's really its name—although it also goes by its Korean name, So Kong Dong) whenever the weather got cold or I started to feel a bit of a sniffle coming on.

Flavored with pork, beef, mushrooms, or seafood in a broth similar to a Japanese dashi flavored with sea kelp and dried anchovies, it's laced with gochugaru (Korean chile flakes) and fermented gochujang (chile wheat paste). The bulk of the dish is made up of tofu of the softest silken variety, which develops an ultra-creamy, smooth texture as it heats in the boiling-hot broth. This version features chunks of daikon radish, mushrooms, scallions, and soft tofu in a dashi-style broth. Soondubu jjigae is typically made in a stone bowl called a *dolsot*, but your wok will do an excellent job here. Sinus clearing, nutritious, and easy to down by the dolsotful, it's perfect restorative fare.

DIRECTIONS

① If using kimchi, drain the kimchi in a fine-mesh strainer set over a small bowl, squeezing to remove as much liquid as possible. Roughly chop the kimchi and reserve the kimchi and juice separately.

② Heat the oil in a wok, stone dolsot, or saucepan over medium-high heat until shimmering. Add the scallions, garlic, and chopped kimchi (if using). Cook, stirring constantly, until fragrant, about 1 minute.

③ Add the kimchi juice (if using), gochujang, and soy sauce. Cook until the vegetables are well coated in an even layer of sauce. Add the gochugaru and dashi. Bring to a simmer and cook until the daikon is tender, about 15 minutes.

④ Add the tofu and scallion greens, stir gently, and heat until boiling. Season to taste with more gochugaru or soy sauce if desired. Break the eggs directly into the simmering broth. You can stir the egg in to make a richer soup or let them loosely poach in the broth, carefully doling out one poached egg per serving.

SPICY KOREAN RICE CAKE STEW (GUNGMUL TTEOKBOKKI) WITH KIMCHI

Yield
Serves 4

Active Time
15 minutes

Total Time
30 minutes

This is the brothier version of Gireum Tteokbokki (page 212) and one of the simplest, most comforting Korean staples. You don't need to add kimchi or pork belly to it, but I like the extra flavor and texture they bring. Rendering out some lard from the pork belly before adding the remaining ingredients to the wok gives the sauce a rich, porky flavor that goes well with the heat and sweetness of gochujang, as well as giving the sauce a gorgeous sheen. To take it over the top, this dish is wonderful with a poached, fried, or soft-boiled egg on top of each portion.

NOTES

Hondashi is powdered dashi that can be found at any Japanese market and most well-stocked supermarkets. While stick-shaped rice cakes are more traditional for this dish, either stick or disk-shaped rice cakes will work. If frozen, defrost the rice cakes in a bowl of cold water and drain just before adding to the broth in step 1. This dish also makes a good party snack when served in a preheated heavy bowl (to retain heat) or a slow cooker next to a cup full of toothpicks.

INGREDIENTS

1 tablespoon (15 ml) peanut, rice bran, or other neutral oil

4 ounces (120 g) fresh pork belly or bacon, sliced ⅛ inch thick and cut into squares (optional)

4 ounces (120 g) kimchi, cut into 1-inch pieces, plus a couple tablespoons (30 ml) kimchi juice from the jar

2 teaspoons (5 g) minced garlic (about 2 medium cloves)

2 cups (475 ml) homemade dashi (pages 519–21) or the equivalent in Hondashi (see Notes)

1 pound (450 g) Korean or Chinese rice cakes (see Notes)

3 tablespoons (45 ml) gochujang

1 tablespoon (5 g) gochugaru (Korean chile flakes)

1 tablespoon (12 g) sugar, plus more to taste

2 teaspoons (10 ml) light soy sauce, plus more to taste

4 to 5 scallions, cut into 2-inch pieces

Freshly ground black pepper

DIRECTIONS

(1) Heat the oil in a wok over medium-high heat until shimmering. Add the pork belly, if using, and cook, stirring, until well rendered and crisped, about 4 minutes. Add the kimchi and kimchi juice and cook until the liquid is dried up and the kimchi is lightly browned around the edges, about 3 minutes. Add the garlic and stir-fry until fragrant, about 30 seconds. Add the dashi, rice cakes, gochujang, gochugaru, sugar, and soy sauce. Adjust the heat to keep it at a brisk simmer until the rice cakes are fully tender, about 10 minutes.

(2) Add the scallions and continue cooking until the stew is reduced to a rich, saucy texture, 2 to 5 minutes longer. Season with black pepper and more sugar or soy sauce to taste. Transfer to a serving bowl and serve immediately.

KOREAN RICE CAKE CURRY STEW

Yield
Serves 4

Active Time
10 minutes

Total Time
25 minutes

NOTES

If using frozen rice cakes, defrost them in a bowl of cold water and drain just before adding them to the broth in step 1. Korean curry powder is a mild curry powder that also contains wheat flour. If you don't have it, you can use 2 tablespoons (15 g) of Japanese-style curry powder (such as S&B Oriental Curry Powder, or your favorite premixed or homemade curry powder) mixed with 1 tablespoon (8 g) of all-purpose flour.

INGREDIENTS

1 tablespoon (15 ml) peanut, rice bran, or
    other neutral oil
1 small onion, cut into ¼-inch slices
1 medium carrot, peeled and diced
2 teaspoons (5 g) minced garlic (about 2
    medium cloves)
2 teaspoons (5 g) minced fresh ginger
    (about ½-inch segment)
3 tablespoons (25 g) Korean curry powder,
    such as Ottogi (see Notes)
3 cups (700 ml) water or dashi
12 ounces (340 g) rice cakes
1 tablespoon (12 g) sugar
2 teaspoons (10 ml) light soy sauce
Freshly ground black pepper

This variation of Korean stewed rice cakes uses a curry-flavored base with the addition of onions and carrots. If you'd like, you can also add bite-sized chunks of chicken or thinly sliced beef or pork.

DIRECTIONS

Heat the oil in a wok over medium-high heat until shimmering. Add the onion and carrot and cook, stirring, until the onion is just starting to brown, about 4 minutes. Add the garlic and ginger and cook until fragrant, about 30 seconds. Add the curry powder and stir until everything in the wok is coated in a layer of curry paste and oil, about 30 seconds. Add the water or dashi, rice cakes, sugar, and soy sauce. Adjust the heat to keep it at a brisk simmer until the rice cakes and vegetables are fully tender and the sauce has thickened into a rich gravy, 10 to 15 minutes. Season with pepper to taste and serve immediately.

Stock-Based Soups and Stews

EVERYDAY CHICKEN AND GINGER STOCK

Yield
Makes about 2 quarts

Active Time
10 minutes

Total Time
1 hour and 45 minutes, plus time to cool

NOTES

When making chicken stock, make sure that the bulk of your chicken is made up of carcasses, wings, and/or leg bones with some meat and connective tissue still attached. If including breast meat, make sure to fish it out and remove the meat as soon as it is done cooking, then return the bones to the wok or pot to continue (breast meat becomes dry and stringy if overcooked).

As with all stocks, this one freezes and defrosts very well, especially if you freeze it flat in quart- or gallon-size zipper-lock bags and use an aluminum baking sheet for faster defrosting (see page 399 for how to freeze things flat and thaw food rapidly). You can also freeze it in ice-cube trays, pop the frozen stock cubes out, then store them in a zipper-lock freezer bag. Each cube is about an ounce of stock and defrosts quickly on the countertop (or even faster in the microwave).

INGREDIENTS

3 to 4 pounds (1.5 to 1.8 kg) chicken parts (see Notes)
2 ounces (60 g) fresh ginger (about six ½-inch-thick slices)
6 whole scallions, roughly chopped
1 teaspoon white peppercorns

This simple stock is the ideal stock to have on hand as the base for a huge range of recipes. Add leftover chicken meat and vegetables to it for a quick and easy chicken soup (noodles or rice can bulk it up). Use it any time a stir-fry recipe calls for chicken stock. Season it with salt and white pepper (and MSG if you like) and sip it from a cup as a soothing broth.

As with Western-style stocks, the more connective tissue and skin your chicken has on it, the more gelatin you'll extract and the richer your stock will be. Meanwhile, the more meat you leave on the bones, the more flavor your stock will have. Oftentimes what I'll do is buy a whole chicken, remove the breast meat for stir-fries, then save the carcass, wings, and legs for broth. After the broth is made, you can pick the meat off the legs to use for soups or salads.

When making more complex stocks, such as the Superior Stock I use for wonton soup (page 549), you can start with this base stock and simply boost its flavor with the added aromatics and other base ingredients.

DIRECTIONS

(1) Combine all the ingredients in a wok, large saucepan, or stockpot. Add enough cold water to barely cover everything. Bring to a simmer over high heat, then adjust the heat to maintain a bare simmer. Cook, skimming scum off the surface occasionally, gently moving the pot contents around to make sure any bits sticking above the top of the water get submerged, and topping up with water if necessary, for 1½ hours total. (If you have any breast meat in there, take it out after 20 minutes of simmering, pick it off the bone and reserve for salads or soups, and return the bones to the stock to continue cooking.)

(2) Strain the stock through a fine-mesh strainer. Pick the meat off any thighs or drumsticks you used and reserve for salads or soups and discard the remaining solids. Allow the stock to cool to room temperature, then transfer it to sealed containers and store in the fridge for up to a week or in the freezer indefinitely (see Notes).

ADD GINGER AND RICE CAKES FOR THE BEST CHICKEN "NOODLE" SOUP

This simple chicken soup is inspired in part by a bowl of *samgyetang* that I had in Seoul on a dreary December day back in 2012 with my wife, Adri, and my mother, Keiko. Although the classic Korean soup—made by stuffing a whole young chicken with rice, simmering it in a broth flavored with garlic, ginseng, and jujubes, and finishing it with a boatload of scallions—is customarily eaten warm on the hottest days of the summer, on that day it seemed to have been custom-made for warming us up from the wet snow and wind outside.

For a Colombian to not love soup would be like a Boston native forgetting what happened on October 27, 2004, or a *Star Wars* fan forgetting that Han Shot First. Even though Adri has been a naturalized U.S. citizen since 2013, I'm pretty sure that there are Colombian bylaws that require her to love soup even after she's sworn her allegiance to another country. I'm not sure what the consequences would be if I failed to provide her with an adequate supply, but I'm not really willing to find out. Over the years I've adapted that soup to a simpler version that's easier to make and easier to eat (and no less warming).

My soup starts with the same whole chicken, but rather than cooking it whole, I hack it into smaller pieces, which allows flavor to be extracted from it more easily. As the pieces finish cooking, I fish them out of the broth and shred the meat, which makes the whole thing easier to eat at the table. I also decided to make the switch from tough-to-find and expensive ginseng root to regular old ginger. I sometimes add leftover rice to the soup, but I prefer using the Korean rice cakes called *tteok*. I love how they plump up in the soothing broth.

Napa cabbage is wonderful simmered in a gingery chicken broth, and thinly sliced onion, scallions, and Chinese yellow chives (you can use regular chives or omit them with no issue), along with some quick-pickled chiles with garlic (page 84) round it all out.

Why so many alliums? I think it's because as a kid, when I had a sore throat, my mother would wrap up a bunch of scallions in a bandana, tie it around my neck, and tell me to lie down without moving. I'm not sure if she really believed this would help or if she was applying some sort of positive punishment to discourage me from my habit of faking colds to get out of school.

Point is, I have no idea if onions are good at curing colds, and a quick internet search reveals that the idea is mostly supported by naturopaths, which automatically makes me dubious. What I do know is that thanks to Pavlovian conditioning, every time cold season comes around, I crave scallions and all of their ilk.

The finished soup is intensely aromatic, warm, soothing, and easy to eat. And most importantly, Adri loves it, which, oddly enough, makes scallions, chives, and garlic key ingredients not just in my soup but in our matrimonial harmony.

CHICKEN AND GINGER SOUP WITH RICE CAKES

Yield
Serves 4
to 6

Active Time
30 minutes

Total Time
1½ hours

NOTES

See page 52 for step-by-step instructions on how to break down a whole chicken for simmering or poaching. You can use Everyday Chicken and Ginger Stock (page 542) and the picked meat from a rotisserie chicken or leftover roast chicken or poached chicken instead of the broth and chicken from step 1 of this recipe. You can omit the yellow or Chinese chives if you can't find them, or replace them with any other tender allium, such as garlic scapes or regular chives.

I like rice cakes in this soup, but you could also add rice stick noodles, udon noodles, or cooked rice. Store-bought pickled Thai bird chiles will work for this, but so will any tangy pickled or preserved chile product, such as sambal oelek or even sriracha. Omit the chiles if you don't want it hot.

INGREDIENTS

For the Broth (see Notes):

1 whole 4-pound (1.8 kg) chicken, cut into pieces for simmering or poaching (see page 52)

2 ounces (60 g) fresh ginger (about six ½-inch slices)

4 medium garlic cloves (10 to 15 g), smashed

1 small yellow onion, roughly chopped (about 5 ounces/150 g)

3 scallions, roughly chopped (about 2 ounces/60 g)

2 teaspoons (8 g) white peppercorns

To Serve:

Kosher salt

4 cups roughly chopped Napa cabbage (about 8 ounces/225 g)

6 ounces (170 g) Korean or Chinese rice cakes (tteok or nian gao; see Notes)

1 ounce (30 g) peeled fresh ginger, cut into very fine matchsticks

2 ounces (60 g) Chinese yellow chives or garlic chives, cut into 2-inch pieces (see Notes)

½ ounce (15 g) roughly chopped fresh cilantro leaves and fine stems (about ¼ cup)

2 scallions, thinly sliced

Store-bought or homemade pickled chiles (page 84; see Notes)

DIRECTIONS

(1) **For the Broth:** Place the chicken, ginger, garlic, onion, scallions, and peppercorns in a wok or large pot. Cover with cold water by 2 inches. Bring to a boil over high heat, reduce to a simmer, and cook, skimming scum and fat from the surface regularly, until the chicken breast pieces are cooked through, about 20 minutes. Transfer the breast pieces to a small bowl, cover, and set aside. Continue cooking the broth until the leg pieces are fall-apart tender, about 1 hour longer. Remove the leg pieces and add to the bowl with the breasts. Strain the broth through a fine-mesh strainer, discard the solids, and return the broth to the wok (you should have about 2 quarts/2 l of broth).

(2) **To Serve:** Season the broth with salt to taste. Add the cabbage and rice cakes. Bring to a simmer and cook, stirring occasionally, until the rice cakes are cooked through, about 8 minutes. When the chicken is cool enough to handle, roughly shred the meat with your fingers, discard the bones, return the meat to the pot, and bring to a gentle simmer. Stir in the sliced ginger, chives, cilantro, and sliced scallions. Ladle into a warmed serving bowl and serve immediately, passing pickled chiles at the table.

EGG DROP SOUP

Yield
Serves 4

Active Time
15 minutes

Total Time
30 minutes

NOTE
If you don't have any Everyday Chicken and Ginger Stock on hand, start with 1½ quarts (1.5 l) of store-bought low-sodium chicken stock and simmer it for 15 minutes with 4 scallions, a few slices of ginger, a teaspoon of white peppercorns, and, optionally, a ham bone before straining it and proceeding as directed.

INGREDIENTS

1½ quarts (1.5 l) Everyday Chicken and Ginger Stock (page 542; see Note)
4 tablespoons (30 g) plus 1 teaspoon (2.5 g) cornstarch
Kosher salt and freshly ground white pepper
4 large eggs
2 scallions, chopped

For the longest time I really disliked egg drop soup, and it's because I'd only ever had it from the Chinese buffets where it'd been sitting out all day on a steam table, slowly reducing into a viscous, mucus-like neon-yellow glop with rubbery bits of overcooked egg floating in it, along with the occasional odd sliced button mushroom.

The best egg drop soup, on the other hand, should have a clear, ever-so-slightly thickened broth with the intense flavor of chicken and egg, with the aromas of ginger, scallion, and white pepper. The eggs should form tender, silken curds, some large, some small, offering texture, sure, but predominantly flavor and richness to an otherwise extremely simple soup.

How do you get there? Well, two simple steps, and the first we've already accomplished: making a flavorful broth. The Everyday Chicken and Ginger Stock is perfect for this soup, though if you want a little more flavor, you could add a ham bone along with the chicken carcass to boost its meaty flavor and add a hint of smokiness.

The second step is adding the eggs. The egg flower, as it's referred to in Chinese, is really simple to do. The key is to swirl the soup in a lazy vortex while slowly drizzling in the eggs, which are scrambled with a bit of cornstarch (the starch impedes protein connections, preventing the eggs from getting rubbery).

The best way to drizzle in the egg is to hold either two chopsticks or a fork across the top of a small bowl and drizzle the egg slowly through the tines. It's essential that the soup be hot, but not boiling, as you do this. You want the egg to set into relatively large curds that you can then break up to the desired size by stirring more or less vigorously after you drizzle it.

DIRECTIONS

(1) Bring the chicken stock to a bare simmer in a wok or saucepan. Combine 4 tablespoons (30 g) of the cornstarch with 4 tablespoons (60 ml) water in a small bowl and mix with a fork until homogenous. Whisk into the broth and bring to a simmer. Reduce the heat to low. Season with salt and white pepper to taste.

(2) Whisk together the eggs, a pinch of salt, and the remaining teaspoon (2.5 g) cornstarch in a small bowl until homogenous. Swirl the soup once with a large spoon or ladle, then, holding a pair of chopsticks or the tines of a fork on the edge of the bowl, slowly drizzle the egg mixture into the soup, shaking the fork or chopsticks back and forth rapidly to flick the egg mixture as it drizzles. Allow the soup to sit for 15 seconds, then stir gently to break up the egg to the desired size. Sprinkle with scallions and serve.

HOT AND SOUR SOUP

Hot and sour soup and I have the kind of relationship that they make movies about. Movies of the kind Adri enjoys watching on plane rides, with fine, soft-spoken British actors and plots that chronicle tender, tragic relationships.

We first met in the flesh at a roadside Chinese restaurant in New Jersey when I was six years old. Sure, I'd caught glimpses of it in the past, inhaled its heady aroma as it was whisked by on the arm of a waiter. It had a previous engagement with the charlatan at table 12, see, but I was intoxicated by its delicate spicy perfume nonetheless. I'd been working up the courage for years to ask for it, afraid that, if I turned my back on the precious wonton soup that I'd loved since before I could remember, I'd risk losing both of them and I'd be stuck like a sucker sipping on egg drop forever.

I must say: it wasn't love at first sip. Slick and thick with cornstarch, the stuff I was served was tasty, but the pungent vinegar and white pepper hit took getting used to for a six-year-old. There was a period when I was around eight years old when my parents made the version in the *Joyce Chen Cook Book* once a month or so. I distinctly remember picking the hard nubs off the soaked wood ear mushrooms that went into it, and the debates we had over whether the herb—not commonly found in New York supermarkets in the 1980s—was called "cilantro" or "coriander."

Since then, my love for it has only grown. The dish is popular in both Beijing (where it's made with white pepper and black vinegar) and Sichuan (where it gets its heat from dried chiles), and I've had excellent renditions in both, but really, the version I love most is the one you find at old-school New York Cantonese restaurants. The kind that's dark and vinegary, packed with white pepper, thickened to a mouth-coating texture with cornstarch, with strips of firm tofu, pork, daylily buds, wood ear mushrooms, and drizzled with eggs. The advantage of making it at home is that while usually the soup you get at those restaurants has been sitting in a warming tray all afternoon, when it's homemade, it stays *fresh*.

In the past, I've eschewed the stir-frying step that some recipes (such as Fuchsia Dunlop's) recommend for developing flavor before adding the broth. I've more recently come around to it, as it's relatively easy and is especially useful if you like extra mushrooms in your hot and sour soup (which I do!).

Thickening with cornstarch is, by the way, not without controversy. In some Chinese traditions, hot and sour soup is thickened (with blood from either a chicken or a pig). In others, it's served thin. I like what I grew up with, however, so I add the cornstarch.

The real key: add in that pepper and vinegar right before serving. They lose aroma fast. In fact, for good measure, it's a wise idea to have a bit at the table so your guests can season their bowls as desired. That fresh white pepper and vinegar hit? That's the difference between the hot and sour soup that's good enough to keep you satisfied in your own company at home and the hot and sour soup that's so good you absolutely must take it home to meet the parents.

It's the hot and sour soup I fell in love with, but I'm not so selfish I wouldn't share it with you all.

Yield	Active Time
Serves 6	30 minutes
	Total Time
	1 hour and 45 minutes

NOTES

If you don't have any Everyday Chicken and Ginger Stock on hand, start with 1½ quarts (1.5 l) of store-bought low-sodium chicken stock and simmer it for 15 minutes with 4 scallions, a few slices of ginger, a teaspoon of white peppercorns, and, optionally, a ham bone before straining it and proceeding as directed. Wood ear mushroom is also sold as "black fungus" and can be found at Asian markets or online, along with dried daylilies. Chinkiang vinegar is also sold as Zhenjiang vinegar in Asian markets. If unavailable, substitute black vinegar or balsamic vinegar.

INGREDIENTS

The Dry Ingredients (see Notes):

¼ cup (¼ ounce/8 g) dried Chinese wood ear mushrooms
¼ cup (¼ ounce/8 g) dried daylily buds

For the Stir-Fry:

1 tablespoon (15 ml) peanut, rice bran, or other neutral oil
4 ounces (120 g) fresh mushrooms, such as thinly sliced shiitake or button or whole trimmed beech mushrooms
6 ounces (170 g) trimmed boneless pork shoulder or loin, cut into 2-inch-long slivers (optional)
2 tablespoons (30 ml) Shaoxing wine

To Finish:

1½ quarts (1.5 l) Everyday Chicken and Ginger Stock (page 542; see Notes)
6 ounces extra-firm tofu, cut into thin matchsticks
4 tablespoons (30 g) plus 1 teaspoon (2.5 g) cornstarch
2 large eggs

To Serve:

Kosher salt
1½ teaspoons (5 g) freshly ground white pepper, plus more to taste
¼ cup (60 ml) Chinkiang or black vinegar, plus more to taste (see Notes)
1 teaspoon (5 ml) roasted sesame oil, plus more to taste
2 scallions, chopped
Small handful of roughly chopped fresh cilantro leaves and fine stems

DIRECTIONS

1 **Rehydrate the Dried Ingredients:** Place the wood ears and daylily buds in a large bowl or measuring cup large enough for them to expand about fourfold. Cover with very hot water and set aside until rehydrated, about 15 minutes. Drain thoroughly. Remove the tough centers from the wood ears, then thinly slice them. Cut the daylilies into 2-inch pieces.

2 **For the Stir-Fry:** Heat a wok over high heat until lightly smoking. Add the oil and swirl to coat. Add the fresh mushrooms and stir-fry until lightly browned around the edges, 2 to 3 minutes. Add the pork (if using) and continue to stir-fry until no longer pink, about 1 minute. Add the wood ears and daylily bulbs and stir-fry briefly to drive off excess moisture. Add the wine by pouring it around the edges of the wok and toss to combine.

3 **To Finish:** Add the stock and tofu and bring to a simmer. Combine 4 tablespoons (30 g) of the cornstarch with 4 tablespoons (60 ml) water in a small bowl and mix with a fork until homogenous. Drizzle into the broth and return to a bare simmer. The broth should thicken.

4 Whisk together the eggs, a pinch of salt, and the remaining teaspoon (2.5 g) of cornstarch in a small bowl until homogenous. Swirl the soup once with a large spoon or ladle, then, holding a pair of chopsticks or the tines of a fork on the edge of the bowl, slowly drizzle the egg mixture into the soup, shaking the fork or chopsticks back and forth rapidly to flick the egg mixture as it drizzles. Allow the soup to sit for 15 seconds, then stir gently to break up the egg to the desired size.

5 **To Serve:** Just before serving, season with salt to taste and stir in the white pepper and vinegar. Drizzle with the sesame oil and sprinkle with the scallions and cilantro. Serve immediately, passing more white pepper, vinegar, and sesame oil at the table to adjust to taste.

THE INGREDIENTS OF SUPERIOR STOCK

Superior stock (also known as "supreme stock") is a Chinese stock that combines chicken, pork, and dried shellfish for a complex aroma and flavor that comes from the way various amino acids and peptides extracted from meat and shellfish interact synergistically, for the ultimate in umami. According to Eileen Yin-Fei Lo, author of *Mastering the Art of Chinese Cooking*, it was developed by restaurant chefs in Guangzhou, where it is known as *seung tong* ("best soup"). This stock forms the backbone of my favorite style of wonton soup, which happens to be one of my favorite soups in the world. It's overkill to use this stock for things like stir-fries or soups with many other strongly flavored ingredients, but in brothy, stock-forward soups, it has unparalleled depth.

There are countless recipes for superior stock, and you can always feel free to experiment with using ingredients like dried scallops and shrimp, Jinhua ham versus fresh pork, aromatics like dried tangerine and dried longans, and anything else that strikes your fancy. So long as you have a combination of meaty bits and oceany bits, it's hard to go wrong.

Here are my usual ingredients:

Chicken Carcasses. Chicken carcasses are inexpensive and provide a modest amount of body and a neutral flavor that can enhance other flavors without overwhelming them.

Pork Bones. I've tried using various cuts, including pork necks and leg bones, but I generally go with trotters, which pack a huge amount of connective tissue that gets converted into gelatin, giving the stock a rich

texture. Because pork trotters typically contain a lot of marrow that can add impurities that will cloud your stock, it's important to first blanch them by covering them with water and bringing it to a boil, then drain and scrub them under running water. You can then start the broth with fresh water.

Jinhua Ham. This is a salted ham from Jinhua province that's been produced since at least the tenth century and is quite similar unsmoked to American-style country hams or unsmoked European hams like prosciutto or Serrano. This is good news if you don't live near a Chinese market that sells it. Unlike its European and American cousins, Jinhua ham is used primarily for flavoring soups and stews, not for eating plain. I learned the hard way that, like country ham, Jinhua ham *must* be blanched before cooking, or your broth will end up unbearably salty. You can blanch the ham right along with the pork trotters. If you can't find either of these, prosciutto or pancetta ends or even a hunk of bacon or salt pork will do the job.

Dried Seafood. Dried scallops, shrimp, or flounder will enhance the umami flavor of meat and cured pork products. In my testing, I found that dried scallops are the best for adding umami without an overpowering seafood aroma, but they're also the most expensive dried seafood and relatively difficult to find. Usually I add sea-based umami in the form of kombu (which I always have on hand), some dried shrimp, and in dishes where I'm going to include fresh shrimp, the fresh shrimp shells.

Aromatics. Ginger and scallions are the basics. I also like to use a few leaves of Napa cabbage (a flavor I consider essential for wonton soup in particular). Many recipes for superior stock also contain ingredients like dried mushrooms (to enhance umami), tangerine peel, or dried longans (for a citrusy or sweet aroma).

SUPERIOR STOCK

Yield
Makes about 2 quarts

Active Time
15 minutes

Total Time
3½ hours

NOTES

Kombu is giant sea kelp. It can be found at most Asian grocers. Yellow chives can be found at Chinese grocers. Dried shrimp or stockfish (dried flounder) can be found at Chinese or other Asian supermarkets. You can omit them. If cooking a recipe that includes shrimp, save the shrimp shells and add them to the stock during simmering.

As with all stocks, this one freezes and defrosts very well, especially if you freeze it flat in quart- or gallon-size zipper-lock bags and use an aluminum baking sheet for faster defrosting (see page 399 for how to freeze things flat and thaw food rapidly). You can also freeze it in ice-cube trays, pop the frozen stock cubes out, then store them in a zipper-lock freezer bag. Each cube is about an ounce of stock and defrosts quickly on the countertop (or even faster in the microwave).

This stock is essential for the very best wonton soup. It has an intensely savory flavor that is suitable for any number of brothy soups.

INGREDIENTS

2 pounds (900 g) chicken backs, wing tips, and/or bones, roughly chopped with a cleaver

1½ pounds (680 g) pig's trotters, split or sliced

3 ounces (90 g) Chinese Jinhua ham, American country ham, or prosciutto or Serrano scraps

½ ounce (15 g) kombu (approximate 4- by 6-inch piece; see Notes)

1 ounce (30 g) dried shrimp or stockfish (optional; see Notes)

4 scallions, roughly chopped

One 4-inch knob (about 1½ ounces/45 g) fresh ginger, sliced

4 Napa cabbage leaves

DIRECTIONS

(1) Combine the chicken, pork trotters, and ham in a large wok or stockpot and cover with water. Bring to a boil over high heat. Boil for 10 minutes, then dump the contents into a colander in the sink and let the liquid drain. Clean the bones and meat under cold running water, rubbing off any scum or blood clots that may appear and using a skewer or chopsticks to clean out any bits of soft coagulated material stuck in crevices in the bones.

(2) Return the washed bones and ham to the stockpot or wok. Add the kombu, dried shrimp or stockfish (if using), scallions, ginger, and cabbage leaves. Bring to a boil over high heat, reduce to a bare simmer, and cook, uncovered, until the broth is deeply flavorful, about 3 hours.

(3) Using tongs, discard the bones from broth. Strain through a fine-mesh strainer into a large saucepan. Defat the broth with a ladle if using the same day (alternatively, cool and refrigerate the stock overnight and skim the solid fat off the top the next day). Allow the stock to cool to room temperature, then transfer it to sealed containers and store in the fridge for up to a week or in the freezer indefinitely (see Notes).

FOR CLARITY'S SAKE: The Importance of Blanching and Scrubbing Large Cut Bones

Oftentimes, stock recipes that include ingredients like pork trotters or large cut beef or veal bones will recommend blanching and scrubbing the bones before making your stock. When working on my wonton soup recipe, I noticed that my finished broths were brown and very cloudy if I skipped this step. This is due to the clotted blood, proteins, and other impurities that are leached out of cut bones during the first few minutes of the simmering process. Blanching the bones briefly in boiling water, then dumping the water, scrubbing the bones, and starting with fresh water will give you a clearer broth with a cleaner flavor.

Don't believe me? Here's what you're trying to get rid of:

Not pretty, right?

The easiest way to do it is to cover your bones with water, bring them to a simmer, then dump everything directly into a large colander in the sink. Then rub the bones all over under cold running water, using your fingertips or a chopstick to get out all of the bits of gunk that are caught in their crevices.*

When you add the fresh water and bring it up to a simmer again, the only stuff that floats to the surface is fat and a small amount of clean, white flotsam. Some folks like to go a step further and meticulously skim away this fat and scum, but I've found that so long as you get rid of the gunky stuff that coagulates within the first fifteen minutes or so, you actually end up with better flavor if you don't skim your broth until after straining it.

---

* It's actually strangely satisfying, like those Dr. Pimple Popper videos on YouTube.

ZHA CAI ROUSI MIÀN (SICHUAN PORK AND PICKLE SOUP)

Yield
Serves 4
to 6

Active Time
15 minutes

Total Time
30 minutes

NOTES

You can use extra-firm tofu in place of pork or chicken (omit the washing step in step 1 and gently toss with the marinade instead of roughly massaging). Zha cai is spicy pickled mustard stem. It is similar to its cousin (pickled mustard leaves) but with a more pungent, radish-like aroma. You can find it either whole in the refrigerated section of a Chinese supermarket, in cans, or slivered in cans, jars, and pouches. If you can't find it, you can use sauerkraut or kimchi in this soup for something that, while different, is nonetheless delicious. This soup is great with or without the noodles added.

This is a simple but classic Sichuan soup made with pickled mustard stem (zha cai), slivered pork, and noodles. The combination of pork, pickled crunchy vegetables, and a starchy supporting actor reminds me an awful lot of *kapustnyak*, the Ukrainian soup of sauerkraut, pork, and potatoes. So much so that on the rare occasion that I don't have zha cai on hand, I find that sauerkraut is the most natural substitute for it.

You can use store-bought chicken broth or Everyday Chicken and Ginger Stock (page 542) for it. Using Superior Stock is definitely not traditional and may feel like overkill, but man is it tasty. Use whatever stock you have on hand; the rest of the dish is very straightforward.

INGREDIENTS

For the Pork:

6 ounces (170 g) pork loin, pork sirloin, or chicken breast, cut into thin slivers (see Notes)

1 teaspoon (5 ml) Shaoxing wine or dry sherry

1 teaspoon (5 ml) light soy sauce or shoyu

¼ teaspoon (0.5 g) freshly ground white pepper

Kosher salt

Pinch of MSG (optional)

1 teaspoon (3 g) cornstarch

For the Soup:

Kosher salt

1 tablespoon (15 ml) peanut, rice bran, or other neutral oil

6 ounces zha cai, thinly slivered into sizes similar to the pork (see Notes)

1½ quarts (1.5 l) Superior Stock (page 549), Everyday Chicken and Ginger Stock (page 542), or store-bought low-sodium chicken stock simmered for 10 minutes with a few slices of ginger and roughly chopped scallions

8 ounces (225 g) bok choy, baby bok choy, Chinese broccoli (gai lan), or Napa cabbage, cut into bite-sized pieces

Freshly ground white pepper

8 ounces (225 g) fresh wheat noodles

3 scallions, sliced

recipe continues

DIRECTIONS

(1) **For the Pork, Chicken, or Tofu:** Place the pork or chicken in a medium bowl, cover with cold water, and vigorously agitate it. Drain through a fine-mesh strainer set in the sink and press on the pork with your hands to remove excess water. Return the pork to the bowl. Add the wine, soy sauce, white pepper, a pinch of salt, the MSG (if using), and the cornstarch. Roughly work the marinade into the meat for at least 30 seconds. Set aside to marinate for at least 15 minutes and up to overnight.

(2) **For the Soup:** Bring a pot of salted water to a boil over high heat. Meanwhile, heat a wok over high heat until lightly smoking. Add the oil and swirl to coat. Add the pork and stir-fry until no longer pink and lightly browned around the edges, about 2 minutes. Add the zha cai and stir-fry for 1 minute. Add the stock and bok choy. Bring to a simmer and season to taste with salt and white pepper.

(3) When the pot of water is boiling, cook the noodles according to the package directions. Divide the noodles between bowls. Divide the broth, pork, pickles, and bok choy between the bowls. Sprinkle with scallions and serve immediately.

THE BEST WONTON SOUP

A few years back, I made it my mission to try every bowl of wonton soup worth trying in New York City (a pretty tall task) and found that when done right wonton soup need not be the cheap appetizer of choice but a worthy dish unto itself. There are the Chinese American roast pork broth versions with thick-skinned wontons sold at barbecue shops, or the kind with large pork- and bok choy-filled wontons served floating in chicken soup with noodles at the Shanghai restaurants. At the city's handful of Fuzhou restaurants you can get broth filled with dozens of wispy, comet-shaped wontons that look like Pac-Man ghosts, with bits of pickle and dried shrimp.

But my favorite version is the rich shrimp and pork version served in Hong Kong. The broth is made with Superior Stock, flavored with pork (and often chicken), dried ham, and dried seafood (typically dried flounder and shrimp roe). The wontons are stuffed fuller than most, folded into little round parcels, filled with juicy pork and shrimp that pop out as you bite through the thin, thin wrappers, the shrimp crunching under your teeth as you chew.

This is the version of wonton soup that I crave, and this is the version that, once you have Superior Stock under your belt, is a simple matter of making the wontons and putting it all together.

THE WONTON FILLING

The filling for Hong Kong–style wontons is generally made with lightly seasoned pork flavored with ginger, yellow chives, soy sauce, and sesame oil, along with some form of shrimp. In the simplest version the shrimp is ground up right along with the pork, but I personally prefer the version in which the shrimp are left intact, each wonton being stuffed with a single plump, crunchy shrimp. You get this by soaking the shrimp in an alkaline brine before adding them to the wontons (see page 143 for more on how alkaline brines make shrimp plump).

For the wrappers, I use store-bought skins (the square kind, not the round dumpling variety) of the thinnest gauge I can find. If you have an option between plain wheat flour wrappers and those that are enhanced with egg yolk, go with the latter, as they stand up to boiling a little bit better, developing a nice chewiness as they cook. (Be aware that some brands of wonton wrappers offer both white and yellow varieties, the only difference being the inclusion of food coloring to simulate eggs.)

You can shape your wontons any way you wish. The easiest are the comet-shaped wontons where you place a wrapper on your hand, add a small dollop of filling and a shrimp, then squeeze it all shut. Almost equally simple is a triangle shape, in which you lay the wrapper flat on a board, add the filling, then fold the wrapper over. In either case, make sure to moisten the wrapper with a fingertip or brush of water before sealing to help it close up tight, and squeeze out as much air as possible before sealing in order to prevent them from blowing out as they simmer.

For a fancier "water caltrop" shape, follow the step-by-step instructions on page 555.

THE BEST WONTON SOUP

Yield
Serves 4
to 6

Active Time
30 minutes

Total Time
40 minutes, plus
time to make the
broth if you don't
have it already

This Hong Kong–style wonton soup has plump pork and shrimp dumplings in a pork- and seafood-based superior stock. If you'd like, add a handful of wonton noodles to each bowl as well.

NOTES

Both the broth and the wontons can be made ahead and frozen. To freeze the wontons, place them on a parchment-lined plate, cover them loosely with plastic wrap, then place them in the freezer until completely frozen, about 1 hour. Transfer them to a plastic bag. They can be cooked directly from frozen; just add 1 to 2 minutes to the cooking time.

Shrimp shells can be added to superior stock while it simmers. Yellow chives can be found at Chinese grocers. If unavailable, green chives or scallions can be used in their place.

INGREDIENTS

For the Wontons:

24 small shrimp, peeled (see Notes)
½ teaspoon (2 g) baking soda
Kosher salt
¼ cup (60 ml) water
12 ounces (340 g) ground pork
2 teaspoons (5 g) minced garlic (about 2 medium cloves)
2 teaspoons (5 g) minced fresh ginger (about ½-inch segment)
2 teaspoons (8 g) sugar
1 teaspoon (5 ml) soy sauce
2 teaspoons (10 ml) roasted sesame oil
1 ounce (30 g) fresh yellow chives, sliced (see Notes)
24 wonton wrappers, preferably the thin variety

To Finish:

2 quarts (2 l) Superior Stock (page 549)
8 Napa cabbage leaves (about 12 ounces/340 g), cut into bite-sized pieces
12 ounces (340 g) wonton noodles (optional)
3 scallions, thinly sliced

DIRECTIONS

(1) **For the Wontons:** Place the shrimp in a small bowl. Add the baking soda, 1 teaspoon (3 g) salt, and the water and mix with your fingers. Set aside for at least 15 minutes and up to 1 day in the refrigerator. Drain when ready to proceed.

(2) Meanwhile, combine the pork, garlic, ginger, sugar, soy sauce, sesame oil, half of the chives, and 1 teaspoon (3 g) salt in a medium bowl. Mix with your fingers until thoroughly combined. To test for seasoning, place a small amount on a microwave-safe plate and microwave on high power until cooked through, about 10 seconds. Taste for seasoning and add more salt as necessary.

(3) Fill the wontons, using 1 tablespoon (about 15 g) of filling and 1 shrimp per wrapper, following the instructions on page 555 to shape them.

(4) **To Finish:** Bring the stock to a boil. Add the wontons and cabbage and cook until the wontons are cooked through, about 3 minutes, adding wonton noodles during the last minute of cooking (if using). Stir in the remaining chives and scallions and remove from the heat. Allow to cool for 1 minute. Serve immediately.

HOW TO MAKE WONTONS

The classic shape for wontons is what Fuchsia Dunlop refers to as "water caltrops" in her amazing book *Every Grain of Rice* (order it now if you don't own it already!). It's made by forming a triangle and folding the two "arms" of the triangle across each other (*choushou*, the Sichuanese term for these wontons, translates as "folded arms").

To form the wontons, place a tablespoon or so of filling in the center of the wonton square.

Here's how it's done:

Step 1 • Place Your Wrapper

To stuff, hold a square wonton wrapper in your hand or leave it flat on your cutting board.

Step 2 • Place Your Filling

Add about a tablespoon of filling to the center of the wrapper (the less you use, the easier it'll be to stuff), then place a single shrimp on top of the filling (if using).

Step 3 • Moisten the Edges

Use your fingertip to add a thin layer of water all around the edges of the wrapper.

Step 4 • Pinch It Up

Pull two corners together and pinch them shut to form a triangle, then seal up the edges of the triangle, making sure to push out as much air as possible to prevent a blowout when you boil them later.

Step 5 • Make the Corners Meet

Moisten the folded corners, then pull them toward each other, making them meet and cross in the center.

The most common mistake I see is to fold the arms across the "belly" of the wonton so that you end up with something nearly cylindrical. Instead, the arms should be pulled downward away from the pointed end of the triangle. This plumps up the belly and creates a crescent shape that's much better suited to picking up sauce.

Step 6 • Ready to Cook

The finished wonton should be plump, like a little sphere wearing a cape.

Step 7 • Repeat

Repeat until you've made all your wontons. They can be frozen for future use by placing them on a parchment-lined plate in the freezer. Once fully frozen, they can be stored in a plastic zipper-lock bag. Wontons can be cooked directly from frozen.

SICHUAN-STYLE HOT AND SOUR WONTONS (SUANLA CHAOSHOU)

Yield
Makes about 40 wontons, serving 6 to 8 as an appetizer or light meal

Active Time
1 hour

Total Time
1 hour

INGREDIENTS

For the Wontons:

1 pound (450 g) ground pork shoulder

2 teaspoons (8 g) kosher salt, plus more if needed

1 tablespoon (12 g) sugar, plus more if needed

1 teaspoon (3 g) finely ground white pepper, plus more if needed

1½ ounces (20 g) minced scallions or Chinese chives (about 2 scallions)

2 teaspoons (5 g) minced garlic (about 2 medium cloves)

2 teaspoons (10 ml) Shaoxing wine or dry sherry

40 thin square wonton wrappers

For the Sauce:

1 recipe Hot and Sour Chile Sauce (page 558)

To Cook and Serve:

2 tablespoons (15 g) lightly crushed roasted peanuts or Fried Peanuts (optional; page 319)

Small handful of fresh cilantro leaves and fine stems, roughly chopped

Sweet and savory. Slippery and slick. Juicy and tender. Hot and sour. Garlicky. So. Freaking. Good.

These are all words that should enter your head as you slide back a bowl of *suanla chaoshou*, the Sichuan-style wontons that come coated in an intensely aromatic sauce made with vinegar, garlic, and chile oil.

I first tasted a version of the dish at Mary Chung's (which she called "Suan La Chow Show"), the longstanding Cambridge restaurant that was one of the early pioneers of Sichuan American cuisine. Her version came on a bed of bean sprouts with a moderately hot chile oil and a hint of vinegar. In the subsequent years I've tried the dish all over the United States and in Sichuan and have come to prefer a version with a bit more vinegar in the sauce and heat in the chile oil. Still, I have Mrs. Chung's success to thank for the wontons in chile oil, Chongqing-style hot and numbing chicken, and mapo tofu that were the mainstay of my diet for the decade that I lived in the area.*

Like many Asian dishes, suanla chaoshou is as much about textural contrast as it is about flavor. The wrappers should be slippery and tender, with a flavor that is almost bland compared with the sweet, mild pork filling (sweet but not cloying, as some versions tend to be). In turn, the wontons as a whole are also bland when compared with the sauce. It's the sauce that brings on the contrasts with its almost overly intense flavor, thanks to Chinkiang vinegar, soy sauce, and plenty of chile oil with crunchy bits of fried dried chiles and, if you're inclined, peanuts or sesame seeds.

For the wontons, I use a simple mix of ground fatty pork (ask your butcher to grind up some extra-fatty pork shoulder for you or look for the whitest, streakiest grind you can find in the supermarket display) flavored with Chinese chives or scallions, a little garlic, white pepper, salt, sugar, and a splash of Shaoxing wine or dry sherry.

---

*   I also have her to thank for the highlight of my very short career as a rock star: the band with whom I occasionally guest-performed played at the All-Asia Lounge in Central Square, a restaurant operated by Mary Chung's daughter and her husband. The band was called The Emoticons. Really.

DIRECTIONS

(1) **For the Wontons:** Combine the pork, salt, sugar, white pepper, scallions, garlic, and wine in a medium bowl and knead and turn with clean hands until the mixture is homogenous and starting to feel tacky/sticky, about 1 minute. Transfer about a teaspoon to a microwave-safe plate and microwave on high power until cooked through, about 10 seconds. Taste and adjust the seasoning with more salt, white pepper, and/or sugar if desired.

(2) Fill the wontons, using a scant tablespoon (about 12 g) of filling per skin and following the instructions on page 555 for shaping.

(3) **To Cook and Serve:** Bring a wok or large saucepan of water to a boil. Cook 15 to 20 wontons at a time until they are completely cooked through, about 4 minutes. Drain the wontons and transfer to a warm serving platter. Spoon the Hot and Sour Chile Sauce on top. Sprinkle with peanuts and minced cilantro and serve immediately. Repeat with the remaining wontons.

HOT AND SOUR CHILE SAUCE FOR WONTONS, NOODLES, OR DUMPLINGS

Yield
Makes about ½ cup (120 ml)

Active Time
5 minutes

Total Time
5 minutes

INGREDIENTS

¼ cup chile oil, homemade (page 310) or store-bought, with its sediment

1 tablespoon (15 ml) roasted sesame oil

3 tablespoons (45 ml) Chinkiang vinegar or a mixture of 2 tablespoons rice vinegar and 1 tablespoon balsamic vinegar

2 tablespoons (30 ml) soy sauce

1 tablespoon (12 g) sugar

1 tablespoon (8 g) minced garlic (about 3 medium cloves)

1 tablespoon (8 g) toasted sesame seeds

Hot and Sour Chile Sauce is the perfect companion to Suanla Chaoshou (page 556). Suanla literally translates to sour-hot, and this sauce is precisely that: a combination of vinegar and chile oil.

OK, it's a bit more complicated than that, but not by much. You can start with a high-quality store-bought chile oil (look for jars with lots of chile sediment packed in deep red oil at your local Asian market), but you'll get better flavor with homemade Sichuan Málà Chile Oil (page 310) or any homemade chile oil with sediment of your choice. The rest of the sauce is a snap: Chinkiang black vinegar and soy sauce are mixed with sugar until the sugar dissolves, then some garlic and sesame oil round out the flavor. Though not strictly traditional, I like to garnish mine with crushed peanuts for some crunch.

Like many Sichuan dishes, the sauce is quite oily—there should be a crimson streak of fiery chile oil on the surface of the sauce. As you drag your wontons up through it, it coats them in a red slick, their nooks and crannies picking up drops of vinegar and bits of crispy roasted chiles and peanuts.

This sauce, incidentally, can be used as the base for a number of other dishes. Adding sesame paste turns it into "Mysterious Flavor" sauce, the essential flavor profile of Bang Bang Chicken (page 568). I also like to use it as a dressing for simple blanched green vegetables and tofu, as in my Asparagus and Tofu Salad with Málà Chile Oil Vinaigrette (page 559).

DIRECTIONS

Combine the chile oil, sesame oil, vinegar, soy sauce, sugar, and garlic in a small bowl and stir until the sugar is dissolved. Set aside until ready to use. The sauce can be stored in a sealed container in the fridge for up to 2 weeks.

ASPARAGUS AND TOFU SALAD WITH MÁLÀ CHILE OIL VINAIGRETTE

Yield
Serves 4
to 6

Active Time
30 minutes

Total Time
30 minutes

INGREDIENTS

For the Sauce:
¼ cup chile oil, homemade (page 310) or store-bought, with its sediment

1 tablespoon (15 ml) roasted sesame oil

3 tablespoons (45 ml) Chinkiang vinegar or a mixture of 2 tablespoons (30 ml) rice vinegar and 1 tablespoon (15 ml) balsamic vinegar

2 tablespoons (30 ml) soy sauce

1 tablespoon (12 g) sugar

1 tablespoon (8 g) minced garlic (about 3 medium cloves)

1 tablespoon (8 g) toasted sesame seeds

For the Salad:
Kosher salt

1 pound (450 g) thin asparagus stalks, ends trimmed, cut into 2-inch pieces

10 ounces (280 g) extra-firm plain, smoked, or five-spice tofu, cut into 2-inch matchsticks

4 scallions, thinly sliced on a sharp bias

Asparagus isn't exactly a Chinese ingredient, but that doesn't mean that it can't find a comfortable home in Chinese food. I love it stir-fried with velvet chicken and lemon or in place of broccoli in classic Chinese American Beef with Broccoli (page 118). China has a food culture that makes use of every available ingredient. I've got no doubt that, if asparagus were to grow in the cool, misty mountains near Chengdu, we'd see it served as a cold green appetizer or side dish on menus in Sichuan.

At least that's how I'd serve it. This recipe—cold and crunchy asparagus tossed with firm tofu in a fiery sweet-hot-sour vinaigrette—is inspired by the cold or warm appetizers you find in Sichuan that make use of chile oil, Sichuan peppercorns, and vinegar. In fact, the sauce itself is exactly identical to the one I use for the preceding recipe, Sichuan-Style Hot and Sour Wontons (Suanla Chaoshou). I really like the way the tofu and the tiny budding tips of asparagus soak up the sauce and the way the textures of the meaty tofu and tender-crisp asparagus play off each other.

Are you going to find this dish on any Chinese restaurant menu? Probably not. But a single bite will transport you straight to those fog-covered hills in Sichuan, and that's a big enough win for me.

DIRECTIONS

1 **For the Sauce:** Combine the chile oil, sesame oil, vinegar, soy sauce, sugar, and garlic in a small bowl and stir until the sugar is dissolved. Set aside until ready to use. (The sauce can be stored in a sealed container in the fridge for up to 2 weeks.)

2 **For the Salad:** Bring a large pot of salted water to a boil over high heat. Add the asparagus and cook, stirring occasionally, until the asparagus is bright green with a tender snap, about 1 minute. Drain in a colander and rinse under cold running water until completely cooled. Transfer to a rimmed baking sheet lined with a clean kitchen towel or a double layer of paper towels and shake to dry thoroughly.

3 Combine the asparagus, tofu, and scallions in a large bowl. Stir the dressing and add to taste, tossing to coat the vegetables. Serve immediately.

Safe (and Juicy!) Poached Chicken Breasts

I love chicken breast meat. It wasn't always this way. For years I was convinced that the only people interested in eating chicken breast were dieters and those afraid of flavor. That was before I discovered that, when cooked properly, breast meat can be every bit as juicy as dark meat, while also providing a perfect canvas for a host of other flavors. The secret is using a gentle, moist cooking technique and paying careful attention to temperatures.

Easier said than done. (We're going to do a deep dive here, so if you prefer to jump straight into the action, skip to "The Short Version" on page 564.)

While poaching is a classic technique for chicken in cuisines across Europe and Asia, it hasn't been met with the same enthusiasm in the United States, where it often feels like if something is not brown and crispy, it's not worth eating. I blame it partly on our fascination with deep frying, a technique that historically gained popularity due to the availability of inexpensive oil and

the natural preservative qualities that frying gives foods (the hot food is encased in a dry, hard shell that is inhospitable to bacterial or fungal contamination). But the bulk of the blame can be placed on the well-intentioned folks at the USDA and their recommendation that chicken be cooked to 165°F (74°C), a temperature at which it becomes dry as chalk, no matter what method you use to cook it.

This is due to the structure of muscles, particularly the muscles that form breast meat. As we all know, poultry has two kinds of meat.

Dark meat is made of slow-twitch muscles. These are muscles that the chicken uses steadily throughout its life, like its thighs, drumsticks, and the muscles along its back. Because they are used frequently, they tend to be high in connective tissue and command a correspondingly large blood supply, giving dark meat a stronger flavor and darker color. Practically in cooking, dark meat tends to stay juicier and is more forgiving during cooking because of the moistening effect that the breakdown of connective tissue provides for it.

Light meat is made of fast-twitch muscles. These are muscles that are used infrequently and in short bursts, including the breasts and wings.* Fast-twitch muscles don't need a strong and steady blood supply and are typically more subtle in flavor and lighter in color. Because of its lack of connective tissue, white meat is also more prone to drying out.

These differences in dark and light meat exist even in wild birds, but with domesticated chicken there's another factor at play that accentuates these differences. Modern chickens are bred to grow extremely fast and

---

* While wings are technically light meat, they tend to have a very high proportion of connective tissue and skin, which makes them behave a lot more like dark meat than light, especially the second segments (which wing lovers call "flats").

to have huge breasts that are low in fat and connective tissue. This makes the breasts of your standard supermarket chicken significantly milder in flavor and more prone to drying out than those on a heritage-breed chicken that has a more reasonably proportioned figure. Moreover, because younger animals tend to have softer bones and more connective tissue than mature animals, the dark meat of modern chickens—typically slaughtered at just 5 to 7 weeks of age—are extremely high in connective tissue.

All that is to say that for folks who don't like breast meat, I don't blame you. Breast meat is almost always dry and flavorless. So why bother with it? Why not just give you a recipe for a whole poached chicken so that you can grab the leg meat and your hapless guests get saddled with the breast? Or better yet, why not just poach chicken legs and forget about the breasts entirely?

Well, it's because I am at the point where I actually *prefer* light meat to dark most of the time, and I believe you may come to feel the same way once you've discovered how juicy and delicious poached-and-dressed chicken breast meat can be.

So how do you keep it moist and juicy? There are a few methods. Using a sous-vide device, a tool that allows you to maintain a water bath at a very precise temperature (within a single degree of accuracy), makes it extremely easy. Given that you can now buy one for under $100, I'll give you instructions on how to use one for poaching chicken breasts. (If you have one of those newfangled steam-injected precision ovens, that'll do the job in the exact same way.)

The low-tech way is to simply use a wok or a saucepan and a thermometer. It takes a little more care and attention, but no more than stirring a pot of polenta or, say, properly brushing and flossing your teeth.

Before we get to the poaching, we need to understand a little bit about food safety.

CHICKEN AND FOOD SAFETY

There is a misconception about what constitutes a safe cooking temperature for meat. If you've ever worked in a restaurant or taken a ServSafe class, you've probably heard of the 40° to 140°F (4° to 60°C) "danger zone," the temperature range in which bacteria supposedly thrive. You've been given urgent warnings to avoid serving any food that has remained within this range for a total time of four hours. You've probably also heard that for chicken to be safe it ought to be cooked all the way to 165°F.

Yet there are modern techniques, such as sous-vide-style cooking, that can take place well below the 140°F mark, in excess of four hours. My own recommendation for chicken white meat is 150°F (66°C), well below the 165°F target we've all learned. What gives? Is 150°F chicken safe to eat?

Here's the thing: Industry standards for food safety are designed primarily to be simple to understand, usually at the expense of accuracy. The rules are set up such that anybody can grasp them, ensuring safety across the board. But for single-celled organisms, bacteria are surprisingly complex, and despite what any ServSafe chart might have you believe, they refuse to be categorized into a step function.

With salmonella in chicken, for instance, what the USDA is looking for here is a 7.0 log10 reduction in bacteria. That is, a reduction that ensures that out of every 10,000,000 bacteria living on that piece of chicken to start, only one will survive. Pasteurization, or the process of destroying pathogens on food through heat treatment, is a function of both time and temperature. The higher the temperature, the less time it takes. Here is a chart from the USDA's own literature that shows the time it takes to safely pasteurize chicken with 5 percent fat content against salmonella, a particularly hardy germ.

Temperature	Time to achieve 7.0 log10 reduction in salmonella
136°F (58°C)	68.4 minutes
140°F (60°C)	27.5 minutes
145°F (63°C)	9.2 minutes
150°F (66°C)	2.8 minutes
155°F (68°C)	47.7 seconds
160°F (71°C)	14.8 seconds
165°F (74°C)	Less than 2 seconds

As you can see, at 165°F, you achieve pasteurization nearly instantly. It's the bacterial equivalent of shoving a stick of dynamite into an anthill.

At 136°F (58°C), on the other hand, it takes a little over an hour for the bacteria to slowly wither to death in the heat. (In fact, if you've got a device that can cook with degree-accuracy, such as a sous-vide circulator or a modern precision steam oven, you can even pasteurize chicken at temperatures as low as 130°F (54°C)—not that you'd want to: chicken at 130°F looks, feels, and tastes raw.)

At 150°F (66°C), that time is 2.8 minutes. Only 2.8 minutes! What this means is that as long as chicken stays at 150°F or higher for at least 2.8 minutes, it is as safe to eat as chicken that has been cooked to 165°F. This is good news if you, like me, like your chicken to be juicy. I've found that, when chicken is poached and pulled out of the water as soon as the center hits 150°F, it will maintain that temperature for several minutes—well beyond the requisite 2.8. Moreover, bacteria is being actively destroyed as it heats from 130°F to 150°F.

SIMMERING QUESTIONS

There's a general principle of thermodynamics that applies to pieces of food you are cooking with heat, which is that, given the same medium (whether that's the air of an oven, the oil in a deep fryer, or simmering water in a wok), the higher the temperature of that medium, the greater the temperature differential you'll build inside the food.

For instance, if you roast a prime rib in a 400°F (205°C) oven until it registers 130°F (54°C) at its very center, its cross section will show a distinct "bull's-eye" pattern, where the outer layers of meat are gray and well done and get progressively rarer as you approach the center. If, on the other hand, you roast it at 200°F (95°C) to the same central temperature of 130°F, that bull's-eye pattern will be almost indiscernible—you end up with roasted meat that is rosy pink from edge to edge.*

The same logic applies to poaching. Drop a chicken breast into a body of vigorously boiling water and its outer layers end up hopelessly overcooked by the time the center has reached 150°F. If, on the other hand, you add your chicken to *cold* water and slowly bring that water up to a subsimmer (the point at which teeny bubbles just start rising from the base of the wok), the chicken cooks far more gently and evenly, retaining its juiciness (and flavor!).

Let the heat drop off as the chicken cooks and you further improve things. The classic Cantonese technique for *bai qie ji* ("white cut chicken") involves adding a whole chicken to hot water, letting it boil, lifting the chicken in and out a few times to ensure that there's no cold water trapped inside (no need to lift the chicken in and out if using chicken parts), then shutting off the heat and letting the chicken cook in the residual heat. I've found that this method adds some unpredictability (the shape and size of the vessel as well as the temperature and air flow in your kitchen can alter the cooking time), but it can be mitigated by keeping the heat on at the lowest possible setting.

Using bone-in and skin-on chicken instead of boneless, skinless chicken also helps. Skin, with its abundance of fat, is an excellent insulator. Indeed, insulation is one of skin's primary functions (see also: waterproofing and keeping insides in). Bones, with their spongy or marrow-filled cavities, are also great at insulating. This insulative quality helps ensure that the heat reaching the meat underneath comes in slowly and gently.

THE EFFECT OF TEMPERATURE ON JUICINESS

I knew that the hotter you cook chicken, the more juice it expels, but I wanted to know exactly what the effect is, both from a measurable, quantitative perspective and from a subjective "How does it taste?" perspective.

To test this, I cooked near-identical chicken breasts using a sous-vide device to temperatures ranging from 135°F (57°C) up to 165°F, measuring the moisture lost to the bag in each sample and tasting the results.

From a quantitative perspective, the differences are pretty dramatic: Ounce for ounce, chicken cooked

---

* Searing the prime rib after this low-temperature roast is the best way to cook a roast. It's a process I've written extensively about in my first book, *The Food Lab*, as well as on *Serious Eats* and in *Cook's Illustrated* magazine. The technique has been dubbed "the reverse sear" by nerds on the internet.

to 150°F (66°C) will release more than twice as much juice as chicken cooked to 140°F (60°C)

Interestingly, I found that the amount of liquid a chicken breast loses does not rise steadily as the temperature increases. Below 138°F (59°C) or so, it loses very little, but there's a big bump right around 139° to 140°F (59 to 60°C). Between 140° and 149°F (60° and 65°C), there's again a steady increase in juices lost, followed by another big bump around the 150°F mark.

Moreover, even though chicken fat starts to melt at around 100°F (38°C), it's not until you hit that second bump at 150°F that liquefied fat really starts to come out, beading on the surface of the juices. When tasted, all of the chicken came out relatively juicy, though the juiciest were those that were cooked the least.

But juiciness is not everything when it comes to texture. Chicken breast also needs to strike the perfect balance between soft and firm, offering resistance to chewing but not so much that it becomes a chore.

THE EFFECT OF TEMPERATURE ON TEXTURE

The texture also changes dramatically as you cook your chicken at progressively higher temps, and, unlike with juiciness, this is a change that's readily apparent when you eat. In the photo, you can see the chicken cooked at a lower temperature (on the left) gets progressively more stringy and dry as it gets cooked to higher temperature (on the right). Just like any overcooked chicken, once you get to around the 155°F (68°C) mark, sous-vide chicken starts to take on an unpleasant chalky, tacky texture (though, again, far less than with conventional cooking methods). Note that these descriptions are for chicken cooked sous-vide. Chicken cooked through

more traditional poaching methods will be less juicy overall.

140°F (60°C) Chicken: Very Soft and Juicy. Chicken cooked to 140°F has a very tender, extremely juicy, and smooth texture that is firm and completely opaque and shows no signs of stringiness or tackiness. It melts between your teeth, which can be a good or a bad thing depending on how much chew you prefer. I find that 145°F is ideal for serving chicken breast hot, but for cold situations, I prefer it cooked to a higher temperature.

150°F (66°C) Chicken: Juicy, Tender, and Slightly Stringy. Once we get over that 150°F hump, things start to look a little more traditional. Your chicken will still be plenty moist and tender, but will also show some of its signature stringiness. This is my preferred temperature for chicken that's destined to be served cold as a salad.

160°F (71°C) Chicken: Juicy but Firm and Stringy. It's hard to accurately describe the texture of well-done sous-vide chicken. Imagine the texture of traditional roast chicken from, say, your high school cafeteria. Now imagine that the chicken is just as stringy, with that tacky texture on your molars as you bite into it, except it's also extremely juicy and moist.

If you are a lover of traditional roast chicken, but have always wished it were moister, then this may be the temperature for you.

OTHER CONSIDERATIONS: AROMATICS, CHILLING, CUTTING

You can poach your chicken in plain water, but I like using the classic Cantonese combination of ginger and scallion added to the poaching liquid. This very mildly perfumes the chicken meat, but more importantly, it flavors the poaching liquid, which, in turn, becomes a very light chicken stock. Use the same poaching liquid to poach a few more chicken breasts or use it in place of water when making fresh stock and you'll only enhance its flavor, or use it in place of water to cook rice to serve alongside the chicken.

You can eat poached chicken hot straight out of the wok when it's done poaching, but I have come to prefer my poached chicken cold, either sliced with a dipping sauce or shredded and dressed for a salad. Chilling the chicken in ice water is especially important if you plan on serving it sliced with the skin on, as it causes the skin to firm up and get an almost crisp texture. Not in crisp-and-firm way that fried chicken is crisp, but in the crisp-yet-flaccid way that, say, cold jellyfish is crisp. (If crisp-yet-flaccid cold chicken skin doesn't sound appealing to you, then you and I may not see eye to eye about many things and we should consider putting our relationship on pause.)

Chilling the chicken also makes slicing it into neat serving pieces easier, as cold meat is firmer than hot meat. While the traditional Chinese approach is to chop the chicken bone and all, allowing diners to remove the fragments as they eat, taking the bones off before slicing is easy and makes eating easier and safer, especially when you've got kids in the house.

THE SHORT VERSION: HOW TO POACH CHICKEN BREASTS

If poaching using a wok on the stovetop:

- Start with **bone-in, skin-on chicken breast**, which is better insulated than boneless, skinless breasts and therefore comes out juicier.

- **Start the chicken in cold water** in order to heat it slowly and gently without and within.

- **Reduce the heat once it reaches a simmer** in order to allow it to cook through as gently as possible.

- **Use a digital thermometer** to monitor the cooking and take the chicken out of the liquid when the coolest part of the largest piece of chicken hits 150°F (65°C; about 25 minutes after you've shut off the heat).

- **Shock the chicken** in an ice bath to halt the cooking and set the skin.

- **Strain the liquid** and use it as a light chicken broth or in place of water the next time you make stock or steam rice.

- **Remove the meat from the bones,** then slice it for serving with a sauce or shred it for serving in salad.

Taming Onion's Bite

Onions get their characteristic pungent bite from a set of chemicals called *lachymators*, from the Latin "to cry," designed to ward off predators who bit into them. These compounds don't exist naturally in onions; rather, onion cells contain precursor chemicals that then combine and form new chemicals when its cells are ruptured and its contents allowed to mix (this is why a raw onion has very little aroma, but that aroma grows the moment you make a cut into it).

Cooking destroys this pungency, but is there a way to control it when eating the onion raw?

There are two techniques. The first is to slice the onion with your knife oriented pole-to-pole, rather than oriented parallel to the onion's equator (the way you'd cut it for onion rings). Onion cells are elongated and aligned pole to pole, which means that you end up rupturing fewer cells when cutting in that direction, and fewer ruptured cells means fewer lachrymators are created. (Letting a sliced onion sit around for a long time before serving it will also increase its pungency. You ever dice an onion, stick it in a sealed container in the fridge, then pull it out a couple days later and open the lid? *Whoof!*)

The second technique is to simply wash away those lachrymators. But what's the best way? I tried a few different methods, with cold and hot water, soaking versus rinsing, and the length of time for the soak.

Soaking doesn't work particularly well unless you use a very large quantity of water to dilute the onioniness. The best method turned out to be the fastest and easiest: just rinse away all those extra-pungent compounds under warm running water. The speed of chemical and physical reactions increases with temperature. Using warm water causes onions to release their volatile compounds faster—about 45 seconds is enough to rid even the most pungent onions of their kick, and to immediately rinse them away.

There's no need to worry about limp onions using this technique either. Even the hottest tap water comes out at around 140° to 150°F (60°C to 66°C) or so while pectin, the main carbohydrate "glue" that holds plant cells together, doesn't break down until around 183°F. After rinsing in hot water, I transfer my onions to a bowl of cold water to encourage them to stay plump and crisp until I'm ready to add them to my salads or sandwiches.

PERFECTLY POACHED CHICKEN BREASTS

Yield
Makes 4
poached
chicken
breast
halves

Active Time
15 minutes

Total Time
40 to 60 minutes

INGREDIENTS

2 whole bone-in, skin-on chicken breasts or
    4 breast halves, 1 to 1½ pounds (450 to
    675 g) total
6 scallions, very roughly chopped
4 coin-sized slices (about ½ ounce/15 g)
    fresh ginger
3 quarts (3 l) cold water

DIRECTIONS

1 Combine the chicken, scallions, ginger, and water in a wok. Place over high heat and heat until the liquid is barely simmering, using tongs to turn the chicken over and around a few times as it heats. The liquid should register around 200°F (94°C) on an instant-read thermometer.

2 When the liquid is barely simmering, reduce heat to the lowest setting and cover with a lid. Meanwhile, set up a large bowl with a few cups of ice and a couple of quarts of cold water.

3 Check on the chicken every few minutes with the thermometer and remove it from the poaching liquid when the thickest part of the largest piece registers 150°F (65°C), about 25 minutes. Transfer the chicken to the ice bath and let chill for 15 minutes. The chicken is now ready to be carved and served or incorporated into a difference recipe.

FRAGRANT SCALLION-GINGER OIL

For years I'd eaten and loved the simple ginger and scallion oil condiment that comes served on the side with Hainanese chicken rice or Cantonese-style white poached chicken, never really thinking about how it's made. I don't remember exactly when or where I learned the technique, but I *do* remember testing it. This was in the old prechildren days, when I could get away with waking Adri up in the middle of the night to taste something that just blew my mind.

She would usually smile, nod, give a thumbs up, and drop back into the pillow. (In case you're wondering, like ancient astronomers and vampire hunters, I do most of my best work at night.) These days, with a preschooler in the house, Adri values her sleep more than feigned sympathetic excitement. On the one hand, this means I have to wait until the morning to share whatever it is I cooked the night before. On the other, it means that there are now *two* captive audience members onto which I can foist my wares, and one of them is way more excitable and enthusiastic than the other.*

This scallion-ginger oil is not only incredibly simple, it's positively magical as far as versatility and flavor go. It's also a heck of a lot of fun to make. Pouring sizzling hot oil over raw ingredients is easily among the top five impress-your-kid-(at-a-safe-distance) cooking techniques.

Incidentally, if you are looking for a full Hainanese chicken rice recipe, I'd suggest checking out Adam Liaw's version, which is, like most of his recipes, outstanding.

Yield
Makes about 1½ cups (360 g)

Active Time
10 minutes

Total Time
10 minutes

INGREDIENTS

1 cup (240 ml) vegetable oil
6 ounces (170 g/about 18 scallions) scallions, sliced (1½ cups)
1 ounce (30 g) minced fresh ginger (about 2-inch segment)
Kosher salt

DIRECTIONS

(1) Heat the oil in a small saucepan over medium-high heat until shimmering (a single scallion slice dropped into it should sizzle immediately). Meanwhile, combine the scallions and ginger in a medium heatproof bowl and season well with salt. When the oil is hot, pour it over the scallions and ginger. It should sizzle for a few seconds. Allow to cool.

(2) Store in a sealed container in the refrigerator for up to several months. Serve with grilled or poached meats, poultry, or seafood, on top of rice or noodles, drizzled onto soup, mixed with soy sauce and vinegar as a dumpling dip, or with anything else you can think of.

---

* This may be changing. The other day I was telling Alicia about the square-cube law and why terrestrial animals have an upper limit on size when she casually held up her hands in the "stop" pose, said, "Papa, it's OK. You don't have to tell me," shrugged her shoulders, and walked away.

POACHED CHICKEN AND CABBAGE SALAD WITH CASHEWS AND MISO DRESSING

Yield
Serves 3
to 4

Active Time
20 minutes, plus
time to poach the
chicken

Total Time
20 minutes, plus
time to poach the
chicken

NOTES

This salad can be made with chicken poached according to the directions on page 565 or with any leftover chicken meat. This dressing can be used for any salad you'd like, though it is especially good with crunchy ingredients like cabbage and radish. If it works in coleslaw, it'll work with this dressing.

INGREDIENTS

For the Dressing:

2 tablespoons (30 g) white or yellow miso
    paste
1 tablespoon (15 ml) fresh lemon juice (from
    1 lemon)
2 teaspoons (10 ml) mirin
½ teaspoon (1 g) dry mustard powder,
    preferably Japanese
1 tablespoon (15 ml) extra virgin olive oil
1 teaspoon (2 g) minced garlic (about 1
    medium clove)

For the Salad:

2 poached chicken breast halves, skin and
    bones removed (12 to 16 ounces/340
    to 450 g total boneless, skinless breast
    meat; see Notes)
12 ounces (340 g) red or green cabbage
    (about ½ head), shredded
2 scallions, thinly sliced
¾ cup (75 g/about 2½ ounces) toasted
    cashew nuts, lightly crushed in a mortar
    and pestle or under a skillet
Kosher salt and freshly ground black
    pepper

The dressing for this simple chicken salad is based on Japanese *nuta*, a simple dish of sashimi-grade tuna dressed with a creamy dressing made with miso and mirin. To that dressing base I add a splash of lemon juice, then toss it together with poached shredded chicken, shredded cabbage, red onion (that I've rinsed in hot water, see "Taming Onion's Bite," page 564), sliced scallions, and toasted cashew nuts that I crush lightly in my mortar and pestle.

This is a versatile salad base that can take on a variety of other ingredients, such as grilled or boiled corn kernels, edamame, cherry tomatoes, cucumbers, avocado, radish, or grated carrots.

DIRECTIONS

(1) **For the Dressing:** Combine the miso paste, lemon juice, mirin, dry mustard, olive oil, and garlic in a large bowl and whisk until homogenous.

(2) **For the Salad:** Shred the chicken meat into bite-sized pieces with your fingers. Add them to the bowl along with the cabbage, scallions, and half of the cashews. Toss everything to combine, season with salt and pepper to taste and toss again, transfer to a serving platter, sprinkle with the remaining cashews, and serve.

BANG BANG CHICKEN

If I'm to trust the results of a Google search, when most folks hear the phrase "bang bang chicken," they think of a Cheesecake Factory concoction with fried chicken and shrimp, rice, and a generically pan-Asian creamy coconut-chile-soy-peanut-lime sauce, which, while possibly delicious, is similar to the original Sichuan bang bang chicken only in that they both contain chicken. I'm familiar with this strategy of ethnic-sounding-food-words co-optation. I once worked for a similar chain restaurant where we served seared tuna with a "ponzu dipping sauce" made with sesame oil, soy sauce, and ginger, a far cry from true ponzu made with citrus juice and dashi. I lasted only a few months in that job.

True *bang bang ji si* gets its name from the sound that a mallet makes when beating the tough chicken breasts of yesteryear into tender submission before being dressed in a sauce known as "mysterious flavor" in Sichuan cuisine, as it combines a wide variety of stimulating flavors: numbing and citrusy Sichuan peppercorns, pungent garlic, toasty sesame paste, sweet sugar, sharp and sweet Chinkiang vinegar, and hot chile oil.

I've been playing around a lot with the method I use to make this classic sauce. My current favorite method is to break out the mortar and pestle, which helps bring out better flavor from all the aromatics as well as combining them into a neatly emulsified sauce. I start by grinding Sichuan peppercorns, raw garlic, sesame seeds, and a touch of sugar into a paste before adding the liquid ingredients and grinding them into a stable emulsion. If I recently poached the chicken, adding some of its strained poaching liquid to the dressing thins it out to a nice saucy consistency.

This same sauce is great on any cold poached meat, on hot or chilled noodles or tofu, or on cool crunchy vegetables like cucumbers and cabbage.

As for the chicken, luckily, our modern chickens don't need the titular bang-bang treatment. All you need to do is remove the bones, then either slice the chicken (with the skin on!) or shred it, toss or drizzle it with the dressing, garnish with scallions and sesame seeds, and you've got yourself the bangin'est unbanged bang bang chicken around. The sauce does so much of the lifting that even store-bought rotisserie chicken will shine here.

Yield
Serves 3
to 4

Active Time
20 minutes, plus
time to poach the
chicken

Total Time
20 minutes, plus
time to poach the
chicken

NOTES

You can use the Sichuan Málà Chile Oil recipe on page 310 for this or use your favorite store-bought chile oil. This salad can be made with chicken poached according to the directions on page 565, with store-bought rotisserie chicken, or with any leftover chicken meat. If you cooked the chicken sous-vide, use some of the liquid from the sous-vide bag in place of the poaching liquid in step 2. If using leftover chicken, you can thin the sauce with homemade or store-bought low-sodium chicken stock or water instead of poaching liquid in step 2.

The Mysterious Flavor Sauce can be scaled to a larger quantity and saved in the fridge for several weeks. Use it on hot or chilled noodles or tofu, boiled wontons or dumplings, fresh crunchy vegetables, or cold poultry or meats. It's especially good on leftover roast turkey the day after Thanksgiving.

INGREDIENTS

For the Mysterious Flavor Sauce:

2 teaspoons (4 g) toasted Sichuan
  peppercorns
1 tablespoon (12 g) sugar
1 tablespoon (8 g) minced garlic (about 3
  medium cloves)
1 tablespoon (8 g) toasted sesame
  seeds
1 tablespoon (15 ml) sesame paste,
  preferably Chinese
1 tablespoon (15 ml) light soy sauce or
  shoyu
2 tablespoons (30 ml) Chinkiang or
  black vinegar or a mixture of 1
  tablespoon (15 ml) rice vinegar and 1
  tablespoon (15 ml) balsamic vinegar
1 tablespoon (15 ml) roasted sesame oil
¼ cup (60 ml) chile oil with sediment
  (see Notes)
2 tablespoons (30 ml) poaching liquid
  from poached chicken (see Notes)

For the Salad:

2 poached chicken breast halves, bones
  removed (12 to 16 ounces/340
  to 450 g total boneless, skinless
  breast meat; see Notes)
2 scallions, thinly sliced on a sharp bias
Additional toasted white or black
  sesame seeds, for garnish

DIRECTIONS

① **For the Mysterious Flavor Sauce:** Grind the Sichuan peppercorns in a mortar and pestle until a rough powder is formed. Add the sugar, garlic, and sesame seeds and pound until a rough paste is formed. Add the sesame paste, soy sauce, and vinegar and grind in a circular motion until a smooth paste is formed. Stir in the sesame oil and chile oil and sediment and the chicken poaching liquid. Set the dressing aside.

② **To Serve the Chicken Sliced:** Slice the chicken with the skin on and transfer to a serving platter. Spoon the dressing all over and around the chicken. Garnish with the scallions, sprinkle with sesame seeds, and serve immediately.

To Serve the Chicken Shredded: Discard the chicken skin. Shred the chicken into bite-sized pieces and add to a large bowl. Add the dressing and half of the scallions. Toss to coat, transfer to a serving platter or bowl, spoon any dressing remaining in the bowl around the chicken. Garnish with the remaining scallions, sprinkle with sesame seeds, and serve immediately.

SPICY CHICKEN AND BANANA BLOSSOM (OR CABBAGE) SALAD WITH FRIED SHALLOTS, GARLIC, AND LEMONGRASS

Yield
Serves 4

Active Time
1 hour

Total Time
1 hour

NOTES

If possible, use smaller, sweeter Thai shallots and garlic for the recipe. If you're using Thai garlic, you can leave the skins on the individual cloves when frying. Makrut lime leaves can be found at Thai supermarkets. Fresh lemongrass can be found at most Asian markets and in the specialty produce section of many Western supermarkets.

Thai chiles can vary in heat. Taste a tiny bit of your chiles before smashing and adjust the quantity accordingly. The dressing should be quite hot to balance out its sweetness. Palm sugar can be found in Thai markets. If unavailable, substitute with brown sugar.

This salad can be made with chicken poached according to the directions on page 565 or with any leftover chicken meat.

Banana blossom can be found at East Asian or Indian grocery stores. It is wonderful in place of the cabbage in this recipe, with a mildly bitter, astringent flavor.

This salad is one that I first made when staying with my good friend Yvonne Ruperti and her husband, Hallam, at their home in Singapore, near the Tanjong Pagar neighborhood. Yvonne and I had spent years together as roommates and coworkers at *Cook's Illustrated*, so I'd be damned if I missed the opportunity to spend some time in the kitchen with one of my favorite people.

Banana blossom and chicken salad is a not-uncommon dish found mostly in the central Thai cooking of Bangkok. You won't find it on every street corner or in every restaurant, but it shows up regularly enough. The classic version is made with poached shredded chicken, thinly sliced banana blossom, raw shallots, coconut, and a hot-sour-sweet dressing flavored with garlic, chiles, palm sugar, and fish sauce. My version starts off similarly but strays a bit, and when I make it at home, where banana blossoms are hard to come by, more frequently than not I'll just use crunchy cabbage instead.

The first thing I did was to add a whole slew of fried shallots to the salad base. They lose some of their crispness once dressed, but in return they give it a unique sweet-savory flavor. I added a bunch of garlic cloves, which I'd quickly smashed in the mortar and pestle, as well as some thinly sliced lemongrass and lime leaves. Into the oil they went (if you can't find them, any citrus leaf will work). Finally, I fried up some peanuts to form the flavor base for my dressing. This left me with a bowl full of fried goodies ("No, Adri, those aren't for eating yet"), plus some flavorful frying oil to add to my dressing for extra flavor.

For the dressing, I decided to forgo the coconut milk—there's already plenty of richness going on here with the fried things—instead making a sweet-spicy paste of garlic, chiles, and palm sugar (props to Hallam for some epic mortar and pestle pounding), then thinning it out with fresh lime juice and sugar.

When making salads like this, it's important to dress things in the right order. I start with the chicken, which is the most absorbent and can benefit from a bit of extra time to soak up flavors between its fibers. Next I add the cabbage along with a handful of fresh herbs (mint and cilantro). Finally, I add the fried things just before serving, saving some to sprinkle over the salad, so that they retain at least a hint of their crunchiness.

INGREDIENTS

For the Fried Aromatics:

½ cup (120 ml) peanut, rice bran, or other neutral oil

3 medium European shallots or 8 to 12 Thai shallots, thinly sliced (about 4½ ounces/130 g; see Notes)

9 medium standard garlic cloves or 12 to 15 Thai garlic cloves, roughly smashed in a mortar and pestle (about 3 tablespoons/30 to 40 g; see Notes)

2 fresh lemongrass stalks, outer leaves removed, pale lower 4 inches only, thinly sliced crosswise (about ¼ cup; see Notes)

4 makrut lime leaves, stems discarded, sliced as thinly as possible (see Notes)

Kosher salt

For the Dressing:

4 to 10 fresh Thai bird chiles, roughly chopped (see Notes)

9 medium standard garlic cloves or 12 to 15 Thai garlic cloves, roughly smashed in a mortar and pestle (about 3 tablespoons/30 to 40 g; see Notes)

3 tablespoons (about 25 g) palm sugar (see Notes)

2 tablespoons (30 ml) Thai fish sauce, plus more to taste

2 tablespoons (30 ml) fresh lime juice (from 2 limes), plus more to taste

1 tablespoon (6 g) dried crushed Thai chile powder (or red chile flakes), plus more to taste

For the Salad:

2 poached chicken breast halves, skin and bones removed (12 to 16 ounces/340 to 450 g total boneless, skinless breast meat; see Notes)

⅓ cup (10 g) roughly chopped fresh cilantro leaves and tender stems

⅓ cup (10 g) roughly chopped fresh mint leaves

1 small head cabbage (about 12 ounces/340 g), cored and thinly sliced, or 1 small banana blossom (about 1 pound/450 g), prepared according to directions

½ cup (about 1½ ounces/50 g) roasted or fried peanuts, roughly crushed in a mortar and pestle

DIRECTIONS

(1) **For the Fried Aromatics:** Heat oil in a large wok over high heat until shimmering (it should register around 375°F/190°C on an instant-read thermometer). Add the shallots and cook, stirring constantly, until golden brown, about 2 minutes. Quickly remove with a fine-mesh strainer or slotted spoon and transfer to a paper-towel-lined bowl.

(2) Repeat the frying with the garlic, followed by the lemongrass, and then the lime leaves, adding each fried aromatic to the same bowl with the shallots. Season the fried aromatics with salt and toss to combine.

(3) **For the Dressing:** Add the fresh Thai chiles and garlic to the bottom of a mortar and pestle. Add 1 tablespoon of the palm sugar. Pound until a nearly smooth paste is formed (this will take a while; be patient). Add the remaining 2 tablespoons palm sugar and pound until incorporated. Add the fish sauce, lime juice, and dried chiles and stir to incorporate.

(4) **For the Salad:** Shred the chicken into bite-sized pieces and add to the bottom of a large bowl. Add the dressing and reserved frying oil and toss to incorporate. Add the chopped cilantro, mint, cabbage, and peanuts. Reserve 2 tablespoons of the mixed fried aromatics and add the rest to the bowl with the salad. Toss to combine, then taste and adjust the flavor with more fish sauce, lime juice, or dried chiles as necessary. Transfer to a serving bowl, top with the remaining fried aromatics, and serve immediately.

How to Prepare the Banana Blossom

Prepare the banana blossom by filling a large bowl with 2 quarts (2 l) water and add ¼ cup (60 ml) white vinegar or lemon juice. Lay a clean kitchen towel on the surface of the water, letting it soak. Peel off and discard the tough outer layers of the blossom until you reach the pale pink inner layers. Split the blossom in half lengthwise, then slice crosswise as thin as possible. Immediately transfer the slices to the bowl and lay the towel over them to keep them submerged. When ready to add to the salad, remove the towel and skim off and discard any tiny buds that float on the surface. Dry the slices on a clean kitchen towel or in a salad spinner and proceed.

How to Make Thai Curries

Often when I approach adapting a foreign recipe for a largely American audience, I do what many publications do: I spend a lot of time working out how to replace tricky-to-find ingredients. My conclusion? If that's what you're looking for, using premade curry pastes is the way to go. They pack a lot of difficult-to-find ingredients into a single, easily purchased jar that lasts virtually forever in the fridge. (I use Maesri or Mae Ploy brand, mostly). Even with store-bought curry paste, you can make a decent curry. That said, nothing compares with the flavor (or muscle- and character-building effort) of homemade curry pastes.

What we refer to as "Thai curry" in the West is what is known as *kaeng* in Thailand, the collective term for dishes made with curry paste and intended to be eaten with rice. While the prototypical Thai curry may resemble a rich soup, there are watery curries, stew-like curries, and even dry curries (such as Pad Prik King, on page 588). Many curries use coconut milk, others use broth or water, some use animal blood for thickening. Thai curries can be long-cooked, meat-packed stews, or they can be quickly simmered dishes with seafood or vegetables.

Perhaps the one unifying trait of all Thai-style curries is the use of a moist curry paste made by pounding together spices and aromatics in a heavy mortar and pestle. And therein lies its difficulty. Doing it the traditional way is tough, forearm-breaking labor, especially if you are aiming for a smooth, fine texture.

But wait, you may be thinking. *Isn't this exactly what technology is for? Why would we bother using a mortar and pestle when we've got food processors and blenders at our disposal?*

I am not the type to be enamored of old-fashioned techniques when modern methods can get the job done faster or better, so I decided to put it to the test.

THE MORTAR AND PESTLE IS CURRY PASTE'S BEST FRIEND

To start, I made a few batches of Thai red curry paste as well as a few batches of Italian pesto side by side in a food processor and in a mortar and pestle, then gave them to tasters for a blind taste test. Certainly the batches made in the food processor came together faster, but tasting them side by side with the version made in the mortar and pestle showed that the food processor batches had a grainier, almost gritty texture, while the batch made in the mortar and pestle had a smoother, silkier texture, albeit with a few larger chunks of aromatics intact. Flavor-wise, the differences were even more stark: the mortar and pestle versions were much more aromatic than the food processor batch.

Thinking that perhaps the food processor just needed a bit more time to break down ingredients, I let the processor run with the curry paste in it for up to a full three minutes. It made no difference. After the first 45 seconds or so, the paste is broken down about as far as it's ever going to break down.

So what gives? Why does a food processor produce inferior results?

Well, it's because a mortar and pestle crushes cells rather than shearing them. Vegetable cells are firm sacs, like inflated water balloons. Inside those balloons is where the flavor is. If it helps, think of your vegetable cells as a stack of shipping containers, each with a shipment of juice. A food processor has a sharp whirling blade that shears those containers apart. It may well cut open a few of them, but more often than not, it simply batters them so that they separate from each other while staying intact individually. It's sort of like a hurricane blowing through the shipyard. A mortar and pestle, on the other hand, is like a full-on Godzilla-style Kaiju attack. It doesn't just separate cells, but totally crushes them, releasing their cargo.

If flavor is your goal, you've got to release your inner Godzilla and crush those aromatics like a Tokyo skyline.

THE FOOD PROCESSOR IS THE MORTAR AND PESTLE'S FRIEND

When exploring ways to make making Thai curry paste easier, my first thought was to use a hybrid approach. Could I start my curry paste in a mortar and pestle to get some of the heavy bashing out of the way, then finish it in the food processor to finish the job? Or perhaps the other way around?

I tried making the same batch of curry paste by four different methods:*

1 • Using only a food processor
2 • Using only a mortar and pestle
3 • Starting with the mortar and pestle and finishing in the food processor
4 • Starting in the food processor and finishing with the mortar and pestle

I timed how long each method took, then tasted the final results. As far as ease of production goes, the food processor wins by a long shot. It can reduce a pile of fresh and dried aromatics to a smooth curry paste in just a couple of minutes, requiring only a few scrapes with a rubber spatula during the process. By contrast, making a curry paste 100% with a mortar and pestle, as I've advised in the past, is a much more laborious process that typically takes at least 5 to 10 minutes, but can take much longer with a smaller mortar and pestle or a paste pounder who isn't 100 percent invested in the process. Fifteen to 20 solid minutes of pounding is not unusual for a very smooth paste.

For the combined methods, I employed a one-minute pounding session along with two minutes inside the food processor.

Flavorwise, there were some clear differences. As expected, the paste formed 100% in the food processor had the least developed flavor. Of the two combinations, the one that I started in the food processor and finished by pounding was almost indistinguishable from the one that was made 100 percent in the food processor. Once those aromatics are broken down and in a semiliquid

---

* In fact, I even tried using an Indian wet mill, designed for crushing grains and pulses into wet batters. Unfortunately, curry paste is too thick, even for their heavy stone mills.

suspension, it's hard to get them to crush underneath the pestle. They end up just squishing out to the sides.

But the version I started with the mortar and pestle and finished in the food processor? That was the one! The flavor was almost but not quite as good as using a mortar and pestle alone (I got plenty of cell breakdown during the pounding phase), but the advantage in time and effort was tremendous.

In the future, I'll be sticking to using 100 percent mortar and pestle when I have the time and energy (or an extra set of kitchen hands to pass the task off to), but on busy nights I'll be pulling out both tools to make curry pastes with almost all the flavor at a fraction of the effort.

THE FREEZER IS THE FOOD PROCESSOR'S BEST FRIEND

I'll cut to the chase instead of burying the lede here: in many cases, freezing fresh aromatics before pounding them in a mortar and pestle will produce tastier results.

I know, I find it hard to believe myself. But hear me out, because there's a good explanation for all of this.

This whole idea came about because my refrigerator was broken. Every couple of weeks, it would decide to kick its compressor into high gear, and everything on the bottom shelf would end up freezing solid. One time it was a knob of fresh ginger and a few stalks of fresh lemongrass. I ended up deciding to use that frozen-then-thawed lemongrass and ginger in a Thai-style curry paste and was frankly surprised at how easily they incorporated into the mix in my mortar and pestle. Then it occurred to me: perhaps freezing aromatics is a good thing?

My reasoning went like this: In many cases, we want our vegetables and herbs to stay relatively bright and intact. We want crunch, we want bite, we want texture. But sometimes we want the opposite—we want our vegetables and herbs to get completely pulverized. We want them bruised, beaten, and squeezed until every single one of their cells bursts open and releases its fragrant juices. So where does freezing come in? Freezing can accomplish something similar

to what the mortar and pestle can achieve. Rather than crushing from the outside, though, it causes cells to tear apart from the inside, as liquid water expands and forms jagged ice crystals. Vegetables and aromatics that have been frozen and then thawed are limp and bruised-looking.

So, I figured, if freezing causes cells to rupture, and rupturing cells is our goal when making curry pastes and pestos, could it actually improve the results? Moreover, could it help produce extra-tasty pastes in the food processor or mini-chopper, no mortar and pestle required?

To test this, I first made three different batches of pesto using my colleague Daniel Gritzer's fantastic recipe (you can find it for free on *Serious Eats*). The first I made the traditional way, using fresh basil and a mortar and pestle alone. The second I made in a food processor, using fresh basil. The third I made in the food processor using basil that I'd placed in the freezer overnight and allowed to thaw for a few minutes at room temperature. (Basil has such a high surface-area-to-volume ratio that it freezes and defrosts in moments.)

The results?

The pesto made in the mortar and pestle was definitely the best of the three, boasting a creamy, emulsified texture and really bright, vibrant basil flavor.[*] The batch made from fresh basil in the mini-chopper was easily the worst, with a sort of gritty texture and muted flavor. I wouldn't kick it out of my pasta bed,

---

[*] I admit, embarrassingly, that in my first book I recommended not just using a food processor for pesto but also *blanching the basil*. The result is vibrant green, but I no longer follow that process. Use Daniel's recipe instead.

but it wouldn't be my first choice for a garlic-breath date night, either. The third batch—the one made with frozen basil in the mini-chopper—was somewhere in the middle. It had the same great, creamy texture as the pesto made with the mortar and pestle, and its flavor was also a big improvement over that of its nonfrozen counterpart, though it wasn't quite as flavor-packed as the version made with the mortar and pestle.

For completeness, I made another batch in which I froze the basil, then crushed it with the mortar and pestle. I didn't find any serious advantages there for pesto, but for Thai-style curry pastes, it made the job of breaking down piles of aromatics into a fine paste significantly faster with no reduction in flavor.

In retrospect, this shouldn't have surprised me: I use the exact same logic when freezing vegetables for my gazpacho, and it works wonders there. This is great news if you don't make frequent trips to the Thai market for those specialty curry paste ingredients. You can buy galangal, lime leaf, turmeric, and lemongrass in bulk, chop it up roughly, and store it in the freezer, where it will not only keep its flavor but actually be easier to incorporate into curry pastes down the line.

POUNDING CURRY PASTE: MY THREE RECOMMENDED METHODS

So where does all this leave us?

I have three recommended methods for making curry paste. All produce perfectly tasty curry paste (that will certainly be better than what you can buy in the shop), but some are easier than others. Here we go:

Method One: The Traditional

Method one is to use a mortar and pestle with fresh or frozen ingredients. When making curry paste, start with any dried spices you may be incorporating and grind them down to a fine powder. Next add firm roots, rhizomes, and vegetables, such as ginger, garlic, cilantro root, dried soaked chiles, and turmeric, pounding them with a pinch of salt, which acts as an abrasive and breaks things down more quickly. Finish with softer ingredients like handfuls of fresh herbs or fresh chiles. Start grinding with an up-and-down pounding motion, making sure to scrape the pestle against the side of the

mortar instead of dropping it dead center. This pushes ingredients down to the bottom to be crushed.

Method Two: The Hybrid

Start your paste in a mortar and pestle the same way as for the traditional. If incorporating dried herbs, you can grind them separately in a spice grinder. Pound your ingredients together to form a very rough paste, then transfer the rough paste to the food processor along with any ground dried spices. Process the ingredients until a smooth paste is formed.

Method Three: The Quick and Dirty

For this method, start by freezing your ingredients. The easiest way is to cut larger ingredients into thin slices or smaller pieces, place everything on a rimmed aluminum baking sheet (aluminum transfers heat faster than most other materials in your kitchen), then place the sheet in the freezer until the ingredients have been frozen solid, at least half an hour. You can transfer the frozen ingredients to a zipper-lock freezer bag to store long term or immediately transfer them while still frozen to the food processor and process into a smooth paste. (In this method any dried spices should be ground and added separately.)

The Mortar and Pestle Is the Most Underrated Tool in the Kitchen

Hey, you! Yes you! The one with that old dusty mortar and pestle that your friend gifted you a decade ago sitting on the windowsill! Do you not know what you have here? Do you not understand the power that is within your grasp?

Picture this: row upon row of plump plant cells, stacked and packed scores deep. Like a massive city block, each apartment packed to the brim by a large family of aromatic organic compounds, each unaware of the smiting you are about to dole out on their comfortable abodes. Suddenly a giant hammer smashes down from the sky, crushing the cells, rupturing their walls, and pouring out their contents. Again and again it strikes, the organic compounds battered and bashed about until their homes are reduced to pulp and the compounds are fully exposed. The pounding has stopped. There is no hope for salvation, for there is nothing left to salvage.

This is the raw, primal power that a mortar and pestle endows you with. The ability to fully extract any and all flavor from aromatic ingredients. When I was in high school, I was proud of the one recipe I had under my belt: guacamole. But the version of guacamole I made back then, with onions, cilantro, and chiles chopped by hand before incorporating into the mashed avocado, is positively bland compared to the version I make these days, with the exact same ingredients crushed in a mortar and pestle. I know; I've tasted them side by side.

But . . . *one does not simply guac in the mortar.**

Here's just a small taste of what I use it for:

Grinding Spices

Pre-ground spices may be convenient, but they lose flavor much more rapidly than whole spices due to their larger surface-area-to-volume ratio. With a few exceptions, I buy all my spices whole and grind them as necessary. I know what you're thinking. Whole spices may *taste* better, but are they worth it? Who wants to pull out, plug in, and clean the spice grinder every time you need ground spices? I'm with you, and I have the answer: don't. Instead, invest in an inexpensive heavy granite mortar and pestle.

Spice grinders are great for large batches of spices, but not for normal recipe-sized amounts. Try to grind a teaspoon of coriander seeds in a spice grinder and tell me what happens.

Go ahead. Most likely, those spices go flying around the jar and bouncing off the blades, refusing to settle down and actually get ground. Spice grinders need at least a few tablespoons of whole spices in them to really work well.

A mortar and pestle, on the other hand, can reduce a few teaspoons of dried spices to a rough grind or powder in under a minute—and that's including the time it takes to pull it out and wash it when you're done. Here's how you do it.

Step 1 • Add Your Spices

Place your whole spices in the bowl of the mortar and pestle. Make sure your mortar is on a firm surface. You're going to be pounding.

---

* I know I promised in the introduction that there would be no further puns, but how could I pass this one up?

Step 2 • Partially Cover the Bowl

Grab the pestle with your dominant hand and with the other cover the top of the mortar so that you create a slot for the pestle to move up and down in. This will help prevent whole spices from flying away.

Step 3 • Start Pounding

Pound the spices, trying to scrape your pestle along the sides of the mortar as you move up and down in order to trap and grind spices against the mortar's walls. Continue pounding until most of the whole spices are at least roughly broken down. This should take 15 to 20 seconds.

Step 4 • Grind

Grind the spices by holding the pestle firmly against the base of the mortar and pushing it around the bottom in a circular motion. Imagine an animatronic witch stirring her witch's brew and you get the idea. As the pestle moves around, it should grind spices efficiently against the base of the mortar. Grind as fine as you'd like.

Step 5 • Sift (optional)

With certain spices—especially hulled spices like cumin or caraway seeds—you might find that the hulls of the seeds don't get ground down as easily as the rest. This is OK. I typically use my spices directly as-is from the mortar, even if a few of those hulls make it into my food. They blend right in. If you prefer to remove them, however, you can tip the contents of your mortar into a fine-mesh strainer, then repeatedly tap the edge to let the ground spice drop through and the husks remain.

continues

Pounding Aromatics

Whether it's just some garlic and ginger for stir-fry, smashed anchovies and garlic for an in-the-mortar Caesar dressing, or a full-blown Thai curry paste, I break out the mortar and pestle any time I want to transform solid wet ingredients into a paste. Here's how you do it.

Step 1 • Precut the Ingredients

Peel and trim your aromatics as necessary, then chop them into relatively fine pieces. With tender aromatics like fresh chiles or garlic, a rough chop is fine. For tougher aromatics like lemongrass or ginger, a fine mince will speed things along.

Step 2 • Salt and Pound

Salt acts as an abrasive, which helps tear up and break down those cell walls. Nearly any recipe that calls for a mortar and pestle will also call for salt, but in some cases (such as Nam Pla Prik (page 257). I use sugar as an abrasive instead.

Start pounding the aromatics, using your free hand to cover the top of the bowl to prevent spillage. Once the aromatics start to really break down you should be able to remove your hand. Continue pounding, aiming at the larger pieces and the sides of the mortar, trying to maximize scraping and contact between the mortar and pestle with each stroke.

Step 3 • Grind

Once a moist paste starts to form, continue to break it down by turning the pestle around the mortar in a circular motion without letting it break contact with the mortar. With drier things like curry pastes, you may need to intersperse this motion with some more up-and-down pounds and scrapes.

Step 4 • Finish in the Food Processor (optional)

If you've got it in you, you can finish up directly in the mortar and pestle, but if you want to take the easy (and nearly as tasty) route, transfer the rough paste to a food processor and finish up by blitzing it until smooth.

Crushing Nuts

The mortar and pestle is easily the best and fastest way to crush or chop anywhere from a tablespoon to a cup and a half or so of nuts (more than that and the food processor starts to look a little more appealing).

Step 1 • Fill the Mortar

Add the nuts to the mortar, keeping them to below around the two-thirds line.

Step 2 • Partially Cover the Bowl

Grab the pestle with your dominant hand, and with the other cover the top of the mortar so that you create a slot for the pestle to move up and down in. This will keep the nuts in the bowl.

Step 3 • Crush

Pound the nuts with the pestle, aiming roughly at the larger pieces so that you end up with an even crush.

Cleaning and "Seasoning" a Mortar and Pestle

When I recommend using a mortar and pestle, many people show a reluctance to use one because they've heard that a new mortar and pestle needs to be seasoned or requires special care when washing. The seasoning process involves grinding the pestle into the mortar to remove any bits of excess grit or rock that might come off into your food. The good news is that of the dozens of mortars and pestles I've owned and used, only one ever actually needed to be seasoned before use, and that was my Mexican basalt *molcajete*. Granite, ceramic, wood, and metal mortars and pestles typically come grit-free and ready to use.

To test whether your mortar and pestle needs seasoning before use, rinse out the mortar, then fill it with clean water a quarter of the way. Grind the pestle into the mortar using a circular motion for a few moments, then check the water. Is it clear? You're good to go. Does it come out cloudy with visible bits of grit? If so, season the mortar by grinding ¼ cup of white rice with a few tablespoons of water, grinding until it becomes a wet paste. Work the paste all over the interior surface of the mortar using the pestle for a few minutes, then drain, rinse, and do the clear water test again. Repeat this process until no grit comes off.

Washing a mortar and pestle is easy. The majority of the time, I just rinse mine out with water and a sponge, sometimes adding a little soap if there is any visible or smellable residue left in the bottom of the mortar.

continues

The Best Mortar and Pestle

If I had to pick three pieces of technology to cook with for the rest of my life, a knife, fire, and a mortar and pestle would probably be it. This makes sense. At 100,000 to 150,000 years old, the mortar and pestle is one of our most ancient culinary tools and indeed, for tens of thousands of years we humans were working with a stone knife, a fire, and a mortar and pestle. They've been our best friends for three times as long as we've had dogs. They are a full order of magnitude older than agriculture itself. They have been used by every civilization in every corner of the globe, and to this day there's nothing better for extracting the best flavor out of vegetal matter (though I'm sure Dave Arnold or Nathan Myhrvold would disagree).

There are all kinds of mortars and pestles out there made out of different materials with different finishes. I own at least a half dozen ranging from an Italian marble mortar with a smooth, lathed wooden pestle to a Japanese ceramic suribachi with a hardwood pestle, to a Mexican-style molcajete. My favorite mortar and pestle, the one that I turn back to nine times out of ten, is my Thai-style granite mortar and pestle. It has a large 3-cup-plus capacity, is heavy enough that it won't move even with the most aggressive pounding, it has a heavy pestle that does a lot of the work for you, and it has an unpolished interior surface, which is what you want for effectively crushing cells. (Just think: would you rather be smashed by a wave against a smooth beach or against craggy rocks? Good. The opposite is what you want for your plant cells.)

I have yet to find one brand that is particularly better than another, as long as it meets the solid granite, 3-cup-plus capacity requirements. You can find them at a good Asian supermarket or online for around $40 to $50.

Once you've got your mortar and pestle home, there's not much you need to do with it. Some sets will have to be "seasoned" by grinding wet dry rice in them before use to pull out any bits of trapped sand or rock and to break off any jagged edges. Most sets these days come preseasoned, so all you need to do is rinse them out and you're good to go. Some folks say not to wash mortars and pestles with soap. I think those folks have never made an oil-based sauce in theirs, or perhaps they don't mind their pesto tasting like curry paste. Wash it however you want. It's a hunk of rock; it's not going to get damaged.

Common Curry Paste Ingredients

Aside from the work involved, there's another tempting reason to buy jarred curry pastes: the shopping list. Unlike many Chinese or Japanese ingredients, which you can buy in pickled, dried, or otherwise preserved forms, Thai curry pastes rely heavily on fresh aromatics. Luckily, curry paste can be made in bulk and stored in the fridge for many months or even years before it goes bad. Curry paste ingredients can also be stored in the freezer. Of the ingredients on this chart, coriander root is among the most difficult to find and to replace. If you grow cilantro in your backyard, you have access to fresh coriander root! Let the cilantro bolt and overgrow, then harvest the roots when you pull the plants.

There is a wide range of Thai chiles, both fresh and dried, and if truly authentic flavor is your goal, that's a deep rabbit hole to fall into. On the other hand, most dishes will taste perfectly fine with more readily available Western counterparts.

INGREDIENT	FLAVOR	SUBSTITUTES
Thai Basil	Like sweet Italian basil but more licorice-like	Italian basil
Coriander/cilantro root	Aromatic and herbal, like very intense cilantro	Cilantro stems
Green *prik chi fa* chiles	Thai green "pointing to the sky" chiles are spicy, grassy, vegetal	Any green chile, such as jalapeño or serrano
Fresh Green or Red Thai Bird chiles	Bright and fruity, very hot	Other green or red hot chiles, such as Fresno, cayenne, or red serrano, or very hot chiles, like habanero or scotch Bonnet
Galangal	Piney and citrusy, with juicy flesh and a peppery flavor	There is no great substitute. Ginger will typically work, but it has a sharper flavor. If using ginger, use half the amount.
Makrut Lime Zest and Leaf	Like lime zest with a hint of yuzu	You can use the leaves of any citrus fruit, such as a mandarin or an orange in place of makrut lime leaf, and a mix of lime of orange zest in place of makrut zest.
Lemongrass	Lemony and mild	Lemon zest or lime zest is an OK substitute in curry pastes. Use ⅛ the amount by weight.
Thai Garlic	Bold and pungent	Thai garlic is smaller but more powerfully flavored than Western garlic varieties, but you can substitute one for the other, clove for clove.
Thai Shallots	Tiny red Thai shallots are sweet like Western shallots but with a garlicky bite.	Equal parts shallots and garlic by weight
Turmeric Root	Earthy, gingery, and slightly bitter	1 teaspoon (5 g) of dried turmeric plus ½ teaspoon (2.5 g) of fresh ginger per tablespoon (15 g) of fresh turmeric
Shrimp Paste	Funky and oceany	There's no true substitute for this, but miso paste will have a similar umami, flavor-enhancing effect.

Thai Curry Pastes

This chart shows which ingredients go into which style of Thai curry paste.

	Red Curry	Green Curry	Yellow Curry	Massaman Curry	Khao Soi
FRESH AROMATICS					
Thai Basil Leaves		x			
Coriander Root	x	x	x		x
Fresh Cilantro		x			
Fresh Thai Bird Chiles	x (red)	x (green)			
Galangal	x	x			
Ginger			x		x
Makrut Lime Leaf	x	x	x		x
Lemongrass	x	x	x	x	x
Thai Garlic	x	x	x	x	x
Thai Shallots	x	x	x	x	x
Turmeric Root			x		x
Shrimp Paste	x	x	x	x	x
DRY SPICES					
Bay Leaves			x		
Cardamom				x	x
Cinnamon			x	x	
Cloves				x	
Coriander Seeds		x	x	x	x
Cumin Seeds		x	x	x	
Dried Red Chiles (large, mild, such as Thai spur, California, or guajillo)	x		x	x	x
Fenugreek			x		
Nutmeg			x	x	
Star Anise				x	
White Peppercorns	x	x	x	x	

FIVE CURRY PASTES TO KNOW

There are countless versions of *kaeng* throughout Thailand, and even more recipes for them. But in the West, there are a few that we see more commonly than others:

- **Red Curry** is made with dried *prik chi fa* (Thai spur) chiles and is typically cooked with coconut milk to form a rich, spicy-sweet soup that is great with seafood, chicken, tofu, or vegetables like pumpkin. Adding ground peanuts to red curry paste is a quick shortcut to a Panang-style curry, which goes great with pork or beef.

- **Green Curry** is made with a host of fresh green ingredients, including green chiles, cilantro leaves and roots, and makrut lime. Like red curry, it is often cooked into a soup with coconut milk, though it is spicier and more strongly flavored. It has a particular affinity for fish, shellfish, and eggplants.

- **Yellow Curry** is a result of the British navy's influence across Asia. It's made with some typical Thai ingredients—shallots, garlic, lemongrass, shrimp paste—but paired with colonial British curry-powder-style ingredients, like turmeric, coriander, cumin, and cinnamon. It's commonly paired with meat and starchy root vegetables, like potatoes.*

- **Massaman Curry** is of Muslim origin and contains a slew of spices that made their way to Thailand via the Malay Archipelago in the seventeenth century. Because of its Muslim origins, Massaman curry is frequently made with chicken and potatoes. Beef and goat are also common choices. Massaman curry is often flavored with a sour element, such as orange juice or tamarind.

- **Khao Soi** is a Chin Haw dish originally brought to Thailand, Laos, and Myanmar by Yunnanese immigrants. It shares a lot of ingredients with yellow curry but is more pungent. It's typically served with chicken or beef, along with raw shallots, pickled Chinese mustard root, and Chinese-style egg noodles.

HOW TO USE CURRY PASTE, STEP BY STEP

Once you've got your curry paste, whether it's homemade or store-bought, how do you make the actual curry? While Thai curries vary greatly in their cooking time depending on what you put in them, the process of incorporating and developing flavor in the curry paste is similar for all of them. Note that none of these steps are hard-and-fast rules, and you'll find many exceptions. However, this is a good basic process if you want to improvise with your curry making.

Step 1 • Heat Up Fat in a Wok

If you're making a coconut-based curry, scoop out some of the rich coconut fat from the top of a can of full-fat coconut milk (do *not* shake the can before opening, or you'll have to wait for the fat to settle out again!) and add it to a wok. If you're making a broth-based curry, you can use any oil here instead. If using coconut oil, cook it, stirring until the fat completely breaks out and the solids start to sizzle (see "Breaking Fat," page 585). If using regular oil, heat until shimmering.

continues

---

* There is another type of yellow curry in Thailand that is also known as "sour curry," which comes from the South, is fiery hot, and gets its sourness from the inclusion of tamarind. Leela Punyaratabandhu has some great sour curry recipes to seek out.

Step 2 • **Add Curry Paste and Stir**

Add your curry paste all at once and stir vigorously. The goal is to sort of "knead" the fat into the curry paste. You should end up with a solid mass of paste with no oil slick on the wok. Continue cooking, stirring, scraping, and smearing the paste around the wok.

Step 3 • **Wait for the Fat to Break**

Keep cooking until you notice the fat break back out of the curry paste. It will appear oily and greasy in the bottom of the wok, and the sound of cooking should become noticeably sharper and more crackly.

Step 4 • **Add Hearty Proteins and Long-Cooking Vegetables**

Hearty proteins like chicken, pork, beef, shrimp, or firm tofu can be added at this stage and fried with the curry paste mixture as you stir to coat every piece thoroughly in the mixture.

Step 5 • **Add Liquids and Tender Ingredients**

Add your liquid ingredients. This may be coconut milk, broth, or a combination. Stir well so that the curry paste dissolves in the liquid, then bring it all to a simmer. Depending on the kind of protein used, the curry can cook for a few minutes (thin slices of tender meat or seafood) or for several hours (tough braising cuts of beef, for instance).

More delicate proteins and vegetables like fish and softer tofu should be added to the curry just long enough to cook through.

Step 6 • **Season and Add Aromatics**

Season the curry to taste with fish sauce, sugar, salt, and citrus juice and stir in any finishing aromatics and crunchy vegetables such as herbs, sliced shallots, fresh chiles, or bean sprouts.

BREAKING FAT: The Most Important Step in Curry Making

Curry recipes frequently tell you to cook until you see "the fat break" from the curry paste or coconut milk. But what exactly does this mean, why does it happen, and why is it important? First, let's quickly review what an emulsion is.

An emulsion is a mixture of two liquids that typically don't like to mix together. In culinary terms, that is almost always a fat-in-water emulsion. Fat naturally wants to cling to itself, and if you simply whisk oil into water, eventually the teeny tiny fat globules will connect with others, form larger and larger drops, and eventually coalesce back into a single layer of oil floating on top of the water. We can make this emulsion more stable through two methods: First, by adding a chemical emulsifier—a molecule that is attracted to water on one side and oil on the other, such as the lecithin found in egg yolks. Second, by adding viscosity to the water—as with the mucilage found in mustard seeds or the starch in a cornstarch slurry—which makes it harder for fat droplets to find each other.

So how does this relate to curry pastes? Well, when you add curry paste to oil in a wok and start stirring it, you'll notice that the oil gets incorporated into the paste—the slick of oil at the bottom of the wok disappears and you end up with a homogenous-looking paste again. The oil has been emulsified into the paste, and it's the viscosity added by the crushed aromatics that are stabilizing that emulsion.

Now, as you continue to cook the paste, water is driven off in the form of steam. Here's the thing: with a fat-in-water emulsion, the less water there is, the more stable and thicker the emulsion will be … until it's not. You'll notice this when making mayonnaise: as you add more and more oil, the emulsion will become thicker and thicker until suddenly the water simply can't hold the amount of oil that is there and the oil all breaks out in a sort of chain reaction, turning your thick, rich mayonnaise into a greasy puddle.

The same thing happens when frying coconut fat or curry paste: as moisture is driven out, the mixture becomes thicker and thicker until suddenly there simply isn't enough water left to emulsify the fat and the whole thing gives. The fat comes out of suspension and "breaks" out of the curry paste or coconut fat and back into the wok.

OK, so we've got the *how*. Now what about the *why*? Why is it important to watch for this to happen? It has to do with flavor. As a curry paste fries, most of the energy going into it is used to evaporate its water content. In fact, until sufficient water has been evaporated, the mixture will have a tough time rising much above the boiling temperature of water. This is not a sufficient temperature to toast the aromatics or trigger any of the Maillard browning reactions (the cascade of chemical reactions that give browned foods their complex flavor). Only once water has been evaporated and the fat breaks out can the curry paste really start frying in earnest, developing deeper, more balanced flavors.

RED CURRY PASTE

Yield
Makes about ⅔ cup (160 ml)

Active Time
20 minutes

Total Time
20 minutes

NOTES

See the chart on page 581 for substitutions for difficult-to find ingredients. You can also make this curry paste using one of the other techniques on page 575. You can use miso paste in place of shrimp paste if you want to keep this vegetarian. If you want to store this in the fridge indefinitely, add another teaspoon of salt (when cooking with it, be very careful not to overseason!). Alternatively, pack the excess curry paste into zipper-lock freezer bags with the air pressed out and store in the freezer indefinitely.

The base of red curry paste is dried chiles soaked in water. *Prik haeng* is the Thai term for dried chiles, and the ones used in curry paste preparations vary greatly. My favorite locally available chiles to use in this recipe are puyas, which have a flavor that lies between fiery árbol chiles and fruity guajillos.

INGREDIENTS

- 3 ounces (90 g) puya, guajillo, California, or pasilla chiles, stemmed and seeded
- One 2-inch knob fresh galangal, peeled and roughly chopped (1½ ounces/45 g)
- 6 fresh or dried makrut lime leaves, hard cevntral stem removed and discarded, leaves roughly chopped (½ ounce/15 g)
- 2 stalks fresh lemongrass, bottom 3 to 5 inches only (2 ounces/60 g), tough outer leaves removed and discarded, tender core finely chopped
- 12 medium garlic cloves (40 to 50 g), roughly chopped
- 2 medium shallots (3 ounces/90 g), roughly chopped
- 2 to 12 fresh red Thai bird chiles, roughly chopped (2 will be hot, 12 will be extremely hot)
- ½ ounce (15 g) cilantro root or stems, roughly chopped
- 1 teaspoon (4 g) freshly ground white pepper
- 2 teaspoons (8 g) kosher salt
- 1 teaspoon (5 g) Thai shrimp paste or miso paste (see Notes)

DIRECTIONS

Place the dried chiles in a heatproof container and cover with boiling water. Cover and set aside for 10 minutes. Meanwhile, combine the galangal, lime leaves, lemongrass, garlic, shallots, fresh chiles, cilantro root, pepper, and salt in a mortar and pestle. Pound into a rough paste. Drain the chiles, add to the mortar, and continue pounding until a smooth paste has formed. Pound in the shrimp paste. Store in the fridge for up to a week (see Notes).

RED CURRY WITH MUSHROOMS, PUMPKIN, AND TOFU

Yield
Serves 4

Active Time
15 minutes

Total Time
25 minutes

NOTES

The coconut fat needs to be in a solid layer at the top of the can, so do not shake the can before opening! You can use any kind of mushroom for this, but it's especially good with shiitake, oyster, or maitake. See page 109 for more on Asian mushrooms and how to prepare them.

There is fish sauce and shrimp paste in this recipe, which makes it unsuitable for vegetarians, but you can omit the shrimp paste and use soy sauce in place of the fish sauce if you'd like. You can use chunks of chicken or pork in place of the tofu.

INGREDIENTS

One 13.5-ounce (400 ml) can full-fat coconut milk (see Notes)

1 tablespoon (15 ml) peanut, rice bran, or other neutral oil

¼ cup (60 ml) homemade (page 586) or store-bought red Thai curry paste

8 ounces (225 g) extra-firm tofu, cut into bite-sized pieces (see Notes)

½ kabocha squash (about 1 pound/450 g), seeded and cut into 1½-inch chunks (see page 200 for step-by-step instructions)

8 ounces (225 g) mushrooms, cut into bite-sized pieces (see Notes)

2 cups (475 ml) homemade or store-bought low-sodium chicken or vegetable stock or water

1 tablespoon (15 ml) fish sauce, plus more to taste (see Notes)

1 tablespoon (12 g) palm sugar, plus more to taste, broken up in a mortar and pestle

1 cup (1 ounce/30 g) Thai or Italian basil leaves

Steamed jasmine rice for serving

This simple curry combines kabocha squash (which can be simmered with its skin on!) with mushrooms and tofu for a hearty, quick-cooking meal.

DIRECTIONS

(1) Scoop 2 tablespoons (30 ml) of thick cream from the top of the can of coconut milk and add to a wok along with the oil. Cook over medium heat, stirring, until the fat has broken out of the mixture and it's shimmering and sputtering. Immediately add the curry paste and cook, stirring, scraping, and smearing the curry paste around the bottom of the wok until you see fat start to break out and the curry paste gets a toasty aroma, about 2 minutes.

(2) Add the tofu and pumpkin and stir to coat in the curry mixture. Add the mushrooms, remaining coconut milk, stock, fish sauce, and sugar and stir to combine. Bring to a simmer and cook, stirring occasionally, until the squash is tender, 8 to 12 minutes.

(3) Stir in the basil leaves, season with more fish sauce or sugar to taste, and serve immediately with steamed jasmine rice.

THAI-STYLE TOFU WITH GREEN BEANS AND RED CURRY PASTE (PAD PRIK KING)

Yield
Serves 4

Active Time
30 minutes

Total Time
30 minutes

NOTE
Store-bought curry paste tends to be very salty, so you can't add quite as much of it to a dish as the homemade stuff.

INGREDIENTS

3 tablespoons (45 ml) peanut, rice bran, or other neutral oil

One 12-ounce (340 g) block firm tofu, cut into 1-inch squares ½ inch thick, pressed firmly between paper towels

1 pound (450 g) green beans or long beans, trimmed and cut into 1½-inch lengths

¼ cup (60 ml) Thai red curry paste, homemade (page 586) or store-bought

1 tablespoon (12 g) sugar

1 tablespoon (15 ml) soy sauce or fish sauce

Handful of chopped fresh Thai or Italian basil leaves

Kosher salt (optional)

Steamed jasmine rice, for serving

Stroll by a curry vendor in a Thai food court and you'll likely see one curry that stands out from the rest: *pad prik king*. Unlike most other curries, which are served with plenty of liquid—be it coconut milk or broth—pad prik king is served dry, its intensely flavored curry paste coating each morsel of food. It can be made with any number of vegetables or meat, but I particularly love the common combination of beans and tofu.

Typically, pad prik king would be made by first searing the chile paste in hot oil, which helps to develop and deepen its flavor, then adding the tofu and beans and tossing everything together. I prefer to get a little more flavor and texture in the dish by first panfrying the tofu until it's crisp, removing it from the pan, blistering the green beans in more hot oil, removing them as well, then finally blooming the curry paste and tossing everything back together.

DIRECTIONS

(1) Heat 1 tablespoon (15 ml) of the oil in a wok over medium-high heat until shimmering. Add the tofu, spread it into a single layer, and cook, occasionally shaking the pan gently, until crisp on the first side, about 3 minutes. Flip the tofu and continue cooking until the second side is crisp, about 3 minutes longer. Transfer to a bowl and set aside.

(2) Return the wok to high heat until lightly smoking. Add 1 tablespoon (15 ml) of the remaining oil and swirl to coat. Immediately add the beans and cook, stirring and tossing occasionally, until blistered and tender, about 3 minutes. Transfer to the bowl with the tofu.

(3) Add the remaining tablespoon (15 ml) oil to the wok and return it to medium-high heat until lightly smoking. Immediately add the curry paste and cook, stirring, scraping, and smearing the curry paste around the bottom of the wok until you see fat start to break out and the curry paste gets a toasty aroma, about 2 minutes.

(4) Return the tofu and beans to the pan along with the sugar, soy sauce or fish sauce, and basil. Stir and toss to combine and coat the tofu and beans in curry paste. Season with salt to taste if desired. Serve immediately with steamed jasmine rice.

GREEN CURRY PASTE

Yield
Makes about ⅔ cup (160 ml)

Active Time
20 minutes

Total Time
20 minutes

NOTES

Thai bird chiles are very hot. You can use serrano or jalapeño peppers or any other green chile to reduce the heat level. See the chart on page 581 for substitutions on difficult-to find ingredients. You can also make this curry paste using one of the other techniques on page 575. You can use miso paste in place of shrimp paste if you want to keep this vegetarian. If you want to store this in the fridge indefinitely, add an additional teaspoon of salt (be careful not to overseason your dishes when cooking with this extra-salty curry paste!). Alternatively, pack the excess curry paste into zipper-lock freezer bags with the air pressed out and store in the freezer indefinitely.

Green curry paste is known as *kaeng khiao wan* or "sweet green curry" in Thailand, a reference to its pale green color, which it gets primarily from fresh green chiles. It is typically spicier than red curry paste and works with a wide range of ingredients, including meat and poultry, seafood, and small Thai eggplants and tofu.

INGREDIENTS

- One 2-inch knob galangal (1½ ounces/45 g), peeled and roughly chopped
- 6 fresh or dried makrut lime leaves, hard central stem removed and discarded, leaves roughly chopped (½ ounce/15 g)
- 2 stalks fresh lemongrass, bottom 3 to 5 inches only (2 ounces/60 g), tough outer leaves removed and discarded, tender core finely chopped
- 12 medium garlic cloves (40 to 50 g), roughly chopped
- 2 medium shallots (3 ounces/90 g), roughly chopped
- 2½ ounces (75 g/about 30) fresh green Thai bird chiles, stems removed, roughly chopped (see Notes)
- ½ ounce (15 g) cilantro root or stems, roughly chopped
- 2 teaspoons (5 g) freshly ground coriander seeds
- 1 tablespoon (7 g) freshly ground cumin seeds
- 1 teaspoon (3 g) freshly ground white peppercorns
- 1 ounce (30 g/about 1 cup) fresh Thai or Italian basil leaves
- 1 ounce (30 g/about 1 cup) cilantro leaves and fine stems
- 2 teaspoons (8 g) kosher salt
- 1 teaspoon (5 g) Thai shrimp paste (see Notes)

DIRECTIONS

Combine the galangal, lime leaves, lemongrass, garlic, shallots, chilies, cilantro root, coriander, cumin, white pepper, basil, cilantro, and 1 teaspoon (4 g) salt in a mortar and pestle. Pound into a fine paste. Pound in the shrimp paste and an additional teaspoon (4 g) of salt. Store in the fridge for up to a week (see Notes).

MUSSELS AND RICE NOODLES IN GREEN CURRY BROTH

Yield
Serves 4

Active Time
15 minutes

Total Time
20 minutes if using store-bought curry paste

NOTE
The coconut fat needs to be in a solid layer at the top of the can, so do not shake the can before opening!

INGREDIENTS

4 ounces (120 g) rice stick noodles
One 13.5-ounce (400 ml) can full-fat coconut milk (see Note)
1 tablespoon (15 ml) rice bran, peanut, or canola oil
¼ cup (60 ml) Thai green curry paste, homemade (page 589) or store-bought
4 medium garlic cloves (10 to 15 g), thinly sliced
1 medium shallot (1½ ounces/45 g), thinly sliced
1½ pounds (680 g) mussels
1 tablespoon (15 ml) fish sauce, plus more to taste
1 tablespoon (12 g) palm sugar, plus more to taste, broken up in a mortar and pestle
1 cup (1 ounce/30 g) chopped fresh cilantro leaves
1 small fresh green Thai bird or serrano chile, thinly sliced
Large handful of mung bean sprouts
1 tablespoon (15 ml) fresh lime juice from 1 lime, plus lime wedges for serving

This simple curry starts with coconut milk and green curry paste, along with some extra sliced shallots and garlic. As soon as it comes to a boil, the mussels go in and the lid goes down. I cook the mussels just long enough to let them open (nobody likes an overcooked mussel, except perhaps my dog Shabu, who seems to like overcooked anything). Finally, some soaked rice stick noodles, a shower of fresh cilantro leaves and sliced fresh chiles, along with a squeeze of lime juice, finish it off.

DIRECTIONS

(1) Place the rice stick noodles in a bowl and cover with hot water. Set aside while you cook the mussels.

(2) Scoop 2 tablespoons (30 ml) of thick cream from the top of the can of coconut milk and add to a wok, along with the oil. Cook over medium heat, stirring, until the fat has broken out of the mixture and it's shimmering and sputtering. Immediately add the curry paste and cook, stirring, scraping, and smearing the curry paste around the bottom of the wok until you see fat start to break out and the curry paste gets a toasty aroma, about 2 minutes.

(3) Add the garlic, shallot, and mussels and stir-fry until the mussels are coated in the mixture, about 30 seconds. Add the remaining contents of the coconut milk can, the fish sauce, and the sugar.

(4) Increase the heat to high and bring the contents of the wok to a simmer. Cover and cook, adjusting the heat to maintain a steady simmer, until all of the mussels are open and the broth is rich and aromatic, about 3 minutes.

(5) Drain the rice stick noodles and add to the wok. Cook, stirring, until the noodles are fully softened, 1 to 2 minutes.

(6) Stir in the cilantro, chile, bean sprouts, and lime juice. Season with more fish sauce and sugar to taste if desired. Serve immediately with lime wedges.

GREEN CURRY SAUSAGE MEATBALLS

Yield
Serves 6
to 8 as an
appetizer

Active Time
15 minutes

Total Time
15 minutes

INGREDIENTS

2 pounds (900 g) freshly ground pork
 shoulder

6 ounces (170 g/about ¾ cup) Thai green
 curry paste, homemade (page 589) or
 store-bought

¼ cup (60 ml) peanut, rice bran, or other
 neutral oil

Fried shallots, cilantro, and thinly sliced or
 hand-torn makrut lime leaf, for garnish
 (optional)

Curry pastes can make a great flavor base for homemade sausage, and making it is as simple as adding curry paste to ground pork. When mixing sausage, the most important part is thoroughly kneading the mixture. This causes pork proteins to cross-link, which is what gives sausage its springy, bouncy texture. As you mix sausage, look for a thin film of pork proteins to start forming on the side of the mixing bowl as an indication that the protein has sufficiently cross-linked.

This mixture can be cooked in a skillet in patties, it can be made into small balls to simmer in curry or soup, or it can be formed into patties or logs and fried or grilled. Serve with Nam Pla Prik (page 257) or Jaew (page 440) for dipping.

DIRECTIONS

Combine the pork shoulder and curry paste in a stand mixer fitted with a paddle attachment. Mix on medium-low speed until the mixture is tacky and leaves a thin film of protein around the edges of the bowl, about 5 minutes. Alternatively, knead thoroughly by hand. Form into patties, balls, or logs and cook as desired.

How to Make Khao Soi

"So that's what it's supposed to taste like" is a frequent thought that goes through my head when traveling. It's what I thought in Chiang Mai the first time I tasted *khao soi*, the Chin Haw dish of chicken and noodles in a coconut and curry broth. It was brought to the North of Thailand, Laos, and Myanmar by Yunnanese immigrants. I mean, I'd tasted the dish many times back home, but it was always through the lens of cooks who had adapted recipes for themselves or for their customers. Tasting the real thing in situ lets you really understand its importance.

Of course, that's all a load of BS. Arguments around authenticity can be interesting and enlightening, but only when they consider that the very concept of authenticity is like trying to shoot a target that is constantly zigzagging, being pulled this way and that. Even in Chiang Mai, there are hundreds of variations of khao soi—and we're talking just the laksa-inflected Thai version here, not any of the other variants, which differ as widely as, say, pizza in the United States does. That said, the best khao sois I had shared some common traits: impeccably fresh and bouncy egg noodles, a richly textured broth so intense that it was served only in small quantities, layer upon layer of flavor made by picking the right aromatics and not being lazy with their treatment.

As northern Thailand's de facto signature dish, it's also one of its most regionally incongruous. Wet curry pastes, made by pounding roots, rhizomes, seeds, spices, herbs, and various fermented seafood products, don't feature heavily in northern Thai cuisine, nor does coconut milk, the way it does in the curries of central or southern Thai. Stretchy, eggy Chinese wheat noodles are also not particularly common.

But it makes sense that khao soi is northern Thailand's most popular export. As Chiang Mai–based American chef Andy Ricker pointed out in the *New York Times*, khao soi "is exotic without being weird and, most important, completely delicious." It's the kind of dish everybody can love.

THE CURRY PASTE

Similar in profile to Muslim-influenced Massaman curry pastes, khao soi paste is made with a combination of moist aromatics and a range of dry spices. You can use the standard process of blooming the curry paste in hot fat, but here's an alternative technique I learned from a local chef in Chiang Mai: roast the aromatics in a foil pouch until charred.

This accomplishes two goals. First, it helps develop an extra layer of flavor as aromatic compounds within the spices break down into smaller parts and reassemble into hundreds of new ones in a process known as the *Maillard reaction*. Second, it softens up the vegetables and begins the process of releasing their aromatics. This makes pounding the curry paste significantly easier (and, indeed, the technique also works for other types of curry paste if you want to add some charred flavor).

THE BROTH

Khao soi is a soupier dish than most other curry-style soups, using a combination of coconut milk and broth. Both chicken and beef are common choices, but I generally opt for chicken as it's faster, easier, and store-bought chicken broth is better than store-bought beef broth. As with other curries, I add chicken directly to the bloomed curry paste before adding the liquid ingredients, then I let everything simmer until the chicken is cooked.

As it cooks, the broth should get thicker and break a little, with tiny droplets of flavorful spiced chicken fat pooling on the surface. It should also smell awesome.

THE NOODLES

Last element: the noodles. In Chiang Mai, khao soi invariably comes with yellow, stretchy, flat egg noodles about ¼ inch wide and ⅛ inch thick. Think fettuccine or linguine, if you will. In the West, you may see khao soi served with lo mein noodles or even fat rice noodles.

I don't know what wacky, crazed mind came up with the idea of serving the noodles two ways in the soup, but khao soi gets a nest of crisply fried noodles perched on top of the slick, boiled noodles underneath. Personally, I'm never one to say no to extra fried things.

Stretchy noodles, crispy noodles, tender braised chicken, rich, warmly spiced broth, sharp shallots and pickled mustard root to garnish, and a squeeze of fresh lime. This crazy combination of flavors and textures is what makes khao soi so exciting.

Working with Lemongrass

Lemongrass has a wonderful aroma, but it is extremely tough and requires a bit of extra attention to make it edible. When shopping for lemongrass, look for healthy-looking stalks with minimal dried edges or spotty brown discoloration. Lemongrass can be stored in a plastic bag in the fridge for a few weeks or in the freezer indefinitely.

How to Use Lemongrass to Season a Broth

If you're using lemongrass to season broth and then discarding it, the best technique is to use the back of a knife or cleaver to bruise and smash the stalk up and down its length so that it releases its flavor more easily to the broth.

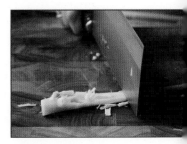

How to Prepare Lemongrass for Curry Paste

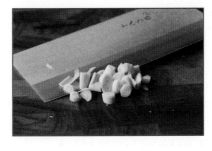

Only the tender, bottom few inches of a lemongrass stalk are edible. Start by peeling off and discarding the outer leaves until you reach a pale yellow tender layer underneath. Next, cut the stalk about 5 inches from the base and check the cross section. If you notice any woody, tough-looking leaves, trim off a little more until all the leaves are tender. Keep the tender stuff and discard the rest of the trim.

Next roughly chop the tender parts and add them to your mortar to be pounded (discard the tough nub at the base).

How to Slice Lemongrass for Frying or Stir-Fries

Peel off the outer leaves and trim as for rough chopping. Then, using a very sharp knife, slice the lemongrass as thin as you can manage. The thinner the better! The sliced lemongrass can be chopped further for stir-fries if desired.

NORTHERN THAI–STYLE KHAO SOI (CURRY CHICKEN AND NOODLE SOUP)

Yield
Serves 6
to 8 as an
appetizer

Active Time
45 minutes

Total Time
2 hours

NOTES

You can use ⅓ cup of store-bought red or yellow curry paste in place of the homemade curry paste, though the flavor will be quite different. See the chart on page 581 for substitutions on difficult-to-find ingredients. You can also form this curry paste using one of the other techniques on page 575. If you want to store this in the fridge indefinitely, add additional teaspoon of salt (be careful not to overseason your dishes when cooking with this extra-salty curry paste!). Alternatively, pack the excess curry paste into zipper-lock freezer bags with the air pressed out and store in the freezer indefinitely.

The coconut fat needs to be in a solid layer at the top of the can, so do not shake the can before opening!

INGREDIENTS

For the Curry Paste (see Notes):

1½ ounces (45 g) dried mild red chiles, preferably Thai spur (pasilla, California, or guajillo would also work)

½ ounce (15 g) cilantro root or stems, roughly chopped

6 medium garlic cloves (15 to 20 g), roughly chopped

1 medium shallot (1½ ounces/45 g), roughly chopped

1 fresh lemongrass stalk, bottom 3 to 5 inches only (about 1 ounce/30 g), tough outer leaves removed and discarded, tender core finely chopped

One 1-inch knob fresh ginger (about 1 ounce/30 g), peeled and roughly chopped

One 2-inch knob fresh turmeric (about 1 ounce/30 g), roughly chopped

3 fresh or dried makrut lime leaves (¼ ounce/8 g), hard central stem removed and discarded, leaves roughly chopped

1 teaspoon (3 g) ground coriander seeds

1 teaspoon (3 g) ground white peppercorns

½ teaspoon (2 g) ground black or green cardamom seeds

Kosher salt

To Cook:

1 pound (450 g) fresh Chinese-style egg noodles

1 cup (240 ml) peanut, rice bran, or other neutral oil

Kosher salt

Two 13.5-ounce (400 ml) cans full-fat coconut milk (see Notes)

4 chicken legs (about 6 ounces/170 g each), split into drumsticks and thighs

1 quart (1 l) homemade or store-bought low-sodium chicken stock

1 tablespoon (15 ml) fish sauce, plus more to taste

1 tablespoon (12 g) palm sugar, plus more to taste, broken up in a mortar and pestle

To Serve:

Sliced shallots

Lime wedges

Minced zha cai (Chinese pickled mustard root)

(1) **For the Curry Paste:** Place the chiles in a heatproof container and cover with boiling water. Cover and set aside for 10 minutes.

(2) Meanwhile, place the cilantro root, garlic, shallot, lemongrass, ginger, turmeric, and lime leaves in the center of a 12-inch square of heavy-duty aluminum foil. Gather the edges up to make a tight pouch. Place the pouch directly over the flame of a gas burner and cook, turning occasionally, until aromatic and wisps of smoke begin to rise, about 8 minutes. If no gas burner is available, place the pouch in the bottom of a wok or cast iron skillet and heat over high heat, turning occasionally, until smoky, about 10 minutes. Allow the contents to cool slightly and transfer to a large mortar and pestle.

(3) Add the ground coriander, white pepper, cardamom, and 1 teaspoon (4 g) salt to the mortar. Pound into a rough paste. Drain the chiles, add to the mortar, and continue pounding until a smooth paste has formed. Set the curry mixture aside.

(4) **To Cook:** Separate out one-quarter of the noodles (enough noodles to make a crispy fried-noodle topping for 4 bowls) and set the remaining noodles aside. Heat the oil in a wok over high heat until shimmering. Working in 4 batches, add the noodles to the oil and fry, stirring and flipping until golden brown and crisp, about 1 minute. Transfer to a paper-towel-lined plate. Season with salt and set aside.

(5) Discard all but 1 tablespoon oil from the wok. Scoop 2 tablespoons of the thick cream from the top of the can of coconut milk and add to the wok. Cook over medium heat, stirring, until the fat has broken out of the mixture and it's shimmering and sputtering. Immediately add the curry paste and cook, stirring, scraping, and smearing the curry paste around the bottom of the wok until you see fat start to break out and the curry paste gets a toasty aroma, about 2 minutes.

(6) Add the chicken pieces and turn to coat in the mixture. Add the remaining coconut milk from the cans, followed by the chicken stock, fish sauce, and palm sugar. Bring to a bare simmer and cook, turning the chicken occasionally, until the chicken is tender and the broth is very flavorful, about 30 minutes. Season with more fish sauce or sugar to taste as desired.

(7) **To Serve:** Bring a pot of salted water to a boil. Add the remaining uncooked noodles and cook until al dente, about 1 minute. Drain the noodles and divide between 4 warmed bowls. Top the noodles with 2 pieces of chicken. Divide the broth evenly between the bowls. Top with fried noodles and serve immediately with sliced shallots, lime wedges, and zha cai on the side.

20-MINUTE CHICKEN RED CURRY NOODLE SOUP

Yield
Serves 4

Active Time
10 minutes

Total Time
20 minutes

NOTES

The coconut fat needs to be in a solid layer at the top of the can, so do not shake the can before opening! I often stir a tablespoon or two of shrimp paste or store-bought Thai chile jam (*nam prik pao*) into this soup as it simmers if I'm in the mood for a little more seafood or chile flavor.

INGREDIENTS

One 13.5-ounce (400 ml) can full-fat coconut milk (see Notes)
1 tablespoon (15 ml) peanut, rice bran, or other neutral oil
¼ cup (60 g) Thai red curry paste, homemade (page 586) or store-bought
2 small boneless, skinless chicken breast halves (about 12 ounces/340 g total)
1½ quarts (1.5 l) homemade or store-bought low-sodium chicken stock
1 tablespoon (15 ml) fish sauce, plus more to taste
1 tablespoon (12 g) palm sugar, plus more to taste, broken up in a mortar and pestle
1 tablespoon (15 ml) fresh lime juice from 1 lime

To Serve:

4 servings of noodles of your choice, such as dry Thai-style rice noodles or fresh wheat noodles, cooked according to package directions
Handful of roughly chopped fresh cilantro leaves and fine stems
1 small shallot, thinly sliced
Lime wedges

This recipe is a fast and easy version of khao soi that is by no means authentic but uses a bunch of shelf-stable staples—Thai red curry paste, store-bought or homemade stock, dry noodles, a can of coconut milk—and combines them with a few fresh ingredients like chicken, herbs, and limes, for a hearty, quick, flavorful noodle soup that's just 20 minutes away. Top it off with some of that crispy chow mein in a can or even canned potato sticks for extra crunch.

DIRECTIONS

(1) Scoop 2 tablespoons of thick cream from the top of the can of coconut milk and add to a wok, along with the oil. Cook over medium heat, stirring, until the fat has broken out of the mixture and it's shimmering and sputtering. Immediately add the curry paste and cook, stirring, scraping, and smearing the curry paste around the bottom of the wok until you see fat start to break out and the curry paste gets a toasty aroma, about 2 minutes.

(2) Add the chicken and turn to coat in the curry paste. Add the rest of the coconut milk, the chicken stock, fish sauce, and sugar. Bring to a boil, then adjust the heat to maintain a bare simmer. Cook until the chicken is cooked through, about 15 minutes. Transfer the chicken to a bowl and tear it into strips as soon as it's cool enough to handle. Season the broth with the lime juice and more fish sauce or sugar to taste if desired.

(3) **To Serve:** Divide the noodles and chicken between 4 large bowls. Divide the broth between the bowls. Serve with chopped cilantro, sliced shallots, and lime wedges.

SIMPLE THAI HOT AND SOUR SOUP WITH SHRIMP (TOM YAM KUNG)

Yield
Serves 4

Active Time
15 minutes

Total Time
30 minutes

INGREDIENTS

For the Broth:

2 teaspoons (10 ml) peanut, rice bran, or other neutral oil

12 ounces (340 g) large shrimp, peeled, shells reserved

1 quart (1 l) homemade or store-bought low-sodium chicken stock or water

2 fresh lemongrass stalks, bottom 3 to 5 inches only (1½ ounces/40 g), tough outer leaves removed and discarded, tender core bruised multiple times with the dull side of a knife blade

One 1-inch knob fresh galangal, peeled and roughly chopped (⅔ ounce/20 g)

3 fresh or dried makrut lime leaves, hard central stem removed and discarded, leaves roughly chopped (¼ ounce/ 8 g)

For the Soup:

4 fresh red Thai bird chiles, more or less to taste

12 cherry tomatoes, cut in half

5 ounces (145 g) oyster or button mushrooms or shiitake mushroom caps cut into bite-sized pieces

¼ cup (60 ml) fish sauce

¼ cup (60 ml) fresh lime juice (from 4 to 5 limes)

¼ cup (60 ml) nam prik pao

½ cup (120 ml) evaporated milk or coconut milk (optional)

Handful of chopped fresh cilantro or culantro (Thai sawtooth herb)

Tom yam soup is a classic Thai dish that can be as simple or as complex as you'd like. The name translates as "boiled mixed" and refers to the wide range of aromatics that are incorporated in its making. Think of it as an aromatic tea. It has a sour-hot flavor from the inclusion of lime juice and *nam prik pao* (Thai chile jam), along with aromatics like lime leaf, lemongrass, and galangal. Many modern recipes include a can of evaporated milk for richness. Add coconut milk and it becomes tom kha.

DIRECTIONS

1. **For the Broth:** Heat the vegetable oil in a wok over medium-high heat until shimmering. Add the shrimp shells and stir-fry until browned in spots and fragrant, about 2 minutes. Add the stock, bring to a simmer, and simmer for 5 minutes. Remove the shrimp shells with a fine-mesh strainer and discard.

2. Add the lemongrass, galangal, and lime leaves. Simmer for 5 minutes. If desired, remove and discard the aromatics, or leave them in and have diners eat around them.

3. **For the Soup:** Crush the chiles in a mortar and pestle. Add the tomatoes and gently pound to break them up slightly, then add the mixture to the soup. Add the mushrooms, fish sauce, lime juice, nam prik pao, evaporated milk (if using), and shrimp. Bring to a simmer and cook just until the shrimp are cooked through, about 1 minute. Stir in chopped cilantro or culantro and serve.

MAPO TOFU

Yield
Serves 4

Active Time
20 minutes

Total Time
20 minutes

INGREDIENTS

1 tablespoon (8 g) red Sichuan peppercorns

2 tablespoons (30 ml) peanut, rice bran, or other neutral oil

1 teaspoon (3 g) cornstarch

1 tablespoon (15 ml) cold water

4 ounces (120 g) ground beef or pork

2 teaspoons (5 g) minced garlic (about 2 medium cloves)

2 teaspoons (5 g) minced fresh ginger (about ½-inch segment)

2 tablespoons (30 g) fermented chile bean paste (doubanjiang)

2 tablespoons (30 ml) Shaoxing wine

1 teaspoon (5 ml) dark soy sauce

2 teaspoons (10 ml) light soy sauce

¼ cup (60 ml) homemade or store-bought low-sodium chicken stock or water

1½ pounds medium to firm silken tofu, cut into ½-inch cubes

¼ cup (60 ml) homemade (page 310) or store-bought chile oil

3 scallions, sliced

Steamed rice, for serving

This is it. My favorite dish in the world and the grandmother of Sichuan cuisine. Translated literally as "pockmarked grandmother's tofu," its totally apocryphal origin story is identical to a half dozen other food origin stories: it starts with hungry crowds and a cook with few ingredients but plenty of creativity. The result is an inexpensive stew that uses simple ingredients—soft tofu, ground meat (traditionally beef, but frequently pork), fermented chile bean paste, a handful of Sichuan peppercorns, and plenty of red-hot chile oil—to create simple, soul-satisfying fare.

I grew up on the sweet-and-salty, heavy-on-the-beef version of mapo tofu that my mom used to make for us (see page 600). When paired with her handmade beef dumplings, it was far and away my favorite meal. Since then, I've had mapo tofu everywhere from Chinese takeout joints in Manhattan to directly from the source in Chengdu.

I very rarely get visibly excited about anything—I'm not sure if that makes me a stoic or an emotionless shell of a human being—but as we sat down at Chen Mapo Doufu, the upscale Chengdu institution that was supposedly built on the fame and recipe of Grandma Chen herself, I got a little giddy.

You can find mapo tofu on the menu at almost any restaurant in China, especially in Sichuan, but this version, served in a screaming-hot cast iron bowl, was easily my favorite. Tender cubes of soft tofu laced with tender ground beef under a bubbling layer of chile oil, fragrant with toasted Sichuan peppercorn and fermented horse beans. It didn't have the blast of chile heat you might expect from looking at it. Rather, it has a more subtle, layered heat with chiles that come through alternately as sweet and hot with the rich, almost raisin-like flavor of dried fruit.

I'm happy to say that the best version I've had in the States, made by Zhang Wenxue, a Sichuan chef at Fuloon, in Malden, Massachusetts (I believe that it has since shuttered), is a near-perfect taste-alike to the one at Chen. I'm even happier to report that he was kind enough to share his techniques and recipe with me a few years back, and I've altered it very little over the years. The only thing I've changed is how I handle the tofu. Traditionally, the tofu is boiled in water briefly before being added to the stew. I've always heard this explained as "to remove the raw bean flavor." Having tasted it side by side, I've never noticed any difference, so I personally skip the step, though I won't hold it against you if you want to preboil your tofu.

There's nothing difficult about the technique other than being careful once you've added the tofu not to break it up by stirring too vigorously. If you can toss with no utensils, do it (see "The Technique" on page 366). Otherwise, carefully slide a wok spatula under the tofu and turn it gently as you cook. Once you've got the ingredients prepared, the recipe takes all of 10 minutes at the stove.

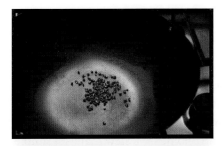

DIRECTIONS

(1) Heat half of the Sichuan peppercorns in a large wok over high heat until lightly smoking. Transfer to a mortar and pestle. Pound until finely ground and set aside.

(2) Add the remaining Sichuan peppercorns and the oil to the wok. Heat over medium-high heat until lightly sizzling, about 1½ minutes. Remove the peppercorns with a spider and discard, leaving the oil in the pan.

(3) Combine the cornstarch and cold water in a small bowl and mix with a fork until homogenous. Set aside.

(4) Heat the oil left in the wok over high heat until smoking. Add the beef and cook, stirring constantly for 1 minute. Add the garlic and ginger and cook until fragrant, about 15 seconds. Add the chile bean paste and cook until the oil starts to turn red, about 30 seconds. Add the wine, soy sauce, and chicken stock and bring to a boil. Pour in the cornstarch mixture and cook for 30 seconds, until thickened. Add the tofu and carefully fold it in, being careful not to break it up too much. Fold in the chile oil and half of the scallions and simmer for 30 seconds longer. Transfer immediately to a serving bowl and sprinkle with the remaining scallions and the toasted ground Sichuan pepper. Serve immediately with steamed rice.

MY MOM'S JAPANESE-STYLE MAPO TOFU

Yield
Serves 4

Active Time
15 minutes

Total Time
15 minutes

INGREDIENTS

1 teaspoon (3 g) cornstarch

1 tablespoon (15 ml) cold water

2 tablespoons (30 ml) peanut, rice bran, or other neutral oil

4 ounces (120 g) ground beef

2 teaspoons (5 g) minced garlic (about 2 medium cloves)

2 teaspoons (5 g) minced fresh ginger (about ½-inch segment)

2 scallions, chopped into ¼-inch pieces, dark greens reserved for garnish

2 tablespoons (30 ml) sake

2 tablespoons (30 ml) mirin

1 tablespoon (15 ml) shoyu or light soy sauce

¼ cup (60 ml) low-sodium chicken stock, dashi, or water

1½ pounds medium to firm silken tofu, cut into ½-inch cubes

Steamed rice and chile oil, for serving

This version of mapo tofu is similar to what we ate growing up, though instead of plain ground beef my mom would use the dish as an opportunity to use up leftover dumpling filling. You could do the same if you have leftovers from a batch of My Mom's Beef and Vegetable Filling for Dumplings (page 417). Unlike the numbing-hot Sichuan version, this one is savory and sweet, with the classic Japanese flavors of soy, sake, and mirin, and comes together even faster, if you can believe it. It's one of my go-to meals for the family when Alicia or Adri is not in the mood for spicy foods and I'm craving saucy soft tofu.

DIRECTIONS

1 Combine the cornstarch and cold water in a small bowl and mix with a fork until homogenous. Set aside.

2 Heat the oil in a wok over high heat until smoking. Add the beef and cook, stirring constantly for 1 minute. Add the garlic, ginger, and scallion whites and pale greens and cook, stirring, until fragrant, about 15 seconds. Add the sake, mirin, soy sauce, and chicken stock and bring to a boil. Pour in the cornstarch mixture and cook for 30 seconds, until thickened. Add the tofu and carefully fold it in, being careful not to break it up too much. Transfer immediately to a serving bowl and sprinkle with the scallion greens. Serve immediately with rice and chile oil.

WATER-BOILED BEEF

Never has the name of a dish been so incongruous with the dish itself. While the beef in Sichuan *shui zhu niu rou* (water-boiled beef) is *technically* boiled in water, a more fitting name would be "Chile-Coated Beef Tenderized by Sauron Himself in the Eternal Fires of Mt. Doom." (If someone could translate that, I'd appreciate it.)

Wanna see more chile oil than you've ever seen in a single place? Order yourself a bowl of shui zhu niu rou and wait for your volcano to arrive. Tender slices of marinated beef are tucked under a layer of angry red chile oil speckled with garlic, chiles, and Sichuan peppercorns. As you lift the slices out from their bath, they drag up through the oil, which gives them (and probably your shirt) a flavorful coating.

For such a complex-tasting and impressive-looking dish, it's remarkably easy. All you need to do is marinate beef, coat it in starch, simmer it in a flavored broth with some cabbage, celery, and scallions, pour it into a bowl, and drizzle the whole thing with sizzling-hot oil to bloom some of the flavors. The starch coating on the beef gives it an ultra-tender, almost slippery texture.

The technique I use is based on Fuchsia Dunlop's recipe from *Land of Plenty* (now re-titled as *The Food of Sichuan*), an essential manual for any English-speaking cook who wants to learn more about Sichuan cuisine. I've adapted it a bit to my own tastes by changing the cut of beef, adding a baking soda marinating step, and adding garlic to the bowl before pouring over the sizzling hot oil, but the basic technique is intact.

Yield
Serves 4

Active Time
25 minutes

Total Time
25 minutes

NOTES

This recipe calls for beef tenderloin. You can also use other lean, tender cuts like flank steak, tritip, or eye of round. The key is slicing very thinly against the grain. A sharp knife helps with this, and if you still have trouble, try throwing the beef in the freezer for 15 minutes to firm it up. You can also buy shaved beef intended for shabu or sukiyaki for this dish. If you don't have Sichuan er jing tiao chiles, you can use other small red chiles, such as árbol, Japones, or chao tian jiao.

INGREDIENTS

For the Beef:
1 pound (450 g) beef tenderloin (see Notes), sliced against the grain as thin as possible
¼ teaspoon (1 g) baking soda
1 tablespoon (15 ml) Shaoxing wine
1 tablespoon (15 ml) light soy sauce
1 teaspoon (5 ml) peanut, rice bran, or other neutral oil
1 tablespoon (9 g) cornstarch

For the Málà Mixture:
3 tablespoons (45 ml) vegetable oil
12 to 20 small dried red chiles, such as Sichuan er jing tiao (see Notes), stems snipped off and discarded, seeds mostly shaken out and discarded
1 tablespoon (5 g) Sichuan peppercorns

To Cook:
1 celery stalk, cut on a sharp bias into 1½-inch segments
2 scallions, white and pale green parts cut into 1-inch segments, greens chopped for garnish
8 ounces (225 g) Napa cabbage, cut into bite-sized pieces
3 tablespoons (45 g) Sichuan broad bean chile paste (doubanjiang)
2 teaspoons (5 g) minced garlic (about 2 medium cloves)
2 teaspoons (5 g) minced fresh ginger (about ½-inch segment)
1 tablespoon (10 to 12 g) Sichuan or Korean chile flakes
2 cups (480 ml) homemade or store-bought low-sodium chicken stock or water
1 tablespoon (15 ml) dark soy sauce

To Serve:
1 tablespoon (8 g) minced garlic (about 3 medium cloves)
¼ cup (60 ml) *caiziyou* (roasted rapeseed oil; see page 18) or peanut, rice bran, or other neutral oil

recipe continues

1. **For the Beef:** Place the beef in a medium bowl, cover with cold water, and vigorously agitate it. Drain through a fine-mesh strainer set in the sink and press on the beef with your hands to remove excess water. Return the beef to the bowl, add the baking soda, and vigorously massage the baking soda into the meat, lifting the meat, throwing it down, and squeezing it for 30 to 60 seconds. Add the wine, soy sauce, oil, and cornstarch and roughly work the marinade into the meat for at least 30 seconds. Set aside.

2. **For the Málà Mixture:** Combine the oil and chiles in a wok. Cook over medium heat, stirring and flipping the chiles constantly until they start to darken in color, about 1 minute. Add the Sichuan peppercorns and continue cooking until very fragrant but not burnt, 30 to 60 seconds longer. Transfer the chiles and peppercorns to a cutting board, leaving the oil in the wok. Chop the chiles and Sichuan peppercorns until they are about the same size as standard red pepper flakes (the kind you put on your pizza). Set aside.

3. **To Cook:** Return the wok to high heat until smoking. Add the celery, white and pale green parts of the scallions, and Napa cabbage and stir-fry until tender and wilted, about 2 minutes. Transfer to the bottom of a large serving bowl, leaving the oil in the wok (if the wok is dry, add another tablespoon of oil to the bottom at this point).

4. Return the wok to high heat. Add the chile bean paste and cook, stirring, until it sizzles and the oil starts to turn red, about 30 seconds. Add the garlic, ginger, and chile flakes and cook until aromatic, about 15 seconds. Add the stock and the soy sauce and bring the mixture to a simmer.

5. Gently lower the beef into the wok one piece at a time so that it doesn't stick. Increase the heat to high and cook, swirling constantly, until the beef is just barely cooked through and the liquid is simmering, about 1 minute. Pour the beef and the broth over the celery and cabbage in the bowl. Wipe out the wok.

6. **To Serve:** Sprinkle the chopped chile and Sichuan peppercorn mixture all over the top of the beef. Sprinkle the minced garlic over the top. Heat the oil in the wok until it is smoking hot, then pour it all over the top of the serving bowl, causing the chiles, Sichuan peppercorn, and garlic to sizzle and release their aroma. Top with the scallion greens and serve immediately.

SICHUAN-STYLE FISH POACHED IN CHILE BROTH (SHUI ZHU YU)

Yield
Serves 4

Active Time
25 minutes

Total Time
25 minutes

NOTE
For this dish I like to use green Sichuan peppercorns, which have a stronger numbing effect and brighter, more citrusy aroma. If you can't find them, red ones will work just fine.

This is one of my dad's favorite dishes. He knows it as "Fei Teng Fish," named after a famous chain of Sichuan restaurants in Beijing. In Sichuan, they call it *shui zhu yu*, or "water-boiled fish." It's very similar to water-boiled beef, but because of fish's more delicate texture and flavor, the broth is a little bit lighter, flavored with scallions and ginger and just a hint of fermented chile bean paste. It also makes the dish even easier to prepare.

INGREDIENTS

For the Fish:
1 pound fish fillet, such as tilapia, flounder, or sea bass, thinly sliced on a bias
1 teaspoon kosher salt
½ teaspoon (1 g) freshly ground white pepper
1 tablespoon (15 ml) Shaoxing wine
1 large egg white
2 tablespoons cornstarch
2 teaspoons (10 ml) peanut, rice bran, or other neutral oil

For the Málà Mixture:
3 tablespoons (45 ml) peanut, rice bran, or other neutral oil
12 to 20 small dried red chiles, such as Sichuan er jing tiao (see Note), stems snipped off and discarded, seeds mostly shaken out and discarded
2 tablespoons (10 g) green Sichuan peppercorns (see Note)

To Cook:
2 teaspoons (10 g) Sichuan broad bean chile paste (doubanjiang)
2 cups (480 ml) homemade or store-bought low-sodium chicken stock or water
2 tablespoons (30 ml) Shaoxing wine
2 scallions, white and pale green parts cut on a sharp bias into 1-inch segments, greens chopped for garnish
8 ounces (225 g) bean sprouts, trimmed
3 slices fresh ginger
Kosher salt

To Serve:
Handful of chopped fresh cilantro leaves and fine stems
¼ cup (60 ml) *caiziyou* (roasted rapeseed oil; see page 18) or peanut, rice bran, or other neutral oil

DIRECTIONS

(1) **For the Fish:** Place the fish slices in a medium bowl. Add the salt, white pepper, wine, egg white, cornstarch, and oil. Stir with your fingers until the fish is thoroughly coated in the mixture. Set aside.

(2) **For the Málà Mixture:** Combine the oil and chiles in a wok. Cook over medium heat, stirring and flipping the chiles constantly until they start to darken in color, about 1 minute. Add the Sichuan peppercorns and continue cooking until very fragrant but not burnt, 30 to 60 seconds longer. Transfer the chiles and peppercorns to a cutting board, leaving the oil in

recipe continues

the wok. Chop the chiles and Sichuan peppercorns until they are about the same size as standard red pepper flakes (the kind you put on your pizza). Set aside.

(3) **To Cook:** Return the wok to high heat until smoking. Add the chile bean paste and stir-fry until fragrant, about 15 seconds. Add the stock, wine, white and pale green parts of the scallions, bean sprouts, and ginger, and bring to a simmer. Cook just until the bean sprouts are tender-crisp, about 1 minute, then transfer the solids from the wok to a serving bowl using a spider. Return the broth to a simmer.

(4) Gently lower the fish into the wok one piece at a time so that it doesn't stick. Increase the heat to high and cook, swirling constantly, until the fish is just barely cooked through and the liquid is simmering, about 1 minute. Pour the fish and the broth over the bean sprout mixture in the bowl. Wipe out the wok.

(5) **To Serve:** Sprinkle the chopped chile and Sichuan peppercorn mixture all over the top of the beef. Sprinkle the cilantro leaves over the top. Heat the oil in the wok until it is smoking hot, then pour it all over the top of the serving bowl, causing the chiles, Sichuan peppercorn, and cilantro to sizzle and release their aroma. Serve immediately.

Braising with Caramel

Like the Maillard browning reactions, caramelization is a complex cascade of reactions that can transform a pure disaccharide like sucrose (aka white sugar) into a complex, nutty, toasty, bitter-sweet syrup, solely with the application of heat (and a normal Earth atmosphere). Some of my favorite classic braised dishes make use of this reaction to pull deep complexity out of a relatively simple ingredient list. The first is Vietnamese Cá Kho Tộ, or caramel-coated fish. The other is Chinese-style red-cooked dishes, such as *hong shao rou* (Shanghai-style red-braised pork belly) and *hong shao niu rou miàn* (Taiwanese-style beef noodle soup).

What I love about these dishes is how simple they are and how much they rely on good technique. Sure, you can make a decent red-braised pork belly by just dumping all the ingredients together in a wok, but if you want *excellent* red-braised pork, you need to nail that caramel. This is something you can practice visually, or you can rely on a digital thermometer, as the temperature that you cook a caramel syrup to is directly related to the color and flavor it acquires.

The easiest way to make caramel is to start with a mixture of sugar and water. If you're keeping track of the temperature, you'll note that it has difficulty getting much higher than 212°F (100°C)—the boiling point of water—for the early stages of cooking. This is because the energy you're adding to the sugar syrup is mostly going toward evaporating the water, rather than further heating the mixture. Only once most of the water has evaporated will the temperature start to climb more rapidly.

A few basic temperature ranges to look for:

325° TO 340°F (160° TO 170°C). Light Caramel. This caramel is mild in flavor, light, sweet, and toffee-like in flavor.

340° TO 345°F (170° TO 173°C). Amber Caramel. This caramel has a light brown color and sweetness that is rounder and fuller. It's great for making caramel sauce for ice cream or for butterscotch.

345° TO 350°F (173° TO 177°C). Dark Amber Caramel. The caramel is beginning to acquire some bitter flavors and losing a bit of its sweetness. It has an intense flavor that is ideal for pairing with meaty braises or for making things like burnt caramel sauce for ice cream or brownies.

350°F+ (177°C+). Very Dark and Beyond. As caramel continues to darken it will lose more of its sweetness and become increasingly bitter.

Once the caramel has hit the stage you want it to, you can immediately add other ingredients to cool it down and prevent it from darkening too deeply. From there, it's a simple matter of building your sauce and adding your main ingredient.

VIETNAMESE FISH BRAISED IN FISH SAUCE CARAMEL

Yield
Serves 4

Active Time
25 minutes

Total Time
25 minutes

INGREDIENTS

For the Braising Liquid:
½ cup (3½ ounces/100 g) sugar
1 tablespoon (15 ml) water
¼ cup (60 ml) fish sauce
½ cup (120 ml) coconut water

To Cook:
1 medium shallot (about 1½ ounces/45 g), thinly sliced
½ ounce (15 g) fresh ginger, thinly slivered
Four 5- to 6-ounce (150 to 180 g) fillets of firm white fish, such as striped bass, sea bass, snapper, or cod
6 to 8 very thin slices lime
1 tablespoon (15 ml) lime juice from 1 lime
1 fresh hot chile, such as Thai bird, serrano, or jalapeño, more or less to taste, thinly sliced
Handful of roughly chopped fresh cilantro leaves
Steamed rice, for serving

Vietnamese fish sauce caramel is used for a variety of braised dishes, but it pairs particularly nicely with fish. In Vietnam, you'll commonly find it paired with snakehead fish, a semi-amphibious freshwater fish with lots of bones and, to some (including me), a distinctly muddy flavor. In the United States, you'll more commonly see the dish made with catfish, a similar freshwater fish with a similar muddy flavor. While I don't begrudge anyone who wants to make it with snakehead (it is, after all, an invasive species), I personally prefer it with the cleaner flavor of cold saltwater fish like striped bass, sea bass, or snapper. Firm-fleshed tilapia is also a fine choice, though it can sometimes have the muddy flavor of farmed fish.

Make sure to have plenty of rice and steamed green vegetables to go with the extra sauce.

DIRECTIONS

1. **Make the Braising Liquid:** Add the sugar to a wok and add the water. Cook over medium heat, stirring frequently, until the sugar melts into a syrup and cooks down to a dark amber color, 5 to 8 minutes total. Immediately add the fish sauce and coconut water and stir until the sugar is dissolved. Cook until the sauce is reduced by half, about 8 to 10 minutes.

2. **To Cook:** Add the shallot and ginger, then add the fish fillets in a single layer. Cook, swirling the pan gently, for 3 minutes. Using a thin spatula, carefully flip the fillets and continue cooking just until they are barely cooked through, 2 to 3 minutes longer. Transfer the fillets to a serving plate.

3. Add the lime slices and lime juice to the wok and continue cooking, swirling constantly, until the sauce is reduced to a syrupy glaze. Stir in the chile, drizzle the sauce and lime wheels over the fish, sprinkle with cilantro, and serve with steamed rice.

RED BRAISED PORK BELLY (HONG SHAO ROU)

Yield
Serves 6 to 8

Active Time
25 minutes

Total Time
2 hours

NOTE

Look for pork belly with a good mix of fat and lean. Pork belly should come clean, but sometimes it'll have a few stray hairs. To remove them, you can pass a blowtorch over the surface and then scrub it under water with a stiff-bristled brush or scouring pad, or you can rub the skin side on the surface of a smoking-hot wok.

INGREDIENTS

2 pounds (900 g) rind-on fresh pork belly (see Note)
2¼ ounces (about ⅓ cup/60 g) sugar
1 tablespoon (15 ml) water
¼ cup (60 ml) Shaoxing wine
2 tablespoons (30 ml) dark soy sauce
2 tablespoons (30 ml) light soy sauce

Aromatics (optional):

2 scallions, roughly chopped
2 slices fresh ginger (5 g)
2 medium garlic cloves (5 g), smashed
1 star anise pod
1 cinnamon stick
1 teaspoon Sichuan peppercorns
1 small dried hot chile, such as Sichuan chao tian jiao or árbol

This homestyle braised dish, popular throughout China, is a prime example of how a few simple ingredients can create complex flavors. The aromatics added to it add an extra layer of flavor but are completely optional. Even with just sugar, dark and light soy sauce, and Chinese wine, you'll end up with a deliciously sweet-and-savory stew with chunks of fatty pork that melt in your mouth. The flavor and texture profile reminds me an awful lot of burnt ends paired with a sticky-sweet barbecue sauce that has caramelized a bit around the edges. (And if you want to lean into that, red braised pork belly goes great with pickles, slivered onions, and some slices of white bread.)

DIRECTIONS

(1) Place the pork belly in a wok and add water to cover. Bring to a boil over high heat. Reduce to a simmer and cook for 5 minutes. Transfer the pork belly to a cutting board and let it rest until cool enough to handle. Meanwhile, rinse and wipe out the wok.

(2) When the pork is cool enough to handle, cut it into 1½-inch cubes. Set aside.

(3) **Make the Caramel:** Add the sugar to a wok and add tablespoon of water. Cook over medium heat, swirling to promote even browning, until the sugar melts into a syrup and cooks down to a dark amber color, about 5 minutes total. Add the pork belly to the caramel and cook, stirring, until the pork is coated all over in the mixture and starting to brown around the edges, about 2 minutes.

(4) Add the wine and stir until the caramel is dissolved, scraping up any browned bits from the bottom of the wok. Add the dark and light soy sauce, then add enough fresh water to barely cover the pork. Add the aromatics (if using), bring the mixture to a boil over high heat, reduce to a bare simmer, cover, and cook, stirring occasionally, until the pork belly is completely tender, about 1½ hours, stirring occasionally to promote even cooking.

(5) When the pork is tender, remove the lid and continue cooking, stirring occasionally, until the sauce has reduced to a sticky glaze that coats the pork. Transfer to a serving platter and serve.

TAIWANESE BRAISED SHORT RIB NOODLE SOUP (HONG SHAO NIU ROU MIÀN)

Yield
Serves 4

Active Time
45 minutes

Total Time
3 hours

NOTES

If you want to omit some of the spices, I've listed them in order of most to least important. At the very minimum you should include the star anise. Another alternative is to use the star anise, along with 2 teaspoons of Chinese five spice in place of the other whole spices. Doubanjiang is a Sichuan fermented broad bean and chile paste. It can be found at better-stocked supermarkets, most Asian markets, or online (the best is from Pixian in the capital city of Chengdu). Ya cai, zha cai, and suan cai are various types of Chinese pickles. You can find them at most Asian markets or online.

Taiwanese beef noodle soup is a red-braised dish with Sichuan origins that has been adapted and adopted as one of the national dishes of Taiwan. Flavored with warm spices, sugar, and fermented broad bean chile paste, it is traditionally made with gelatinous beef shins and tendons, giving the broth a sticky richness. The flavors and technique are perfectly suited for meaty short ribs, which come out meltingly tender and moist.

INGREDIENTS

For the Braising Liquid:
3 tablespoons (12.5 g) dark brown sugar
1 tablespoon (15 ml) water
2 cups (500 ml) homemade or store-bought low-sodium chicken stock or water
1 tablespoon (15 ml) doubanjiang (see Notes)
1 cup (240 ml) Shaoxing wine
3 tablespoons (45 ml) dark soy sauce
2 tablespoons (30 ml) light soy sauce

For the Beef:
3 pounds (1.3 kg) meaty bone-in beef short ribs (about 4 large rib pieces)
Kosher salt
1 tablespoon (15 g) peanut, rice bran, or other neutral oil

For the Aromatics:
8 to 10 medium garlic cloves (25 to 35 g), unpeeled, smashed with the side of a cleaver or knife
One 2-inch knob fresh ginger, cut into rough ¼-inch slices
3 scallions, roughly chopped
3 small hot dried chiles, such as Thai bird or árbol, split open
1 medium yellow onion, roughly chopped
2 Roma tomatoes, roughly chopped
Kosher salt

For the Spices:
2 star anise pods
2 teaspoons (5 g) fennel seeds (optional; see Notes)
2 teaspoons (4 g) coriander seeds (optional; see Notes)
2 teaspoons (4 g) Sichuan peppercorns (optional; see Notes)
2 teaspoons (4 g) black peppercorns (optional; see Notes)
1 cinnamon stick (optional; see Notes)
2 dried bay leaves

To Serve:
2 tablespoons (30 ml) Chinese black or balsamic vinegar
Kosher salt
1 pound (450 g) baby bok choy, Chinese water spinach, Napa cabbage, or other tender greens
1 pound (450 g) fresh Chinese egg noodles or wheat noodles
Chopped preserved ya cai, zha cai, or plain old sauerkraut (see Notes)
Handful of roughly chopped fresh cilantro leaves and fine stems

(1) **Make the Braising Liquid:** Add the sugar to a wok and add the tablespoon (15 ml) of water. Cook over medium heat, stirring frequently, until the sugar melts into a syrup and cooks down to a dark amber color, 3 to 5 minutes total. Add the chicken broth and stir to dissolve the sugar. Stir in the doubanjiang, wine, and soy sauce. Transfer to a bowl and set aside. Wipe out the wok.

(2) **Sear the Beef:** Season the short ribs lightly with salt on all sides. Heat the oil in the wok over high heat until shimmering. Add the short ribs in a single layer and cook, turning occasionally, until well browned on all sides, about 8 minutes total. (Reduce the heat as necessary if the oil smokes excessively during searing.) Transfer the short ribs to a large plate and set aside. Do not wash out the wok.

(3) **Add the Aromatics:** Add the garlic, ginger, scallions, dried chiles, onion, and tomatoes to the wok, season lightly with salt, and cook, stirring frequently, until the vegetables are starting to brown around the edges and the tomatoes are breaking down, about 4 minutes.

(4) **Bloom the Spices:** Add the star anise, fennel seeds, coriander seeds, Sichuan peppercorns, black peppercorns, and cinnamon stick and cook, stirring frequently, until aromatic, about 1 minute.

(5) Add the braising liquid to the wok, scraping up any browned bits from the bottom. Return the short ribs to the wok and add enough water to barely cover them (about 2 quarts/2 l—it's OK if parts of them poke out a little bit). Add the bay leaves, bring the liquid to a boil, adjust the heat to maintain a bare simmer, cover, and cook until a toothpick or skewer inserted into the meaty part of the largest short rib shows very little resistance, but the meat is not falling apart, 2 to 2½ hours.

(6) Carefully transfer the short ribs to a plate, then strain the braising liquid through a fine-mesh strainer into a fresh pot and skim off most, but not all, of the fat from the surface with a ladle and discard.

(7) Pick any stray spices or aromatics off the short ribs and discard. Return the short ribs to the braising liquid. For best results, allow the short ribs to cool in the liquid on the countertop, then refrigerate overnight.

(8) **To Serve:** Reheat the broth and short ribs to a simmer. Add the vinegar and season the broth with salt to taste. Add the greens and remove from the heat. Bring a large pot of salted water to a boil and cook the noodles according to the package directions. Drain the noodles and divide between 4 serving bowls. Place a short rib on top of each, divide the greens evenly between the bowls, and ladle the broth over the top. Place a small pile of chopped Chinese pickled vegetable or sauerkraut on top of each short rib, sprinkle with chopped cilantro, and serve.

Stew Science: Yes, It's Possible To Overcook Braised Meats

As anyone who has ever tried to eat at a dozen Nashville hot fried chicken joints in the course of one day can tell you, you absolutely can have too much of a good thing.

I used to be of the mind-set that if cooking a stew for a long time is a good idea, then cooking it even longer is a better idea. I remember my mother requesting a beef stew one winter while I was visiting home. I spent the first day making a veal stock—high in gelatin, rich in texture, the perfect base for a luxurious stew. The second day, I seared boneless short ribs, carefully constructed my broth, and set it all in the oven to cook for the entire afternoon before fishing it out for dinner. The house smelled amazing, and I just knew that the beef was going to be insanely tender and juicy after its long stay in the oven.

What emerged was beef that dissolved into a dry, pulpy mass in your mouth as soon as your jaw moved. The flavor was there, all right, but the beef was totally destroyed (along with my mom's dreams of stew and my ego).

Turns out you definitely can overcook beef stew. But how do you know when it's done? What sort of changes in the meat should you look for? I set up an experiment to figure this out.

CUBED STEAK

Using a precise scale, I cut two slabs of top round into forty identical 20-gram cubes. I then added all of the beef to a pot of stock that I maintained at 190°F. After the first 2 hours, I removed four pieces of beef, blotted their surfaces on paper towels, weighed them, then stored them wrapped in plastic wrap. Every half hour after that, I removed another four cubes and repeated the process. I averaged the weight loss in each set of four cubes to arrive at a number that was representative of moisture loss relative to time in the simmering water. I also tasted one cube out of each batch.

Now, here's the interesting part. Beef that's been simmered for five hours tastes distinctly drier in your mouth than beef that's been simmered for only three hours. Yet, when I weighed each cube of beef after cooking, every single one of them ended up at between 11 and 12 grams (for a moisture loss of around 40 to 45 percent), regardless of how long it had cooked. Longer cooking time does not equate to more moisture loss.

So what accounts for the difference in how juicy it tastes?

There are a couple of reasons. First off, our perception of juiciness is not perfectly correlated to actual, measurable juiciness in a piece of meat. Other factors, such as how much fat it has and how much saliva we are producing (and, by correlation, how hungry we are),[*] can affect how juicy something feels to us. In the case of the beef, there are other physical phenomena at work as well: the juices in the three-hour beef are thicker than those in the five-hour beef, and they're held more firmly in place.

When connective tissue in the beef first breaks down, it creates a very concentrated zone of gelatin within the meat. This gelatin thickens juices, which helps them stay put inside the meat along with helping them to coat your tongue and mouth. More importantly, as the muscle structure continues to break down within the meat, it has a hard time hanging on to the moisture it has. Think of it as being like the difference between a net full of water balloons and a net full of sponges. Both may have the same amount of moisture, but press down on the sponges and that liquid comes gushing out all at once, leaving behind a dry shell. The water balloons, on the other hand, take a little more effort to break, releasing their juices in discrete bursts—in the same way that juicy meat should release juice steadily as you chew, not gush out all its moisture at once.

---

[*]   Interestingly, this means that if we think something is going to be juicy, it will actually taste juicier. Neat!

Visualizing Texture

For the next test, I wanted to get a good visual representation of the difference in texture I was feeling in my mouth. To do this, I placed a small plate on top of each cube of beef and placed a can of tomatoes on top of it, letting the weight of the tomatoes deform and break down the beef cube. This should ensure every beef cube is pressed with equal force. I then removed the plate and compared the crushed beef.

Here's how it looked, with the two-hour beef in the upper left corner and beef cooked for a full six-and-a-half in the lower right:

You can see a pretty clear indication of how the beef breaks down over time. This is not unexpected. What is surprising is that this breakdown seems to come in three distinct phases. From two hours to three and a half hours (the first four pieces), the beef looks pretty similar. Then there's a big jump between three and a half and four hours. The next three pieces look quite similar, then another big jump occurs between five and five and a half hours. I refer to these discrete jumps as the primary, secondary, and tertiary breakdown of beef.*

Primary breakdown occurs when the large swaths of connective tissue that run through a piece of stew beef break down and convert to gelatin. Individual cubes will still hold their shape very well but will show tenderness when you bite into them. There is no chewiness in the beef, but neither does the beef shred readily.

Secondary breakdown is when the tissue holding together individual muscle fibrils (the long, skinny bundles of muscle cells that give meat its distinct grain) breaks down and the fibrils easily separate from each other. At this stage, the beef is very easily shredded—even vigorous stirring will do it. This is the stage you're looking for in dishes that are meant to contain shredded meat, like Cuban ropa vieja, or beef barbacoa for a taco, or meat that may become a ragù for pasta.

Tertiary breakdown is when those individual muscle fibrils themselves break down, turning from distinct, juice-filled strands into pulpy mush. At this stage, your meat is beyond overcooked. The dogs are gonna get a nice treat for dinner, but you won't.

Of course, all of these phases are timed based on the assumption that you're cooking your meat gently, at a bare simmer. Rapidly simmering or cooking at a lower temperature will hasten or slow down the rate at which the meat reaches each stage. Different cuts of meat will also undergo changes at different rates, depending on the ratio of fat to lean to connective tissue, as well as how tough or distinct the individual muscle fibers are.

My advice? Use the timing in any stew recipe as a guideline. Start checking your meat when you hit around 80 percent of the total recommended cooking time and stop cooking as soon as it reaches the stage at which the meat is tender but not falling apart—so, if a recipe says to cook the stew for two and a half hours, start checking it around the two-hour mark.

---

* Partly because it's accurate, and partly because words like "tertiary" make you sound smart.

6

SIMPLE, NO-COOK SIDES

—

The good news with many wok-cooked dishes is that as long as you add a side of steamed rice and stir-fried greens, you've got yourself a complete meal. If you don't feel like wokking two dishes in a row, here are a few simple suggestions for some no-cook side dishes that you can throw together just before you start stir-frying your main course.

LEFTOVER VEGETABLE SALAD WITH SOY-DASHI DRESSING

Yield
Serves 4

Active Time
5 minutes

Total Time
5 minutes

This salad came about when I had a half cup or so of leftover Soy-Glazed Mushrooms (page 183) and Stir-Fried Kabocha Squash with Sake and Miso (page 199), but it works well with virtually any leftover simple stir-fried or roasted vegetable, such as carrot, celery, squash, or zucchini. All I did was combine the roasted vegetables with a big handful of washed watercress (any strongly flavored salad green will do, such as arugula or mizuna) and dressed them with some soy sauce, dashi, mirin, and sesame seeds.

INGREDIENTS

2 tablespoons (30 ml) homemade dashi (page 519–21) or Hondashi
1 tablespoon (15 ml) shoyu or light soy sauce
2 teaspoons (10 ml) mirin or ½ teaspoon (2.5 ml) honey or agave syrup
1 tablespoon toasted sesame seeds
1 medium garlic clove, minced
1 tablespoons (15 ml) extra virgin olive oil
1 teaspoon (5 ml) roasted sesame oil
6 to 8 ounces (170 to 225 g) leftover roasted or stir-fried vegetables, such as Soy-Glazed Mushrooms (page 183) or Stir-Fried Kabocha Squash with Sake and Miso (page 199)
4 ounces (120 g) spicy salad greens such as watercress, arugula, or mizuna
Kosher salt and freshly ground black pepper

DIRECTIONS

Combine the dashi, shoyu, mirin, sesame seeds, and garlic in a large bowl. Whisk in the olive oil and sesame oil. Add the vegetables and greens and toss to coat. Season to taste with salt and pepper and serve.

SICHUAN SMASHED CUCUMBER SALAD

Yield
Serves 4

Active Time
5 minutes

Total Time
5 minutes

Smashed cucumbers with garlic are a classic side dish throughout China that can be made in just a couple minutes. Smashing English or Persian cucumbers causes them to split open, which lets them absorb plenty of dressing while staying fresh and crisp.

INGREDIENTS

For the Dressing:
2 teaspoons (8 g/about 2 medium cloves) minced garlic
1 teaspoon (4 g) sugar
1 teaspoon (5 ml) roasted sesame oil
1 tablespoon (15 ml) light soy sauce
2 teaspoons (10 ml) rice vinegar.

For the Salad:
1 large English or 4 small Persian or Japanese cucumbers (about 1 pound/450 g total)
1 tablespoon (10 to 12 g) toasted sesame seeds
Handful of chopped fresh cilantro leaves and fine stems
Kosher salt
2 to 3 tablespoons (30 to 45 ml) Sichuan Málà Chile Oil (page 310) or any other chile oil (optional)

DIRECTIONS

(1) **For the Dressing:** Combine all the dressing ingredients in a large bowl.

(2) **For the Salad:** Place a cucumber on your cutting board. Using the side of a cleaver, a Chinese chef's knife, or the bottom of a skillet, pound the cucumber all along its length until the skin has split open from end to end. Roughly chop into bite-sized pieces.

(3) Transfer the cucumber to the bowl with the dressing, add the sesame seeds and cilantro, and toss to combine. Season with salt to taste, drizzle with chile oil if desired, and serve.

CUCUMBER AND DILL SALAD WITH YOGURT AND CHILE OIL

Yield
Serves 4

Active Time
5 minutes

Total Time
5 minutes

INGREDIENTS

1 large English or 4 small Persian or Japanese cucumbers (about 1 pound/450 g total), chopped into bite-sized pieces

2½ ounces (75 g) red onion, thinly sliced

Big handful of fried (page 319) or roasted peanuts (optional)

Big handful of minced fresh dill fronds

2 tablespoons (30 ml) extra virgin olive oil

1 tablespoon (15 ml) white wine or rice vinegar

Kosher salt

½ cup (120 ml) Greek yogurt or labneh (any percentage fat)

A few tablespoons Sichuan Málà Chile Oil (page 310) or any other chile oil

The flavor combination of yogurt and Sichuan Málà Chile Oil (page 310) is one that I can't get enough of. It's great on everything from hamburgers to meatballs to roasted carrots to grilled vegetables. It's also excellent with cucumbers that are very lightly dressed with plenty of dill. Fried peanuts are also great in this salad.

DIRECTIONS

(1) Combine the cucumbers, onion, peanuts, dill, olive oil, vinegar, and a big pinch of salt in a large bowl and toss.

(2) Spread yogurt over the bottom of a serving platter. Pile the cucumber salad on top of the yogurt, then drizzle with chile oil. Serve.

THREE SIMPLE MISO DIPS FOR VEGETABLES

These simple dips can be served with any number of raw or steamed-and-chilled vegetables for a snack, side dish, or party finger-food, such as cucumbers, asparagus, snap peas, carrot sticks, or celery sticks.

SWEET AND SPICY MISO DIP

Yield
Serves 4

Active Time
5 minutes

Total Time
5 minutes

INGREDIENTS

¼ cup (about 60 g) red or brown miso paste

1 tablespoon (15 ml) roasted sesame oil

1 tablespoon (12 g) sugar

¼ teaspoon (1.5 g) powdered Japanese or Chinese mustard, or 2 teaspoons (10 g) Dijon mustard

2 teaspoons (10 ml) chile sauce, such as sambal oelek or sriracha, more or less to taste

Crunchy vegetables such as cucumbers, radishes, lightly blanched snap peas and asparagus, or bell peppers, cut as for a vegetable platter

DIRECTIONS

Combine the miso paste, sesame oil, sugar, mustard, and chile sauce in a small bowl and stir until homogenous. Serve with vegetables for dipping. Store unused sauce in a sealed container in the refrigerator for up to several weeks.

HONEY MUSTARD–MISO DIP

Yield
Serves 4

Active Time
5 minutes

Total Time
5 minutes

INGREDIENTS

3 tablespoons (about 45 g) white or yellow miso paste
2 tablespoons (about 30 g) Dijon mustard
2 tablespoons (about 30 g) honey
1 teaspoon (10 ml) rice wine vinegar
1 tablespoon (10 ml) rice bran, vegetable, or canola oil

DIRECTIONS

Combine the miso paste, mustard, honey, vinegar, and oil in a medium bowl and whisk until homogenous. Serve with vegetables for dipping. Store unused sauce in a sealed container in the refrigerator for up to several weeks.

MISO-YOGURT RANCH DIP

Yield
Serves 4

Active Time
5 minutes

Total Time
5 minutes

INGREDIENTS

2 tablespoons (about 30 g) white or yellow miso paste
¼ cup (about 60 g) Greek-style yogurt
1 teaspoon (about 2 g) granulated garlic
½ teaspoon (about 1 g) granulated onion
1 medium garlic clove, minced (about 1 teaspoon; 2 to 3 g)
½ teaspoon (about 1 g) freshly ground black pepper
Handful minced fresh dill fronds
2 teaspoons (10 ml) fresh lemon juice
Pinch Korean chile flakes (gochugaru) or cayenne pepper
Kosher salt to taste

DIRECTIONS

Combine miso paste, yogurt, granulated garlic and onion, fresh garlic, black pepper, dill, lemon juice, and chile flakes in a medium bowl and whisk to combine. Season to taste with salt. Serve with vegetables for dipping. Store unused sauce in a sealed container in the refrigerator for up to 2 weeks.

SOM TAM

Yield
Serves 4

Active Time
15 minutes

Total Time
15 minutes

NOTES

Green papaya can be found at well-stocked Asian supermarkets and is best shredded with a special shredding tool that looks like a Y-peeler with a wavy blade. This tool is available at Southeast Asian markets or online. Alternatively, use the shredding attachment on a mandoline or julienne by hand: Start by peeling it, split it and discard the seeds, cut into lengths, then julienne the same way you would a cucumber (see page 99).

Or if that's all too much trouble, you can use 6 ounces (170 g) shredded cabbage with 1 to 2 ounces (30 to 60 g) each of peeled carrot and daikon radish grated on the large holes of a box grater in place of the papaya. It'll still be great, I promise.

INGREDIENTS

3 medium garlic cloves (8 g), roughly chopped

1 to 6 fresh Thai bird chiles, roughly chopped

1 tablespoon (12 g) palm sugar, plus more to taste

2 tablespoons (30 ml) fish sauce, plus more to taste

2 tablespoons (30 ml) fresh lime juice, plus more to taste

Small handful of dried shrimp

½ cup (2 ounces/about 60 g) Fried Peanuts (page 319) or roasted peanuts

3 ounces (85 g) yard-long or green beans, cut into 1-inch segments

6 to 10 cherry tomatoes, cut in half

8 to 10 ounces (225 to 290 g) shredded green papaya (see Note)

Handful of roughly chopped fresh cilantro or basil leaves

This is a classic Thai-style papaya salad that can range widely in flavor from fiery hot and fresh to funky with fermented crabs or other seafood. This version is simple and clean, with just a bit of funkiness from fish sauce and dried shrimp.

Som tam is typically made in a deep wooden mortar and pestle. The dressing ingredients go in first, followed by the vegetables, which get lightly bruised to absorb more dressing. If making som tam in a smaller mortar and pestle, just work in batches and combine everything in a salad bowl.

DIRECTIONS

(1) Combine the garlic and chiles in the mortar and pestle and crush into a paste. Add the palm sugar and continue crushing until smooth and sticky. Grind in the fish sauce and lime juice, then scrape the mixture out into a large, sturdy bowl. You don't need to wash out the mortar and pestle.

(2) Add the shrimp to the mortar and pound until lightly crushed. Add the peanuts and pound until the peanuts are broken up. Add the green beans and crush until lightly bruised. Add the tomatoes and crush until they are juicy and broken up. Scrape out the contents of the mortar into the bowl with the dressing.

(3) Add the papaya to the bowl with the dressing. Holding the pestle in one hand and a large spoon to toss with the other, pound directly in the large bowl, tossing the salad until the papaya is slightly limp and faintly pink from the tomato juice. Toss in the cilantro or basil. Season with more fish sauce, lime juice, or sugar to taste and serve.

MIXED GREENS WITH SAVORY SESAME-GINGER VINAIGRETTE

Yield
Serves 4

Active Time
20 minutes

Total Time
40 minutes

INGREDIENTS

¼ cup (60 ml) shoyu or light soy sauce
2 tablespoons (30 ml) rice vinegar
2 tablespoons (30 g) red or brown miso paste
1 teaspoon (4 g) grated fresh ginger
1 medium garlic clove, minced (about 1 teaspoon; 2 to 3 g)
1 tablespoon (12 g) sugar
1 tablespoon (8 g) toasted sesame seeds
½ cup (120 ml) vegetable or canola oil
¼ cup (60 ml) roasted sesame oil
4 to 5 ounces (115 to 145 g) mixed salad greens
Other crunchy, fresh vegetables
Kosher salt and freshly ground black pepper

My grandmother always had a jar of homemade soy sauce and sesame oil–based salad dressing in her refrigerator, which my sisters and I loved. She unfortunately passed away before passing on the recipe. And when I asked my mother about it, she responded, "I grew up with it and thought it was just regular old salad dressing." She never knew how good she had it!

She was able to piece together that the recipe contained soy sauce, rice vinegar, and sesame, along with garlic powder and MSG. From there, I relied on my own memory of the flavor to put together a dressing that hit the right notes. In place of the garlic powder, I prefer fresh garlic, and swapping out the MSG for miso paste lends the dressing the same umami punch while also helping it to emulsify a little better.

This dressing now holds a permanent spot in a small mason jar in my refrigerator, just like my grandmother's did in hers. It's perfect for a simple mixed green salad, though you can feel free to add any crunchy fresh vegetables you'd like.

DIRECTIONS

(1) Combine the soy sauce, vinegar, miso paste, ginger, garlic, sugar, and sesame seeds in a large bowl. Whisking constantly, drizzle in the vegetable and sesame oils. The dressing can be stored in a sealed container in the fridge for several weeks.

(2) In a large bowl, dress the greens and other vegetables with a few tablespoons of dressing. Season with salt and pepper to taste and serve.

HIYAYAKKO (JAPANESE COLD DRESSED TOFU WITH SOY SAUCE AND GINGER)

Yield
Serves 4

Active Time
5 minutes

Total Time
5 minutes

INGREDIENTS

3 tablespoons (45 ml) homemade dashi (page 519–21) or Hondashi

1 tablespoon (15 ml) shoyu or light soy sauce

2 teaspoons (10 ml) mirin or ½ teaspoon (2.5 ml) honey or agave syrup

One 12-ounce (340 g) block soft or medium silken tofu

A marble-sized dollop of grated fresh ginger

A big pinch of toasted sesame seeds

1 scallion, very thinly sliced

A big pinch of katsuobushi

Silken tofu is wonderful lightly dressed as a side dish, and it can be served straight from the fridge. Tofu with soy sauce and a sprinkle of katsuobushi was one of my favorite snacks growing up (and my daughter loves it now), and it's so simple I'm not even going to offer a recipe. Just put the block of tofu on a plate, drizzle it with soy sauce, add a sprinkle of katsuobushi, and serve with a spoon.

If you do feel like dressing it up a bit more, you can start by cutting the soy sauce with a bit of dashi and mirin and from there take it in any number of directions by pairing it with other sauces or fresh seasonal vegetables.

DIRECTIONS

(1) In a small bowl, combine the dashi, soy sauce, and mirin.

(2) Place the tofu on a serving platter. Drizzle with the dressing. Garnish with the ginger, sesame seeds, scallions, and katsuobushi and serve.

Cold Tofu with Fresh Corn, Tomatoes, Olive Oil, and Basil

Combine 3 tablespoons (45 ml) of dashi, 1 tablespoon (15 ml) of light soy sauce or shoyu, 2 teaspoons (10 ml) of mirin, and 2 tablespoons (30 ml) of extra virgin olive oil in a medium bowl. Add the kernels from 1 ear of fresh corn (or cut off the kernels from some grilled or boiled corn that's been in the fridge overnight) and 5 ounces (140 g) of cherry tomatoes split in half along with a thinly sliced scallion and a handful of finely chopped fresh basil leaves. Spoon this mixture over a 12-ounce (340 g) block of silken tofu and serve.

Cold Tofu with Fermented Chile-Bean Sauce, Cucumber, and Peanuts

Combine 3 tablespoons (45 ml) of dashi, 1 tablespoon (15 ml) Sichuan doubanjiang, 1 teaspoon (5 ml) light soy sauce or shoyu, and 1 tablespoon (15 ml) vegetable, canola, or light olive oil in a small bowl. Spoon this mixture over a 12-ounce (340 g) block of silken tofu. Garnish with a big pinch each of slivered cucumber, sliced scallion, chopped cilantro, and lightly crushed peanuts and serve.

JAPANESE SIDE SALAD WITH CARROT AND GINGER DRESSING

Yield
Makes 1½
cups

Active Time
5 minutes

Total Time
5 minutes

This is the classic bright-orange dressing used for side salads at casual Japanese bento or sushi restaurants, typically served as part of a set meal. It's easy to make and has lots of vegetables. Excess dressing can be stored in the fridge for a few weeks.

INGREDIENTS

For the Dressing:

4 ounces (120 g/about 1 small) carrot, peeled and roughly chopped

2 ounces (60 g/about ¼ small) yellow onion, roughly chopped

1 ounce (30 g/about 2-inch segment) fresh ginger, peeled and roughly chopped

1 small garlic clove

2 tablespoons (30 g) yellow or white miso paste

1 tablespoon (15 ml) honey or agave nectar

½ cup (120 ml) vegetable or canola oil

¼ cup (120 ml) rice vinegar

Kosher salt and freshly ground black pepper

For the Salad (all optional; mix according to taste):

Chopped crunchy lettuce like iceberg or romaine

Thinly sliced red onion

Grated carrots

Sliced cucumbers

Sliced bell peppers

Mung bean sprouts

Blanched green beans, snap peas, or snow peas

Shredded red cabbage

Cherry tomatoes

DIRECTIONS

1. **For the Dressing:** Combine all the ingredients in a blender or food processor and blend until it's as smooth as you like it. Adjust the seasoning with salt and pepper.

2. **For the Salad:** Arrange the salad ingredients on a wide, shallow serving platter and drizzle the dressing on top. Serve immediately. Store extra dressing in a sealed container in the fridge for up to a week.

acknowledgments

This book started as a single chapter in my first book, *The Food Lab*, which my editor, the great Maria Guarnaschelli, very smartly suggested we cut from that manuscript—not because it wasn't any good, but because she saw potential in it for a future project. She passed away before the manuscript for this book was finished, but her mark is all over it. I cannot write without thinking: "What would Maria say?" She was brutally honest, wickedly sharp, and, most of all, fiercely supportive and loyal, and I miss her greatly. Thank you for everything, Maria, I constantly strive to live up to the pride you showed in your writers.

I did not think that anyone could fill the enormous (and comfy) shoes left behind when Maria passed away, but working with Melanie Tortoroli has been nothing but joy. Thank you, Melanie, for putting up with me through countless changes, redirections, rewrites, and late nights, and for never being anything but supportive and understanding, no matter how many extensions I ask for. I can't wait to get started on our next project together (more children's books, please!).

Without great editors, designers, and artists, a book is just a messy wall of text. Thankfully, copyeditor Chris Benton and project editor Susan Sanfrey were here to get my text into shape, while designer Toni Tajima and art director Ingsu Liu made the whole thing beautiful to look at, comfortable to read, and functional to use. Thank you, Chris, Susan, Toni, and Ingsu!

Will Scarlett is a great publicist specifically because he is a genuinely great human being: Kind, caring, and enthusiastic in his work. Thank you, Will, I'll see you on tour.

I'd like to thank my agent, Vicky Bijur, and her husband (and my former boss) Ed Levine. More than just colleagues, Vicky and Ed are better editors,

advocates, cheerleaders, and friends than anyone could hope for.

I owe a huge debt of gratitude to all of the Asian immigrants who came to the United States and brought their food and culture with them, both to those who strove to maintain that food and culture as authentically as possible and to those who embraced adapting it to Western sensibilities. Every one of their stories, both sung and unsung, are worth hearing. Thank you.

I greatly admire the pioneers of Asian cooking education on television, especially Joyce Chen, the first woman of color to host a cooking show and whose book, *The Joyce Chen Cookbook*, was responsible for a huge number of delicious memories from my childhood. Martin Yan's showmanship and energetic teaching style gave me my first glimpse of what goes on behind the kitchen doors in Chinatown. As a role model for Asian American chefs and writers, Ming Tsai showed a generation of cooks the beauty of combining Asian and Western techniques and ingredients, smashing cultural stereotypes in the process. His *Blue Ginger* cookbook was the first book I bought with my first paycheck from my first restaurant job. It has truly blown my mind that I've had the opportunity to meet him since then, and he's as kind and supportive as he seems on TV. Thank you, chef.

Grace Young's cookbooks have inspired and enlightened me for decades, but even more inspiring is her work with uplifting the Asian American community. She is kind, caring, passionate, and tireless in her efforts to help others and to advocate on behalf of those whose voices need amplification. Thank you so much, Grace.

I'd like to thank Eileen Yin-Fei Lo; Fuchsia Dunlop; Elizabeth Andoh; Andrea Nguyen; Hooni Kim; Leela Punyaratabandhu (who volunteered her proofreading services for all of the Thai romanizations and recipes in this book); David Chang; Adam Liaw; Christopher Thomas and Stephanie Li; Namiko Chen; Mark Matsumoto; Wang Gang; Maangchi; Hyosun Ro; Pailin Chongchitnat; Elaine from China Sichuan Food; Bill, Judy, Sarah, and Kaitlin from *The Woks of Life*; Brandon Jew; Irene Kuo; Irene, Margaret, and Andrew Li; Pim Techumvit; Alvin Cailan; Leah Cohen; Mandy Lee; and countless others for their work in celebrating and teaching Asian cuisine to Western audiences. Their books, columns, shows, and videos are the first places I turn when I have questions about Asian cookery. They are insanely generous with their time and knowledge and cooks around the world benefit from it. Thank you to every one of you, and the many others I missed.

My grandmother Yasuko was the kindest, funniest grandmother a kid could ask for. She, without my even noticing it, instilled in me a sense of Japaneseness that only later in life, after her passing, did I realize was a foundational element of my own sense of self. My grandfather Koji taught me that you can be serious about your work without being too serious about life, and that it's really hard to work on something if you're not having fun doing it. Thank you, Kachan and Jita.

I want to thank my father, Fred, whose love of Chinese, Thai, and Mexican food is unparalleled. From my early childhood days scouring New York's Chinatown with him for great Cantonese food, to seeking out the best Sichuan cuisine in the suburbs of Boston, to introducing me to the secret Thai-language menu at Monsoon, his passion for great food is paralleled only by his passion for science (and fishing). Thanks, Fred.

I want to thank my sisters, Aya and Pico, whose love of Chinese food trails only behind Fred's. I tested and wrote a lot of these recipes for you, and I expect detailed reports back on exactly how the chow fun is not as good as at Kwok Wah, and why the Pepper and Salty Shrimp can't live up to the legendary version at Phoenix Garden (it's not and they can't). Thanks Poojack, thanks Bub.

I want to thank my mother, Keiko, for the years of tireless work she put into raising me and my sisters, for always being present in our lives, for making sure that we had dinner as a family nearly every single night (if it wasn't home-cooked it was take-out Chinese or pizza), and for walking that difficult tightrope of raising Japanese American kids as a first-generation immigrant. Thanks, ma.

I want to thank Alicia for all her help and patience through the process of writing this book, which has been in progress since she was born. She was a wonderful assistant photographer (if you see a photo in this book with my hands in it, that was my daughter behind the camera pushing the shutter release!), a voracious taste tester, a truly helpful kitchen assistant, and a wonderful cheerleader (yes, Alicia, I *finally* finished the noodle chapter.) I am blown away and inspired every day by what a smart, funny, thoughtful, and caring a human she is turning into. Thank you, Alicia.

I want to thank Koji who, even in the womb, inspired me to want to do better. Thanks, Wombat.

Most of all I want to thank my wife, Adri, who, despite knowing what writing a book involves, supported me through it all once again, this time while juggling a job, a toddler, and a pregnancy. She not only makes me want to be the best version of myself I can be, but she helps me figure out what that is and how to get there, and I love her. Thank you, Adri.

resources

Here is a very incomplete list of the many excellent resources available to learn more about Asian home cooking and woks. I've included books, websites, and video channels, as well as some online resources for sourcing ingredients and equipment.

BOOKS AND WEBSITES

Chinese and Chinese American

Beyond the Great Wall
Jeffrey Alford and Naomi Duguid

The Breath of a Wok
Stir-Frying to the Sky's Edge
The Wisdom of the Chinese Kitchen
Grace Young

Chef Wang
  (https://youtube.com/channel/
  UCg0m_Ah8P_MQbnn77-vYnYw)
Wang Gang

China: The Cookbook
Kei Lum Chan and Diora Fong Chan

China Sichuan Food (www.chinasichuanfood.com)
Elaine

Chinese Cooking Demystified (https://youtube
  .com/c/ChineseCookingDemystified)
Stephanie Li and Christopher Thomas

The Chinese Kitchen
Eileen Yin-Fei Lo's New Cantonese Cooking
Eileen Yin-Fei Lo

Double Awesome Chinese Food
Margaret, Irene, and Andrew Li

Every Grain of Rice
The Food of Sichuan
Land of Fish and Rice
Revolutionary Chinese Cookbook
Fuchsia Dunlop

Everybody's Working
Martin Yan's Chinatown Cooking
The Yan Can Cook Book
Martin Yan

Florence Lin's Chinese Regional Cookbook
Florence Lin's Chinese Vegetarian Cookbook
*Florence Lin's Complete Book of Chinese
  Noodles, Dumplings, and Breads*
Florence Lin

Joyce Chen Cook Book
Joyce Chen and Paul Dudley White

Mister Jiu's in Chinatown
Brandon Jew and Tienlon Ho

A Taste of Chinatown
Joie Warner

Vegetarian Chinese Soul Food
Hsiao-Ching Chou

Japanese

At Home with Japanese Cooking
*Kansha: Celebrating Japan's Vegan and
    Vegetarian Traditions*
*Washoku: Recipes from the Japanese Home
    Kitchen*
Elizabeth Andoh

Cooking with Dog
    (www.youtube.com/c/cookingwithdog)
Francis the Dog

Izakaya: The Japanese Pub Cookbook
Mark Robinson

Japan: The Cookbook
Japanese Farm Food
Preserving the Japanese Way
Nancy Singleton Hachisu

JapanEasy
Tim Anderson

Japanese Cooking
Emi Kazuko, with recipes by Yasuko Fukuoka

Just One Cookbook: Essential Japanese Recipes
Just One Cookbook (justonecookbook.com)
Namiko Chen

*Kaiseki: The Exquisite Cuisine of Kyoto's
    Kikunoi Restaurant*
Yoshihiro Murata

Korean

*Korean Bapsang: A Korean Mom's Home
    Cooking* (koreanbapsang.com)
Hyosun

Korean Home Cooking
Sohui Kim, with Rachel Wharton

Maangchi's Real Korean Cooking
Maangchi (maangchi.com)
Maangchi, with Lauren Chattman

My Korea
Hooni Kim, with Aki Kamozawa

Thai, Vietnamese, Philippine, Other Southeast Asian

*Amboy: Recipes from the Filipino-American
    Dream*
Alvin Cailan, with Alexandra Cuerdo

Asian Dumplings
Asian Tofu
Into the Vietnamese Kitchen
Vietnamese Food Any Day
Andrea Nguyen

Bangkok
Flavors of the Southeast Asian Grill
Simple Thai Food
She Simmers (shesimmers.com)
Leela Punyaratabandhu

Burma: Rivers of Flavor
Naomi Duguid

The Food of Northern Thailand
Austin Bush

*Hot, Sour, Salty, Sweet: A Culinary Journey
    Through Southeast Asia*
Jeffrey Alford and Naomi Duguid

*Hot Thai Kitchen: Demystifying Thai Cuisine
    with Authentic Recipes to Make at Home*
Hot Thai Kitchen (hot-thai-kitchen.com)
Pailin Chongchitnant

*Kiin: Recipes and Stories from Northern
    Thailand*
Nuit Regular

Lemongrass & Lime: Southeast Asian Cooking at Home
Leah Cohen, with Stephanie Banyas

Night+Market
Kris Yenbamroong, with Garrett Snyder

The Original Thai Cookbook
Jennifer Brennan

Pok Pok: The Drinking Food of Thailand
Pok Pok: Food and Stories from the Streets, Homes, and Roadside Restaurants of Thailand
Andy Ricker, with JJ Goode

Other Asian, General Cooking

Adam's Big Pot (adamliaw.com)
Adam Liaw

The Art of Escapism Cooking
Mandy Lee

Blue Ginger
Simply Ming
Ming Tsai

Cooking at Home
David Chang and Priya Krishna

Momofuku: a Cookbook
David Chang and Peter Meehan

Seonkyoung Longest (www.youtube.com/user/ SeonkyoungLongest)
Seonkyoung Longest

INGREDIENTS AND EQUIPMENT

I do the majority of my shopping at Chinese, Japanese, and Southeast Asian supermarkets, which stock pantry staples; specialty meats, vegetables, and seafood; and a selection of fresh noodles that far outstrips what you can find in a Western supermarket (and at better prices). If you don't have access to Asian markets, here are some online resources.

H-Mart (www.hmart.com)
General Asian pantry ingredients

The Japanese Pantry (https://thejapanesepantry.com)
Artisanal Japanese ingredients

The Mala Market (www.themalamarket.com)
Premium Sichuan specialty ingredients and other Chinese pantry staples

Nihon Ichiban (anything-from-japan.com)
Japanese ingredients and pantry staples

Seoul Mills (seoulmills.com)
Korean ingredients and pantry staples

The Wok Shop (www.wokshop.com)
Professional- and home-grade woks, accessories, steamers, mortars and pestles, hand tools, rice cookers, steamers, knives, tableware, and more

Yami (www.yamibuy.com)
Japanese, Korean, and Chinese pantry ingredients

index

Note: Page references in *italics* indicate recipe photographs.

N

U